# The Courting of Marcus Dupree

## Books by Willie Morris

NORTH TOWARD HOME

YAZOO

GOOD OLD BOY

THE LAST OF THE SOUTHERN GIRLS

A SOUTHERN ALBUM (With Irwin Glusker)

JAMES JONES: A FRIENDSHIP

TERRAINS OF THE HEART AND OTHER ESSAYS

THE COURTING OF MARCUS DUPREE

GOOD OLD BOY AND THE WITCH OF YAZOO

HOMECOMINGS

FAULKNER'S MISSISSIPPI (With Photographs by William Eggleston)

AFTER ALL, IT'S ONLY A GAME

# The Courting
# of Marcus Dupree

---

## WILLIE MORRIS

UNIVERSITY PRESS OF MISSISSIPPI
Jackson and London

First published in 1983 by Doubleday & Company, Inc.
Copyright © 1992 by Willie Morris
Postscript copyright © 1992 by the University Press of Mississippi
All rights reserved
Manufactured in the United States of America
95  94  93  92    4  3  2  1
The paper in this book meets the guidelines for permanence and durability of the Committee on Production Guidelines for Book Longevity of the Council on Library Resources.

*Library of Congress Cataloging-in-Publication Data*

Morris, Willie.
    The courting of Marcus Dupree / Willie Morris.
      p.   cm.
    Updated ed. of the work first published in 1983 by Doubleday.
    ISBN 0-87805-610-6. -- ISBN 0-87805-585-1 (pbk.)
    1. Dupree, Marcus.  2. Football players--United States--Biography.  3. Southern States--Social Conditions.   I. Title.
GV939.D86M67   1992
796.332'092--dc20
[B]                                                                                                   92-27510
                                                                                                           CIP

*British Library Cataloging-in-Publication data available*

*To David Halberstam,*
*Charles Henry,*
*and*
*Irwin Shaw*
*. . . who understand the eighty-yard runs*
*and*
*to Harold "Hardwood" Kelly,*
*my real coach through life*

# Contents

8               CONTENTS

# PREFACE

It has been ten years since my beloved Black Labrador Pete, long since departed to the Lord's infinite Heaven for the finest and bravest dogs, and I started going down to Neshoba County to follow Marcus in his senior season in high school. My old comrade and collaborator from our *Harper's Magazine* days, the writer David Halberstam, subversive as Socrates, had really been the instigator. On a visit to Mississippi from the East, he had said: "We've heard about Dupree in New York City. Do a magazine piece on him, Morris."

I signed to do 15,000 words with *Esquire.* Yet the more time I spent in Neshoba, the more I became immersed in the young man's unforgettable artistry, in his personal and family circumstances, in the vivid cast of people of all ages and races surrounding him: a veritable *melange* of modern Dixie and America in their individuality and flamboyance and contradiction. This was nothing if not serendipitous. Crucial, too, of course, was the seductive and obsessive character of Neshoba itself, a locale taut in its complexity and darkness and symbolism for America. Writers by the nature of the calling must husband their resources, for time is our enemy, and I did not know at the moment that the project would grow into a book and take almost two years of one's life.

I had ambivalent feelings then about this commitment, but in old time's retrospect I am glad I did it, for I learned much about my native ground after many years of being away from it, and about America, and about the horrific pressures placed by its society on the young Marcus Duprees.

Among other things, he was quite simply the greatest running back I and many others had ever seen. He was a funny, kind, complicated kid who happened to be black in Neshoba County, and he carried a big burden. But the old elusive tale, I pray, goes much deeper than that, which is why I hope the tale itself will survive beyond football and the 1980s in the Deep South.

On June 21, 1989, the twenty-fifth anniversary of the Neshoba killings, there was a memorial service at the Mount Zion Church, sponsored by the white, black, and Choctaw leaders of the community. The families of James Chaney, Andrew Goodman, and Michael Schwerner were there. Dick Molpus, the young Secretary of State of Mississippi, who was born and raised in the town, was one of the speakers. "We deeply regret what happened here twenty-five years ago," he said. "We wish we could undo it. We are profoundly sorry that they are gone. We wish we could bring them back. Every decent person in Philadelphia and Neshoba County feels that way."

We asked Billy Watkins of the *Clarion-Ledger* of Jackson, Mississippi, a personal friend of Marcus and a reporter of his legend, to provide a detailed postscript describing the events of Marcus's life after the narrative of this book closes, which he has done responsibly and with immense feeling, including his account of one of the most dramatic personal comebacks in the history of American sports, evocative in its own way of the movie *Brian's Song.*

Near the end of my book, in 1983, after Marcus's first year in college, I wrote:

> *And so the story of Marcus continued . . . And someday—I hope only in the infinitely distant future—his skills would fail him. Perhaps the way he coped with that would prove the final measure not of the boy, but of the man. He had not faced the half of it yet, the pain and discouragement. He was going to be with us for a long time— a name of our generation to be remembered. Perhaps through his struggle and hopes to fulfill his monumental promise, we Americans could understand much in ourselves.*

As athletes, as writers, as people, we all have much to cope with. This is our common strain as human beings, because we are all in it together and all in for a tough time. I shall stand by his greatness as a boy. I shall never forget him then, for he was magic. And I shall forever wish him well.

Willie Morris
Jackson, Mississippi
May 1992

# *The Courting of Marcus Dupree*

# 1
# *More Than Football Itself*

On this hot September night, Number 22 walked through the door of the gymnasium with his fifty or so teammates. He stood there beyond the end zone and waited with them to run onto the field. They were a small-town Mississippi football team.

The stadium behind the old brick high school was crowded with four thousand people. There was a pale quarter-moon on the horizon. A train whistle from the Illinois Central echoed across from Independence Quarters, and crickets chirped from a nearby hollow. The grass was moist from yesterday's rains.

He was big. He was carrying his helmet, which he put on now over a copious Afro haircut kept in place by a red hairnet. He was seventeen years old and he was wearing glasses.

A group of children had gathered near him, and a few dogs. "Get 'em, Marcus!" a little white boy shouted. He acknowledged this injunction with a slight wave of his hand. Under the helmet his glasses reflected the lights of the stadium.

From the grandstands the home band burst into an off-key fight song. The team sprinted onto the field through a large papier-mâché sign with the words "Go Tornadoes!" The crowd stood to cheer.

There was more behind his entrance on this night than football itself.

I had heard about him for many months, ever since I came back from the North to live in Mississippi. Going into his senior year, he was the most sought-after and acclaimed high school football player in America, a swift and powerful running back whom many were already comparing with the legendary Herschel Walker of Georgia. The town of his past and his people—Philadelphia, Mississippi, in Neshoba County—as in the Biblical sense certain places sometimes are, was suffused with its remembrance of self-destruction. Its history evoked for me as a Southerner those lines of Yeats:

> Mere anarchy is loosed upon the world,
> The blood-dimmed tide is loosed, and everywhere
> The ceremony of innocence is drowned;
> The best lack all conviction, while the worst
> Are full of passionate intensity.

His great-great-grandparents had been slaves, and he was born one month less a day before three young men, two New York Jews and a Mississippi black, were murdered seven miles from his birthplace and buried fifteen feet under an earthen dam. The two young whites had been shot once each in the heart with .38s, and the black had been shot three times. Their names were Michael Schwerner, Andrew Goodman, and James Earl Chaney. Their disappearance, along with the harassments, beatings, burnings, and mob cruelties—not only in that haunted summer of 1964 but in the months which followed—attracted the attention of the nation and the world and became a symbol of the entire civil rights movement and of the recalcitrance which greeted it. The names Lawrence Rainey and Cecil Price, the sheriff and deputy sheriff, would become inscribed on the national consciousness, just as in those days the names Bull Connor and Jim Clark had been, and Emmett Till, Rosa Parks, Medgar Evers, Ross Barnett. The town remained for a long time in the grip, as James Silver described them, of "anxious, fearful, marginal white men." The FBI inspector who led the investigations subsequently called the Neshoba Klavern of the White Knights of the Ku Klux Klan "one of the strongest Klan units ever gathered and one of the best disciplined groups." Neshoba County, he later observed, did not need a Klan, for the people were the most conspiratorial he had ever encountered, and Assistant United States Attorney General John Doar said that the town and the county had, for all practical purposes, closed ranks after the murders. Two years later, on the anniversary of the killings, Martin Luther King came to Philadelphia to give a sermon and to lead a memorial march. "This is a terrible town, the worst I've seen," he said. "There is a complete reign of terror here." Not long before his death, he said his visit to Philadelphia was one of only two times that he ever feared for his life.

An observer writing in 1964 would say that among all of Neshoba County's twenty thousand human beings, perhaps not many more than a hundred were capable of the planned murders of three unarmed young men, and of the officially organized domination of the town which these deliberate murders symbolized. But Reinhold Niebuhr, speaking for much of the American sentiment of the day, as Lyndon Johnson's Civil Rights

Act was being passed and before the great riots in the Northern cities, would indict a place in which "the instruments of justice are tools of injustice" and where "there are no limits to inhumanity, cruelty, and sheer caprice once social and communal restraints are no longer in force. Mississippi's standards can sink so low that only the legal and moral pressure of the larger community can redeem them—just as only the pressure of the British Commonwealth can save Northern Rhodesia from becoming another South Africa." And Hodding Carter III, along with his father a principal voice of racial moderation in the Deep South of that time, would write: "The FBI's records indicate that, on the whole, Mississippi is one of the most crime-free states in the nation. The brutality, the bombings, the terror, and the murders can be accurately attributed to the silence of good men, bound by a system which in the name of self-preservation dictated public toleration of the excesses of the vicious and the ignorant."

No moderate white leadership came forward in those hard days in Philadelphia and Neshoba. The dissenters were largely a handful of "ladies," in the Southern essence of that word, much like Miss Habersham in Faulkner's *Intruder in the Dust*, who out of her tenacious and indomitable Southern womanhood felt so strongly for justice that she would help a white and a black child rob graves at night to absolve a black man of murder. There were a few other dissident voices. The risks may have been high, but one is not sure *how* high. Few in the town seemed to have read or appreciated the dreadful nuances of our history—of slavery, the Civil War, Reconstruction, the Klan in the 1920s—and sensed the cadences of doom. It is not difficult, of course, to be brave from such a horrific remove, in time as well as geography, just as it is facile to misjudge the genuine anxieties of a local population over the organized integrationists, many of them outsiders, of the 1960s. Yet unlike Oxford, Mississippi, two years before, which was a university town and had its James Silvers and Duncan Grays in the wake of the James Meredith Riots, in Philadelphia there seemed to be no men of courage, but especially of *wisdom*, who would stand up for the larger community in the name of civilized values, indeed of civilization itself. Where were the Sartorises?

In the town's most agonized times, there were the few notable exceptions, particularly a forty-year-old woman named Florence Mars, descendant of one of the old and distinguished families of the town. She had attended Millsaps in Jackson, which Hodding Carter had called "the most courageous little college in America" because of its stands in the 1960s. After having lived elsewhere, she had come home to stay in 1962. She began raising Hereford cattle and owned the Neshoba County stockyards. She became active in the First Methodist Church, where she sang in the choir and taught a women's Sunday School class. "The church," she remembered, "offered the best hope as a moderating influence." In its moments of crisis she spoke out against what was happening to the town. The community began to regard her as a "Communist agitator," and the White Knights of the Klan succeeded in a boycott of her business. Later the LSU Press would publish her memoir, *Witness in Philadelphia.* "I learned . . . how Nazi Germany is possible in a 'law-abiding Christian society.' And I learned, too, that society will act against its own best interests to protect itself from the truth."

Turner Catledge, who was born and raised in Philadelphia, took his first newspaper job with *The Neshoba Democrat,* and later became managing editor of *The New York Times,* would write of his home:

> Our reporters told me that my friends and my relatives, although greeting them politely, would rarely discuss the murders with them. They closed ranks against outsiders. Worse, within the community few voices were raised to condemn the murders. The "good people" of the community were intimidated. They feared both physical violence and economic retaliation if they denounced the murders or the Klan, which was responsible for the murders. A friend in Philadelphia wrote me a long troubled letter several months after the murders, describing the atmosphere there. The local attitude, she said, was to cry "hoax" when the three civil-rights workers were said to be missing. And then "they asked for it," after their bodies were found. As newsmen flocked to the town, it came to see itself (not the dead men) as the "victim" of the affair, and to blame the news media for once again lying about the South. I was told that some of my old friends thought I had let the town down because of *The Times'* extensive coverage of the murders. But I felt the town had let me down. Or perhaps I had just expected too much.

Nearly three and a half years after the civil rights workers disappeared, eighteen men went on trial in federal court for conspiracy. They included the sheriff, the deputy sheriff, the former sheriff and sheriff-elect, a city policeman, and the Imperial Wizard of the White Knights of the Ku Klux Klan.

Gradually, almost imperceptibly in the years which followed, something would begin to stir in the soul of the town. A brooding introspection, a stricken pride, a complicated and nearly indefinable self-irony, all but unacknowledged at first, would emerge from its dreadful wounds. A long journey lay ahead, marked always by new aggrievements and retreats, yet this mysterious pilgrimage of the spirit would suggest much of the South and the America of our generation.

When Marcus Dupree was a child in the Independence Quarters section of the town, he began attending the Baptist church down the street from his house. It was called Mount Nebo. When he was eleven years old, a memorial was erected in front of his church to Schwerner, Goodman, and Chaney. Later, in 1982, as throughout Mississippi and the Deep South, his high school graduating class would be the first in which young whites and blacks had gone through all twelve grades together.

# 2

# *Red Hill Peregrinations*

I have always had a love for American geography, and especially for the landscapes of the South. One of my pleasures has been to drive across it, with no one in the world knowing where I am, languidly absorbing the thoughts and memories of old moments, of people vanished now from my life. It was no accident that in my thirties I developed a passionate romance with Haiti, for the images of that bewitched and tragic nation reminded me so intensely of the Mississippi of my childhood. As with many Southern writers, I believe that the special quality of the land itself indelibly shapes the people who dwell upon it.

Countless times over the next several months I would make the long drive, one hundred and twenty-five miles, from Oxford, in northeast Mississippi, to Philadelphia, which lies in the east-central part of the state. Amid the slow changing of the Dixie seasons, summer to autumn to winter into the earliest spring, I grew to regard the unique landmarks, the lineaments of the earth, the towns and villages along the way as one honors estimable companions. Often I would drive down alone. In those moments, all about me the sights and sounds of an isolated, rural, poor America that the fashions of this catastrophic age seem to have all but forgotten, I could sometimes, in a reverie, feel life tenderly slipping away, as in the words of a popular song I heard on the car radio one forenoon of a glorious October: "Time goes by so slowly, and time can do so much." Often I would travel there with Pete, my black Labrador, or with interesting and bizarre comrades going down to see Marcus play ball, who will inevitably be part of this narrative too.

The geographers call this region the North Central Hills or, more commonly, the red-clay hills. Going south out of Oxford, the land gradually changes from light orange to the deepest red I have ever seen—"the somnolent hills and indolent populace of East Mississippi," as a Neshoba writer once described the texture of these locales. All this is a long way from the Delta in the western part of the state, that rich alluvial flatland, licentious and reckless, where the big planters are still gamblers against the elements. Shelby Foote, a Deltan by birth and rearing, from the re-

markable river town of Greenville, had observed that people who live in
the Delta do not worry much about the future because the soil is so rich
—like Hawaiians, one would surmise, who, when they get hungry, reach
up and pull a pineapple off a tree. "Out in the hills of Mississippi you will
see people canning vegetables and doing all kinds of things looking forward to a hard winter. Down in the Delta they just go to the supermarket
and buy a can of beans." I grew up a Delta boy, and I recognize this everlasting dichotomy of the spirit. The hill country of Mississippi is impenitent and contained for me; its people are a little intimidated by the histrionics and the broad horizons of the more aristocratic Delta, although
they will dip over into the flatlands ever so often for the drinking, which
has forever been done with a ritualistic flair.

William Styron, who had been down to Mississippi on several visits,
especially to help bring in its riotous springtimes, always remarked on the
empty spaces, the vast skylines, the long stretches of nearly unpopulated
terrain, the dearth of movement on the roads. In its desolation and pride,
he said, it reminded him a little of Russia. The highway, State 9 and later
State 15 at Ackerman, forty miles or so north of Philadelphia, is two lanes
all the way from Oxford, an anomaly for traveling Americans accustomed
to their Interstates, and the journey itself is a trip into the Southern past.
The rugged, primitive hills sometimes soar to dizzying heights, then
stretch downward into low-lying valleys and bottomlands where the cotton, soybeans, and corn have always prospered, and the splendid pines
and hardwoods in both the hills and the bottoms lend a fine beauty to the
hard earth.

Among the many lessons I acquired from my heroic friend Ronnie
Dugger in our long-ago *Texas Observer* days, journeying as we did
across that phantasmagoric country in the young writer's calling, was how
to take notes while driving a car, the secret being to use the steering
wheel as a prop or, if you will, a makeshift desk, then rely on your periph-
eral vision. Dugger once claimed to have written a five-thousand-word
short story between Waxahachie and Austin, and once I myself perfected
this talent I saw little reason to disbelieve him. As the captain of a great
seagoing vessel would keep his log, I began jotting down, in an inchoate,
impressionistic kind of way, a small catalogue of the sights which greeted
me in these comings-and-goings, in the Oxford to Neshoba adventure. I
ask the reader to let me present just a few of them as I scribbled them, in
the moment's passionate observance:

"Barefoot black kids shooting baskets near unpainted houses" . . .
"Ruined shacks with rusty tin roofs under the shade of tall pines" . . .
"Old black man in mule-drawn wagon followed by several nondescript
dogs, one with three legs" . . . "Empty towns drowsing in summer sun—
97 degrees today" . . . "Young cotton blossoming in August—poor-look-

ing cotton to me" . . . "Loblolly pines along road as far as eye can see"
. . . "Sign says: 'Welcome to Choctaw County, Home of Cheryll Prewitt,
Miss America, 1980'" . . . "Crape myrtles along sleepy lanes" . . .
"Parched corn growing right up to Main Street" . . . "Little girls picking
apples" . . . "Country baseball field with chicken-wire backstop" . . . "I
think I just crossed Chickasaw-Choctaw nations' dividing line" . . . "Soy-
beans and kudzu turning yellow in early autumn. Colors deepening.
Golden-reds on roadside" . . . "Cotton bolls along road. More and more
truckfuls of cotton" . . . "Tombigbee Forest—dark and gloomy" . . .
"Negroes always waving at me" . . . "Whites wave too, all ages" . . .
"Tractors at 10 m.p.h., derelict pickups with junk in back and blinkers sig-
naling wrong way, log trucks of all sizes, 25 m.p.h., logs stacked haphazardly—hope they won't tumble off and crash into windshield" . . .
"Catfish restaurants—Mississippi's major industry?" . . . "Abandoned cars
on dusty front lawns—fine cars, too—check G. W. Carver quote" (I later
did. George Washington Carver, admonishing blacks of the Delta many
years ago to be good, frugal citizens: "I've seen Buick automobiles in the
yard of a house where you can study botany through the floor and astronomy through the roof.") . . . "Intersection with great Natchez Trace"
. . . "White women in print dresses in front of country church" . . .
"Unpainted dogtrots with wash on line, old washing machine on porch—
Walker Evans" . . . "All this could be two generations ago" . . . "Never
saw so many country dogs" . . . "Greyhound to Memphis takes up most
of road" . . . "Mississippi State football bumper stickers" . . . "No beer
signs since I left Yoknapatawpha" . . . "Downtown Eupora looks rugged"
. . . "I'm a long way from commuter express to Brewster out of Grand
Central" . . . "Service station sells fried chicken" . . . "What would ma-
tron (Calhoun City) staring in shoe-store window make of Fifth Avenue
shops? Hamptons boutiques?" . . . "Dead possum in middle of highway"
. . . "Gnarled old men whittling in shade of pecan tree (Pittsboro)" . . .
"More old people than young in towns" . . . "Fewer blacks than in Delta"
. . . "Shafts of sunlight on Skuna bottomland" . . . "Just saw two In-
dians on a tractor" . . . "This drive is lonesome . . ."

I remember one afternoon in particular. I had just passed a frame
cabin with smoke curling upward from the chimney on a brisk September
day, then a modest cotton field where a black family—the father and
mother and several little children—were picking cotton, the burlap sacks
of yesteryear draped over their shoulders, so that one small fellow seemed
at the mercy of the bag, which dragged along behind him as if in afterthought. One never sees this anymore, I reflected, this scene from my
childhood, with the mechanization that inspired the largest migration of a
people in the history of the human race. The family owned this cotton
patch and they were picking their own crop. The hill country cotton was

scraggly and impoverished, and this tableau of the family bending over it in the monumental old ritual, silhouettes against a darkening sky, reminded me in that instant of who I was, and where my people and I came from.

Suddenly, as I continued a little farther down the road, the very atmosphere began to change. Purple clouds descended. A terrific wind sprang up, followed by lightning and thunder. It was midafternoon, yet an ominous darkness enveloped the land. The sinister kudzu vines growing on the trees and telephone poles and almost onto the highway itself assumed ghostly shapes, making me remember James Dickey's horror poem about kudzu, where snakes "weave themselves among its lengthening vines" and killed cattle "as the vines, growing insanely, sent great powers into their bodies . . ." Then the rain came, in such torrents that the loblolly pines bordering each side of the road appeared as a dark, misty tunnel out to the horizon, swaying eerily in the wind and rain. I had to stop the car on the side of the road. With the next clap of thunder my dog Pete, who was on the backseat, jumped down and crouched on the floor, his large brown eyes seeming to ask: "What have you got us into this time, you old fool?" We were trapped hopelessly there in the stormy, claustrophobic gloom for a long time. I wrote in my notebook, the words in front of me now: "There are no halfway measures in *this* state."

The route of these scenes would take me through the little hardscrabble towns which, on these driftless journeys, would come to tug strangely at my heart . . . Paris, a lazy hamlet in southmost Lafayette County once noted for the difficulties it caused the federal voting-rights registrars, where one sees stacked firewood on the front porch of the post office, and where the old men play dominoes all day in a forsaken store. The Hollywood people liked to come here to film Faulkner locales, and here one afternoon, as I paused to borrow a little water for the engine of my car, an elderly farmer approached me and asked if I had seen his big red dog, named "Red," in fact, who had run away two days before. The man and I became engaged in a lengthy conversation, as strangers do in this society. He had fought with MacArthur in the Philippines. "I liberated that Manila," he said. "That damned Red may've run off to my cousins" . . . Bruce, a lumber-mill town on the Skuna River, which was not founded until the 1920s because of the timber . . . Pittsboro, a curious county-seat town, the tiny political capital of Calhoun County which a Baptist preacher once told me had the purest strain of Anglo-Saxon people in the world. The courthouse here actually resembles a warehouse, and in the post office across the road, where I once had reason to stop for a special-delivery stamp, the postmaster said: "I ain't got a single one. I ain't even been *asked* for one in two years" . . . Calhoun City, with the poignant sign of welcome at its outskirts, THE CITY WAITING FOR TOMORROW, its one-story businesses located around a large central square which, in the words of a local historian, "has been hopefully preserved since the town was laid out awaiting the time when Pittsboro will relinquish the county seat and courthouse." One of the businesses is a storefront chapel called The Manna Assembly of God . . . Bellefontaine, a crossroads hamlet once noted for its saloons, which the natives pronounce, of course, Bell Fountain . . . Walthall, another minuscule county seat, where the courthouse of Webster County looms suddenly in the middle of a field next to a half-collapsed house with a precarious tin roof . . . Eupora, a substantial town with wide streets and tawdry exteriors, once noted for its feuds and killings which might have put *Huckleberry Finn* to shame, and where, I learned after many nocturnal drives back to Oxford, the late-night boys hang about in T-shirts in front of a service station near the highway junction . . . Ackerman, an old sawmill and courthouse town, the Choctaw County seat, stretched out along the railroad tracks. There is an ancient railroad hotel by the courthouse, splendid with its broad front gallery, empty now and going slightly to decay, where one could picture William Jennings Bryan, played by Fredric March in galluses, swatting flies and drinking ice water and discoursing with the gentry while waiting for the train . . . Louisville, a hill-and-prairie town for farms and lumbering, seat of Winston County . . . and, finally, Noxapater with its desolate little main street, the hallowed village of the Choctaws, of their sacred Nanih Waiya, which that people look upon as the birthplace of their race. From here one traverses the stunningly red earth, past the small farms and distant ridges and pasturelands and rural settlements, on over the Pearl River into Neshoba County and Philadelphia, which, because of a seventeen-year-old black boy with eyeglasses who was six feet three and weighed 230 pounds, was to become, for a time, a home for me.

I came in a soft, still twilight of July. A large sign on a marquee in front of a store near the city limits greeted me:

SLAB BACON
WORMS
WHOLE HAMS

I had not been here in many years, ever since our baseball team came over from Yazoo City, ninety miles due west, to whip the locals. If memory served me, that was 1951, and I ambiguously recalled the town from that distance, enveloped in the red soil and perched at the crest of these vermilion hills, so different from the humming black earth of my Delta— a harsh-looking town as I remembered it from then. But now the residential streets in the central parts of town were more settled and prosperous than I had expected, and the Courthouse Square, as with many villages of the Deep South of our day, had a tidier, less raw aspect than a generation ago. The Square was largely deserted at this hour, its façades caught in the orange of the sunset, and two sizable water towers, not far away from the Square itself, were darkly outlined against the sky.

I got out to walk around. The courthouse itself, which had once been the suzerainty of Sheriff Rainey, was more modern than most Mississippi courthouses, having been built, the cornerstone informed me, in 1928—a solid structure of red brick with two fairly contemporary wings. At each corner of its lawn was a magnolia, and on the northeast side was the monument to the Old Confederacy, towering above the greensward, the marble comrade in uniform gazing from his pedestal northward across Beacon Street. The inscription in the stone said:

1861–1865

Love's Tribute to the Noble Men Who Marched
'Neath the Flag of the Stars and Bars, and
Were Faithful to the End.

C.S.A.
Our Heroes

The names under the words—Yates, Salter, Gamblin, and others—were names I would come to know in the town.

Three young Choctaw men wearing football jerseys emerged from their car and disappeared around the block. Some old black men from the back of a pickup without a muffler waved at me. Several teenage girls sat chatting away on the hood of a Riviera in front of a drugstore, and I knew it was a daddy's car. A boy their age came to a screeching halt; their exuberant greetings echoed back to me. That had not changed, I thought. The sound of the crickets filled the lingering dusk, and the mournful call of a train whistle reverberated from down the hill.

I tarried around the Square. On the north side the sidewalks and the buildings were much higher than the street. Mr. Herbert Garrett of the town would later explain this for me: "Back in the wagon days, groceries and feed were stacked out on the sidewalk with the person's name on them. Then when they were ready to leave town, the wagon was brought from the wagon yard, where Dees Department Store now is, and the merchandise was loaded on the sidewalk, being the same height of the wagon, and the barrels of flour, feed, et cetera, would be loaded up without having to be lifted up." This made eminently good sense to me, and the elevated structures which survived gave now to the Square in the shadowy light a patina of the older days. It was a working courthouse square:

Robinson Sporting Goods, the Patio Ice Cream Parlor and Sandwich Shoppe, Cato, Seward's, House of Fashion, Kenwin on the north side; J. C. Penney, Thompson Drugs, David Lee's, Busby's Jewelry on the west; on the east, Ben Franklin (quartered in the old dull gray Masonic Temple, but now sadly bereft, for the sign said it had gone out of business), Hamill Drugs, City Jewelry, T.W.L., Mars Brothers ("Since 1892") Department Store; and on the south, the Bank of Philadelphia, Yates Drugs, Clark's, and Turner Hardware, the latter with its display: "Limited Time Only. 12 Mo. Free Financing on Shotguns and Rifles."

As I drove about the languid summer streets, Poplar Avenue came before me quite by happenstance, and in a rush it evoked my own past for me. Almost every substantial small town in Mississippi has a Poplar Avenue. In Greenwood it is Grand Boulevard, in Yazoo City it is Grand Avenue, in Oxford it is North and South Lamar, the graceful thoroughfares of the old money, of the progeny of the settled mercantile class, which may yet outlast the new subdivisions at the edges of town with their sprawling ranch-style establishments. These are the streets for the fortunate white children of the South to grow up on, to "play out," as we once called it, in the dew-wet grass, pursuing the phantoms of summer nights. The turn-of-the-century houses with the big porches and verandas and rocking chairs and swings, the dark foliage and the forests of crape myrtles, the children barefoot on the lawns with the lightning bugs in random drift, were a chord in the memory. So was Holland Avenue, paralleling Poplar, with the same rococo multistory houses, including one of the most impressive Victorian dwellings I had seen in the lower South. It belonged to the father-in-law of Archie Manning, the fabulous quarterback, I would later be informed.

But the town, of course, would not all be Poplars and Hollands. Along most of the streets in the white section were the more unprepossessing bungalows and brick ranch houses, many of them with late-model pickup trucks in the driveways. Farther out would be the latter-day subdivisions, the enclaves and cul-de-sacs with the luxurious modern houses, a large number of them owned, I was to learn, by the more recent arrivals, the executives of local industries.

It was a town for trains. The railroad tracks were only a few blocks from the Square, and people sat and waited in the long lines of cars while the interminable diesel freights and flatbeds stacked with logs moved laboriously by. A young man of Philadelphia would advise me that when the teenage couples started dating and went out to park behind the Episcopal Church or at the dead end of the Woodland Hills Subdivision, the boy would bring the girl home late and tell her parents they had been waiting for a train to pass. This was precisely our kind of deception too, in the Yazoo of a generation ago, which had the same long trains in the best part of town. I waited now as an Illinois Central Gulf whose caboose may have just been leaving New Orleans rumbled past. I gazed about me. This part of Philadelphia had an unsettled, countrified appearance, a feel of the authentic boondocks, and the men drifting in and out of a coffee and hamburger place wore blue jeans and khakis, T-shirts and plaid shirts, work boots and tractor caps, and their women wore simple dresses and had distrusting eyes. The domain of the subsistence farmers, of the plain little wooden houses and mobile homes, of the swamplands and the pine and oak forests and the unrelenting red earth, which I would grow to comprehend profoundly over the next months, as if I did not know it already in my soul, was not very far from the Poplar and Holland avenues. Like a Roman outpost in ancient Gaul, the town was enclosed, physically and in the spirit, by the old basic and inchoate elements of life, of suspicion and survival, fear and toil, hope and longing. Civilization is precarious everywhere, I know, but here, as in so much of the small-town South, the vivid contrasts of a fragile human nexus encompassed by the imponderables of the Old Testament would grow more and more palpable for me.

I continued my drive in the fading light, swinging around town as the unknown interloper. Families sat on front porches; young men and women gathered around the ubiquitous pickup trucks in the shopping-center parking lots. The neon beer signs were everywhere. Youngsters of the high school age, white and black, were congregating about the Pizza Hut. There was a baseball game at the Northside Park. At the A&J drive-in of the Valley View Shopping Center, there must have been the beginnings of a party, for a large-breasted girl in her twenties wearing a "Coors Country" shirt had reached into the back of a pickup and was passing a gallon jug among her companions. I admired their shouts and laughter and wondered if this were a concoction of the famous Neshoba moonshine.

Once again I found myself at the Square, for all the roads led to it, as if by simple magnetism alone it had survived, as some town squares of the South had not, the encroachment of shopping centers. I made the right onto Byrd Avenue, past the Downtown Motor Inn, actually the old, refurbished hotel of the town, just a block off the Square. It would soon become as familiar to me as my bungalow on the Ole Miss campus in Oxford. Much football drama would subsequently transpire in the Downtown, for Marcus would be discussed and bartered here, although in that moment I could not have predicted it.

There, not far beyond the Downtown Hotel, was the high school, a meandering two-story red brick structure at the rise of a hill, across from a little bakery called The Fillin' Station. I respected its location in such proximity to the focus of life, only two blocks off the Square, unlike so many modern high schools of the South, which had been situated in the farthest reaches of the new suburbias. I strolled down to the football field. It seemed carved right out of the earth and was one of the most attractive, in a functional sort of way, I had ever seen; it had the feel to it of an amphitheater. The gymnasium and field house were set slightly behind the south end zone, and beyond the north goalpost, where the land inclined sharply downward, was a serene cluster of pines and elms and oaks and sassafras. Dogs howled from a dark hollow immediately to the west of the field; even these frisky hybrid country dogs I would subsequently get to know. On the home side a large grandstand of concrete blocks, some twelve rows high with an undersized press box in the middle, stretched from end zone to end zone, curving inward to the south; directly behind it was one of the brick outbuildings of the school with a sign on it which said Go Tornadoes! sponsored by Dr. Pepper. On the opposite side were three sets of open bleachers. Even this early they were getting ready, for several water-sprinklers were dampening the dark-green turf. I stood there in the grandstand in the preternatural quiet, remembering the football field of my own boyhood, the misbegotten mayhem and glory.

There was just enough light for another drive, for there was a section of the town I had yet to see. Across the tracks to the northwest, near Railroad Avenue, I moved toward it as if by instinct, out of the primal inheritance of my upbringing, and I knew from the same impulses that I would be drawn back here time without number. Why?

Independence Quarters. The sights and sounds and smells enveloped me, recognizable as my own heartbeat. There was the row upon row of dilapidated shacks, some collapsed and abandoned, others peopled by hordes of the young and old. The old ones sat on the sagging porches, on the steps or in straight-backed chairs, while children played on the dusty lawns, swinging from tires roped to the branches of trees, scrambling on and off the fenderless cars. There was high laughter, and music from some of the houses, and the aroma of cooking, and wash on the fences, chickens and dogs in the yards and on the roads, little vegetable gardens out in back, basketball hoops on the trees, tiny cemeteries with flowers on the graves. Old women shuffled along a lane which ran by the sawmill, the logs stacked high up to the sides of the road, sprinklers spraying the logs with water. Ever so often, in the middle of a line of shacks, one or more inviting new brick houses would come into view. Sometimes several of the bright new houses would stand out in their enclaves, then yield once again to the ruined, unpainted exteriors. I sighted the Jesus Saves Temple, and then the Jerusalem Temple where, I was to learn, people wailed, rolled on the floors, and spoke in tongues, and could be heard from a long way off.

Over on "The Hill," the little business district of the Quarters, a notice was nailed to a tree:

BIG CARD GAME AT GUYS AND DOLLS
THURSDAY NIGHT
$1.00 A COUPLE

And in front of Connor and Willis, another hand-painted sign:

GAS
BREAD
MILK
OIL AND GREASE JOB

My directionless ride took me down silent, gloomy lanes with only the deserted shipwrecks of houses, then without warning onto brightly lit streets with crowds of people of all ages moving about everywhere. I drove by the Green Grocery and Barber Shop, the Latimer Metropolitan Funeral Home, the Guys and Dolls Amusement Center, and the Busy Bee Grocery and Record Shop, where dressed-up young blacks smoking cigarettes loitered about a marquee with the words:

BUSY BEE OVER THE HILL GANG
SAYS GOOD LUCK MARCUS DUPREE!

Nighttime had descended. It was a little cooler than it had been. I paused in front of a square two-story brick establishment down from the Busy Bee. It was boarded and empty. My gaze was drawn to a faded wooden sign hanging high from the front: it said COFO, and, under the letters, a white and a black hand were clasping one another.

Farther north, on Carver Avenue and beyond, the scene abruptly changed. This was a substantial neighborhood of modern dwellings, block after block of them, with blacks milling about in front and men mowing their lawns. They were federally subsidized units, I would learn, and were as pleasing as many of the houses I had seen in the other parts of town. Not far from here I came upon a recreation area, which a sign identified as the Westside Community Center, with a swimming pool, a large central building, and a park with a lighted baseball field. A game was being played here also. Across the road was another cemetery, with seven or eight new graves among the older ones decorated with artificial wreaths.

I looped south once more. Four barefooted young boys were lazily throwing a football in an empty field. Several men sat in a circle on the ground under a tree. I turned onto Davis Street. My headlights illuminated a mailbox, and on it the words: REV. MAJOR DUPREE. It was a simple frame house, white in green trim, with a refrigerator on the porch and a young magnolia in the front yard, and English vine, schefflera, and red princess along the sides. The lights were on and an old man was sitting with a little boy holding crutches on the front steps.

Only a hundred yards or so from here, I made a left again onto Carver. On the corner was a modest brick building—the Mount Nebo Missionary Baptist Church. My lights caught another object in front. I sensed what it might be, and I parked the car and got out to examine it. The monument was about three feet high and five or six feet long, slightly obscured by a chicken-wire fence. Three crudely retouched portraits stared out at me, and under each the inscriptions:

ANDREW GOODMAN             JAMES EARL CHANEY
Nov. 23, 1943                      May 30, 1943
June 21, 1964                      June 21, 1964

MICHAEL H. SCHWERNER
Nov. 6, 1939
June 21, 1964

There are thirteen Philadelphias in the United States. They mean, of course, cities of "brotherly love." There are Philadelphias in New Mexico, Virginia, New York, Illinois, Indiana, and Missouri. There are two in Arkansas and three in Tennessee. Philadelphia, Mississippi, was the second largest, next to the one in Pennsylvania. Its population in 1981 was 6,434, with 1,832 blacks, roughly 28 percent of the total, most of whom lived in the Quarters. The names on the storefronts and in the telephone book, which contained forty-two pages, suggested pristine Anglo-Saxon blood, but this was deceptive, for, in truth, it was a town of three races—white, black, and Indian. More than four thousand Choctaws, descendants of the warriors who in 1830 refused to relinquish their land to the United States Government and migrate to the Oklahoma Territory, resided within a forty-mile radius. About fifteen hundred lived on a reservation six miles from the Square; they contributed an exotic diversity to the passing scenes of the town. Among the Anglo-Saxons there had been considerable intermarrying ever since these intrepid pioneers and their families arrived in the early nineteenth century from Alabama, Georgia, and the Carolinas; even into the late twentieth century there were many blood relationships, so that, as one citizen would advise me, "You have to be pretty careful what you say about people."

The town and county derived sustenance from organized religion, which was both tenacious and manifold. There were, in 1981, no less than thirty-two Baptist churches in Neshoba County, six Churches of God, six Pentecostal, four Catholic, four Methodist, three Presbyterian, two Latter-

Day Saints, and one Church of Christ, Assembly of God, Mennonite, and Episcopal. Having read Walker Percy's *The Second Coming,* in which the protagonist was concerned that all the Jews were leaving North Carolina, I once asked a friend how many Jewish people there were in Philadelphia.

He thought for a moment. "Well, none," he finally said.

"Not one?" I asked.

"Not one I can think of, and *I'd* know. Hell, we only have about fifty Episcopalians."

Florence Mars, writing of the 1920s, had observed that the prospects of hell were so horrible that an inordinate number of people in Neshoba County considered themselves to be saved. "There was an oft-repeated saying that 'a Methodist is a Baptist who has learned to read; a Presbyterian is a Methodist who has moved to town; and an Episcopalian is a Presbyterian who has gotten rich.' There were no Episcopalians in Neshoba County and, literate or not, there were far more Baptists than members of all other denominations combined." This was approximately true, also, of the Yazoo of my boyhood.

As with many small towns in Mississippi and the lower South, with their promise of a benign climate, cheap labor, and the absence of unions, Philadelphia since the 1950s had lured a number of big factories. U.S. Electrical Motors, a division of Emerson, came in 1962 and grew from an original fifty employees to more than seven hundred. Wells Lamont, which produced cotton gloves, arrived in 1966, followed by Richardson and then Garan, plants which made battery equipment and sportswear. Fifty-six percent of the county was forest land, and the whistles from the lumber mills swept across the town almost as frequently as the more basso horns from the Illinois Central. In 1966 Weyerhaeuser bought out the A. DeWeese Lumber Company, a homegrown industry which had been founded by the legendary entrepreneur Ab DeWeese in 1897. Half the timber processed by Weyerhaeuser came from small private landowners. Molpus, a large privately owned lumber company, began as a lumber yard in 1905, with the coming of the first railroad, and grew steadily; it opened a huge hardwood mill in 1969. Weyerhaeuser, Molpus, and the others sent out 74 million board feet of lumber every year. More than it ever had been, Philadelphia in 1981 was a blend of farm and factory, the older, intransient South merging subtly with the imperatives, and the dislocations, of the new. The small farms had traditionally been at the core of its rather torpid, insular values—the cotton, corn, and soybeans, and later the cattle-raising—and many of its young over the years, the whites, that is, were seldom prone to leave. In the later times, however, more than a few of its graduates had migrated to Jackson, eighty miles to the west, or to the Gulf Coast, a hundred and fifty miles south, to work for six hundred dollars a month on the oil rigs. "But it's funny," a home expert once said to me over catfish in the restaurant of the Downtown Hotel, "almost all of them seem to come back sooner or later. This town stirs up strange loyalties."

The feeble national economy of our day would take its toll in Philadelphia. During one of my many sojourns there U.S. Motors laid off 135 of its 700 workers, citing "the lower sales in the electric motor industry." Weyerhaeuser discharged a substantial number of wage and hour employees because of the high interest rates and the dubious housing market. Unemployment figures for the county in the early months of 1982 would fluctuate between 12 and 20 percent.*

Here are a few rather idle things I would learn about Philadelphia:

Everyone knew everyone's business.

The young country people favored a drink called "jungle juice" made from the moonshine.

It was a town of jazzy pickup trucks, and pickup trucks without mufflers. The bumper stickers said: GOD BLESS JOHN WAYNE, BULLDOG BLITZ, HONK IF YOU LOVE JESUS, and CAUTION WHEN PASSING—DRIVER CHEWS TOBACCO.

The high school girls drove fine cars.

There was some homegrown marijuana; cocaine had been inhaled in direst secrecy.

The nearest bar was Ed's Beer Joint, eighteen miles away, approximately ten inches across the Lauderdale County line. The nearest liquor store was in Meridian, thirty-six miles south.

It was a sports town, especially for football. Among its graduates had been Blondy Black, the all-American halfback for the Mississippi State Bulldogs in 1940, and Randy Griffin and Steve Breland of State; Bill Richardson, Frank Trapp, Jim Parkes, Larry Thomas, and Jim Haddock of the Ole Miss Rebels; Bobby Posey and Pat Green of the Southern Mississippi Golden Eagles; Alex Dees of the Memphis State Tigers; and Bill Greenleaf of the Delta State Statesmen.

Its celebrated Neshoba County Fair was the oldest county fair in the United States. It was held in rare pride and affection. This backwoods bacchanalia and political jamboree was one of the most unusual events in the nation. The home people were gratified when the *National Geographic* ran a handsome spread on the Fair in 1980. It was the first time in many years that an article on Philadelphia, Mississippi, had appeared in a national publication without once referring to "The Troubles."

* Among the 82 counties of Mississippi, the poorest state in the nation, Neshoba County with its 23,789 people ranked thirty-fourth in per capita income at $5,868. The percentage of families below the poverty level was 18.9. The average teacher's salary was just over $11,400.

# 3
# *The Marcus Legend*

---

Years ago in London, in a pub in Chelsea after the Oxford-Cambridge rugby match, a literary chap from Williams College pointedly asked me: "What's it like in Mississippi? Why do they live there? Why do they live at all?" In the course of the evening, my righteous *convive* discussed in singular detail the bread-and-circuses of ancient Rome. "The match we just witnessed was in some degree an expression of civilization," he suggested, "but football down in your part of the country is a device to detract people from your problems."

The exact idiom of my reply will not be recorded here. Yet one learns much about a place from its bread-and-circuses, which can be of both symbolic and substantive interest. I have often discovered myself viewing the grand and golden spectacles of football as a metaphor for the larger society, especially in the South. "In the East, college football is a cultural exercise," Marino Casem, the venerable coach at Alcorn State University, known to many as "The Black Godfather of Mississippi," observed. "On the West Coast, it is a tourist attraction. In the Midwest, it is cannibalism. But in the South it is religion, and Saturday is the holy day." Much the same held true for the high school football of our region and, especially in those towns where the racial integration of the public schools had worked well, Friday night was still, as it was in my boyhood, the holy *night*. Often on these pages I find myself pondering the remarkable importance which the rituals of the sport had for the people of Dixie, not as the flamboyant Williams College misanthrope might judge them, but rather as an observer of the human adventure, with an eye out, I trust, for the ironic and picturesque detail and for the shadow behind the act. "Football is like sex," a college football coach's wife once confided to me. "They both bring intense relief."

The Marcus Legend, if I may call it that, was already flourishing when I came back home from my village by the sea on eastern Long Island in 1980. People were talking about him all over Mississippi. Clyde Goolsby, the black bartender in our favorite saloon in Oxford and the most powerful man in town because, like Nick Carraway in *The Great*

*Gatsby*, he was privy to the secret griefs of wild, unknown men, was the first to mention him to me. "Have you heard of that Du*pree?*" he asked, more a challenge than a query. Subsequently I would hear him discussed in the Governor's Mansion in Jackson, Doe's Eat Place in Greenville, the lobby of the Peabody in Memphis, the Revolving Table at the hotel in Mendenhall, the Delta National Bank in Yazoo City, and an ambiguous establishment now mercifully defunct called the Chit-Chat near Catfish Row in Vicksburg. A couple of months after my confrontation with Clyde Goolsby, I found myself at the bar of the nightclub in the Sheridan Hotel in Baton Rouge, Louisiana, where the New South rushed upon me from all quarters—the plastic decor, the gurgling fountains, the polyester suits, the garish lighting, the mod-country music. Had William Tecumseh Sherman walked in, I would have given him a box of matches. I started a conversation with an immaculate young black fellow sipping an immense strawberry daiquiri at the next stool. He turned out to be the proprietor of four funeral homes in the neighborhood. He had inherited them from his father. Business was good despite the recession, he said. He had just bought $25,000 in new equipment.

"What kind of equipment?"

"Oh, you know—the standard stuff."

My curiosity momentarily flagged.

"Where are you from?" he asked.

"Mississippi."

"Say—where's that Du*pree* goin' to college?"


Entering his senior year, in September of 1981, he was considered by many the best high school football player ever to play in Mississippi; if so, that would embrace a notable roster. Others were judging him the finest high school player in the United States. An efficacious prophet named Joe Terranova, the most highly respected source of information on college football recruiting in the country, had already named him the supreme prospect in America. "I've seen a lot of recruiting lists, and every one of them starts with him," one college scout said, adding in the volatile parlance of his trade: "He's got it all. He's *numero uno*. He's a franchise. Every major college in America will be camped on his doorstep before we write *finis*." *Inside the Blue Chips*, a Zoroaster among national football recruiting publications, ran his picture on its front cover early in 1981, and published this cryptic assessment:

> Marcus Dupree is without doubt the number one player in the United States. His size, 6'3", 222, and 4.3 speed are simply amazing . . .

His average per carry is almost 13. Still Dupree's greatest ability may be as a kick returner. Last year he returned five kicks, four of which went for touchdowns. Some scouts describe him as a somewhat more elusive Herschel Walker.

Running backs wear what are called "tear-away jerseys," made of a fragile fabric which rips off easily. In his junior year, when Philadelphia was playing an aggressive team from New Hope, a big consolidated country school near the Alabama line, he swept around right end for about twenty yards. Several New Hope players finally maneuvered him out of bounds. One of the defenders grasped his jersey on the play. Part of it tore off, and the enemy defender tossed the shred of red cloth onto the ground. Then, on reflection, he retraced his steps, picked it up, and put it down the front of his pants, presumably as a relic. White children of prominent families in town would have similar remnants of his tear-away jerseys displayed on the walls of their rooms. One white girl in junior high school dispatched a message to him that she wanted a sliver of one of those torn jerseys, and he sent it to her by a water boy. One of his most memorable plays, as a town alderman would describe it for me, occurred in his sophomore year. He took a kick on his own forty-yard line, moved left to the fifty, was trapped near the sidelines, then circled back to his thirty. The hapless defenders, as they grabbed at him, came up with handfuls of his jersey. Finally, as he raced down the opposite sideline for a touchdown, he did not have a jersey left, only his shoulder pads. Those tear-away jerseys, in fact, would hurt the team on occasion, for he would be on the sidelines changing in critical situations. One of the opposing coaches, I was told, had even admitted that it was part of his strategy or "game plan," as football tacticians and old Watergaters called it, to encourage his players to tear off Number 22's jerseys as often as possible.

People outside Neshoba County began to hear of him in 1979 when he was a freshman. He was clocked in the hundred-yard dash in 9.5 and the forty in 4.4; he weighed 210 pounds. Archie Manning, the quarterback with the New Orleans Saints of professional football, was visiting Philadelphia, his wife's hometown. He started playing catch with a big black boy wearing glasses. "He'd just gotten out of the ninth grade," the irrepressible Archie would remember. "I asked him if he'd catch a few long passes. Then he timed me in the forty and I timed him. He ran a 4.6 in blue jeans and tennis shoes." There was a famous photograph in the Mississippi papers in the spring of that year. The fourteen-year-old from Philadelphia was in the finals of the hundred-yard dash in the state track meet. A young man named Calvin Smith, a senior in high school from the town of Bolton, won the championship with a time of 9.3, the fastest time by a high school runner in Mississippi history. The photograph showed the youngster from Philadelphia being nipped at the wire, finishing second to Calvin Smith by inches.*

As a freshman Marcus had played split end on the football team and scored twelve touchdowns. Seven of these were on kickoff or punt returns, including a seventy-five-yard return for a touchdown the first time he touched a football in a high school game. He moved to running back as a sophomore, when he rushed for 1,850 yards and scored twenty-eight touchdowns. In his junior season he gained 1,550 yards and scored twenty times. Philadelphia, a single-A school in the state's four-bracket system, finished that season undefeated and was chosen number one in Mississippi by the Jackson papers. He was selected to both the *Playboy* and *Parade* magazine all-American teams, the only high school junior named to either, and to the Adidas All-American team; he was named Football Player of the Year in Mississippi.

Now, beginning his senior year, as a weight lifter he could bench press 360 pounds, squat 600, and dead lift 700, and these were portentous statistics for someone whose expertise was running with a football. His high school coach was telling the outlanders who were sojourning in Neshoba County in behalf of various universities noted for taking an interest in such matters that he had lost very little speed with his added size. He had also successfully performed for three years in basketball, baseball (he was first baseman and catcher, and hit .481 his sophomore year) and, of course, track, in which he not only did the sprints but long-jumped twenty-three feet.

As the '81 season began, the sports people of Neshoba were swift to remind the outsider that Number 22's statistical achievements would have been even more notable were it not for the arcane matter of punts and kickoffs. Even the black undertaker from Plaquemine, drinking his strawberry daiquiri in that New South *milieu,* had apprised me of this egregious injustice. In his sophomore year, at age fifteen, he had become virtually impossible to defend on punts and kickoff returns. Opposing coaches had begun to confront this truth, and soon they were dealing with the problem. They ordered out-of-bounds punts and shallow kickoffs, or mean little "squib" kicks which bounced harmlessly across the grass like summer bugs against a fluorescent light. In his sophomore year the Tornadoes, having won nine games and lost only two, were invited to compete in the Mississippi Bowl against a superior team from Pearl. The Pearl Pirates built up a three-touchdown lead and, intoxicated perhaps by the alacrity of this margin, decided at that juncture to challenge the young halfback with an authentic kickoff. When he returned it ninety-five yards for a touchdown, the Pirates once more reverted to the vainglorious

* Calvin Smith was destined, as a sprinter for the University of Alabama in 1983, to break the world's record in the 100 meters at 9.93 seconds.

"squib." In his junior year he fielded only five kickoffs, returning four for touchdowns, a fifth touchdown having been called back by an infraction.

There was another heroic challenge in view. After his three high school years, he had recorded sixty touchdowns. That Herculean presence, Herschel Walker, who had played for the high school in Wrightsville, Georgia, had scored eighty-six career touchdowns. Marcus Dupree, who already felt intensely competitive with Walker, would need twenty-seven touchdowns in the 1981 season to break his impressive high school record. With a young and inexperienced offensive line in front of him, and with his reputation eliciting the most fierce aggressions from rival tacklers seeking a small piece of history, this quest would prove arduous and dramatic, culminating subsequently in one of the most impassioned athletic events I had ever witnessed.

Haphazardly at first, I began keeping a file from the papers in the summer before the '81 season. John Williams, the football coach at Mississippi College, had seen Marcus play several times. "I don't believe we've ever had a bigger, faster kid come out of this state," he said. "The thing that impressed me was the three or four passes he caught in one game I saw. He's got the good hands to go along with everything else." Tom Goode, an assistant coach at Ole Miss, said, "He's not as fast as Herschel Walker but he's bigger. He's not as big as Earl Campbell but he's faster. He's in that category." Johnny Draper, his offensive backfield coach at Philadelphia, admitted he sometimes had trouble directing such "God-given talents," as he called them:

> He's so fast that we have to tell him to hold back when he gets the ball so the holes can open up on the line. But when he gets into the secondary and into the open field, you can get ready to hear that scoreboard jingle. Not many people can stop him. As far as I can tell, he has no weaknesses. He can run, catch, block, and throw the ball sixty yards on the option. He'd make a great quarterback, but we think we'd be wasting him there. There's no question he's got more potential, in terms of raw ability and instinct, than any back in the state in high school and college that I've seen recently. Really, we don't know how good he is yet, and neither does he.

From my seclusion in Oxford, languishing in the first Deep Southern summer I had known in years and working on other things, I found myself ineluctably drawn to the accomplishment and promise of the young man, not to mention the tortured locale which had produced him. In my idle moments, gleaning and gathering like a squirrel, I continued to accumulate my dossier from the press. Long before I saw him play or got to know him, however, I began to fret over the perfervid words about him, and particularly the comparisons some of his more intractable advocates were making with Georgia's Herschel Walker, who was surely the greatest runner to emerge in college football in a generation, and whom many considered the best ever to have played the college game. Some of the words would remind me later of the storm in which my dog Pete and I were trapped in one of those journeys to Neshoba—for in rhetoric, as in most other things, nothing truly was ever done halfway in this state. It struck me that a considerable burden was being placed on a small-town black boy who had barely turned seventeen. This mood coincided with the observations of one Tony Misita, a former coach at Ole Miss who had recently moved to Tulane, identified in the clippings as "an eighteen-year observer of Southern football talent":

> I think that would be putting too much pressure on him, to say that somebody could do what Herschel Walker has done in two years. Well, I don't know if *anybody* can ever be another Herschel Walker.
> But I'll say this: Marcus Dupree has all the potential in the world. He's got the body of a Cadillac—now all he has to do is turn the key. But it won't be easy. Big-time college football figures to be a lot tougher than the caliber of competition he's been going against in high school. The kids he's been going against aren't the best—they aren't the worst either —but college is a whole other story.

Still, the litany was so impressive that I began talking around with a few people. Billy Watkins was the young sports editor of the *Star* in Meridian, the closest large city to Philadelphia. He and his staff covered the sports of the whole southern and east-central sections of Mississippi, as well as the college games. Billy Watkins had kept hearing about the running back from Neshoba, so he drove over in 1980 to see for himself. He arrived just in time for the kickoff, which Dupree forthwith returned for a touchdown. At a later game that season, Watkins was standing on the sidelines with Joe Wood, the Philadelphia head coach. Philadelphia had the ball on its own twenty-yard line. Wood sent in a play, then turned to Watkins and said, "This oughta go for a TD." "It was a simple off-tackle handout," Watkins remembered. "And he scored. An eighty-yard run. How often do you see *that?*"

We were sitting in the deserted newsroom of the *Star* on a late summer afternoon, and as we talked Watkins grew more and more ebullient. "I tell our readers we've got a kid thirty miles from here that they'll hear about the rest of their lives. It's hard to write about him because people are gonna say *nobody's* that good." He tossed his head to stress a point. "If he gains just ten yards with five men on him, it's a disappointment. People think he's *got* to score. He's the kind of player you have to see to believe how good he is. The main knock on him now is that he plays against small schools. But I've been covering Big Eight football for years —those are the biggest high schools in Mississippi, you know—and I've never seen a Big Eight player who could touch him."

This perception was to be confirmed by the Mars Boys, James and Daniel, two brothers from Philadelphia who were attending the Ole Miss Law School that summer. Their father was Mont Mars, a lawyer in Philadelphia, and they were cousins to Florence Mars, who had stood up to the Klan in 1964; the Mars family were the Sartorises of Neshoba County. James was a year older than Daniel, and they had graduated from high school in the late 1970s. Both had played football. "James was solid," a friend of theirs had advised me. "He was at his best when he was pissed off. Dan could knock you senseless. He was the fastest white boy we had." These were no dilettantes, then, whom I invited to my cottage on the wooded fringes of the campus for beer one August evening.

"He's the greatest football player I ever saw," Daniel said, with the mystical authority of an expert authenticating the bones of a medieval saint.

"In my opinion," James said, "nobody one-on-one in an open field can stop him. When he gets going, just say goodbye."

"I've seen him come at two players almost next to each other and make a move right between 'em," Daniel said. "Everybody's mad when he only gains five or six yards. People get mad when he doesn't score. Right now Herschel Walker and Earl Campbell are the best running backs in the country. If he had their blockers, he's got as much talent to be just as good."

Against the Union Yellowjackets the previous year, my young companions told me, he broke into the open on a run. Three players hit him on the fifty-yard line and bounced off. Two others tried to tackle him a little later and failed. Then he ran over the referee and went on to score. Against the Winona Tigers during the same season, a teammate lateraled to him on a kickoff. He was trapped by several players on the sidelines at about the twenty. He reversed the entire width of the field and scored without anyone touching him.

In that lingering twilight on the Ole Miss campus, the ardor of the Mars Boys was contagious. Even my dog Pete, who was a courteous listener, got up and stretched and began moving about, as if he himself were ready to return a kickoff against the loathsome Winona Tigers.

Both James and Daniel were members of the Pi Kappa Alpha fraternity at Ole Miss. Marcus had come up for the spring football game the previous year and they took him to the Pike house afterward for a social. "People were all over him," James said. "Tree and Michael were there also."

The reference, I learned, was to Tree McAfee and Michael Smith, two black football players from Philadelphia who, having graduated the year before, had been given scholarships at Ole Miss and were about to begin their freshman season. They were Marcus Dupree's best friends.

"Did Ole Miss give Tree and Michael scholarships to lure Marcus here next year?" the disenchantment of my brushes with Texas politics led me to ask.

"Well, they're good players," Daniel said. "Some people think that, of course. The three of them have been working out back home this summer."

"Michael and Marcus are more introverted than Tree," James said. "Tree's really a good talker. If you see the three of them together, Tree will go on and on. Michael will be very polite. Marcus will look at the ground and not say anything."

"Marcus won't let anybody know who he's leaning to," Daniel said, summoning on his own a fateful subject.

"He talks about Steve Sloan and Buford McGee a lot," James added. Steve Sloan was the head football coach at Ole Miss, a fine fellow from my occasional conversations with him, and Buford McGee was a black running back. "He thinks Sloan is a real honest, straightforward person, and he likes the atmosphere at Ole Miss."

We talked on into the night, about football and other subjects, in the spirit of what we once called "bull sessions" in the college dormitories of the 1950s.

"When we integrated the schools back in '70," Daniel said, "I was ten years old. Some of my best friends were black."

"I can remember sitting at our house," James said, "and visitors saying, 'What are y'all gonna do?' When I first went to school after the integration, I thought: We've lived together for hundreds of years and we've got to stop hating each other. It was an awakening for us."

"When we started playing football in high school," Daniel said, "we'd go to parties together, or we'd buy some beer and take it to our friends in the black section. Our black friends on the team would just be hanging out on the side of the road and we'd turn on the stereo in the car and have a good time and nobody would think anything about it. It was nothing like the things I'd heard about '64 and '65. I guess to live together you've got to go to school together."

My casual interrogations led me to believe Marcus had not had an easy upbringing. His parents had separated when he was little. He was raised by his mother in the house of his grandparents. He had taken the surname of his grandfather Dupree, who was a truck driver and part-time preacher. He had little relationship with his father, Thomas Connor, who was a janitor in the public schools. "Dad never paid me any attention until a year ago," he would tell a Birmingham paper. "All of a sudden he comes around and Mom says it's because of who I am now. My mother went through all the pain of bringing me up." His only sibling was a younger brother, Reggie—nine years old—who was crippled by cerebral palsy. Reggie had had several operations and had been in a body cast, from his neck to his feet, twice, for three months at a time. Reggie adored Marcus. Could Hollywood conceive such a story?

Marcus was born on May 22, 1964, in a decade which had begun with the great vision of John F. Kennedy. The Civil Rights Act was moving through Congress. The Voting Rights Act, under the prod of Lyndon Johnson, was a year away. In the week of his birth, the largest headline in *The Neshoba Democrat* read:

T-MEN SEIZE 1,749-GAL.
WHISKEY STILL IN BARN

The editor, Jack L. Tannehill, wrote in his front-page column:

> This writer saw his first big moonshine whiskey still Monday of this week, and it was quite a sight. The first thought that struck our mind was the filth that prevailed in the making of the moonshine. After the still was destroyed by T-Men, a couple of the cows in the adjoining pasture got to the dumped mash and carried on just like humans do when they partake of such. Didn't know where they were going and didn't care at that time.

The Ellis Theater right off the Square was showing *Move Over Darling* with Doris Day and James Garner and *Safe at Home* with Mickey Mantle and Roger Maris. A new Bible School was opening at Harmanuel community. Not until one month later would this headline appear in the *Democrat*:

MISSING AUTO OF TRIO
FOUND BY FBI TUESDAY

Marcus was baptized just around the corner from his grandparents' house at the Mount Nebo Baptist Church, which would soon be opening its doors to the outside civil rights workers. Football was the thread of his early years. He played in his backyard with the other children from the Quarters. One Christmas all of them got football suits. When he was five his mother enrolled him in the first grade, on the first day the Philadelphia public schools totally integrated.

In the fourth grade he began playing organized flag football. Each boy had a flag, or a large handkerchief, in his belt, and an opponent's pulling out the flag was the equivalent of a tackle. From the fourth grade on, the people of the town, white and black, began to know about him. He weighed sixty pounds, and he scored a touchdown whenever he wanted to. "We were just discovering him then," Tom Turner, who assisted his father in Turner Hardware, would remember. "He was something to watch. Even when he was that little, he reminded me of Gale Sayers—that smooth motion. He could change gears without the defensive backs knowing it." Steve Wilkerson, a young town alderman, was a referee in the flag football competition and had his first glimpse of the precocious runner at age nine. "I told the high school coach, Danny Gregory, that he could play high school ball right now. I remember one kickoff that year. It must've been about 1975. He went to the left and three boys fell down. Then he went to the right and the same thing happened. He ran all the way for a touchdown. He was the first fifth grader I ever saw to give a head fake. He scored every time the other team kicked off. After about the sixth game, the other coaches decided to kick out of bounds. When he was in the sixth grade he had a black coach who was such a nice guy he was afraid he'd get criticized for favoring Marcus. He didn't let him run very much. I think Marcus was a little dejected that year." Danny Gregory, the high school coach who later became principal, first saw him in the seventh grade. "Coach Owen tried to get him to stop reversing the field so much because it wasn't sound football. The problem, of course, was that he scored every time." Gregory thought he had matured early physically and that the other boys would catch up with him. "I went away for a couple of years and came back in his junior year in high school. By then I was worried that by the time he was a senior he'd be too big for a running back." And so the talk went. In the fifth grade he was a little too heavy and he began lifting weights every other day, but he did not get serious about the weight lifting until the seventh grade. He joined the Cub Scouts and played Little League baseball, won the local Pass, Punt, and Kick competition three times, and started gaining so much weight that by the eighth grade even he was concerned that this might slow him down. It was a gratuitous fear. In the ninth grade he made the starting high school team as a receiver. He continued to participate in the other sports. An Ole Miss student named Rocky Miskelly saw him play Ripley in a championship basketball game during his sophomore year. "He played inside most of the night, but once he stole a pass and broke for the goal. Just past half-court he combined a stutter step with a head fake and left our quickest player standing still. He then breezed in unmolested for a lay-up. I was stunned and thought to myself, 'Gee, I know a lot of *football* players who would like to have that move.' That was when I got interested in him."

"My mother was scared for me to play football," he would remember. "She thought I was just a baby and that those big ol' boys
would hurt me. She thinks the same thing today."

Was this seventeen-year-old black youngster, as A. J. Liebling might
have put it, an American Universal? Beneath the surface, what did the
town of his birth really think of him? I found myself curious to know.

A visitor from Jackson, in the summer before his senior year, found
him in blue jeans, a green surgeon top, and white basketball shoes—"an
ordinary teenager who likes to spend his time like most seventeen-year-old
guys: fishing, playing basketball, checking out women, and listening to
music."

Almost every Sunday morning he would walk the block and a half
from Davis Street in the Quarters to the Mount Nebo Baptist Church.
What did he make of the memorial to the three slain young men in front
of his church?

He was making B's and A's in high school, and he had a well-
deserved reputation for not saying very much. "He's very quiet and shy,"
Daniel Mars had forewarned me. "You may have to work to get him to
talk." Daniel had sat with him in the stadium at the Ole Miss intrasquad
game the previous spring. "He went down to the sidelines and all the little kids recognized him. They came up and surrounded him, about fifty of
them. That seemed to embarrass him."

He liked children, I was to discover, and after his high school days he
would work with little Mississippi whites and blacks in a project called
the Outreach Program. "Most kids are growin' up in the wrong way," he
would say. "The more kids you can help, the better. I don't like to see
kids get away from doin' right. I owe them that." His timid way with
words, nonetheless, was destined sooner or later to get him into an
occasional difficulty with the big-time reporters—"the nationals," as I
called them. A year or so after he graduated from high school, when a
brief contretemps was to surround him in a national magazine, a white
man of the town who knew him well said: "Through all the controversy
and stuff, he's concerned about people. A lot of times he says things short,
hoping people will understand him. I hope it won't affect him. He's just
the way he is. He's quiet. That's his personality."

Marcus had told Billy Watkins, the sports editor from Meridian:
"Some people think I have the big head, but I don't think I do." Around
those he trusted, I would learn, or in a raucous cadre of teenagers at the
Pizza Hut—the Elaine's of Philly—he was not without a rather sly sense of
humor, which usually caught one unaware and was fine as rain.

"I'm just another high school senior that happens to play football," he had said. "I work hard to keep my body in shape, but all I can do is listen to the coaches and try to do my best. The team, especially the offensive line, made it possible for me to do well. I just try to go for it on every play." Earlier, of the recruitment process, he had said: "It's getting nervewracking, but I'm lucky to be in a position where all these schools are interested in me. If I can do well in college ball, I'll be able to help my family. I just want to go to a good school and I want to play. My dream is to finish college and make the pros. If I can do that, I can take care of my momma and my little brother." Yet the aching middle-age cynicism of the writer did not wish him to be *too* good. Who wanted a character from *Hoosier School Days* in blackface who happened to have pushed himself religiously with the weights and the sprints? It was more than refreshing, then, to read from my Oxford retreat that he was envious of Herschel Walker's eighty-six high school touchdowns and had ambitions of surpassing that stunning mark in 1981, and that the purposeful gang-tackling of earlier seasons had elicited a vein of anger if not righteousness. "Some people expect you to score every time you get the ball. They don't know what it's like to have six or seven guys hanging on you every play. You can't have a great game every time." And I nearly wept with deliverance after I considered this revealing self-assessment: "I think I'm a little like Earl Campbell, O. J. Simpson, and Walter Payton rolled into one. If they don't get out of my way or if I can't dance around them, then I'll run right over them." As Dizzy Dean said: If you can do it, it ain't braggin'.


It was during the summer before his junior year, 1980, that the colleges had started making their contacts. The list was staggering and numbered more than a hundred schools, including, of course, every major college football power in America. Southern Cal, UCLA, Oklahoma, Penn State, LSU, Texas, Arkansas, Alabama, Ohio State, Texas A&M, Nebraska, Michigan, Tennessee, Pittsburgh, Georgia, Notre Dame—they and all the others were paying their deferences to a sixteen-year-old with two more years remaining in high school. The three larger state rivals—Ole Miss at Oxford, Mississippi State at Starkville, and Southern Mississippi at Hattiesburg—were preparing for one of the most strenuous recruiting wars in history, and they were already advising the young man and his mother that he should remain in his native state. So were the predominantly black Mississippi schools, Alcorn and Jackson State, which had produced so many professional players. Later in this narrative I will explore the follies, histrionics, and complexities of the college football recruiting of our day, especially as they reflect many of the excesses of our contemporary society, for it was a world unto its own, and that world was coming to Neshoba County. The object of their solicitations was, in the terms of the trade, a "franchise." Bear Bryant, that towering personage at the University of Alabama, in a notable autobiography on his coaching life that was not reviewed by Mary McCarthy or Lillian Hellman in *The New York Review of Books*, discussed his philosophy of the "franchise"— bring in a remarkable athlete and build around him. "College coaches do that all the time. Find the talent and relate to it. It's not like the pros, who draft players to fit a system. That's why the college game is never stereotyped, and never will be. Every four years there's a complete turn-over in personnel."

As for the young athlete himself, in various moments during his junior year, he had claimed to be leaning to Alabama, Oklahoma, Texas, Southern Cal, Ole Miss, and Mississippi State. This, however, was academic, since by the regulations of the National Collegiate Athletic Association he could not sign with a school until after the football season of his senior year in high school. The "national signing date" would be February 10, 1982, although he would not necessarily have to make his decision and sign the papers on that date. By then, as I would witness it, he would have changed his mind countless times about these and other colleges.

Now, in the late summer of '81 as he was beginning his final season, the recruiting activity was quiescent. The NCAA rules precluded personal visits from college representatives from the beginning of the season until December 1. During that period the colleges would be limited to telephone calls and letters. There was one exception. An athlete was allowed an "official visit," with all expenses paid and for the duration of forty-eight hours, to six college campuses of his choice; he could visit any campus he wished at his own expense. After December 1, a recruiter would be allowed six visits with the athlete—three at his school, three at his house.

The latest intelligence from the catfish rendezvous and coffeehouses of Philadelphia, where Nietzschean philosophy, the Romantic poets, and onomatopoeia were rarely discussed before lunch, was that he would narrow the field gradually as the football season neared its end, and that he would wait until the season was over before making the official visits to the campuses of his choice.

In Stribling's Drug Store just off the Square, where the white merchants traditionally congregated for coffee from two to ten times a day, depending on the tide of commerce, the gossip during this period centered on the question of whether he should choose Ole Miss, Mississippi State, or Southern Mississippi. The sentiment was emphatic that, for reasons nearly mystical in sweep, he should remain in Mississippi for his collegiate career, and this was not merely a question, as the town burghers conceived it, of "loyalty." As one of them told me, "He's just a small-town colored boy. I'm scared if he goes out of state to one of those big places he'll be unhappy and want to come home and get himself messed up and lose a year or two of eligibility. He's the sort of boy who should stay real close to home, just stay right here in poor ol' Mississippi." Another observed: "In terms of Mississippi, which doesn't have all that many people, he's a once-in-a-lifetime. He won't come along again in many years, a classic, powerful running back like that. Mississippi needs him. If 'Bama doesn't get him, Ole Miss will. Wait and see." Yet another explained to me that Philadelphia was very much a Mississippi State town. The power structure and the flow and distribution of money were largely controlled by the State people. The new mayor and the mayor before him were faithful State graduates, and so were most of the members of the city government. The boards of directors of the Citizen's Bank, the Bank of Philadelphia, and the Peoples Bank of Mississippi were, with certain exceptions—the lawyer Mont Mars, for instance, was an active Ole Miss alumnus on the board of the Citizen's Bank—in the hands of State men. "But the Ole Miss people are diehards, and don't count out Southern," I was advised.

On the face of it, there were strong attractions for the youngster in each of the three Mississippi schools. Although Ole Miss had been losing of late, its last winning season having been 1975, Steve Sloan and his first assistant Tom Goode were respected men; it was also to Ole Miss, the capstone state university, that his comrades Tree McAfee and Michael Smith had gone to play football. Mississippi State, the traditional land-grant college, which had been fielding successful teams—it had won eight and lost three in 1980 and went to a bowl game—used what was known as the "Wishbone" formation, with a variation called the "Wingbone." Indeed, its coach, a saturnine figure named Emory Ballard, had created the Wishbone while at the University of Texas, a discovery more pleasing to some Longhorns than the vaccine against cholera. As for Southern Mississippi, its resourceful young coach, Bobby Collins, a native of Laurel who had played for Mississippi State, was establishing a wining tradition and had defeated both Ole Miss and State regularly in the recent past— four wins in a row over State, two out of the last three over Ole Miss. And a former Southern Mississippi star, later the football coach at both Philadelphia High and Neshoba Central and just elected chancery clerk, was a persuasive Southern representative in town. His name was Bobby Glen Posey, a gentle and perceptive fellow, and already there were predictions that "Coach" Posey, as he was called, would intercede at the last moment and convince young Marcus of the cultural and athletic advantages of Hattiesburg. "We can do anything we want to at the University of Southern Mississippi," Bobby Collins, the head coach, said that summer. "We can be national champions. We can have a Heisman

Trophy winner. We qualify. We're Division 1-A just like the other major colleges. We can do anything we want to if we're willing to pay the price."

There were, of course, many football subtleties involved in all this. A number of the teams actively recruiting Marcus—Mississippi State, Alabama, and Oklahoma among them—used the aforementioned "Wishbone" formation, as, for that matter, did the Philadelphia High Tornadoes. Would Marcus choose to go with a Wishbone team in college? *The Jackson Daily News* put this alternative succinctly: "If proof is needed that the Wishbone is statistically not the system for producing individual greatness, look at this—of the top 10 rushers in career yards in NCAA history, only Earl Campbell (ranked number 10) played in the Wishbone. But on the other hand, the team record for most players gaining 100 yards or more in a game, for highest average gain per rush, for most yards per game rushing, for most rushes per game and for most touchdowns rushing per game are all held by Wishbone teams." These considerations were of no small consequence.

The rivalry among the Mississippi schools was particularly rigorous. There were three major football powers—not including the black universities—seeking the same talent in a state that ranked thirty-first in population; this was exacerbated by the fact that more and more colleges were coming into Mississippi each year to recruit. In recent years, many of the best players had gone out of state, to Pittsburgh, Alabama, and elsewhere.

For a time, the Stribling's Drug Store nucleus reported to me on the long-distance wires, "the talk is nothing but 'Bama, 'Bama." Bear Bryant, on his way to winning more games than any college football coach in history, was only 160 miles from the Neshoba County Courthouse. Bobby McKinney, a forester for Molpus Lumber, was a former defensive back for the Crimson Tide, and Tim Allen, of a pulpwood company, was a charismatic Alabama alumnus known in some quarters as "the Bear's man in Philly." In fact, when Marcus had pulled a hamstring muscle while running in the state finals of the hundred-yard dash in the tenth grade (he still finished second), none other than Bobby McKinney took him to Tuscaloosa to have the Alabama team doctors examine the injury. Bear Bryant observed his team practices from a ninety-foot tower, where he had reigned for years like the Old Testament Jehovah assaying the whole of His Creation. A Philadelphia man happened to be at a 'Bama practice one afternoon. "I looked up at the top of the tower, and I saw Bear Bryant and Marcus Dupree." It was further said that Coach Bobby Glen Posey, the chancery clerk and Southern Mississippi man in town, received telephone calls now and again from Bear Bryant about young Marcus, and what did one make of that?

Among the numerous visitors that summer, I had likewise been informed, was Fred Akers, the attractive young coach at the University of

Texas, which happened to be my alma mater. The splendid pull of Austin, where the South and the West converge in those enraptured violet hills, would be difficult to deny, as would the splendid fight song, "The Eyes of Texas," which to this day brings tears to my eyes, and which Coach Darrell Royal once claimed was worth three points in any close contest.

I have always admired the company of sportswriters, preferring their companionship to existentialists, vice-chancellors of universities, computer technocrats, condominium developers, and the jolly Madison Avenue sort of fellows of the Lowenbrau beer commercials of our day. They have seen much of life on this planet as it takes its whirls out at the edge of the universe, and they have learned to tolerate existence, though sometimes barely. Wines and spirits have abetted them in their quest of the human heart in conflict with itself, and the best of them are poets of the night, nor is it mere accident that more than a few fine American novelists began as sportswriters. They can be the most loyal of friends, and will share with you what they see. Down South, they have an institution known as the Southeastern Conference Skywriters. They take a plane in a large group and touch down at each of the ten colleges of the SEC just before the start of the football season. This gives them the opportunity to evaluate the prospects of the teams before any of them have been defeated, as well as to go to bed early each night. One of their number described for me a dialogue which took place in Athens, Georgia, home of the University of Georgia, in late August of 1981.

The Skywriters were talking with Vince Dooley, the Georgia head coach, who had won the national championship the previous year. In the shank of the night, in the hospitality suite, two of the writers had wedged Dooley between the bar and the door and would not let him leave the one to go through the other. He was staying late anyway, since he seemed to want to savor the last sweet days of being the national champion.

"Vince?"

He looked up. They had not been talking about football.

"You recruitin' this kid, Marcus Dupree? From Mississippi?"

Dooley gazed at his inquisitor with a touch of condescension.

"Marcus Dupree is the sort of player who comes along who you *have* to recruit," Dooley said.

"Have you met him?"

Dooley shook his head. "But I talked to him on the phone."

All three put down their drinks.

"What did you say to him?"

"I said, 'Marcus, how would you like a challenge?' "

He was serious; this was precisely what he had said on the telephone. He did not need to explain to the sportswriters that Georgia's running back for the next three seasons, unless he managed to turn professional, would be Herschel Walker, who the previous year had gained more yards than any freshman in history and had finished third in the balloting for the Heisman Trophy, which is awarded each year to the outstanding player in the country.

Young Marcus himself, on the eve of his senior year, was more or less noncommittal. "A good environment is important," he had told one of the many reporters who had already been to Philadelphia, "and a winning tradition. It wouldn't bother me to play a long way from home. And it wouldn't matter if they changed coaches before I got there. One day me and my mother will sit down and talk about where I should go to school. I won't rush into anything." He and his mother had not yet started taking the telephone off the hook, although they were getting countless long-distance calls a day, each call ranging anywhere from five to fifteen minutes. Some recruiters were telephoning regularly, and others only once in a while. They usually asked him how he was doing, or what he was thinking. Ole Miss and Mississippi State, for instance, were calling and sending letters once a week. "I don't hang around just waiting for the phone, either," he said. Numerous letters were arriving every day with postmarks from all over the nation.

Earlier in the summer, the town was somewhat agitated by a strange trip that he and his two comrades from Philadelphia, the black players Tree McAfee and Michael Smith, who were soon to depart for Ole Miss on football scholarships, made to Los Angeles. Their expenses were paid by an enigmatic gentleman named Marty Gamblin, an effervescent young man in his thirties who was a show business promoter in L.A. but had grown up in Philadelphia. Marty Gamblin had spent some time in college at Mississippi State and was a partner for a while in a sporting goods firm across from the Philadelphia courthouse. Later he moved to Nashville and became an entertainment promoter and a friend of Jim Weatherly, a famous country singer who had once played quarterback for the Ole Miss Rebels. When Gamblin emigrated to Los Angeles, he established close contacts with UCLA, which, along with everyone else, had been drawn to the talents of Marcus Dupree. Gamblin was in Philadelphia in the summer of '81 cultivating Marcus.

He and Tree and Michael stayed in a house in Malibu for several days, just down the road from the blond starlet named Farrah Fawcett. He met not only Miss Fawcett, but also Cheryl Ladd, Erik Estrada, John Schneider, Richard Roundtree, and Toni Tenille. He sat behind the dugout at a Dodgers baseball game and chatted between innings with the mayor's wife. He also went out to the UCLA campus. Terry Donahue, the UCLA football coach, was in a meeting. "But when we got there," Marcus said afterward, "he came right out. He showed us around. It was nice."

It is fascinating to envisage the three young black boys of poor families from a small town in the hills of Mississippi on their first real trip from home as they mingled with the golden stars of the television age, walked the beaches of Malibu, and absorbed the opulence of Beverly Hills. It must have been as alluring to them as Memphis was to me on my first genuine journey from Yazoo City when I was a boy, and equally as resplendent. But the effect of their trip was electrifying. All over America college recruiters, whose intelligence network, some felt, rivaled the Israeli secret service, heard about it. A buoyant football publication called *Leonard's Losers*, which covered the South with its predictions and insights, soon reported: "UCLA has the early lead on the recruiting of this year's Herschel Walker, that is Marcus Dupree of Philadelphia, Miss."

Yet surely there was a compelling logic here. David Halberstam, one of the best of American reporters, wrote:

> UCLA was a beautiful school, one of the loveliest in the country; its faculty and intellectual climate, as America's power and affluence steadily moved westward, had been continually on the rise. It was also one of the first major American colleges to go after black athletes. Long before Jackie Robinson had starred in major league baseball, he and Kenny Washington had starred in football at UCLA. It was, moreover, situated in an ideal place, gentler of climate, and less rigid of lifestyle, than many areas blacks now wanted to forsake. The pull of California upon blacks was not to be underestimated.

The cornucopia of UCLA with its thirty-five thousand students in the stately precincts of Westwood, and the attraction of its triumphant football tradition, were exotic and powerful in Neshoba County, yet must have seemed a world away. There could be no denying that Coach Terry Donahue and the Golden Bruins, not to mention the hospitality of Marty Gamblin, had scored early and dramatically. But could they, from their three-thousand-mile remove, maintain their impetus?

The rumors, that summer, abounded in Philadelphia, and they would intensify in the six or so months leading to the NCAA's national signing date. In Stribling's Drug Store, Turner Hardware, the corridors of the high school, the Busy Bee Grocery and Record Shop, the Guys and Dolls Amusement Center, the Mount Nebo Missionary Baptist Church in Independence Quarters, and the lobby and restaurant of the Downtown Hotel the speculations would continue to germinate, spreading eventually to all corners of the sovereign state of Mississippi. Much of the gossip at this juncture was spurious, but it intrigued me, nonetheless, for sometimes it was rather revealing. One such rumor had it that Marcus Dupree was really twenty-five years old. Another was that, being from a poor background, he was highly susceptible to money. Roman Catholic priests all over America were telephoning him in behalf of the Fighting Irish of Notre Dame.† He was wearing a jeweled watch which had been given to him by Ole Miss. His uncle Curlee was on the payroll of the University of Southern Mississippi, but that institution was about to be placed on probation by the NCAA for recruiting violations. Alumni of Mississippi State were raising a secret slush fund to entice him to the environs of Starkville. He had pledged to go to Alcorn University, the black college in the woods near the Mississippi River, because his mother had attended school there. Ohio State was beginning to come on strong. Jackie Sherrill, the coach at the University of Pittsburgh, had promised him a condominium in proximity to Three Rivers Stadium. Three of his six "official visits" would be to Ohio State, Michigan, and Texas. Coach Wood and Principal Gregory of the high school were prevailing upon him to play for their alma mater, Mississippi State. Coach Akers of the University of Texas would report UCLA to the NCAA because of his vacation in Los Angeles. The University of Texas had guaranteed him an $80,000-a-year job if he went out there but got hurt playing. His last six choices would be Alabama, Ole Miss, Mississippi State, UCLA, Southern Cal, and Oklahoma. The University of Oklahoma was talking about a couple of oil wells. On an early visit down there, I drove into a service station. The attendant, a young man with the look of the backwoods about him, said: "He's great. They can't tackle him. They say he's goin' to Alabama. He's drivin' a new Alabama car and everything. Ain't that awful?"

He was, indeed, driving a car, a 1980 Delta 88 Olds with chrome wheels and tinted windows. I would see it often that year parked behind the school gymnasium with a decal on the window which said "22". "I bought it working at school after hours," he said. "And my grandfather helped me." It was commented that he had put Mississippi State and Southern Mississippi bumper stickers on it. One prominent citizen, going around the Square, saw him from a distance and later confessed to someone that he could not help circling the Square again to see what kind of car he was driving.

Our seventeen-year-old black youngster, then, could hardly avoid a growing awareness that he was being *watched*. His every movement—putting on bumper stickers, conversations with strangers—was subject to the

† "If I wanted a kid bad enough," Bear Bryant of Alabama once said, "I used every trick I could think of. Frank Leahy used to tell everybody that when I was at Kentucky I dressed our manager, Jim Murphy, in a priest's outfit to recruit Gene Donaldson away from Notre Dame. Maybe Jim Murphy did tell Donaldson he was a priest. Shucks, I'd have told him Murphy was Pope Pius if I'd thought we would get Donaldson that way."

most intense scrutiny. "He's got to be scared," a young woman who had taught teenaged blacks in the integrated schools of Mississippi said to me. "Who's advising him? I have a seventeen-year-old boy—he's *white*—and I know the natural adolescent complications *he's* going through. I feel sympathy for your Philadelphia boy."

And, increasingly, so did I, especially as I would grow to know and like him and eventually to care very much for him. There must be no misjudging that college football in the America of our time was an awesome business, and becoming more and more so with the importance and significance of big television money. He was to be, indeed he already was, an object in a contest of the highest stakes, an invaluable commodity upon whom the reputations of many grown men he had never even met, and never would, might succeed or fail. I sensed it was not going to be easy for him.

Amid this Marcus-watching, I would soon discern among some in the white community certain ambivalent feelings about him, qualifications to the general awe—that he was lazy, spoiled, slow to get up, that he was not as good as his clippings. I was afforded an insight into this and other matters on a journey down there in late July of that year when I met three pillars of the local economy, all congenial figures, as Mississippi as the Tallahatchie River, who had had their confrontations with visiting writers in the sensitive years and were willing to talk, though not to be identified. Because of their wishes, and their fellowship, which included a considerable quantity of ice-cold beer, there was a large part of the discourse that I have not recorded. The Neshoba County Fair was to begin in a few days, and we drove leisurely through the countryside out to the Fairgrounds, where people who were cleaning and repairing their gaily painted cabins near Founders' Square shouted their greetings. Then we returned along country lanes to a modern ranch-style house for steaks and baked potatoes and the frosty mugs which were fine antidotes to the oppressive humidity. One of my companions was a Mississippi State man, the second, Ole Miss, and the third, Southern Mississippi, and their jibes and banterings reminded me all over again that football talk in a small town of Dixie in the summertime was an expression of something deeper—a source of comradeship and enmity, status and ambition, pride and belonging, suspicion and insecurity.

I had brought along with me a "To Whom It May Concern" letter from a friend of mine, Warner Alford, the athletic director of Ole Miss, which in effect disowned me, declaring that, although I was at the time a writer-in-residence at that institution, I would be a dispassionately neutral observer in the recruiting of Marcus Dupree. This letter, in fact, would prove to be absolutely necessary for me. Many of the collegiate recruiters had long since, in their indeterminate profession, grown wary of spies, informers, and the general breed of charlatans and fakirs, and although I believed myself to be of innocent demeanor, inspiring considerable trust in my encounters with strangers across America, Alford's letter of disclaimer, perhaps because of the respect in which he was held among football people, served to soften those innate suspicions. The only dangerous moment might have come when I presented this document much further along to a representative of the University of Oklahoma, an institution noted for its rivalry with the University of Texas. I had forgotten that one of the sentences said: "He is not only not an Ole Miss man. Far from it. He graduated from the University of Texas." The Oklahoman, however, had the grace to be amused, and to invite me into his room in the Downtown Hotel for a glass of Kool-Aid.

In much this spirit, the Mississippi State and Southern Mississippi men accepted my portfolio, as if I might have been an officer in a peace-keeping force of the United Nations.

"He's the greatest high school athlete I ever saw," the host said, and the others agreed.

They had heard, of course, of the odyssey he had made to California in the company of Tree and Michael, the house in Malibu, the introductions to the golden girls of television, the visit to UCLA. They dwelled at some length on the local boy, now West Coast entertainment promoter, Marty Gamblin, in words that would have flattered neither Mr. Gamblin nor the West Coast. "He was hanging around town tryin' to spend as much time as he could with him," one of them said. All of them were partners in the xenophobic yet curiously affecting emotion I have reported. "He should stay in Mississippi. He'll probably be comin' back to live in Mississippi someday when it's all over. The blacks are comin' back home now. We need him more than California does.

"I got a call just the other day from a coach up at the University of Nebraska. He wanted to know if the kid was as good as all the reports they had. 'He's good,' I said. 'Should we recruit him, or are we wastin' our time?' 'You've been lookin' at him for more than a year.' 'Should we continue to be interested?' 'Yes, you should. No harm in tryin'.'"

There was laughter over this, and then the dialogue turned grave as they took turns talking. "The Alabama approach is low-keyed right now. They really want him. The ol' Bear thinks he can *mold* him. What if they bring in the Bear at the right moment, say in February?" This gave me visions of Bear Bryant, descending on Valentine's Day from a Victorian carriage driven by eight white horses in front of the Confederate Monument, asking one and all, as he did in a well-known Bell Telephone television commerical of that time: "Have you called your momma lately? I wish I could call mine."

"Look at all the attractions being offered the boy. How can a seventeen-year-old think about the future? What can he know about being twenty-five? And thirty-five is around the bend."

"Well," I asked, "what people does he trust for sound advice? What's going through his head?"

They considered this. I believed I had touched a nerve. One of my confreres attended to the sirloins in the oven. Another fetched the beer. The third went out the back door to relieve himself under a sassafras tree. "It's better outside, the way God intended it," he said on returning. They congregated once more around the table.

"Jackson State is really losin' out. More colored kids in Mississippi are goin' to white colleges. Look, Walter Payton"—an outstanding running back in professional football from Jackson State—"wasn't all that recruited in his time."

"Right now he's with Steve Sloan and Tom Goode in Jackson on an official visit. A dollar to a doughnut it's Ole Miss. Ole Miss turns out all the influential people in this state anyhow."

"To hell with Ole Miss. They don't have an offensive line. That quarterback—what's his name?—*John Fourplay*—runs the ball all himself. He'll pick State for the Wishbone. State's a hell of a lot friendlier than Ole Miss. Rich men's kids! Damned *party school!*"

The two dissidents glared at one another, then exchanged short, vivid words in chorus.

"Both of you don't know what you're talkin' about. *Southern's* the place for him. Look here—Coach Collins is a great molder. He had a scrimmage one time down there and about three quarterbacks came down hurt—dislocated shoulders, everything. Then Reggie Collier comes in, leads the offense down the field, keeps gettin' hit hard. He's just a kid, came as a superstar, and it's his first scrimmage, you see. He takes an awful lick and is lyin' there on the ground. Nobody comes over and says, 'Reggie, are you okay? Reggie, can I help?' His teammates who just plastered him say, 'Aw, come on, Reggie, get up.' Tough! That's what he needs."

As his friends and rivals, in their turn, glowered contemptuously at the Southern Mississippi advocate across the table, I sensed a different resonance to the talk at hand, something lurking there, as yet unspoken.

"Well—he's not too popular in the Bottoms. Some of the people in the Bottoms think he's got the *swell head.*"

"The big question I've got is, is he *tough* enough? Does he have the discipline? I hear he's been spoiled by Coach Wood. He takes himself out of games when he wants to come out. Joe Wood's lettin' him off too easy. The coaches wanted to put him in on the kickoff team in the second half last year against Northwest Rankin, and I hear he refused."

"Wait and see if he doesn't *telegraph* his runs off the veer this season."

"Can he take orders?"

"Can he adjust to college ball? It's a bone-crusher. With all the attention, he may *really* be spoiled. He looked lazy in spring practice. We scrimmaged Neshoba Central in the spring game. He kept gettin' whacked, really *whacked*, by a 240-pound tenth grader named Woodward. After the game he came up to Woodward and said, 'Hey, man, you *hurt!*' Woodward said somethin' and walked away. He walked after him and pulled on his jersey. Woodward got him under the chin even with the helmet on and knocked him down."

"What's gonna happen in college when he's just another number? In high school he's so big and quick, he can turn the corner on anybody. Then he breaks free in the secondary and the first man at him is a 160-pound defensive back with fuzz on his cheeks. In college that first man who gets to him in the secondary is a 230-pound linebacker who'll go right at his chest with his helmet. What does he do then?"

I was led to recall what Bear Bryant had once said about the incipient hazards to a young athlete whom everyone wanted. "You take a boy and wine him and dine him and he has to be pretty solid to stand it. Then he gets to college and finds out he's just another guy."

"I can tell you this," one of my hosts said, "his senior year is gonna be his hardest yet. With all his publicity, the other big ol' tough boys are gonna be out to get him. He'll face some good teams, too, and don't think they won't try to wrack him up."

This reminded me of a talk I had had not too long before with a college coach who expounded to me his "the bread ain't baked yet" theory. "The first really strong team on the schedule of his freshman year is a completely different ball game from high school," the coach said. "The defensive opposition will be so much bigger and quicker than anything he's ever seen before in high school—they hit so hard. I've seen some kids who never get over that first encounter. They're almost *shell-shocked.* I'd bring him along gradually as a freshman. Giving him the ball twenty or twenty-five times against the first really good team like Alabama or Georgia or Florida would be unfair to him. But some teams will do it. And so much will be expected of him his freshman year. He'll only be eighteen."

I had mentioned the coach's theory to Mr. Silas Gault, a garrulous soul who worked for the post office, a couple of afternoons later with the boys in Shine Morgan's Furniture Store on the Square in Oxford. "Hell," Silas said, "when I was eighteen I was crawlin' across Europe on my belly, dodgin' bullets and mortars."

All this talk with my three Philadelphia friends had been sudden and torrential, and it abated as swiftly now as the thunderstorms of the Mississippi springtime. We talked of other things—of the Neshoba Fair, the soybean crop, life among the Choctaws, a moonshine raid, the trial docket at the courthouse, a great Neshoba team of the past, the coming of divorce to Philly, the best place to eat catfish.

As we were about to adjourn, the eldest of the number returned briefly, tenderly almost, to the subject at hand, in the tones of the ancient resignations and inferiorities of our Mississippi.

"California . . ." he mused. "It's got to have an attraction for a poor kid like him . . . The tailback system at Southern Cal, UCLA, the TV, the weather, the lights, the wealth." He shook his head. "*California*," he repeated, as if he himself had one day wished to go there from these tenacious hills and never quite made it. Then, he added: "Don't believe ninety percent of what you hear about where he's goin'. It'll go down to the wire."

He did not know how right he was.

In August *The Neshoba Democrat* published its football spread on the forthcoming season. There was a large, formal photograph of the 1981 Philadelphia High Tornadoes, suited out and sitting together in the bleachers. I counted fifty of them. Number 22 was the second from the right on the front row, between Number 21, Monty Lang, and Number 23, Willie Rush.

Up in Oxford, a junior high school student who was the son of friends saw the photograph in my living room and examined it closely. He had a class assignment to describe briefly some object which had interested him. He wrote:

> There were as many black teammates as white ones. They really looked like a team, too. The guys on the front row all had their clenched fists resting on their knees, like they were ready and they were sharp. Each player stared straight ahead, with a peripheral vision that kept each one in touch with the other. Yet they were distinct individuals, with an obvious

separateness that kept them apart in that instant that the photo was taken. I think they had a sensitivity to Number 22 who was with them in the bleachers, but did they really know it?

The team, it was reported again, had lost its entire offensive line from the previous year. Joe Wood, the Philadelphia coach, would say at the end of that season: "Losing the line hurt. Plus the fact that everybody we played was sky-high for us and always keying in on Marcus. You just wouldn't believe it. There would be ten or eleven on the line and they would just wait." I myself would soon see how a school playing Philadelphia was obsessed not so much with winning a game as with beating the runner with the glasses and the red hairnet under his helmet, the one his mother had knitted for him.

So the circumstances which had become clarified for me, then, as the 1981 school year began, were of a young man who had touched all aspects of his town, a town which had once been scourged in its fear and blood. Flag football, the Cub Scouts, Little League, the Mount Nebo Church, high school basketball and baseball and track, the images of him with his schoolmates at the Pizza Hut and with his crippled little brother at the ice-cream parlor—all these had made him an integral, almost mythic presence there. Ever since he was fourteen, subscribers to *The Neshoba Democrat* had been reading of his accomplishments. White and black, the young boys of Philadelphia had been emulating the way he walked, his distinctive bouncing gait. A prominent white lawyer, speaking of his teenaged daughter, had told me: "She's genuinely concerned about his well-being and has never once even mentioned the fact that he's black." At the football games, where many had come only to watch him, a white bank president sitting next to a black carpenter had turned and said, "How about *that* play?" His high school coach had taken him to a local restaurant where a few black executives from Emerson had started coming for lunch, and among the regular patrons, I was told, "he was treated like the governor." A black factory worker had said: "Remember, he was born in 1964, the same year as the murders. I think he's a gift. A gift from God, a gift to us. Martin Luther King really brought something to this town. He has too." The mayor had said: "I'm downright thankful for him." The alderman who had seen him play as much as anyone would say: "He's been accused of not putting out one hundred percent. But here's a kid who runs a 9.5 hundred, a 4.4 forty, how can you say he's not giving it everything? A lot of older people in this town would like to see him go away and fail. Every day I hear someone say, 'Aw, he's not *that* good.' It's not because he's black. It's all the attention."

I remembered the description from my readings of history of the "slave athletes"—the mulatto fighters soaked in brine on whom the white planters had gambled. I remembered, too, what a college recruiter from an adjoining state had said to me: "If he breaks his leg this season and never plays again, he'll be just another colored boy from a small town in Mississippi . . ."

Was the white community using him? Or did the truth go further— that the parents, students, teachers, teammates there had intuitively *adopted* him? Was there a need for expiation in the town? And was he saving its soul? I wished to find out; I would become part of the boy and the town.

# 4
# *The Basement Is Not Deep*

"In Neshoba County, Mississippi, the basement of the past is not very deep," Florence Mars wrote in *Witness in Philadelphia*. "All mysteries of the present seem to be entangled in the total history of the county." DeSoto passed over the northern boundary of what would become Neshoba in 1539. In 1830, with the Treaty of Dancing Rabbit Creek, the Choctaws ceded their lands east of the Mississippi River to the expansionistic United States. Several thousand of them were removed to the Oklahoma Territory. Under the treaty, those who chose not to migrate to Oklahoma could remain, and Neshoba was designated the capital of the Choctaw Nation. Soon after that, the white pioneers moved in from Alabama, Georgia, and the Carolinas. Those wooded red hills were not sufficiently blessed to accommodate the white-pillared mansions of the more classic Deep South, or the Deep South of myth. It must have been unrelenting country, and the early settlers fought for a living in cotton and subsistence farming. The native Indians who had stayed behind, the pioneers found, lived mostly on fishing and hunting, and they were skilled in wood-carving and clay-modeling.

Neshoba County, from the Choctaw for "gray wolf," was formed in 1833. The immigrants settled at first in tiny hamlets built around churches—Emuckalushia ("our people are there"), Coffadelhia ("sassafras thicket"), Cushtusha ("fleas are here"), Waldo, Hope. Later settlements would bear such names as Hemlock, Jewel, Pilgrim, Nearby, Damascus, Fusky, King Bee, Barfoot. Philadelphia was little more than a tree-covered hill until 1837, when the county seat was moved from a village called Camden. The ancient Indian village near the site of Philadelphia was known as *Aloon Looanshaw* ("bullfrog place," or "burnt frog"). The early white population was almost entirely Anglo-Saxon Protestant, although a few Catholic families named Kenna and Rush arrived in the late 1830s from County Down, Ireland. "The Negroes of the county were as a whole an uncontaminated black," one chronicle would note, "and among the Choctaws there were few half-breeds. There had been no infusion of alien breeds from foreign lands . . ." In 1840 there were 2,683 whites and 744 slaves in the county; in 1850, 3,393 whites and 1,355 slaves; and in 1860, 6,131 whites and 2,212 slaves, the forebears of the modern-day Independence Quarters thus comprising about 28 percent of the population at the outbreak of the Civil War.

As with the black slaves, the hardship of the Choctaws was part of young Marcus' heritage.

Their sacred ground was Nanih Waiya, just north of the Neshoba line. They called it "Great Mother" and looked upon it as the birthplace of their race. Out of this mound hundreds of years ago, they believed, first came the Muskogees, Cherokees, and Chickasaws, who sunned themselves on the mound until dry, then moved on. The last to come were the Choctaws. They settled around the "Great Mother," who warned them that if they ever left her they would die.

Nanih Waiya, the capital of the nation for more than a thousand years, had a population of twenty-five thousand in the early nineteenth century before the advent of the white settlers. In our day it would become a state park, surrounded by fields and pasture.

The authority on the southwestern Indians believed the Choctaws were once to have been envied. "They loved war less than truth and truth less than oratory, and were slow in all things save horticulture and diplomacy. Like the meek, they were slow inheriting the earth because their neighbors could not compete with them economically."

In the three decades before the Treaty of Dancing Rabbit Creek in 1830 they tried to accommodate themselves to the United States. It was said that they never broke a single covenant with the state or federal government.

Their efforts to gain fair treatment would fail. When the last of the Choctaw land was lost in 1830, many of those who migrated to Oklahoma died along the way. The several thousand who remained in the neighborhood of Neshoba became tenants to white landlords. "For them treachery came soon," a tribal historian wrote, "and hope died fast." They lived an impoverished existence as squatters and sharecroppers on their former land, and they were under constant harassment to move west. From a population of 19,200 in 1830, only 1,200 remained in 1910. At the time of their first removal, the Choctaws were believed to have one of the finest school systems in the South. A Catholic mission founded in 1884 was their only educational institution to survive into the twentieth century. The Choctaw children were excluded from the white public schools, and their parents were not willing to send them to Negro schools. Not until 1930 would there be elementary schools in all seven Choctaw communities of the vicinity, and a high school education was largely out of the question until 1963.

In April of 1861, according to Mary Ann Welsh in the centennial issue of *The Neshoba Democrat*, the people of Philadelphia gathered around an old oak at the corner of what would become Main Street and Center Avenue and watched as fifty-three men were mustered into the Neshoba Rifles, Company D, Eleventh Mississippi Infantry. Other Neshobans were posted to other commands, but the Rifles fought under Robert E. Lee in the Army of Northern Virginia and were engaged at First and Second Bull Run, Seven Pines, the Seven Days, Antietam, Fredericksburg, Gettysburg, the Wilderness, Spotsylvania, Cold Harbor, and Petersburg—a roll call of the bloodiest battles of the war. The Neshoba Rifles took fifty-five men into Pickett's charge at Gettysburg, and ten returned. At Appomattox, parole records indicated that fewer than twenty men of the Mississippi Eleventh surrendered there, and only one private answered the final call for the Neshoba Rifles.

Philadelphia was selected as the object of a cavalry raid under Colonel Benjamin H. Grierson in 1863, part of the daring march behind the Confederate lines which John Wayne and William Holden would fictionalize for Hollywood in *The Horse Soldiers*. As the Union troops approached, most of the livestock and valuables were hidden in the hills and reed brakes. The dauntless Colonel Grierson, in the words of one account, found "little of value to destroy in Philadelphia."

Reconstruction brought the usual bitter suffering. Bridges, buildings, and crops had been destroyed, and Confederate bonds were worthless. The loss of men was stunning, and in some instances the freed slaves remained with the farmers until the crops of 1865 were in. With the long federal occupation and the arrival of the carpetbaggers, the freedmen flocked to Independence Quarters and for several years ran the local government. As elsewhere in the devastated South, economic conditions remained miserable. "The courthouse," one gentleman later wrote, "was all cracked open and fastened together with long iron rods. There was a big white thing on the top of the building which they called a cupola." The first white public school, established in 1870, occupied a log cabin, at what would become the corner of Pecan Avenue and Columbus Road. The town remained virtually landlocked. Ox carts and mule teams brought merchandise over nearly impassable roads from Meridian, thirty-eight miles away, and the trip took a week; there was practically no migration into the locale except from adjoining counties, and the one-crop cotton had severely depleted the soil. At the turn of the century Philadelphia was a somnolent hamlet of several hundred citizens with no electric lights, running water, telegraph, or telephones. It was known as one of the most isolated backwoods villages in Mississippi. Goats ambled through the courthouse, which had dirt floors where old men sat on benches spitting tobacco juice, and one side of the Square was a cornfield.

"There was nothing new," an observer of later years would note, "in the non-observance and non-enforcement of the law in Neshoba County." Violence was so endemic that the grand jury of 1904 reported:

> We find the general conduct of the county in a serious condition. Crime is on the increase. It is a sad fact that this year . . . has recorded more homicides and more attempts at homicides than any one year in the recollection of anyone now living. We believe that the cause is the fact that all kinds of intoxicating liquors are being sold throughout the county. The pistol is a baneful curse that follows in the wake of this destroying force. The moral manhood of the county is being ignored by the rough element and our young men debauched by the common curse of liquor and pistols.

The year 1905 was marked by the arrival of the M. J. and K. C. Railroad, as critical a juncture in the history of the town as the summer of 1964, the integration of the schools in 1970, and, a few years later, the coming of age of Marcus Dupree. Overnight the struggling crossroads village was accessible to the outside world. New settlers began arriving, and with them all the appurtenances of the unknown life. A *Neshoba Democrat* of 1906 announced: "For the first time in its history, Philadelphia will be visited by a big railroad show Thursday, March 22, and there is no doubt it will attract many to town. Monster elephants, roaring lions, fierce tigers, and such wild beasts will prove real novelties here, and many people of this city will see them for the first time."

Miss Margaret Hester, born and raised in Philadelphia, was my high school history teacher and senior class sponsor when I was coming up in Yazoo in the 1950s. Behind her back we called her "Red" for her lovely flaming hair. She was the best girls' basketball coach in Mississippi in that day, when the girls' game was played on two separate sides of the court, and only two dribbles were allowed. The Women's Movement helped do away with that most leisurely approach. "Red" taught us all the nuances of States' Rights, her hero being, as I remember, U.S. Senator Pat Harrison. She recalled those horse-and-buggy days of Philadelphia in the first two decades of this century. Almost every house on Holland Avenue had a paling fence around it to keep out the horses and cows, and a barn in back with a horse and cow and a loft for hay. The son of the family would take the cow to Welch's pasture every day. There was a chain link fence around the old courthouse, where people in town from the county tied their mules and horses. They usually stayed all day, she said, so they also brought a feed sack for the animals. There was a gazebo bandstand on the Square where the local musicians would congregate every Sunday afternoon to perform. One of "Red" Hester's earliest memories was of seeing the Confederate veterans, who were affectionately called "the Old Soldiers," at their reunions around the Square, reminiscing in their gray coats and hats of those tempestuous times. I have before me now a photograph from *The Neshoba Democrat* of the dedication of the Confederate Monument on a hot July day of 1912. There are the whiskered and goateed old men gazing out proudly from under a tattered Stars and Bars, and the ladies in long dresses carrying parasols, and a few saddled horses here and there, and far in the background, near the walls of the courthouse, several old black men watching the proceedings, just as they had watched every conceivable activity on the courthouse lawn of the Yazoo of my boyhood, including the fiery addresses of Theodore G. Bilbo exhorting them with atavistic gestures under his high, sweaty forehead to go on back home to Africa.

The 1920s in Philadelphia were dominated by a memorable individual named Clayton Rand. He was a graduate of the Harvard Law School and editor of *The Neshoba Democrat* from 1920 to 1925. Stanley Dearman, who would become editor in 1968, called Rand "the most unusual, most energetic, most ambitious, most industrious, and most vocal of all the *Democrat* editors. Certainly he was the most colorful. And he was completely fearless." Turner Catledge, who as a young man worked for Rand and later became managing editor of *The New York Times*, said he was "one of the most remarkable men I ever knew."

"Nothing is as disturbing as truth when put into print," Rand once wrote. "You can criticize a community in spoken words without serious offense, but print it and the curse of the crowd is upon you." Neshoba County could have used Clayton Rand in 1964, the year of Marcus Dupree's birth. What was a newspaper's purpose if not to lead in the ways of civilization, for this was the American journalistic heritage, at least as it came down to us, to those young writers of the South of my generation who cared passionately for our native ground and were nurtured by Hodding Carter, Harry Ashmore, Jonathan Daniels, and Ralph McGill, not to mention William Faulkner. The moral collapse of *The Neshoba Democrat* in the 1960s would be symbolic of the abdication of those years in the town. A distinguished editor would have performed a salvation, as Rand said, through "truth as put into print."

Rand was a funny, ironic man. Just after World War I, the Southern Baptists were part of a campaign to send money for the economic and spiritual regeneration of Europe, especially Belgium. "Neshoba County came out financially ahead on the money raised for 'The Poor Belgians,'" he wrote. "For three quarters of a century the Belgians had maintained a Catholic Choctaw Mission in the county at Tucker, for the purpose of Christianizing the Indians. And while we were sending nickels to the Belgians they were sending dollars back to us to redeem our 'savages' for civilization."

There was something touching in his paean to small-town life, for one did not hear this very much in America anymore, except in a cultist way, although I wish we did: "Villages lack the cold indifference of the metropolis where one doesn't know one's neighbor in the next apartment and has no inclination to cultivate him. The small town may suffer some inconveniences, but one need not be lonely there. One's joys and sorrows become the joys and sorrows of the whole community. A faithful dog is struck by a car and every child in the community is grief-stricken. A noble steed goes to his last reward and men and women are sad. Sentiment, like trees and flowers, thrives best in the less populated places."

Given the fierce struggle led by Rand against the Ku Klux Klan in Philadelphia in the 1920s, Neshobans of the 1960s would have been well advised to read his words on fathers, sons, and the fragilities of history:

> Early in 1917 my father lay at the point of death and the war was one of the reasons he gave for not wanting to die just then. He reminded us of the Civil War, with its aftermath of Reconstruction, and the drastic changes it wrought in a reunited country. He believed that peace would usher in a topsy-turvy world. Father wanted to live long enough to witness some of the excitement that he expected in the wake of the world conflict.
>
> We thought he was a little addled at the time. One of life's anomalies is that we seldom appreciate the wisdom of our fathers until we have sons of our own. Unfortunately, each generation has to learn all over for itself. As Hegel, the German philosopher, put it, "We learn from history that we learn nothing from history."

Turner Catledge, whom I knew well and cared for enormously, would have agreed with much of this. I liked this description from Catledge: "Those two papers, *The Neshoba Democrat* and *The New York Times*, which consumed so much of my life and love, were different only in the size of figures. They had the same joys and the same frustrations, the same aspirations and the same annoyances. Above all, they had the same purposes, namely to mirror for their readers what was happening in their day and in the process make a record for those who chance this way in the years to come." When I was editing *Harper's* and he the *Times*, we would congregate with our Northern friends in his apartment on Park Avenue. He would tell stories of his boyhood in Philadelphia, of the picnics and revival meetings he covered for Rand and the *Democrat*. He also signed people up for subscriptions and often accepted hams, chickens, and molasses in lieu of cash, so that the newspaper office practically turned into a produce center. When Catledge went on too long with his Neshoba stories, I would counter with bizarre tales of my Yazoo days. Often the two of us talked simultaneously, while the New Yorkers gathered around and tried to make sense of it, usually with little success.

Here is Clayton Rand's description of the town on a day in 1918, which reminded one of the hamlets that Huck and Jim encountered along the river many decades before:

> The first time I climbed the steep, muddy hill on a boardwalk from the railroad station to the town square, I beheld [Philadelphia] as a village of squalor.
>
> A dilapidated brick courthouse, ready to tumble, was surrounded on four sides by rows of stores, banks, and shops that flanked and faced the square. Watering troughs were conveniently placed at each corner of the courtyard, around which an iron-pipe, one-rail fence served as a hitching post for horses and mules. Merchandise was being loaded into wagons, and a milling crowd in overalls, corduroy, and gingham, passed greetings along the curb or gabbed in friendly groups. The courthouse lawn was worn bare by the treading of many feet and was stacked with wood which was carelessly piled in high, truncated pyramids. Wooden benches, unpainted and well occupied, were propped against the walls of the courthouse or parked under the trees. In one corner of the courtyard, its rear exposure facing a cafe and bank, was the county privy, a frame structure rank with disinfectants. And off the square were livery stables, blacksmith shops, mule lots, an inn, churches, and a newspaper office.

One of his maiden editorials had to do with the deplorable sanitation conditions. Merchants dumped rotten produce on the streets. Mules and horses, tied at random, evacuated on the Square. "Unclean stables; and people housing pigs in dirty pens; and stench whiffed on every passing breeze . . . People's teeth falling out because of Riggs' disease, and the public cup unprohibited. Abandoned wells breeding mosquitoes and open closets breeding flies. Citizens with contagious diseases in their families careless and unquarantined. Tuberculars and others spitting on the walls and floors of public places—a courthouse plastered with spit."

The merchants, as everyone else, were slaves to King Cotton, "perpetuating an agricultural serfdom that impoverished the soil and pauperized those who tilled it." There were no hospital facilities, no trained nurses, and Rand himself owned the only microscope. Most of the doctors died during the influenza epidemic of 1918, and the people who were not sick were building coffins and digging graves.

A farmer named Uncle Jeff Cato said one day, "Editor, we ain't Delta planters with landlords; we're white dirt farmers. With our women and children we dig a living out of the soil, and then we spend our spare time eatin' dust and wadin' mud. I don't believe the good Lord intended us to be earthworms, but the span of our lives is from dust, through dust, to dust."

> The native whites were pure Anglo-Saxon, the angular, raw-boned, calcimine type. The first observation I made to Judge Wilson Rogers . . . was that all the people resembled one another. He explained, "They have married and intermarried until they look as much alike as coons," and the judge himself was no exception.

There was a sad moment in the 1920s, more than half a century before a young black running back would perform his feats on the same field. A boy on a visiting high school football team was killed during a game. The small-town South of that and later years was marked by such tragedies during football games. When I was a child I saw a boy killed on the field in Yazoo; an Oxford boy died in a game in 1953 and lies now in St. Peter's Cemetery not far from William Faulkner under a tomb with the stone carving of a football player and engravings of his high school sports letters. Clayton Rand wrote of the death in Philadelphia with ironic undertones for this narrative:

> He was the only son of a doctor who had come to see his son play, and as he bent over the lad's limp form, helpless to save him, it was the kind of heart-rending scene men and women never forget . . . There wasn't any enthusiasm for football in Neshoba for several seasons. I paid glowing tribute to the father's self-control on that occasion, and wrote at length on the pity of such a costly sacrifice on the altar of sport.

The fabulous Neshoba County Fair, the nation's oldest county fair, was flourishing in the teens and twenties. The grounds covered twenty acres in a beautiful wooded valley. People called it the "World's Fair," and it most certainly had an aura of the world's largest family reunion. Its focus, then and in our day, was Founders' Square, that and a speaking pavilion with a dirt floor, open on three sides with a broad stage and homemade wooden benches. Its dates traditionally coincided with the dog days, between the cotton harvesting and the Democratic Party primaries; children of the generations grew up there, loved those days more than Christmas, brought their own children and grandchildren, and watched with their eyes the South in its changings. The Fair was always a combination camp meeting, picnic, recital, amusement park, music jamboree, race track, and political rally, and there was no institution quite like it in America; one could not conceive of it in Wilkes-Barre, Pennsylvania. Whites, blacks, and Indians flocked to it from all over the hill country.

In the pavilion, anyone who wished could make a speech. This was the historic Mississippi forum for announcing for statewide office, and the rhetoric became essential to the legend. One candidate called his opponent "a willful, obstinate, unsavory, obnoxious, pusillanimous, pestilential, pernicious, and perversable liar," without a pause for breath. One contemporary observed that even his enemies removed their hats. James K. Vardaman, an incorrigible reprobate and grandiloquent white supremacist, was a favorite. He would arrive at the Fair wearing a white linen suit and sitting in a logging wagon driven by white oxen. He would recite Tennyson's "Locksley Hall" and Markham's "The Man with the Hoe" before launching into his perorations. The violence of the language sprang straight from the red hills themselves, and there was never a dearth of fistfights.

It was at the Fair that Theodore G. "The Man" Bilbo, who had earlier announced his candidacy for another term as governor of Mississippi from a jail cell, was accused by one of his opponents of being a jailbird. "My children," this other old renegade replied, "I'm not ashamed of having gone to jail, for I remember that St. Paul, that great soldier of the Cross, went to jail. It was also while serving sentence in prison that John Bunyan wrote his *Pilgrim's Progress*, that inspiring story of a Christian's triumph over sin. Jefferson Davis, President of the Confederacy and matchless statesman of the Lost Cause, also went to jail. Following the conflict between the states, Jeff Davis was put in irons at Fortress Monroe by the Yankees. Yes, my friends, Bilbo went to jail, and Bilbo is proud of his company." Ronald Reagan, who delivered his first speech in his campaign for President at the Fair in 1980, must have found it difficult to match that prose from the cosmos and confection of Southern California.

Mrs. Kate Williams, one of the elderly widowed ladies of the town, touched this vagabond heart with her memoir of the Fair in a *Neshoba Democrat* of 1981. Her first recollections were of going with her parents in a wagon covered with a bow-frame. They brought trunks full of apple juice, custard and jelly cakes with jelly between the layers, and homemade bread in loaves. They carried their best clothes starched stiff and also packed in trunks. She especially remembered keeping "a lace-trimmed voile to wear on Thursday with my large leghorn hat with red roses on the side and streamers down the back." Her parents told her and the other children that they must stay in Founders' Square; when the pine-knot fires near the pavilion began to die, they knew they were to come at once to the tent or wagon. "It was a wonderful day when we would get ice cream and soda pop instead of the lemonade made in the zinc tubs and when the big sound truck was brought out so we could really hear the programs. And having electric lights instead of pine-knot fires."

Mrs. Kate was of my own grandmother Mamie's generation, children as they were of defeat, impoverishment, and devastation. The resurgence, in the Mississippi of Mrs. Kate's twilight days, of the party of Lincoln, Grant, Sherman, Sumner, and Thaddeus Stevens—and of the young captain of infantry who destroyed my grandmother's father's printing presses in Raymond in 1863—baffled her as much as it had my own grandmother. Something in Mrs. Kate's spirit moved her to write:

> I don't think we are keeping the spirit and respect due to the founders of the Fair who fought in the War Between the States for our Southern way of life. Most of them went through the suffering during the siege of Vicksburg. They were all real Democrats, and no Republican had ever been on the program until recent years. I can't understand why people have forgotten all those things. Personally, I don't think any Republican should be on our program, regardless of who he is or what he is running for. It is not in keeping with the people who worked so hard to make the Fair a success.
>
> Regardless of all the different opinions and lack of loyalty, I am just as patriotic and loyal to the Fair as I have ever been and feel I must do all the cooking I am up to and see that food gets down there to try and help feed the entertainers and special visitors and friends and be ready to give a glass of cold water in the heat of the day.

During the Prohibition days and beyond, as Florence Mars would remember, Neshoba County remained "one of the wettest counties in the dry state of Mississippi." In her childhood two drugstores on the Square served wood alcohol in milkshakes. Bootleggers did a flourishing trade, just as they would under the continuing Mississippi prohibition of my own boyhood. The moonshine of Neshoba was famous throughout the area and would remain so into the 1980s. As in the words of the gentleman serving a certain wine to his guests in the James Thurber cartoon, "You may not appreciate its vintage, but I think you will admire its presumption." The well-to-do drank bonded whiskey while the poor relied on homebrew and "corn." Clayton Rand explored these social complexities:

> The bankers, lawyers, and politicians usually had good stuff, while the undertakers relied on "embalming fluid" and the barbers drank hair tonic. Neshoba County consumed "white lightning," synthetic gin, antiseptic, and Jamaica ginger. Our stills produced a concentrated product that was the quintessence of kick. Good whiskey usually had a mellowing effect on one's affections, but the stuff we distilled and lapped up in the Hills had fight in every drop. Fortunately, it usually produced nausea before its victims had delirium. We staged a stag banquet for a prominent Neshoban on the eve of his wedding, at which was served liquid corn that had been aged in a charred keg for six months. Everybody got so sick that it was necessary to postpone the wedding.

As in other Southern towns of the time, morphine addiction was a reality, especially though not exclusively among certain prominent but secretive white ladies. Morphine had been declared illegal in 1914 but was easy to obtain. "In the 1920s," Florence Mars remembered, "a small group of prominent young men became addicted, and this, plus the reputation for frontier violence and widespread bootlegging, gave the county an unenviable reputation; Philadelphia, especially, was referred to as a city of sin and was held up as an example of a present-day Sodom in revivals held in neighboring counties. Needless to say, the reputation was deeply resented in Philadelphia."

At one point in the twenties, over a period of twelve months, there were twelve killings in the county and no convictions. Fixed juries were commonplace. This apposition of savagery and friendliness was striking. "There were men in Neshoba County so religious they would ask the blessing before they took a chew of tobacco," Rand wrote, "but who would shoot at you just to see you jump. There were those who would burn down your house because they didn't like you, though your neighbor would rebuild it." During one four-year interval in which there were thirty-three homicides, only two of the murderers paid their debt to society; those two hanged themselves in their jail cells. For many years juries almost never convicted a white man of murder.

A local official who had been accused of embezzlement once knocked Editor Rand to the ground when he was not looking. He carried a gun and terrorized everyone in the town—"a big, two-fisted bully with a vindictive reputation." He was beyond the law; jury after jury refused to convict him. Four decades later the town would know similar bullies.

Within the old paternalistic context, the relationship between the whites and blacks of the town was largely easygoing and affectionate.

Frank Stennis, Marcus Dupree's great-grandfather on his mother's side, was beginning to farm a plot of land out in the country. The leading citizens, Florence Mars recalled, "were protective of Negroes and tried to help them . . . These citizens were not intimidated by the attitudes of those who were mean . . . Neshoba County also prided itself on its 'good Negroes,' those who worked hard but knew their place. Any Negro who wasn't appreciative was considered a troublemaker." When I was coming up in the 1940s, I was always mystified by the importance the white churches placed on raising money to send missionaries to Africa to save the lost souls. "Yet brotherhood seemed to end there," Miss Mars wrote of the Philadelphia of her girlhood, "and I saw no real concern shown for the souls of the 'Africans' who dwelt among us. If Negroes were thought to have souls to be saved after their journey from Africa, it did not seem to be our concern in Neshoba County."

Miss Mars remembered, when she was quite young, how glad she was not to be a Negro, and the sorrow she felt for the maids and domestic workers. There was a servant house in her backyard, and the mournful singing which she heard from there was saddening to her. The Negro maids walked to work six mornings a week and left before supper. "I wondered how they made ends meet. I knew that the custom of allowing the kitchen help to take leftovers from the table must have helped . . . After finishing up in the white kitchens, maids carried the dirty clothes home with them to be boiled in iron wash pots, scrubbed on washboards in the zinc tubs out in their yards, and then pressed with flat irons heated on wood stoves or in front of the fireplace. Although most white families in town had electricity, none of the Negroes in town owned their homes and none of them had electricity."

The attitude of the best Neshobans, and Southerners, of the day toward Negroes was epitomized by the reformer Clayton Rand:

> The Negro has few anticipations and is not harassed by the uncertainties of the future; he lives in the present and lets the white man do his worrying . . . Like the commoners of England, the Negro knows that he can never be king, while every white child born in the United States is a potential President. By virtue of the pigment of his skin, the Negro may be America's pariah, but he is sublime in his humility. Neither slavery nor discrimination has crushed his spirit . . . The Negro by instinct is gregarious. But a few centuries removed from barbarism and not long up from servitude, like a child he is only content with his own kind. Isolated from his crowd, he becomes as bewildered as a goose lost from the flock.

For me one of the powerful scenes in American literature was the "battle royal" the white men staged among the young blacks in Ralph Ellison's *Invisible Man.* Clayton Rand described a similar event on the Square in Philadelphia in the 1920s; I would not forget this one, either, as

I watched the integrated high school football games in the same town in the 1980s.

A prize ring had been improvised on the Square, an elevated, roped-off platform. Eleven Negroes qualified and at the sound of the gun went to work. In battle royals the last in the ring gets the gold and it is customary for several of the weaker contestants to gang up on the stronger ones, eliminating them first.

Preacher Jim outstripped the others in size, strength, and popularity and by the time he had thrown several of the contestants over the ropes, the remaining ones concentrated on him in the blood-spattered arena. The spectators, unfamiliar with the rules, resented the procedure with a vengeance that verged on mob violence, and as master of ceremonies I was forced to call off the fight.

Is there any doubt that young Marcus Dupree, a boy of the 1920s, would have been in the ring?

From the perspective of 1964, the Ku Klux Klan in Philadelphia in the 1920s was a taunting study in similarities. As in the later era, its membership in Neshoba County then, in Rand's account, was "a strange conglomeration of religious bigots, decent citizens, visionaries, and bootleggers." In both cases, the fury of the vigilantes divided the community against itself.

"How the Klan ever germinated in Neshoba is still a mystery to me," Rand would write.

In its perverted patriotism it concentrated on Jews, Catholics, Negroes, and aliens. Kaplan, the only Jew we had in the county, a splendid citizen, had moved to Louisville, Kentucky, to open a wholesale dry goods house, and had left his Neshoba store in charge of a pious Presbyterian. We had a mere handful of Catholics in the county, most of whom were Choctaws domiciled at the Tucker Mission . . . Of a total population of 19,303, there was one alien in the county, a Chinese laundryman named Charlee, and he never bothered anybody. The five foreign-born residents of Neshoba were all naturalized law-abiding citizens. There wasn't a Communist in the county. If some radical stranger invaded Neshoba and began preaching wild-eyed isms, he was usually warned to leave town or was ridden out on a rail . . .

I doubt if white, black, and red men lived in more complete accord than in Neshoba. The county's most commendable attribute was the preservation of its racial unities. Negro, Choctaw, and Anglo-Saxon had lived together for more than a century, keeping their respective racial strains intact.

In relation to the pervasive terrorism, within the Philadelphia community there were two significant differences between the twenties and the sixties. One, *The Neshoba Democrat*, in the person of Clayton Rand, took a firm and consistent editorial stand. Two, a group of the most influential citizens refused to give in. There were about a dozen men in this latter group, and they and the newspaper made it so difficult for the konclave that it eventually had to move its meetings from the Masonic Hall to an abandoned livery stable. Ab DeWeese, who owned the DeWeese Lumber Company (it would be sold to Weyerhaeuser in 1966), wrote a letter which occupied almost a third of the front page of the *Democrat*: "I take the position that [the Klan] is acting in opposition to constitutional government. It assumes to indict, to represent the jurors, and to judge, and then to execute, and this power and right should only come through the constitutional government. And furthermore it acts behind a mask and does not come out in the open . . . A man should not put his light under a bushel and hide his good deeds." Another stalwart businessman in an open letter argued that every town needed men of courage to stand up for what they believed, and he regretted that "so many weak-kneed politicians and preachers had become intimidated to the point that they were afraid to express their honest convictions on the Klan issue." In 1964 such language would be noticeably missing.

With this determined opposition, the Klan finally ran its course in Philadelphia, and retired to await a more propitious day. After this, the white establishment sponsored public meetings of whites and blacks. A black educator from Meridian was asked to address one such gathering. "You Negroes shouldn't try to steal," he said, "because you don't know how. When you steal it's usually a chicken or some trifling thing that won't pay your fine. Only white folks know how to steal. When they steal, it's a bank or a railroad." He told them to be proud of their color, and he asked the whites for more understanding.

Clayton Rand reviewed the lessons of the struggle:

> To those of us who fought for freedom, the Klan was a monstrous menace, a serious threat to our inalienable rights. There is nothing fixed in freedom. Men gain it, now and then, as they travel down the corridors of time. Periodically, the tyranny of mobs or the autocracy of despots destroys it, but like eternal truth, crushed to earth, it will rise again. Freedom is a blessing for which a people must fight over and over. It is gained by one generation to be lost in another.

Beneath its surfaces, the decade of the twenties was in some ways a time of progress for Philadelphia and Neshoba. Farmers' cooperatives came into existence for those laboring against erosion and the boll weevil, and the United States Government finally acknowledged that the Choctaws were not going to leave for Oklahoma.

"Prejudice, neglect, and injustice," in the words of the tribal historian, had continued to leave many of the Indians of the area destitute. In 1917 a congressional committee heard testimony that one in five had perished in the influenza epidemic during World War I. Their wages for sharecropping and other labor was fifty cents a day. One Indian testified before the congressmen that a farmer had sold him a cow and then taken it back. The chairman asked if all white people acted that way. "No, not all of them," he replied. "Mighty few. But them that wears the fine clothes is going to beat you every time."

Over the next several years the Bureau of Indian Affairs bought land for a reservation. These purchases in seven major areas of the neighborhood were sold to Choctaws on loans to be repaid from farm income. Between 1920 and 1930 medical facilities and several elementary schools were established. These schools, however, included only the first eight grades, and a few Choctaw children attended high school at Indian boarding schools, mainly in Oklahoma. Many of the Indians would remain sharecroppers and day laborers until the early 1960s.

By the late twenties many of the streets in the white section of the town were paved. The Square was filled on all four sides with one- and two-story brick establishments with wooden awnings covering the sidewalks in front. Toward the end of his editorship, Clayton Rand revised his description of the place as he had first glimpsed it in 1918:

> From a hick town with few of the comforts and conveniences of modern civilization, [Philadelphia] became a spick-and-span, up-and-doing community with pavements, concrete walks, electric lights, and modern plumbing. The village finally boasted a new courthouse, an inn, and two hospitals. Self-help and private initiative had transformed a dump on a hill into a thriving, bustling trading center.

Marcus Dupree's aunt worked as a domestic at one of the big houses on Holland Avenue. His grandfather was a teenager, earning money at the hard and menial tasks.

# 5

# *Moist Talcum and Drugstore Perfume*

*Recruiting is about the same. Been getting a pretty good amount
of calls at home. Especially the first part of every week. Also getting
Mailgrams from all over. Ohio State, UCLA, Alabama, Texas, Mississippi State, and Georgia are the ones that stand out in my mind. Everybody says about the same thing. Got personal calls from Coach
Donahue (UCLA) and Coach Bryant (Alabama).*

I arrived at the stadium early to observe its first stirrings. The teachers
who sold the tickets and the game programs and the parents who volunteered for the concession stands were already there, as well as the little
boys who have always, in my memory, chosen to come to the field three
hours before the kickoff. I asked a young woman who sold me a ticket
why they called it Harpole Stadium. "Well, after Ol' Man Harpole," she
said, and that was the end of that.*

I had driven down that afternoon from northeast Mississippi. The
flashing sign in front of the bank in Calhoun City had said ninety-seven
degrees. I had checked into the Downtown Hotel, which would be my
domicile for many weeks, and then drifted around the Square. I dropped
into the courthouse to pay my greetings to Bobby Glen Posey, the new
chancery clerk who had played halfback for Southern Mississippi a generation ago and later coached at both Philadelphia High and Neshoba Central. "Eupora's usually solid on blocking and tackling," he told me.
"They've always been tough country boys. See if you think he oughta be
running out of the Wishbone."

Now, as I settled briefly into a seat in the deserted concrete-block
grandstand, I perused the game program. I remembered the passage from
my ever-faithful Federal Writers' Project *Guide to Mississippi* which I

---

* Actually it was named after Jeff Davis Harpole, a pharmacist at Turner Drug
Store who organized the first football team in 1906.

had earlier paused to read at the Sonic Drive-In in Eupora about that
community.

> . . . a neat town with wide paved streets shaded by tall hardwood
> trees . . . It now has a peaceful, smoothly flowing life antithetical with
> that of its past. At one time it was notorious for its feuds, killings, and
> lynchings. In the latter part of the nineteenth century feuds were constant
> and difficulties were settled without assistance of the law. Property rights,
> wills, love, and marriages were topics of violent family controversy; hot
> tempers were cooled by gunfire and arguments settled by a rope attached
> to the limb of a tall oak tree. The bloodiest feud was that between the
> Gray and Edwards factions—a feud that grew out of a dispute over prop-
> erty rights and ended years later with the wholesale murder of the Grays.

There were no Edwardses or Grays on the roster of the Eupora Eagles
on this night. Perhaps they had not lasted long enough for children.

There was a stupefying contrast in the weights of the big boys and the
little fellows, which as memory served me had always been true of high
school football in Mississippi. Charles Summers of Philadelphia, a tackle,
weighed 240 pounds; Dickie Sistrunk, a back, weighed 105. I prayed for
Sistrunk that they would not sooner or later collide, even if they *were*
teammates.

There was no particular emphasis on the player I had come to see.
His blurred individual photograph, one among many gazing out hazily
from the pages, carried the longest caption, however: "Height—6-3.
Weight—222. Position—RB-S. All Conference, 1979 and 1980. Most Val-
uable Back, 1979 and 1980. All South, 1980. All State, 1980. High School
All-American, 1980. MSWA Player of the Year, 1980. *Clarion-Ledger*
Player of the Year, 1980."

I studied the 1981 schedule for the Philly Tornadoes. I did not know
then that I would become so absorbed in the performances of Number 22
that I would journey down to every match except one (plus to the Choctaw Bowl which was as yet, of course, unlisted) and that I would soon become as familiar with his movements, gestures, lackadaisical pauses,
unhurried reverses, phantom-like bursts of speed, as his coach or his
mother or his brother—as familiar too with the coaches, cheerleaders,
band members, flag bearers, water boys, and mascots as to know their
every whim and eccentricity. The musical repertoire of the marching band
would become my repertoire, and I would soon be able to predict each
cartwheel of my favorite cheerleader as accurately as I could the echo of
the trains from beyond the hollow in the field named in memory of Ol'
Man Harpole.

The stadium slowly began to fill. The western sky was a blend of soft
blue and orange from the setting sun, and there was the beginning of a

# 1981  PHILADELPHIA  TORNADOES

| No. | Name | Pos. | Wt. | Grade | No. | Name | Pos. | Wt. | Grade |
|-----|------|------|-----|-------|-----|------|------|-----|-------|
| 10 | Justy Johnson | QB | 141 | 12 | 49 | Doug Donald | B | 155 | 10 |
| 11 | Greg Smith | QB | 154 | 11 | 50 | David Kohler | T | 175 | 12 |
| 12 | Greg Nowell | QB | 121 | 10 | 51 | Wyatt Waddell | C | 200 | 12 |
| 14 | Mike Sampsell | SE | 155 | 12 | 52 | Steve Molpus | C | 185 | 11 |
| 16 | Cleveland McAfee | SE | 165 | 10 | 53 | Mike Green | G | 219 | 11 |
| 18 | Cecil Price | SE | 140 | 12 | 54 | Harold Blocker | C | 185 | 10 |
| 20 | Jay Graham | TE | 170 | 12 | 55 | Carl Lee Smiley | T | 195 | 11 |
| 21 | Monty Lang | TE | 165 | 12 | 56 | Rob Robinson | G | 170 | 11 |
| 22 | Marcus Dupree | B | 222 | 12 | 60 | Ricky Stewart | G | 182 | 12 |
| 23 | Willie Rush | B | 130 | 10 | 61 | Mike Donald | G | 175 | 12 |
| 24 | Terry Hoskins | B | 150 | 9 | 64 | Scott Carter | G | 166 | 10 |
| 25 | Nathan Horne | B | 151 | 10 | 67 | Richard Sockey | G | 141 | 10 |
| 28 | Mark Burnside | B | 175 | 12 | 68 | Wayne Williams | T | 175 | 11 |
| 29 | Donny Shannon | B | 139 | 10 | 70 | Eddie Willis | G | 132 | 11 |
| 30 | Daran Jackson | B | 205 | 12 | 71 | Roe Ross | T | 220 | 12 |
| 31 | James Henson | B | 135 | 11 | 73 | Jim Fulton | T | 170 | 12 |
| 32 | Ken Griffin | B | 140 | 11 | 75 | Brad Permenter | T | 200 | 11 |
| 34 | Thomas Booker | TE | 127 | 10 | 77 | Charles Summers | T | 240 | 10 |
| 35 | Danny Skipper | B | 145 | 11 | 78 | Roderick Sutton | T | 220 | 12 |
| 36 | Michael Groves | SE | 141 | 11 | 79 | Wydell Fulton | T | 150 | 12 |
| 39 | Otis Smith | B | 150 | 10 | 80 | Shay Daly | SE | 120 | 12 |
| 40 | Dickie Sistrunk | B | 105 | 10 | 81 | Trey Burkes | SE | 115 | 10 |
| 42 | Scottie Wilson | B | 160 | 9 | 82 | Mike Sanders | TE | 175 | 11 |
| 43 | Mike Bassett | B | 161 | 11 | 86 | Don Huddleston | TE | 130 | 10 |
| 44 | Carl Johnson | B | 152 | 12 | 87 | Terry Rush | TE | 145 | 11 |
| 45 | Alan Moorehead | B | 151 | 10 | 88 | William Burnside | SE | 147 | 10 |

Coaches:  Neil Hitchcock, John Draper, Joe Wood, Kenneth Cook, Danny Howell

Managers:  Alan Burnett, Randy Hill, Daran Leach, Doug Jones, Mark Fulton, Jason Fulton, William Bassett, Erick Huddleston, Rodney McLendon, Fred McAfee

Superintendent:  Therrell Myers

Principal:  Danny Gregory

Band Director:  Dathan Hart, Nancy Williams, Assistant

Cheerleaders:  Stephanie Griffin, Yvonne Burnett, Dee Dee Morgan, Tonya Alexander, Suzette Blacks, Rhonda Allen, Gayle Vines, Nancy McNair, Lori Sharp

Cheerleader Sponsor:  JoAnn Davis

quarter moon. The heat lay heavy on the grass of the field, which glistened from yesterday's rains, and a faint veil of mist rose from the puddles along the sidelines. Two or three dozen little white and black boys wearing red T-shirts with "Philly" emblazoned on them were playing tackle in the end zone abutting the gymnasium. The Philadelphia band members arrived, singly and in groups. One black youngster in his red band uniform and top hat looked to be five feet tall and twelve years old. As he ambled across the flat lawn above the highest seats of the grandstand carrying his trumpet, a white man caught him by the elbow and said, "I want you to blow that horn good, now." "I sho' will," the boy replied. Three old yellow school buses pulled into the parking lot behind the bleachers on the opposite side and the Eupora band emerged; the crackle of snare drums and one lonesome bass echoed in the stifling air. A slouching figure came onto the empty field and placed three tear-away jerseys with Number 22 on them on the Philadelphia bench. "Hey, Coach!" a little boy shouted. "Them for *Marcus?*"

The crowd was pouring in now, white and black people of all ages, some carrying cushions, with their children and babies and game programs and binoculars. In the seats between the twenty-yard lines, I noticed, the white and black townspeople sat together, and the rows where the students sat was a sea of white and black, but as the concrete grandstand curved toward the south end zone, the patrons were almost entirely black people. The Eupora bleachers on the west side were filling, too; it promised to be a capacity crowd, perhaps four thousand or more. The Philadelphia cheerleaders, six white girls and three black, came onto the field.

As I sat there in my solitude, I was suddenly overwhelmed with memories of my own high school days—the cheerleaders and majorettes, the yellow school buses, the little boys in the end zone, the parents sitting on cushions in the grandstand, the snare drums and trumpets, the heat mirages shimmering from the grass, the squeaky public-address system. I could have closed my eyes and been sixteen again, in Crump Stadium in the Yazoo of the Korean War years. The pretty blond majorette sitting with the band could have been my plantation girl of a generation ago; the band director, distracted and askew, could have been Mr. Stanley C. Beers; the coach with the tear-away jerseys could have passed for my old coach, Oscar "Buck" Buchanan; the couple seated on the fifty-yard line, the woman in a red summer dress and the man with the legal pad and pencil, might have been my own parents, now lying under a mimosa on the last hill before the Mississippi Delta.

Suddenly the two teams sprinted onto the field for their early warm-up drills, Eupora in maroon, white, and gray, Philly in red with white numerals. Seven or eight dogs of indeterminate pedigree had wandered up from the hollow and were sniffing around the field; one was lying on his back with all four legs straight up, and another was scratching a flea behind his ear. Several boys proceeded to chase them unceremoniously away. One of the dogs, small and rust-colored, wished to linger, but when he saw he was alone, he scurried through a small hole in the fence and under the Eupora bleachers.

I strained for my first glimpse of Marcus Dupree. Finally I sighted him near midfield as he waited motionlessly to catch a punt. He was not difficult to find, for he was one of the three or four biggest players on the field. He caught the punt and glided casually to his left, then returned to his original spot. He walked gingerly on his toes; there was a languid grace to the way he moved. He dominated the surroundings, like a soldier ant among aphids.

On the row in front of me, a visitor sat with a local who had a fine crop of red hair.

"Where is he?"

"Right there—see?"

"Hey! Look at them *legs!* Look at that *butt.* Can he run?"

"Shit, man."

All eyes were on him as he returned another punt. Then he walked back a few yards and began shaking hands with a few of the white and black Eupora players, towering over them. Others of the young Euporans came over for a handshake.

I counted fifty-two players for Philadelphia, thirty-three for the visitors, each of the teams about equally white and black. When they departed for the gymnasium before their final entrance, I explored the stadium. The odor of inexpensive perfume wafted up from the grandstand. It was easy to tell the town people from the ones from the country; the instincts of my upbringing had taught me to sense the difference. One man wore a red tractor cap with the words: "I'm a Redneck and Damn Proud of It."

"He better put on a show," the man was saying to his companion.

"They'll have six guys on him ever' time," his friend said.

All through the crowd were the rippling words . . . *Marcus, Marcus.* A group of elderly women in straw hats were clapping to the rhythms of the hometown band. A man with sparse hair plastered wetly to his skull held a child licking a lollipop and tried to converse with a neighbor about the Ole Miss vs. Tulane game the next day. Men stood about in clusters in their sleeveless shirts with open collars, and the talcum on the necks of the women in their gay print dresses was moist with perspiration. "If he get in the open, he go!" a black youngster shouted to some friends. Many of the blacks were in their Sunday best, and a few of the women wore jaunty little hats, Dresden figures of gaiety. Others of the black men wore the day's work clothes, still sweaty from the farm or lumber mill. There seemed a preponderance of little black children, ages three or four or five, who bounced up and down the steep aisles or eyed their diminutive white contemporaries with dark, sleepy eyes. I worked my way down to the door to the field house, and gazed upward through the diaphanous heat mist at the moiling Neshoba humanity.

At that moment the Philadelphia team came single file through the doorway. The children gathered around Number 22. The players waited restlessly as the Eupora Eagles, at the other side of the end zone, made their entrance onto the field to the somewhat dissonant strains of the Notre Dame fight song. Then their band burst into its "Hail to the Varsity," the fight song which Philadelphia High shared with the University of Michigan.

> *Hail to the conquering heroes,*
> *Hail to the victors valiant,*
> *Hail, hail to Michigan,*
> *Champions of the West.*

The players, led by their lithesome cheerleaders, sprinted through the papier-mâché sign with its words Go TORNADOES! onto the field.

From my station at the top of the grandstand again, I listened to the invocation on the loudspeaker by the Reverend Rudolph Whitehead, pastor of the Goodway Baptist Church. From the cadences of the language, and especially from the pronunciation of the words *ask* and *strength*, I knew that Reverend Whitehead was black:

> This evening, our heavenly Father, we are gathered here tonight to enjoy an evening of activity and fellowship with each other. Heavenly Father, help us to keep in mind the spirit in which we have gathered here tonight. Please have mercy on each player as they use their body physically here tonight in the great competition. Have mercy on the coaches of both schools who have trained the minds of these young people to be able to perform such a physical task. Father, we know that both teams cannot win tonight, so we ask you to give the team that lose the spirit to accept being a loser. Give them the strength to play a clean-cut game that each person here tonight can enjoy and be proud of. And when the game is over, guide us safely back to our different homes in peace. We pray in your name. Amen.

"And bless our offensive line," the man with the red hair on the next row said to his visitor.

Now both teams, Philadelphia in front of us and Eupora on the far side, circled around their coaches for their own prayer. As they did so, the cheerleaders gathered to one side and prayed too, finishing as if on cue just as the teams did. Then the co-captains, one white and one black for each team, met in the center of the field. Philadelphia won the toss of the coin and chose to receive the kickoff.

Allow me to arrest my narrative here for a brief elucidation. Although I appreciate the tactics and strategies of football, and in my lifetime have witnessed hundreds of high school, college, and professional games, I am not an authority on this sport, nor have I ever wished to be. However, I admire the game, if not the questionable values and aggrandizements which have threatened to damage it as it is played in the colleges of America; I honor the intelligent team struggle and the flair and distinction of the individual performance. Nor have I intended this to be "a book about football" (no more, say, than The Great Gatsby is a book about bootlegging, or "The Eighty-Yard Run" a story about a blocking back), and if it so turns out to be, then I will have failed even the most indulgent reader.

With apologies for that, I must now say that on this first occasion I watched young Marcus play, discounting as best I could all I had heard of him, I felt in the presence of true greatness—those composite elements of grace, discipline, power, and courage which, in their different contexts, shape the great musician or artist or teacher or poet. He was not merely a joy to watch—the unearthly speed in a human being so large, the felicitous deceptions and pirouettes, the horrendous authority when trapped or outnumbered, the spirit to rise time and again when crushed at once by three or five or seven opponents. There was something more dramatic and imperishable, and that was the recognition he evoked that at any given instant *anything could happen*—the highest note ever struck, the finest painting of a generation, the instantaneous seventy-yard run whose very effortlessness would disguise its virtuosity. It was this quality of potentiality which enveloped him, this awareness that on the next snap of the ball he might go all the way as no runner had ever done, that like the lighted fuse to the explosive he could ignite at any moment, that would distinguish him as long as he could carry a ball. Even the criticisms of his "laziness" had a certain logic for me; I perceived from this first game that whenever he got up slowly from a tackle, or moved indolently into a huddle or off the field, or dallied between plays, he was—in the words of the Gershwin brothers—merely biding his time, awaiting that instant flickering of time when he was free, open, and gone. So that from the beginning I was telling myself, as many others would say: If he does not get hurt he will go down as one of the great ones ever. This divination would magnify for me as the weeks went by.

Not that he reached immortality against the Eupora Eagles on this night, far from that. He suffered several leg cramps, prompting some of his local detractors to accuse him of being physically out of shape. He slipped a few times on the wet grass. More than once he was thwarted near the line of scrimmage, and only one time did he negotiate what football people call "the big play." The group tackling, or "gang tackling," was effective against him for long intervals. There would be subsequent games, two in fact, in which he would not score a touchdown, and two in which he would fail to carry the ball for the magical figure of one hundred yards. But it was that aura of the infinite possibility which always remained, and the fruition of which, time and again that season, that made my long drives south worthwhile, and my implicit trust in his future gratifying.

The absence of an experienced offensive line was obviously damaging to him in that first game. The blocking was careless and at times nonexistent, although those youngsters would gradually improve until they became an effective unit in the final games of the year. I could not help but reflect to what lengths he might go with a huge, mobile offensive line in college in front of him. And the fact that the Eagles of Eupora were the big, aggressive country boys I had been told they would be, anxious to test his formidable reputation, meant that at least three, often more, of those opponents "keyed" on him on every play.

That team strategy against him was apparent from the opening kickoff. As he stood deep to receive, the kicker bounced the ball about thirty yards. A Philadelphia player bobbled it, then held on to it and lateraled it to Marcus back on the twenty-yard line. By the time he had it, three men were on him, and he returned to the twenty-seven. The same happened on two subsequent kickoffs, and the Euporans never once punted to him, preferring shorter kicks out of bounds.

At first he was making modest yardage—four-, six-, eight-, ten-yard carries with powerful moves and swerves, taking three or four defenders with him. A black fullback named Daran Jackson usually alternated with him in carrying the ball. The visitors had an audacious tackler named Lopez Jones, who was not even listed in the game program. Could he have been a ringer from Slate Springs or Alligator?

Throughout much of the first half the teams moved up and down the field within the two twenty-yard lines. Penalties and fumbles negated any sustained drives. It seemed to me that Philadelphia's "Wishbone" offense —the fullback lined up directly behind the quarterback, with the two halfbacks to the sides of the fullback and slightly behind him—was severely restricting his running room from left half. In the fourth game of the season, the Philadelphia coaches would change their offense to the "I" formation, which would put their runner deeper behind the line of scrimmage with more space to maneuver and, in their idiom, "to pick his holes." It is fascinating to note that, almost precisely a year later, one of America's great college coaches would switch to the "I" formation for him, and for the same reasons.

Number 22 for a four-, six-, twelve-, and a fifteen-yard pass reception. The cheers from the Philadelphia side, full of their black rhythms, grew apace: "*Philly, you can do it, you can do it, you can do it tonight!*" But after another penalty, on a Philadelphia punt, the Eupora runner raced from his own thirty-yard line to the Philadelphia three. Two plays later Eupora scored, missed the extra point, and led 6–0 with seven minutes remaining in the first half.

With three minutes left in the half, he broke through the line from the Eupora thirty-eight-yard line for an eight-yard gain. As five tacklers converged on him, he was one step away from breaking into the open. The next play was revealing. Justy Johnson, the little quarterback, kept the ball on what was known as the "bootleg," moving alone to his left as Marcus faked into the right side of the line. Justy went untouched for six points while the defenders were tackling Dupree. With the failure of the conversion, the score was 6–6.

The home team got the ball again just before the end of the half. On a pitchout he broke three or four tackles and sprinted for twenty-one yards to the Eupora thirty-two-yard line before being driven out of bounds. On the last play of the half he went fourteen yards to the eighteen-yard line.

At the halftime I wandered around the stadium again. The dogs who had fled the field before the game were sitting in a group now in a corner of the south end zone observing the human proceedings with expressions of chastisement. Michael Smith, the hometown black who was now a freshman player at Ole Miss, had come back for the weekend and was surrounded by a throng of admirers. There were Mississippi State, Ole Miss, and Southern Mississippi caps and T-shirts in the crowd. The whites and blacks in the grandstand were milling about exchanging comments. "Better pitch it to him outside—he ain't gettin' it enough outside." As the Eupora band played "Ghost Riders in the Sky" on the field, I spoke with Mr. Joe King, a discerning Philadelphia sportsman who was enjoying a respectable dip of snuff. "Lots of rumors," he said, "but it's pretty quiet. Of course, the recruiters can't even talk to him during the season." Fred Akers of Texas was here recently, he reminded me. Also a Nebraska assistant, and an LSU fellow. Joe Paterno of Penn State had been telephoning, and of course there was the trip to Los Angeles and the house on Malibu. The spot for the most enterprising sports gossip, I discovered, was near the doorway to the gymnasium and dressing rooms, where the white and black citizens who knew their football congregated at halftime. "Nothing new," one of their number said. "It's the lull before the storm. There ain't even any scouts here tonight. They already know what he can do. They'll be in later on, though, that's for sure." Another volunteered: "He'll break loose. They got trouble with the offensive line. But he always picks up more yards than you think."

In the midst of the swirl and dervish of end-zone talk, the Philadelphia Tornado marching band had taken the field. I noticed young Kim Kilpatrick, the pretty teenaged daughter of friends, striding briskly and playing her flute. The flag bearers waved their colorful flags in the still, humid night and then, for the first time and by no means the last, the band burst into "New York, New York."

> *My little town blues*
> *Are melting away,*
> *I'll make a brand new start of it*
> *In old New York . . .*

Eupora took the second-half kickoff and drove for a touchdown, missing the point and leading, 12–6. Throughout the second half, Marcus was gaining six, seven, nine yards every time he carried the ball up the middle. But the Philadelphia team appeared ragged. The blocking was listless, and there were additional penalties. He limped off the field with a leg cramp in the third quarter and rested on a small table behind the bench. "I think he's got lazy," a man said. With his football helmet removed, the red hairnet covered his Afro haircut, and white and black children came up to the fence just behind the table and stared at him.

Late in the third quarter, the Philadelphia quarterback, on the same "bootleg" play, went for ten yards as the opponents swarmed as before on Number 22. After that, Marcus lunged straight ahead for eight.

Suddenly, with fifty-five seconds left in the quarter, on a counterplay to the left side from the enemy forty-two-yard line, he ran over three tacklers and was open. When the last defender had bounced away, he accelerated the now familiar mincing, gliding motion and simply outran the entire secondary by several yards. The grandstand came to life again with shouts and hugs and the band followed with "Hail to the Varsity." With another unsuccessful kick, however, the score stood 12–12.

From his defensive safety position, he intercepted a Eupora pass on the Philadelphia six-yard line in the fourth quarter. After punting, the home team stymied a Eupora drive on the seventeen-yard line, after which he made gains of ten, seven, and sixteen yards, all on power plays to the middle.

Regulation time ended in the 12–12 tie. But under new conference rules for a "sudden-death" playoff, each team was given the ball on the other's ten-yard line with an equal opportunity to score on four attempts. Philadelphia kicked a field goal from the five before Eupora failed in its four times. Philadelphia 15, Eupora 12.

His statistics were twenty-two carries for 179 yards and one forty-three-yard touchdown. "You didn't *see anything*," Daniel Mars, one of the Mars Boys who had philosophized with me in Oxford in the summer, said as we were leaving.

In my room in the Downtown Hotel that evening, I put down a few notes for myself in the staccato idiom of football: "Eupora was big, hard-hitting . . . The opposition will be ready for him and all over him this season . . . The way they pitch back to him on squib kicks, even when he's trapped, and he makes yards . . . He actually starts running forward from the goal line on kickoffs . . . The whole defensive line went after him on two quarterback bootlegs . . . His power on slants and plays up the middle . . . His breakaway speed on his touchdown run—nobody will catch him in the open . . . Little room to maneuver in the Wishbone . . . Who is Number 18, the white player who helps him on the sidelines with his tear-away jerseys? . . . The great affection of the blacks at the game for him . . . The mingled awe, affection, and suspicions of 'laziness' and 'lack of discipline' among some of the whites . . . I hope he doesn't get hurt this year with all the keying-in . . . I'm going to follow him on through . . . Maybe a room with a better view next week?"

I drove back to Oxford on a splendid morning of September. The cotton bolls lined the roads and there was a nimbus of early autumn on the land.

In Eupora, which was the halfway point of those journeys, I stopped at the Texaco station on Main Street to ask directions to the high school. I wanted to talk with the Eupora coach about last night's game. As all small-town coaches are on the Saturday mornings of the fall, he was sure to be in the gymnasium washing football uniforms.

As I was conferring with the proprietor of the service station, a sun-wizened old sinner in khakis chewing a great wad of tobacco walked up to me. He must have seen my Lafayette County license plates.

"You been to that game down there last night, ain't you?"

"Yessir."

"If you're a football scout for Ole Miss, tell 'em not to get that nigger halfback."

"Why not?"

" 'Cause he ain't no good, that's why. Get a white boy."

It pleased the old gentleman that I took down his name and address and told him that Coach Steve Sloan of the Ole Miss Rebels would be calling him tomorrow for that and other counsel.

# 6
# *Tensions*

In the 1930s a visiting writer described the Philadelphia region as "a neighborhood of earth-rooted individuals who know and understand one another and who collectively face an industrial revolution with hoes grasped tightly in their clay-stained hands." It was a lull before the restlessness of World War II in America, which would touch the towns of Dixie. The population of Neshoba County in the early 1940s, including Philadelphia, was 28,000; in 1964 it would be 20,000. The country hamlets and the rural terrain, as in other neighborhoods of the South, would become more and more bereft. Much of the loss of population in Neshoba in those years, of course, would be blacks migrating to the great cities of the East, the Midwest, and the West Coast—to Chicago, New York, Detroit, Los Angeles. But the blacks were not all. As in the rest of Mississippi, Philadelphia in that time would also lose ambitious young whites seeking better opportunities and cultural advantages elsewhere, so that the state became noted for its superior class of exiles.*

The disparity between white and black facilities in Mississippi in the thirties and forties was nowhere more evident, of course, than in the public schools. In the rural areas many of the black schools were one- or two-teacher institutions with disgraceful equipment. In the 1930s, 1,440 out of the 3,753 black public schools in the state met in churches, lodges, garages, stores, or tenant houses. Five months was the average school term for rural blacks. The average salary for rural black teachers was twenty-five dollars a month, thirty-five for teachers in city schools. Sixty percent of all the blacks in the public schools were in the first three grades, and only 5 percent in the high school grades. In Philadelphia as in the rest of the state there was one school board, composed of whites, for the city's white

* As a result of the continuing exodus, by 1970 an estimated 800,000 blacks who were born in Mississippi would be living outside the state. "The majority of these blacks," the Ole Miss historian David G. Sansing wrote in *Mississippi: Its People and Culture,* "were middle-aged adults who were just entering upon their most productive years. Out-migration was almost as significant among whites as it was among blacks. In 1970 approximately 650,000 white Mississippians were living outside their native state . . . These white out-migrants, like their black counterparts, were young, well-educated, and potential leaders. The loss of productivity which Mississippi has sustained because these young black and white people left the state is immeasurable."

and black schools. So much for the doctrine of "separate but equal" established by *Plessy* v. *Ferguson* in 1896.

The relative affluence brought about by World War II was tangible in Philadelphia. A country club and golf course were soon established. In those childhood years of Marcus Dupree's mother, there was more money in Neshoba County from shipbuilding jobs on the Gulf Coast, payments to servicemen, and an increase in long-term federal loans. The number of white tenant farmers dropped drastically. "This was the beginning," Florence Mars observed, "of a major change in the social fabric of Neshoba County. No longer would there be an enormous class of tenants who were poor and dependent on a small number of landlords for their livelihood and for loans." The condition of the black farmer also improved somewhat. The number of black tenants declined, though not as dramatically as among the whites. A substantial number of both whites and blacks continued to leave the county in the 1950s, but the black population remained at about one fourth.

In the mid forties a white businessman bought a large area of land across the tracks on the northwest fringes of Philadelphia and began selling it to blacks in small lots on credit. Many of them moved from their dilapidated rental houses to that neighborhood, which was Independence Quarters. In 1947 the town built a twelve-grade black school there and named it Booker T. Washington. Florence Mars remembered:

> Independence Quarters was annexed to the city, though it was more primitive than most areas in town. There were no sidewalks, the roads were poor, and there was no running water, sewer system, or garbage pickup until the mid-1950s. (There was no mail delivery until much later.) It was, however, a great improvement in the rental property. Despite the gradual improvement in the Negroes' circumstances, the overriding fact was that the Negro race had a certain place, separate and inferior to that of the white race.

The general population decline would likewise continue. From 1950 to 1960 the whites decreased from 19,064 to 15,026.

Throughout the South in the early fifties there was a deepening fear that the federal courts would intervene in the segregation of the schools. In Mississippi there was a desperate effort to improve the black schools to forestall that action. In the school year of 1952–53, these were the comparative figures in the appropriation of funds for white and black schools:

| Category | White | Black |
|---|---|---|
| School Enrollment | 272,549 | 271,856 |
| Transportation | $4,476,753 | $1,179,826 |
| Instruction | $23,536,002 | $8,816,670 |
| Average Teacher Salaries | $2,109 | $1,153 |

Every county in the state was required to survey its white and black schools. The results of the study in Neshoba County were emphatic: "Separate but equal" had meant "separate and unequal."

> Most of the school plants for white pupils in this county show planning, are well adapted to the needs of the school and community, and have been erected with local district funds . . .
> Due to inadequate financing the colored school buildings are generally small, the furniture and other equipment obsolete, and the surroundings unattractive.

The reports across the state, and in Neshoba County, cited the coal fires, wells, and outdoor toilets.


In Philadelphia, Mississippi, as throughout the South, the 1954 Supreme Court decision on the integration of the schools introduced a new day fraught with tensions. For many whites it spelled doom. I myself vividly recall reading the newspaper headlines in the old cafeteria across from Breckenridge Hall at the University of Texas, and my own feelings of surprise and unsettlement. The savagery of public discourse in the Philadelphia of the middle fifties would worsen with time. In Philadelphia and elsewhere, the years immediately following *Brown* v. *Board of Education* were dark and violent. At stake was the soul of the South, and meaningful dissent was all but impossible.

The Citizens' Council, a wholly legal organization composed largely of prominent professionals and businessmen, was formed shortly after the court decision. (Hodding Carter, Jr., would call the Council "the Ku Klux Klan with a clipped mustache.") "We want the people assured that there is responsible leadership organized which will and can handle local segregation problems," a Council member declared in a statement that would return to haunt Mississippians and Neshobans. "If that is recognized, there will be no need for any 'hot-headed' bunch to start a Ku Klux Klan. If we fail, though, the temper of the public may produce something like the Klan." There was an active Council chapter in Neshoba County. There, as elsewhere, refusal to join was viewed as treachery. Tut Patterson, one of the founders of the organization in the state, said: "There won't be any integration in Mississippi. Not now, not one hundred years from now, not six thousand years from now—maybe never."

I remember attending the first meeting of the Citizens' Council in my hometown in this period. I was home on vacation from the University of Texas; at that remove, and as editor of *The Daily Texan*, I sensed the portentous stirrings of those days. James J. Kilpatrick was espousing a doctrine called interposition, which sounded, to the bearer of adolescent loins, obliquely sexual. I recall the rage on the faces of the fathers of my contemporaries at that meeting, and an aura of disaffection almost palpable in its intensity. Since I loved my town very much, I could not reconcile my tender boyhood solicitudes with the scene before me. The NAACP had sponsored a petition demanding the integration of the public schools. Several dozen black citizens had signed it. Any employee who failed to remove his name would be fired immediately. Anyone renting property would be evicted. Anyone trying to buy groceries would be turned away. My neighbor from across the street rose. He had an unlikely name—Few White Ball. "I agree with everything you're doing," he said, "but I work for a national corporation. This is unconstitutional. It's against the Consti—" Few White Ball was peremptorily hooted down. "Sit down, Few, you old fool!" Within days, only one name remained on the petition, and he left town on the bus for Chicago.

In the spring of '54, one Tom P. Brady, a circuit judge who later became a Mississippi Supreme Court justice, wrote a book called *Black Monday*, which was published by the Citizens' Council. He argued that the court decision on segregation was part of a Communist plot and was not valid or binding. He urged that state officials work against its implementation. In Philadelphia and other towns of Mississippi, Brady's book was an accurate reflection of the predominant white attitude and became nothing less than a bible of defiance:

> The American negro was divorced from Africa and saved from savagery. In spite of his basic inferiority, he was forced to do that which he would not do for himself. He was compelled to lay aside cannibalism, his barbaric savage customs. He was transported from aboriginal ignorance and superstition. He was given a language. A moral standard of values was presented to him, a standard he would never have created for himself and which he does not now appreciate. His soul was quickened. He was introduced to God! And the men of the South, whether we like it or not, were largely responsible for this miracle . . . The veneer has been rubbed on, but the inside is fundamentally the same. His culture is yet superficial and acquired, not substantial and innate . . .

> The great barrier to the integration of the races has been segregation. It is also the greatest factor for peace and harmony between the races. The NAACP realizes that until the barrier is removed in the schools, churches, and in housing districts, integration of the races will be extremely difficult. For this reason, education on the grammar school level was the center of the target. You cannot place little white and negro children together in classrooms and not have integration. They will sing together, dance together, eat together, and play together. They will grow up together and the sensitivity of the white children will be dulled. Constantly the negro will be endeavoring to usurp every right and privilege

which will lead to intermarriage. This is the way it has worked out in the North. This is the way the NAACP wants it to work out in the South, and that is what Russia wants.

Six months after the Supreme Court decision, the citizens of Mississippi approved by a five-to-one margin a constitutional amendment tightening voting requirements; the amendment, in effect, made it virtually impossible for blacks to register to vote. There was little need for the new law in Neshoba County. Although a handful of blacks had registered there in the 1940s, the circuit clerk reported to Florence Mars that none registered while he was in office from 1948 to 1956, "and the clerk from 1956 to 1960 said she was certain that not more than eight Negroes were on the books when she took office and that not over four were registered when she went out. None of the Negroes who had been registered since the 1940s voted in the 1950s."

As a further result of Citizens' Council lobbying and the hardening of public opinion, in December of '54 the voters of Mississippi approved another constitutional amendment which authorized the state legislature to abolish the entire public school system if this were deemed necessary to prevent desegregation, either locally or statewide. Mississippians endorsed this amendment by two to one, and the voters of Neshoba County by five to one.

Something valuable was being destroyed in the South. In Philadelphia, it was noted, after the Supreme Court ruling, blacks stopped attending the Neshoba County Fair. "By the end of the year," Miss Mars would write, "I knew the old relationship between white and Negro was over, at least for a long, long time."

> The easy interchange on street corners could no longer be risked by whites for fear of being called "nigger lovers." I was sad that the unself-conscious openness of the Negro population was being lost to white Mississippians in their frantic resistance to the granting of constitutional rights. Because I knew the street scenes of Philadelphia would soon begin to change, I bought a camera and an enlarger, built a darkroom, and began to snap thousands of pictures.

In May 1955, fifteen months after its watershed decision, the Supreme Court ordered full compliance with its school desegregration ruling, but with "all deliberate speed"—in other words, with no specific deadline. The massive integration of the public schools, in Philadelphia and much of the South, would not take place for another fifteen years—the year Marcus Dupree was in the first grade.

Much suffering was to come in Mississippi. After the murder of Emmett Till, the fourteen-year-old Negro boy from Chicago who had whistled at a white woman in the Delta and the subsequent acquittal of the men accused of the killing, there would be the Meredith Crisis at Ole Miss with two deaths and scores of injuries. There would be Medgar Evers; and Schwerner, Goodman, and Chaney; and Martin Luther King; the harassments, burnings, and mob cruelties; the Raineys and Prices and Connors and Faubuses and Barnetts and Wallaces (or should we say, in 1982, the *old* Wallaces?); and the more muted yet effective defiances. "We speak now against the day," William Faulkner had said in 1955, "when our Southern people will resist to the last these inevitable changes in social relations, will, when they have been forced to accept what they at one time might have accepted with dignity and good will, will say: 'Why didn't someone tell us this before? Tell us this in time.'"

By the early 1960s Mississippi, and especially Neshoba County, seemed emotionally on edge. A decade of fear, suspicion, intimidation, and violence—both rhetorical and physical—had induced a perilous tautness of the spirit. On a single night in the spring of 1964, shortly before a future running back was born, twelve crosses were burned in Neshoba County—one on the courthouse lawn.

# 7

# Recruiting: the Real, the Sad, the Bizarre

Given the intricacies of college football recruiting in this nation, and the many aspects of it I did not particularly admire, I knew I needed an unimpeachable source, neutral yet discerning, shadowy yet authoritative, a figure I could call upon on the bleakest midnights for counsel and sustenance—a Deep Throat, if you will, whom I might trust as implicitly as Bob Woodward and Carl Bernstein trusted theirs in the unraveling of Watergate a decade before. I found him early on, a friend of friends who had played, coached, and recruited in college, and I shall protect his identity even on pain of incarceration in the Mississippi State Penal Farm in Parchman. I shall call him Temple Drake.

I met him in the lobby of the Peabody, that grand old mistress of the South which had recently been restored in all her grace and luster. I had driven up to Memphis that afternoon through an implacable thunderstorm, and I found him under the high-vaulted ceilings near the Travertine marble of the fountain nursing a George Dickel on-the-rocks. He was behind a man-sized potted plant, and he was peering out at me through the foliage. I suspected he might have read his Graham Greene.

"You're late," he said. "I got tired of watchin' these damned birds." With an impatient gesture of the forearm he dismissed the famous Peabody ducks as they waded about in the fountain.

I would confer frequently with Temple Drake during the next several months. Despite his exuberance for the colorful distinctions, I found him to be right almost every time, and on those few occasions he was wrong, everyone else was wrong too. I learned from him, as I did from others, that college football recruiting in our day was a subculture all its own, suffused with its own homages and rituals, a fraternity with its own codes and crescendos, a brotherhood of the skeptical and homeless, curiously united in both fellowship and distrust. The profession of the recruiter involved zany deceits in the night (and some not so zany), shadowing other recruiters like private detectives in pursuit of the lovers' tryst, hiding recruits from other recruiters, cultivating withered old grandmothers and cousins on the take. The recruiters themselves sometimes went berserk, and one could vouchsafe them that, for it was a dark and lonely calling; but as long as things were what they were, Temple Drake said, someone had to do it.

We dallied for a moment over our drinks, gazing out at the ebb and flow of the rich Delta wives who had come up for the day to shop on credit. My friend reminded me of the Englishman I once had met in Paris who was married to an Iranian oil heiress and felt he had to tell me first what *oil* was.

"College football is what it is because the American public wants it so bad," he said, examining me closely to see if our mutual friends might have overestimated me. "Everything else proceeds from there. Now why the public wants it so much is a question for the public. Right?"

I enthusiastically agreed.

"Now—this Dupree. I saw him play down there when he was in the ninth grade, and I told people he could've played college football right then. My only worry is that he could've matured too early. I've always looked for a kid who'll *progress*. But this kid's got it."

He could judge a boy, he said, by watching him play volleyball, touch football, or just running. "Hell, I don't even have to see him in a game. As long as he's got the ability, he can be tougher."

A tall blonde came by our table on the way to the bar. She wore a chartreuse dress and carried a Gucci bag. "I used to know her ex-husband," he said. "She's from Nashville and a pain in the ass. Height, weight, speed." At first I thought he was talking about the blonde from Nashville. "You can start with these three because they can be easily ascertained. The four hidden factors are character, education, ability, and desire. I've graded every kid on a one-two-three system, three being the highest. Most recruiters will agree, you've got to know a kid on these four hidden factors. Now, let's take my breakdown for backs and receivers on the tangible things." He reached into a pocket of his polyester jacket and brought out a pencil, then began to write on a Peabody napkin. I have the napkin before me now.

*Height*

| 5′10″ to 5′11″ | — 1 point |
| 5′11″ to 6′½″ | — 2 |
| 6′½″ up | — 3 |

*Weight*

| 165 to 175 | — 1 point |
| 176 to 180 | — 2 |
| 180 up | — 3 |

*Speed in 40*
4.8 to 4.75     — 1 point
4.7 to 4.65     — 2
4.65 and under  — 3

Along about here I was getting a little lost. "Is all this really relevant?" I asked, then immediately regretted saying it.

"You damned well better believe it!" he said. "Everybody goes about it in different ways, but it comes down to all this. One step further—any kid who grades less than five overall in all three categories put together, shit, I wouldn't even check him out." He looked at me again for a moment, as if I had scored far below five.

"Now, on *education*, for instance, if he scores seventeen on the ACT test, I'd give him one point, progressing on up from there. Then I'd send in the following to talk to the kid who scored high in these categories— the position coach, the area recruiter, then the head coach. But a combined five on height, weight, and speed, and only seventeen on the ACT test—he won't make it. Why waste your time?" He shrugged petulantly and took a sip from his drink. "You don't ride a jackass in the Kentucky Derby.

"Don't underestimate these football camps, either," he said. "Every major power has camps in the summer. They're great for the coaches. You get to see fifty to seventy-five kids from ten-year-olds through juniors in high school. You know about these boys when they're fourteen. It's a regular network.

"Of course, you gamble on some kids. Don't make the charts hard and fast. Now, you got some questions?"

I said I wanted to know about the recruiting itself. He hesitated momentarily. Was he reluctant to begin because he knew too much? As he sat there, the ducks left the fountain to the strains of a Sousa march and waddled across the lobby toward an elevator. He did not appear to notice. A large man at a nearby table, undoubtedly a Delta planter discouraged by the incessant rain, said to his companion: "I'm givin' up Mississippi for Lent." The pianist had just come to work, and he exhausted his entire Cole Porter repertoire before my confidant had finished. I had not heard such an eclectic *tour de force* since I was stranded years before in the airport in Montgomery, Alabama, and listened to Norman Podhoretz discourse on American letters. I have recorded this response as it was presented to me, and in its precise sequences, for I would not wish to lose the flavor of its circuitous edification.

"If you're smart," he began, "you won't stop with the parents. You'll go to the grandparents. Sometimes they've got more influence than the parents, especially the grandmothers. A friend of mine that I outrecruited on a blue-chip because I got in with the grandmother said he wanted to write a book called *American Football and the Grandmama*. If a kid's taller and bigger than his parents, then look at his grandparents—little things like that add up."

"Bear Bryant says the best thing you have going for you in recruiting is a boy's mother," I said.

"Well, that's true in most cases," Temple Drake replied. "But sometimes the grandmother advises the mother. And you've got to find out what the people at the drugstore and the pool hall think of him, also his coach and classmates and teachers and teammates. That's the character angle. I remember one boy who missed two appointments and we didn't give him a scholarship. He lasted two weeks at one little college, and four days at another little college with no trees and grass and on such a steep hill the buildings are gonna slide off someday. He's gone now. Everybody lost track of him. He's probably out on the streets sniffin' funny stuff. 'Yes' and 'no' in recruiting don't mean a damned thing. The boy changes his mind constantly under the pressure. Sometimes he gets so confused he says 'no' when he means 'yes.' You're sittin' in some town at 5 P.M. drinkin' coffee with the other recruiters, being real friendly and talkin' about everything but the kid, but the next day if one of you is missin', you go look for him. We used to steal each other's motel messages. You'll know where everybody else is going that day. You follow each other in cars." He interrupted himself to cast some disparaging judgments on a rival recruiter whom he did not particularly admire, an individual who had only recently retired. Carlyle, I remembered, had once called Emerson "a gap-toothed and hoary-headed ape . . . who now in his dotage spits and chatters from a dirtier perch of his own finding and fouling." Temple Drake's description of his own adversary was considerably more earthy and graphic, involving body orifices, appendages, and functions. Then he continued:

"You get lonesome. You haven't seen your family in about a month. You forget what grade your children are in. You're in a dry county way out in the woods and you just ran out of bourbon. One night I said what the hell and phoned the desk for two cold beers. The gal said, 'What are you, buddy, a dreamer?' Sometimes you're in a motel that's got black-and-white TV and doesn't take messages and the messages on the door disappear. All the times I've gone into a bathroom that's so small I sit on the commode and hit my head on the damned sink.

"Something will turn a kid. Sometimes it's the least expected thing, especially when he's highly recruited—a girlfriend, an uncle you didn't know existed who's gettin' ten thousand dollars. A favorite teacher is sometimes very important, sometimes more important than the coach. I remember a recruit that the shop teacher hid away for two days. You court the coach, court his friends. Who are the people in touch with the parents? Who's the banker? Who holds the loan? Who do the mom and dad work for? The grandparents?

"Bluff and win, bluff and lose. Small towns are tougher because everybody knows what you're doin' and what everybody else is doin'. The whole damned town knows. All the recruiters are keepin' up on everybody else's personal visits.

"It's changed a lot. When it went to the thirty limit, you began missin' a lot of boys who could've played for you. You miss the hell-raisers, the fighters who'll fight for you in every way. The worst mistake you can make is to take a kid so dumb he won't make the grades. Some of 'em mature too early. They won't get any better, and then the injuries come along and they fall apart. They've never encountered failure. This happens time and again.

"You want to know what's goin' on down in ol' Dupree's town? Find the most popular coffee shop closest to the motel and high school and the recruiters will all be there, bein' friendly and deadly. If I were a coach, I'd have invited Dupree's coach to the summer camp. I'd give him access to everything he wanted—our playbooks, weight programs, anything.

"For a big football power, there's a network of alums for hundreds of miles who know where every outside coach will be at any given moment —and they'll know where I am. I tell you, it's kind of spooky.

"It's different recruitin' a black kid from a white. You can usually trust the white boy's answer. A black coach may say, 'I'll produce him for a thousand dollars.' A black coach will sell out before a white one will. The NAACP may not like this, but I ain't a moralist, and that's the way it is. A black kid will tell you what you want to hear. He never wants to say no. His parents won't tell you anything. His grandparents will hide in the toilet. You knock on the door of a black house. 'Is Alvin Jones here?' 'Who? He don't live here.' They expect the law, or a bill collector.

"Payoffs . . . There's been very little bidding in the last three or four years. The green was really flyin' back then. Everybody's lookin' at everybody else more than ever. Everybody's scared of somebody findin' out. There's a hell of a lot of snitchin' going on. A few years ago in the South you could've bought who you wanted. It's still being done, but people are more careful. It has to be hidden cash, and after the boy reports to the campus for the first year. Otherwise, you'd probably lose your money. If alums give a boy what he wants after he graduates from college, so what? There ain't no way to stop that. You got long-range deeds of credit, long-range personal loans through other parties. Promissory notes on cars or houses, paid off mysteriously three or four years later. Then you've got the ticket deals. It's easy. I know one school that specializes in ticket deals. They'll give a good prospect fifty tickets a game, a great prospect a hundred tickets a game, and if he's *unreal*, two hundred a game. So this can't be traced, they'll call up some big rich alums and say, 'In addition to your X tickets a game, we want you to buy ten more—the extra are for Leon.'

Then they mix up the seating, and the ticket agent sells them for Leon. Ten dollars a ticket, that mounts up.

"It used to be simple. Put the cash in an old suitcase and tell 'em to bury it under the chinaberry tree in the backyard and spend it twenty dollars at a time. I was once all ready to sign a kid, and at the last minute he went with somebody else because of fourteen hundred dollars. One boy got paid off with a brand-new shotgun stuffed with hundred-dollar bills. If you got whipped as a recruiter, you either didn't do your groundwork or you got outbid by somebody. I'll tell you, about the worst I ever ran into . . . There was this running back with fifty coaches standin' outside his door. His mother was a laundress and lived in a shack. She got forty thousand dollars for a house and a forty-acre farm. He got a hundred thousand for a trust fund when he graduated from college. And he didn't even turn out to be that great anyway!"

With this Temple Drake laughed uproariously—the laugh itself a poetic retribution against all the unfairness and chicanery in the world—and people at other tables glanced our way. The pianist was playing "Dixie," and two men at the bar stood up and sang the words.

"Every college football recruiter's got his stories," he said. "Remember that old television series that everybody liked? 'The city's full of a million stories. This is just one of them.'

"I'll predict one thing, and you mark my words. When it gets down to the lick-log along about next February, just before the national signin' date, you're gonna see two or three recruiters who think they got him down in Philadelphia start gettin' a little crazy—*irrational*.

"Keep your eyes and ears open, kid. Maybe they don't like Marcus because he's colored. Maybe they only like him because he wins on Friday night. Here's a kid who's got the chance someday to put Philadelphia on the map all over the country, after all the stuff that happened down there. What if he tears up his knee in the fourth game of his senior year and can't ever play anymore? Wait and see how quick he'll be just another seventeen-year-old nigger again." He had uncannily echoed the words of another recruiter.

He stood up, shook hands, and wished me well. "I may not know as much about this as ol' Bear Bryant," he said in farewell, "but I damned near do." Then he drifted into the crowd and was gone. Cynic or realist, he had struck an apprehensive chord.

"Ol' Bear Bryant," to whom Temple Drake had paid his homage, likely knew more about college football than any living man.* He remem-

---

* The Bear had all but admitted that he bordered the thin line of ethics when he coached at Texas A&M. Right after A&M won its first Southwest Conference cham-

bered the days when coaches would hide boys out in the natural order of things—on boats or hunting trips or in luxury mansions with deluxe entertainment—to keep them away from enemy recruiters. Before World War II, recruiters would raid another campus in the middle of the night and virtually kidnap a talented prospect. When the Bear was head coach at the University of Kentucky another college came into Lexington and whisked away two youngsters from his freshman roster. "The raider accidentally left the bottom of a five-hundred-dollar check from a company . . . that happened to be in the school's hometown. The money paved the way for the detection. I called the school's athletic director about it. He confessed. He said they were starting a new program and he was desperate.

"He said, 'Bear, we just had to have them.'

"Hell yes, he did. They were the two best prospects around that year. I still have the bottom of that check."

The recruiting pressures grew more rigorous after the war. When Bear Bryant first got into coaching, he and a couple of his colleagues might swing through Pennsylvania, or Arkansas, and perhaps visit a prospect one time each. ". . . now you might see that same boy fifteen times. Besides that, you go, watch him play, and you have his coach send you films. The real good one who might have had one or two schools interested now has every school in the country after him. It takes a lot of character to cope with that kind of pressure."†

An exultant gentleman named "Tonto" Coleman, who was commissioner of the Southeastern Conference a number of years ago, once wrote:

What is football?

It is a wild and wonderful combination of intelligence, dumbness, speed, agility, and a large helping of violence.

It is a rugged game, almost brutal, for men only. Every weekend it might demand a fresh blood sacrifice. It is gallantry personified, the closest thing to gladiatorial combat that a supposedly merciful society permits. It is mock warfare, stern and awful, yet strangely stimulating. Its mystique is largely muscular but its appeal can be intellectual . . .

Football is not an original game. It was put together of equal parts of soccer, rugby, and genuine American spirit. It has absolutely no hold on

---

pionship in 1956, the Aggies were placed on probation. Doug Barfield, the former coach at Auburn, once said: "Go on as you have been and eventually get fired. Cheat more and survive. Or quit." Barfield was fired.

† *Bear* by Paul W. Bryant and John Underwood is required reading on recruiting, among other things.

foreigners. Even Canadians, who ought to understand us and our games if anyone in the world should, don't think we play football with enough men. To the English it is a dreadful bore, too many time-outs, not enough continuous action, don't you know, old chap? . . .

For all its bravado, football is at the mercy of the infidels, high school boards and college alumni who manipulate multimillion-dollar enterprises. It is a captive of its own ability to turn the masses into yowling drooly jawed wolves . . .

"Tonto" Coleman was right. I have often suspected that grown men and women turned out in such numbers, and with such abandon, for college football (and, in differing degrees, for professional football and baseball) out of almost primal wants: frustration, loneliness, boredom, fear, the need to belong. When human beings are alone and bored and full of *ennui*, they are known to become obsessed with their children, their marriage, their money, not to mention the inevitability of death. A stirring game on a lovely afternoon with all its accompaniments postpones with zest and purpose the last Appointment in Samarra. The wife of the college coach who told me that football is like sex because it brings relief was closer to the elemental truth than she may herself have known. Recently a football partisan of Louisiana State University wrote a letter to a Baton Rouge newspaper suggesting that LSU fans be allowed to be buried beneath the stands of Tiger Stadium. This arrangement, the writer said, "would go far toward satisfying the ultimate longings of loyal Tiger fans everywhere while simultaneously filling the void in athletic department coffers. The most obvious plan would call for the construction of burial vaults in the open space beneath the seats. Cost to the prospective interee would vary according to location, with crypts nearer the fifty-yard line commanding higher prices." ("It's hard to imagine a better place to try out [this] idea than LSU," *Sports Illustrated* observed. "Because of the storied inhospitality of the school's rooters to visiting teams, Tiger Stadium has long been known as Death Valley.")

Shortly after my clandestine conference in the Peabody with Temple Drake, I found myself with three voluble cohorts in the catfish place in Taylor, Mississippi, a sleepy little hamlet a few miles outside of Oxford where Faulkner had set *Sanctuary*. One dined there at long tables in the back of a general store surrounded by walls which bore three generations' scribblings of Ole Miss students and country folk: "Well, Daddy, we did it! Love, Mama . . ." "The Southern state of mind is another word for *Lutkenism* . . ." "Larry L. (Whorehouse) King et catfish here . . ." "If you ain't from Georgia, you ain't shit . . ." "Here lies one whose name

was writ in water. Love, D.T. . . ." "Bull Pussy Kirkpatrick . . ."
"Rudyard Kipling wrote of the American that he had a cynical devil in
his blood that bids him flaunt the law he makes, that bids him make the
law he flaunts."

Over a bottle of Old Charter whiskey I asked my companions why,
indeed, football was more important around here than other values.

"What are the other values?" one of them asked.

"I'll tell you what," another interrupted, "it's *pride*. Back in the
1950s and '60s when Mississippi was so down and out, and everybody was
dumpin' on us, Ole Miss was *winnin'*! At least we had somethin' to look
to."

"That's it," the third said, and he went on to describe a fistfight
which took place between two proper white businessmen in Clarksdale,
over in the Delta, two years before over whether Buford McGee, a black
halfback from Durant High School, was going to Mississippi State or Ole
Miss.

"The biggest football fans," another cryptically suggested, "are
bankers who don't get along with their wives."

One of my friends pointed out that the most didactic football people,
in his experience, often turned to intensive Bible studies in their mid
fifties. "And the *recruiting*, you see, is just like leadin' your people into
the Promised Land."


The process of recruiting, as my companion had said, had always
been essential to the delirium, and a hard core of football people had followed the recruiting rivalries involving their alma maters with a nearly
maniacal diligence. Temple Drake's assertion in the Peabody that there
was a web of alumni who knew at any given moment the whereabouts of
their own and enemy recruiters was no mundane exaggeration, and any
coach at Notre Dame or Nebraska, Penn State or Florida, would testify to
their alumni's disquieting though sometimes useful presence. One such
zealot at one of the Mississippi universities kept elaborate charts on individual prospects during the recruiting season and, as he subsequently told
me, received a number of telephone calls a day from others like him in
Biloxi or Jackson or Natchez seeking the latest intelligence. The usual sal-
utation in 1981 and early '82, he would inform me, was: "What have you
heard about Marcus Dupree?" In time this would be shortened to the
more manageable "What have you heard about Marcus?" and finally to
the simple "What have you heard?" I was granted access to his notebook
for that period on other recruiting prospects, and I pass along a few of

his enigmatic assessments here in the spirit of humane reserach, with the names disguised.

Smith: *Brother, leave him alone.*
Jones: *MSU. OM didn't offer "dog."*
Johnson and Edwards: *State doesn't want them real bad.*
Ledbetter: *Southern, maybe Tulane. Tulane can't get him in school.*
Louis: *We're worried. Has his hand out.*
Thompson: *Vandy, Bama, us. Vandy says can't pass freshman English.*
Benson: *State. Ghetto kid not a bad player.*
Baker: *Got off him early. Memphis State or Valley.*
Applewhite: *May score out of ghetto.*
Felix: *A little slow and wants stereo.*
Sutter: *If we want him.*
Gaston: *State, Jackson State, LSU. Mother hates Ole Miss.*
Paulson: *Us or Penn State.*
Davis: *Much $. Tenn. or Bama.*
Emmett: *4.5 40. Got picked up for pot.*
Fields: *Clemson, Auburn, us. Smart-aleck.*
Atkins: *Ark., Texas, O. State, not for us. Won't play hurt.*
Buss: *Little sis wants scholarship.*
Williams: *Will mature. Good risk. Us, Bama, Northern schools.*
Lester: *Bad back. Talks a storm. Still all systems go. Watch Bama, Tenn.*

In this esoteric context, before we move on, there were certain basic rules of recruiting, policed by the National Collegiate Athletic Association, which should be set down straightforwardly for the reader who was never moved to conduct such an intelligence system himself.

1. A recruit could make one official visit, for forty-eight hours and with all expenses paid, to each of six schools, and as many unofficial visits to various campuses as he wished on his own.

2. With the exception of the official visit, recruiters could not have personal contact with a prospect from the start of his high school football practice until December 1. They were allowed, however, to telephone or write the athlete as often as they wished. Most schools encouraged selected alumni and co-eds to telephone their prize frequently.

3. After December 1, recruiters could visit the prospect three times at his house and three times at his school.

4. Absolutely no gifts were allowed, from cars to cowboy boots to money.

5. The national signing date would be February 10, 1982. A prospect could not sign the formal papers with a school before that date, although nothing prevented him from announcing his choice unofficially at any time. Only his signature on the official papers would be binding. A pros-

pect did not have to sign on February 10. He could postpone his decision indefinitely if he wished.

6. Head coaches could actively participate in the recruiting but under a new rule would not be permitted to participate in the formal signing.

7. A school could give no more than thirty football scholarships each year, and the aggregate number of players on scholarships at any time must not exceed ninety-five.

This latter regulation, along with other strictures, had been designed in 1973 to give smaller colleges a reasonable chance to share the high school talent. In that year, also, freshmen were allowed to participate with the varsity, a change which encouraged many high school players to choose smaller schools where they might play immediately. For these reasons, teams like Boston College, San Jose State, West Virginia, and Tulsa were beginning to reach the Top Twenty in the national football polls. Before that, the most powerful teams had signed players they may never have planned to use simply to keep them away from rival schools. Johnny Vaught of Ole Miss was known to do this regularly at the apex of his success, as were many others. In 1973, just prior to the new emphasis on parity, Johnny Majors of Pittsburgh, later of Tennessee, signed sixty-nine freshmen in one year, which led to a national championship.

For poor families, of course, a football scholarship was more often than not of crucial importance. In the Southeastern Conference, for instance, a grant-in-aid in 1981 was worth approximately five thousand dollars—free room and board, tuition, and books. It was the constant possibility of additional inducements, from recruiters themselves and school alumni, which had prompted the beleaguered NCAA from its offices in Shawnee Mission, Kansas, to institute for the first time two new investigative programs. One, in the paramilitary language of football, was called "Operation Intercept," under which NCAA investigators would come into a "sensitive situation" to discourage transgressions, if possible, before the fact. The other, "Operation Big Brother," provided for NCAA representatives to advise the most valuable high school prospects and keep them out of undue difficulties. Beginning in 1979, the investigators made a list of the most sought-after high school football and basketball players in the country, then went out to observe firsthand what was going on. Each investigator tried to get acquainted with the athletes, their families and coaches, as well as to look into the actual recruitment.

For there could be no denying, in the autumn of 1981, that, on ethical grounds if nothing else, college football, along with other college sports, was deeply troubled. It was rife with questionable admission practices for athletes, transcript irregularities, cheating scandals, the failure of athletes to graduate, and blatant recruiting violations. The burgeoning power and control of television over college football seemed to go unchallenged. Court fights over multimillion-dollar television contracts served to jeopardize the future of college sports, especially football. Only a last-minute compromise with the NCAA averted a secession of the major football schools into their own self-aggrandizing organization, the College Football Association, which would bring in larger television revenues at the expense of the smaller colleges.

Not since Sputnik in 1957 had there been such a vociferous national debate on education. Yet big-time football continued to menace the priorities of higher education, but with television as its ally—or, one could say, as television's *adjunct*—the threat was now on a more ominous scale than it had ever been. "Loneliness in today's America, adrift in time," Theodore H. White wrote, "is a disease almost as perilous as inflation. It is the lonely who are particularly vulnerable to television, to its personalities, its fragments of reality." Many lonely people, and others not so lonely, were demanding the fervor of televised college football. The winning teams got the largest share of the TV revenues. Considerable money was out there to be made on the talents of athletes between the ages of eighteen and twenty-two. College football had become a vast and lucrative industry. "The only president who's ever been fired at Alabama was against football," Bear Bryant once said. "Any new president cuts his teeth on it, and he better be for it. Because if he's not, they won't win, and if they don't win, he'll get fired."

"You've got to be a winner, brother," the director of athletic fund raising for Texas A&M would say in 1982. "It's not everything, it's just life and death." The stress on winning, buttressed by the infusion of the television money for the successful, had at many colleges become all-consuming. Coaches' salaries and the fringe rewards had risen to six figures and more at many schools. The pressures from rich alumni were likewise growing. The athletic director at Vanderbilt would criticize those alumni who viewed educational institutions as athletic franchises. "They'll get the message," he said, "when coaches begin side-lining star quarterbacks because they've flunked English literature exams."

The athletic director of Vanderbilt had made a notable point. The failure of many college football players to complete their degrees, or to get a degree with little semblance of an education, may have been, in simple human terms, the most critical shortcoming of all. John Underwood's researches for *Sports Illustrated* served especially to expose those failings.

Lou Holtz, the disarming coach of Arkansas, said of one of his players, "He can do anything with a football but autograph it." The comment of Terry Donahue, the UCLA coach, on a judge's order that one of his ex-players learn to read and write while serving a jail sentence, was candid: "Gee, there's a lot of courses in this school where a student doesn't have to do much reading."

At another school, the success of one outstanding athlete whose thirteen hours of courses included Fundamentals of Recreation, Recreational Leadership, and a freshman geology course known as "Rocks for Jocks," prompted his academic advisor to say, "We're really making strides." Digger Phelps, the basketball coach at Notre Dame (which had one of the highest graduation rates among athletes in the country), believed the largest injustice was the failure of so many athletes to get a degree, or to graduate with a major that meant little or nothing.‡ "I don't think there's a school in the country where the academic requirements for admission of the regular students is the same for the athlete. There are certain situations now where you need a 2.0 average to graduate and a 1.9 average to be eligible to play. Now what are we doing to that kid? He's eligible to play sports, but he's not eligible to graduate." In most cases, Phelps had said, high school athletes reach college without sufficient college preparatory units—history, English, math. "We're saying we've got to go to a progressive plan, from eight college prep units to ten or twelve so that five years from now students coming out of high school will have a fundamental academic background."

In his memoirs Paul Brown, owner and coach of the Cleveland Browns, and later with the Cincinnati Bengals, described the changes in professional football after he returned to that sport in 1968. "We were getting a different type of player from the colleges," he wrote, "and a certain percentage of them were not what I considered college material. They had been exposed to education, but not actually educated. One player of mine, for example, said, after he retired, that he wanted to return to his university to get his degree—but that it would take him three and a half years to get it. That man had already completed four years of college when he had been drafted, and I can't imagine what he had been doing during that time. His type of athlete was becoming increasingly common."

Not too long before his death, the incomparable Red Smith published in his column in *The New York Times* an essay written by a football player at a major university. "He is an attractive young man," Smith

‡ A survey by the NCAA of the years 1975 to 1980 disclosed that only 42.9 percent of college football players graduated. In a similar study *The Sporting News* reported that 45 percent got degrees, ranging from 100 percent in the Ivy League to 16.7 percent in the Southwest Conference. Another study by *The Shreveport Journal* of five Louisiana universities discovered that 31.6 percent of the players who received football and basketball scholarships in 1977 and 1978 went on to graduate. Tulane University raised the average, but the figures for LSU were 18.2 percent and for Louisiana Tech 16.6 percent. In 1981 six of ten seniors playing college basketball in the U.S. did not graduate.

wrote, "short months away from graduation, the best wide receiver in the school. One of his professors, who happens to be a football buff, asked him why his teammate, John Doe, never played first string although he was a better passer than Richard Spelvin, the starting quarterback. The young man said he would write the answer 'like it was a quiz.' What follows is an exact example of the young man's answer. That is, it is exact except for the names" (including the team name *Yankees*):

> People (Some) feel that Doe did not have the ability to run the type of offense that the yankys ran. He also made some mistakes with the ball like fumbling.
>
> As a wide receiver it didn't make me any different who quarterback. But I feel he has the best arm I ever saw or play with on a team. Only why I feel the way I do about the quarterback position is because I am a receiver who came from J.C. out of state I caught a lot of pass over 80 and I did not care a damn thing but about 24 in one year.
>
> Spelvin is my best friend and quarterback at my J.C. school. Spelvin has an arm but when you don't thrown lot of half the time I dont care who you are you will not peform as best you can. Spelvin can run, run the team and most of all he makes little mistakes.
>
> So since they didn't pass Spelvin was our quarterback. But if we did pass I feel Spelvin still should of start but Doe should have play a lot. Tell you the truth the yanky's in the pass two years had the best combination of receivers in a season that they will ever have. More—ask to talk about politics alum Doe problems just before the season coaches hate?

"The importance of disguising the names of these student athletes and the identity of the university is obvious," Red Smith wrote. "It would be unforgivable to hold a kid up to public ridicule because his grip on a flying football was surer than his grasp of the mother tongue. He is only a victim. The culprit is the college, and the system."

> The young man's prose makes it achingly clear how some institutions of learning use some athletes. Recruiters besiege a high school senior with bulging muscles and sloping neck who can run 40 yards in 4.3 seconds. The fact that he cannot read without facial contortions may be regrettable, but if his presence would help make a team a winner, then they want his body and are not deeply concerned about his mind.
>
> Some colleges recruit scholar athletes in the hope that the scholar can spare enough time from the classroom to help the team. Others recruit athletes and permit them to attend class if they can spare the time from the playing field. If the boy was unprepared for college when he arrived, he will be unqualified for a degree four years later, but some culture foundries give him a degree as final payment for his services . . .
>
> Where outside of pro football can our wide receiver go? He can pump gas. He can drive a truck. He has seen his name in headlines, has heard crowds cheering him, has enjoyed the friendship and admiration of

his peers and he has a diploma from a famous university. It is unconscionable.

Unconscionable, too, at least for me, was the practice of dropping
players from their grants-in-aid scholarships, which were renewed at the
end of each year, for being marginal on the football field, even though
they may be doing well in class.

And what would happen to the big linemen and backs who were
directed to gain ten, thirty, or fifty pounds through the organized weight
lifting—euphemistically called "the strength program"? I was strolling
one afternoon outside the Ole Miss football stadium with Josiah Bunting,
the president of Hampden-Sydney College in Virginia, who was down on
a visit. We stood for a moment and watched the football players exerting
themselves with the heavy weights.

"I feel sorry for them," Bunting said. "They gain all this brawn to
play football, and then football is over and they stop weight lifting. It's
physically unhealthy." What would you do, I asked. "I'd encourage them
to swim," said Bunting, who was an all-American swimmer in college. "I'd
get them in the routine of swimming. At least they could carry *that* with
them."

In the winter of 1983, as this book was being completed, the seventy-
seventh convention of the NCAA, meeting in San Diego, approved a
sweeping plan to stiffen entrance requirements on athletic scholarships.
Known as Proposal 48, the new rules stipulated that a college athlete
must have a C or 2.0 grade average in high school, a "core curriculum" of
three years of high school English and two each of social science, math,
and physical or natural sciences, and a minimum score of 15 on the American College Test (ACT) or 700 on the Scholastic Aptitude Test (SAT).
These reforms would take effect in 1986 and would apply to the 277 Division I schools. A loophole specified that athletes who failed to satisfy the
requirements would be allowed a scholarship but could not play their first
year, losing also a year's eligibility.

The "core curriculum" was a key part of the new rules, since equal
consideration had been given to the athlete who took high school vocational-technical courses along with the student who had completed English, history, and physics. The problem lay in the specific required number on the SAT and ACT scores. The scores of 700 and 15 on those
standardized tests usually excluded the lower third of high school seniors.

Some one hundred and twenty-five college presidents rather than the
usual twenty-five or thirty attended the convention which adopted the

proposal. Joe Paterno of Penn State, an honorable man, took the lead among the football coaches. Arguing against the "exploitation" of college athletes, he charged that black players in particular had been "raped" by a system which utilized their talents without giving them an education. "We can't afford to do that to another generation."

A substantial number of blacks, especially from the predominantly black colleges of the South, immediately called the new regulations racist. The standardized tests, they said, were biased toward fortunate whites and discriminated against young blacks from poor backgrounds. Jesse Stone, the president of Southern University, the largest predominantly black college in the country, was a fierce opponent. Jesse Jackson, the civil rights activist, called the rules "short-sighted and mean-spirited. They used literacy tests to deny us the right to vote. Then they want to use standardized tests because white boys are inferior athletes to blacks." *Sports Illustrated* commented: "Colleges could do a far better job of providing a real education to the disadvantaged athletes they lure onto their campuses . . . Instead of Proposal 48, the NCAA should adopt and *enforce* proposals that will require its member schools to educate those athletes they now only exploit."

The academic counselor for the athletic department at Iowa State, Dr. Gerald Gurney, reported that tests showed 95 percent of the athletes in a single, unspecified freshman class at that university had reading levels below the tenth grade and 10 percent were functionally illiterate. This situation was probably the same at other major colleges, he said, because of poor classroom programs in high school. In many cases, he argued, the athletes had average or above-average intelligence but were not being given a serious educational program. He cited the remedial program at Iowa State for these unprepared students. "There's a great deal of concern that the rule will keep many black athletes out of college. ACT scores aren't a fair measure of predicting academic success for minorities. But for white Anglo-Saxons, it's a good measurement."

Many in the academic community considered collegiate athletic reforms long overdue. Yet some thoughtful people had pause. "I believe the black student has an average of 12 on the ACT or 694 on the SAT," Eddie Robinson, the longtime coach of Grambling, said. "One coach said he wasn't concerned about the numbers. He just wanted some criteria. I don't believe I could confront a young man who hadn't scored 15 or 700 that he couldn't play football when somebody else who didn't make those scores was still in the band. And if it's good for Division I, why isn't it good for Division II or III?"* A friend of mine, a white woman whose

* The latest figures showed blacks averaging 707 on the SAT and whites 927. Only 28 percent of blacks who took the ACT in 1982 surpassed the NCAA minimum of 15. Tom Osborne, the football coach at Nebraska, agreed with Eddie Robinson

teenaged son played sports with young blacks in high school, shared Robinson's concerns. "Let's include the cheerleaders, the pep squad, the band," she said. "How about the sorority girls who don't know what a book is and never came close to a 2.0? What about the high school *teachers?* If we penalize the black kids being raised by their grandmamas, let's at least know what we're doing and don't stop there." The reforms likely had to come, one admitted. But they touched on the broader academic malaise. The issue was fraught with the deep and anguished American complexities.


A number of critics believed there was more cheating in college football and basketball than ever before because the rewards for winning had grown so immense. In the autumn of 1982 a record seventeen major colleges were on NCAA probation, and another thirty-five were under investigation. Research by Robert Heard of *The Texas Alcalde* revealed that in the three decades since its member institutions granted the NCAA authority to sanction transgressors, at least 114 major schools had been penalized by the NCAA at least 171 times. (The NCAA was secretive about those figures, but other sources said the number was 250.) "These are not penitentiaries we're talking about," he concluded. "Nor even competing business enterprises. These are institutions of higher education. They should be expected to cheat about as often as churches." Twentynine schools had been punished more than once. Southern Methodist had been caught five times, Miami of Florida and Wichita State four each. These had been on probation three times: Arizona State, California, Florida State, Indiana, Kansas, Michigan State, Mississippi State, North Carolina State, Oklahoma, UCLA, and Southern Cal. Fifteen schools had been sanctioned twice. In football the NCAA punishment had included bans on televised games, bowl games, or other post-season competition, ineligibility to appear in the United Press International's weekly poll of the country's best twenty teams, and occasionally the loss of a certain number of scholarships. In early September of 1981, at the start of Marcus Dupree's senior year in high school, the NCAA informed the University of Southern Mississippi, which was one of the many schools seeking to enlist him, that it had begun a preliminary inquiry into the Southern athletic department for recruiting violations.

---

that the new rule was discriminatory: "You might have two individuals with the same basic intelligence. If one had not been in a good school system, had not been in a home where there were books, where a certain vocabulary is in use, that person will not test as well." Harry Edwards, the black sociologist at Berkeley, who specialized in race and sports, also disagreed with blacks' opposition to rule 48 arguing that the academic standards were not high enough. See his forceful essay "Educating Black Athletes" in *The Atlantic Monthly*, August 1983.

"The real hypocrisy," District Court Judge Philip Baiamonte said in a ruling, "is when colleges across the country maintain and establish professional ball clubs in the guise of amateur rules." But, in 1981, the job of the NCAA in trying to enforce these regulations was an impossibly difficult one. The NCAA Enforcement Division in Shawnee Mission had only eight full-time field investigators, two assistant directors, a director, and an "assistant executive director" charged with guarding the rules. Forty former FBI men, who had been working as arson investigators for an institution called the National Fire Association, were about to join this group on a part-time basis. "I hope they bring their fire hoses," one football cynic said. Lacking the power of subpoena or to obtain bank and financial records—it could not deal with criminal law, only with its own regulations—the NCAA had traditionally relied on tips from disgruntled coaches eager to inform on their rivals, reporters, and parents of athletes who were being recruited.†

The NCAA was beginning to devote more time and money to enforcement and was trying to simplify its procedures. David Berst, the director of its enforcement arm, believed that as the sentinels were becoming more diligent and sophisticated, so indeed were the transgressors. He told the Associated Press:

> In the early 1970s . . . you might have a head coach just walk up and offer somebody, say, a Pontiac GTO. There might have been a head coach or two who figured they would do that and, if the NCAA did hear about it, it was unlikely the NCAA would ever get around to investigating. And if they did get around to investigating that it was unlikely anybody would ever get punished. We nailed a couple of people in cases just like that. And then we noticed that cars started showing up titled through a prospect's sister-in-law, or grandmother, or whatever. And bank loans came into play. We've had to learn a lot about banking procedures. We've grown more savvy, but so have the cheaters. I guess you could say we've grown up together.

The difficulties in adequate enforcement had been complicated in some measure by the sweep and complexity of the NCAA rules and procedures themselves, which in some cases appeared niggardly. A college could give a young football player a paid forty-eight-hour trip to its campus and a full scholarship, but a cheeseburger away from the campus, a T-shirt, a pair of school sneakers, or presumably a package of bubble gum or a novel by Harold Robbins were violations, at least technically.

Otis Singletary, a distinguished friend from my earlier Mississippi

† Digger Phelps rocked the sports world in 1982 when he claimed that a number of colleges were paying $10,000 a year to basketball players. Although he did not identify the schools, he said that the payoffs usually came from assistant coaches, fans, and alumni. My own conclusion was that a great deal more cheating was taking place in college basketball than football.

and Texas days who was president of the University of Kentucky (which itself had been on NCAA probation in the middle 1970s), cited "these petty-fogging little things" as one of the three most significant problems with the serious athletic schools, along with the recruiting process and the academic failings. The NCAA and its rulebook, he argued, should be simplified and college presidents should involve themselves more actively in reforming their own houses. More important, Singletary declared, he would not be surprised if coaches and athletes themselves were to be punished in the future for violations of the rules. In the past, only the offending colleges had been made to pay. Walter Byers, the executive director of the NCAA, had likewise argued that college presidents should try to wield more control in the policing of athletic transgressions, although many presidents might find that hazardous. "You may end up directly opposed to one of your most influential alumni, some of your highest donors, your state legislature," Byers said. The penalties for violations should also be more stringent—taking away more scholarships, prohibiting the football coaches from recruiting away from their campus for a year. "I'm for something dramatic in this situation." Digger Phelps had advocated a policy under which an athlete who had accepted a scholarship but violated a rule while being recruited should lose his eligibility. "He keeps the scholarship but he can't play anymore. The school and the coach should go on automatic four-year probation. If the coach leaves the school, the probation follows him." Bill Bradley of Princeton and the New York Knicks who was elected in 1978 to the U.S. Senate from New Jersey advocated an even more drastic policy. "I've long felt," he said, "that college athletic programs simply should operate on two different tracks, semi-pro and amateur." It was an intriguing notion:

> Colleges that elected to go the semi-pro route would accept and pay the star athletes who are uninterested in academics but eye careers as professionals.
> These colleges could say to the athletes, "All right, if you want to take the thousand-to-one chance you eventually will make the grade professionally, we'll do our best to prepare you for it." Such athletes would be enrolled in special programs, centered on courses that could help them in their professional sports careers.
> I favor there being some semi-pro programs because colleges should not have to make the pretense that all athletes are in college to gain an education when, obviously, many of them are not.

Bear Bryant of Alabama told of a college which offered a high school player $15,000, and lost him to another school. Another offered a young man $48,000 over a four-year period and he went elsewhere. "The athletic departments aren't doing it, of course, because that would be suicide.

They let the alumni do it." Could anything be done about all this? he asked in his book:

Sure. Do a net worth on every kid and his parents when he's in the eleventh grade—I'm talking about the kid who is a skilled athlete, the one schools are going to be after—and then do another net worth on them when he's a junior in college and see what they have earned in the meantime. That includes clothes, automobiles, everything. You would either end the gossip or find some interesting things.

Can the NCAA do such a thing? Hell, yes, if they want to. And if they get a boy or a school who won't tell where the goodies came from, or if they turn out to be crooks, ban the boy for life and ban the coach, too. Make 'em both ineligible. A kid knows. A parent knows. An alumnus knows when he gives something. But nothing happens to them.

It's stupid to punish the school. Some people who cheat want to win, period. They don't care if they're on probation, they just want to beat somebody's tail. Ban that kid for life, and kick the coach out of the conference, and you won't have to ban any more. You'll put the fear of God in them.

Beano Cook was known by some as the conscience of college football, if anyone on television could be called that. He loved the game but perceived its problems; he considered it a finer sport than baseball or professional football. When the American hostages from Iran were given lifetime passes to major-league baseball games, he asked, "Haven't they suffered enough?" Nor did he think college football was a farm system for the National Football League. "The colleges were there before the NFL. If you ask me which of the two will be around a hundred years from now, I'd say college football. College football will always be there. College football's problems are off the field, not on. It's a more interesting game than pro football because the colleges play to win instead of not to lose." When Beano Cook began his commentaries for ABC-Television in 1982, *Sports Illustrated* said: "Cook isn't always right, but you do have to admire his independence. No longer can ABC be accused of shilling for the NCAA TV committee."

To Cook, as to many others, the game was not what it had been ten or twelve years before. With the threat of the College Football Association, the new lobbying group composed of the 60 most entrenched football powers from every major conference except the Big Ten and Pac-10, Walter Byers, the director of the NCAA, had lost much of his base of power, and with that much of his idealism. "With what's happened in the last six or seven years in college sports," Cook argued, "with so many players not graduating, the average fan has become more cynical about college athletics." He proposed NCAA penalties to deal with such abuses; a college should graduate a specific number of players on pain of losing a certain percentage of its athletic scholarships. More basically, the monetary rewards for college football had gotten much too high. "Too many college presidents," he believed, "have sacrificed the principles of what a university stands for because of the TV money."

In 1982, CBS and ABC were paying the NCAA and its member institutions $263,500,000 for television rights to college football for four years. Five more minutes of commercial time—from twenty-three minutes to twenty-eight—were allowed for each game. It had become apparent even to the most casual observer that television, with its stress on the values of show business, on the *event*, or the message—to paraphrase the mystic of the 1960s, Marshall McLuhan—was a principal menace to college football. The arrogance of moving kickoffs to 11:30 A.M., of encouraging night games in stadiums with their daytime tradition whose administrators found it appropriate to bring in portable lighting, of interrupting scoring drives with long official time-outs for commercials would have been disquieting enough. "If during the sixties," David Halberstam wrote, "the great story for a serious sports journalist was race, in the seventies it was more and more what television and concurrent big money had done to sports . . . the excess that television had wrought upon sports, of the assault upon civility and texture that the tube with its need for action and event demanded."

College football, as other institutions in American life, likewise seemed a potential victim of the development of the new, sophisticated technologies of cable and pay television. The College Football Association, the organization of dissident football powers, sensed these burgeoning revenues available from television when it demanded in 1982 that its members receive most of the TV money on threat of seceding from the NCAA. The NCAA acquiesced; the television revenue would no longer be divided among the other Division I schools but only among the 60 members of the CFA and their opponents. For these purposes the Division I colleges were reduced from 137 to 97. A new classification, 1-AA, was established, and included the poorer kin of the Missouri Valley Conference, the Mid-America Conference, and the Ivy League, who would no longer share as much as they had previously in the TV contracts. Also in 1982, a federal judge ruled that the NCAA's TV package— its contract with the networks under which the major teams could only appear on television a certain number of times a year, while some smaller teams in the lower divisions would occasionally have their turn—was in violation of the antitrust laws, and that each school could negotiate on its own with network and local television. The ruling was subsequently upheld by the Tenth U.S. Circuit Court of Appeals and would likely go to the Supreme Court; if sustained there, it could bring chaos. The Alabamas and Oklahomas would make all the television money, and the smaller schools would, in effect, be excluded from TV exposure. A dozen or more of the traditional football giants would have most of the television revenues all to themselves, and this might lead to the destruction of college football. As Marcus Dupree began his senior year, the sport was at a critical juncture.

Under these circumstances, the gravity of recruiting was more pointed than ever, and the demands on the individual recruiter to sign the superior prospect had increased. As Temple Drake would say to me, "Better watch out. Better keep the losses down. You ain't got no tenure."

The temptations to cheat were always there, especially as the high school talent became more skilled and better coached. The boys were getting larger and faster. The possibilities were always high that the recruit would stand one up and eventually go to another school, in which case he might lose fifteen pounds and a full second in the hundred-yard dash overnight, and acquire an abrupt history as a thief of stereo equipment and cashmere sweaters. On the other hand, there were no scrupulous or mathematical assurances that a transcendent high school athlete like Marcus Dupree, whom one had followed for months and finally signed, would fulfill his promise. The world of college football was rich with tales of the Duprees who had, in Temple Drake's words, "matured too early," or quit, or gotten hurt, or become the stand-in for a less glamorous young man who has never attracted half the attention.

Little surprise that Bear Bryant would say, categorically, "I hate to recruit," or that Darrell Royal of the University of Texas would stress his distaste of recruiting as one of the main reasons he retired in his prime. "Recruiting has never changed and it never will," Emory Bellard of Mississippi State said. "It's the same thing. You're going night and day." Here is an unspectacular vignette from a piece by Jerry Potter of the Jackson, Mississippi, *Clarion-Ledger:*

> On Sunday Tennessee football coach Johnny Majors returned to Knoxville from a week on the road. He unpacked, repacked and hit the road again Monday morning.
>
> In between, his wife Mary Lynn told him, "John, if you die before I do, I'm going to bury you in a travel bag."
>
> Last Thursday, Majors answered a message to return a call.
>
> Coach, where have you been?
>
> "From the East Coast to the West Coast in the last three days," he answered.
>
> Where are you now?

"In the Midwest, at Chicago."
How much longer are you going to be out?
"At least another week," he said.

Much of the active recruiting had devolved upon the assistant coaches who handled, again in the terminology of the trade, "the groundwork," while the head coaches often came in to "close out the deal." The rituals had become so complicated and highly charged that most of the big schools had a "recruiting coordinator" who remained on the campus and supervised his men in the field. (The names Jerry Pettibone of Texas A&M—he was the first full-time recruiting coordinator, at Oklahoma in 1971—Ken Dabbs of Texas, and Scott Hill of Oklahoma were often mentioned as prototypes in this executive category.) He kept detailed records on the candidates, organized the assistant coaches' travel plans, oversaw the official campus visits, and ascertained whether the prize at hand, during the period when personal contact was disallowed, was receiving the usual letters and telephone calls of solicitation. Often he encouraged alumni and students to write or telephone the prospect. Some schools organized well-spoken co-eds to use the long-distance telephone.‡ One partisan of Southern Mississippi in Philadelphia, Mississippi, circulated the story that Marcus Dupree had received a call from a black co-ed who was a "Rebel Recruiter."

"What are your major interests?" the co-ed asked.

"Sports and women," the diffident young running back was said to have replied.

"Well, there are plenty of sports at Ole Miss, and I'm a woman."

There were peculiar risks, of course, in the use of co-eds as recruiters. When an athlete arrived at a campus on his forty-eight-hour "official visit," he would often be escorted here and there by a designated co-ed, not unlike, in the principle of it, baseball's designated hitter. "You have to be careful that our girl, or girls, don't make the boy's girlfriend back home jealous," a Southern coach told me. Or as Temple Drake put it, "The girls have to be diplomatic if the situation calls for it."

There were other, minor perils in the official visits. Larry Rea told of two prized recruits in Tennessee who were advised they could order whatever they wished during their stay at a select hotel and charge it to the university. Their first order included two sizable steaks, potatoes, a whole chicken, two slices of cream pie with ice cream, and a chocolate cake. The bill came to $155. The two young men were entertained until late at night, then returned to their rooms and selected steak, eggs, pancakes, and ham. After a tour of the football stadium the next day, they came back and or-

‡ One recruiting coordinator said: "In the course of their phone conversations, the girls find out things that maybe the recruits don't tell our coaches. So when they do come visit us, we can show them the things they are most interested in."

dered dinner for two for $112. Breakfast in the morning was steak and eggs. Their hotel food bill for the forty-eight-hour sojourn—bless the gluttony of growing boys!—was more than $300.

At the most ambitious schools, recruiters were divided into two classifications—"evaluators" and "salesmen"—the former usually being a coach who analyzed the films of the player in action and composed the critiques of how successful he might be in college. The magazine *Inside Sports* named Bill Rees of. UCLA as an example of one of the best "evaluators" in the country, while among the "salesmen" it was difficult to outwit Bill McCartney of Colorado. For an insight into the criteria of the "salesmen," here was the magazine's assessment of McCartney:

> He gained his reputation at Michigan, where he was an assistant coach. McCartney was in charge of the Wolverines' recruiting in Florida, where he found Anthony Carter and Stefan Humphries. As many as a half-dozen Florida products are expected to contribute at Michigan this year, including freshman place-kicker Pat Moons. It's not easy to sell a high school player from Florida on moving 1,250 miles away from home to play in the snow, but McCartney hopes his technique continues to work at Colorado, where he was named head coach this summer. He was listed in "20 Questions" last year as one of the five best defensive coordinators.

I did not know that I would soon be on friendly terms with, among others, such persuasive salesmen as Tommy Reaux* of Texas and Lucious Selmon of Oklahoma, who would enliven this narrative more than I might ever have foreseen.

At the heart of this system, giving blood and substance to its immense hierarchy, were the assistant coaches in charge of the "groundwork." They were usually in their late twenties, thirties, or early forties; more often than not they were unsung, underpaid, and overworked, and after observing them at their multitudinous labors I believed they deserved to be organized into a trade union. They bore the most onerous burdens, as Temple Drake had described them to me, of the premises of big-time college football. They were active coaches—of linebackers, or cornerbacks, or interior linemen, or running backs, or receivers, or offensive linemen, or quarterbacks, or "special teams." In this capacity they worked from dawn to late at night supervising their charges in practice, studying endless footage of film, contributing to "game plans," scouting enemy teams, wandering the sidelines in concentration at the games themselves. Only the most unvarnished love of the game must have kept them true to these pursuits, this and the omniscient hope that someday they too might

* Pronounced Ra'-yo.

have "the head job" somewhere. During the football season they might attend a high school game hundreds of miles away to study a player, returning just in time for the team breakfast on their campus before an important game. When the season was over—from December 1 to the middle of February—they would be constantly on the road courting the high school boys to whom they had been assigned. In this capacity they would combine the provinces of private detective, evangelist, family counselor, and lawyer, and the volume of their telephonic communications with their "recruiting coordinators," head coaches and alumni, would have mystified the *Wehrmacht*. In these interminable periods, filled with much doubt and tension, they seldom saw their wives and children. Their job security was at the mercy of the head coach, who hired and fired them on the whim of a winning or losing season, and when the head coach himself was dismissed, they too usually found themselves adrift. In these times they would alert their friends and acquaintances in the trade, or attend the National Coaches Convention in January, which was no less a slave market than the national conventions of the Modern Language Association or the American Historical Society. The incidence of their leaving football entirely for the insurance business, or real estate, or high school administration was always formidable.

In the Southeastern and Atlantic Coast conferences, their existence had been even more disarranged before the NCAA's policy of a "universal signing day" in February was established in 1981, coinciding with Marcus Dupree's final year in high school. Before that change in dates and the concurrent ban on personal visits during a recruit's football season, the recruiters in the South had to sign their prospects to local "letters of intent" in mid December. Those contracts were only binding locally, or to the conference membership. After that the Southern recruiters had to concern themselves with getting signatures on the national grants-in-aid in February; then they were in competition with every school in the country outside their own conferences. That meant that during the football season they had to be away from their campuses from Thursday afternoon after practice until the Saturday morning before a game. "From Thursday till Saturday," a former Ole Miss assistant coach told me of those days, "we'd call on maybe five towns in the state, or adjoining states, visiting coaches, watching films in the coach's office, going to the Friday night games. One fairly typical Thursday we had five coaches and a pilot in a private plane. We had to make it eventually to Athens, Georgia, on Saturday morning where we were playing Georgia. We landed in McComb, Meridian, Hattiesburg, Gulfport, and New Orleans. Everybody got off one-by-one in these towns. This gave everybody more than twenty-four hours in each place. Then in the wee hours Saturday morning the plane came back to every town to pick us up. We landed in Athens, Georgia, at 5 A.M. There weren't any cabs, and the car rentals were closed tight. We found an airport vehicle, hot-wired it, and got to the motel, then sent some kid back to the airport with the vehicle. We all got two hours' sleep and made it to the team meeting at 9 A.M. We were happy to see the old conference 'letter-of-intent' abolished."

All this would be eliminated during the new 1981 season. College recruiters would be in evidence at the Philadelphia High School games, but only because Marcus Dupree was such a gilt-edged commodity. Under the altered regulations the coaches could not talk with him, but they wished him to know they were there just the same.

In those ceaseless perambulations, the recruiters had always been subject, as Temple Drake advised me, to "very specific rules, which, after we looked around to make sure nobody was looking, tried to *bend* a little." Predominant among those, until the NCAA became much more exacting on it, was the notorious "Bump Rule," around which a recruiter's folklore had grown. If a prospect accidently "bumped into" a recruiter, or vice versa, at a practice, or in the gymnasium, or somewhere in town, the recruiter might talk with him briefly, and this would not be charged as an "official visit." As Temple Drake recalled it, "Some coaches would wait around all day to get *bumped* into. Hell, they'd wait at a bend in the corridor in the schoolhouse knowin' the kid would be comin' that way after a class. Then they'd literally bump into each other. Or they'd spend half the afternoon in the coach's office, because the boy would come in there sooner or later. Some friendly coaches would *make* a bump for you. If that fellow I told you about ever writes that book *American Football and the Grandmama*, I hope his next one will be *A Guidebook to the Bump*. Of course, that's pretty much gone now, and I never did it anyway."

I had heard tales also of recruiters bringing in their wives to help. Eddie Crawford, a former assistant coach at Ole Miss, had a lovely, willowy wife named Shirley. Many years ago, there was an important prospect who lived with his numerous siblings in a poor farmhouse in the hills of northeast Mississippi. Eddie and Shirley Crawford sat on the front porch of the cabin while the mother of the young man went about her arduous chores. "Ain't it hard?" the woman said. "Churnin' buttermilk and cookin' and ironin' and sewin'—the way they mess up clothes." Crawford gingerly nudged his wife, who had played eighteen holes of golf the day before and attended a bridge club. "Ain't it, though?" Mrs. Crawford said. "Yesterday I churned five gallons of buttermilk and sewed till sunset." She got up and helped with the ironing.

Tom Goode, Coach Steve Sloan's main assistant at Ole Miss in 1981, became an archetype for me of the overworked recruiter. He was forty-two years old, and he had been recruiting Marcus Dupree for a very long time.

In the tenth grade Marcus' highest ambition was to play for Ole Miss, Goode believed—the historic capstone university of the state as, say, Chapel Hill was to North Carolina, or UVA to Virginia. That was true well into his junior year in high school, for he had attended the summer football camps at Ole Miss and was given much expertise and attention, almost as if it were *expected* of him to go to the University of Mississippi, where his talent might come to fruition on native ground and for the example he might afford all blacks, not to mention whites, in Mississippi.

I would see Tom Goode at the Philadelphia High School games that autumn of '81, standing behind the end zone with other recruiters, or with those who remembered him from his playing days—a huge man, kind and considerate, only the scars on his face reminding one of the violent contests of his past. He was always traveling about the countryside. I grew fond of him and appreciated the difficulties of his calling. He had worked hard at it, and he thought Marcus Dupree would eventually come to Ole Miss. "I'm as tough as a two-dollar T-bone," Tom Goode once said, but I knew that toughness had to be consciously summoned. He had been an all-American lineman at Mississippi State and was All-Pro with the Miami Dolphins. He had delivered the snap from center for the winning field goal when Baltimore defeated Dallas in Super Bowl V, and he had written a book called *Guts, God, and the Super Bowl*. I would see much of the early recruiting of 1981 through his sensibility. From him and others among the assistant coaches I would learn it was a difficult business, Darwinian in its unfolding. "The terrible thing about recruiting," he once told me, "is the brush fires you have to put out all over the place—the rumors, the gossip, the falsehoods, everybody tryin' to hurt everybody else." Recruiting, I would discover, was Faustian in its unreality, full of comedy and pain, all of it leading to the golden pageantry of the American stadiums on Saturday afternoons.

We were Southerners, of course, and in 1981 we knew a little of the drama and intricacy of relying upon the black athlete in the colleges of the native South. We knew where the future lay, and also something of the irony of our past.

Kentucky, in 1967, was the first Southeastern Conference school to have a black football player.* Bear Bryant and Alabama came along fairly

† The first black athlete in the Southeastern Conference, embracing the states of Mississippi, Tennessee, Kentucky, Alabama, Louisiana, Georgia, and Florida, was a basketball player named Perry Wallace. He played for Vanderbilt in 1966. On road games, especially in Mississippi and Alabama, he suffered untold abuse. *The Los Angeles Times* recently asked him if he would do it again. "I don't know. Probably not. But a son of mine? God, no. Never. I'd never put him through something like that."

late in 1971. Southern Cal visited Birmingham in the first game of the 1970 season and defeated all-white Alabama, 42–21. The black fullback for Southern Cal, Sam "The Bam" Cunningham, scored three touchdowns that night and gained over two hundred yards. One of Bryant's assistant coaches remarked to him that Sam Cunningham did more for integration in the South in sixty minutes than Martin Luther King had in twenty years. After Bryant integrated his Alabama teams, he said, "I don't believe you are better because you're black or because you're white. But some of the blacks now are like I was when I came out of Arkansas. They don't want to go back to what they came from." Bo Schembechler, the coach at Michigan, advised Bryant before he began seeking black players, "They won't quit you. They got nothing to go to."


Bear Bryant began recruiting blacks after the Southern Cal game of '70. He played two blacks in 1971 and a few more with each passing season. His teams won fifty-three regular-season games and lost two over this five-year span.

After Bryant's retirement and shortly before his death in 1983, Howell Raines of *The New York Times*, a native of Alabama and a graduate of the university, wrote a moving, introspective article in *The New Republic* in which he posed the question: If the Bear were such a saint and hero, why did he wait until 1971 to integrate his teams?

> Before he is enshrined forever as an Icon of Sports, it is worth remembering that Paul William Bryant, Jr., was also a public man who lived in a poor and troubled state at a grim time. The year 1958, when Bryant fielded his first Alabama team, was also the year in which George C. Wallace made his first campaign for governor. Throughout the 1960s and 1970s, these two men were the dominant figures of public life in Alabama and the state's main representatives to the nation. In that time, they so dominated the consciousness of the state that it is only in relation to Wallace that we can understand the service that Bear Bryant did Alabama and how, like so many lesser men, he also failed that state in the midnight of its humiliation.

Nonetheless, Raines said, the record was fairly strong that Bryant felt contempt for Wallace's brutalizing racist politics. He worked behind the scenes with the university president to try to soften some of Wallace's behavior. In 1963 he warned Bull Connor, the police chief of Birmingham

---

Seven years later, in 1973, Coach C. M. Newton of Alabama had four black starters on his basketball team. In 1982 in the Southeastern Conference, considered by many the best basketball league in the country, forty-two out of the fifty starting players were black.

who had become a television celebrity when he turned the fire hoses on children, that if tickets were not made available to blacks at Alabama games in Birmingham, and if they were not treated with courtesy, then 'Bama would not play any more games in Birmingham. "Bryant and his teams provided a diversion from the old compulsions. They gave the state at least one thing to be proud of when Wallace was making it an object of approbrium. If Bryant never stood up to Wallace as he might have, he at least forced the little man to share center stage, and the coach's huge, calm presence made Wallace look small and shrill."

The early 1970s, coinciding with the massive integration of the Southern public schools, were revolutionary for college sports in Dixie. The exodus of black players going from the South to the North was ending. The all-white colleges had suddenly opened to blacks. States like Mississippi, Georgia, Alabama, Louisiana, Tennessee, and Texas, which in the recent past had permitted their native blacks to perform on the West Coast or in the Midwest, were now inducing them to remain at home, not at the smaller all-black schools like Alcorn, Jackson State, Tennessee State, and Grambling, but at the principal state universities. The white fans cheered their black players, who became authentic campus heroes and began to be held in as much affection as their white contemporaries. The first black football player at Ole Miss, for instance, Ben Williams of my hometown Yazoo City who would later go on to the Buffalo Bills of the National Football League, in his senior year was elected by the student body "Colonel Rebel," the highest honor for a male student. There was a perfunctory query in Mississippi in our day regarding any promising high school player. "Is he white, or black?" Marcus Dupree of Philadelphia, Mississippi, would be a foremost legacy of those indwelling changes of the seventies.

It was indicative of the importance of the Southern black schools athletically before those changes that 197 alumni of Grambling in Louisiana went on to play professional football over the years. The record of Jackson State, Alcorn, Tennessee State, Southern University, and the others was also impressive. The professional football scouts were spending less and less time at the black schools. In 1968 the National Football League drafted eleven players from Jackson State. Eleven years later the entire Southwestern Athletic Conference, of which Jackson State was one of seven members, had only five players selected.

Eddie Robinson, the coach at Grambling for more than four decades who in 1981 was second only to Bear Bryant in his number of victories, understood the implications of this newly integrated South. "There was a time when a black player worried about being recruited just by a Grambling or a Jackson State or an Alcorn," he said. "Now, he's got a lot of schools interested in him. Yes, it's tough on the coaches. But more than anything, it's tough on the athlete. Now that same black player worries about adjusting to a predominantly black school because he probably came up through an integrated system." Marino Casem, the coach at Alcorn, which was located in the woodlands north of Natchez not far from the Mississippi River, also remembered the days before integration: "Quite naturally when we had carte blanche with the black athletes in our area, if a kid wanted to stay in the state he stayed with us. We had more players to choose from and we got the cream of the crop. Now the predominantly white schools are recruiting the cream of the crop. And the recruiting is more intense." One never sees more blacks than whites sitting on the bench at the primarily white colleges, he would add. Jake Gaither, who coached for years at Florida A&M in Tallahassee, predicted those transformations a long time ago. "Kids used to hitch rides in here," he said. "Now I have to go out and pay air fare for them."

The trend at the three predominantly white universities in Mississippi was obvious. In 1981 the Mississippi State and Ole Miss football rosters were roughly half white and half black. Southern Mississippi had established itself as a football power by persuading black players to come there rather than to the traditional black shools.‡ The enticements of expensive facilities and playing before large audiences had not been lost on those outstanding young blacks. Johnnie Cooks, a black linebacker from the Delta town of Leland, Mississippi, who was an all-American at Mississippi State in 1981 and a first-round choice in the professional draft, had been recruited by several black colleges before he decided on State. "I've got to live with white people," he said. "I went to high school with them. I've lived with them all my life. I didn't see why I should make a big jump and go to an SWAC school. If you have the ability and go to the big-time schools, you'll do well. And you'll get more publicity than you'd get if you'd gone to the black schools. That's going to give you a big edge."

The descriptions of the college recruiters going into the homes of poor black families were heartrending and legend. Every recruiter in America had his stories about those experiences. At one conference in a bar near the Mississippi River in western Tennessee, Temple Drake told me he once almost cried in front of a recruit and his family. He was sitting in a straight-backed chair in a tenant shack talking with a big tackle. It was a few days before Christmas and the house was cold. There was cardboard in the windows. The grandmother was wandering about in a

‡ I am very grateful to Jerry Potter of The Jackson Clarion-Ledger for his help and writings in this largely neglected area, as well as to Temple Drake and other knowledgeable recruiters.

torn nightgown and old tennis sneakers with holes in the toes. The little brothers and sisters were sitting on the bare floor looking up at him and saying nothing. They had just had a dinner of cornbread and water. They all slept on blankets on the floor in two rooms in the back. The father was in one of the back rooms coughing. The mother was out somewhere working as a maid. "I felt so sorry for them I didn't know what to do," he said. "I'd seen a lot of bad places, but it was Christmas, and there wasn't a toy in the house for those kids. There wasn't even a television. I talked to the boy for a while, but my heart wasn't in it. When I got up to leave I looked in my wallet. I had seventy-five dollars and needed twenty-five dollars to get home. I went into the back room and gave the father a fifty-dollar bill for Christmas. Sure it violated the rules. Some payoff! To hell with the damned NCAA. You're a human before you're a coach."

John Merritt, the football coach at Tennessee State in Nashville, had three brothers named Richardson who played for him when he was coaching at Jackson State:

There was Willie Richardson, who played for Baltimore for a while, and one played with the Cleveland Browns and Kansas City, and the other played with New England. They lived in one of these shotgun houses, a slender house with one room right behind the next one. You got a living room and right behind that is a bedroom and right behind that is a kitchen and right behind that is the outdoor toilet. And, of course, those boys were able to build their mother and father a new home and give them and that family a whole new outlook. Their brothers and sisters, who weren't athletes, got a college education. Before that, college wasn't even in their future. To me, this is the wonderful thing that happens in football. But it's depressing at the time, when you see it recruiting. And, oh Lord, there's so much of it, so many people living like that, more than most people can ever imagine. Most people are sheltered from that kind of thing. They don't know it's even going on. They never see it.

One recruiter told me of the young man who had large blisters on his feet because he was wearing his older brother's discarded shoes, which were three or four sizes too big. His mother said she hoped the facilities at the university were good ones; her son had used an indoor toilet for the first time in the Head Start Program. Bill Canty of Ole Miss described the shack on the Gulf Coast that was so crowded with people the boy had to go out to an abandoned car in the backyard and study his schoolbooks by flashlight. Eddie Crawford spoke of a boy with alcoholic parents and six or seven brothers and sisters in a tiny house. He had a sleeping bag and slept in the back seat of an old car. The tales abounded among the recruiters of going into the bare cold-water apartments in the city ghettos and being both saddened and afraid.

A gentleman named Bill "Bull" Bolton told a story about basketball recruiting. Bolton was an assistant coach at Florida State. He was from a small town in Tennessee and had played for Ole Miss during the Meredith times. He went to New York to recruit a six-foot-eleven black boy who lived in an impoverished ghetto of the Bronx. He decided to buy a long leather jacket so he might blend into the environment. He wandered through the crumbling neighborhoods but could not find the prospect's apartment. As he stood dubiously on a street corner, six large young black men approached him. One was carrying a portable radio of the type known as a "ghetto-blaster." "I'm in trouble," Bolton said to himself.

The young blacks came up to him and began touching his new leather jacket. "Hey, man, we like this coat," one of them said.

"Bull" Bolton told them he was a basketball coach at Florida State University and gave them the name of the young man he was looking for. "We want him to play basketball in Florida," he said. "I'm trying to get him out of here."

The six blacks escorted him to the apartment and introduced him to his man.

One assistant coach in the South recounted visiting a little concrete-block house and sitting next to the young athlete in front of a wood fire. He remembered it was during the off-season, and the fire was not big enough to heat the whole house. While they talked, the boy's stomach kept growling.

"When was the last time you had anything to eat?" the coach asked.

"Yesterday."

"What did you have?"

"A bologna sandwich."

"What about your brothers and sisters?"

"Yesterday too."

The coach took all of them to a restaurant for hamburgers. The bill came to about twenty dollars, which was also against the rules.

The coach was prompted to add a footnote. "The kid's father was about six feet two and 140 pounds, thin as death, with only four front teeth that went in all directions. When I saw the father again a month later he had gained about twenty pounds and had a new set of teeth. I knew then I'd lost the kid."

One young man from a poor family, a promising cornerback, arrived as a freshman at the school he had chosen. He was an immediate disappointment. He was running slower than his recorded speed and he could not lift weights very well. The coaches sent him for another physical examination. The doctors discovered that his mouth was riddled with abscesses. He had never been to a dentist.

A few years ago in a dilapidated house in Vicksburg, Mississippi, the father of the athlete did not like what a recruiter from Mississippi State was saying. He drew a pistol on the visitor and ordered him to leave, which the recruiter did with no further encouragement.

A Texas coach remembered waiting for two hours for a top prospect to meet an appointment. He sat in a sad little shack watching television with the parents and a number of younger children. While an infant urinated in his lap, two dogs began using his legs as sexual objects. When the young athlete finally arrived, he said, "Coach, I'll be back in a few minutes." From a window, the recruiter saw him drive off in a car with "Texas A&M" on the door. "That's when I decided to retire," the coach said.

One coach, whom I knew to be a consummately straightforward man not given to exaggeration, brought in a junior college player from Los Angeles and met him at the Memphis airport. "I decided to take the scenic route down to school, kind of show him the area. We were driving along on a back road around Sardis and he asked, 'What's that?' I told him it was a cow. He said he'd never seen a cow before. He was amazed." He also went somewhere else, the coach explained.

In one black family in Mississippi, several of the sons had grown up picking cotton and had gone on to excel in sports. The youngest, a senior in high school, was a superb football player. The word around the recruiter's network was that an out-of-state school had offered a substantial amount of cash. A Mississippi recruiter, who knew and admired the father, discussed this with him. "Coach," the father said, "I've raised seven boys, and I ain't sold any of 'em yet."

We were getting into a day in the South and elsewhere, one must add, in which black assistant coaches were beginning to go into white households and recruit white athletes. There would be a literature to that, too, for I had learned that the best people among the recruiters were not least of all chroniclers of the heart.


I would get to know a black man in Philadelphia, Marcus' Cub Scout leader and Little League coach, who in smaller measure had been the "Marcus Dupree" of his time there. He was an excellent running back for Booker T. Washington High School. He missed by less than a year the integration of the public schools, and the integration of the football teams at the majority white universities of Mississippi by two or three. He came from a poor family and decided on East Central Junior College, where he got hurt and languished with injuries. Yet even had he been as superlative an athlete as his protégé was to become, the options of his day in the South were few. Much had happened since the late sixties.

The alternatives available to Marcus at age seventeen would be exceptionally varied, encompassing not just Mississippi or the South but the whole of America. His mother was a graduate of Alcorn University. Coach W. C. Gordon of Jackson State, which only a few years before had produced the great running back Walter Payton of the Chicago Bears, was earnestly pursuing him. With all the methodical encouragement that he remain in his native state, would the black Mississippi schools make a provocative argument? Or, in 1981, was it too late for that?

# 8

# A Dollar to a Doughnut

*I gained 179 yards in 22 carries against Eupora. Ran pretty good but leg cramps bothered me. Got cramps in both legs in second half. Wasn't just me, however, all the backs got them.*

*Also I couldn't cut like I wanted to. The field was wet, and just couldn't cut like Coach Wood taught us to.*

*Recruiting is about the same. Been getting a pretty good amount of calls at home. Especially the first part of every week. Also getting Mailgrams from all over. Ohio State, UCLA, Alabama, Texas, Mississippi State, and Georgia are the ones that stand out in my mind. Everybody says about the same thing.*

*Got personal calls from Coach Donahue (UCLA) and Coach Bryant (Alabama).*

The Tornadoes of Philadelphia were at home again in the second game of the season against the Winona Tigers. I drove down from Oxford a couple of days before with Ed Perry, the ebullient State representative from Lafayette County who, as chairman of the Appropriations Committee of the Mississippi House of Representatives, was sometimes described as the third most powerful man in the state. When the wines and spirits and the convivial political and sports talks were well flowing on an ice-cold night, his friends in Clyde Goolsby's bar in the Holiday Inn in Oxford, right off the Square and down the road from Mr. Bill's grave, would affectionately call him Third Most. Ed Perry had to go to Jackson for some budget meetings. "I don't know why I'm going," he said. "Mississippi ain't got no money." He deposited me in Philadelphia and promised to return in time to watch Marcus on Friday night. Since there was no mass transit system in Philly, I would, in the most un-American manner, walk to my appointments. This presented no difficulty, since my quarters were precisely at the nucleus of everything anyway.

This Philadelphia home for me for the next few months was the Downtown Motor Inn, but since it had all the character and appurtenances of the old-style, small-town Southern hotel, only recently refurbished, I shall call it the Downtown Hotel, or, in moments of affection, merely the Downtown. Originally it was the old Benwalt Hotel and was widely known in the red-hill country of Mississippi until it fell upon rather toilworn days, one local wit saying that it looked like an "exhausted spinster." Then an ingenious native named Morgan Hardy bought the property and did it over with his own hands, room by room, so that it was blessed now with all the modern conveniences. But, thankfully, its shop-worn legacy could not be fully denied. Its elevator worked, and its rooms were as comfortable as any chain motel, and it had the dial-out telephones so requisite to writers, reporters, and football recruiters, and color television hooked to the cable networks of the era, but one could close one's eyes and tangibly feel its encrusted turn-of-the-century past. Imagine an approximate cross between old whipped-down Dixie and Perth Amboy, New Jersey.

I was never sure why Morgan Hardy called it a "motor inn," since there was no parking lot, and the only parking spaces were in front of the time meters outside on Byrd Avenue. I do not want to be argumentative about this, however, for I would grow attached to the Downtown and its variegated people, especially since on subsequent trips they allowed my black Labrador, Pete, to stay as an honored guest.

The Downtown was situated only a short block from the Courthouse Square, the hub of Neshoba County. Another short block or so south was Philadelphia High School and the football stadium. Two doors north was Dr. Skipper the optometrist, and just across a narrow street called Myrtle was Wizard's World, where the younger generation of the town, white, black, and Indian, could partake of such intellectual stimulants of our day as Centipede, Berserk, Super Cobra, Pac-Man, and Asteroids Deluxe. The modest little house where the most acclaimed high school football player in America lived, with his grandparents, mother, and little brother, was only a five- or six-minute drive over in Independence Quarters, and his coach's office was a minute's stroll away in the gymnasium by the stadium. This general proximity made it inevitable that when the recruiting wars intensified after the first of the year, as everyone in town knew they inevitably would, the Downtown, the eyes of the American collegiate sports world upon it, would be the center of jostling intrigue.

From the outside, full-face, the Downtown was remarkably unprepossessing. From a distance one could see an enigmatic aluminum dome, painted blue, which served as its roof, four floors above. I could never comprehend what purpose this dome might have served, or what might be under it, and neither could anyone else, but when the reporters began arriving from all over the South and the Southwest after the '81 football season, it was not impossible to convince some of their number that under this blue dome was nothing less than the Grand Ballroom where, in the halcyon years, Ted Weems and the Dorseys had once performed. All around the front and side of the building were balconies on each floor, so that, on the unseasonably warm evenings of that autumn, the people in domicile might be sighted, much like the residents of New York's Lower East Side in July, leaning on the iron railings while looking down listlessly at the activity along Byrd Avenue and in Wizard's World.

There were plate-glass windows on each side of the front door, which opened into the lobby. Sofas and easy chairs in plastic upholstery were scattered about the room, dominated by an immense color television. In the normal hours this room was filled with animation. People dropped in to gossip or to watch the television. A crowd assembled there one morning that fall to watch the wedding of Prince Charles and Lady Diana. As Diana was being escorted into Westminster Abbey by her father—a rather large man who seemed to be breathing heavily—one observer in the lobby (a soybean farmer, I was later told) said: "I don't think that ol' fella's gonna make it." A middle-aged black man named Alexander, who could frequently be seen walking around town praying to himself, stopped often in the lobby before resuming his travels, punctuated by many visits to the coffee shops; it was said that this boulevardier prayed several times a day over cups of coffee. In fine weather a gnarled and decrepit old man, thin as a straw, would move a straight-backed chair onto the sidewalk outside the door and sit there motionlessly for long hours gazing out at nothing. Another man, not quite so ancient, sat dozing in an easy chair in a corner of the lobby all day, his head hunched on his shoulder. This was Mr. Presley Snow, the retired night clerk, who had a room in the back.

Next door to the Downtown, with entrances both from the sidewalk and from the lobby, was the restaurant, which was one of the most active places in town for breakfast, lunch, and the interminable cups of coffee for which Southern towns have forever been distinguished. The signs on the front window said:

CHITTERLINGS—ALL YOU CAN EAT—BOILED AND FRIED—$5.50

CATFISH—ALL YOU CAN EAT—$5.95

The breakfasts there were excellent, and so also was the talk, so natural and native as I eavesdropped upon it. One of the regular patrons would say to an old man eating alone: "Mr. Drew, you got it all figured?" Or to the postman, dining on the boiled chitterlings: "Hello, mailman, you treatin' yourself good?"

The principal topic in my time there, of course, was young Marcus Dupree, how he had performed on the previous Friday, where he might go, and the scale of the speculations ranged along many of the human emotions: bafflement, envy, curiosity, pride. On my very first visit into the Downtown Restaurant I overheard this exchange, among a long table of white men who were farmers, truck drivers, carpenters, shopkeepers, which, later, I hurried back to Room 24 to write down:

"He looked lazy last Friday. He better take some *pep pills*."

"Aw, he's out of shape."

"Yeah, I wish *I* was that out of shape."

"You know his daddy—ol' Thomas Connor. He's a janitor at the school. The boy's not too much bigger than the daddy."

"Well, he's goin' to UCLA. They treated him pretty good out there. He wants them *bright lights*. I saw him the other day wearin' a T-shirt that said 'Gold Club Spa of California.' They give him that."

"What's a 'spa'?"

"Like Hot Springs, Arkansas."

"He went to a party with that gal in 'Charlie's Angels.' "

"Shit." Guffaws and other whispered oaths.

There was a brief silence. Then one wrinkled artisan who had not previously spoken—of indeterminate age, with a young old face, as spare as hard tack, and you knew he would have been with the Neshoba Rifles under Stonewall when he outflanked Joe Hooker—said: "Well, he's the only player I ever saw, on TV or anywhere else, who looks like he can run as fast as he wants to. All this publicity may be goin' to his head, but it ain't yet. I run into him last week over by Thompson's. He had his crippled brother with him. I never talked to him in my life. He's bigger than he looks. I asked him where he was goin' to college, and he was pretty nice about it. He said he didn't know right now."

The group absorbed this for a while.

"Well, here's a dollar to a doughnut he plays for Alabama."

"I say State."

"Joe Wood better give him the ball more."

"Ole Miss—a dollar to a doughnut."

"Wait till February. He won't know where he's comin' or goin'."

And so it went, day after day in the restaurant of the Downtown.

There were other topics, of course. One strange, foggy morning before the Winona game a young man in overalls was watching the network news on the TV. Only he and the white waitress and I were there. "I don't know why everybody's jumpin' on the South Africans," he said to the waitress. "All they tryin' to do is keep the spades out." The word *spades* had an exotic quality. I had barely heard it since the intellectual salons of the Upper West Side of New York City in the 1960s. The waitress agreed. Moments after the young man departed, a large black woman, perhaps in her late thirties, came in and sat at the counter with a deep, expiring sigh.

"Hello, Shirley, how are you?" the waitress asked.

"I just give some blood to the blood bank."

"Eeeeew!"

"I feel awful. I ain't never gonna do that again. Let 'em bleed to death."

"Oh, poor Shirley," the waitress said, touching her in light commiseration on the arm. "Let me get you some coffee."

"Give me some *blood*, honey."

"All I got's coffee."

As the days passed, my best friend at the Downtown Hotel was a lean, rawboned soul named Roy Tingle, the night clerk. Roy was sixty-two years old, so slight and meager that I sometimes worried if he were eating enough, but I soon learned that, like the drifting sands of Kuwait, he had untold reserves of energy He worked in the Oliphant Furniture Store just off the Square during many of the daylight hours. He had prominent features, especially a fine nose that could not go unnoticed, deep wrinkles, and soft gray eyes that suggested a most tender pain. He usually wore an old blue Windbreaker. Every time I checked in at the desk, he would shake my hand and say, "You come to see our boy?" and he would telephone me in the room three or four times a day to ask if everything were functioning properly. Roy Tingle and I, being nocturnal creatures, shared beer or coffee in his sparse room on the ground floor. "I enjoy people," he once said to me. "They relate their selves to me. I listen to their words and needs. When I try to give anybody advice, it's like Sears Roebuck. You can take it or send it back." He was divorced, and, as it turned out, his daughter was married to a young man named Rocky Felker, who had been an exceptional quarterback for the Mississippi State Bulldogs and was now an assistant football coach at Memphis State University. "Rocky says send the kid up to Memphis," Roy said. "He says they might be able to fit him in, although it could take a little *jugglin'*." He became one of my valued confidants in Philly, for he was a good football gossip. "I'll feed you what I hear," he said, "and leave it up to you to make sense out of it, if there is any." He added in a conspiratorial whisper: "As of now it's UCLA." Sometimes he would telephone me late at night when I was back in Oxford. "It's mighty slow in the ol' Downtown tonight. I hear some Texas millionaires are flyin' in. One of them *Lears*." Need I add that when the situation grew tense in February, Roy at his switchboard was not ethically above listening in on the conversations of the recruiters for me? "I think they got a code language," he said.

I soon discovered that the only spot in town which stayed open all night was the House of Barbeque, down the hill on West Beacon and across the tracks, and it beckoned me time and again. The late lonely nights I would spend in the House of Barbeque! Edward Hopper would have been drawn to it—the pale, wasted nighttime faces, the stale breath of beer hovering about its patrons, the swirling haloes of cigarette smoke, the $1.75 plate special with slaw and pickles. At the beginning even I, who had frequented exotic late-night establishments all across Europe, the Caribbean, the Eastern Seaboard, San Francisco, the border towns of Mexico, and Centex, was intimidated. The whites and blacks and long-haired Choctaws often sat at the vinyl tables among themselves glowering wordlessly at one another, in mute testimony to the infallible compulsions of segregation in our land. Yet on other nights in the House of Barbeque there was a kind of violent camaraderie to the ambience, a gruff cheer that somehow uplifted me after a long day's work.

"*Du*-pree. That his name?"

"Uh-huh. And a big 'un."

"Say, Jimmy, you got any beer out at your trailer?"

"None for you, you cross-eyed son of a bitch!"

"He goin' to State?"

"Shit naw—he's goin' to *Decatur!*"\*

"This pork tastes like the tail-end of a dead pig's ass."

The waitress, who had one eye, would shout, over this bedlam: "Number 81! Ticket Number 81! Better come git it or I'm gonna eat it."

A lanky son of the earth wearing a green tractor cap yelled back at her: "I can teach you in half a night what you can't have in three weeks."

It was the songs on the jukebox in the House of Barbeque that held its driftless incumbents together. The jukebox was the parliamentary gavel, the ceremonial mace, the conch shell in *Lord of the Flies*—the elemental country words of anguish, pain, and betrayal, yet always of possibility, a Neshoba poetry. "Still Doin' Time" by George Jones, "Take This Job and Shove It" by Johnny Paycheck, "Older Women" by Ronnie McDowell, "She's Got a Drinking Problem" by Gary Stewart, "When a Man Loves a Woman" by Percy Sledge, "Looking for Love" by Johnny Lee (sung by the Eagles), and, of course, "Help Me Make It Through the Night" by Willie Nelson. The most popular paean of all in that autumn of '81 seemed to be Johnny Duncan's, about the fellow making love to his best friend's spouse:

> *It couldn't have been any better,*
> *It couldn't have been any sweeter,*
> *It couldn't have been any better*
> *If we'd climbed to the top of the world.*

\* The home of East Central Junior College.

Waiting for my order on those long smoky nights of the football season, I would peruse that debonair weekly prediction sheet which they gave away at the counter, *Leonard's Losers*, so faithfully digested throughout the Southland by petty gamesters such as myself:

### ARKANSAS vs. TEXAS

Fred Akers drives his Thundering Herd of Longhorns into Fayetteville Saturday afternoon and they'll run up on a slick bunch of Hogs that'll be determined to dehorn the Cattle before they can get back to the safety of their Lone Star Ranch. But the Porkers had better have some heavy duty dehorning equipment or they could get the lard knocked out of 'em in the process. Lou Holtz always has a couple of surprises in store for the Big Bulls, but neither one of 'em will have anything to do with the scoreboard.

### NOTRE DAME vs. MICHIGAN STATE

The Big Green Machine from East Lansing ain't been hitting on more than half of its cylinders for the past few years but when they crank up to go to South Bend this Saturday they'd better have everything in working order or they'll stall down before they get started. The Pope's Pupils ain't feeling very benevolent after getting knocked off in a Boiler Room last weekend and it's doubtful if the Spartans will have any fun at all on this trip.

Then, driving back up the hill on a deserted side street to the Downtown Hotel at 2 A.M., as if from nowhere there would suddenly be the growl of a car not far behind. One knew from old Yazoo instincts that it was the police car, and of course it was. As the vehicle pulled broadside, recollections of Sheriff Rainey entered one's head. Then the car passed, and the cops waved.

After breakfast one morning that week in the restaurant of the Downtown, where I imbibed the latest football rumors, I went over to the Neshoba County Library. It was new and well appointed and would grace any town. The libraries of little American towns, like their graveyards, had always touched me with assurance and serenity, perhaps because both evoked for me the feeling of time; even in the most irresolute surroundings, libraries were the custodians of civility. With all its newness, this library greeted me with the wonderful musty smell of well-worn books, an odor so durable and distinct from those rainy-day afternoons in the Ricks Memorial in the Yazoo of my childhood that I felt I was in a familiar place. This emotion was all the more affirmed when I was warmly greeted by the librarians, who had read some of my sentences and were curious as to why on earth I was in Philadelphia. When I told them, one of their number pointed to a black woman behind a desk. "That's Mrs. Sutton. She works with us. Her son Rod plays with him." She too came over. "Well, we're all proud of Marcus," she said.

I wanted to browse through a few of the recent Philadelphia Public School yearbooks merely to get a feel of that institution. One of the ladies said she did not have the latest ones on hand but could get them for me from a student's mother in thirty minutes. And she did.

I began with the Nanih Waiya of Marcus' sixth grade and proceeded from there. The photographs of him were in individual and classroom and sports poses. There he was wearing his glasses and the Afro, and from year to year he kept getting bigger and bigger. I examined the pages of the 1979–80 book, his sophomore year, more thoroughly. Many of the class officers were black students. "Most Likely to Succeed" was Dwight McWilliams, black, pictured with Leeanne Marshall, white, with their hands inexplicably holding the top of a shovel. "Neatest" were Juawarkita Griggin, black, and Rayford Manning, white, standing by a flower bush. "Best All Around" were Terri Cox, white, and Shay Daly, white, next to a piano. "Best Athletes" were Terri Cox, white, and Marcus Dupree, black, reclining on the railing of a wooden bridge. In the 1980–81 yearbook I counted seven blacks out of thirty-nine on the high school faculty. The senior class had forty-six whites and twenty-nine blacks; Marcus' junior class was composed of fifty-four whites and twenty-two blacks. As one dipped into the lower grades, there were more black faces. The first grade had sixty-seven whites and fifty-nine blacks, a vivid reminder of the dropout rate among blacks as they got older, and of the fact that Mississippi alone of the states did not have a compulsory school attendance law.

I was the most taken, nonetheless, by the handwritten inscriptions in the latest yearbook, which had obviously been written to the boy who owned it by his classmates. They could have sprung full-born from my own copy of the 1952 *Mingo Chito of Yazoo High.* "Dear ————":

> I'll never forget our good times at ol' Philly High. You're cute and the neatest. Always had a little crush. Remember the night after the Kosciusko game behind the Pizza Hut? Ha! Ha! I won't tell. Love ya, ————.

> They won't forget us at Eddie's Beer Joint. You're the finest, sweetest boy. The biggest honor I ever had was wearing your football jacket. Sorry we had to break up. I can't believe our days at Philly High are gone. Please don't forget me. Love ya, ————.

> We busted some ass, didn't we? Best damned team Philly ever had. You're the best teammate a guy could have. Neshoba Central thot [sic]

they was *hot shit*, didn't they? They didn't know what hit 'em. Hope you
bust ass all thru life, ol' buddy. Your pal since the first grade, —————.


There was an institution in town called Peggy's, a frame house
right off the Square which served as a restaurant for the lunchtime trade.
Peggy's had a buffet table with country Southern dishes, all you could eat
for three dollars, and the customers paid as they departed on the honor
system, leaving their money in a big bowl. Peggy's never once made me
miss the business lunches at the Four Seasons or L'Argenteuil, not even
the martinis. It was there that I first met Tom Turner, a spry young man
of smallish frame, auburn hair, and freckles, who was to become one of
my trusted comrades in Philly. Tom was an Ole Miss man, one of the
most loyal among a loyal and rhetorical breed. He was a scion of an old
Neshoba family—a distant cousin of Turner Catledge—and he worked
with his father at Turner Hardware, which occupied much of the south
end of the Square.

We sat with our fried chicken, collard greens, black-eyed peas, and
cornbread amid the buzz of talk about commerce, crops, and Dupree.
Tom Turner always had an ear to the ground for me, and so did his wife,
Molly, who taught in the high school. I told him what Mont Mars, the
lawyer and Ole Miss alumnus who was the writer Florence Mars's cousin,
had said to me earlier that morning: "I've been tempted to say things to
the right people, but I'm a little afraid. The Ole Miss coaches want you
to help, but then they want to control it, too. It's ticklish."

"Well, if we win seven games this fall," Tom said, "the Rebels are
gonna get him." His confidence on this point never waned.

"For a long time it was all 'Bama. He used to wear a T-shirt to
school that said 'On the Eighth Day God Made the Tide.' But he's been
tellin' some of the kids at school he's goin' to State. He went up to my
wife, Molly, in school the other day and said, 'Bulldog Blitz!' She asked
him why, and he said, 'Because State's winnin'.' I sure hope it doesn't
split the town. Last year Molly was walking down the hall in school and
Marcus stuck his head out the door of a classroom and said, 'I hate Ole
Miss.' He's always teasin' her this way. Molly went into the room to talk.
The teacher had gone out for a minute. One girl said, 'You don't like Ole
Miss because they don't *want* you.' 'Oh yes they do,' he said. A black girl
said to him, 'You're gonna end up at *Hill University*.' The Hill is the
business section of Independence Quarters, you see. There's a lot of interest in town about the cars he drives, of course." Much of the bad talk
about him comes from Neshoba Central, he said—the rival county consolidated school built on a former goat field. The Philly Tornadoes always
played Neshoba Central in the last game of the season.

"He's a quiet kind of kid. One of his teachers tells me he blossomed from the tenth to the eleventh grade. In the tenth he was like a statue, but in the eleventh he got a little more lively. I sure wish Joe Wood would put in the 'I' formation for him, like they do for Herschel Walker. In the 'Wishbone' he's so close to the line of scrimmage, when he tries to break outside they're already all over him. Watch the defensive cornerbacks. They go right after him whether he's got the ball or not. In an open field he's *free*." Three or four businessmen at the next table agreed. (In Peggy's they finished your sentences for you.) "Free as a bird!" one man said.

"I'll tell you one thing," Tom said, stressing his point with a chicken leg. "He's dominated the conversation in *this* town for three years."

"That's the truth," another gentleman at the next table said. "It's gettin' kind of dull."

"I remember when he was in the tenth grade," Tom said, ignoring his corroborator. "Up at Kosciusko, they had this one big defensive player named Dennis Williams assigned to Marcus wherever he went. In the fourth quarter he kept gettin' up slower and slower. Some drunk ex-football players for Kozy kept laughin' and hootin'—'Look at him now!' Can you imagine, belittlin' a tenth grader like that? I still say, if we win seven we got him."

"But you ain't gonna win seven," a man two tables over suggested.

I left them with this discourse over dessert and strolled across the Square in the autumn sunshine to the Philadelphia Motor Company, which was part of the view from my quarters in the Downtown. I had an appointment with the owner, Allan King, who had been the mayor of Philadelphia from 1968 until his retirement a short time before.

I had had slight difficulties in arranging to see the former mayor. The day before, I had looked up his number in the telephone book and called, asking for Mr. King. This was King, the voice said. I was writing something on Marcus Dupree, I explained, and identified myself. Could I come see him and talk about it? "I don't think so," he told me. Taken aback, I asked, "You won't see me?" "I sure won't," he said.

This was the first time anyone in Philly had spurned me, and I was angry. I did not need him. In my lifetime, I had dined with Hedy Lamarr, Lauren Bacall, Shirley MacLaine, and Lena Horne, and once received a four-page handwritten letter from Ali McGraw. I had eaten escargots in Maxim's and strolled through the gardens of Worcester College, Oxford, with Vivien Leigh. Toots Shor had introduced me to Leo Durocher, and I had once had tea with Alexander Kerensky. I had lunched in the Century Club with John J. McCloy, dined in the Players' Club with Frank Sinatra, discussed money with John Kenneth Galbraith, and shared a podium with Arthur M. Schlesinger, Jr. I had consumed a fifth of Wild Turkey in the VFW bar in Provincetown with Norman Mailer and eaten health food in a spot on East Thirty-third Street with Upton Sinclair. In Oxford, England, I had conversed whenever I wished with my fellow student, King Constantine of Basutoland, and on several tropical nights had closed down the bar at the Gran Hôtel Olaffson in Port-au-Prince with Barry Goldwater. I knew this was going to happen here sooner or later. To hell with the former mayor of Philadelphia, Mississippi. But then I examined the telephone book again. I had called J. T. King's Auto Parts on Highway 16-W and gotten the wrong King. My disappointment was immediately assuaged when the right man told me to drop by any time.

I had been taken with some observations of Mayor King that summer in a fine piece by Art Carey in the magazine of the *Inquirer* in the other Philadelphia—the one in Pennsylvania: "We integrated before you did. People thought we'd have a heckuva time, but we didn't. One private school was started,† but it went out of business . . . I believe in segregation, I'll be honest with you, but, hell, I've grown up with them, played with them, had 'em work for the city." My friend John Leslie, the popular and erstwhile mayor of Oxford (who wished his constituents to call him "Your Worship"), had spoken well of King. He led me into his office off the display room. He was a large, graying man of fifty-five, hospitable though cautious. "He's had a good effect on the town," he volunteered at the start. "You don't see an athlete like this come along very often." He was also fortunate, he believed, to have "high caliber people" like Superintendent Myers, Principal Gregory, and Coach Wood in the school.

In one regard Mayor King was typical of the older generation of white Neshobans: At first they were ill-at-ease with the outside writer, and would go to considerable lengths to avoid any reference to the dark days of the 1960s. "Everyone always wanted to interview me about 'The Troubles.' I stopped doing it. Enough was enough. I just won't talk about 'The Troubles.' "

There were three blacks on the police force, he said, and three in the fire department, and one black each on the park commission, the school board, and the utilities board. "We needed their input. We've been fortunate. We haven't had any racial disturbances since those days. We've paved all the streets over there, put up streetlights, and collect the garbage. A big number of black people own their own houses. If you live in Philadelphia now, you get the same treatment. Even before our board had a black alderman, we tried to be fair. This is a little town with not much money. The city is solvent. If you live in a country town like this, and it's grown over the years, we had blacks that lived right behind us. Whites, blacks, and Indians—we all worked together for the city. You want to be fair and honest with 'em, and that's what we wanted to do. Try to be fair to whites, blacks, Indians, and all."

† The Pioneer Academy lasted three years.

The public school bond issue, one of the first in all of Mississippi after the integration of the schools in 1970, passed decisively. "I was proud of that. I think our town has done real well." There was a new water treatment plant and the runway at the airport had been lengthened. The latest bond issue for a vocational-technical school, which would have many black students, likewise was passed by a huge majority. "Our kids here need that. All of 'em won't go to college."

Ronald Reagan launched his campaign for President at the Neshoba County Fair in 1980. "I was pleased there was no heckling in this Democratic country. I was tickled to meet the President. I introduced myself to him as the mayor of Philadelphia. 'PA?' he asked. 'Nossir, Mississippi.' "

When he stepped down as mayor, he said, the town officials gave him a watch. A black policeman, who formerly had been deputy sheriff, joined a group of people who came up to him after the ceremony to wish him well. The two of them had grown up together in the same neighborhood many years before. The black policeman shook his hand and said, "We go back farther than the rest of them."


The block letters on the marquee in front of Philadelphia High School said: PHILLY VS. WINONA, FRIDAY NIGHT, ROLL TORNADOES! and right beneath those words: IN AMERICA EVERYONE IS CREATED EQUAL WITH THE RIGHT TO BECOME UNEQUAL.

The sunshine had yielded to a misty overcast. From far in the distance, from behind the school, came the strains of "Hail to the Varsity," and I caught a quick glimpse of unfurled flags. Mr. Dathan Hart's band was getting ready for Winona.

When I walked into the main corridor of Philadelphia High School for the first time, I sensed I was entering a special cosmos. The integrated public school of the small-town Deep South was, in no small measure, a world unto its own. Right down the street might be the feed store–seed store–courthouse-square aura of the older South which, with all its enormous deferences to the new day, still responded deeply to many of the social rhythms of a generation before. But inside the school building itself one perceived on all sides the results of the contemporary Southern revolution. I arrived there during a class change. Small groups of white and black students walked together down the crowded hallway. A white boy who must have been late to somewhere collided with a black girl, who dropped her books; he stooped to pick them up and said, "Gee, Ann, I'm stupid." A white and a black teacher stood to one side talking earnestly. A thin white boy walked between two huge blacks; they wore football jackets emblazoned with "P," and suddenly they stopped and began wrestling among themselves for something, screaming loudly, until after much arm-twisting the white surrendered what appeared to be a ball-point pen. A white and a black girl sat together on the first step of a stairway examining a page of a textbook. The surroundings resounded with interracial squeals and chatter. With little warning whatever a young white boy in a T-shirt that said "Fly Delta to Dallas" and a black girl in a sweater and blue jeans confronted me.

"Are you a coach?" the boy asked. I would be challenged with this question a dozen times in my visits to Philly High, so that after a time I began identifying myself as a representative of the University of South Dakota at Vermillion.

"No," I said.

"Well, you look like one."

It rather surprised me that I felt flattered.

"Come to see *Du*-pree?" the girl wanted to know.

"Yes. Eventually."

"Everybody comes to see *Du*-pree," the boy said. "I wish I was *Du*-pree." And then they vanished, like pebbles in a pond. Suddenly the rest of the manswarm had vanished too, and as the school bell rang there was silence in the hall after the previous turmoil, broken here and there by the echo of a closing door, of tardy footsteps.

"Are you a coach?" The query this time came from an elderly black man holding a broom. He was wearing an Ole Miss jacket.

"No."

"Lookin' for Marcus?"

"Well, yes and no."

"I got no complaints about Marcus. He's the best they is."

"Are *you* a coach?" I asked.

He looked down at his jacket. "Aw, no! I'm the janitor. Henry." It was the first of several exchanges with Henry Moore, who usually ended his conversations with the same exclamation: "That boy's a *runnin' fool!*"

The times I spent in that building never failed to bring back for me the sights and smells of Yazoo High of the 1950s, which in fact it resembled to a remarkable degree. At any moment in the stampede of the class breaks I expected to see Muttonhead Shepherd and Daisye Love Rainer and Barbara Nell Hollowell and Big Boy Wilkinson and Werdna Dee Phillips and Henjie Henick and Tomcat Sanders and Nettie Taylor Livingston. The boys and girls of Yazoo High—where have you gone?

I especially would admire the school building on the morning of a game. Banners on the walls proclaimed CAGE THE TIGERS! or ROAST THE GOATS! or WHIP THE WHIPPETS! or NO HOPE FOR NEW HOPE! or NO GUTS, NO GLORY! The cheerleaders, already in their uniforms, would stroll along together rehearsing their yells. Justy Johnson and Carl Lee

Smiley and Wyatt Waddell and Rod Sutton and Marcus Dupree would stroll down the hall to the shouts of encouragement from their contemporaries: "*Git 'em, Du*-pree!"

I presented my letter from Warner Alford to Therrell Myers, the superintendent of schools, who lit a menthol cigarette and studied the words closely. He leaned back in the chair behind his desk and welcomed me to Philly High. He seemed eager to please. He was so young-looking that I had to ask him his age. He was twenty-nine, and formerly the principal. "We've had a lot of people in. Of course, we have to be completely impartial. The pressure could get pretty bad. My main interest is that the kid gets a good college education. He's a nice kid. We like him here. I find something touching in his loyalty to his family, especially his little brother. He's crippled, you know."

The fellow who was keeping tabs on everything, the superintendent said, was the high school principal, and he took me down to meet Danny Gregory.

Principal Gregory was rather wary with me at first. In one of our early conversations I believed I heard the whir of a tape recorder. In such moments I assumed an air of innocence which I had acquired from the Methodist Youth Fellowship. Danny Gregory and I, in fact, although neither of us knew it in his office that day, would soon be sharing much together, so that to a degree we became collaborators and allies. When I was not in Philadelphia, we would sometimes stay in touch by telephone, as I did with Roy Tingle at the Downtown Hotel, and before it was over we found ourselves exchanging from time to time our expanding dossiers of gridiron information.

He looked almost as young as Superintendent Myers. He was thirty-four, a native of Ecru in northeast Mississippi, not very far from Oxford. He had graduated from Mississippi State, where he had been an athletic trainer. The route to becoming the school principal and later the superintendent often began, as one knew in the South, in coaching, and Gregory had been the Philadelphia High football coach a few years back. There was a suggestion of piety to Gregory on that first day, something of the Sunday School deacon to his voice and gesture, but the game in Philadelphia was for high stakes, and initially he may have suspected me of espionage.

The main concern he expressed to me that afternoon was the alumni of the various colleges. "I'm not so worried about the coaches, like Tom Goode at Ole Miss and Wesley Reed at State, but the alums showing up here in town or at the school." A couple of people, he complained, seemed to have taken it upon themselves to recruit for Alabama. "We don't want Marcus to get caught in anything that would affect his eligibility, or to have anything hurt our school."

An assistant coach from a college in another state was sitting with Gregory at that desk not long before. "Danny, do we have a chance?" the coach asked. Then he began inquiring about such matters with the Dupree family as car payments and house payments. At that point Gregory became rude. Then the coach quickly said, "Well, we don't do that sort of thing, but some other schools do." Gregory said to me, "I guess we're getting all the good ones, because they all say they don't do that kind of thing."

He warmed to the subject of Marcus, who, he felt, had become a folk hero to the children of the town, as well as to many older people. He himself was proud to have Marcus' autograph, and his four-year-old boy, John Henry, wore Number 22 and once told his father, "I'm gonna be a white Marcus Dupree."

"They won't have to worry about him staying eligible. He does his work and won't give anybody any trouble. He's punctual and in general is a good student. This summer he had a little 'air' about him. But once school started, it's been much better. He's been brought up to say, 'Yes, sir' and 'No, sir,' and he's only seventeen years old. The school hasn't had any experience with all this, but I can tell you we want to do what's best for him." Bill Ross, for years the sportswriter for *The Tupelo Journal* whom Gregory had read as a boy in Ecru, visited Marcus and said he was unlike so many high school athletes of great promise he had met over the years; far from being cocky and arrogant, Ross told Gregory, he was quiet and shy. "I honestly think one reason he's kept a perspective on this is his little brother, Reggie—that he has the God-given attributes and his brother doesn't. The family is extremely close. That could influence his final decision." He had the feeling, however, that his father, who was divorced from his mother, would not participate in the decision. "I've told the recruiters not to think they'll be coming into a shack where they'll hear jive talk."

One of the problems this year with the team would obviously be offensive blocking. The squad lost thirty-two players. "The blocking, compared with last year's, may be, as Emory Bellard says, 'like an ace over a deuce.' Last year he'd be seven or eight yards beyond the line of scrimmage before they got to him. Also, we had a good running back named Leach—he went over to East Central—who took some of the pressure off.

"We're expecting anything," he said. "We're getting more letters here addressed to Marcus than we do on school business. That's why we've set up some strong guidelines. Marcus' mother and Coach Wood and I sent them out to all the recruiters last week." He reached into his desk and withdrew some mimeographed sheets. I read them later over boiled chitterlings in the restaurant of the Downtown. The guidelines were firmer than the chitterlings:

There has been a great deal of interest expressed by a number of universities concerning Marcus Dupree. Realizing the great deal of information needed by these universities, but also realizing the need for Marcus to have as near as possible a normal senior year, the following guidelines have been established for everyone to use in his efforts to recruit Marcus:

1. Marcus will not want any visits from college representatives from the Monday of his first game until the conclusion of his season.

2. Visits may be made until that Monday and telephone calls may be made during the season, but no visits.

3. Telephone calls may be made to Philadelphia High School and a message taken, but Marcus will not be called out of class to receive telephone calls.

4. Philadelphia High School will not release any records or transcripts without written authority by Marcus and his parents.

5. Philadelphia High School does not allow any visitors on campus without first securing approval.

6. Any representative from any college will be required to sign a form in the principal's office when he arrives on campus indicating who he is, who he is representing, and what the purpose of his visit is.

7. Marcus will wait until the end of the season to make any official visits.

8. Mrs. Cella Dupree, Marcus' mother, will handle all the scheduling involved in Marcus' official visits.

9. Coach Joe Wood, athletic director and head football coach, will handle all correspondence.

We hope that by establishing these guidelines everyone will understand the expectations of Philadelphia High School and Marcus during his recruitment. We want this to be as enjoyable for Marcus as possible, and we certainly do not want anything to happen that would affect Marcus or his eligibility.

> Sincerely,
> DANNY GREGORY
> Principal
> Philadelphia High School

"I feel he has the potential to win the Heisman Trophy." How many times would I hear this? The speaker this time was Kenneth Cook, a young black man of twenty-seven, one of the four assistant coaches for the

Philly Tornadoes and the eighth-grade math teacher. His wife taught learning disabilities. I had walked down the hill to the gymnasium for my first meeting with Joe Wood, the head coach. On the football field some little white and black boys were trying with dismal success to place-kick a football through the goalposts. "I ain't big enough yet," one of them who had kicked too low shouted. A black boy yelled: "Jimmy's a *Caucasian!*" Wood was on the telephone in his office with the people at Ohio State, and then Tennessee, and while waiting I chatted with Cook. We sat precariously on a low bench in the empty dressing room. Practice would not start for another hour. Barbells and weights were scattered here and there, and the odor of analgesic balm, the Mississippi cure-all—known to help anything from tuberculosis to hemorrhoids—stung the nostrils. On the walls were several large handwritten signs: No EATING—BY ORDER OF COACH JOE WOOD; IF YOU THINK YOU ARE BEATEN, YOU ARE!; ON FRI. NIGHT YOU CAN DO YOUR THING; IF YOU DON'T THINK YOU CAN WIN, SOMEBODY WILL DO YOU IN!

"I went to college at Jackson State. He reminds me a lot of Walter Payton,‡ who was two years ahead of me there. If Payton can't go around you, he'll go over you. He gets a lot of yardage on his own. He can stop on a dime. Marcus is even bigger and faster. Since I'm an alum, I'd like to see him go to Jackson State. He could break all of Payton's records. Of course, he couldn't win the Heisman there—not enough publicity. I'll never forget the first time I saw Marcus play when I came here last year. Fantastic. Awesome. Everything they'd said about him was true. We joke around a lot. He's an all-round kid. He always gives his linemen credit. All backs should do that."

A couple of fiercesome adolescents raced through the room toward the basketball court, knocking over a table. "Hey! Hey!" Cook shouted. "Cut it out." Then he told me of all the coaches who had already come to the school. He found this rather exciting. He had even gotten some sound advice from several of them on defensive alignments. "We got 'em down on paper—how to cover people in different sets. We're gonna put some of that in. I like pickin' their brains. It hasn't cost a cent."

What about the relationship between the white and black boys on the team? "Oh, no problems at all. They're a good bunch. They hang out together, you know. Study together. They go into each other's homes."

At that moment the door to the tiny office swung open with a thud. A figure emerged who might have been a somewhat older version of Robert De Niro, who played the country catcher from Georgia in *Bang the Drum Slowly.* This was Joe Wood, Mississippi High School Coach of the Year in 1980, of whom another coach had said, "You may not agree with

‡ Payton, a native of Columbia, Mississippi, would go from Jackson State to the Chicago Bears of the National Football League.

his game plans sometimes, because they're pretty weird. But ol' Joe's a winner."

Coach Wood, I would soon learn, was a connoisseur of country songs and snuff who could spin a long tale, and a source of mischief and inane giggles—a red-hill country Mississippi boy if ever one existed. We were destined to become friends as the weeks of football passed on into the recruiting season, and we subsequently even made an eighteen-hundred-mile drive together into the farther reaches of America, a description of which will come in due course. He was always diagramming plays for me which he would use, and I was fascinated by how articulate and self-possessed both he and his famous running back would become with the passage of time.

"Let's go down here where we can have some *privacy*," he said, and he led me across the basketball floor to a small hideaway office.

The first thing that drew my attention to Wood was the ring of keys he carried on his belt. There were dozens of them; in aggregate they must have weighed about five pounds. As we walked through the gymnasium, they made a ponderous jingle not unlike the rattling of a chain. He always had a slow, rather crouching walk, like a ship at a slight list, which he later told me may have come from having milked so many cows when he was a boy, although I believed the weight of the keys may also have contributed. Every high school football coach I ever knew was the keeper of the keys, which would unlock every secret recess and closet in the entire school, and with this always went a concomitant recognition of power, both ceremonial and real. Wood now browsed through his keys looking for the one to the hideaway office and he found it as swiftly and unscientifically as W. C. Fields, the bookkeeper, had located a long-forgotten document on his cluttered desk in *My Little Chickadee*.

We sat down in chairs next to a scarred old table. He pulled up a wastebasket into which he might expectorate his snuff. "Just a normal day," he said. "Recruiters callin' from everywhere." The sounds of the students in their physical education class in the gym, the cries of prepubescent boys and girls, drifted our way as Wood began telling me about himself and Marcus Dupree.

He was thirty-six years old and had graduated from Ackerman High School in 1963. He lived on a farm five miles out from Ackerman in Choctaw County, with a family of seven sisters and four brothers. "From the time I was nine years old, I'd get up at 4 A.M., then I'd work till the school bus came at 7:15 A.M. I also worked when I got home, except during football season. That's one reason I love football. We had about fifty-five cows, which was fifty-four too many." The family also raised corn and a little cotton. His parents still lived in the same house, though they had sold the farm; his father at age seventy-five was a lumber checker for

Sturgis Lumber over in Ackerman. His parents were both Baptists. "I joined a little ol' Church of Christ because all my friends went there." Later he switched back to the Baptists because his wife was one, and he became a deacon in the First Baptist Church of Philadelphia. He played football from the seventh grade on but was too small for college. He was the biggest man on his high school team—a tackle and 160 pounds. The end and guards played at 120. "We had a teacher in the high school named Prof Adams who always said, 'Tut! Tut!' For a long time some of the ol' boys thought this was cussin'."

There was a knock on the door, and a black student appeared. He needed the key to a certain closet near the dressing room. The coach took a key off the chain and handed it to the young man, then spit into the wastebasket and continued.

He went to Holmes Junior College, in Goodman, Mississippi, for two years, then transferred to Mississippi State, where he majored in physical education. He saw a little of America while working on pipelines in the summers, which paid his way through college. After Mississippi State, he took his first job as the junior high school coach and general science teacher in Kosciusko, then became an assistant high school coach under a man named Art Nester, who taught him everything he knew about football. "I enjoy workin' with kids—love goin' out there on Friday and tryin' to beat the other guy. I like the sound of the band, the noise from the crowd—all that." He paused here, pondered what he had said, and disposed of some more Skoal, as if he feared he might be waxing a little too poetic. "I especially like workin' with the younger kids. They're so enthusiastic. As they get older, they lose a lot of this enthusiasm." He gestured in mild provocation. "That's just the way it is. I'm a very low-keyed kind of fellow. I believe in bein' *positive* about it. If a boy does something wrong, I don't jump all over him in front of the others. I try to show him how to do better."

"Coach, Jimmy cut his hand." Another student had appeared in the doorway.

"Is he okay?"

"Oh, just a scratch. We need the iodine."

He peeled another key off the ring, as a Jersey *consigliere* might peel off a hundred-dollar bill for an honored Bronx hit man. "Bring it back," he said.

"I came here in '79. The head job had opened here. I felt I was ready for it." His team won nine and lost three in his first year and was unbeaten in 1980 and the poll in the Jackson papers named them the best team in the state, so that with the victory over Eupora last week his record stood at 20–3. His wife taught the first grade, and he worked the usual long hours of a high school coach, arriving at seven-thirty each morning and not getting home until long after practice. There were the ninth-grade games on Tuesday night, the eighth-grade on Thursday, the varsity on Friday, and the cleaning chores in the dressing room Saturday. "I got no complaints. It beats milkin' the cows." For all this his base salary was $14,000 a year.

When did he first see Marcus?

"In his freshman year, when Kosciusko played Philadelphia. He was a wide receiver. He broke a kickoff in that one for about ninety yards. I knew he was good, but I didn't know he'd turn out to be *this* good. He was big in the ninth grade, but not overpoweringly big—maybe about 200. I got him on a weight program in the summer of '79. He gained twenty pounds that summer. This year he's playin' at 230, although we got him listed at 222. It's a play on numbers, you know. The kid likes the number 22.

"The first time I met him was in our spring practice his freshman year. He was real quiet. You'd ask him somethin', and all he'd do was shake his head. Before this year, all anybody he didn't know ever got out of him was a *yes* or *no*. He's the best natural athlete I've ever seen. He can kick off, pass, run, catch, punt—anything you want him to do, he'll do. He's a solid team player and a leader. I've never heard him criticize another player. Look, I'm not gonna exaggerate. All you got to do is watch him. He'd got three or four scores last Friday if the grass hadn't been so wet. So many of his runs stand out in my mind. Two years ago, for instance, he broke six or seven tackles on a kickoff return, and it was called back. There were a lot of TD's like that called back. He's a four-sport man. He's twenty-two feet eight inches in the broad jump. He missed the North Mississippi 220 record last year by .4 of a second. He's a hard worker. Every evenin' after wind sprints before the season started he'd run half a mile, and sometimes run the steps.

"I used to worry he'd get hurt. I hate to see eight or nine people get at him, and he gets tired toward the end. But he's so big and strong. If he was gonna get hurt, he'd have been long before now. We'll open up this week. He'll gain his yards. It's deceivin'. You're sittin' there before he breaks the long one, and you don't think he's gettin' all that many yards. But he is. He always gets the two or three extra."

A student in gym shorts and a T-shirt had his head in the door. "Long-distance call, Coach." He departed to the sound of the jangling metal, which I could still hear from far down the hall. The student briefly remained.

"You a coach?"

"University of South Dakota at Vermillion."

"Oh."

Joe Wood returned momentarily. "Tommy Reaux of Texas," he said.

"He says he's comin' over for a couple of games. I don't think Marcus and his mama know how bad it's gonna get. Wait till the season's over and they *all* come in." He was an assistant at Kosciusko when everyone was recruiting a player named Jeffrey Moore, who later went on to Jackson State and Seattle of the National Football League. "I hope it won't get that way. Ole Miss thought they had him, and they stood guard in his yard. Then State did the same thing. One would stake out the house, then the other would. I've tried to use all this to build our team up. I tell the others—*you* play good, and one of these recruiters will give you a scholarship too.

"It's been a good experience watchin' him, and how well he's handled all this. I was afraid he might change with all the attention. He's the same ol' Marcus, except he talks more. He don't expect any special treatment, and we don't give him any." They were at a track meet in another town last year. Some children came up to Marcus for his autograph. He later said, "Coach, I sometimes wish I could be average." "Watchin' him grow up has been worth it all."

He shook his head in disbelief. "Havin' somebody like him has really been somethin'. He was blessed by the Good Lord. Number one, size, those powerful legs that make him such a great runner. Number two, the speed of a sprinter. Number three, that great, quick cutting. The Lord gave him so much, and little Reggie has this disease and uses a wheelchair and crutches. I think this has humbled him, helped him handle the pressure—the awareness that, you know, it's not him on the crutches. My wife Renee has this idea to get in touch with the Easter Seal people who do the big TV program and get him and his brother on it."

Then Joe Wood giggled to himself, for I would soon find he was not one to be exorbitantly sentimental. Had the milk cows in Choctaw County restrained him? "I never saw anybody who could *eat* more," he said as he locked up the office. "He'd done somethin' to his leg, and one day I drove him to State for the doctors to have a look at it. 'Coach, I'm a little hungry,' he said on the way home. We stopped at McDonald's. He had two Big Macs, two big fries, one apple pie, one apple danish, one large Coke, and one milk shake. When he finished he looked like he wanted more, but by then I had him back in the car."

The signs in the Independence Quarters on Thursday said:

BOOKER T. WASHINGTON GYM
BIG DISCO DANCE
AFTER THE FOOTBALL GAME

I had appointments with two of the high school teachers that day. I found Sarah McKay in her classroom during her free period. She was a widow, a graduate of Mississippi University for Women, who had been in Philadelphia High School for six years.

The role of the high school English teacher, I knew, was important in America. Usually she was a woman, and if she were a good teacher her dedication to words and to literature was heartfelt. Most of the students might not comprehend this commitment, but to the best young people she could be a salvation, for this was their first genuine confrontation with language and its possibilities after their lifelong bombardment with the easy flickering images and facile injunctions of television. Several people had told me that Sarah McKay was that way, and her enthusiasm on my visit was effervescent as a bubble. "I enjoy these kids," she said. "I teach my heart and soul out. I'm crazy about Marcus Dupree, but then I'm crazy about all of them. Marcus Dupree and I are buddies."

In the South there are certain names—the Christian and the surname in combination—which are often pronounced almost as one. There have never been any rules to this; some names demanded to be used in full. So it was with Mrs. McKay, and quite a few others in Philadelphia, with *Marcus Dupree*. "Marcus Dupree's no problem in a classroom. He doesn't mind talking, but so far as *volunteering* information, he doesn't. He doesn't really like to talk in class. In our third-period English class, I do call on him every now and again, and he'll always do his dead-level best to answer. If I explain something in class and he doesn't understand it, he won't ask a question there. He'll come to me after class and ask his questions."

She did not know him until last year, not even by sight, she said. His friend Michael Smith, who had gone to Ole Miss to play football, was in her homeroom that year, and Marcus and Tree McAfee would spend time in her room visiting Michael. On the first day of school this year, Marcus was assigned someone else's homeroom as a senior. Yet he came to her first meeting. "You're not in my homeroom, Marcus," she said. "Yes I am, Miz McKay. I was in here all last year. I don't know why I have to change now."

She described how touched she was by something that had happened at the start of the semester. She also taught two classes in speech, and Coach Wood had suggested to her before school began that she try to get Marcus to sign up for the speech course. She asked Joe Wood why he had made this suggestion. "Well, you know, all these reporters and TV folks he'll have to talk to . . ." She asked him to register for the course. "No, Miz McKay, I can't do that," he said. "I can't stand up there and give a speech." But he began sitting in on at least one of her speech classes every day. "I wish I'd have enrolled in the course," he said to her later. But he was coming to the class, diligently listening to the other students and to her critiques of delivery, poise, inflection.

"He's handling all the attention exceptionally well," she said. "He's taken some serious and painful needling from some of the kids. Some of them can't stand all the attention he's getting. Of course they're jealous. He's had some catty remarks directed at him, but I've never once seen him get perturbed or upset."

On the street where she lived were two white second graders, John David Williams and David Adkins—her neighbors' children. They loved football, and they had uniforms, shoulder pads, helmets. After school they used their front yards and part of hers for their games. "They don't play football. They play *Marcus Dupree*. They don't even fuss about who's Marcus Dupree. They both are. One day I told him about this. He said, 'You talkin' about David and John David? I know those kids. I drive up your street all the time. Sometimes I stop and talk to 'em.' "

Sandra Luke, the marketing and fashion merchandising teacher, met me for coffee in the restaurant of the Downtown. She was a very good-looking, blue-eyed, blond, Noxubee County girl. I was reminded of the Baudelaire poem about meeting a girl so beautiful that she frightened him. I retained my wits, especially when I saw the wedding ring. When I later escorted her outside to the street corner and returned to the lobby of the hotel, my confidant Roy Tingle almost tripped over Mr. Presley Snow, the retired night clerk who always slept in an easy chair. He did not say anything, merely raised his eyes to the ceiling.

Marcus was in her marketing class, she had emphasized—not fashion merchandising. "He's an average high school kid who dislikes tests and school in general," she said. He once wanted to feel her new frizzy hairdo; when he came into class with a brand-new wristwatch, he did not want to show it to anyone. "His handwriting is like a girl's—a beautiful feminine hand." She gave them ten new words a week to spell—such as *cancellation, erroneous, connoisseur*. (When I was writing these in my notepad, she looked down and exclaimed: "You just misspelled *connoisseur!*" And indeed I had.) Every time she would turn around in the marketing class, the other students were giving him the spellings.

There were two large double tables rather than individual desks in her classroom. Because of his size, Marcus sat at the end of one table and stretched out. "Marcus Dupree, you can't do that!" she said. To which Daran Jackson, the 205-pound black running back, replied: "Do you know who you're talkin' to? The *great* Marcus Dupree."

"The kids are making a lot out of all this. The blacks here really build him up. But there *is* a little jealousy among the blacks." Last year, the other back, William Leach, gained over eight hundred yards, "but he was sort of bitter because Marcus Dupree ran the ball so much. He's handling it well. He's not loudmouthed, not conceited. The other kids help him study for his tests." About the only time she had seen him lose his temper was in the Eupora game the previous week. Philadelphia was backed up near its own end zone. She overheard a black youngster who was a school dropout yell, "Come on, *Du*-pree! Break loose and *do* somethin'!" He shouted back: "I can't. I don't have any blockin'."

How would she describe the white-black relationship in the school? Her slightly clipped response was typical: "We don't have any prejudices." I would hear this from everyone in the school. "We don't think in terms of race," Sarah McKay had said. When I later asked Danny Gregory, the principal, he was equally emphatic. I put down his words:

> The only time in our school that race plays a role is at the beginning of every school year when we have to turn in a report to the State Department of Education—statistics on black boys, black girls, white boys, white girls in each class. You see, they're doing that to check on whether you're segregating in your own schools. Other than that, I really think our students and faculty and community have accepted the unitary school system.
>
> Philadelphia got such negative attention in the 1960s that it was determined to make this work successfully. In the two years I've been principal, there's not been a single race-related incident. I'm proud of that, and if it weren't true, I wouldn't stay here another day. Because we have so many problems other than race.

The early morning of the second game was humid and foggy, with dark purple clouds at the eastern horizon. But by midafternoon the sun had broken through, and it was hot.

Winona, my WPA guide reminded me, "on the line between the swampland to the east and the Mississippi-Yazoo Delta to the west, is the small center of a fertile hill-farms district. Its families are old." James K. Vardaman, the "Great White Chief," governor and senator, had started out there. "Vardaman, with his long white hair, wide-brimmed hats and frock coats, was a picturesque figure. He drove about the countryside in a buckboard during his campaigns and never failed to arouse his constituents with his cry of 'Nigger, Nigger,' symbolic of his racial prejudice."

I settled into the home grandstand early again and watched as the local people and the visitors came in. Ed Perry, the Oxford state representative, had come in from Jackson and we sat among the Philadelphia partisans. In the game program I noticed that the Winona Tigers had a 170-pound tackle named "Trae Dance," which sounded like a racehorse to me.

The white and black boys of Winona, in their red and gray uniforms, were never in the game. Marcus opened the first quarter with runs of thirteen, six, seven, and twelve yards. On the latter, as he carried several defenders with him, Ed Perry said, "God A'Mighty."

He scored from two yards up the middle with 6:27 left in the first quarter.* Later he turned the corner from his own five-yard line, skirting the sidelines for thirty yards to the Philadelphia thirty-five. On a six-yard gain two Winona players were injured tackling him. With 10:14 left in the first half he scored again on a ten-yard run to the outside. Mark Burnside added a one-yard touchdown soon after that. Eupora had had its Lopez Jones on the previous Friday. The Lopez Jones of Winona on this night was Bubba Smith, likely one of sixteen thousand Bubba Smiths in Mississippi, a scrappy end who fought and clawed his way all over the field. He too was hurt trying to bring Marcus down.

At halftime I went over to the concession stands and bought a box of popcorn from quarterback Justy Johnson's mother, a pretty blond divorcée. As we talked, the Philadelphia band from its marching formation on the field burst into "New York, New York."

> *These vagabond shoes*
> *Are longing to stray,*
> *And step around the heart of it,*
> *New York, New York*

In the second half, Marcus kept getting his jerseys torn off. As he sat on the table behind the team bench getting another replacement, one of the water boys tossed shreds from the jerseys to the little children who had gathered behind the fence.

With 9:53 remaining in the third quarter, he broke free on a pitchout, ran over two defensive backs, and scored from twenty-six yards, his sixty-fourth high school touchdown. Daran Johnson contributed a final score in the last period. Joe Wood began clearing his bench, and Philly won, 32–12. Marcus' statistics were three touchdowns and nineteen carries for 205 yards. At the final whistle, the Winona players gathered around him to shake hands.

When Representative Perry and I reached Calhoun City on the long dark drive back to Oxford that night, we encountered a Highway Patrol roadblock. The representative had misplaced his driver's license during the recent Ole Miss–Tulane football weekend in New Orleans, and it was

---

* High school football games in Mississippi had twelve-minute quarters, compared with fifteen minutes in college.

incumbent upon him to explain those embarrassing circumstances. The policemen examined the trunk of the car before their flashlights caught the state legislature sticker on the front window. We confronted four more roadblocks in the next fifteen miles; Highway Patrolmen with shotguns were stationed at each, and at each the representative described the loss of his license. "Well, I hope ol' Dupree is worth all this," the third most powerful man in the state said as we departed the last roadblock. "This is the most serious driver's license check I ever saw." The next day we learned that the constabulary had been searching for a citizen who had kidnapped a woman and put her in the trunk of his car; he later murdered her. Such were the nocturnal hazards that autumn of Highway 9-W from Philadelphia to Oxford.

# 9
# *Summer of Darkness*

At the beginning of 1964, the twenty-four square miles of Neshoba County's pine woods and pastures was starkly isolated from the civil rights struggles of the day. The county's population of some twenty thousand was composed of fifteen thousand whites, twenty-five hundred blacks, and twenty-five hundred Choctaws. Roughly half the whites and half the blacks lived in or near Philadelphia; most of the Choctaws dwelt on the Pearl River Reservation six miles from town. The Philadelphia blacks lived largely in Independence Quarters and in another neighborhood known among the whites as Shaky Ground. ("If you go over there at night, you're on shaky ground.") Their rural contemporaries lived in several enclaves off the main roads, where they owned a little land and had their own country churches; many of them received relief checks and gifts from relatives in the North.

The Mississippi legislature, sensing that the summer would bring turmoil, passed a number of stern laws dealing with picketing, riot control, curfews, boycotts, and violation of local ordinances. Paul Johnson, the governor, had surprised many by the moderation of his inaugural address, which discouraged any violence that might incite a direct confrontation between the federal government and the state. "You and I are part of this world, whether we like it or not. We are Americans as well as Mississippians . . . hate or prejudice or ignorance will not lead Mississippi."

These were idle words, unfortunately, for the Mississippi and the Philadelphia of 1964. The national civil rights campaign was beginning to focus on the state. Its leaders, who had previously been fragmented into several dissident organizations, were unifying to make Mississippi a symbol in the effort to dissolve the restrictions against the registration of its black voters; slightly more than twenty thousand of its four hundred thousand Negroes were registered to vote. The segregation of public facilities was under attack and sweeping civil rights legislation was pending in the United States Congress.

The Council of Federated Organizations, COFO—composed of CORE, SNCC, the NAACP, and Martin Luther King's Southern Christian Leadership Conference—had set late June as the time to begin a massive program in Mississippi. COFO announced it was sending a thousand or so students from all over the nation, led by veterans of "The Movement," into the state to establish black community centers and "freedom schools" and to conduct voter-registration drives. Actually about eight hundred would eventually come to Mississippi, ranging from age eighteen to the late twenties. Most of them were college students from Berkeley, Wisconsin, Stanford, Chicago, the Ivy League, and elsewhere. There was a large proportion of young women.

For years there had been little Ku Klux Klan activity in Mississippi. But the White Citizens' Council, the organization of businessmen and professionals which had espoused the retention of segregation without violence through rearguard paralegal action, had all but collapsed, both in the state at large and in Philadelphia. Emotions were taut over the expected influx of "Reds" and beatniks, and the moment was ripe for the extremists. In 1963 the Klan had been revived in a series of Klaverns in southwest Mississippi, which were associated with the Original Knights of the Ku Klux Klan of Louisiana.

A man named Sam Bowers was the founder of the Mississippi Klansmen. When they broke away from the Louisiana organization, he became the Imperial Wizard of the White Knights of the Ku Klux Klan of Mississippi, which was to be the most ruthless, disciplined, and furtive klan cell in the Deep South of the twentieth century. He was thirty-nine years old and owned a vending machine business in Laurel, Mississippi, called the Sambo Amusement Company. He claimed to be a Biblical scholar and seemed to have unlimited funds. His grandfather had been a U.S. congressman from the state early in the century. Sam Bowers "was pretty much a loner," Don Whitehead wrote, "and he frequently mystified acquaintances with his peculiar habits. One story was that he was seen to put a swastika emblem on his arm, draw himself to stiff attention before his dog, give a Nazi salute, and say, 'Heil, Hitler!'" In the spring of 1964 he addressed three hundred armed Klansmen in a secret meeting outside of Raleigh, Mississippi, seventy miles from Philadelphia: "The military and political situation as regards the enemy has now reached the crisis stage. Our best students of enemy strategy and technique are in almost complete agreement that the events which will occur in Mississippi this summer may well determine the fate of Christian civilization for centuries to come . . . We will, of course, resist to the very end the imposition of martial law in Mississippi by the communist masters in Washington."

Bowers further advised his members that they would be justified in killing any civil rights workers "caught outside the law."

The recruiting for the White Knights in Neshoba and Philadelphia was rigorously secretive. Sam Bowers' agent there was a part-time Baptist minister and sawmill operator known simply as "The Preacher." That spring the Knights proclaimed their presence in Neshoba by burning the twelve crosses—six in the county in mainly black settlements, five in Independence Quarters in town, and one in front of the courthouse. No citizen attempted to tear down this latter cross; no police officer said he had seen it placed there. *The Neshoba Democrat* cryptically reported: "Sheriff Lawrence Rainey said it was believed that outsiders came through this area and burned the crosses and were gone before anyone could see them. He said he definitely felt that the burning was not done by local people and that it was an attempt by outside groups to disrupt the good relations enjoyed by all races in this county."

Lawrence Rainey had been elected sheriff of Neshoba County in August of the previous year. His campaign slogan was: "The Man Who Can Cope with the Situation That Might Arise." He finished first in a field of ten with 63 percent of the vote. Florence Mars, among others, believed at the time that the 37 percent for his opponents was more a protest against Rainey than anything else, although this disaffection, though strongly felt, was not openly expressed. In Mississippi the office of sheriff had always been an extraordinary personal and political fiefdom, for he was not only the main office of the law but also the tax collector, with a lucrative income from commissions. The stories abounded in my boyhood of the wealth that a resourceful sheriff could accumulate.

Rainey was forty-one years old. He was six feet one and weighed 240 pounds; he was seldom without a wad of chewing tobacco in his jaw. He had attended a county school for eight grades, then went to work in Philadelphia as a mechanic. He was later hired as a policeman in Canton, a town sixty-five miles to the west near Jackson, where he made a reputation for being brutal to Negroes. He returned to Philadelphia as a city policeman, and from 1960 to 1963 was the deputy sheriff of Neshoba County. In this period in Philadelphia two blacks were killed "in the line of duty."

After Rainey was elected, he appointed Cecil Price as his deputy. Price was twenty-seven, only slightly less formidable than his superior. He had come to Philadelphia when he was nineteen from Canton and traveled the back roads of Neshoba as a dairy supply salesman. Later he was a part-time policeman and a fireman.

Florence Mars wrote in *Witness in Philadelphia*:

> Previously, sheriffs of Neshoba County had seemed to be a pretty even-tempered lot. They wore regular suits, and most of them had other interests such as farming. Their guns were inconspicuous. Rainey and Price outfitted themselves in identical uniforms, the first western-style

suits ever worn by the Neshoba County sheriff's office in my lifetime. They wore boots, cowboy hats, and each had a six-shooter hanging from one hip and a blackjack and nightstick hanging from the other. Rainey cruised around town in his 98 Oldsmobile, which had four antennas and a large gold sheriff's emblem almost covering each front door. Price was considerably less ostentatious; he drove a plain Chevrolet equipped with a police siren and a blinking light.

Since 1954 the editor of *The Neshoba Democrat* had been Jack Long Tannehill, a relative of the Longs of Louisiana. On April 9, 1964, only a few days after the cross burnings—and two and a half months before the disappearance of the three civil rights workers—he wrote in a front-page editorial that would inevitably become notorious: "Outsiders who come in here and try to stir up trouble should be dealt with in a manner they won't forget." Given the neighborhood's long history of incipient lawbreaking and violence, and the xenophobia of much of the citizenry over the impending civil rights summer, that was nothing more nor less than an invitation to anarchy.

A few weeks after the people of Neshoba received this advice, printed circulars were distributed throughout the area, and to every white residence of Philadelphia, listing twenty reasons for joining the White Knights of the Klan—including their policy of secrecy and their opposition to Negroes, Jews, Catholics, and Communists:

> The issue is clearly one of personal, physical SELF DEFENSE for the American Anglo-Saxons. The Anglo-Saxons have no choice but to defend our Constitutional Republic by every means at their command, because it is LITERALLY their life. They will die without it.
>
> If you are Christian, American Anglo-Saxon who can understand the simple Truth of this philosophy, you belong in the White Knights of the KU KLUX KLAN of Mississippi. We need your help right away. Get your Bible and PRAY! You will hear from us.

The town and the state were explosive with hostility. The press reported the fight for the Civil Rights Bill in Congress as the apocalypse of civilization. Through May and into June the newspapers* warned against the "Mixers" and "Commies" who were on their way to Mississippi and carried the frequent exhortations of Ross Barnett, the hero of the 1962 Battle of Ole Miss:

> We are facing the most critical hour in the history of our nation. We must either submit to the unlawful demands of the pressure groups or stand up like men and tell them, "Never!"

* Not the least of which were the two Jackson papers, the *Clarion-Ledger* and the *Daily News*, at that time perhaps the most race-baiting newspapers of any substantial size in America. Seventeen years later, these papers would be among the most progressive, enlightened, and professional in the entire South, and the *Clarion-Ledger* would win a Pulitzer Prize for public service.

Mississippi has been the special target of the Communists and the Mixers because Mississippi has given this nation and the world the shining example of successful segregation. We will never abandon our time-honored and workable patterns of race relations. We will never yield to the Mixers.

Michael Schwerner and James Earl Chaney were beginning to make nighttime forays from Meridian into the black communities of Neshoba County. At a secret meeting in May, the Klansmen decided they would get Schwerner.

In Philadelphia, on May 22, a future running back was born.

For an insight into Klan activity in Mississippi in that period, this verified list of black churches destroyed or damaged by fire or bombings between June 15 and September 17 made a memorable catalogue:

June 15: Hattiesburg, Rosary Catholic Church (auditorium gutted by fire after meeting of Negroes who discussed means of averting racial violence).

June 16: Philadelphia, Mount Zion Baptist Church (leveled by bomb after local whites beat three Negroes).

June 21: Brandon, Church of Christ Holiness (bombed by Molotov cocktail; destroyed in early August).

June 25: Ruleville, Williams Chapel (Molotov cocktail).

June 26: Clinton, Church of the Holy Ghost (extensive damage from kerosene).

July 6: Jackson, McGraven-Hill Baptist Church (kerosene fire, slight damage).

July 11: Browning, Pleasant Plan Baptist Church (burned to ground).

July 13: Kingston, Jerusalem Baptist Church (leveled by fire).

July 13: one mile east of Kingston, Bethel Methodist Church (totally destroyed by fire).

July 17: McComb, Mount Zion Hall Baptist Church (moderate damage).

July 19: Madison County (on Highway 51, between Ridgeland and Madison), Christian Union Baptist Church (burned to ground).

July 22: Pike County (six miles east of Magnolia), Mount Vernon Baptist Church (completely destroyed by fire).

July 24: McComb, Rose Hill Church (moderately damaged by fire).

July 30: Meridian, Mount Moriah Baptist Church (leveled by fire).

August 5: Finwick (near Natchez), Mount Pilgrim Baptist Church (burned to ground).

August 11: Gluckstadt (near Canton), Mount Pleasant Church (severely damaged by fire).

August 12: Brandon, St. Matthew's Baptist Church (heavily damaged by fire).

August 22: Itta Bena, Perry's Chapel (burned to ground; local fire department deemed building out of its jurisdiction).

September 9: Aberdeen (on Route 45), Mount Moriah Baptist Church (parts destroyed by dynamite).

September 12: Aberdeen, Daniel Baptist Church (porch burned off).

September 16: Valley View (eight miles from Canton), St. John the Baptist Church (totally destroyed by fire).

September 17: Madison County (seven miles east of Canton on Route 43), Cedar Grove Baptist Church (church leveled by fire; only stone steps remain standing).

September 18: Near Philadelphia, a Negro church and a Choctaw Indian church severely damaged by fire.

The civil rights organization CORE had set up an office in the summer of 1963 in Canton, the county seat of Madison County, where the population was almost three-fourths black but where only a few Negroes were registered to vote. In the following months the advance guard of the COFO "Freedom Summer" arrived in Meridian, the second largest city in Mississippi, with a much less repressive atmosphere than Canton. Meridian, in Lauderdale County, was thirty-eight miles from Philadelphia, and was to be the beachhead for the civil rights campaign in east-central Mississippi in the summer. A black community center had been started there in January 1964, directed by two white New Yorkers, Michael and Rita Schwerner.

From Meridian in the early months of '64 the Schwerners reported directly to the statewide headquarters at 1017 Lynch Street in Jackson, where Bob Moses, a young Eastern black with a Harvard master's degree, was the catalyst for the hundreds of students who would arrive in Mississippi in June. Moses, a quiet and gentle man, had come to the state three years before; he was the saint of The Movement. Isolated totally from the white power structure of Mississippi, he had tried to encourage the blacks to exercise their rights and not to be afraid.

Unlike Philadelphia, the white leadership in Meridian largely abhorred the Klan (although the White Knights were growing strong there) and controlled the police, and for this reason the Schwerners had not been jailed or abused physically. But their early time there was not easy. There were threatening telephone calls; their utilities were turned off from time to time. Many black adults feared that their projects would stir up trouble. The Schwerners began concentrating on the younger blacks. With books donated from the North they established a library where blacks came to check out books; they inaugurated story hours for the children and sewing classes for the adults and recruited bright teenage blacks to tutor the younger children in reading, math, and history. They canvassed the black community and held twice-weekly classes on voter registration, held sit-ins at the lunch counter of a bus depot, and led a boycott against several stores. Those activities did not go unnoticed in the rest of the state, including neighboring Philadelphia. With the burgeoning of the Klan in both Neshoba and Lauderdale counties, Schwerner soon became a symbol of the Klansmen's hatred and fears. He was an outsider and a troublemaker. They called him "Goatee."

His name was Michael Henry Schwerner, but he went by Mickey. He was twenty-four years old, buoyant and compact, sunny-dispositioned, the grandson of European Jews and the younger of two boys. He was born in New York City but grew up in suburban Pelham. His father was a wig manufacturer and his mother taught high school biology. He loved W. C. Fields, the New York Giants football team, the Mets baseball team, and animals, and he went to Cornell to study to be a veterinarian, later switching to rural sociology. He became involved with The Movement as a social worker in the welfare department in New York City. "Mickey was the gentlest man I have ever known," a close friend from New York later said. "But he was far from shy. If he differed with you, he never pretended agreement, but he was tolerant of difference . . . What caused him to go South was Birmingham. He has been deeply affected by the photographs of Negroes sprawling under the dogs and the fire hoses. The sight of Bull Connor or Governor Wallace on television saddened him. The slaying of Medgar Evers shook him. So when the four little girls were murdered in church on September 15, 1963, he decided that nothing short of a complete commitment to The Movement would satisfy him. This doesn't mean that he thought the white people of Alabama and Mississippi were any more evil than people everywhere. The man was free of hate: he didn't hate any Ku Klux Klansmen in Alabama, Mississippi, or anywhere. What he recognized was that the hardest-core problem existed in those areas."

During his first weeks in Meridian, he wrote the national office of CORE:

> The Meridian Community Center, of Lauderdale County, Mississippi, *must* succeed. The Negro population has suffered too long with insufficient education, high infant mortality rate, low dietary level, and lack of job opportunities. Sure, the task looks hopelessly large, but we must not fail if the South is to take its rightful place in American society . . .
> In low-income areas there are insufficient library facilities to the

young, and Negroes are denied access to many of the existing facilities. Recreational and culturally uplifting activities are nonexistent in the rural areas. Expenditures for education are far below the nation's average; and money spent for the education of each Negro child is less than half of that spent for the education of each white child . . .

With story hours, games, and music, we are doing everything possible to attract to the Center children who are five and six years old. These children are Mississippi's best hope. They are the ones who, if assisted, can improve most and contribute most . . .

I have a photograph of him before me now, taken two months before his death—short hair, round cheeks, chin whiskers—a very Jewish face, reminding me of some of the Jewish boys, a little older, whom I once knew in New York; yet, strangely, with the sunny innocent features of the Jewish boys of the South of a generation ago, or of my friends among the Sigma Alpha Mu's at the University of Texas, except for the eyes, which are sadly dark and brooding.

His closest colleague in Meridian was a twenty-one-year-old black, a school dropout from a broken family named James Earl Chaney. He did odd jobs as a painter and a carpenter. "He'd go hungry and do all the dirty work," a worker there remembered, "just for the chance to stay around the Center where he felt like something was going on. I guess with The Movement he found his first sense of participation. Mickey knew how to put him at ease, so Mickey could count on Jim Chaney to walk through hell with him."

In mid June the Schwerners and Chaney drove to Oxford, Ohio, to participate in a training program for the COFO students who were soon coming to Mississippi. While there they met another young man, Andrew Goodman, who had volunteered to return to Meridian with them.

Andy Goodman was twenty years old, the middle of three sons, a student at Queens College—"fine, intelligent, unassuming," Rita Schwerner described him. His father was a civil engineer and contractor and his mother a psychologist in Westchester County. Like Mickey Schwerner, he had been born into the liberal Jewish tradition. "Andy knew he had enjoyed most of the good things of life," his mother later told William Bradford Huie. "He was secure in the affection of his brothers, his parents, and his larger family, including his grandparents, his uncles, aunts, and cousins. He had been reared in an atmosphere of love, respect, and culture, with books, music, paintings, appreciation of learning, appreciation of individual effort to improve the human personality . . . He was a happy, well-adjusted, lighthearted young man who knew how and when to be serious. He joined The Movement for two main reasons. He felt it was unfair for him to enjoy so many good things without making some modest effort to help those who were unjustly deprived. And he felt that he had much to learn from the people in Mississippi. He never thought he had all the answers."

While in Ohio, Schwerner learned that a black church which he had visited in Neshoba County had been destroyed. He, Goodman, and Chaney drove back to Meridian.

The black community of Longdale, long respected by the whites of the county, was eight miles east of Philadelphia off Highway 16. There was an abandoned school there, a couple of Negro graveyards, and the Mount Zion Methodist Church. The farmers in the neighborhood, mostly older blacks whose children had long since gone away, eked out a living raising chickens, pigs, and cows, and some corn and cotton. Earlier that spring Schwerner and Chaney had driven there from Meridian to persuade the members of Mount Zion to let them use the church as a COFO center for rural Negroes during the summer. There had been several meetings in houses. On Sunday, May 31, Schwerner had addressed about forty or fifty people in the church. He spoke about their registering to vote. "Before this happens, someone may have to die. I may be the one, but if I do, it will be better for these little children," he said, pointing to some youngsters in the church. The Mount Zion people decided they wanted a freedom school.

On June 16, while Schwerner was in Ohio, the Klan held a secret meeting in an old school gymnasium in the Bloomo community. Later that night they drove to Longdale, where a meeting in the church had just dispersed. They severely beat several elderly blacks, and later burned the church to the ground.

A death warrant was out on Mickey Schwerner. The conspirators had been waiting for a long time to get him outside of Lauderdale County.

In the early afternoon of Sunday, June 21, a bright, hot day, Schwerner, Goodman, and Chaney left Meridian in their blue Ford station wagon to drive to Longdale to investigate the burning of the Mount Zion Church. Andrew Goodman had been in Mississippi less than twenty-four hours. In Washington the U.S. Senate had just approved the Civil Rights Bill.

They went directly to the Longdale community, saw the ruins of the church, and talked with a number of the blacks, including one who had been beaten. Then they departed in the direction of Philadelphia. Chaney was driving. They were arrested on a busy street at the outskirts of Philadelphia by Cecil Price, the deputy sheriff. At 4 P.M. Price jailed them, booking Chaney for speeding and holding Schwerner and Goodman for investigation of the church burning. They were in the jail for more than six hours. At about 10:30 P.M. Price released them on payment of a twenty-dollar fine. He accompanied them from the jail to their station wagon and told them to get out of the county as fast as they could.

What follows are the words of a federal grand jury indictment returned against eighteen men: "It was part of the plan and purpose of the conspiracy that Cecil Ray Price, while having Michael Henry Schwerner, James Earl Chaney, and Andrew Goodman in custody in the Neshoba County Jail located in Philadelphia, Mississippi, would release them from custody at such time that he, Cecil Ray Price, Jimmy Arledge, Horace Doyle Barnette, Travis Maryn Barnette, Alton Wayne Roberts, Jimmy Snowden, James E. Jordan, Billy Wayne Posey, Jerry McGrew Sharpe and Jimmy Lee Townsend could and would intercept Michael Henry Schwerner, James Earl Chaney and Andrew Goodman upon their leaving the area of the jail, and threaten, assault, shoot and kill them . . .

"Pursuant to the conspiracy, and in furtherance of the objects thereof, the following defendants committed the following overt acts within the Southern District of Mississippi:

"On June 21, 1964, Cecil Ray Price detained Michael Henry Schwerner, James Earl Chaney and Andrew Goodman in the Neshoba County Jail located in Philadelphia, Mississippi, after sundown on that day until approximately 10:30 P.M.

"On June 21, 1964, Billy Wayne Posey drove an automobile south on Highway 19 from Philadelphia, Mississippi.

"On June 21, 1964, Cecil Ray Price drove an automobile south on Highway 19 from Philadelphia, Mississippi.

"On June 21, 1964, Cecil Ray Price removed Michael Henry Schwerner, James Earl Chaney and Andrew Goodman from an automobile stopped on Highway 492 between Highway 19 and Union, Mississippi, and placed them in an official automobile of the Neshoba County Sheriff's office.

"On June 21, 1964, Cecil Ray Price transported Michael Henry Schwerner, James Earl Chaney and Andrew Goodman from a place on State Highway 492 between Highway 19 and Union, Mississippi, to a place on an unpaved road intersecting Highway 19 south of Philadelphia, Mississippi.

"On June 21, 1964, Billy Wayne Posey drove an automobile bearing the bodies of Michael Henry Schwerner, James Earl Chaney, and Andrew Goodman from a place on an unpaved road intersecting Highway 19 south of Philadelphia, Mississippi, to the vicinity of the construction site of an earthen dam, located near Highway 21, approximately 5 miles southwest of Philadelphia, Mississippi."

Signed statements by two subsequent FBI informers, corroborated by information from other members of the White Knights, described what happened that day. One of the informers was James Jordan, a thirty-eight-year-old drifter who worked in a trailer court in Meridian and had been administered the Klan oath by a sergeant on the Meridian police force. The other was Doyle Barnette, a twenty-six-year-old Meridian auto parts salesman and Klansman.

I shall rely here, in paraphrase, on the well-documented account by Don Whitehead in his *Attack on Terror: The FBI and the Ku Klux Klan in Mississippi.*

During the time that the three civil rights workers were in the vicinity of the Mount Zion Church that Sunday afternoon, Deputy Sheriff Cecil Price received a tip that they were there. He sighted their station wagon coming toward Philadelphia on Highway 16 as he was speeding toward Longdale. He turned around and caught up with them in Philadelphia. After he charged them with speeding and left the jail, the Philadelphia and Meridian Klansmen soon learned that Schwerner was a prisoner. "The Preacher" and two friends drove from Philadelphia to a cafe near Meridian. A number of telephone calls were made. James Jordan, among others, volunteered his services. The group met at a trailer court with pistols and rifles. They filled two cars with gasoline and bought brown cotton gloves. The Meridian volunteers included Doyle Barnette; James Jordan; Wayne Roberts, twenty-six, a window salesman; Jimmy Arledge, twenty-seven, a truck driver; and Jim Snowden, thirty-one, a driver for a laundry. Besides the Preacher, there were two others from Neshoba County: a seventeen-year-old high school dropout and a twenty-one-year-old worker for a pulpwood supply firm.

The eight drove in their two cars from Meridian to Philadelphia. Doyle Barnette, driving a Ford sedan, parked on the Courthouse Square. The Preacher left, then returned shortly and said, "They're still in jail." He led Barnette's car to a warehouse. "We've got a place to bury them and a man to run the 'dozer to cover them up." When he found out which way the three prisoners were going, he said, he would let Barnette know. Barnette dropped off the Preacher and returned to the warehouse. Shortly another man drove up to them and said, "They're headed down Highway 19."

At about 10:30 P.M. Cecil Price took Schwerner, Goodman, and Chaney from the jail to their station wagon. When they departed, he got in his patrol car with another police officer and followed the station wagon to the city limits. Then he drove back to the police station and let the other officer out. Price then drove onto Highway 19 toward Meridian. Just south of Philadelphia there were three cars parked on the side of the road. One was a Highway Patrol car, the second was Doyle Barnette's, and the third was a red sedan driven by Billy Wayne Posey, twenty-eight, a service station operator. Three young men were with Posey. Cecil Price pulled in beside those cars. When the patrol car headed away toward town, Posey talked with Price, then told the others: "The Deputy Sheriff's going to stop them."

Price drove onto Highway 19 again, and behind him were Posey in the red sedan and Barnette in his Ford. In a few minutes they approached the taillights of the station wagon. Chaney tried to outrun them. The red sedan developed mechanical trouble and stopped at the side of the highway, but Barnette remained behind Price. The station wagon turned off Highway 19 onto a narrower highway toward the town of Union. Price turned on his flashing red light and followed. Chaney pulled off the highway and stopped. Price halted his police cruiser and got out just as Barnette stopped behind him.

"I thought you were going back to Meridian if we let you out of jail," Price said.

"We were going," Chaney replied.

"You sure were taking the long way around," Price said. "Get out of the car."

Then he opened the door and pulled Chaney out from the steering wheel. Schwerner and Goodman got out of the station wagon and into the back seat of Price's patrol car. When Chaney started to follow them, Price hit him over the head with his blackjack and pushed him into the car. He told Jimmy Arledge to drive the station wagon and to follow him in the patrol car. James Jordan got into the front seat with Price.

Price drove back to Highway 19 and turned north toward Philadelphia. Barnette's car followed, then the station wagon. They drove slowly. When they reached the red sedan which had been parked because of mechanical trouble, they stopped. The teenager working on the engine said for them to go on. "I'll catch up later." Wayne Roberts and two other men got into the two other cars. Soon Price turned onto a dirt road. That was Rock Cut Road, about four miles from the spot where the three had been taken from their station wagon. After less than a mile Price halted at a place in the road where clay banks rose on both sides. Doyle Barnette was behind him. It was before midnight.

At this point Jordan and Barnette's accounts differed. Jordan said that when the cars reached Rock Cut Road, he stopped to wait for the red sedan:

> During the fifteen- or twenty-minute period I waited at this intersection, I heard the cars stop, the motors stop running, and the car doors shut. I could not hear any conversation but could make out muffled voices . . . I heard a volley of shots, approximately six or seven, followed by two separate shots. At this time I called out, "Is everything all right?"
>
> As I appeared around the right bend of the road . . . someone said,

"Yes, help us get these empty shells." Someone, sounding like the same person, said, "I've already got mine . . ."

The Negro was lying in a ditch on the left side of the road, face down, headed west, and the body more or less parallel to the road and about a car length behind the station wagon and a car length in front of Price's car. Goodman was . . . lying face down in a crumpled position . . . Schwerner was lying face down in a position similar to Chaney . . .

Barnette's story, however, had James Jordan at the murder scene:

. . . Before I could get out of the car Wayne Roberts ran past my car to Price's car, opened the left rear door, pulled Schwerner out of the car, spun him around so that Schwerner was standing on the left side of the road with his back to the ditch, and said, "Are you that nigger lover?" and Schwerner said, "Sir, I know just how you feel." Wayne had a pistol in his right hand, then shot Schwerner.

Wayne then went back to Price's car and got Goodman, took him to the left side of the road with Goodman facing the road, and shot Goodman.

When Wayne shot Schwerner, Wayne had his hand on Schwerner's shoulder. When Wayne shot Goodman, Wayne was standing within reach of him. Schwerner fell to the left so that he was lying alongside the road. Goodman spun around and fell back toward the bank in back.

At this time Jim Jordan said, "Save one for me!" He then got out of Price's car and got Chaney out. I remember Chaney backing up, facing the road, and standing on the bank on the other side of the ditch, and Jordan stood in the middle of the road and shot him. I do not remember how many times Jordan shot. Jordan then said, "You didn't leave me anything but a nigger, but at least I killed me a nigger" . . .

From the evidence, including ballistics reports, the FBI was convinced Jordan had fired the bullet that went into Chaney's abdomen, and that the pistol which killed Schwerner and Goodman also fired the bullet which entered into Chaney's brain.

Don Whitehead would graphically describe the burial:

. . . Imperial Wizard Sam Bowers' elimination order had been carried out. The execution was swift and without ceremony—swift, brutal, and efficient. When it was over, Billy Wayne Posey said, "All right, let's load these guys in the station wagon and take them to the spot."

Schwerner and Goodman were loaded first into the station wagon through the open tailgate, and then Chaney's body was tossed in on top of them. Posey got behind the wheel of the station wagon and said, "Everybody follow me. We'll go the back way."

Price turned his car and drove back toward Highway 19 to return to Philadelphia. The others moved north over dusty back roads. Barnette could scarcely see the station wagon's taillight through the swirling clouds of brown dust. They skirted the edge of Philadelphia and went on to the

Burrage farm. They passed through the gap in a barbed-wire fence and moved across the rough terrain to the dam. The klansmen saw that the dirt fill was only a few feet high. Two bulldozers stood nearby.

"I wonder where the bulldozer operator is?" Posey said. "Somebody better go and get him." Three klansmen left to look for the operator. Jordan and Snowden were posted as guards in the woods. A few minutes later a low whistle sounded. Wayne Roberts walked from the woods with the bulldozer operator, who had been waiting in a car parked a short distance down the road.

The bodies were pulled from the station wagon, Chaney first and then Goodman and Schwerner. They were dragged onto the dam. The bulldozer operator started the engine of the machine and moved it into position. One steel tread passed over a portion of Chaney's body, and anyone standing close enough might perhaps have heard the crunching of bone. The blade bit into the clay and within minutes the bodies were buried. The klansmen had no fear that the bodies would be found. Bulldozer operators were due to return to the site early in the morning to continue building the dam.

The little group left the dam and met Snowden and Jordan at the gap in the barbed-wire fence. Posey said, "They'll be twenty feet under before this is all over."


When the three young men did not return to their office on Monday, the word of their disappearance spread quickly from Meridian to Washington. On Tuesday morning Florence Mars visited the beauty parlor, the drugstore, and the grocery. "Wherever I went, the disappearance was the topic of animated conversation. The mood of the town was jovial; everyone thought it was a hoax. Although the rest of the country might fall for it, Neshoba County knew better: 'COFO arranged the disappearance to make us look bad so they can raise money in other parts of the country.'" The editor of *The Neshoba Democrat* voiced the same belief.

On Tuesday afternoon, June 23, their station wagon was found, a burnt-out shell, in the Bogue Chitto swamp twelve miles north of town. "COFO must have burned their own car to make the hoax look convincing," someone said. When the station wagon was discovered, Miss Mars knew the boys were dead. "Even if they had wanted to stage a disappearance," she remembered thinking, "they would not have burned their only means of escape . . . There was no response from the city administration or from church groups expressing even perfunctory sympathy for the missing young men or concern for their welfare. A few days after the disappearance I went to see the mayor, an old family friend who impressed me as being a man with a strong sense of justice. I asked him why there had been no official statement, and he said he didn't know of his own knowledge what had happened and thought it would be presumptuous to assume that a crime had been committed. After that remark, there didn't seem to be anything to say."

On Monday afternoon J. Edgar Hoover had ordered the FBI office in Meridian to begin an investigation. They questioned Sheriff Rainey. "They were here all right," he said. "Price arrested the nigger for driving seventy miles an hour in a thirty-mile zone and he held the other two for investigation. When they paid a twenty-dollar bond for speeding, Price told them not to hang around Philadelphia, but to be on their way. And they drove out of town." Rainey said he had gotten his information from Deputy Price. He himself, he reported, had been at the hospital in Meridian where his wife was a patient, and had not returned to Philadelphia until midnight. Cecil Price told the agents that when he saw the station wagon leaving for Meridian he had come back to town, but no one could place him in Philadelphia in the critical time between 10:30 and 11:40 P.M.

A group of twenty black civil rights leaders, including the comedian Dick Gregory, announced they were coming to Philadelphia Wednesday. On that day the courthouse was surrounded with city policemen, state troopers, and deputized guards wielding rifles, shotguns, and pistols. A small delegation of the civil rights people was permitted to talk with officials in the courthouse.

There began now a forty-four-day search for the missing young men in which the eyes of the world were on Philadelphia. After the burned station wagon was discovered, President Johnson announced that the federal government would expect every effort to solve the case, and he dispatched Allen Dulles, the former director of the CIA, to Jackson to discuss law enforcement with Governor Paul Johnson. A regional FBI was established in Jackson, and J. Edgar Hoover came for the opening ceremony.

The FBI soon inundated Neshoba County, the first wave of a force which would increase to some hundred and fifty agents. They began making a house-to-house investigation of the county and set up roadblocks and a communications center. Helicopters dotted the skyline, and there was even a photo-reconnaissance jet. By late June, four hundred sailors from a naval air station in Meridian were searching the Bogue Chitto swamp where the station wagon had been found a few yards off Highway 21—a murky, treacherous territory infested with rattlers and water moccasins. When nothing was found there, their explorations took them through most of the woods and fields of Neshoba County. Their efforts were hampered by the oppressive heat, rainstorms, chiggers, mosquitoes, and snakes. Each squad of sailors was accompanied by a state highway patrolman, whose responsibility, the governor said, was "to be certain that the people's houses and property of this area are protected at all times."

Four boats dragged the Pearl River, one young local calling out from a bridge: "Throw a relief check out there in the river and that nigger you're lookin' for will come up and grab it!" Sheriff Rainey was critical of the meddling outsiders; *The Jackson Clarion-Ledger,* which also took an exceedingly dim view of this activity, observed:

During the past seven days, Neshoba Countians have seen hundreds of federal agents, highway patrol personnel, and even members of the U.S. Navy trampling over the countryside. They have heard the President of the United States talk about their town. They have read about a visit by Allen Dulles to Mississippi to discuss their town. They have seen one of the largest groups of news media personnel ever to gather in Mississippi. They have seen their town Philadelphia through the eyes of national television; they have heard about their town on radio; they have seen their town through the "eyes" of newsprint and pictures.

They have seen their town tried and found guilty by many outsiders . . . an observer can hear phrases of displeasure, particularly concerning national television personalities who have . . . attempted to outdo each other.

An observer . . . immediately gets the feeling that Philadelphia would rather just be left alone. "If people would 'tend to their own business, everything would be all right," one old courthouse sitter said. "If it was boiled down to gravy there wouldn't be much in it, nohow," another responded.

"I don't know, maybe I was wrong," the father of Andrew Goodman said in New York. "When our son first suggested he wanted to go down there, we spoke frankly of the dangers, the realities. But we also spoke of the values we have held in our home. Here was a twenty-year-old boy who was deeply conscious of a moral right . . . He wanted to go. We let him go." Mickey Schwerner's father said, "It's perilous just to cross the state line in Mississippi. They're animals down there. The police don't protect people, they beat them and persecute them." Leaders of the NAACP in Washington passed a resolution that the federal government take over the administration of the state of Mississippi.

The town was swarming with reporters from the national and international press and from the television networks. A large room in the Benwalt Hotel, destined one day to be the Downtown, was specially equipped with teletypes and telephones. The media people, more than the FBI, suffered from the hostility. Much of the local sentiment still held that no crime had been committed; if so, it had been provoked by outsiders.†

† William Bradford Huie, who was on the scene, made an interesting point. "In a murder case where every knowledgeable survivor is guilty, and where every living witness is a murderer, you obtain information from informers, and you obtain evidence by inducing one murderer to witness against another. And where every witness is under a real threat of death from his fellows if he talks, a witness can be a problem.

"Sheriff Rainey is the bravest sheriff in America," Circuit Judge O. H. Barnett said, and by all accounts he was expressing the majority view.

Rita Schwerner, the twenty-two-year-old wife of Mickey Schwerner, had gone to Jackson four days after her husband had vanished to try to see Governor Paul Johnson. The next day she drove to Philadelphia to confer with Sheriff Rainey. She later filed this affidavit with the United States Court of Appeals:

On June 25, at about 3 P.M., I went to the State Capitol building in Jackson with John Robert Zellner, a Student Nonviolent Coordinating Committee field secretary, and Reverend Edwin King, the Tougaloo College chaplain. I attempted to see Governor Johnson to ask for his promise of help in the search for the three men. We were told by Senator Barbour that the governor was out for the afternoon and could not be contacted. He was extremely rude in his treatment of me. We then walked over to the Governor's Mansion, arriving just as Governor Johnson walked up the steps with Governor Wallace of Alabama. We followed them up the steps and Mr. Zellner introduced himself by name to Governor Johnson and they shook hands. Mr. Zellner then turned towards me and introduced me as the wife of Michael Schwerner, one of the three missing men. He said that I would like to speak for a moment with the Mississippi governor. The moment Johnson heard who I was, he turned and bolted for the door of the Mansion. The door was locked behind him and a group of Mississippi highway patrolmen surrounded the three of us. An officer with the name plate "Harper" refused to allow us to request an appointment with the governor. Harper said that he would not convey our request to Johnson.

On June 26, 1964, when I went to Neshoba County to speak with Sheriff Rainey, the car which I was in was followed by a blue, late-model pick-up truck without license plates. There were two white men in the truck. At one point the truck blocked us off in front and a white, late-model car blocked us from behind. We turned our automobile around and were able to get by the white car; the pick-up truck followed us awhile farther. We reported this to the FBI agents who were working in Philadelphia on the investigation. After I spoke with Sheriff Rainey, who denied knowledge of the circumstances of the disappearance of the three men, we obtained permission from Rainey and the FBI to follow the sheriff's car to the garage where the station wagon (which the men had driven on June 21) was being kept, in order that I could see it. Several

---

"In this, in fact, Mississippi is no different from New York. When, because they fear involvement, thirty-eight 'decent' New Yorkers neglect to call the police while an innocent woman is murdered before their eyes, how can 'decent' Mississippians be expected to witness against terrorists? Bodies hidden by the Mafia and other gangsters are as hard to find as those hidden by Mississippi gangsters; and a thousand murders committed by gangsters have gone unpunished in the United States because 'decent' citizens declined to take the risks of giving testimony."

young white men, who I believe were workers at the garage, laughed and made screams which are usually referred to as rebel yells when they realized who I was. When we left the garage the sheriff's car was close behind ours, and the blue pick-up truck once more followed after us to the outskirts of town, with the sheriff making no attempt to stop it or question the occupants about the lack of license plates.

As the search continued far into July, it became more and more apparent that with such vast stretches of countryside to be explored, and with a native populace which out of fear or belligerence remained uncooperative, the bodies would never be found without the services of an informer, or informers, and that is what eventually happened. A rumor had been circulating that the FBI would pay up to twenty-five thousand dollars for information leading to the gravesite. But the silence of the general citizenry was not unanimous. A few respectable people in the town felt the FBI was serving as a buffer between the law-abiding citizens and the Klan and they were quietly encouraging the investigators and inviting them to their houses.

The community was particularly disturbed by the nightly network news shows, and such indictments as Walter Cronkite's ringing epithet, "Bloody Neshoba." The town was being scorned and humiliated before the entire country, it was felt, with a daily barrage of unflattering comments and film clips. Florence Mars recounted the hysterical anger which followed an NBC interview with a Neshoba eccentric, one Buford Posey, who told the nation he believed the police had something to do with the disappearance of the three civil rights workers and that he, Posey, would likely be run out of town for having said it. The town still remembered Buford Posey's open support of Harry Truman in '48 instead of the Strom Thurmond–Fielding L. Wright Dixiecrat ticket, and that he had once challenged the editor of *The Neshoba Democrat* to a duel. "Anybody could have told them that Buford Posey doesn't represent the thinking people of Neshoba County," one woman complained. She told Miss Mars she was so angry that she beat her hands on her television set.

There were a small handful of others who believed a murder had been committed with the collusion of the local authorities. One was Florence Mars's mother. Another was her Aunt Ellen Stendrup, a tall, gray-haired woman who was outspoken in her criticisms of the police and of the abdication of the town's leaders. Aunt Ellen was the first person in town to entertain some of the FBI agents. A third was "Boots" Howell, a contractor whose progenitors were prominent Neshobans and who argued with the members of the Rotary Club, including the mayor and the editor of the *Democrat*, that the officers of the law were involved in the disappearance and that they should not be protected. In addition, there were a few women here and there who were vocal in their disdain. This report of Florence Mars was especially revealing:

> It seemed that most of the people who could see what must have happened were women, and of them, a large percentage were Catholic. Catholics generally may have been less inclined to believe in the hoax theory because they had long been a minority and had been a Klan target themselves in the 1920s. Catholic women may have felt freer to speak their minds than other women because no Catholic woman could fear that her husband was secretly a Klan member. Virtually no Negroes believed in the hoax theory.
>
> The friends I talked with were all disturbed by the common attitudes of "they got what they deserved" and "they had no business down here." One woman said, "The idea of these people trying to defend murder," and another said, "I was taught that murder is wrong and I never dreamed the community would try to defend it." When we publicly expressed the view that this was no hoax, we were all met by a common response: "Are you for COFO?" One was either loyal or one was not.

The main question among these few, as Miss Mars and the others discussed it, "was not who had actually committed the murders, but how high the Klan membership went in the community's structure." They noticed that a sizable group of men, many of whom were employed in stores around the center of town, had been organized to check license plates from outside the county and to identify all outsiders, especially journalists, and do what they could to annoy them. All day long there were strange meetings taking place in a certain restaurant and in drugstores and barbershops. "My friends and I did not doubt that these men knew a murder had been committed, and that it was 'theirs.' Yet, they claimed as loudly as anyone that it was a hoax and probably helped convince the town that it was." A more direct source of vigilante activity was the auxiliary police. Earlier in the year the state legislature, in a series of actions to help deal with the COFO campaign, had established machinery for home-guard organizations, and the Philadelphia auxiliary became a legitimate arm of the Klan and congregated openly. Miss Mars and the others felt that, no matter what they thought of COFO, "a few men of influence would eventually be able to see the principle of justice involved":

> FBI agents told me they were having trouble finding people who would talk with them. What puzzled agents was the attitude of Philadelphia's businessmen. Executives in the privacy of their offices were as cool and noncommittal as the man on the street. They especially wondered why the man who was generally acknowledged to be the most influential and powerful businessman in the community was not really cooperating with them.
>
> After this conversation with the agents, I went to talk with the man

they were referring to, a prominent citizen and an old family friend, who had earlier sent a telegram of protest to Walter Cronkite. I thought perhaps he had reacted with understandable civic loyalty to the insulting misnomer of the county but hadn't realized the strength and danger of the Ku Klux Klan. I thought if anyone had the courage to stand in opposition to the Klan, it was he. When I told him the FBI thought they had a Klan murder on their hands, he seemed surprised. He said he had been busy and hadn't given it as much attention as he should have but he certainly was interested and would look into it.

I said the FBI would be glad to talk to him and I was sure they could tell him more than I could. He said, "Well, that's all right. I've got some contacts of my own that I can check." I left thinking he would look into it and possibly take some action. After a few weeks I knew that he was aware of the strength of the Klan and that he had taken no action.

Several months later he told a New York Times reporter, "We were just the tragic victims of chance. I have never felt a guilty conscience about this thing for the simple reason that I know our people here are as good as people anywhere else. The rest of the country thinks it has been tense in Philadelphia. But we've just been free and easy—business as usual."

During the FBI's search, the U.S. Congress passed the historic Civil Rights Act, with its provisions on equal rights in voting, employment, public accommodations and facilities, and education. Its enactment served to exacerbate the local temper even further, as did the rioting which was erupting in several Northern ghettos.‡

Six weeks had passed. It seemed impossible that the three boys would ever be found. The people of Philadelphia began preparing for the Neshoba County Fair.

On Monday, August 3, acting on the tip of an informant, the FBI sought and was granted a search warrant by a federal judge to enter the old Jolly Place, a 250-acre farm about five miles southwest of Philadelphia, to excavate an earthen dam. Monday night a bulldozer and a dragline were brought in by truck from Jackson.

‡ Later that summer, after the passage of the Civil Rights Act, the board of directors of the NAACP had a meeting in Jackson. Then they traveled all over the state testing motels on the public accommodation clauses. They arrived in Philadelphia and had a meeting with local officials at the courthouse. David Halberstam of The New York Times was there; he recalled the intimidating atmosphere. Robert Carter, the NAACP lawyer—a black man from New York—did much of the talking. The county attorney treated him with great condescension. He kept calling him "Robert." As Halberstam remembered it, Carter responded: "Well, George, if you really feel that way," —or whatever the official's first name was—or "I see it this way, George." Halberstam said: "This was when I first realized the Old South was ending."

On Tuesday afternoon, under eighteen feet of clay, they found Andy Goodman and Mickey Schwerner lying face down in the red earth, arms stretched above their heads. Schwerner had been thrown on top of Goodman. Jim Chaney lay on his back next to Goodman.

A famous photograph showed Deputy Cecil Price helping with the plastic bags.

"The discovery," Florence Mars remembered, "shattered Neshoba County's hoax rationale and was met by silence or muted conversation." Hodding Carter III wrote in *The Delta Democrat-Times* of Greenville, Mississippi:

> . . . Now that the three missing civil rights workers have been found, brutally murdered, in Neshoba County, many of us in Mississippi need to take a . . . long hard look at ourselves . . . We could begin by altering the sorry record of interracial justice which we have made over the last decade. In celebrated case after case involving the murders of Negroes . . . we have been seemingly unable or unwilling to find the guilty parties, try them and convict them. The roll call of the dead is long. The list of those convicted is still a blank page.
>
> Now there is going to be another opportunity for justice. The three civil rights workers did not kill themselves . . . Someone murdered them, and it is a safe bet that the FBI will in the near future make an arrest.
>
> Thereafter the task will be up to our fellow Mississippians. Let us pray that this time, if the evidence is clear, a jury will find it in themselves to convict. It is irrelevant what passions stirred the men who shot down the three young men. What is relevant is that justice must prevail. Who are the guilty? They are numerous. They are the people who did the killing, those who conspired with them and those who helped create an atmosphere in which anything is preferable to change . . . But those who committed the crime and those who conspired in its commission are answerable to the law.
>
> And this time, if they are indicted and tried and a Mississippi jury frees them in the face of conclusive evidence, all the world will see what they really mean when they talk about states' rights down there.
>
> They mean the right to commit murder and get away with it.

The corpses were taken to Jackson for autopsies. Goodman had been shot once in the right chest, Schwerner once in the left lung. Chaney had been shot three times, in the back, abdomen, and head. Because the bodies were so decomposed, it was not possible to tell if they had been beaten.

The Neshoba County Fair was taking place two miles south of the earthen dam. Governor Paul Johnson said, to applause at the political rally: "Some news media have tried hard to run down this section of our state. They jump on an isolated incident but ignore 804 unsolved cases of murder and missing persons in the state of New York."

The bodies were released to the families. Separate services were held in New York for Schwerner and Goodman. Andy Goodman was buried in Mount Judah Cemetery, in Cypress Hills, Brooklyn; Mickey Schwerner was cremated. The eulogy for Goodman was given by Rabbi Arthur Lelyveld, who described Andy as "a proud and self-accepting Jew." He said:

> These are the young men who are patiently instructing the old and the young in their citizenship rights; who are offering fellowship to the dispossessed; and who, as they go from door to door for voter registration or teach in freedom schools, give to the Negro community of Mississippi the assurance they are not alone.

Jim Chaney was buried on a hill south of Meridian shortly after his body was returned from Jackson. In a gathering darkness there were fifteen mourners and no flowers in a new burial ground. That night, however, after Chaney's burial, two hundred blacks and a few whites marched through Meridian for a memorial service for Chaney in a Negro Baptist church. The marchers were jeered and bottles were thrown at them. There were seven hundred people in the church. David Dennis, a black man who was an associate of Bob Moses with COFO in Jackson, one of the distinguished men associated with The Movement of that day, gave the eulogy, which contrasted deeply, his friends said, with his earlier optimism about change in Mississippi. The cameras caught this unforgettable speech. "I'm sick and tired of going to the funerals of black men who have been murdered by white men," Dennis said. "I'm not going to stand here and ask anyone not to be angry, not to be bitter tonight. We've defended our country. To do what? To live like slaves." His voice rose. "Don't just look at me and go back and tell folks you've been to a nice service. Your heart is just beginning. And I'm going to tell you deep down in my heart what I feel right now. If you go back home and sit down and take what these white men in Mississippi are doing to us, if you take it and don't do something about it, then God damn your souls! I don't want to go to another funeral like this. I'm tired of it!" Then he stepped back from the pulpit and broke down, sobbing and crying.

Shortly after this, on August 16, 1964—two months to the day after the church was burned—there was a memorial service for Schwerner, Goodman, and Chaney in the ashes of the Mount Zion Church in Longdale, Neshoba County. The black people sat on wooden benches under the trees. Sheriff Lawrence Rainey and Deputy Cecil Price stood to the side and watched. James Chaney's eleven-year-old brother made a speech, closing with: "I want us all to stand up here together and say just one thing. I want the sheriff to hear this good. *We ain't scared no more of Sheriff Rainey!*"

A black preacher, the Reverend Clinton Collier from Neshoba, said: "All the cops in Neshoba County will not be able to kill this cause. This Heaven which the white man has made for himself in Neshoba County, it's hell for us. Lord, give us the strength to make a Heaven for ourselves here too."

# 10

# *"I Run for Both of Us"*

*I ran better this week, picking up 204 yards on 19 carries against Winona. Offensive line played better too. They're really young and last week didn't have assignments down. This week the guys really came on. Thought I ran pretty good. Field was dry and was making cuts a lot better.*

*Got more Mailgrams from same people. I really don't mind all the cards and letters. No phone calls really stand out in my mind.*

*Georgia has been calling. I wouldn't mind running in the same backfield with Herschel Walker.*

*Right now leaning toward UCLA. I really like it out there. It's a nice environment and I made a lot of friends out there this summer. I like Texas a lot, too.*

The Philly Tornadoes, two-and-nothing but with problems—blocking and the Wishbone—were moving on the road against the unbeaten Newton Tigers, one of the strongest teams in that area of Mississippi. I myself knew Newton High School, from a generation ago and in the white era, to be a tough town with superior athletes—mean, hardened, and with nothing to lose. In the words of our day, "They'd just as soon shit on you as look at you." It would be a difficult night for Marcus, one of the three of his senior year.

As I checked into the Downtown this time, my informant Roy Tingle proudly showed me some photographs of his new grandson in Memphis.

"He's handsome, Roy."

"Don't he just look like a linebacker?"

"His dad will make him a quarterback."

"Say, watch out for *Texas*. That's the word."

The football players, white and black, and a few other students and their dates had parties after the games in private houses. Last Friday night, after the Winona game, the party was at Justy Johnson's, the quarterback. Justy's mother, the pretty blond divorcée, served Cokes and sandwiches and they danced to disco records. After the party one of the white boys, a senior who was not on the team, was killed in a car wreck. In the funeral parlor a couple of days later someone saw, among all the flowers, a spray with a long black streamer with "⚡22" printed on it, and attached to it a sympathy card from Marcus Dupree.

One hot, muggy night on this visit I was driving randomly through Independence Quarters, absorbing its varied scenes, observing the crowds of black people entering or leaving the churches, standing on the street corners, drinking beer beyond the open doorway of Guys and Dolls to the tune of discordant music. Going over my notebook later, I found that for some reason I had scribbled to myself that night: "My feelings of *Ecclesiastes*—just human beings trying."

I was drawn to the Busy Bee Grocery and Record Shop, possibly because of the sign that was on its marquee almost every day that autumn, in rain or shine, victory or defeat:

NUMBER 22
MARCUS DUPREE—PLAYER OF WEEK
CONGRATS FROM OVER THE HILL GANG

I parked the car by the marquee and went inside to get a Coca-Cola. It was a cluttered, haphazard establishment, with newspaper clippings about Marcus on the walls and on a big cash register. A lively young black man stood behind the counter talking with three or four children.

"Hi there," he said. "You a coach?"

Only a writer, I replied.

"Writin' on you-know-who. *Marcus Dupree!* Hey, man, he lives right around the corner. He's shy all right. He's young! Everybody in the Busy Bee's crazy about him. He comes in here and buys Cokes and signs autographs for the little kids. He comes from a fine family. You know— Reverend Major Dupree. That's his granddaddy. He's a *preacher*. Dupree's the greatest in the world, man." He pointed to the clippings. "Look at all this stuff. They just keep pourin' in."

His name was Larry Walker, a native of Philadelphia and a graduate of Neshoba Central who went right to work. Another native of the town named Marty Stuart, a singer who traveled with Johnny Cash, had recently composed an album of "progressive folk" with the title *Busy Bee Cafe* named after this distinctive landmark.

I asked him where he thought his hero might go to college.

"Not to any of these Mississippi schools. They ain't good enough for Marcus Dupree. Hell, he better go to *California*. It's glamorous out there, right? I never been. U.C. and L.A. or Southern Cal, that's where. That Marcus Allen, he's a senior this year—our Marcus can step right in as the tailback. He'll be an instant success. Maybe the Texas Longhorns. Not Notre Dame. They just lost two in a row. Marcus, he got to go with a *winner.* None of this rebuildin'. None of these Mississippi schools either. He's made for better relationships in *this* town. Marcus Dupree shows it depends on the individual, not the color of the skin. We had a bad name. People away from here would fill up with gas way down the road before drivin' through Neshoba County. But Marcus Dupree helped everything around here. He's a *winner!* He's gonna shine for us. He won't never let us down."

I knew it was time for me to meet the young man.

I used the pay telephone up the block. His grandmother answered. He was not there. He and Reggie and their mother could be found at the junior high football game. I drove down to the stadium behind the school and got out. The country dogs from the hollow who were perpetually being chased off the field during the high school games greeted me. At the moment, twenty-two violent adolescents were going at it in the neighborhood of the forty-yard line. The concrete grandstand and the bleachers under the lights were all but deserted.

I spotted him in the end zone on the gymnasium side. He was playing touch football with several children. Watching from a few yards away were a little black child on crutches and a large, heavy-set black woman.

I had written him and his mother a letter a few days before, and now I introduced myself. "Marcus, we just *scored!*" a boy shouted as we talked. He took me over to meet his mother and his brother. I had brought along a few books I had written by way of introduction. We arranged to have a long meeting the following night. As I drove away, I noticed him leaning against the wall of the gymnasium perusing the books. Sarah McKay, his English teacher, later told me he brought them to school to show them to her.

It was a small frame house, white with green trim, with two young magnolias in the side yard. There was a refrigerator on the front porch, and sitting next to it in a straight-backed chair was a big, imposing man perhaps in his seventies. This was the Reverend Major Dupree. "Go right on in," he said in a strong bass.

Marcus' mother, his brother Reggie, and another little black boy were sitting in a cramped front room. A baseball game was on a color television in the corner. A carpet covered the linoleum floor. There was an inexpensive sofa and easy chairs scattered about, and on a coffee table by the sofa was obviously the day's mail; I noticed envelopes and letterheads from the Universities of Oklahoma, Alabama, Pittsburgh, Tennessee, and Georgia. On one wall was a UCLA football poster, and on shelves on another, above a bed—Marcus' bed, Reggie later told me—were a large number of trophies and plaques. There was a shelf on the floor with encyclopedias and some graduation photographs.

The other child was a cousin named Rock, a sprightly figure wearing glasses. Rock's responsibility that night was to answer the telephone, which rang every two or three minutes.

Marcus' mother's name was Cella Connor,* her married name. Her sons had taken the surname of her father. She was in her late thirties, with a broad, pleasant, open face. She too wore glasses.

"Marcus had to go down the street. He said to tell you he'd be back in a minute. We got your letter. You were editor of *Harper's* magazine. I know that magazine. I've read it."

I told her I planned on seeing all the football games this year except one. "You *are?* All the games?"

The telephone interrupted. Cousin Rock picked it up, then handed it to Marcus' mother. She listened intently. "You're still on the list," she said, then listened some more. "We beat Winona last week . . . Well, he did all right."

While she talked, I got up and looked at several photographs of Marcus and Reggie. Reggie was reclining in an easy chair. He gazed up at me. "I remember the day those pictures were taken," he said. "June 12, 1981." I asked him how he remembered. "Because I had to go into the hospital the next day."

I began telling him all about my dog, Pete, whom I intended to bring on my next visit.

"How big is Pete?"

"About ninety-five pounds."

"Wow! How much does he eat?"

"As much as he can get."

"What's his favorite food?"

"Fried chicken livers."

"Is Pete smart?"

"He can drive a car."

"Say, Rock," he shouted at his cousin, "his dog, Pete, can drive a car!"

Marcus' mother joined us again after this alexandrine exchange. She taught "secondary English" in a public school—West Kemper—in the adjacent county, she said. She drove over in a car pool every day. About 75 percent of her students were black, she said. She was born in Philadelphia, attended Coahoma Junior College in the Delta, and graduated from Alcorn State University. Then she returned to the area to teach. Her father worked for the Cole Brothers wholesale grocery and also had a church in

* Various members of the family had spelled the name differently from time to time, sometimes Conner, sometimes Connors.

Kemper County which Marcus occasionally attended. Her father came from Alabama. Her mother's people, she said, were Mississippians. She herself had no memories of her grandfather Frank Stennis, a farmer out in the county. He died the day she was born.

The phone rang. She sighed in amiable exasperation and threw up her hands. Young Rock, who was plainly enjoying his duties as surrogate secretary, again answered. "He ain't here," then gave the phone to her. "You're on the list. We'll give it a lot of thought." She returned with apologies.

She gave him the name Marcus, she said, from Shakespeare's Marc Antony. She could tell he was an athlete since he was small, as early as the first grade, even though he had to wear glasses by the time he reached second grade. "He was always bigger and could run faster than the other children. Oh, how he could run! Sometimes I'd look out the window and see him runnin' by himself down the road."

"He sure can run, can't he, Rock?" Reggie said from the easy chair.

"He sure can," Rock assented.

"The other children would just be playin' around," she continued, "but Marcus always wanted to play football, always wanted a football in his hand." Once, a white man who was a school official drove up to the house, she recalled, and asked for Marcus. She went to get him. "What have I done wrong?" he asked his mother plaintively. The man wanted him to play football for the grade school flag-football team he coached. So he was the first recruiter.

As we talked, Reggie pulled himself out of the easy chair. He did not have his crutches. He hobbled in a crawling posture into an adjoining room.

"He went out for the high school varsity team in the spring practice of eighth grade," she said. "He didn't tell me. He was afraid I'd be worried."

I asked her what was her single favorite play he ever made. "Oh! I remember it so well. Marcus was in the ninth grade. It was against Kosciusko. Marcus and Michael Harmon were the big stars. Michael was a senior. He plays for Ole Miss now, you know. They gave Marcus the ball and he just outran Harmon for a touchdown, about sixty yards. I've seen him do quite a few."

I do not intend to describe every telephone call in this visit. Cousin Rock would jump at the first ring. "There it goes again," he would say, then pass the phone along to Cella Connor. The telephone company was realizing a return on its investment in long-distance communications in the Dupree household that evening.

"I know we'll have pressure," she said. One way they planned to deal with that was to be candid with those schools in which they had no interest by telling them so, the intention being that those schools would then take themselves out of the running. She also wanted to try to limit the recruiters from each college to only one official visit in their house, although the NCAA allowed three. She hoped he might stay in Mississippi, she said, but it depended. "I've talked to him about Alcorn, but he says he ain't goin' to a college out in the woods." She laughed heartily.

I asked what her hopes for him were.

"I'd want him to have a good life. Somebody once said to me, 'One of your sons is a hero and the other is a cripple.' I don't care. I love them both." She made a movement of her hand toward her heart. "I love them so much. I love them equally. I want them both to have good lives." Reggie, she said, went to Jackson frequently for surgery, the last time to have a plate adjusted in his hip.

Reggie came back into the room and sank again into the easy chair. He had a photograph in his hand which I had sent him earlier of my dog, Pete. He held it up for us to see.

She gestured toward the younger son. "They're very, very close. They joke each other a lot. Reggie's gained a little weight, and Marcus kids him about that. Reggie kids him about his girlfriends."

"I talk to those girls on the phone," Reggie said.

"So do I," Rock said.

"It makes me feel proud and happy," she continued. "I'm proud my son is amountin' to something here, makin' something of himself. It gives me a good feelin' down here." Again she placed a hand on her breast.

"There was a white lady over at the Wal-Mart this afternoon who asked me, 'Please, can you get my little boy just one little Number 22 jersey that you don't want?'" She burst into another throaty laugh. "'Okay,' I said, 'I think I can get you one.'"

At that moment the young man himself walked in the front door with his spry, bouncing gait. He shook hands and said he was sorry for being late, then sat in a chair and listened seriously as his mother and I talked.

He was an authoritative physical presence in the tiny room. With his Afro haircut and his glasses he looked older than his seventeen years. He was very dark, with smooth features and his mother's open face. Sometimes he spoke so softly that it was difficult to hear his words. He laughed more easily than I thought he might, less a laugh than a deep chuckle. At first he did not talk any more than was necessary. He was extremely polite, and exceedingly bashful. Later, as I came to know him, he seemed to grow more well-spoken, with a sense of humor, almost of self-irony, as if he were considering the day-by-day consequences of his prodigious talent. Yet he remained gentle and self-effacing. He always tried to respond thoughtfully and honestly. This serenity was genuine, I would learn, yet it somehow seemed in contradiction with the redoubtable prowess he exhibited on the athletic field, that and a flair for the histrionic which somehow seemed necessary for him. I grew to sense a well of complexity in him that he was not yet ready to face. What seventeen-year-old ever is? I sometimes wondered if he ever pondered what he might have been doing in Mississippi a century and a quarter ago. Fifty years ago? I never asked him. He would have time for that. I wondered, too, if he knew that the great mythical cities of the North would one day beckon him, as they had me, and if he ever listened to the train whistles from the Illinois Central at night and thought of the faraway mysteries of Chicago, Boston, Manhattan. I recalled the words of William Styron—"the shade of Thomas Wolfe must be acutely disturbed to find that his earthly stock has sunk so low"—and although I knew Marcus Dupree had likely never picked up a book by Thomas Wolfe, I knew too that there had forever lurked in the breasts of all small-town Southern boys, white or black, that yearning for the eternal attractions of the Yankee manswarm.

He was always at his most animated when talking about running with a football. In such moments his dark eyes would lighten, his grave expression soften, his natural humility assume an edge of confidence and assertiveness, as on this night when I asked him right at the start about the great running backs.

"I watch 'em on TV," he said. "I watch 'em for how they move, how they run. Then I get out and try to do it my way." Earl Campbell, Walter Payton, Tony Dorsett, Billy Sims—he did not have any favorites.

I asked if he had ever seen any film clips of a running back named Jim Brown, of the Cleveland Browns quite a few years ago.

"Oh, yeah. I watch him for his moves. He's super." And Gale Sayers? "Oh, he was great."

By now young Marcus may have thought he had underestimated me. I was not talking with him about where he was going to play in college, but about the one thing he instinctually knew best.

His hero was Herschel Walker. In fact, as the weeks went by, I would note in Marcus not merely a healthy respect for Herschel, but a profound competitiveness—not just to follow in the footfalls of the immortal Walker, not merely to break his records, but even more. Could this be possible? As for now, sitting in the room of the little house on Davis Street, and speaking with relish, he considered Walker "one of the greatest." Not too long after this, he went up to Oxford to see Walker in the Ole Miss–Georgia game and was introduced to him in the Georgia dressing room afterward. "Herschel talked to me about how I was gonna get the pressure," Marcus would tell me, "and to handle it right. He went through it." As for Walker the runner, "It seemed like he was just tippin', you know, and then he'd break."

Were they similar or different as runners? I asked him on that occasion. "We're *similar*. He can fly! It was like watchin' myself."

I learned other, eclectic matters from him that night—that he wore Number 22 because he was born on May 22, that the local hangout for the ballplayers and their girls was the Pizza Hut, that his mother would be his most trusted advisor on where he went to college, that he was accustomed to the way the opposing defenses keyed in on him and that he was not bothered by it anymore, that he did not know what he wanted to study in college, that his favorite high school teacher was Sarah McKay in English, that his closest friends were the ballplayers Tree McAfee and Michael Smith at Ole Miss, that he never wanted to be a quarterback or a receiver. "I just always liked to run the ball, ever since I was a little boy." He and his mother, as well as Reggie and Rock, laughed when I reminded them he only needed 23 touchdowns in the next eight games to break Herschel's high school record.

Cousin Rock, between telephone rings, brought out a scrapbook. "Here's Marcus in the eighth grade," he said. We all examined the picture.

Through this evening there was a great deal of banter between Marcus and Reggie. It was apparent that between the two brothers lay something deeper and more binding than obligatory sibling affection. Once at the school, as Reggie hesitated before some steps, I saw Marcus bodily lift him over them, then gently put him down. Later that year, in the hideaway office in the school gymnasium which Coach Joe Wood always let me use, Marcus said something to me, almost in passing it seemed, that stunned me with its touching simplicity. "I guess I run for both of us," he said.

After the ball games, I wondered, what did the players on the other teams say to him when they came up to shake his hand? "Well, they tell me to keep my head up, that they hope I make it, that they want to see me play on TV." As for his nemesis at Kosciusko, the fellow who over the high school years had always been assigned to go after him on every play: "He was bigger than I was for a while. Now he's about 6 feet and 210. He always came up later to wish me well." After the team practices during the week, "I'll lift some weights, see some girls, ride around town some, listen to some music—I like the beat of it. Sometimes I go out in the country and ride a little horseback."

Rock answered the telephone. It was for Marcus. I heard him whisper: "I can't talk now. We're talkin' to a *writer*."

I asked if he were religious. "Yes, I believe in the Lord." He went to church about every second and fourth Sunday around the corner at Mount Nebo Missionary Baptist, and had been going there, his mother said, since he was a little boy. "He's religious," she said, "but, you know, not in an open way, not *extra* religious. I think he prays more during the football season.

"Most of the recruiters and coaches from all the schools say what Marcus has is a God-given talent," she said, "but it doesn't really come from any emphasis on it. It just comes *natural*. It comes from God."

Did he agree with that?

"It just all comes. It just came to me."

From the darkness outside, I heard a child's voice: *"Grandmama, Miz Evers says thank you for keepin' Prissy!"* I was conscious of subtle movement: big Reverend Dupree in the side yard, the grandmother from a small room behind us.† The sounds of the Quarters, as old and familiar to me as anything I ever knew, yet forbidden and exotic as always, wafted into the room—music from down the street, the babble of secret laughter, voices in the night, the crying of babies, a dozen dogs barking, the rumble of a train. For the first time some emotion deep in me told me I had truly come home to live, home again at last.

I was talking again to Marcus. He sat straight in his chair, gazing toward the floor. He saw the memorial on Sundays in front of his church, he said, the one to Schwerner, Goodman, and Chaney. After their deaths, Martin Luther King had preached for equality in his church. Was he aware of what happened here in 1964? He did not reply. "*Civil Rights Movement,*" his mother whispered to him, with a soft and knowing chuckle. "I don't know," he finally said. "It's been on TV before. I really don't think much about that."

His mother nodded, whispered again: "*Troubles.*" She was nineteen when Marcus was born in 1964, she said. "Those were frightening times." She continued: "A lot of people look at Mississippi as bein' fifty years behind the times. It's progressing, little by degrees. A lot of the changes began before Marcus started playin'. But I'd like to think my son's had something to do in helpin' bring whites and blacks closer together."

We talked in a desultory way about other things. As I was about to leave, I stood on the porch with Marcus and Reggie, who had his crutches. What if he got hurt badly tomorrow night against Newton and could never play again, I asked Marcus.

† Temple Drake's earlier warning about the importance of grandmothers in football recruitment would not apply to Marcus'. Gladys Dupree was a gentle old woman who had never seen him play because the night air aggravated her arthritis, and she always worried he might get hurt. She would tease the mailman about all the letters he brought to the house. "I'm going to set a big can out here," she said, "where you can drop the mail in because the mailbox just won't hold it all."

"I just like horses and cows and the outdoors," he said. "I like bein' free."

"Bring that dog, Pete, around here sometime," Reggie said.

The historical marker at the train depot in Newton said: "Here at Newton Station, on April 24, 1863, Federals under General Benjamin H. Grierson struck the Vicksburg-Meridian rail route, tore up tracks, and burned the depot."

It was an exemplary night for football—cool, clear, in the mid fifties. The cars moved slowly to the stadium in long lines in the dusty twilight.

At the game I was meeting one of my best friends, Glynn "Squirrel" Griffing, who was driving over from Jackson.

Squirrel was a Mississippi legend. He had been named "Squirrel" by "Dog" Brewer, the Ole Miss quarterback before him. He grew up around Vicksburg and lived for a time in a little house on the battlefield, and when the spring rains came he and his brother would go to the creeks and collect the minié balls that had washed down from the hills. Once, when he was digging the earth for a vegetable garden, he found the bones of a human hand. He was the All-American quarterback and captain of the Ole Miss Rebels in their glory days of the early sixties. His teammates included "Bull" Bolton, "Possum" Price, "Snake" Elmore, "Mule" Jones, "Hoss" Anderson, "Bird" Partridge, "Catfish" Smith, "Bear" Brown, "Dog" Brewer, " 'Boon" Alford, and the more mundane "White Trash" Champion. In '62, a few days after the Meredith Riots, he threw four touchdowns in the first half in a game in Jackson, and during the half-time ceremonies Ross Barnett stood on the fifty-yard line with his Stetson on his heart and the band playing "Dixie" and spoke of the fortitude of the sovereign state of Mississippi.

Unusual things always happened to Squirrel. Shortly before the '62 Cotton Bowl against the Texas Longhorns, he had a vision in a dream of a big scoreboard reading: 12–7. Late in the fourth quarter Ole Miss was deep in Texas territory, but on a fourth down and two yards to go, Squirrel was thrown for a loss and knocked unconscious by a huge Texas lineman, who was also knocked out. When Squirrel came to he gazed up and saw through his haze: "Texas 12, Ole Miss 7." He later told me: "That's one of them déjà-vu's." Then he spent some time with the New York Giants and threw a touchdown pass in the championship professional game of '63 to Frank Gifford.

One night in Memphis, Squirrel and I were sitting on the first row watching a college game. "Those drunk fellows who sit eighty rows up and cuss out the players when they do bad ought to be sittin' down here and see how young these big boys look—they're really just young kids."

Some ex-athletes did not know anything about football. Squirrel knew the game as well as anyone I ever met. I was anxious for his studied appraisals.

He and I wandered the sidelines before the kickoff saying hello to the people I knew from Philadelphia. The stadium was packed, perhaps four thousand people, and they spilled out of the grandstand and bleachers almost onto the field itself. Temple Drake had forewarned me that in some Mississippi towns after integration, with strong private schools (or "seg academies") to rival the public schools, only six classifications of whites attended the public school games. "One, parents of players," he had said. "Two, parents of cheerleaders. Three, parents of band members. Four, teachers. Five, outside coaches. Six, the local poolroom guys." But this was public school country, and the crowds here reminded me in spirit of the high school games in Mississippi of a generation ago. The spectators seemed equally divided between whites and blacks and here, as in Philadelphia, the little black children were everywhere. The unbeaten Newton Tigers were about 30 percent black. They came onto the field through a papier-mâché sign with the words "Reach Out for Victory," just as dozens of blue balloons were set adrift and blew away toward the burnt-orange horizon. Then the Philly Tornadoes came onto the field.

Walking about under the dim stadium lights, Squirrel Griffing and I absorbed the sideline talk.

"Where's he at?"

"Right there. Look at them *laigs!*"

"Say, which one's *Du*-pree?"

"He's that one. Man, he big."

"That Number 22. He's *bad.*"

And with this, there was the usual rumble of talk here and there about State, Ole Miss, Southern, Alabama, LSU.

Swirls of dust hovered over the field at the kickoff. Philadelphia received the customary squib kick. Coach Joe Wood's protégés were still running from the Wishbone. On the first play from scrimmage, from deep in his own territory, Number 22 came within one step of breaking free. He gained nine yards. On the next play he picked up ten yards with literally seven defenders on him before he went down. Then on a pitchout he went for thirteen. Then seven.

"God A'mighty!" Squirrel Griffing exclaimed. "I can already tell. This kid's the best runnin' back I ever saw." Two plays later he ran for nine yards.

"Fantastic!" I had not seen the Squirrel this excited in years. "I want you to watch somethin'. He comes out runnin' *ass-high.* Most big men run upright. He runs low for a big man. That makes him harder to hit."

The game settled down into a tough battle between the thirty-yard lines, the Newton star being a blithe little halfback named Yogi Johnson.

The scoreboard broke down in the second quarter and we were without downs, yards, and time. Philadelphia was hampered all through the evening by costly penalties. The tackling was savage and the defensive keying-in on Marcus Dupree merciless. It was one of the two games that season in which I feared for his physical safety. None of this was lost on Squirrel Griffing.

"If only he had an offensive line to give him a little runnin' room. The offense ain't right. The Wishbone doesn't give him enough space." His enthusiasm was unabated, however, on the six-, eight-, eleven-yard gains, and then a thirty-five-yard run that was called back for clipping. The score at the end of the first half was o–o. A young black man standing next to us turned to his companion as the half ended and said: "Time to go get that woman, huh?"

During the halftime ceremonies, in fact at the precise moment the Philly band began "New York, New York," an angular gentleman in khakis with a chew of tobacco in his jaw began talking with us.

"I'd have him at tailback carryin' the damned thing ninety percent of the time," he said. "Do they know what they *got?*"

"He comes out ass-high," Squirrel repeated.

"Say, you fellas coaches?"

"Right," Squirrel said. "Ohio State."

"You ain't gonna get him. I drove all the way from Mendenhall to see him. How's that ol' Woody Hayes?"

He could not break the big play in the second half. He came close on two. He was gang-tackled with even greater consistency, and every time he hit the hard Mississippi earth the Newton crowd roared more and more enthusiastically. Taunts began to fill the dusty air.

"How about *that*, Dupree?"

"You ain't gonna get up from *that* one!"

"How'd *that* feel, you motha!"

Suddenly, quick as a thunderbolt in the waning seconds of the third quarter, Newton exploded with an eighty-yard touchdown pass. The game ended that way, 7–0. Marcus' figures: no touchdowns, 19 carries for 140 yards. In the parking lot, I heard a black Newton fan tell his wife: "Yessuh, he knows he's been hit tonight."

\* \* \* \*

*Lost to Newton. Our line didn't play too well. Kind of felt there was a little cheating. Every time we got down to their ten, we got a fifteen-yard penalty.*

*I should have had a real good game, but it was only average. I felt good running the ball. The line just had a couple of breakdowns.*

*This wasn't the first time our offense has been shut down. Our offense hasn't scored touchdowns a couple of times, but we'd kick a field goal. I don't remember us being shut out. The defense played real well, but we just had one mental breakdown for one long play.*

*I think the defense will help us. We're going to switch up the offensive line a little bit. I believe we needed to lose a game. There was a lot of pressure from last year, and going 10–0. This ought to bring us down to earth.*

*I hope to have a good game this week. It's homecoming against Northwest Rankin.*

*Recruiting hasn't changed much. Got letters from a couple of "new" schools—North Carolina and SMU. Also got calls from UCLA, Texas, Alabama, and Georgia. Right now my only "official" trip planned is to UCLA sometime in December. I also plan to visit Georgia and Texas.*

*Might go and see the games (State-Florida, Ole Miss–Arkansas) in Jackson this weekend. I hope to see both games.*

*       *       *       *

During the Newton game, as at the earlier ones, whenever Marcus came off the field for a new tear-away jersey or a rest, I noticed little Number 18. He was a substitute end who did not play much, but he helped Marcus with his shoulder pads and his jerseys, sometimes bringing him a cup of water and sitting next to him, an arm casually draped over his shoulder, on a table behind the main bench.

After the game, as I was waiting in my car for the traffic to thin out in the parking lot, I turned on the light and looked at the Philadelphia team roster in the game program. Number 18 was Cecil Price, Jr.

Young Price was born in October of 1964 while his father was deputy sheriff, two months after the grave was discovered in the earthen dam at the old Jolly Place. He and Marcus, I learned, started the first grade together in the year the schools integrated. His father returned to the town after his four years in a federal penitentiary. He worked now for a gasoline company, and his mother in a drugstore on the Square. They did not make themselves available to writers. They had the choice twelve years before of enrolling their son in the abortive segregated academy, but decided that if there was going to be an integrated society, "it's better for him to be brought up in it."

In 1975, when Cecil Price, Jr., was in the fifth grade, CBS Television showed its documentary on the murders in Philadelphia based on Don Whitehead's *Attack on Terror*. The next day young Cecil was beaten up by several black students. "That film had a big impact on the town," one citizen told me. "It was absolutely unreal for Marcus and the other black kids. They'd never been exposed to that kind of raw violence and hatred."

"You can't blame the kids for what the parents were involved in," Marcus' mother had said. "That happened a whole generation ago. The kids now don't pay attention to color, it's not a big thing. They go to class together. They play ball together. But what happened seventeen years ago has to be remembered. It should always be remembered." Cecil and Marcus had become friends during their years in school together. They visited each other at home. "I like him and he likes me," Marcus said. "It's not hard to understand. I don't know his father. I only met him once or twice."


I was in town early in the week for the homecoming game against the Cougars of Northwest Rankin. There had been some grumbling about the shutout loss to Newton—some condescending remarks from whites, I was told, about Marcus. The recruiting rumors had quietened somewhat, and even the Downtown Hotel was more somnolent than usual, as drowsy as Mr. Presley Snow in his perpetual sleep in the easy chair in the lobby.

I made my usual rounds of the Square and paid another visit to the library. While I was perusing some local history, a handsome woman in her forties came over and introduced herself. She was Seena Kohl, an anthropologist on leave from Webster College in St. Louis. She had been serving as Neshoba County's scholar-in-residence under the Mississippi Committee for the Humanities. More stunning to me was that she was the cousin of Joseph Heller, the author of Catch-22, who had been my neighbor on eastern Long Island. I believe the last person on earth I would have expected to run into on a slow autumn's forenoon in Philadelphia, Mississippi—with the exception perhaps of Clare Boothe Luce, Gloria Vanderbilt, Ahmet Ertegun, or Leonard Bernstein—was Joseph Heller, for some people and some terrains in America simply do not go with one another, and meeting his cousin here was not unsurprising either. She and I arranged to meet for coffee in the restaurant of the Downtown in late afternoon.

I had been alone at a corner table overhearing a couple of farmers talking about the expensive tastes of Mrs. Ronald Reagan.

"All them plates and stuff in the White House ain't good enough for her," one of them said.

"She ain't bad," his friend said. "Leave her alone."

Seena Kohl came in and sat down. "Oh, for a martini before the commuter train," I said, and she agreed. She had been born and raised in the East before moving to St. Louis and she had not known about the liquor laws down here before she came, she said.

She discussed her project with the library. It was called "Diverse Origins, Common History," and one of its purposes was to encourage the blacks, whites, and Choctaws of Neshoba to learn their separate and common histories. The very existence of such a project, she believed, said a great deal about Philadelphia, Mississippi—racial relationships here, she had learned, were as bad and as good as in any Northern city of our day. What had struck her deeply was the *defensiveness*, "not just here, but all over Mississippi."

This reminded me, I told her, of a recent conversation in the Warehouse Restaurant in Oxford. The company consisted of three good Mississippi fellows and Winthrop Jordan, the distinguished American historian, author of *White over Black*, who was at Ole Miss on leave from Berkeley. We had been discussing various Mississippi matters. "Why is everything so *complicated* here?" Jordan asked. The others bristled at this, though in a polite way, but I defended his question. "Even though I'm a native of this state, a seventh-generation Mississippian," I said to Mrs. Kohl, "it's still the most complicated place *I've* ever lived. Everything affects everything else. Everything makes waves." She was fascinated with Mississippi and intended to return, she said, after her project on Neshoba was done. The subject of Marcus came up. She understood. "Football as a metaphor for what's happening deeper," she said. Another side of that, she said, were the separate white and black baseball leagues for the young boys in the summer, which caused me to reflect that the further one got away from the aegis of the public schools, the more some things reverted to the older patterns.

This happened to be a topic which intrigued me, and after the discerning Yankee anthropologist departed from the Downtown Restaurant with its lingering aromas of catfish and chitterlings, I was eager to talk with a black man I had heard much about. His name was Jimmy Lee Shannon, and he had been elected to the board of aldermen and was active on the sports scene in town.

Shannon was waiting for me on the front porch of a small frame house just across the road from the sawmill in the Quarters. We sat in chairs on the porch in the twilight amid the clean odor of newly cut pines. He wore a shirt and tie with the collar unbuttoned, an inspiriting young man of thirty-one who had been elected alderman three months before from Ward 4, which had about six hundred registered black voters and one hundred whites. He was the second black elected to the board. Before that he had served on the school board. His parents, grandparents, and great-grandparents had all been born and raised in Neshoba County; his great-grandfather lived to be one hundred and ten. Shannon himself grew up in a house in the same block on Davis Street where Marcus now lived. "We were very, very poor," he said. He now worked in "production control" at the U.S. Electrical Motors plant.

Abruptly he went into the house and returned with a photograph, which he proudly showed me. It was the Little League team which he coached when Marcus was eleven years old. They were called "The Knockouts." "He was somethin' in baseball. He was so big in the last year he was eligible, they wouldn't let him play." He was also the scoutmaster of the Cub Scout troop. "We had a barbecue every year for the kids. When Marcus was nine he could eat two chickens and ask for more. They'd let him run with the Boy Scouts in track and he'd outrun 'em all." Besides Marcus, he had Mark Burnside and Daran Jackson, two black running backs on the present Philly team, on his Little League teams and in the Cub Scouts, as well as Michael Smith, who had gone to Ole Miss last year on a football scholarship, and Dwight McWilliams, who was playing basketball for Delta State. "Dwight was captain of the Philadelphia High basketball team, real humble and smart. I just act like they're my kids. I'm like a daddy to 'em. They're real respectful, amenable boys. Michael's the brightest of the group. He'll do fine at Ole Miss, play ball and be an honor student."

The sun's fading glow caught the tall stacks of timber across the way. Two children with several dogs on their trail ran by pushing an old tire.

I had been advised that Jimmy Lee Shannon had been the Marcus Dupree of the last days of the segregated schools in town, and with his stockiness and nimble movements as he paced the front porch he still had the look of the running back. I asked him about this.

Yes, he said, he had been a halfback at Booker T. Washington High School. He weighed 180 pounds and ran a 9.9 hundred. He scored twenty-six touchdowns his senior year. He had gone over to Philadelphia High when integration came in January 1970, so that he spent the second semester of his senior year in the integrated school and was in the first graduation class of whites and blacks. Both Alcorn and Grambling approached him on football scholarships.

"I didn't want to get too far from home," he said. "I didn't have nobody to really push me." He paused, as if he had considered that many times. "It was different back then," he said. He went to East Central Junior College on a football scholarship, got hurt, and that was that.

"Yeah, I've thought about it a lot. The black players have so much more possibilities now. I might've come along about two or three years too early. I'm not bitter about it. The Lord's blessed me. I've got peace of mind—about myself, my family, my community. The Lord's blessed me all right."

When Marcus' own future came up, Shannon brightened. "This is the first time we've had anything like this," he said. "You hear of this in *other* towns around the country. The white uptown will tell you, 'He's our kid, he's our boy.' He belongs to both of us. You go around town in

the coffee shops and the whites say, 'Our boy, our boy.' The whole town
—everybody's got the college of their choice. But the feelin' is, wherever
he go, he'll do good. Myself, I'd like to see him stay in Mississippi. He
was born and raised in Mississippi. Me, I love Mississippi. I've been up
north in Detroit for a year and a half in the eighth grade with my father.
That kind of life . . . I guess I just don't go for that environment. I like
to set down and reason and come together and be peaceful. Up north you
hear sirens all the time.

"But these big schools like UCLA, Southern Cal, Alabama, Texas,
Oklahoma, they're at him and they have a lot to offer. Goin' north, to a
big city like Pittsburgh, wouldn't hurt him. He can take the hardness, the
chewin' out. The coach at Pittsburgh is a Mississippian. That's good. No
matter who he signs with, I imagine his friends Jackson, Burnside, or Sutton would be included in a package. If he was to come and ask me, I'd
say, 'Now, you're gonna have to live with this, you're gonna have to
make your own decision.' But wherever he go, I'm goin' to see him—live,
and not on TV."

With this he got up again, walking the length of the little porch.
"Think of a great big offensive line in front of him somewhere! You're
gonna see seven, eight yards at a time. I just hope he keeps his head
screwed on right. Just keep his head, that's the main thing. Just be plain,
just be plain." A few years back, he said, there was a black running back
from Philadelphia named Randy Griffin. "He went to Mississippi State
to play ball, got in a fast crowd, and dropped out. Marcus is a big boy.
You forget he's just seventeen. He didn't even start courtin' girls till after
the eleventh grade. He hadn't had all that exposure to runnin' around and
all that. Right now his girlfriend is my wife's sister—Katrina. Katrina's in
the eleventh grade and plays basketball."

When we got to "The Troubles," his voice was subdued. "We've
come a long way," he said. "A long way since '64. Since integration. It follows us everywhere. We don't like even to talk about the murders. We're
tryin' to make a better community. We need a lot more industry. Housin'
is too high. But we all know each other. We have blacks from Northern
cities come in here and tell us they can do this and they can do that and
they live among the whites and all that. But there's more discrimination
up there than down here. Down here a white man will tell you right away
what he thinks. Integration worked better here than there, and they
pushed it down here.

"The black people in this town are very politically active. We can go
to a white politician and tell him what we want. Three years ago the
NAACP had its district meeting at the courthouse, just like anybody else
who wanted to meet. Five months ago we had an NAACP banquet out at
Westside and there was as many whites as blacks. We got a bond issue

passed for a vo-tech school that will cost the city and county $900,000. It carried ninety percent in the city and eighty-five percent in the county. This is mostly for poor kids to learn a trade and make an honest livin'. We're able to cope with our problems—discussin' 'em in nicer ways, not in a nasty way. Ain't got to fuss and raise sand about it.

"We have the problems. We don't have enough black doctors, lawyers, big-time businessmen, black people thought well of financially. We need more principals, coaches, teachers. Year before last we only had four black faculty here. Now it's about eight or nine."

It was almost dark now in Independence Quarters. The piles of timber were like ghostly pyres against the sky. From inside the house came the smell of something frying.

I asked if he had any fears about Marcus. "The only thing I can do is pray for him. I remember his sophomore year, against Neshoba Central. He scored a touchdown, then strutted a little in the end zone. I got on him for that. He's a fine kid. He'll be okay.

"All these boys I had in the Scouts and Little League—Marcus' parents got divorced when he was small, Daran Jackson's father died when he was little, Mark Burnside's parents got divorced. All these boys have wonderful mothers. I guess they've always leaned on me a little. I tell 'em I hope if they live and I live, they'll come back home and have a nice house and raise a fine family and have me over, and I'll sit at the table and kick my heels up, I'll be so happy.

"So many of the young blacks here think life is just like a TV picture. I tell 'em life ain't just a holiday. There's a time for everything, to let your heels go and have a good time, and a time to work hard and show respect.

"My boys—Marcus, Daran, Mark, Michael up at Ole Miss, Dwight up at Delta State—I'm proud for them. They worked hard. Dwight would walk to the school at 5 A.M. every day and shoot baskets for two hours in the gym. I don't want just Marcus to have everything. I want my other boys to have it too."

We stood in the yard as I was leaving. "I tell Marcus the one thing I want him to do is be himself," he said. "Watch his friends and be sure he gets that education. And I tell him don't forget where he came from—Philadelphia, Mississippi—and the people who care about him."

That Thursday afternoon I walked from the Downtown to the stadium to watch the team practice. It was hot and bright, and the concrete grandstand was empty except for a few of the high school girls.

The team was at the north end of the field going through its drills without pads. Coach Joe Wood was experimenting with the "Shotgun" formation, with Marcus as the deep back throwing passes. He was connecting on long and short ones with considerable accuracy to Cleveland McAfee, Jay Graham, Mark Burnside, and Cecil Price, Jr.

"Hey, Rodney," one of the assistant coaches shouted, "bring some water!" The girls in the grandstand were discussing their dates for tomorrow night.

Suddenly there was panic on the gridiron. The players began running in all directions, their yells filling the air. Was this a mutiny against the Shotgun formation? Nothing so simple. A swarm of yellowjackets had descended on the unwitting Tornadoes. Then, just as swiftly as they had come, the invaders returned to their hive near the ten-yard line. When practice resumed with the second-team backfield running the offense, Marcus casually went over to the yellowjackets' nest and bent down to examine it.

Joe Wood blew his whistle. "Git on over here!" he shouted to the team. From my own experience I knew this would be a speech, so I left the grandstand and walked down to listen. Marcus saw me and waved.

"Now, tomorrow's homecomin'," Wood said. "School's lettin' out at one for the parade. There's gonna be a lot of *distractions*. We don't plan to have the pallets in the gym or the pregame meal in the cafeteria. So after the parade, go home and rest. Start thinkin' about the game. If you forgot an assignment, ask somebody. Ask your mama to fix you a steak or somethin'. Nothin' greasy. I don't want you wanderin' all over town."

When he had finished, I got in step with him on the way to the gymnasium. "We plan to open up some tomorrow if we have to," he said.

I was on the Square the next afternoon for the parade. The merchants were drawn from their stores, and the sidewalks and courthouse lawn were lined three or four deep with white and black spectators.

The band appeared playing "Hail to the Varsity." The homecoming maids, white and black and in the Sunday best, came by in sleek convertibles, followed by students in pickup trucks with signs that said: CAN THE COUGARS! and FEAST ON COUGAR MEAT. Some of the players stood on the high sidewalk in front of the ice-cream parlor and shouted at the girls. Several modest little floats drifted past, and cars carrying the officers of various clubs, and a number of golf carts decorated in the school colors with the cheerleaders inside. Bringing up the rear were the dogs from the hollow by the stadium, including the rust-colored one with red-and-black crepe tied loosely to his neck. In all truth, the parade did not last very long.

It was a clear, warm night of late September in Harpole Stadium. The signs on the visitors' side proclaimed: TAME THE TORNADOES!, COU-

GAR BLITZ!, and BITE THE DUST, MARCUS! Northwest Rankin, half white and half black, had only twenty-eight on its traveling squad, including a substitute end who weighed 122 pounds, and its band wore matching T-shirts and trousers.

Earlier in the day, at the Downtown, I had arranged to meet two other friends who had driven from Oxford. Both were intrepid followers of football. Russell Blair, known as "The Commander," was a lawyer who had played sports at Annapolis in the late thirties and was on the U.S.S. *California* at Pearl Harbor on December 7, 1941. Charles Henry was an insurance man, a Deltan who had grown up on the Coldwater River between Sledge and Darling. Commander Blair and Charles Henry were as curious as Squirrel Griffing and Representative Perry had been to observe Marcus for the first time.

There was no scoring in the first quarter. Marcus had runs of four, six, seven, eight, nine, and twelve yards. Early in the second quarter he broke off tackle out of the Wishbone for a fourteen-yard touchdown. Less than two minutes later Mark Burnside scored from forty-one yards out to put Philly in front, 12–0. Marcus, directing the kickoff team with timing signals, came over to the sidelines and raised his arms to solicit yells from the home crowd. The fans stood in unison, clapping and shouting.

He was gaining substantial yardage. My companions from Oxford expressed their pleasure with terse, clipped comments and an occasional flamboyant oath. Then he headed up the middle on a long run. Number 10 of the Northwest Rankin Cougars, whose name was Jessie Bilbro, caught him by the shirt and the top of his football trousers and held on with great tenacity. Marcus pulled him another ten yards, but Bilbro refused to let go, sliding along on the ground until two of his teammates finally made the tackle after a fifty-two-yard gain. This unusual feat was a little like mixing sex with booze; it was not poetic, but it worked. The home crowd laughed, then applauded young Bilbro's accomplishment in a spirit of sportsmanship. The Navy's Blair and the insurance man Henry were equally impressed. "Number 10 will remember when he's an old man," one of them said, "holdin' on to Marcus Dupree's shirt like a man holdin' on to a wild mule." A little later, with 5:33 remaining in the first half, he ran over half a dozen defenders, including the indomitable Jessie Bilbro, on a forty-seven-yard sweep for a touchdown. Philly 19, Northwest Rankin 0.

As was my habit, I wandered about the stadium at halftime chatting with Principal Gregory, "Boots" Howell, Superintendent Myers, young Amy Kilpatrick, and others, to the strains of the Philadelphia band addressing itself to making it big in the city that does not sleep.

The homecoming queen and maids were then presented. The white and black girls were escorted to the center of the field by their fathers as the voice on the loudspeaker made the introductions. "First in our line of royalty is maid-at-large Betty Hampton." There was general applause. She was a black girl in a yellow evening dress, and she was cited as a member of the Society of Distinguished American High School Students. Another black girl, Teresa Stribling, was introduced as president of the senior class, five-year honor student, and "most intellectual girl" her senior year. Similar homage was paid to the other beaming girls of both races in the Tornado court of royalty.


During these ceremonies, merely in the mood of casual inquiry, I walked over to the visitors' side of the field. The cheerleaders of the visiting team and of Philadelphia had congregated in a little semicircle near the empty players' bench to exchange the traditional felicities. And with this I must be indulged a brief digression of the most academic nature.

I immediately took notice of one of the visitors' cheerleaders. She was so stunningly beautiful that the sight of her was like a sudden blow in the back of the neck. She stood there among her fellows in a pose of studied nonchalance; I knew she was very aware of her beauty. She was one of those willowy blond lovelies in whom the sovereign state of Mississippi had forever abounded and been justly famous. Her soft, clean features stood out in the festive Neshoba evening. Without warning, in that instant, I was overcome with an emotion of sadness. What would become of this splendid young creature? Where might she be twenty years from this night? In the suburbia of Greater Atlanta or Birmingham? On the field the Philadelphia band was playing again:

> My little town blues
> Are melting away,
> I'll make a brand new start of it
> In old New York . . .

Would she have a long, happy life? Surely she would not grow old and die! As she detached herself momentarily from her companions, for little reason at all she performed a ginger cartwheel, then a tender arabesque. I sensed as I always had the worm in the lilac, remembering anew the lines of Emily Dickinson:

> This quiet Dust was Gentlemen and Ladies
> And Lads and Girls—
> Was laughter and ability and Sighing,
> And Frocks and Curls.

She returned to the friendly semicircle. She looked up into the bleachers, tossing back her long golden hair. Behind me some county fellows in Coors T-shirts and tractor caps were snickering about her. "She is one of those village beauties of which the South is so prodigal," Walker Percy said in *The Moviegoer* about Binx Bolling's secretary in New Orleans from Eufala, Alabama. "No one marvels at them; no one holds them dear. They flush out of their nests first thing and alight in the cities to stay, and no one misses them. Even their men pay no attention to them, any way far less attention than they pay to money. But I marvel at them; I miss them; I hold them dear." Binx Bolling marveled likewise that, twenty years ago, "practically every other girl born in Gentilly must have been named Marcia. A year or so later it was Linda. Then Sharon. In recent years I have noted that the name Stephanie has come into fashion."

Had only Binx Bolling been with me in my travels in that imperishable autumn of 1981 to the high school football stadia of east-central Mississippi studying the cheerleaders. Philadelphia itself had *Stephanie* Griffin, as well as *Yvonne* Burnette, *Dee Dee* Morgan, *Tonya* Alexander, *Suzette* Black, *Rhonda* Allen, and *Lori* Sharp. I would not, unfortunately, match the black or white faces with the names, but 1964 must have been an auspicious year for Europe, and especially France. Might Jacqueline Kennedy have had an influence here? Eupora featured *Jacqueline* Gary and *Corinne* Hooper, Newton had *Denise* Cumberland, and in time I would see and admire *Denise* LeFlore of Carthage and *Renee* Thompson of New Hope. My favorites included *Falisia* Fullilove of Winona, *Nina* Glaze and *Sonya* Bounds of Newton, and *Vonda* Bowie and *Angle* Stephenson of Ackerman. Otherwise the rosters would include *Misti, Christi, Lori, Terri, Sherri, Wendi, Vicky,* and *Cindi; Cissy, Starry, Tammy,* and *Sandy; Debbie, Berdie,* and *Connie;* two *Pams,* a *Malissa* and a *Melissa;* and one each of the more utilitarian *Sharron, Dorice, Tina, Kim, Ilean,* and *Jimmie Lyn.* God bless them every one.

"High school football games are great for fathers of teenaged daughters who are cheerleaders," a father of just such a cheerleader in Oxford, Mississippi, had told me. "Teenaged daughters love to scream. This gets them out of the house to scream, and in a good cause." He produced for me his cheerleader-daughter's shopping list before the first game of the season, done in her own hand:

    1 nautical blue eyeliner
    1 shell white eyeshadow
    1 Burgundy Blush
    1 Cinnamon Blush (Covergirl)
    1 Plum Berry Blush (Revlon)

"The 'Blushes,' you see, are lipstick," he explained to me. "She's been experimenting before the games."

Throughout the season, as I followed the fortunes of Marcus Dupree, I discovered that the styles of all the cheerleaders in the various towns, when placed under rigorous scrutiny, seemed rather similar. This led one to suspect that most of them had attended the Ole Miss Cheerleaders' Clinic in the summer. Strolling across that campus one afternoon the previous July, I had been exposed to the most bizarre spectacle—a scene from Fellini. Walking up the street or through the Grove toward their mass convocations, the cheerleaders from each school would be clustered together, wearing their school colors. As they strolled along they were practicing their favorite or most difficult yells. One group of little nymphets in matching blue and gold were actually perched in the limbs of an elm tree doing their routines. Another was on the roof of a sorority house. Some of the squads were half white and half black. Others had only one or two black girls in their number. I counted one group with ten blacks and two whites. Several were all white—the private academies, no doubt, from Jackson or the Delta. Imagine, if you will, regardless of your sociological bias, walking innocently across the Ole Miss campus with your beloved dog Pete, and then being bombarded from every direction by hundreds upon hundreds of screaming teenagers, strutting to various beats, yelling their different yells in the fashionable black cadences, one battalion of them disappearing down the hill while another—echoing from the distance—appears suddenly from around a bend, louder than the one before.

The next week, one knew, the high school twirlers would arrive for the Ole Miss Baton Twirling Clinic. The twirlers would be quieter, more sedate. But there were other differences as well, almost existential in substance. As I stood on the North Rankin side of the Philadelphia stadium at halftime on this night, investigating the cheerleaders of both teams, I remembered what an especially perspicacious law student had told me not many days before. "Baton twirlers are more thoughtful and deliberative," he had explained. "I believe they have a more lonely calling than cheerleaders. In the South, and especially in Mississippi, many of the twirlers' mothers were twirlers. That's an unconscionable burden, you know. The mothers get their daughters started in twirling at an early age. They want to relive their own youth as twirlers through their daughters. How often do you see that among cheerleaders? One girl I know of—her mother was a twirler in the 1950s at Copiah-Lincoln Junior College, they called them "Co-Letts"—started twirling when she was two or three years old. She was the featured twirler at Brookhaven High School and later tried out for the main job at Southern Mississippi. She didn't make it. It was sad."

My advisor continued: "Cheerleaders don't suffer the way twirlers do. Twirlers aren't in a group all the time. They're the last of the individualists. But it's all changing. The trend now is toward a drum-and-bugle-corps style, twirling rifles and flags and God knows what else. It's the damned Pentagon influence. The individual twirler is out now in Mississippi, but who knows? Toynbee had it right. Twirling comes and goes in cycles." I appreciated the law student's wise counsel. From that night I began to look on both professions with a new eye.

I settled in again with my companions in the home grandstand. Joe Wood was letting Burnside and Jackson carry the ball much of the time. Philadelphia was in possession on its own thirty-seven-yard line with 7:53 left in the third quarter. Marcus took the ball on a pitchout to the right. He hammered over two linemen, then sidestepped a cornerback, and outran everyone else for a sixty-three-yard touchdown. There was no one within fifteen yards of him when he crossed the goal line.

Late in that quarter I witnessed one of the two or three most spectacular runs I had ever seen in a football game. Philadelphia had the ball on the enemy's forty-four-yard line. He took the ball to the left side of his line and was immediately hit by two defenders. Both bounced off. Moving farther to his left, he was hemmed in near the sidelines. Then he completely reversed his field, making a wide arc far behind the line of scrimmage. He reached the sidelines in front of us, broke another tackle that nearly sent him out of bounds, and outraced three or four other defenders while tightroping the boundary.

"Did you see what I saw?" Commander Blair of Annapolis asked.

That was all for Marcus. He spent the rest of the game sitting on the little table behind the bench with the children competing for his attention on the other side of the fence. Philly 32, Northwest Rankin 0. His statistics: 12 carries for 241 yards and 4 touchdowns on runs of 14, 47, 63, and 44 yards. He carried the ball two times in the second half for 107 yards and two touchdowns.

In the room at the Downtown later, my companions and I poured a drink and I listened aimlessly to their agitated talk.

"He could've gained five hundred yards tonight."

"Dooley was six and five when he signed Walker."

"Ole Miss has a shot. Tom Goode recruits mamas and daddies."

"Your allegiance is to the school where they cut your hair short."

"He's got the super-star air about him already. See how he goes and sits behind the bench on that table?"

"If he came to Ole Miss I'd give him a *throne* to sit on."

The next morning, before departing, I dropped by the dressing room in the school. I observed once more the activity of a Saturday morning in a small-town gymnasium after a football game. Dirty uniforms were strewn all about. The laundry machines whirled and rattled, and young boys were at work sweeping the floor. Coach Wood was in his office with a couple of assistants. "Did you see how that new play worked?—the fake to Burnside up the middle and the pitch to Marcus on the sweep!"

I was taken, I told the coach, by the way he reversed the whole field on that one touchdown.

"You ain't seen nothin' yet," Joe said, aiming a little snuff at the wastebasket.

# 11

# *He That Loseth His Life...*

Not long after the discovery of the corpses in the summer of '64, Sam Bowers—the Imperial Wizard of the White Knights—was heard to say: "This is the first time in history that Christians have carried out the execution of a Jew." During the Neshoba County Fair that August, the White Knights distributed copies of their official publication all over the fairgrounds:

> . . . Schwerner, Chaney, and Goodman were not civil-rights workers. They were Communist Revolutionaries, actively working to undermine and destroy Christian Civilization. The blatant and outlandish National Police activity surrounding their case merely points up the political overtones of the entire affair. Hundreds of people disappear and are killed all over the U.S. each year with little or no National Police Investigation . . .

Ten days after the bodies were found, while the Fair was still on, COFO set up an office with about a dozen volunteers to encourage voter registration in the old two-story Evers Hotel in Independence Quarters. It had been owned by Charles Evers, brother of Medgar Evers and later mayor of Fayette, Mississippi, who left town in 1956 when his life was endangered. From mid August into September 1964, mass violence was feared. White businessmen met secretly to explore methods of getting the COFO people out of the county. Economic pressures and firings were suggested. But, finally, as before, the extremists took the lead with night-ridings and threats. Black men in the Quarters soon began to arm themselves.

Here are five entries obtained from CORE documents of that period, quoted verbatim to suggest the mood of that tormented city:

### August 18

The always-present sentiments of violent suppression in this community are once again bursting to the surface. Shortly before 11 P.M. Saturday night (August 15) a car stopped across the street from the Freedom School headquarters here and the driver kept a single-barreled shotgun pointed at the office for approximately 5 minutes, left, and returned a second time. When two Freedom School teachers filed a warrant about the incident with the District Attorney, the official put on it that the party was a COFO worker who made $9.64 a week, "lives off the people in the community, and has no other visible means of support." Freedom School coordinator Ralph Featherstone refused to sign the affidavit with the addition, while his companion, University of California at Berkeley student Walter Kaufman of 1123 Kieth Avenue, Madison, Wisconsin, did sign the complaint. The name of the man with the gun is known; action on the case is awaited.

Sunday night (August 16) a rumor began spreading that the office and the motel across the street from it, where workers eat, would be bombed. By last night the rumor was widespread; the woman at the motel was threatened and told workers she could not feed them anymore. FBI watched the office all night; local police took no action.

This morning Deputy Sheriff Price, the officer who arrested James Chaney, Michael Schwerner, and Andrew Goodman, came to the office and took films of all the workers; he came by three times. He has reportedly been questioning local Negro citizens as to the workers' activities.

Today a local Negro citizen was beaten by a white man when he went into a store with a Negro girl. Philadelphia staff reports the man could be taken for white and was probably thought to be a project worker. He came to the office after leaving the doctor's office where he had treatment for injuries sustained during the beating. The man was frightened, and refused to contact local police. The FBI was contacted, and the man was questioned for approximately one-half hour. One agent was reportedly "very hostile."

### August 19

Increased harassment and intimidation efforts continue at the Evers Motel headquarters of the Neshoba County mobile Freedom School here. Between 8:55 and 9:15 this evening two carloads and one truck of white men with rifles visible parked outside the headquarters on the outskirts of Philadelphia; Deputy Price was observed smiling as one carload of whites told him, "We're gonna get the job done tonight." While the carloads of whites parked or the occupants milled about in front of the office and other cars cruised in the area, threatening 'phone calls were received at approximate intervals of five minutes stating "Your time is up." 'Phone calls continued until 4 A.M.

### August 20

Neshoba County law enforcement has used a questionable building lease to try to evict COFO workers from the newly opened COFO office in Philadelphia. The office, located on Adkins Street near the Booker T. Washington High School, is the old Evers Hotel which has been entirely leased for use as a Freedom School and office base. At about 11 A.M. this morning Deputy Cecil Price, Sheriff Rainey, and District Attorney Walter Jones presented an eviction notice, indicating that the six COFO workers then in the office would be arrested if they had not left the premises by 1 P.M. The law officers claimed the building lease was invalid, and that old tenants still held the lease. Police, both city and county, appeared frequently at the office from about 1 P.M. to 3 or 4 this afternoon. It was reported police did have warrants for the arrest of the six workers on trespass charges. The former occupant of the building came to the office late this afternoon and agreed to terminate his hold on the building and to have all his property moved out within five days.

COFO workers indicated their determination to stay in Philadelphia despite legal or other types of pressure. According to 25-year-old Washington, D.C., Negro and Philadelphia Freedom School coordinator Ralph Featherstone, a local Negro woman told one of the workers this morning: "If you all leave us now, they'll kill us. They'll pile our bodies one on top of the other."

Headquarters in Jackson stated additional staff had been moved into Philadelphia by late afternoon, and more would be sent as soon as needed, "to keep our pledge to the local people."

Today's legal harassment followed several tense hours last night as the Philadelphia office was surrounded by carloads of armed whites.

Following the eviction notice, local Negro citizens came to the office and provided "a fabulous dinner for us all."

### August 27

The first voter registration meeting in this vicinity since the killing of three COFO workers on June 21, 1964, was held in Philadelphia this evening at the Hotel Evers. The meeting attracted 24 local people. Sheriff L. A. Rainey and Deputy Cecil Price watched the proceedings from outside.

### September 2

A number of Alabama cars seen, one of them with Sheriff Rainey inside. At 8 A.M. a 15–20 car procession drove by COFO headquarters, revving motors, with high beams, kicking up dust and gravel. About 15 minutes of this, until FBI cars appeared. Earlier these cars had run two Negro youngsters off the road into a ditch nearby the office.

Eighteen local blacks, accompanied by several white and black COFO workers, tried to register to vote in the courthouse in September. The sheriff's office had been forewarned that they were coming, and they were greeted by a large crowd of jeering whites. One white COFO worker was arrested by Deputy Cecil Price. The applicants were lined up outside the courthouse and allowed inside one by one. Through the hot afternoon they were taunted by the crowd. Three of the eighteen were permitted to register.

By this time, aided by several informants, the FBI had compiled a voluminous report for the Justice Department on the murders, the beatings and burnings at the Mount Zion Church, and the activities of the law enforcement officers. The investigation disclosed how pervasive the Klan was in the county. It further revealed a consistent pattern of mistreatment and intimidation of Negroes. "First thing we knew, everyone who'd been in there [the jail] got the hell beat out of them," an FBI agent said. One after another the signed statements of the victims told the grim story of abuse of authority—abductions, threats, beatings with blackjacks and long leather staps, pistols put to heads, knives to faces, innocent people driven out of town.

Both the governor and the state attorney general announced that no charges would be preferred in the Mississippi courts. Under law the federal government could not seek indictments for murder, but only for violations of Constitutional rights.

In early December 1964 FBI agents arrested twenty-one men on conspiracy charges arising from the murders of Schwerner, Goodman, and Chaney. The list included Sheriff Rainey and Deputy Price, both of whom paid bond and were back on their jobs the next day. A lengthy and complicated legal struggle lay ahead, which would not end until October 1967—three years and four months after the murders. First, a U.S. Commissioner would refuse to accept a signed confession in a preliminary hearing. Next, Federal Judge Harold Cox, a conservative Mississippian, convened a federal grand jury which returned indictments against eighteen of the men; Judge Cox, however, would rule in early 1965 that they could only be tried under misdemeanor charges. Only as late as 1966 would the U.S. Supreme Court reverse this decision, ruling that the defendants could be tried for felony—for conspiracy to deprive the victims of federally guaranteed rights.

For weeks, months, years, there were no charges outstanding against a single person. No jury in Mississippi had ever returned convictions in a civil rights case. The moderates of Neshoba County had pause to wonder. And their community would continue to suffer through arduous times.

Shortly after the first arrests in December 1964, the Neshoba County Ministerial Association made a statement which was broadcast on the radio:

There is an element of shame to all that there would be among us those accused of such a crime; nevertheless, we desire to see justice prevail.

We dedicate ourselves to the task of giving leadership to our community so that through this damaging and deteriorating experience of the past five months the result may be stronger character and a deeper appreciation for those basic elements of democracy that have made our nation great.

We have confidence that the law-abiding citizens and leaders of Philadelphia and Neshoba County will respond to the present situation with respect to the cause of justice.

This statement was written by the Reverend Clay Lee, minister of the First Methodist Church in Philadelphia. He had assumed his appointment only a few days after the disappearance of the three civil rights workers; he became increasingly concerned about the response of the town, and its surrender to the terrorists. He began conferring frequently with the chief FBI investigator, Joseph Sullivan, and with his fellow ministers. He and the minister of the First Baptist Church, Roy Collum, delivered sermons after the arrests on the atmosphere of the town. Lee spoke of the "evil resistant force which rises to destroy truth and love," of "the bigot [who] cannot stand in the face of restraint and courage, [but] must be able to bully and dominate to be sustained." As a community defense fund was being raised for Rainey, Price, and the others, Lee supported a more modest campaign to help raise money to rebuild the Mount Zion Church, which had been burned the previous June. "We are faced with a conspiracy of evil," he said in a sermon at the end of 1964, "which cares nothing for the health and wholeness of the community." He became a focus for the decent elements of the town. "I felt deeply moved," Florence Mars later recalled of his words, "as though a great weight had been lifted off of me. Friends told me they shared this sense of relief. Finally, someone speaking for the community had taken a stand against the Klan."

On the first anniversary of the murders, sixty blacks and several whites marched from Philadelphia to the ashes of the Mount Zion Church. They sang "We Shall Overcome." "Fifty paces from the crowd," Don Whitehead reported, "Deputy Sheriff Cecil Price sat at the wheel of a truck, smoking a cigar as he listened to the singing and the speeches that followed. A gun rack behind Price's head cradled a submachine gun and an automatic shotgun."

The Klan's strength in mid 1965 had not noticeably diminished. At a large rally near Meridian in July, Sheriff Rainey received a standing ovation and gave a brief speech. A few days after that Rainey and Price were introduced at another sizable rally in Greenville.

Two months later, in September 1965, under the "freedom-of-choice" plan, three black girls enrolled in the twelfth grade of Philadelphia High School, and twelve black children in the first three grades. In a public statement, the school superintendent declared that Philadelphia would comply with the law and tolerate no trouble. "There was a great sense of community pride in his stand," Florence Mars recalled, "and he immediately received phone calls thanking him for taking a strong and positive position. However, it was commonly known that he also received a number of threatening phone calls, and for a few nights the police guarded his home." The three black girls went through the twelfth grade "in an atmosphere of almost total hostility. They were constantly subjected to humiliating remarks and the physical harassment of shoving, having objects thrown at them, and books pulled from their hands." The few white youngsters who tried to befriend the girls were criticized as "COFOs." One boy in particular encouraged most of the difficulties. When the superintendent, whose name was Hurdle, attempted to discipline him, the boy's father, a well-known member of the local Klan, began a campaign of threats and obscene calls against the superintendent. One night, finally, the Klansmen fired a shotgun into the superintendent's house.

The weeks passed. The long Mississippi seasons came and went.

Marcus Dupree was a toddler in the Quarters when Martin Luther King came to Philadelphia on June 21, 1966, the second anniversary of the murders. King and some two dozen others had left a march of leading civil rights workers protesting the shooting of James Meredith in his solitary walk south of Memphis. King's group was joined in Independence Quarters for the memorial demonstration by one hundred and fifty Philadelphia blacks. They moved from the office of the Freedom Democratic Party toward the courthouse two miles away. "Trouble began about half a mile from the Square," Florence Mars remembered.

At that point, cars and trucks with their motors roaring came racing down the hill, aiming into the line of marchers. Most veered off, but one truck did hit a boy. The marchers did not break rank, but continued up toward the square. All along the route angry whites stood shouting and shaking their fists. I stood on a corner of the square and watched in stunned silence as people I knew shook their fists and shouted insults. The city police did nothing to restrain the crowds. When people in the crowd recognized Negroes they had known all their lives, they became even more enraged. Mary Batts, a Negro woman from the Stallo community, told me of a friend of hers who looked over into the crowd and saw a white woman whose kitchen she had worked in for years shouting and pointing at her. The Negro woman, equally outraged, shook her fist and shouted back, "Yes! It's me and I've kept your children. I could've spit in their milk for all you know!"

Cecil Price blocked King from going onto the lawn of the courthouse. As he spoke from a curb, the whites surrounded the marchers and mocked the speaker's every phrase. "Sometimes they listened and screamed so carefully," a Northern reporter wrote, "that Dr. King appeared to be leading them in a responsive reading." As the group marched toward Independence Quarters again, a number of whites, encouraged by the auxiliary police, began to strike the blacks with their fists and to throw stones, bottles, and firecrackers. Only when the younger blacks started fighting back did the police step in. "This is a terrible town," King said in the Quarters, "the worst I've seen. There is a complete reign of terror here." A few hours later, night-riding whites fired gunshots into the Quarters. Once more the blacks fought back, and a white man was injured. "There isn't anything to it," Mayor Clayton Lewis told reporters the next day. "It's just those rabble-rousers, a bunch of foreigners that came in here."

Three days later, on June 24, King returned with three hundred marchers. He delivered a sermon in the Mount Nebo Baptist Church in the Quarters, and then the group moved toward the Square along the same route as three days before. Again they were heckled. This time there was concern over greater violence, and state highway patrolmen separated the demonstrators from a crowd of some fifteen hundred onlookers. When the Reverend Clinton Collier, who had given the eulogy to Schwerner, Goodman, and Chaney in the ashes of the Mount Zion Church in the summer of 1964, began a prayer, the crowd threw eggs and bottles. "The people that are gathered around us," Stokely Carmichael said, "represent America in its truest form. They represent a sick and resisting society that sits in the United Nations and gives lip-service to democracy." Carmichael had only recently launched in Mississippi the clarion of "Black Power," and King's words were conciliatory.

Stephen B. Oates, in his *Let the Trumpet Sound: The Life of Martin Luther King, Jr.*, described this confrontation:

> As he and Ralph Abernathy approached the courthouse to pray, Sheriff Lawrence Rainey intercepted them. "You can't go up these steps," he drawled menacingly. "Oh yes," King said, "you're the one who had Schwerner and the other fellows in jail." Rainey was proud to say he had done that all right. King looked behind him at a white crowd gathering around the courthouse, and he thought for sure he was going to die. As he and Abernathy knelt to pray, King said under his breath, in reference to the slain civil-rights workers, "I believe the murderers are somewhere around me at this moment." "You damn right," Rainey said, "they're

right behind you." King and Abernathy rose, walked away from Rainey and the mob at the courthouse, and somehow got their people out of Philadelphia without mishap. With aides later, King recounted the scene at the courthouse steps, with Rainey and all those whites behind him. "And brother," King said, "I sure did not want to close my eyes when we prayed." He grinned. "Ralph said he prayed with his open."

The conduct of many of the whites during King's two marches had a lasting effect on the blacks who had participated in the first civil rights demonstration of their lives. "It revealed Philadelphia to me," one elderly black woman told Miss Mars two years later. "I just couldn't believe it. We all lives here, was raised here, my foreparents stayed here all my days. It don't make me feel good walking up the streets now. Folks looking for us to trade with them even treats me nicer than before, but I'll never feel the same again."

Yet beneath these smoldering surfaces, there were indications that the disposition of the town might be changing. The solidarity of the White Knights of the Klan, Don Whitehead noted, "dissolved in bickering, mutual distrust, wrangles over money, and the fear that anything said in a meeting would soon be known to FBI agents." When a county grand jury failed to indict the Klansman who had been badgering the school superintendent, the school board called a large public meeting of church and business leaders who denounced the Klansman; *The Neshoba Democrat* covered the meeting. After a Mennonite church was bombed for the second time in 1966, a white citizens' committee was established in Philadelphia. "It is the hope of our committee," a statement on the front page of the *Democrat* said, "to give citizens of Neshoba and surrounding counties a means of registering a protest against such wanton brutality, and at the same time serving as a means to make a concrete expression in favor of these Christian people." The work of Clay Lee and Roy Collum, the Methodist and Baptist ministers, also continued.

At long last, however, it was the new conspiracy indictment by a federal grand jury against eighteen men in February of 1967 which buttressed the changing mood of the community. With three exceptions, the defendants were the same men who had been indicted two years before. There was no indictment this time against Jimmy Lee Townsend, but added to the list was former Sheriff E. G. "Hop" Barnett and, more significantly, Sam Bowers, the Imperial Wizard of the White Knights. Because of a technicality involving jury lists, the trial was delayed until October 1967. The nine defendants from Neshoba County were Sheriff Rainey, Deputy Sheriff Price, Barnett, city policeman Richard Willis, Edgar Ray Killen,

Billy Wayne Posey, Jerry McGrew Sharpe, Herman Tucker, and Olen Burrage. They, along with seven men from Lauderdale County and Sam Bowers, were indicted with conspiring to "injure, oppress, threaten, and intimidate Michael Henry Schwerner, James Earl Chaney and Andrew Goodman, each a citizen of the United States, in the free exercise and enjoyment of the right and privilege secured to them by the Fourteenth Amendment to the Constitution of the United States not to be deprived of life or liberty without due process of law."

The most important question, of course, was: Could the federal government successfully prosecute its case before an all-white Mississippi jury? Many of the defendants did not appear to think so. They frequently joked and laughed among themselves. There was a famous photograph by Bill Reed of *Life* magazine, subsequently published around the world, of Price and Rainey seated next to each other during the trial in their uniforms, broad grins on their faces, Rainey reclining in his chair with a booted leg propped up as he dipped into a package of Red Man Chewing Tobacco, their comrades on the row behind them equally amused.

John Doar, head of the Civil Rights Division of the Justice Department and a veteran of the Southern struggles of the early sixties, was the government's main prosecutor. He said in his summation:

> [This crime] has no precedent anywhere . . . this was a calculated, cold-blooded plot. Three men, hardly more than boys, were the victims. The plot was executed with a degree of self-possession and steadiness equal to the wickedness with which it was planned . . . The deed was accomplished smoothly, quietly, effectively, efficiently. The object of the conspiracy achieved . . . the participants believed themselves safe, safe because the crime was committed in Neshoba County and Neshoba law was involved.
>
> . . . Much has [been] and will be said about the extraordinary methods in discovering the guilty. Should it have been otherwise? Was this a State to be forgotten? Was this not a case for the maximum effort of the FBI? Could the Federal Government have succeeded in any . . . way other than rewards, payment for information, tending to expose the band of murderous conspirators, the midnight killers, to bring them to the bar of justice . . . ? Ladies and gentlemen of the jury, there could be no justice if your Federal Government had not tried to solve this crime . . .

On October 20, 1967, three years and four months after the murders, the jury announced the verdicts. Those convicted from Neshoba County were Cecil Price and Billy Wayne Posey, and from Lauderdale County Alton Wayne Roberts, Horace Doyle Barnette, Jimmy Arledge, and Jimmy Snowden. Imperial Wizard Bowers was also found guilty.* It was

---

* James Jordan pled guilty in a federal court in Atlanta and was subsequently sentenced to four years.

noted that, with the exception of Bowers, the jury apparently based guilt on actual participation in the murders, not on participation in conspiracy to murder. Those acquitted from Neshoba County were Sheriff Rainey, Richard Willis, Herman Tucker, and Olen Burrage. Three Neshobans were released on mistrials: Edgar Ray Killen, Jerry Sharpe, and Hop Barnett. Two months later Judge Harold Cox sentenced Bowers† and Roberts to ten years in prison. Price and Posey were given six-year terms, and Snowden, Arledge, and Barnette three each.

"The convictions were a turning point for Mississippi," Florence Mars wrote. "This was the first time a jury in the state had returned a guilty verdict in a major civil rights case since Reconstruction, and the convictions marked the end of the long chain of widely publicized and unpunished racial killings that began after the Supreme Court decision of 1954." No longer could Klansmen rely perfunctorily on Mississippi juries, and responsible Neshobans and Mississippians believed the convictions would severely deter the organized terrorism which had so wracked Philadelphia. In this surmise they were right.

In the mid 1960s, the influence of the federal government was beginning to be felt in Neshoba. In late 1965, Federal Judge Cox, who later presided over the conspiracy trial, ruled that the facilities of the county courthouse be integrated; the old "White" and "Colored" signs came down. The U.S. Congress had passed the Voting Rights Act in April of 1965, and by the end of that year more than seven hundred blacks in the county had registered to vote, some four hundred of that number by federal registrars. A voters' league chartered by the state was established in the county in 1970, and the blacks of Neshoba who had secretly joined the NAACP‡ in the 1940s and '50s openly joined other blacks in vocal encouragement of voting. Blacks began to work at the polls. By 1972 roughly two thousand of the thirteen thousand registered voters in Neshoba were black. Black registration continued to increase dramatically throughout the 1970s.

After the long nightmare, the moderate element in the white population began to exert itself in those years. Disturbed that Mayor Clayton Lewis' name had been mentioned in the federal trial for attending a meeting of the Klan, a descendant of one of the oldest families ran against

† On his release from prison in 1976, Imperial Wizard Bowers had become an ordained Lutheran minister.

‡ When a new editor, Stanley Dearman, took over The Neshoba Democrat, that paper began to cover the county NAACP meetings. "People outside the area may not put much significance in that," the editor said, "but I do. Back in the sixties, the NAACP was the worst thing anyone had ever heard of."

him for mayor and won. Upon his death he was succeeded by Allan King —"a quiet, decent, civilized man," as one native described him to me— who would be elected to three consecutive terms before he retired. Lawrence Rainey's term as sheriff expired in late 1967, after which he moved elsewhere.

With the perceptible softening of tensions, there were strides in many areas, including the industrial expansion cited earlier.* After the Civil Rights Act of 1964, the national plants gradually began to hire blacks for other than menial jobs. There was a sharp drop in those years in black tenant farmers, and the decline in black population was not as high as it had been. Federally subsidized housing came to Independence Quarters, and an attractive community center with a swimming pool and sports facilities was built with a federal grant in 1971. This facility was called Westside Park, and in the mid 1970s a lunch program for the elderly was established there. Each day more than a hundred men and women, about half of them white, would gather in the assembly hall. When I visited there one day, I was taken with the sight of old white and black people sitting together at the tables in conversation. There was talk among them of Marcus Dupree, and one gray-haired black man was trying with scant success to explain to his companions why Coach Joe Wood had switched from the Wishbone to the "I" formation. A sign on the wall said: FAITH, HOPE, AND LOVE, BUT THE GREATEST OF THESE IS LOVE.

In human measure, the most sweeping change in the history of the town, as in many other Deep Southern towns, came in January of 1970 with the massive integration of the public schools. This came five and a half years after the civil rights murders and sixteen years after the Supreme Court school decision of 1954 and was the result of a federal court order from the U.S. Fifth Circuit Court of Appeals. The national reporters and network television news returned to Philadelphia on that bitterly cold January morning expecting violence and mayhem, but the revolutionary transformation could not have been more peaceful. Had they had prescience, the cameramen that day could have taken some early shots of a five-year-old black child, a future running back, entering the biracial first grade.

In the words of The Neshoba Democrat, the staffs of the white and black schools "had worked hard and diligently to make the transition a smooth one. Efforts by students, faculties, and parents were rewarded by a successful unification." Organized opposition was absent on this day, and only 3 percent of the white students left the public schools to attend the Pioneer Academy. (It closed after three and a half years.) The superintendent praised several white church congregations, as well as black par-

* There would be crippling layoffs during the economic recession of the early 1980s, however. The unemployment rate for Neshoba County fluctuated between 12 and 20 percent.

ents whose children would be leaving Booker T. Washington and George Washington Carver, for contributing to this momentous change. A year later Roy Reed of *The New York Times*, who had reported the events surrounding Martin Luther King's march in 1966, returned to write: "Philadelphia has abolished segregation as thoroughly and with as little friction as any place of its size and racial makeup in the South." And six years later, in 1976, by a margin of almost nine to one, the people of the town approved a $375,000 public school bond issue. It was in this week, too, that the high school graduating class had its first integrated party at the Philadelphia Country Club.

Much of this emerging tone of moderation in the town could be attributed to the latest editor of *The Neshoba Democrat*. At thirty-four, Stanley Dearman had become the editor of this paper with its complicated and distinguished past in November of 1966, six months after Martin Luther King's marches, two and a half years after the murders; he had bought the *Democrat* in 1968. He was a native of Meridian, an Ole Miss man who had been elected editor of the student newspaper, *The Mississippian*, and he had degrees in journalism and English.

I grew to know Dearman well in my many trips to the town, and we spoke frequently in the *Democrat* offices in the white-porticoed building which had once been the funeral home. I grew to trust him deeply. When I visited him and his wife Carolyn in their house, he would sometimes sit down to his baby grand and play a little Chopin. "There is a corporate guilt," he had reflected in 1972, "something that very much involves the life of the town. They could have reacted differently, but there was no leader."

Dearman was rather shy and reserved, and not one to talk much about personal courage. Once when I asked if he had ever feared for his personal safety, he confessed that three or four times he had. One time in particular was a December day of 1964, right after Sheriff Rainey had been arrested by the FBI. He was doing the story for *The Meridian Star*, where he then worked. He walked into the Neshoba courthouse with his camera and notepad. The corridors were crowded with Rainey's supporters, and there was an air of imminent violence. A woman who worked in the chancery clerk's office got him inside and tried to persuade him to hide his camera and notepad, but he was on a story and would not do so. There were other fearful moments that he wished not to talk about.

We Americans usually pay ritualistic deference to the value, indeed the *necessity*, of freedom and civilization, not to mention decency, order, restraint, humanity. A courageous and enlightened newspaper is vital to these qualities, and often even more so in the small towns where the people one writes about are the people one sees every day. There are times when an editor must risk his life. I do not say this lightly, or moralistically, for I have thought about these things, and as a young editor in the Texas of the late 1950s and '60s experienced more than a few hazardous moments. I remembered of those difficult years the story of the man who challenged Big Hodding Carter with a .45 automatic in the offices of *The Delta Democrat-Times* in Greenville, Mississippi, and Hodding, whom we did not call "Big" for nothing, simply wrestled the .45 off the gentleman.

The abdication of its responsibilities by *The Neshoba Democrat* before and during "The Troubles," I would become convinced in retrospect, helped send the town to its doom. "Outsiders who come in here and try to stir up trouble," it had editorialized in April 1964, "should be dealt with in a manner they won't forget." Yet the pivotal moment for the paper and the town, a newspaperman from Jackson who had covered Neshoba in those days once argued to me, came two months after the editorial, with the burning of the Mount Zion Church and the beatings of the blacks there. Bill Minor, a courageous Mississippi reporter, had broken the story for *The New Orleans Times-Picayune.* Yet even after that, the editor of *The Neshoba Democrat* refused to report what had happened, instead supporting the sham that the beatings and burning were a hoax perpetrated by outsiders. Five days later Schwerner, Goodman, and Chaney, after their visit to the destroyed church, were arrested. "If the editor had covered that story as a diligent *reporter*," the Jackson newspaperman believed, "the thugs might've had reason to pause in plotting the murders and everything that followed. What's a newspaper for?"

"Stan Dearman is so quiet and reserved," a college graduate in the town once said to me, "that you might be tempted to think he wants to avoid controversy. This isn't so. He's without a doubt one of the three or four bravest small-town editors in Mississippi. He's taken our town through integration, several bond issues, a beer referendum, and a lot of other things. He's stood up for his convictions every time. Like Clayton Rand and Turner Catledge, he loves the town. And like them he's an honest, decent, educated man."

All this gave reason to consider, from the perspective of the years, what might have happened, or might *not* have, had Dearman been the new young editor of *The Neshoba Democrat* in 1964.


"It's amazing," an FBI investigator would reflect, "that a state could be torn apart by so few people. But it happened." The same could be said of the town. Much of the crowd which had been associated with the flourishing local bootlegging industry had moved into the Klan; it must have been an easy adjustment. "In the whole of Neshoba County," a trustworthy source who had been involved in the federal conspiracy trial said, "there were maybe a hundred people who were involved peripherally with the Ku Klux Klan. There were probably fifty of that number who knew that something was going on when the three men disappeared. And of that number, a dozen people had direct information. Six knew where the murders had been committed, who did it, and where the bodies were buried."

Into the modern day there would be a deep touchiness, a pervasive defensiveness that the town had been mercilessly tormented by outsiders, and this was perhaps understandable. The people of Neshoba were unfailingly courteous to this writer who insinuated himself on their town, yet the darker past always seemed to exist there silently for them in the shadows. A decade after the conspiracy trial, in the late 1970s, Florence Mars noted the lingering hostility to any reference to "The Troubles" and the resentment that everything written about the community mentioned the murders. "They make no connection, apparently, as do the blacks, between these three deaths and the changes that have taken place in the community."

Here is a brief catalogue, a few diverse words told to me or others:

Jimmy McWilliams, a black mechanic, one of about a dozen black Vietnam veterans in the town: "My mother breast-fed most of them." In Vietnam, white and black soldiers "slept in the same beds, drank out of the same canteens, wore the same clothes, ate the same food, shared each other's blood. Why can't we do that here?"

Clifton Judan, a thirty-five-year-old black: "In the sixties, blacks didn't have a chance. If you went to a movie, you better not be on the streets after dark. They'd slap you upside of the head. In the old days, every light had to be out at ten o'clock. If you got caught outside, you got your ass whipped. Now, if you ain't bothering the police, they won't be bothering you. Pickin' on you just to be pickin' on you, they don't do that anymore."

Charles Judan, Clifton's brother who came back to town after having lived for ten years in Chicago: "Since I left, it's improved a helluva lot. Black people got paved roads, a park, a swimming pool, a recreation center. People can buy houses now. It used to be you couldn't buy no houses. You couldn't go to the bank and get a loan without getting Miss So-and-So to sign for you, or putting up a little land. Now, you can get anything you want if you have the money."

Glenda Greer, a black leader: "The big difference is education. The white folks are more educated now. They still feel the same way about us, but they've learned how to handle their feelings, keep them inside."

Kermit Stribling, a black Vietnam veteran: "As far as prejudice goes, I don't think Marcus Dupree has had any effect on the town. He's an individual and he's made good, but this won't have nothin' to do with me at all. The interest about where he goes is more in the white community than the black. They want to see him go to one of their schools. The blacks just want him to do good and keep goin'.

"It was tryin' times here. I was goin' from school and was stopped by the police force. I was abused pretty good. I left right after that and went to New York. Naturally you can't compare prejudice now to what it was then. There's no way you can do that. But it's still here. I think you have as much prejudice in the black against the white as you do in the white against the black.

"Prejudice still exists here, but it's much better in a lot of ways. I think my kids today have a better opportunity than they would've had in '64. Being black still has its drawbacks. I found this out in the service—no matter where you go or what you do, you're still black. You can't get away from that fact. Just do the best you can at what you got to do."

Polly Cumberland, white, director of the county welfare department: "Common courtesy is the term we use around here. Honest to goodness, they [the civil rights workers of '64] gave off an odor. Their hair was dirty and stringy and they presented themselves as the lowest type of people. Appearance, of course, doesn't justify what happened."

Dan Turner, white, undergraduate at Ole Miss from Philadelphia: "It's a town whose past was permanently stained by the actions of a few and whose future holds great promise—a New South that will produce state, national, and world leaders. I think people are basically unforgiving. There always will be people who will blame an entire section of the country for the violence that took place. Sadly, there are still a few who are proud of these happenings. Maybe to an extent we stifle our own progress."

Stanley Dearman, white, editor: "Philadelphia, Mississippi, is a symbol—I don't know what of—but it certainly involves self-righteousness. Pointing the finger at us makes everybody feel better, I suppose, but what happened in '64 would have happened somewhere else sooner or later. In my opinion, there had to be a tragedy of this kind to make it clear to certain elements in our society that they couldn't use force anymore.

"I think race relations are better today than they've ever been. There haven't been any incidents or demonstrations. The reason, I'd say, is the congenial relationship that exists between the black leaders and white leaders here. That's not to say that everything's perfect, but for the amount of trouble this town has had, and in view of where it's been, I think things have moved along very smoothly. One of the big hurdles was school integration in 1970. It came off without any incident whatsoever, and there was almost a tangible sense of relief that this had finally come about.

"The Klan is more active in Illinois, probably Pennsylvania, Texas, and California, than it is here. I don't know of a single incident. Every three or four years, someone will paint 'KKK' in white letters on the road, but that usually happens in other counties, not here, and I think it's just pranksters . . ."

Robert Greer, black, grocer in the Quarters: "I travel about some—and wherever I go, people ask me where I'm from. Even in other parts of Mississippi their reaction is the same. They say, 'Philadelphia? Isn't that where them three civil rights workers were killed?' And it's been that way everywhere I go for the last seventeen years. But now, for the first time in my life, people are saying something different. Instead of 'Philadelphia, where them human rights people was killed,' it's 'You're from Philadelphia—Marcus Dupree's hometown.' He's erasing an image of this town that's been here for twenty years."

The years of young Marcus Dupree's lifetime had witnessed a subtle revolution in the Deep South, and in the America of which it was a part. This time was "bannered with the slogans of liberty and hope," Theodore H. White had observed, and "had affected life-styles, sex relations, race relations, manners, morals." Born six months after the assassination of John Kennedy, who in his brief time had helped liberate those hopes, and one month before the Freedom Summer of '64 in Mississippi, Marcus and his contemporaries in Philadelphia had grown up into the quieter yet equally demanding time of the 1980s. In between there had been much suffering, and much had been lost to fear.

On my early visits to the town I could not help but remember the stories many of my friends and fellow writers who had been there in the 1960s had told me of the fierce hostility and suspicion they had so often encountered. One morning I went out to my car, which had been over-parked in front of the Downtown Hotel. There was a green card on the windshield, and I knew I had a parking ticket. I looked at it. On one side were the words: "For Out of Town Autoists . . . this card entitles you to park your car as long as you please in PHILADELPHIA, MISSISSIPPI." And on the reverse side, in words just as bold: "Welcome Visitors! To Our Growing City . . . Philadelphia Extends to You a Cordial Welcome, and Hopes You Will Return Often—Police Dept. . . . For General Information on any matter—Call City Hall."

On December 12, 1976, the year of the public school bond issue, there had been a historic moment at the Mount Nebo Baptist Church around the block from Marcus' house in the Quarters.

A local organization had raised money for a monument to Mickey

Schwerner, Andy Goodman, and Jim Chaney bearing replicas of their photographs on the FBI's "missing" circular of '64. The funds had come exclusively from white and black residents of the county, and the speakers at the dedication were all local people. Clinton Collier, the black preacher who had suffered the organized intimidations of the 1960s, was one of the last to speak. Dr. King, he reminded the crowd, had said in this church that people must keep alive the memory of the slain young men until the blood of all the Negroes killed in Mississippi has dried up. He concluded with Matthew 10:39:

*"He that findeth his life shall lose it: and he that loseth his life for my sake shall find it."*

# 12

# In Residence with
# My Brother Pete

---

*Played all right, got 241 yards on 12 carries (in the victory over Northwest Rankin). Line really did a lot better job. I wish I could run the ball more, but the coach wouldn't let me.*

*I would like to average about 20 to 25 carries a game. I felt if I had played a little more I could have gained 300 yards. Coming in I felt I could have a big night.*

*My goal still is to break Herschel's high school touchdown record. He's got 86, and I've got 20 more to go. With six games left, I feel it's possible. If we win our next two, we'll get in the playoffs and my chances will be a lot better.*

*I'm getting a little bit tired of being the center of attention. I really don't understand why. But it's not hard to be myself. I'm just acting like it's an everyday thing.*

*Nothing new in recruiting really. Didn't get a chance to see the games in Jackson. Hope to go to Tuscaloosa and see Alabama and Ole Miss this weekend.*

*Still like UCLA the most. Plan to visit Ohio State later. I like the in-state schools; we run the Wishbone like Mississippi State and I like that.*

In early October, Philly was on the road again against the Trojans of New Hope, a big consolidated country school over near the Alabama line. I planned to spend three or four days in Philadelphia before driving to the game Friday afternoon.

I had decided I would start bringing my dog, Pete, with me on those sojourns in Neshoba. My neighbor Frances Mitchell on Faculty Row at Ole Miss had looked after him when I was gone and had even written a book of verse about their daily walks about the campus, but I had missed him. The proprietors of the Downtown Hotel had told me he would be a welcomed guest any time.

Pete was destined to become friends, at least tentatively, with the dogs who lived in a pack behind the football field. Coach Joe Wood, Marcus, and some of the other players grew accustomed to seeing him taking his walks around the stadium and the hollow, and so did the most persistent college recruiters. The denizens of the Square eventually thought nothing of the sight of his gingerly relieving himself in some prickly shrubs in front of the Peoples Bank of Mississippi, and he became almost as familiar a presence in the lobby of the Downtown as Mr. Presley Snow asleep in his chair. Later on, we would be hopelessly snow-bound in the town, and then we would observe at close quarters the fever-ish last days of recruiting. So, since Pete is an essential character in this book, one should perhaps know a little more about him.


Pete and I had not been together always. Rather, we sought each other out, two vagabond bachelor hearts. I was drawn to him from the moment I saw him—a splendidly handsome black Labrador retriever, per-haps three years old, who spent much of his time with the boys in the ser-vice station in our village on eastern Long Island. As the semiofficial mayor of the town, known to all as "Your Honor," he patrolled its streets and its schools and its beaches and its graveyards and its whole backyard world of gardens and orchards and barns by day. He always met the 1:27 train from Manhattan. At night he slept in bars or in pickup trucks. He belonged to no man. Yet I perceived he was beginning to look me over. Whenever I drove into the station for gas, he would get in my car. As we rode across the lush fields and sand dunes of the great Eastern lit-toral, he would sit there quietly, looking as if he were reflecting on me. Soon he started visiting me at my house, each visit longer than the one before.

One afternoon, however, he did not leave. "Go back, Pete," I said. "They expect you." He refused to go. It was a moment of rare conse-quence, for we have been inseparable ever since.

When, a couple of years ago, I decided to leave the village of Bridgehampton on Long Island and return to live in my native Missis-sippi, I felt guilty for taking Pete, a Yankee dog if ever there was one, from his home ground. But tell me: Had I a choice? The car was loaded and I was ready to depart, for I had made my own painful farewells. Pete ruminated for the briefest instant, one transitory moment of profound Labrador reflection, then jumped inside. Did he have a choice?

What is the mysterious chemistry that links a human being and a dog? I only know that the friendship between me and Pete, like the few truly fine things in life, was as God-given as Marcus' running ability, solidified by shared experience and fidelity and a fragility of the heart. I grew up—from childhood through adolescence and to maturity—with honored dogs. Pete, the dog of my middle age, was the best of them, for he had endless kindness, imagination, and good cheer.

He had brown eyes, floppy ears, and a shining ebony coat. We were together constantly. Every morning he awakened me with his cold wet nose, and he nuzzled me again at night as we separated to sleep.

I was forever impressed by what I felt sure was his extraordinary intelligence. To the most remarkable degree he comprehended words, unspoken fears, joys and desires. One night at a hunting lodge far in the woods outside of Oxford—the odors of autumn on the land, and the deep quiet, and the muted outside sounds of the first frost, and other country dogs baying in the distance—several of us were sitting on the back porch exchanging stories. Pete had been rummaging about in the kitchen. After a time, he came and and stood at the door, looking out at us for a long while. In this pause, he seemed to be saying: "I am almost one of you."

He eavesdropped on my telephone conversations. If we had not seen my son in several months, and I said, "David is coming tomorrow," Pete rose and stretched and was ready to go to the airport. We had a private language—often not words so much as gestures, expressions, and intuitions. We shared ancient affinities.

When I was feeling silly or mischievous, he walked right up to me and joined in my spirit. When he was sad or depressed, I was a little downtrodden too. In moments when we were alone, I talked to him. One night, as we drove to the all-night grocery, for strange reasons I told him about the loss of love. I heard myself chattering inanely into the night. Back home, we sat in the yard among the windswept leaves. We watched the sliver of a moon play with the clouds. We knew our moods.

I called him "Hans" (for "Handsome"), "Pierre," "Pedro," and "Pedro Borbon" (inexplicably, after a journeyman major-league pitcher, now retired). I knew he liked chocolate bars, pistachio nuts, and raspberry ice cream. In his stocking at Christmas, he found fried chicken livers. When I set his dinner down and he finished, he sought me out and thanked me by nudging my hand.

Tricks were beneath him. Ask him to shake hands, and he would look at you as if you were out of your mind. Despite the injunctions of his bloodlines, I had yet to see him retrieve anything, and even in his younger days he was seldom in much of a hurry. On one of our recent strolls, a strange lady paused to admire him. "What a fine dog," she said. "Can he count or subtract like those canines on television—anything like that, you suppose?" The question was undeserving of an answer. Pete did not care for arithmetic or professional acrobatics. Character was surely enough.

When requested to do so (he did not take orders, only requests or, better, suggestions), Pete would wag his long tail in a continual circle, to the delight of his many friends who were children. But the children loved him most of all, I suspected, for his gentleness. Once, having been invited with him to a classroom at the schoolhouse in Oxford, I watched as dozens of fifth graders surrounded him, then formed a line to pet him; he stood there wagging his tail benignly in a circle. He even allowed his best friend, "Cap," seven years old, to ride on his back. When we went in our car about town, an incomparable Deep Southern town, the children would sight him perched regally in the backseat. "There's ol' Pete drivin' around!" one of them would shout. In the cemetery in Philadelphia one day, his tenderness met a singular test. A yapping, mean, inconsequential little dog circled him in shrill ambuscade, then dashed in and bit his tail. Unappreciative as he was of this monumental presumption, Pete turned and walked away, tolerant as always of the failings of others.

At the same time, Pete was a most independent dog. After our long years together, I understood that he must have time to himself. What he dwelled upon in those private moments I did not know—his early years, perhaps? His mother and father? The fields and dunes of eastern Long Island? Old angers and laughter? Death? He knew I would not intrude. Our maid, an amiable and discerning personage named Pearline Jones who had put three children through Ole Miss, once exclaimed: "Pete's the only dog I ever knew who has his own bedroom!" That was correct. When we had visitors, sometimes after a while he would discreetly retire to his room. "There goes Pete to think things over," a friend observed.

He had adjusted to Dixie, bless my Pete, although Mississippi was removed from Long Island in much more than miles. He had taken to the beauty and serenity of the Ole Miss campus. In the summer, he had his own watering spot, a little place in the woods where he sat twice a day in the stifling humidity for a very long time. He ate catfish and collard greens and ham hocks, and I thought I discerned a hint of "y'all" in his bark.

As I write these words, I reflect on particular moments Pete and I shared. We had been trapped in New England blizzards—trapped together, too, at the lawn parties of politicians and heiresses and movie actresses. We had been chased by copperheads in the wooded hills behind William Faulkner's house. In melancholy times late in the nights, we had sat and watched the fire. We had waded in the Bloody Pond on the Shiloh battlefield. We had watched baseball games from the left field bleachers. Together we had investigated courthouse squares, junkyards, saloons, the governor's mansion of Mississippi, and the lobby of the Waldorf-Astoria in New York City. We had attended stock-car races and gone deep-sea fishing. Once we took off in my battered Plymouth in the flowering of springtime and nonchalantly toured Mississippi for a week. I found some of my long-dead forebears in the cemetery in Port Gibson, and later we traversed the land between there and the River—the shadowy woods and precarious embankments, the Spanish moss in the gnarled trees, the ruins of the ghost towns and plantations. We had been together at birthdays, Christmases, and New Year's Eves. We had loved the same friends and suffered the same fools.

Shortly after we came South, Pete ran away. More accurately, he got lost. For hours I drove around looking for him. At night I left my back door open, listening sleeplessly to each rustle and sound. I contacted the mayor, the dog warden, and the constabulary. I telephoned the governor. Was Pete disoriented in the impenetrable Mississippi woods? Lying dead in a ditch? Kidnapped? On the fourth day, stricken and hopeless, I sat in my house with a friend who comprehended my terrible broken heart. She and I consumed a bottle of scotch.

Suddenly, from the crest of the hill outside, something flickered briefly in the corner of my eye—a silhouette. I went outside and peered through the mist. Pete was faltering down the hill. Then he saw me. As in a vintage Hollywood film, we walked slowly toward one another, old as time. He was wet, filthy, and bleeding. I embraced him there, in the middle of the road.

The only time Pete was ever frightened was in thunderstorms. Trembling, he came to me, and I tried to comfort him. I put my arms around him and told him it was all right. I fed him and gave him a warm place to sleep and searched him for ticks during the Dixie tick season and took him to Dr. Shivers when he was sick or hurting. For me there was an abiding recompense, for Pete knew when I was sad or hurt, and his friendship eased the times of loneliness and guilt. And whenever I returned home from someplace, he was there, welcoming me.

I find myself staring at him now, lying on the carpet of our room in the Downtown Hotel . . . the web paws, the wet black nose, the graying whiskers on his distinctive muzzle, the keen eyes—and I wonder where he came from . . . wonder, too, at the fate that, out of the incalculable void, brought the two of us together in our mortal moment on this earth. I was glad Pete was going to be with me from here on in down in Philly, and watch the recruiters come and go.


I had acquired the usual bits of intelligence. Temple Drake had advised me that 'Bama might be on the wane, UCLA was up, and to keep an eye out for Oklahoma and Texas. There had been a wry exchange on the radio. The new football coach at Auburn University, named Pat Dye, had a call-in program which went out all over Alabama.

"Hey, Pat. You're doin' a great job."

"Where you calling from?"

"Up in Gadsden."

"How's the weather up there?"

"We need a rain."

"We do too, but not Saturday. We don't need LSU and rain too."

"Pat, I wanted to ask you what you know about recruiting?"

"I know a lot about recruiting." You could hear Dye chuckling.

"Well, who you gonna sign?"

"I said I knew a lot about recruiting. I didn't say I was going to tell you anything. You'll know when we sign 'em in February."

"Tell me about one boy."

"You'll know in February."

The gentleman in Gadsden would not give up. "Well, how about this boy over in Mississippi? *Dupree*? You gonna recruit him?"

"No," Dye said.

The man in Gadsden was too surprised, apparently, to say anything.

"I hear he's a great athlete," Dye said. "But we got enough outstanding backs in Alabama and Georgia and Florida to keep us busy. We're not going to Mississippi to recruit Dupree."

There was another development which confirmed the pervasiveness of the rumor system. On the Saturday morning after the previous home game, the two friends who had come with me were having breakfast in the restaurant of the Downtown. The restaurant was crowded and noisy with football talk. The sports pages had much advance coverage of the game between Penn State and Nebraska in Lincoln, Nebraska, that afternoon. I walked into the restaurant, shouting in a mood of mischief to my companions: "Coach, be sure and phone Coach Paterno in the Holiday Inn North in Lincoln. The bus leaves for the stadium in half an hour."

The crowd became silent and attentive. "Don't worry," one of them alertly replied, "I'm going back to the room and call Joe right now."

As I left the restaurant again, I could hear the excited whispers among the tables. Three days later Squirrel Griffing telephoned me in Oxford. He had just been in a bank in Vicksburg and a lawyer came up to him and said, "Squirrel, did you know Penn State was in Philadelphia last week watchin' *Du*-pree?"

On a bright, cool morning of October I went to see Florence Mars, author of *Witness in Philadelphia*. I had talked with her several times on the telephone; she had been dividing her time between Philadelphia and a cabin in the mountains of North Carolina. Her house was one of the old ones on Poplar Avenue, and she was waiting on the porch for me. She led me inside to the kitchen and introduced me to her mother, who was slicing pears for a salad. Then we settled down in the parlor.

I had just read an interview she had had with a Northern writer, Art Carey of *The Philadelphia Inquirer*, in which she had softened some of her earlier assessments of her town: "It turns out that we really don't have a corner on prejudice, but that's not what's selling newspapers, and still isn't. People have a way of not looking at themselves. I think there's more truth to what people say—that folks up North are just as prejudiced as we are. When these murders happened, the Northern cities had not burned. Later, it didn't seem a big deal that the police were involved in this sort of thing. I guess originally there was a lot of naïveté."

She was a small, energetic woman, quite warm and gracious, who was full of amiable curiosity about her visitor. Her speech was swift, in a certain matronly Southern mode. "I talk too much," she said. "It's nervousness, I suppose." Courage comes in unexpected formats.

We spoke about the changes in the town. The telephone rang as often there as it had in Marcus Dupree's house. A lady named Gladys called about houses for sale or apartments for rent. It could have been my own mother talking. Their telephone conversation swerved toward other Southern things—cousins, in-laws, places of Philly, a neighbor who drowned in 1931. As she talked, I lazily looked out the window at the broad sweep of Poplar Avenue, the graceful lawns, the houses of another era.

We discussed her book, how much I had admired it. The young people in town these days, she said, sometimes complained they could not find out what had happened by asking their elders, then they discovered her book. She had kept adding stories to the manuscript, she remembered, and got some good editorial help from the LSU Press. She was glad she wrote it, she said.

We returned to the kitchen to chat with her mother. She pointed to the large backyard. Her cousin Mont Mars, the lawyer, lived in the big house right across from there. Esther Connor, Marcus Dupree's grandmother on his father's side, lived in a small house just off this yard when she was working for Mont Mars's family years ago.

Miss Mars had become interested, she told me, in an abandoned cemetery in town which had just been cleared from a dense tangle of underbrush. She had found the grave of one Jonas Backström, born in Sweden in 1776, died in Philadelphia in 1840. This was the oldest tomb she knew of in the county. Jonas Backström had migrated from South Carolina and owned two thousand acres, which was considerable since there were no large plantations in the area then. I told her I had heard of "Foots" Baxtrum, an elderly black trumpet player from the town. The names were spelled only slightly differently. "Oh, yes," she said. "There was quite a stir in the late sixties when his band played in the gym at Booker T. Washington." Some of the white boys in the high school came to play in the band or to listen to the music. "One of the DeWeese boys went—his father was running for mayor." So young DeWeese's visit to Booker T. got into politics.

She asked if I would like to accompany her to the cemetery. I followed her in her Volkswagen to the outskirts of town. I could see how the tiny graveyard had been so obscured to the living generation. Even with most of the underbrush removed, it was a secret kind of place, still bosky and tangled with vines. I enjoyed watching Florence Mars as she examined the ruined tombs of the early people in the sunshine.

Later, standing near her car, I asked her about Lillie Jones, an old black woman she had described in her book—Lillie Jones who had raised ten children and worked in the fields and become active with the COFO workers of 1964 because, as she said then, "I didn't have nothing and didn't want nothing but my freedom."

"She still lives alone in the Quarters," Miss Mars said. "Want to go see her?"

We drove to a frame, shingled little house at 241 Carver Avenue, two blocks from the Mount Nebo Church. The front yard, enclosed by a wire-mesh fence, was filled with plants and shrubs, and in the back some chickens pecked in the grass. Directly across the street was the Busy Bee Grocery and Record Shop, and next to that the cement-block building with boarded windows. Florence Mars pointed to the structure, which I had driven by many times, the COFO headquarters in the 1960s. In front was the wooden sign with the faded initials "COFO" and the white and black hands clasping one another. This may be the last extant sign like that of those years, Miss Mars said.

We were met in front of the house by an old woman, brown-skinned, with a deeply lined face. She wore steel-rimmed glasses and a green apron over a bright print dress. She and Florence Mars greeted each other affectionately. We stood there talking; Miss Mars asked after several people who lived in the Quarters.

"How old do you think I am?" Lillie Jones asked me.

"Seventy?" I replied.

"Ninety-one. I'll be ninety-one on January 5—that's what it seems like I remember."

An elderly black man crossed the street from the Busy Bee. "Hi, Florence," he said. "Hi, Miss Lillie." This, it turned out, was the Reverend Clinton Collier, who had given the eulogies at Mount Zion and read the Scriptures at the unveiling of the monument at Mount Nebo. He now had a church over in Leake County.

We talked of Marcus Dupree. "I remember he was playin'," Lillie

Jones said. "But I didn't know he was *this* good. I don't know much about ball."

"I know all about him," Collier said.

In the luminous sunshine a car full of young blacks wearing sunglasses drove by, glancing our way. When Collier departed, Florence Mars said: "He doesn't look too good."

"No, he don't," Lillie Jones agreed. They described to me how the Klan had burned crosses on his lawn and later destroyed his church and tried to take away his land. "It's his nerves," Miss Mars said.

She had an appointment in Jackson. "I'm always running late," she explained, and with that she gave us a bustling goodbye and was gone.

There was a gas fire in the front room of the house, a sewing machine, and chairs, and from the kitchen the aroma of baking, perhaps a pie. Lillie Jones already had a visitor, a black woman in her sixties, fancily dressed, who was sitting in one of the chairs. This was Queenie Esther Calloway, who was a sister-in-law. "Lillie has the same name as my maiden name," she explained.

"I imagine he don't remember as far back in the county as I do," Mrs. Jones said of young Marcus. "'Cause, you see, I'll soon be ninety-one years old and I have saw a heap of changes. One thing, we wasn't allowed to vote, wasn't allowed to register to vote. I saw that change and it was a terrible change. The day I went down to register—in '64—I could've went in, but I left my glasses and couldn't see how to write. Gettin' off in a hurry, you know."

As she sat in a rocker, gently answering my questions, she reminded me of someone from my past, just as Florence Mars talking on the telephone had earlier reminded me a little of my mother, but I could not for the moment place the similarity.

She said she always thought back in those days that she was going to be able to vote before she died. She returned to the courthouse a year later to try to register. "The man that was takin' our register—the head man, I'm goin' to say it like that—when I walked in, he just act like I had been a dog walked up on the porch. 'What do you want?' I say, 'I want to register.' He said, 'What do you want to register for?' I said, 'So I can vote.' 'Well, what do you want to vote for?' 'So I can help put such as you out and put somebody better in,' I said, 'that's what.'"

The gas hissed in the heater and Queenie Esther Calloway sat listening as we discussed Martin Luther King's two memorial marches in Philadelphia in 1966. She was seventy-five then. She remembered the white people pushing and cursing them in the Square. While she stood praying, a little white boy of about twelve turned a water hose on her. She noticed an old white man looking on, and she later told her friend Florence Mars that if the man had been "a right kind of person" he would have scolded the boy. But Minnie Herring, the wife of the jailer, did make the boy stop.

Dr. King was a good friend of hers, she said, and visited her in this house. "He was just tellin' us to be encouraged and don't let nobody discourage us, 'cause what we were doin' ought to have been done years ago, and now it's just on its way." Some of the COFO people sometimes came back to see her, she said. "Mrs. Chaney's daughter, she was here this year. She lives in Washington. She was just askin' how was we progressin' here in our undertakin' in '64 and '65. I told her that we was doin' fair. We didn't even have the opportunity of drinkin' at the fountain up at the courthouse until we went to Meridian. We had to go to Meridian to help get that—up at the federal court."

Someone was singing over by the Busy Bee as the two sisters-in-law talked about Marcus Dupree's family, his mother and grandmothers and grandfathers. They remembered his great-grandfather Frank Stennis, who farmed on the west side of the county—"a light-skinned man who married a dark-skinned woman." They talked about the Reverend Major Dupree's Baptist church over in Kemper County and how popular he was in the community.

"My house burned out east of here, out Berefield, about ten years ago," the sister-in-law said, "and he was livin' down here in the Quarters then."

"He was livin' down here when I moved over here," Mrs. Jones said, "which has been twenty-one years."

Queenie Esther Calloway brought up her sister-in-law's ninety-first birthday in January. "She is active," she said. "Would you believe she walks down to my house?"

"I think I could walk to town if I wanted to," Lillie Jones said.

"When they marched out to the Mount Zion Church, back in '65, do you know Sister Lillie walked out there and wouldn't ride? The elder ones could ride 'cause it was a little over eight miles. I just thought that was remarkable for her. It didn't stove her up."

Lillie Jones sat in her chair and smiled.

"Sixteen miles there and back!" her sister-in-law said.

"I was a little younger then than I am now, though."

She could probably do it now, it was suggested.

"If she wanted to," the sister-in-law said.

From the backyard a rooster crowed. "You know, that book of Florence Mars," Mrs. Calloway continued on a new theme. "She just don't know how many miles that book has gone."

"I sold a lot of her books that went to New York and Washington and Penn," Mrs. Jones said. "I told them that I had the books here to sell."

"She's been many places," Mrs. Calloway said.

"I have been to Washington two or three times. I went to ask for our mail delivery. I went to the Justice Department—in '65, I believe. Mr. John Doar, do you remember him? I went before him. I told him how far we had to walk, that's what I went for. Mail wasn't delivered here, and we had to walk all the way to the post office in town. They wanted to know what happened to the money that they would send down here for such things as that. I told them, when they started it from up there it was green, and when it hit Mississippi it turned white, and that was the end of it for us. After I come back, they let us know right away to buy us some mailboxes, 'cause we was fixing to get mail delivery." And the other changes since that time? "I knowed something had to happen. I knew it had to get worse or better one. I knowed it had to be one of the two."

I asked about the integration of the schools.

"It seems like the youngsters get along well," Mrs. Calloway said. "As far as I know, I haven't heard of any disturbances."

"I was just expectin' for them to have all kinds of trouble every which-a-way," Mrs. Jones said, "on account of the way the situation was. But it worked out nice, I think, to what I was thinkin'."

Lillie Jones remembered the three boys, Schwerner, Goodman, and Chaney. "They were good boys." She knew they were dead from the moment they were reported missing. "I couldn't sleep, it hurt so bad." She rustled for a moment in her chair, then was still again, her hands clasped on her lap. She had been active in the local organization which raised the $850 for the monument to the three in front of Mount Nebo, and she had spoken on the afternoon of the unveiling. She had recalled on that occasion what James Chaney's mother had told her he had said the day he left Meridian for Neshoba County on June 21, 1964: "Momma, I got to do something that my flesh is not willing to do because it's weak but my heart is willing." Now, she said, white and black people who come to see the monument sometimes drop by to visit her.

"Now, when you walk in the stores, between the races I mean, they will ask what they can do for you. And you used to walk in and if there was a white person in there they didn't say nothin' to you till they left. You had to stand there and wait for your turn. But now it's not like that. You walk in there, somebody meet you and want to know what can they do. Well, that's better than it was. And it's better for coloreds in the factories, too."

"All my kids up North," Mrs. Calloway said, "they left after they had went to Jackson State and come home and didn't have nothin' to do. They went up there to work. They had to go to the big-time work. Everybody couldn't get in the mill. Now they are stayin' here much better, because they have somethin' to do. Anywhere there is a vacancy. They can put applications in anywhere. It has been here for years."

Lillie Jones and I left the warm room and went outside. She retired for a moment to see about the chickens, then we stood briefly in the yard and gazed across at the movement in the Busy Bee, which, as I grew to know, was indeed perpetually busy. She told me her father died about sixty years ago. I asked where all her people were buried.

"Well, they are just scattered around," she said. "Some of them are at Hopewell, about three or four miles from here, and some of them are out there at Mount Zion, where the church was burned, and some of them are at Poplar Springs." She paused, then said, "They are all buried in Neshoba County, you can say that."

Only when I was at the football stadium later, with Pete taking his walk, did I finally recognize whom she brought back for me. In her gentleness, the soft detachment, the way she held her hands in her lap as she summoned the past, she had reminded me of my own grandmother, Mamie, in the parlor on North Jefferson in Jackson those years ago; they were of the same time, and the same place and people. In just such as this, Neshoba was bringing me back around.


"He's a real intellectual," someone had described Lovett Weems to me. Weems was the pastor of the First Methodist Church, which was established in 1837 not long after the founding of Philadelphia and was the first church in the town. Clay Lee, the Methodist pastor who had come in shortly after the killings and been a moderating influence in Philadelphia, had moved on to the Galloway Memorial Church in Jackson, just south of the State Capitol, which had been my mother's and grandmother's church and where I had been christened as an infant.

I remembered an eloquent essay Lovett Weems had written in a Mississippi publication in the late 1960s which was partially a review of my first book, *North Toward Home*. He had said then of his generation of Southern whites:

> Born following World War II, we finished high school in the mid-1960s at the height of Southern racial violence. There were, for us, few alternatives as to how we could view our traditions . . . We could either accept and defend unquestionably what a few had been allowed to define as the Mississippi Way of Life or we could reject this style of life and thought. Obviously, with the issue so polarized, there was only one choice acceptable to those who were opposed to the many injustices being practiced—total rejection.
>
> This rejection of our culture led to an unhealthy one-sidedness. This view was especially prevalent among Mississippians who . . . were "liberated" without leaving the state. We were blinded to those aspects of our past and present which were quite decent. It also led to a certain naïveté.

We thought things were right everywhere else and that we should try to become "like them." One had to remember that this was a time of national naïveté, when we thought prejudice and discrimination were almost completely limited to the South. One can scarcely blame those of us who had never left Mississippi for believing this.

One fairly common response was what Robert Penn Warren has called "self-hatred—sometimes self-hatred disguised as liberalism." This self-hatred is not unlike that felt by many Negroes, especially in years past, who could not accept their blackness. It should not be surprising if a renewed appreciation of the values of Southernness corresponds with the black man's pride in his blackness. Both movements arise from minority groups which have been saddled with the notion that they are inferior. Just as the black man has always been told, or at least made to feel, that he is inferior—so has the Southerner. No one who is sensitive to the repeated assurances that he is receiving an appallingly inadequate education in the poorest, most backward state in the country, can escape this feeling. For the white this self-hatred is greatly intensified by a tremendous burden of shame and guilt.

I met Weems in his study at the large, imposing church building on East Main. (On the street directly in front, Schwerner, Goodman, and Chaney had been arrested for "speeding" on that afternoon of seventeen years ago.) He was a handsome, thoughtful man of thirty-five who had been the pastor for six years, beginning in 1976. He had finished high school in Forest, Mississippi, in the fateful year 1964, and had later graduated from Millsaps in Jackson.

He talked of Marcus. "His effect on the town has been good. It's brought some progressive things to the forefront that were already beginning to take place. But it's not representative of a black kid growing up here. A lot of what's coming Marcus' way is because he's an achiever, a good kid, and people want to acknowledge that."

His children were in the fourth and sixth grades. "School integration is working here. Yet I see so many children starting out with so many disadvantages."

I asked had he been surprised by anything in particular when he first came to Philadelphia. "Yes," he said. "The latent progressive feelings. A lot of progress had taken place before then. I had real reservations about coming here because of the history." From the beginning, he said, he had asked the congregation, "Are we going to be a church, or a private club captive to its culture? I believe people get excited by a church standing up for something." There was guilt among some whites, he said, but not among others. "But the general feeling was that we've got to do better."

There had been no integrated meetings in the church before 1976. In the early 1960s the First Methodist Church had passed a written policy that it would not accept black members and that no blacks would be admitted to services. This policy was rescinded before Weems came to Philadelphia. There was an organization called the County Council on Ministries, composed of all the Methodist churches in Neshoba County—eight black, two "native American," the rest white—which among other things trained the Sunday School teachers, and the first year he was here there were integrated services celebrating the two-hundredth anniversary of the Sunday School program. Four people from each congregation in the county come to these quarterly meetings. Before the first one, a black minister said to Weems, "You don't know the history of this church and this town. We're going to come if I say it's all right. But we're going to bring a lot more than four. We're afraid to come with such a small group."

This organization posed the question to the representatives of all the congregations: "What can we do better together than separately?" Florence Mars, a member of Weems's congregation, told him at the time, "You need to realize this sort of thing won't happen in your lifetime or mine." On the night of the very first integrated meeting, it so happened that the documentary *Attack on Terror: The FBI Against the Ku Klux Klan in Mississippi* was on national television.

After that, Weems said, whites started attending black services occasionally. An elderly white woman at a Sunday night service in Weems's church stood up and said, "I just went to a black church for the first time today," and went on to describe to the rest of the congregation how moving this visit was to her. When the Methodist bishop came to Philadelphia not too long ago, Weems said, "we had a well-integrated service here." He added: "This was symbolic, not typical." Both the Episcopalians and the Roman Catholics of Philadelphia also have some black participation, he said.

From outside were the shouts of children playing, and the echo of an old hymn from my childhood on a piano from down the corridor. "There's so far to go. The battle for 'openness' was just a first stage. There's a long way to go." He dwelt on the word *inclusiveness*. "I still think that inclusiveness tends to be more token. Sensitive persons on the inside of things know that racism is still going on. But it's not the old racism. There's so much you want to affirm. But I know a lot of limitations—that element of racism that has to be dealt with. The public arena has run faster than the church arena."


On an oppressively hot night of that October, I was driving around town with a friend, a white man from Meridian who knew the county and its people well. The streets were dark and almost empty, and at 11 P.M.

the town was closed down as irrevocably as any place of six thousand souls in America could be. The establishments that remained open were the ones with the neon beer signs, which threw little garish patches of color into the still evening.

We drove into the Quarters and decided to buy a six-pack of beer. We stopped at one of the beer places. Outside were several young black men with goatees. One of them was barefooted. "You got a quarter for me, mister?" I gave him two quarters. We bought the beer and were returning to the car. The same young man came up to me again. "You got *another* quarter for me, mister?" In the car my companion told me this young man had just served a stretch in Parchman on a marijuana charge.

Driving up Carver near the Mount Nebo Church, we saw a new blue jeep in front of us, driven by a black woman in her twenties. I noticed it had been cruising slowly around the block. "She's got all these colored. men mad," he said. "That jeep belongs to a white man she's friendly with, and *they* know it. She's driving around like that to make them jealous."

It was midnight now, and a shimmering half moon was low on the horizon. In a gathering breeze the dust eddied along the streets of the Quarters. My friend had agreed to show me where the murders had taken place, and then the earthen dam.

The Courthouse Square was deserted in this hour. We headed down East Main, then southeast on Highway 19 toward Meridian. No cars were out.

I had been to the site of the murders once before, with Pete in a twilight of the early autumn. Rock Cut Road was the place, five miles or so from town and right off Number 19. I had come with a map, but those roads were unmarked. I had asked a Negro man in front of a store for Rock Cut Road. He had looked at me knowingly: "Second on the right." After the turn, not far up the road, were the prominent clay banks on each side. I had stopped the car here. The orange of the sunset and the red of the earth among the shadows had blended into a fiery glow.

My friend and I reached this spot. We sat there wordlessly for a moment in the darkness.

Then we circled back toward town and took Highway 488. After a time we stopped just off the road. He pointed. "The dam is right over there," he said. "You can see it in daylight."

On the drive back to town again we talked about those times. "Florence Mars," he said, "she was the one who stood up against it, a little woman."

The *rage*, I said, that had to go into the killing of those boys. And it only happened seventeen years ago—Marcus' lifetime; and the changes that had taken place here.

I remembered in that moment what the mayor of Biloxi, Mississippi, had once said: "They had targeted Mississippi—COFO and all that was an attack on Mississippi's pride, and many of your ordinary day-to-day people who don't ordinarily engage in racist diatribes and savagery felt put upon. The guy that runs a little drugstore that has a little counter, all of a sudden he's the target of a national movement, and so he would tend to vent his emotions. But that subsides pretty quickly . . . It was the murders that did it, I think. The murders, the death of those three guys was not in vain . . . The decent people of Mississippi, I think they felt a revulsion of that, and that was . . . a turning point."*

My companion considered this. The Kennedys and then Johnson knew they had to make the town a *symbol*, he said finally—given what was happening then in the South, FBI informers, a Mississippi judge, a Mississippi jury. "My children are more and more liberated from what we were. In another seventeen years we'll probably have integrated marriages. I tell my children, that's where I draw the line."

But what happened? I asked again.

"Hell, it was federal *law*, federal *legislation*. The federal government finally got into it." He was silent again, then he added: "And the good people responded."

I knew he was right, of course. But was that all? And how much further was there to go?

On the Friday morning of the Philly–New Hope game I left Pete in the Downtown watching a rerun of "Sesame Street" and strolled to the school for the pep rally. I stood in the back of the auditorium with two or three of the teachers and watched the interracial scene. I was greeted by clamoring noises and undulating bodies. As the band played "Hail to the Varsity," the cheerleaders were doing a dance number on the stage. The football players were wearing their red jerseys. I spotted Number 22 squeezed uncomfortably into a row of seats next to Burnside, Johnson, and Sutton. When the music subsided, the students shouted spontaneously: "*No Hope for New Hope!*"

Coach Joe Wood took the microphone to tumultuous cheers. "We're up against a mighty fine team tonight," he warned in the accents of Choctaw County. "I been talkin' to coaches all over that section of Miss'ippi and they tell us to expect the *pass*. I expect those ol' boys to throw the ball fifty times tonight. They'll be ready!" He asked the starting defensive team to stand up. They did so to applause. Then the coach in-

* Hank Holmes's interview with Gerald H. Blessey, Mississippi Department of Archives and History.

troduced the co-captains appointed for that night's game—Roe Ross, a white tackle, and Jay Graham, a black end. Shuffling their feet nervously, they gave the same speech that high school football captains have been giving at pep rallies since the birth of the game. "Well, uh, we appreciate your support, and, well, we gonna *whup* 'em."

Suddenly the band broke into a black-rhythm number. On the stage the cheerleaders—Stephanie and Yvonne and Dee Dee, Gayle and Nancy and Lori, Tonya and Rhonda and Suzzette—began swaying their hips and waving red, white, and black pompons. The crowd in the audience stood up and clapped in unison, weaving and dipping to the music. Then everyone turned toward one of the aisles. A small black boy was in the aisle dancing to the beat of the band, snapping his fingers and tap-dancing. Everyone cheered him wildly; the noise must have been heard to the Courthouse Square. Perhaps it was good they did not know what evil awaited them on the fields of New Hope.


The New Hope school, several miles east of the historic town of Columbus, was somewhat sequestered. Not far from the football field, a sign in front of a store said: BUY YOUR POSSUM FEED HERE.

The little stadium was packed half an hour before the kickoff, with hundreds standing on the sidelines and the traffic still coming in. I conversed with a local wag, who advised me that the eastern goal line was also the Alabama state border. The New Hope team, which came out in black-and-yellow uniforms, was 3–1 on the season, big and fast.

During the pregame drills, the public-address announcer, who sounded a little like a backcountry James Cagney, said: "Don't let your lady fix supper for the game next Friday. Please don't! Bring her over here to eat. Mrs. Sprayberry says they're gonna have homemade biscuits with the beef stew and three different pies. Stew, biscuits, and pies! So come on over at five before the game and don't make the lady work."

As the New Hope band played "Dixie," the Philly cheerleaders led the visiting crowd, who had driven eighty-seven miles for this game, through the yells:

> *We got Mar-cus, we got Mar-cus! . . .*
>
> *Who dat? Who dat?*
> *Who dat tryin' to beat our Philly?*
>
> *We got the fever*
> *We got the fever*
> *Yes we are . . . Tornadoes*
> *Right on!*

It proved to be a reenactment of the Newton game. Joe Wood's Wishbone was sputtering, and the gang-tackling was more pronounced than ever. Marcus took a lateral on the opening kickoff and returned it twenty yards before being hit by five or six defenders. Just after that a yellow dog, more tenacious than his Philadelphia counterparts, came onto the field and it required some twenty people and two or three minutes to chase him away. Then Marcus broke on a forty-two-yard gain on a sweep, then eight yards, then a fourteen-yard pass reception. "Hold him now, Jeff!" one of the New Hope fellows carrying the yardsticks shouted. "He's loafin'!"

There were several fumbles, and neither team could move the ball consistently. The Trojans of New Hope called for the pass on every other play, and Joe Wood was using Number 22 on defense at length for the first time in two years. In fact, from his position at safety he seemed to develop a camaraderie with Number 82, a tall black end named Eddins whom he covered on the pass routes, slapping him on the back after each play, helping him up when he was on the ground. Once, after he had hit young Eddins on a jarring tackle and Eddins lay motionlessly on the turf, Marcus hovered around the trainers and walked with him toward the bench when he was helped off the field.

The Tornadoes led 3–0 at the half, but the hometown squad roared back after the intermission, frequently blasting their famous adversary on or near the line of scrimmage as the partisans cheered their gratification. Philadelphia was inside the enemy fifteen-yard line four times but could not score, while New Hope launched a sustained drive for a touchdown in the third quarter, adding another in the fourth to win, 14–3. It was the second and last game of the season in which Marcus Dupree failed to score a touchdown. He gained ninety-six yards on nineteen carries, putting him at 849 yards for five games. It was the first time he had not gained more than a hundred yards in a game since his sophomore season.

The Tornadoes now stood at 3–2, with their venomous rivals, the Kosciusko Whippets, coming up next. Joe Wood had about decided on a new offense. "We got to give him more *room*," he confided to me.

# 13

# *Mississippi!*

---

In Oxford, too, the talk was often of Marcus, for he had come to represent something in this state, and grown men and women could talk assiduously in the Sizzler or the Warehouse or Clyde Goolsby's bar in the Holiday Inn or the Hoka late at night about what his future might hold. To Mississippians, in other words, the story involved more than football, and appealed to their histrionic nature. There was a curious logic to all this, and all of it seemed to have something to do with my coming home.


My people settled and founded Mississippi—warriors and politicians and editors. On my mother's side they descended from a heroic figure, Captain John Harper of Alexandria, Virginia, my great-great-great-great-grandfather, a landowner and shipping merchant who conducted his fleet of ships from Harper's Wharf on the Potomac River, at the foot of Prince Street in old Alexandria. He had twenty-nine children by two wives, and there was considerable intermarrying with the Lees and the Washingtons; both he and his son Captain William Harper, my great-great-great-grandfather, were friends of Washington and were mentioned in his diaries. Captain William crossed the Delaware with Washington in December 1776, fought in the battles of Trenton, Princeton, Brandywine, and Germantown, and was at Valley Forge. He commanded the artillery company which accompanied Washington to the laying of the cornerstone of the U.S. Capitol and fired the salute in the ceremony. Afterward Washington and the others retired with Captain William to the Harper estate in Fairfax County for what one of his biographers, my cousin Admiral Frank O'Beirne of Arlington, called "a sumptuous dinner," and Washington christened his land "Federal Hill" that day. Captain William later commanded the artillery which fired the minute guns at Washington's funeral.

My great-great-uncle Cowles Mead was the first acting territorial governor of Mississippi and the organizing colonel of the First Mississippi Infantry (which Jefferson Davis later led at Buena Vista); it was he who arrested Aaron Burr near Natchez in 1807. Another great-great-uncle, Henry S. Foote, was U.S. Senator from Mississippi—he delivered the dedication address at the laying of the cornerstone of the Washington Monument and defended, in those days after the Compromise of 1850, "the Grand Old Union, sage fruit of our immortal ancestors"—and defeated Jefferson Davis for governor in 1851. He called my great-grandmother his "favorite niece." My great-grandfather George W. Harper migrated to Mississippi from Virginia in 1844—just after the decade when cotton quadrupled in Mississippi and the slave population increased by nearly 200 percent to compose for the first time a majority of the state's human beings; he was a leading newspaper publisher and Whig politician of the era. He vigorously opposed secession, but later became a major in the Confederacy, and was one of the first white men elected to the Mississippi Senate in the latter years of Reconstruction.

The past, its responsibility and thrall, had always beguiled me, but one man's genealogy is another man's *ennui*; I do not cite the family pantheon to impress the Colonial Dames of America. But this narrative, much as an act of the subconscious, has really become a book about two small-town Mississippi boys—a seventeen-year-old black and a middle-aged white, and the young black's odyssey into the greater world would coincide, or almost did, with the middle-aged white's return from a long exile. Perhaps there was an ironic logic in this too—that while the white man's progenitors were marching with Washington, laying cornerstones, and establishing the state of Mississippi, the young black's forebears were crossing the ocean in boats from Africa and toiling in cotton under the eternal sun. Each of the two sprang from a most radically different heritage—yet from a mutual one, too.

I was born and raised into this heritage, growing up in a town half delta and half hills, before the television culture and the new Dixie suburbia, absorbing mindlessly the physical beauty of the land, going straight through all of school with the same white boys and girls. We were touched implicitly, even without knowing it, with the schizophrenia of race and imbued in the deep way in which feeling becomes stronger than thought with the tacit acceptance that Mississippi was different, with a more tenacious inwardness and impetuosity and a darker past not just than that of New York, or Ohio, or California, but of Arkansas, Tennessee, Alabama, and Louisiana, which were next door. This was a long time before anyone deigned to think that a Southerner could be elected President of the United States with everything that this would imply—not only elected in large measure with Southern votes but, four years later, in 1980, turned out resoundingly with Southern votes as well. As they said of the heavy-hitting but weak-fielding outfielder for the old Chicago Cubs, who once hit a three-run homerun in one inning and contributed three enemy runs with errors in the next, Hack Wilson giveth and Hack Wilson taketh away. It was a long time too before I myself, a native son, could comprehend retrospectively just how isolated we were, how starkly separate from the national impetus.

I went away to college in Texas, and in England, and ran a newspaper in Texas, and sojourned in California, and edited a national magazine in New York City and, having served my time in our cultural capital as many of us must, moved out to the eastern tip of Long Island to the village by the sea.

In *The Last Gentleman*, Walker Percy says that most Southerners have a cousin who went off to New York. I was one of the cousins. I dined in The Four Seasons and the Oak Room of the Plaza and the Sign of the Dove and the executive suites of the skyscrapers, and mingled with the scions of the Establishment in the Century, and sipped Bardolino with the movie girls in Elaine's, and performed on the talk shows, and stood on the balconies of the apartments on Central Park West and tinkled the ice in my glass and watched the great lights of Manhattan come on. Like the cotton candy at the county fairs of my youth, it was all so wonderfully sweet, yet dissolved so swiftly.

I often dwell on the homecomings I have made—the acutely physical sensations of returning from somewhere else to all those disparate places I have lived. To the town of my childhood—Yazoo—it was the precarious hills looming like a mountain range at the apex of that triangle known as the Mississippi Delta, the lights of the town twinkling down at night in a misty rain. To the city of my college days—Austin—it was the twin eminences of the University Tower and the grand old State Capitol awash in light from very far away. To the citadel of my young adulthood—Oxford University—it was the pallid sunlight catching all in filigree the spires and cupolas of that medieval fortress on its estuary of the Thames. To the metropolis of my ambition—New York—it was the Manhattan skyline which seemed so forbidding, yet was at once so compact and close at hand. To the village of my gentlest seclusion—Bridgehampton—it was the Shinnecock Canal opening onto that other world of shingled houses, flat fields and dunes, and the blue Atlantic breakers.

It was in the East that I grew to middle age. I cared for it, but it was not mine. I had lived nearly twenty years there, watching all the while my home ground from afar in its agonies, perceiving it across the miles, returning constantly on visits or assignments. The funerals kept apace, "Abide with Me" reverberating from the pipe organs of the churches all too much, until one day I awoke to the comprehension that all my people were gone. As if in a dream, where every gesture is attenuated, it grew upon me that a man had best be coming back to where his strongest feelings lay.

I was away during much of the dark times. I was a senior at Texas during the Emmett Till trial and the Montgomery bus boycott, and in England when Ross Barnett was elected governor of Mississippi. I was back in Austin again, editing *The Texas Observer*, when the Meredith Riots erupted at Ole Miss. I was a young editor in New York when Medgar Evers was murdered in 1963, and it was from that distance that I witnessed the events of Philadelphia, Mississippi, in 1964. Those days back home for me were all shadows and *déjà-vu's*. There was even a song of that period with the title "Mississippi, Find Yourself Another Country."

I remember, too, amid my images of those years, a nocturnal conversation with Richard Wright in Paris. I was twenty-one then, a student in Europe. I had found Richard Wright's telephone number. I knew he was a native of Mississippi who had left as a young man. I had been reading his books, I told him. I wondered if I might buy him a drink. His voice was cool and aloof. I said I was from Yazoo City, Mississippi. "You're from *Yazoo?*" he said. "Well, come on over." We retired to an Arab bar on the Île St. Louis and got a little drunk. He was curious about everything in Mississippi. His friends had been urging him to come back home. I asked him if he would. "No," he said. "I want my children to grow up as human beings." When I later tried to describe our meeting, I recall a silence fell between us, old as time. Or was it my imagining?

Many Americans, to express it boldly, had remained afraid of Mississippi. I witnessed this fear time and again in the East, and I see it to this day, into the 1980s. I recall sitting in a coffee shop across from my offices in New York City, hearing Bob Moses, the civil rights leader, describing in his gentle way what he had lived through in Mississippi. He had spent more than three years in the state, urging the blacks to seek the vote. Six people had been killed in the summer of '64, eighty beaten, two wounded by gunfire, more than a thousand arrested, and dozens of Negro churches destroyed. He had been in solitary confinement in a Mississippi jail for seventeen days.

A few years later, in the autumn of '69, I read a brief wire service story on an inside page of *The New York Times* about the federal court order out of New Orleans that sixteen years after *Brown* v. *Board of Education*, certain key areas in the Deep South, including Mississippi, must massively integrate the public schools after the Christmas vacation. I resolved from a suite on Park Avenue that I must go home to write about Mississippi in its most challenging moment of change. Some 92 percent of the total student enrollment in the state returned to the public schools. In the book I wrote, I believe I was largely right in my assessments. I misjudged, however, the long-range efficacy of the private academies in certain places, especially the Delta and the city of Jackson.

I have a friend named "Wissie" Dillard, who had been a halfback at Ole Miss in the 1950s, a flamboyant and beloved figure. Once at the halftime of a game in which Ole Miss was being soundly beaten, he said to his teammates, "Our problem is field position. We showed up on the wrong field." At another, similar, halftime, he observed, "Boys, the trouble is our kicking game. We're gettin' our tails kicked."

In 1970 Wissie Dillard was the principal of the public high school in Itta Bena, a Delta town in a county that was nearly 70 percent black. Overnight, because of the exodus of the whites to the private academies in that vicinity, the enrollment in his school changed from almost 100 percent white to almost 100 percent black. He was experiencing some problems in being accepted by the black students. A few days after the "integration," he and a new black teacher were touring the empty schoolhouse after hours. They entered a deserted classroom, and on the blackboard a student had written: "Mister Dillard is a jackass." The distraught black teacher reached for an eraser. "No!" Dillard shouted. "Leave it up! He called me 'Mister.'"

I like Calvin Trillin's tripartite definition of a big city—where no member of the city council comes to meetings in white cardigans, where there are at least two places to buy pastrami, and where people eat supper after dark and call it dinner. Oxford, Mississippi, will not qualify. Years from now it may be one of the very last, the last of the way things were here in the lower South. Even now I keep an eye cocked toward the catastrophic suburbs of Memphis only seventy miles away, spreading southward into Mississippi. Despite the shopping centers and chain stores on the edges of town, there is still a patina of time in the graceful streets and wooded open spaces, in the quiet nights of one's childhood with the katydids chirping and the rustlings of the trees and the cool dew on the grass. "Things seem on a human scale here," C. Vann Woodward said when he came to visit me. It took me a time to understand that my coming back home had a great deal to do with the importance of memory, of holding on to memory, of my experience deep down with my own memory. Walker Percy called this living in some authentic relation to the main events of one's life. It was a matter too of the eternal rhythms, of a relationship with the land, of the accessibility of solitude, of the chimes on each hour from the courthouse, of watching the children of one's friends growing up, of the football and basketball and baseball, of the banter between the old whites and blacks, of the funerals and the graveyards and the way people care for the dead. From what other state university town in the nation could you drive a little over a mile into the countryside and find a road colloquially called Dead Pecker Hollow, so named because the people who lived there never had any children?

"Optimism, perseverance, patience, and an eager view of the distant horizon have always been a gift of the earth to those who stayed close to it," Hugh Sidey once wrote in one of his distinguished essays for *Time*. Not that we were agrarian sons and daughters of the soil; but the real enveloping earth was often a strength and solace as one grew older in a land one loved. A mean and shifty-eyed fellow from, of all places, *The Washington Post*, of a careless and deracinated breed of modern America which I had come to call "groovies," slipped into the town and wrote, for whatever purposes, "a big piece" for a nexus of American intellection called "Style," ridiculing my friends and me for caring nothing about the outside world beyond football, for apparently not reading books, for drinking too much, and for talking to our dogs. The mucilaginous little man, who consumed much himself of the hospitable wines and spirits, comprehended little of one's deep, hard-earned equilibrium in America after all of it, and it probably never occurred to him that we preferred talking to my aging dog, Pete, and to Dean Faulkner Wells's undeceitful and vivacious beagle, Lion Faulkner Wells, than to such as he. I am sure he felt he had performed with valor, and perhaps by his lights he had.

The campus is only a few blocks down University Avenue. Here the town and Ole Miss seem to merge, little outpockets and cul-de-sacs of youth and age. The campus does not have the intense, self-contained beauty of Washington and Lee, or Sewanee, or Chapel Hill, or the University of Virginia, but it almost does. There is a loveliness to it, an unhurried grace, with its gently curving drives, its shady bowers, its loops and groves and open spaces crowned with magnolias, oaks, and cedars and lush with forsythia and dogwood and Japanese magnolias and the pear trees in the early spring; the ancient Lyceum at the crest of the hill, the new library with its inscription in the stone, "I believe that man will not merely endure . . . he will prevail," the football stadium only a stone's throw from all this and named Hemingway Stadium (after the law professor, not the writer) in Bill Faulkner's hometown.

At Smitty's, where I go for breakfast, the talk during the intermina-

ble coffee breaks, among the merchants of the Square, and the legions of
lawyers (why do small Southern towns have so many lawyers?), and the
farmers from the farthest reaches of Lafayette County is about Afghani-
stan, the crazed Khomeini, the hostages, the Russkies—one morning,
coffee toasts were exchanged to the American ice hockey boys—and the
next Ole Miss game, basketball or baseball, or how Steve Sloan, the young
football coach, had just recruited two enormous white twins from Lynn,
Massachusetts, and a black flanker from the Delta who ran the one hundred in 9.6 and made straight A's in the integrated high school, and an
ambidextrous black quarterback from Bruce, a few miles south on the
Scoona River. At five o'clock, some of the merchants go to the back of
Shine Morgan's Furniture Store, behind the ovens and refrigerators, for
drinks and Ole Miss sports talk before winding on home. They drink, not
bourbon, but vodka, so their wives won't know. This is the Courthouse
Square metaphor for the commuters' pause at the Madison Avenue bars I
once knew around Grand Central before the rush to the trains.

The air of youth, tonic, breathless, sexual, touches the Square. It is a
contagion. On the afternoon of a game there will be Alabama or LSU or
Vanderbilt pennants on the Square, streamers on the out-of-state cars in
alien colors, cheerleaders in the buoyant sunshine, exuberant shouts punctuated here and there by the hometown Rebel yell. The SAE's or KA's,
celebrating early before a game, as is their wont, emerge from the Gin or
the Gumbo or the Warehouse. "Hotty Toddys" reverberate off the old
façades, and more Rebel yells. Mercedes-Benzes mingle on the Square
with dusty pickup trucks from out in Beat Two, Snopes country. The
most beautiful co-eds in America drive down to shop at Neilson's or The
Image; Delta cotton money is present among the sunburnt old boys in
khakis and overalls. The girls come to the Square with a sense of purpose,
with sunswept hair and smiling faces. In the midst of the toenail painting
on Sorority Row, a voice down the hall had proposed a traditional way to
get through the afternoon: "Anybody want to go buy some shoes?" As
they browse through the shops facing the courthouse, there is a languor-
ous ardor in their selections amounting almost to foreplay. When the moment of crisis finally arrives and the purchase of Pappagallos or Capezios
consummated, they negligently toss their parcels in the backseats of baby
blue Oldsmobiles and compare notes, with practiced irony, on their beaus.
Their mothers would be proud of them. What would Marcus Dupree of
Neshoba County make of all this?

As I strolled across the Ole Miss campus in the beginnings of the
Southern autumn, in those times when I was back from Neshoba, it was

difficult to conceive the chaos and mayhem of almost twenty years before
—the gunshots and burning vehicles, the bricks and tear-gas canisters, the
federal marshals and National Guardsmen and airborne troops confront-
ing the mob. Two people died and scores were injured. This was less than
two years before the events in Marcus' hometown in 1964, and it was the
Last Battle of the Civil War, the last direct constitutional crisis between
national and state authority. James Meredith, an Air Force veteran, was
enrolled as the first black student at Ole Miss the next day.

One of the sadnesses was that many Mississippians believed the assurances of their leaders that defiance could succeed. "What are you going to
do now, Leander?" Earl Long of Louisiana had asked the states rights
conservative Leander Perez of Plaquimenes Parish. "The Feds have the
H-Bomb."

A close friend here named Billy Ross Brown, of impeccable Mississippi lineage—his great-grandfather was wounded in the charge at Gettysburg—was the captain of a national guard unit which was federalized that
day. Once we were standing on the back porch of my bungalow on the
edge of the campus. He gazed out toward a beautiful wooded terrain.
"This was where we dug in," he said. "This was the left flank of our pe-
rimeter. We went all the way up to the Law School." What impressed
him the most, he said, was that the country boys under his command
were against everything Meredith and his advocates were trying to do, yet
they were completely loyal to the American flag. He said, tenderly almost:
"I guess it must've been the discipline they'd learned in the military."

Faulkner died less than three months before the Crisis. The events of
that September, and of the summer of '64 in Neshoba, would likely have
broken his heart. "The white people have already lost their heads," he
said of those years. "It depends on whether the Negroes can keep theirs."


In 1981 there were approximately seven hundred black students at
Ole Miss out of an enrollment of ten thousand, or 7 percent. The University actively recruited blacks and encouraged their participation in extra-
curricular activities. Whites and blacks strolled across the campus green-
swards together, and sat on the grass studying their books together in the
Grove. Yet the subtleties abounded and required the discerning eye.
There were only seven full-time undergraduate black professors. Money
was one problem, and black professors and administrators were often lost
to larger schools. The rural backdrop was another, as was the absence of a
sizable middle-class black community here. The Black Student Union and
the Associated Student Body, which, in effect, had been the student gov-

ernment, had recently merged. But the pervasive sorority and fraternity system remained segregated; the blacks had their own chapters.

Many black students complained that they did not feel they were a significant part of campus life, and that there were in fact two cultures juxtaposed here. I witnessed this emotion in a small class I taught. I had encouraged the young whites and blacks to be candid about the realities of their relationships here. Everyone began talking at once, as if an ancient burden had been lifted. The blacks said they found it difficult to consider this *their* university. The whites said they were trying to understand. One white youngster was especially disarming. "I have nothing against you," he said. "In fact, I like you. I think if there were *more* of you the situation would be better."

I had heard other stories. In a freshman zoology class of thirty-six students, mostly white sorority girls, with only one black male student, no one chose to be the black's laboratory partner. Finally, after an embarrassing interval, a white girl who was not in a sorority volunteered. In a history class which was discussing the Meredith Riots, a black student argued: "Only the vocabulary has changed. How many black professors are there? How many administrators?" A white private academy graduate replied: "If things are so bad, why are you here?" During this discussion, it was noted, two white sorority girls were thumbing through *Vogue* magazine.

It was a sensitive dialogue, enveloped with consequence. Both the white and black students were largely the "aristocrats" of their races in the state, and they were imbued with a fierce pride. "There are only five or six black students I can call by name," a young white said. "I average one black a semester in my classes." Another said: "It's like they separate themselves from us." A graduate student argued: "The blacks on this campus permit tokenism and the whites promote it." A professor cited the products of the rigorously ideological private academies which emerged after the integration of the public schools—roughly 20 to 25 percent of the student body by his calculations. "They don't even know their black contemporaries the way we did in the *segregated* South," he said. A black teacher said: "For many whites and blacks, rapport is not the natural thing it may seem. People have to learn it."

A final contention lay in the traditional symbols of the Old South. Many blacks complained of the school fight song "Dixie," the mascot "Colonel Rebel," and the waving of the Confederate flag at athletic events; the flag was by far the most inflammatory. The first black cheerleader in Ole Miss history attracted considerable attention by announcing he would not carry the flag on the field. His wishes were understood by both the administration and most of the students, although he was the recipient of considerable hate mail. National reporters, who swiftly came down believing Mississippi was on the brink of another Armageddon, were impressed by the dignity of the young black man. A columnist in *The Daily Mississippian*, young Dan Turner of Philadelphia, Mississippi, addressing himself to a few disgruntled alumni, wrote: "I have one piece of advice to all those amazed with our selection of cheerleaders. Grow up. We did." As for "Dixie," the Ole Miss band, which had many black performers, had perfected a song called "From Dixie with Love," which was a stirring blend of both "Dixie," and "The Battle Hymn of the Republic." This rendition, played at all games, would have touched the soul of a Massachusetts abolitionist.

The institution was a blend of everything the Deep South was and is. Many of the white students lived the most sheltered of lives. Their proximity with their black contemporaries seemed both mystifying and exhilarating. They were both grown-up and rowdy children. They still got hopelessly drunk at the Gin or the Warehouse or the Abby, and I sometimes wondered how many of them read books.* Yet others of them came to the Hoka at midnight for coffee to discuss those things which were inherent to a university town—literature and history, the human race. Allison Brown, daughter of an old Mississippi family, honor student and campus beauty who was the editor of the Meredith anniversary issue of the *Ole Miss Magazine*, would write in her editorial: "We are of a generation in Mississippi that knows first-hand that blacks and whites can actually work together, grow up together, and share common experiences. Even at Ole Miss, where tradition hangs on until the very last thread, much progress has been made . . . Our generation can do something about it. We can work toward the inevitable changes that will make Ole Miss a better place for people of all races."

In the spring of 1983, however, as I was finishing this book about Marcus, a number of sorrowful events served to cut through the assumptions many of us had had about racial enlightenment at the state university. In three years I had learned much from my young black students. The Ole Miss blacks, in response to the publishing of several photographs of the Ku Klux Klan in the new yearbook, came out with a set of fourteen demands, including the abolition of the Confederate flag, the mascot "Colonel Rebel," and "Dixie." (The Chancellor, Porter Fortune, had already decided to withdraw any official sanction of the flag, and made that announcement later in the week. He received several death threats.) One night several hundred white students, a thousand of them by some estimates, marched on a tiny black fraternity house, in such contrast to the palatial white sorority and fraternity residences, where one of the black

---

* It was interesting to note, however, that Ole Miss had produced twenty-two Rhodes Scholars, eighth among American public universities, compared with one for Mississippi State and none for the University of Southern Mississippi.

student leaders, young John Hawkins, the cheerleader who had refused to wave the Rebel flag at ball games, lived. The ten or twelve black youngsters in the fraternity house were confronted by this mob, which yelled "Nigger night!" and "Save the flag!" An Ole Miss spokesman later called this an expression of "spring fever." The police arrived in time to surround the house. In the days following, many white students taunted the blacks on the campus and the streets of town by waving the flag in their faces and demanding to know why they were not at Jackson State. "What kind of people must have raised these kids?" someone asked.

The party-loving sorority and fraternity students, representatives of an entrenched social system rife with philistinism, were at the core of this shameful outbreak, and of the emotions which prompted it. It was an exercise in penultimate nihilistic Mississippi self-destruction, as if these young whites neither knew of nor cared for the delicate progress of twenty years, neither understood nor even acknowledged the presence of an outside world, of Auschwitz and the choice Sophie had to make, or Selma or Neshoba in '64, or the Tet Offensive, or all the assassinations, or the very flow of human history; or the reluctant American civilization itself trying to deal with our darker impulses. "The girls are gorgeous and the boys are sleek young hounds," a friend of mine who knew and was concerned for them said. "Their disaffection is frivolous and unearned. We've failed them somehow." "It's a time warp," commented Leon Daniel, a much-traveled wire service reporter who had covered the Meredith Riots and the Vietnam war. "I haven't seen kids like these since the 1950s." Dean Faulkner Wells, the novelist's niece, herself a writer and a graduate of Ole Miss, said: "It takes a certain kind of human being to come here and stay happy. It's a haven from the rest of the world. A very safe place. Moonlight and magnolias. They really do believe that *Gone With the Wind* was real. It was real to their mamas and real to their grandmamas. This is a continuation of the security they've had all their lives. All of the clichés come to mind; 'Daddy's rich and mama's good-looking.' Unless they're crossed they're perfectly harmless."

In the autumn of 1981 Ole Miss was anxious to have Marcus Dupree. "Is he going to come here?" everyone asked me. "He should."


The Ole Miss football team was roughly half white and half black. The Rebel partisans cheered their black players as enthusiastically as they did the whites, and the outstanding ones were campus heroes—Hammerhead and Buford, Michael and Carlos, Freddy Joe and Chico. It was one of the endless ironies of this complicated setting that the white fraternity boys with their Rebel flags who might march on a dozen unsuspecting blacks would show an unqualified pride in the black athletes and appreciate their friendship. What manner of state was ours? "We all love Mississippi," the historian David Sansing once said to me, "but sometimes she does not love us back."

Michael Harmon, a pass receiver who had played in high school against Marcus Dupree, grew up in Kosciusko. He was one of nine children. "We all picked cotton growing up," he said. "It's pretty rough work, but we did it together as a family. We didn't mind. A lot of times we'd get up at dawn and pick cotton until school started. We'd go to school and then come home and pick cotton until dark. I used to miss twenty or twenty-five days of school a year picking cotton. On Saturdays we'd take a radio to the fields and listen to the games. I liked Ole Miss and I liked Coach Sloan," he said. He was a good student and he married the first girl he dated on the campus. "I wouldn't change anything about it, except maybe what people think about Ole Miss," he said. He actually had black football recruits ask him if they beat black players at Ole Miss with chains. "Can you believe that? Chains!"

This touched upon an interesting point, germane to this narrative. The competition for high school football players in Mississippi between Mississippi State, Southern Mississippi, and Ole Miss had become suicidal. In the successful days of Ole Miss football under Johnny Vaught, when the team was consistently one of the national powers, Ole Miss got most of the Mississippi players it wanted. "When I was coaching at Alabama," Coach Steve Sloan of Ole Miss said in the summer before Marcus' senior year in high school, "Coach Bryant used to tell us that we had to get at least 75 percent of the players in the state of Alabama to be a great football team. This is true of any state in the Southeast and especially in Mississippi, where we don't have as many people as most states. Prior to integration, Ole Miss did this in Mississippi. After integration, we began to split the players. In some years, especially before the seventies, we were dominant in this state. That's why I refer to Ole Miss football in terms of B.I. and A.I., before integration and after integration."

The problem athletically at Ole Miss had much to do with recruiting the great black players from the state. The rival recruiters from other schools, especially Southern Mississippi, were telling the black players and their parents that Ole Miss was a slave factory, harkening to the plantation days. The traditional symbols of the older South at the state university were only a part of this campaign. This systematic elaboration of the alleged treatment of black students at Ole Miss was relentless and often persuasive.

All three schools, naturally, were avid to have Marcus. Herschel Walker, after all, had made the University of Georgia a national contender almost overnight. And Marcus was a Mississippian. State and

Southern had been fielding winning football teams, and both had excellent coaches and good small-town environments; Ole Miss had been losing. I myself admired much about the people of State and Southern; the jousting among the three schools for the young athlete was a source for me of a nearly obsessive fascination.

In the summer of '81, the case could be made that Ole Miss had an inside track. Marcus had attended the Ole Miss summer football camps in his high school years. From these he knew the coaches and the coaches knew him. His two closest friends had chosen to attend Ole Miss on football scholarships. And there was the additional challenge, in the language of the world of football, of "turning the program around."

But all this, of course, was involved with something broader.


James Meredith had always intrigued me. He was a mystic, I sensed; one could not fault him his courage. It was gratifying that Ole Miss invited him back to give the keynote speech at the observance of the twentieth anniversary of his stormy entrance to the university. When I was living on the Upper West Side of Manhattan in the late 1960s and he was a student at Columbia, by exceptional fate my telephone number was identical to his except for the last digit, which was one different. I got more than a few of his calls and I presume he got some of mine.

Not too long ago he said:

> Man, let me tell you something. It's true I was born in Mississippi, but that's not why I'm here. Mississippi is the center point, the apex of the system that brought blacks and whites together. Mississippi is the perfection of the merging of blacks and whites. The merger took place because of economics. The system was slavery. No place was this system more perfected than in Mississippi. That means this is the turn-around point. This is where the turn-around has got to come. That makes Mississippi a land of opportunity. That's why I'm here.
>
> In terms of just living, Mississippi is by far the best place in America to be. You have more integration in Mississippi than you have anywhere else by far, North or South. You can go anywhere in Jackson, Mississippi, tonight and see blacks and whites eating, dancing and having a good time together.
>
> But that doesn't mean there's anything to celebrate. I think Mississippi has decided to standardize the social pattern in this state. They want to set the standard for the South and for the nation. And that's going to take place. The only question is what that standard is going to be.

The most horrific specters of the state had always been racism and poverty. Ed Perry, the chairman of the Appropriations Committee of the

Mississippi House of Representatives who had accompanied me to see Marcus play in Philadelphia, recalled what his grandfather, who was a farmer down in the hard land of Choctaw County not far from Neshoba, once told him: "Mississippi was the first state the Depression hit. It was so poor people didn't even know they were in a Depression. They were in a Depression before there was a Depression."

The returning son needed little to remind him. The shacks and the unpainted façades still abounded, and although the paved streets and public housing in the older black sections of the towns seemed prolific in contrast to the 1940s, a random drive through the rural land or the larger cities revealed much of that same abject impoverishment, mainly black but white as well. Out in the Delta, where time often seems not to have moved, the extremes haunted one as they always did (the homes of many of the rich white planters, it must be said, would be cottages in East Hampton, Long Island), but the very land itself seemed bereaved with the countless half-collapsed, abandoned tenant shacks set against the boundless horizon.

Near the end of his life Martin Luther King had stopped in the town of Marks in the Delta. In *Let the Trumpet Sound* Stephen B. Oates described the visit:

> He saw scores of Negro children walking barefoot in the streets, their stomachs protruding from hunger. Their mothers and fathers were trying to get funds from Washington, but nothing had come through yet. They raised a little money here and there trying to feed their children, trying to teach them something. Some parents were unemployed and had no source of income—no pensions, no welfare checks, nothing. "How do you live?" King asked, incredulous. "Well," they said, "we go around—go around to the neighbors and ask them for a little something. When the berry season comes, we pick berries; when the rabbit season comes, we hunt and catch a few rabbits, and that's about it." Sometimes, though, it was really bad. Sometimes they couldn't get any food at all, not even for the children . . . When King heard that, he broke down and cried.

On a recent drive through the upper Delta, I saw a number of haphazard concrete-block structures, now used for storage in the flat fields. These were the rural Negro schools which had been built in the late 1940s in an effort to give substance to the doctrine of "separate but equal." I came upon the hamlet of Falcon, an all-black town which had recently been incorporated and had a brand-new water tower and hydrants—a municipal water system constructed under the Carter administration with federal money. It was a Sunday afternoon, and I drove down the dirt main street paralleling the railroad. The lean-to shacks, the sagging stores, the people reminded me of Haiti.

Signs of the economic recession of the early 1980s were everywhere in the state. White and black tramps carrying their pathetic bundles hitchhiked on the roads between Oxford and Philadelphia. I stopped in one small town en route to Philadelphia to buy something in a drugstore; two drugstores on the main street were closed in the middle of the afternoon. When I asked a fireman sitting in front of the firehouse why they were not open, he said: "Because they ain't doin' no business." At the corner of Mill and Amite in Jackson, a scene I remembered from my childhood in the Depression was re-enacted in our day—the dozens of black men, seated on buckets, waiting for people to drive by looking for day laborers, indicating with their fingers how many workers were needed, and the scramble that ensued.

"Since the Civil War," John Emmerich, one of the state's perceptive editors, wrote not too long ago, "the history of Mississippi has been the story of two races of people—black and white—trying with difficulty to live together, one dominant, the other suppressed, the two often in conflict. Both really have been disadvantaged—first by military defeat, ultimately by economic decline, recession, depression, rural poverty, and enormous social, educational,† and economic problems beyond our ability to overcome. That is why Mississippi today is the poorest, the worst educated, the most dependent on the federal government of all the states —and the list on which Mississippi is at the bottom goes on and on . . . It's an old story in the history of mankind: economic greed perpetuated oppression. Today we continue to pay for the sins of our forefathers."

The figures were there to see, and they were emphatic—unemployment for blacks in the state running two or three times higher than for whites, most black families existing below the recognized poverty level, more than one fourth of all black families fatherless (compared with 56 percent nationally). Mississippi was last among all the states in black median family income, which was less than half that of Mississippi whites.

Yet in Marcus' lifetime one was witness to the decline in the urban civilization of the North. The black riots of the late 1960s led in city after city to the continuing massive flight to white suburbia and the white abandonment of the public schools. The statistics on this exodus of the 1970s were remarkable. Examining them, Theodore H. White would conclude: "Big-city schools are now more segregated in fact (though integrated in law) than ever before." One of the ironies of contemporary

† Governor William Winter of Mississippi, one of the most enlightened leaders of the modern South, steered through the legislature in 1982 his Education Reform Act. Among other things it established a compulsory school attendance law (more than 40 percent of those who started school in the state did not finish) and public school kindergartens. Mississippi had been the only state without public kindergartens.

America was that institutionalized racial integration among the young, with all its human implications, was working best in the small to middle-sized towns of Dixie. Who would have predicted it?

What had happened in many of these places of the South? I had posed the question to my friend the night we left the earthen dam in Neshoba. The cup of bitterness at last drained? The old basic decency freeing itself before it was too late? What would Faulkner make of these changes in Mississippi and much of the South since his death less than two months before the Meredith confrontations of '62? If I chanced across him on the Square in Oxford tomorrow in his old tweed jacket with the leather elbows in front of Shine Morgan's Furniture Store and he said, "Let's go sit on the front porch, Morris, and drink some whiskey . . . I want to know what's been goin' on"—what would I tell him?

I believed I would begin with his sixteen-year-old great-nephew whom we know as "The Jaybird," grandson of his younger brother Dean. One night recently I was sitting at the old table in the house on South Lamar where Dean Faulkner Wells, The Jaybird's mother, and her husband, Larry Wells—publisher, editor, and janitor of the Yoknapatawpha Press, located over the Sneed Ace Hardware Store, now lived. Much of *Absalom, Absalom* had been written on this table, during Faulkner's grief over his brother's death. The Jaybird had just departed to play in the high school basketball game. I was talking with Miss Louise—Faulkner's sister-in-law, Dean's widow. "Miss Louise," I asked, "if Mr. Bill were sitting here tonight and knew that The Jaybird was the only white boy on the starting five for Oxford High School, what would he think?" Miss Louise thought for a while. "I think," she finally replied, "he'd be honored that The Jaybird made the team."

To me The Jaybird's warm comradeship and day-to-day proximity under the official auspices of the public schools of Mississippi with Top-cat, The Hawk, Toad, Scott, Calvin, and the others went to the heart of a different South.

Sitting on the front porch with Mr. Bill, I would have to go from there. I would suggest that since his departure the very context of our dialogue—the dialogue itself—had altered drastically. Public kindness, courtesy, and regard were surely not inconsequential qualities, and much of the malevolence of the language had disappeared, and the rhetoric of the most belligerent of the white supremacists was no longer fashionable. Would I advise him that the immense tide of legislative accomplishment and judicial decree which emerged from the struggles of the 1960s—the Second Reconstruction, as C. Vann Woodward and others called it—had helped save the South from itself? The Civil Rights Act of 1964, the Voting Rights Act of 1965, the whole crescendo of decisions from the federal courts, such as Judge Frank Johnson's in Alabama, and Judge William Keady's in Mississippi, had achieved results that were tangible now.

The author of Go Down, Moses and The Unvanquished would be intrigued, yet by no means surprised, to learn of one of the most splendid periods in our history when the bravery of the black Southerners of the 1960s and those of The Movement—in Neshoba County and elsewhere—demanded equality under the law for themselves and their progeny, and their traditional allies among the white Southerners grew in number and derived an incalculable sustenance from their example. Leaders like Martin Luther King, as a young black once said, "made it possible for them to believe they could overcome."

In 1965, writing in a special issue of Harper's on the one-hundredth anniversary of Appomattox, Walker Percy, I might have told Mr. Bill, described Mississippi as "a fallen paradise," which had spurned all civility. What Percy found tragically absent in Mississippi, and implicitly in much of the lower South of the mid 1960s, was a sense of "public space" in which people might let one another alone for the sake of civilizing values. I believed Mississippi and the South in the years which followed rediscovered the necessity of such a noncombat zone. For whatever reason, the flourishing of independent expression here in recent times—the tolerance of the hopes and fears of others, the awareness that words used carelessly can be the most inflammatory of instruments—and with this the articulated recognition in the broader context of the necessity of universal access to public institutions—had served our deepest traditions well. On the front porch, sipping the sour mash, Mr. Bill may have been listening, so that I might have asked him to drive down to Philadelphia with Pete and me the following week to watch Marcus Dupree.

# 14

# The Judge
# Was Misinformed

*Played defense for the first time . . . it was all right. New Hope
had a pretty good receiver, No. 82, and I mainly stayed on him. He
didn't catch any passes.*

*Playing defense affected my running a little bit, but not much. I
only got 86 yards, but the main reason was because they were keying
on me. It's kind of frustrating, but there was nothing I could do. I
have to take everything all in stride.*

*This week's going to be a big game. If we win over Kosciusko it'll
be a tie between us and them in the district. We need this game if
we want to go to the playoffs. It's a must game.*

*I'm planning to go see Georgia–Ole Miss this weekend. The
coach of Georgia wants me to meet Herschel. I'm also still interested
in Ole Miss. It's got a good tradition, good coaching and good environment all around.*

*Got letters from Mississippi State, Ole Miss, UCLA, Georgia,
Oklahoma and Texas last week. Also got call from Oklahoma. I doubt
I'll visit Oklahoma.*

*I know I'll visit Texas, not sure of the date.*

The Tornadoes' road game against the Kosciusko Whippets on October 9 was the only Philadelphia match I missed during the '81 season. It
was an Ole Miss football weekend, a weekend of high spirits and demen-
tia, catfish and champagne. The Rebels, though well on their way to another losing year, were playing the University of Georgia Bulldogs, who
were the defending national champions, and it was rumored they were
bringing with them a sophomore running back named Herschel Walker.
Marcus would be watching from the sidelines, and my literary agent,
Sterling Lord, was flying down from New York.

I had first met Sterling Lord almost twenty years before, in one of
those vaguely ambiguous bars which share the lobbies of Upper East Side
hotels, where agents and editors sit eternally in the shadows and discuss

writers. I was a few minutes early for our appointment. A gentleman in London tweeds walked by. "Are you Sterling Lord?" I asked. "No," he replied, "but I know him. Everybody in this town knows Sterling Lord." The right man finally came in, and it was the beginning of a long and enduring friendship. Among other things, I would learn of him, he loved and enjoyed sports; he himself had been nationally ranked in amateur tennis, a ferocious Iowan out of Grinnell College. Although he was too much the gentleman to put this into words, my intuition was that he was coming all the way to Oxford, Mississippi, to see Herschel Walker first, and his client second. Who could blame him for that?

In the autumn of 1981, Herschel Walker was already a national monument, perhaps the greatest running back in collegiate history. In the previous season he had gained the most yards ever for a freshman, 1,616, and he should have won the Heisman Trophy. "He's one of the few God puts on this green earth now and then," Johnny Majors, the University of Tennessee coach, had said. "We have seen the future of speed," *Inside Sports* observed, "and his name is Herschel Walker. Big men, six feet and 220 pounds, who can maul you and fool you and outrun you, all in one blast." Bud Wilkinson, the TV commentator and former Oklahoma coach, said: "I've seen a lot of great running backs over the years, but I don't believe I've ever seen one as good as Herschel Walker." His coach in high school had said, "We didn't coach him, we just aimed him."

In a splendid article by Terry Todd in *Sports Illustrated*, the track coach at Walker's high school remembered: "Herschel was 12 when he came to me wanting to know how to get big and strong, and I told him what I told the other kids who asked me. 'Do push-ups, sit-ups, and run sprints,' I said. He just thanked me quietly and walked away. To be honest, I didn't give it much thought. Herschel was short for his age and he wasn't particularly fast, even though he had some older brothers and sisters who were excellent athletes."

He would run long races through the countryside with his older sister Veronica. "One of the things I used to pray for every night," he said, "was for God to let me beat Veronica. I promised that I'd train hard and live a Christian life if only he'd let me get faster." Finally, after his sophomore year in high school, he beat Veronica. "I cried all night and then decided to quit track," Veronica said, "but Mama talked to me and helped me see that it had to come sometime, Herschel outrunning me."

He was, by all accounts, an ingratiating young man, as was Marcus Dupree, and there were other similarities between the two. Both were shy and rather humble. Both sprang from poor black families with strong mothers. Both were from small towns of the Deep South—Herschel from Wrightsville, Georgia, which had a recent history of serious racial troubles; Marcus from Philadelphia, Mississippi, whose racial violence was inextricably associated with the 1960s. Both were the most sought-after football players in the United States in their senior year of high school, and for both there was competition for them to remain in their native states. Both were big, strong, fast running backs; Herschel was thought to be a little less than a stride faster, but Marcus was two inches taller and, despite the printed statistics, between fifteen and twenty pounds heavier. Both were self-disciplined in their boyhood years, Herschel on his "push-ups, sit-ups, and sprints," Marcus on his running and weight lifting. Both had a languor about them getting off the ground or between plays which the novice might mistake for laziness. There were similarities and differences in their styles of running with a football. Herschel probably accelerated a little quicker and was in full speed with the first stride, cutting away when a defensive hole closed. Marcus, in his own words, was "a little more a finesse type." Enemy defenders keyed on both. Both could run over a defender with incredible power, and routinely get an additional two or three yards after everyone thought they had been stopped, and both were gone the moment they got in the clear. In this regard, Marcus may have been the more explosive of the two—likely to be contained near the line of scrimmage more consistently, but (as his college freshman performance might someday suggest) with a greater propensity for the sudden long, dramatic, spectacular run. In the autunm of '81 the great Herschel was the largely unproven Marcus' hero.


Before Herschel Walker of Georgia and Sterling Lord of Manhattan came into town for this October weekend, I did some reading of an unscholarly nature on the subject of *speed*. Is speed, for instance, God-given? "The idea gives pause," Terry Todd admitted, as did I. "Physiologists and sprint coaches agree on one thing—the ability to run truly fast is a natural gift; training is said to only marginally enhance performance. A physically mature individual can expect training to provide little more than a five percent improvement in sprinting speed—from a 10 flat 100-yard dash to a 9.5, for example."

How did such a "genetic predisposition," then, relate to intangibles like upbringing and aspiration? Granting them their physical gifts, would Herscel and Marcus have been a step or two slower if, say, they were sons of a white dentist from Shaker Heights specializing in root canals, or a stock analyst who commuted from the Pelhams? It was a seductive topic for speculation.

I knew at least three people who had considered the subject outside the laboratory; Temple Drake's philosophy was succinct. "There are certain kids," he told me, "who grow up in places they want to run from fast. That shaves some seconds off the time clock."

Ron Shapiro took the more historic view. Shapiro, a Midwesterner by upbringing, was one of the few Jews in Oxford, Mississippi—the proprietor of an institution called the Hoka, a late-night movie house and coffee emporium, who traveled to Philly three times to see Marcus play. "You know that Eastern philosophy, Karma?" he said one night over hippie tea and bagels at his establishment. "What goes around comes around. People believe the Jewish people have prospered so much because they suffered so much. Hell, Walker Percy said that in *The Second Coming*. Maybe these super black runners are a Karma of their suffering. Maybe there's a great God who has a balance sheet and evens everything out somewhere along the line—cuts about three tenths of a second off the forty-yard dash when he wants to."

Ron Shapiro continued: "Maybe the black man's time has finally arrived. The Jewish people over the last two or three generations worked hard, you know, in business, finance, medicine, law, the arts. The blacks have done well in music and sports. Also, I've noticed around this town— the black kids who live out in the country in, say, Toccapolla, or Taylor, come into town on bicycles. They take labor jobs for spare money. They're always *active*. They get all that coordination. The white kids are driving cars and standing around in front of video games."

Judge Tom Brady, the Mississippian who wrote *Black Monday* for the Citizens' Council back in the 1950s, claimed that one of the reasons the Negro was inferior was because he had flat feet. I always disputed the judge's scientific hypothesis every time I saw Jim Brown, Bob Hays, or O. J. Simpson running with a football on television. Simpson once said the legs of many black running backs were built for speed.

David Halberstam, in his book *The Breaks of the Game*, wrote that many black athletes themselves believed there were physiological differences. "Yet sociologists and black leaders were reluctant to accept such explanations. Not only did it tend to diminish the achievement of the athlete himself, but it opened the door to other arguments of genetic difference. Black sociologists preferred instead to point out that athletes were the only obvious role models for millions of ghetto youths."

Nonetheless, Halberstam reported of professional basketball, many coaches "were struck by the differences they saw between the black bodies of basketball players. Some coaches thought it an odd and ironic genetic legacy of slavery; slave hunters, they believed, had picked out the best physical specimens possible, and then bred them for even greater physical excellence. Only the strong had been able to survive the hard labor of slavery, creating in the end a generation of very powerful young men and women in the post-slavery South." In any event, in the National Basketball Association, black players described someone who was a step and a half slow as having "white man's disease."

My informal researches on speed led me beyond the encyclopedias to an informative study by Leonard Shapiro of *The Washington Post* in *Inside Sports*, one of those good magazines whose lot it was to fold. Why, for instance, had the forty-yard dash become the timing measure in football? Who decided on this distance, Shapiro said, was a mystery. Some believed Bear Bryant started it at Alabama. Others thought it was a man named Eddie Kotel, a scout for the Los Angeles Rams; or that Paul Brown, who later owned and coached the Cleveland Browns, first used it in the 1930s; or that Gil Brandt of the Dallas Cowboys initiated it in 1961. Whatever, it was a distance that did not induce many pulled muscles. "Oh hell, I can remember timing guys in the forty back in college, and that was in the mid-1940s," said Sid Gillman, the old quarterback and coach. "We used to run them at fifty yards, but someone decided they'll hardly ever run fifty in a game, so they cut it down to forty. Then we'd put two watches on them; one to get them at twenty to check the burst and then at forty to see how they did over the long haul." Jim Brown, one of the game's finest running backs, was 230 pounds and could run the forty in 4.45. Herschel Walker at 220 pounds had been timed on the forty in 4.3, Marcus Dupree at 230 pounds in 4.3.

The fastest running backs in the National Football League ran at 4.6 or better, and Leonard Shapiro, edifying me further, listed the five most speedy backs of our day in the pros, in order, as Curtis Dickey of Baltimore, Tony Dorsett of Dallas, Billy Sims of Detroit, Joe Cribbs of Buffalo, and Wilbert Montgomery of Philadelphia. The five fastest "Big Boy Backs"—weighing 215 pounds or more with between 4.5 and 4.7 speed—were Randy McMillan of Baltimore, Mike Pruitt of Cleveland, Ottis Anderson of St. Louis, Chuck Muncie of San Diego, and Earl Campbell of Houston. More specifically, Speed Professor Shapiro advised that running backs needed "quick-start speed" because the opening in a defense was only there for a second. Tony Dorsett of the Dallas Cowboys, who weighed 190, considered "speed and quickness" his means of survival. He could go "from a quick stop to instant acceleration in slivers of a second."

Two of the best running backs in the professional football of our era were Walter Payton of Chicago and Wilbert Montgomery of Philadelphia—both of them blacks from Mississippi. "What I have is an ability to accelerate," Payton described his genius to Shapiro, "which is the most important thing for a running back because football is a game of five- and ten-yard sprints. I played tag as a kid and I didn't want to get caught. So

I'm running and feinting and sliding under and jumping over people and just trying to get away." Wilbert Montgomery's reflections supported Temple Drake's theory, for he remembered "needing all his speed as a kid to escape a farmer firing buckshot at him for whipping his pigs with a stick." In the off-season Payton and Montgomery, those two Mississippi boys, stayed in shape running sprints up the levees of the Mississippi River. The very sight of the two of them, Payton and Montgomery, racing on the levee, the cotton fields all around them and the eternal River in the distance, would be worthy of the film *Chariots of Fire.*

Then there was Marcus Allen of Southern California, who would star as a rookie for the Los Angeles Raiders. "What Allen does better than anybody," *Sports Illustrated* wrote, "is make the opposition miss; he's a mirage in low-cuts." One of his coaches said, "His body is relaxed but his eyes are intense. The only time I saw his eyes light up during recruiting was when we would talk about him becoming a great player. He liked that." Another of his coaches, asked about his running style, said: "I can't describe it, but he sure has one."

In the virgin days of professional football, an old team called the Brooklyn Dodgers was coached by a scholarly colonel named John McEwan, who also taught English at West Point. One of his running backs sought his advice on a certain play. "Young man," the professor replied, "dispatch yourself with utmost precision and proceed as far as your individual excellency will permit." The Galloping Ghost himself, Red Grange of Illinois, told Dave Anderson of *The New York Times* not too long ago: "It's hard to know what you did when you were running a football. If you stop and think about it, you'll get tackled. No running back really knows what he does, he just does it. And whatever he does is always different than what the other runners do. If you ask me what I did, I don't have any idea. I had speed. Beyond that, I just ran."

That may have been the most provident observation of all. As with many of the fine things in life, one surely must be wary of the overdefinitions. Who wants to parse a Wallace Stevens poem? As Marcus once said to me, "It just all comes."

In this unexceptional little treatise on speed, drawing on some of the experts, I noticed that all these runners, who comprised the modern lineage of Herschel and Marcus' talent, were black. So much for Judge Brady, *Black Monday*, and flat feet. As with Bogart's coming to Casablanca for the waters, the judge was misinformed.


On an aureate, windswept afternoon, Sterling Lord and I went out to the stadium. I saw Marcus on the sidelines with some of the high school recruits. When the Georgia band broke into the tender strains of "Georgia on My Mind," I thought of my departed friend, the writer James Jones, of how much I missed him and had learned from him, for this was his favorite song. And when the Ole Miss band eased into "The Battle Hymn of the Republic" in the middle of "Dixie," Sterling Lord said, "What's going on down here?"

A few days earlier, Coach Steve Sloan of Ole Miss had said his team was considering leasing a truck to prepare for the game with Georgia: "We feel this would effectively simulate Herschel Walker for our defense."

It was one of the most consummate athletic performances I had ever witnessed. Running from the "I" formation, Walker gained 265 yards on forty-one carries. He was everything everyone had ever said about him. There was one especially unforgettable moment. Well on their way to a one-sided victory, the visitors had fourth down on the Ole Miss two-yard line. Walker took the ball and, just before reaching the line of scrimmage, dove high into the air. He was struck in midair by several defenders, landed on his feet, and trotted into the end zone. Then he casually gave the ball to the referee and jogged to the sideline. It was no mere circumstance that in the subsequent Philadelphia High Tornadoes games, Marcus would begin perfecting his own high dives near the goal line.

In the Georgia locker room after the game, the players were singing "Glory, Glory to Old Jawga." A Georgia assistant coach led Marcus Dupree to the bench where Herschel Walker was putting on his socks and shoes. Marcus stood there nervously, waiting for Herschel to look up. Then Herschel stood up and they shook hands. No one had to introduce anyone. They were an awesome pair standing there. The Georgia players stopped singing to watch.

"Yeah, you'll get tired of all the attention," Herschel said.

"I already have," Marcus said.

Vince Dooley, the Georgia coach, happened by. "Herschel, you did a good job today," he said. "A real good job. Your best yet. Gettin' better."

"Thanks, Coach."

Dooley turned to Marcus and they talked about recruiting. "I'd like to give it to you twenty-five times a game," he said, "and to Herschel twenty-five times a game." As Dooley departed, the beneficiaries of this strategy smiled, then sat down together on the bench.

"How much you weigh, anyway?" Herschel asked.

"About 220," Marcus incorrectly said. Herschel said: "I don't know how much I weigh. One day I weigh this and one day I weigh that. I know how tall I am. People say that I'm six feet one, and six feet two, and six feet three. But I'm six foot, one-quarter inch."

Fully dressed now, he was wearing a tawny-colored leisure suit. "Hey, isn't there an airport around here? We've got to bus to Memphis, then fly to Atlanta, then bus to Athens."

A Georgia official walked up. "Let's go, Big Timer," he said. "We've got a plane to catch."

"Okay. Say, have you met Marcus?" They both stood again at the same time. "Man, you're big enough right now," Herschel said, looking up at Marcus. "I'm way down here."

A couple of highway patrolmen told Herschel they would take him to the bus. They planned to whisk him around the field house so he could avoid the crowds waiting outside.

The two shook hands again. "You come up to Athens," Herschel said. "We'll have fun together."

"Maybe we could play in the same backfield," Marcus said.

"That would be great," Herschel said, and then he was gone, out into whatever a twenty-year-old American does in our time to cope with fame.

# 15
# He Runs Wild

*I didn't even ask to see the stats (19 carries for 80 yards in a loss to Kosciusko). I didn't want to see them. I got a slight injury when I slipped down on the wetness, my side went in and hurt my hip. But it's OK. I went in later in the game.*

*The main problem was that they were keying on me pretty heavy. They were after me, plus the field was wet and it made it hard to run.*

*Met Herschel after the Ole Miss game. He was surrounded by news reporters, but we talked briefly afterward. Talked about little stuff, like how big he was and how big I am. Also, talked about the possibility of playing in the same backfield. He asked me if I was getting tired of recruiting, I said a little. He really had no words of advice for me.*

*I watched him during the game. He's super. Seems like we're in the same situation. People key on him just like keying on me. . . . His play for the TD, I'd never seen a play like that before in my life. Met Coach Dooley.*

*Think I'm going to visit Georgia. Trips are still planned now to UCLA, Texas, Georgia and Oklahoma. Backing off a little from Ohio State. Can't explain why. I like Oklahoma a little now. Just a change of heart.*

*Ole Miss was all right. Saw Mike and Tree. They're playing junior varsity this year.*

Joe Wood had finally spurned the Wishbone and installed the "I" formation in the Kosciusko game. In the "I," the deep back is positioned about six yards behind the offensive line, giving him more space to choose his moves than the quick-run-oriented Wishbone. After heavy October rains, the Kosciusko field, Joe said, "was so wet all you could do was slide and wallow." The Tornadoes lost, 18–7, to drop their record to 3–3. Marcus scored Philadelphia's only touchdown on a forty-yard run, the sixty-ninth of his high school career, but he was held to less than a hundred yards for the second straight game, and there was an undercurrent of criticism again in town. Was he merely going through the motions? Was he bored with high school football, waiting his time for the larger glory?

"It was always a matter of the right moment," the loyal country coach Joe Wood would say. "We *really* had to get the offense together. It wasn't workin' for him. Our offensive line was so young, and the kids were a little intimidated by him. And I was worried about the gang-tacklin' on him."

A long time later, as Wood and I were returning late in the night from one of Marcus' college road games, he driving and I riding next to him with the black coffee between us, the deep American dark on the windshield, and our companions asleep in the backseat, Joe would talk with me about that time in October of '81. Much before then, of course, I had learned that Wood was one of those unexpected people among our fellow Americans. The white thirty-six-year-old farm boy's fidelity to the seventeen-year-old black had been unqualified.

"I was a little concerned then," he said. "I knew I had a responsibility to Marcus—he was so great. I didn't know much about the 'I.' I was a Wishbone man, you know, from Mississippi State. But I knew we had to put in the 'I' for him. Even he was a little reluctant. Philadelphia had a black running back in Marcus' freshman year who got beat up pretty bad. I wanted to get him through his senior year—to do good and not get hurt. All the big-time coaches kept callin' me on the phone. I just wanted to do right by him, but then not playin' *favorites*. Kids are funny. They really loved him and were honored to play with him, but there's always that little jealousy. Can't do nuthin' about that. Anyway, we put in the 'I' against Kosciusko, and if it hadn't been so wet and sloppy, he'd have gone wild. You saw what he did with it later. Listen, I just got tired of the gang-tacklin'. The 'I' was so good for him, I felt guilty I hadn't put it in sooner. Don't think he ain't an 'I' back."

In the school the young recruit was still walking up to Molly Turner, an Ole Miss alumna, and teasing her with the State clarion, "Bulldog Blitz!" He had put bumper stickers on his car which said "It's Bulldog Country," "Bulldog Blitz," "USM Eagles," and "Luv the Eagles." Temple Drake telephoned just before Pete and I were leaving for Philly. "Keep an eye out for a Texas U. recruiter—a big black fellow. I'd say Texas has played it coy. They're smart. Also, keep watchin' for Southern. Those boys are *reckless*."

As usual, Temple Drake was right. An NCAA investigator named Mike Glazier dropped by the high school a few days earlier to visit Joe Wood. He asked Wood's permission to watch practice. At the football field that afternoon was Bootsie Larsen, an assistant coach and recruiter for Southern Mississippi. He should not have been there because he might have made contact with Marcus, which was against NCAA rules during the high school season. Glazier of the NCAA and Larsen started talking. Larsen asked the visitor where he was from. "Kansas City," he replied. They continued their conversation. Finally the coach asked Glazier what he did for a living. When he said he worked for the NCAA, someone nearby who had been observing this scene said, "That coach's face turned white as ash and he just took off."

That Friday the Tornadoes, in their seventh game of the season, journeyed to Carthage, the seat of neighboring Leake County, a lazy town of church steeples and frame buildings and shady lanes. I left Pete in the company of Roy Tingle at the Downtown—they intended to listen to the game and watch the all-sports network on TV in Roy's room—and drove over alone in a tender, misty dusk.

The Carthage Tigers, four and two on the season, played in a little stadium directly behind their school building. Inside the gate the white and black Carthage girls were selling candied apples, sandwiches, and homemade cakes. Swarms of bugs, brought out by the warm weather, flitted about the pale stadium lights. I chose a place at the top of the visitors' bleachers. A large crowd of white and black Neshobans had come over despite Philly's three losses. Again I imbibed the Friday-night aroma of talcum and drugstore perfume. I waved to Jimmy Lee Shannon, the black alderman, and Marcus' little brother Reggie, and some other people from around the Square.

There was a capacity crowd by the time the Carthage band played "The Star-Spangled Banner." Then, in their usual separate clusters, the teams and the cheerleaders and the officials bowed their heads and prayed.

Philly received, and Marcus began with runs of six, eight, and twelve yards. He was working out of the "I," the first time I had seen him in that formation, and I liked the way he looked in it, for it seemed to give him the latitude he needed.

He went nine yards on a pass reception while tiptoeing the line, then dragged five or six defenders with him for seven more. A garrulous white fellow in a T-shirt and Atlanta Braves cap was sitting to my left. He had driven over from Canton, Mississippi.

"Hell," the man said, "he can get nine yards just slantin' down and turnin' sideways."

"He'll break some tonight," I said.

The man glanced at my notebook. "You a coach?"

"A friend of the family."

"I seen him in four, five games. He's the best I ever saw in *this* state, and I been goin' to games since the war."

Philly had a drive going, and midway through the quarter Daran Jackson broke through on a short run for a touchdown. "Hail to the Varsity" sallied forth from the Tornado band. The inevitable yellow dog came onto the field before the next kickoff, a candied apple in his mouth, which he settled down to enjoy, prompting the customary laughter, then cheers when the head linesman chased him away.

To my right next to me were three black men from Philadelphia. They were talking about some of the white boys on the team, using their first names—"Justy," "Roe," and the others. For the hundredth time I was struck by how the black people cheered the white boys, the white people the black. The Carthage Tigers had a black quarterback, one of several I would see during the season. They came back with a touchdown with fifteen seconds left in the first quarter and took the lead, 7–6.

It was Number 22 at his best now, the brutal, piercing runs with defenders all over him, the deft pass receptions on Justy Johnson's lobs and spirals. When Marcus moved in this way, a subtle electricity seemed to seize a crowd, as if the witnesses to it knew they were part of something that had magic in it, yet so fragile and swiftly gone.

He ran over several defenders on a ten-yard pass. Then, from the Carthage twenty-four, he sped straight up the middle, breaking three tackles, for his seventieth touchdown. Philly connected on a two-point conversion and led 14–7 at halftime.

I left my loquacious Canton companion and explored the little stadium during the intermission. I stood on the sidelines and talked with Sandra Luke, the Philly High teacher who had with her an infant just learning to walk. A soft breeze came in from the south, making riplets among the bugs at the lights, and there were the smells of peanuts and popcorn and the freshly-cut grass of the field. Beyond the concession stands some little boys with "Philly" on their T-shirts were playing tackle with a miniature football. The Philadelphia band was performing "New York, New York."

In the end zone I saw Tom Goode, the Ole Miss assistant coach. The Rebels were playing the Bayou Bengals of LSU in Jackson the next afternoon.

"What do you hear?" he asked.

"It was quiet in Philly," I said.

"Well, it'll heat up after December 1. A kid starts out enjoyin' it, but then it gets pretty old, all the pressure. The 'I' formation's suited for Marcus. It makes all the difference. Steve and I've told him if he comes with us we'll put in the 'I' for him."

I asked if any LSU coaches were here.

"I don't think so. You'd know if they were. They wear their colors, you know."

A corpulent policeman walked up to us. "Didn't you play pro ball?" he asked Goode.

"Yeah. Sure did."

"Who'd you play for?"

"Well, Miami and Baltimore."

"Sho' nuff? I thought so. I swear. It's an honor." He shook Tom Goode's hand.

I stood on the Philadelphia sidelines for the second half. Marcus' running was the best I had seen so far. On the first possession of the half he negotiated a thirty-two-yard sweep with four tacklers holding on. He was running low and powerfully. From the two-yard line, he took the ball as Herschel had a few days before and dove high for a touchdown.

I noticed, a few yards from me on the sidelines, a man in a light orange sports shirt with U. OF MIAMI on the pocket. He seemed excited, and in fact appeared to be talking to himself. I began watching him every time Marcus carried the ball. He jumped up and down two or three times, then walked around nervously. Soon we found ourselves standing next to one another.

"You a coach?" he asked.

No. Was he? He was the defensive end coach for the University of Miami Hurricanes, who were playing Mississippi State in Starkville the next day.

Marcus ground out a twelve-yard gain. "Did you see that? That boy's a *franchise!* I tell you somethin', he's the best *I've* seen."

We introduced ourselves. His name was Christ Vagotis, and he had played under the Bear at Alabama in the mid 1960s. Later, when I got back to Oxford, I did some research on him. He had once been the head coach at Killian High School in Miami. He had dramatized one pregame pep talk by biting the head off a live frog.

Another fine moment was at hand. Carthage had just scored a touchdown and was kicking off. Marcus was near the goal line in the deep receiving position. The kicker approached the ball and booted it in a long high arc.

"My God!" I said to Christ Vagotis. "They're kicking off to him!"

"What?"

"Other teams don't kick off to him."

Before our eyes, scant yards away, Marcus lovingly gathered in the ball, as if it were a gift from the Magi. He moved in our direction. On the fifteen-yard line, near the sidelines, a Carthage defender tried to tackle him. He ran over him with such force that the young man caromed off him with a frightening thud and landed at the feet of Christ Vagotis.

Then Marcus continued down the sidelines, breaking three or four other tackles, swerved to the right, jumped right over a man, outran the others, and went ninety-five yards for the touchdown.

It was called back on a clip.

"Never mind!" the Miami coach exclaimed. "*Did you see that!* That guy bounced five yards off him. That wouldn't have happened if he only weighed 190. Hell, that boy's 235! Don't give me any of that 222. See that speed? I tell you, he's in the franchise range—like Herschel."

A little later he broke another touchdown, this one for forty yards, with a quick weaving movement that had him free just beyond the line of scrimmage. "You see what I mean there?" the coach said. "He sees the first hole and he's gone." Then, almost to himself, a little guiltily: "I never saw him play till now, but we heard about him ever since he was a sophomore."

He was an enthusiastic fellow, and he was talking rapidly now. "He runs like a Mack truck goin' through a caution sign at a hundred miles an hour. The only difference between him and the Mack truck is that he looks *smooth*. He's like the other really great backs—on his first 'read' he breaks away easy. His second and third 'read' can be taught. You know, how to use all his great attributes."

On the field Marcus had just gained another ten yards. "Look at that. All great running backs have the same thing—lookin' lazy between carries. He reminds me of Jim Brown."

Christ Vagotis turned to me. His eyes gleamed. "You know, we play our home games in the Orange Bowl. It'd be great seein' him in the Orange Bowl. Under the moonlight, the palm trees wavin' in the breeze. Dupree in the Orange Bowl! Our band would be playin' 'Moon Over Miami.'" He paused in this deathless fantasy. I envisioned the swaying palm trees, the tanned Florida beach girls waving pompons. "I can just see it now," the coach said.

"The question is, can he keep his head on?—the way Herschel has. You think we have a chance? What do you hear?"

When the game ended, Vagotis shook my hand, then rushed onto the field to introduce himself to Joe Wood.

Philly had won, 28–19. Marcus gained 216 yards on twenty carries, plus five pass receptions. He scored three touchdowns, with the ninety-five yard one called back. He now had seventy-two touchdowns, fourteen away from tying Herschel's record, with four games remaining.

Sid Salter now enters this narrative. He would soon become as central to the tale as Marcus, Joe Wood, Pete, and the college recruiters.

Sid was twenty-three years old, a sixth-generation white Neshoban, a dark and quizzical young man with the eye of the hunter peering through the undergrowth. I met him at the Carthage game and we talked. I admired some of the things he said about his hometown, and his intelligent perceptions of it. We arranged to continue our conversation in Philly the following week.

Sid Salter was just finishing the semester at Mississippi State. He had gone there on an academic scholarship, where he had read literature, history, and political science, and had written a column for the student paper. Now he was returning to Philadelphia to become the associate editor of *The Neshoba Democrat* under Stanley Dearman. There he was joining the *Democrat* tradition of Rand, Catledge, and Dearman; I could soon tell he was a natural reporter of the old school.

I was glad of that, for we were to become collaborators in the story of Marcus. Soon he was calling me "Woodward" and I, of course, was calling him "Bernstein," and although our story may not have had the manifold implications of the bigger one, it indubitably would be more fun.

Sid Salter possessed what T. S. Eliot called "an experiencing nature." He was a young man of serious countenance who sought the curious and the theatrical. He loved women, dogs, writing, football, Mississippi State University, and the red earth and piny hills of Neshoba. He drove a vintage pickup truck which blended well into the landscape, and he had a good memory. The name of his great-great-grandfather Samuel Salter was inscribed on the Confederate Monument on the Square. He came likewise from a family of teachers. His father was the principal of Neshoba Central High School, the other school in the county out on the fringes of town, when the integration came in 1970. "I'd be a pretty fool if I wasn't scared," his father had said before the day came, "but I'll tell you this. We are going to have school at Neshoba Central. I don't care how much law enforcement we've got to get out there, we are going to have school." And despite the rudeness of some national television crews wishing violence on that day for the sake of a story for the evening news, they had school.

Sid had a grandfather he loved whom he called Papaw, who lived on the family farm near the swamps of the Pearl River Basin. Papaw was a hardworking survivor of the Great Depression. His hands were rough and gnarled; he rolled his own cigarettes from OCB papers and a tin of Prince Albert tobacco, and he liked Old Charter whiskey. Sid was five years old in the summer of '64. He remembered Papaw talking about "the troubles with them civil rights boys." He would listen to the radio or watch the television reports and grow angry. Then he would go out and sit on the porch alone late in the evenings and roll enough cigarettes to calm himself.

"I can remember that look of violation and betrayal on people's faces," Sid would tell me. "I wondered why people were so angry when the FBI and sailors were here in '64 looking for the bodies." He still had a sailor's cap from that time. He went with his father one day that July to a country store. With the help of his father, he reconstructed the scene as he best remembered it.

"How's things over at the school?" he remembered a man in a railroad cap asked his father.

"Busy like always," his father said. "I'm trying to get the football field in shape, but the sun's about to kill all the grass we planted."

"Boy, that's a sharp cap you got there," the owner of the store said to him.

"Those navy boys were through here today looking for the civil rights workers," his father explained, "and one of them must have dropped his cap. I tried to find somebody later to give it back to, but their bus had already pulled out. So I let the boy have it as a souvenir."

"I know they were here," the owner said. "I sold more Vienners and saltine crackers today than I've sold in a month of Sundays. Most of them Yankee boys didn't even know what they were."

One of the men asked his father, "Mr. Salter, what do you think happened to them civil rights boys?"

"I really don't know. Since they found the car, I imagine they're probably dead. But I don't know if we'll ever really know what happened. The governor said on TV last night the whole thing is a fake."

"Well, if they're dead, they got what they deserved," the man said. "They shouldn't be down here stirrin' up the niggers in the first place."

"That may be true, but nobody deserves to be killed," his father said. "If somebody did kill those boys, they're no better than the civil rights workers. You can't take the law into your own hands."

With that they left the store and started walking home. Sid said the expressions on the faces of the men had always stayed with him.

Sid knew Marcus and his family well. He remembered Marcus when he was in the fifth grade. "It was the last time he was awkward. He was a gangly, rawboned kid with glasses, who smiled all the time." When Marcus was in the seventh grade, three or four of the seniors on the football team would work with him and the other young boys after school. "Even then he was several inches taller and ten or fifteen pounds heavier and light-years faster than the other kids. Most of the plays were Marcus left and Marcus right. Then he was more of a curiosity than the phenomenon he became. But Coach Danny Gregory knew how far he could go. Even then it was very unusual for a kid, either white *or* black, to say 'yessir' to anybody. He said 'yessir' to me when I was a senior in high school. He was respectful and willing to learn. He took it very seriously.

"He has less of a sense of black and white than any kid I've talked to. This may be because he's the first to go through all twelve grades in the integrated system. He talks about school, family, team. I don't think he has any appreciation whatsoever that he's being embraced by a town that was such a symbol of racial trouble. He doesn't fit any of the stereotypes. Even his taste in music is unusual. Usually young blacks like the funk sound, the disco sound. I think ol' Marcus kind of drifts toward the heavy metal—R.E.O. Speedwagon, Rush."

One late autumn evening Sid and a couple of his friends from high school and I slipped into the House of Barbeque to talk. Although most of the town was slumbering, the whites, blacks, and Indians were out as always. A pale white girl in blue jeans and a Southern Mississippi shirt was poised before the jukebox buttons.

"Play some Jimmy Buffett!" a man with grease on his tractor cap shouted from a table.

"Oh, shut up, Billy. I was goin' to."

A couple of the fellows at the next table were discussing why on earth Dupree would want to go to Ohio State. I went to the counter and picked up that week's *Leonard's Losers*, that Godzilla of football intelligence reports:

L.S.U. VS. KENTUCKY

Fran Curci and his Big Blue Cats head into the Bayou for a visit with their Cajun Cousins Saturday evening and this could be a long night for one group of Felines. The Purple Bengals have shown signs of coming to life once in a while only to lay down and die before anything can happen, and if they ain't on their best behavior they'll get scratched up pretty bad by the Claws from Lexington. This could go either way but the Little Smart Pill Machine is turning deep purple and vibrating so that can mean only one thing.

We ordered some coffee; Sid and his high school mates began talking about the integration of the schools. They were in the fifth grade then. There was a photograph in a statewide paper of two exhausted Philadelphia High football players, one white and one black, after a ball game. They were using the same towel at the same time to wipe the sweat off their faces. To Sid and others this was a small symbol of the "harmony" which had begun to exist among the young people of the town at that time.

"Everybody in the country had this image of Philadelphia being a hellhole of race relations," Sid said. "Several of us boys hung around a lot together. We were all closet smokers. That was the height of sin. We'd get a package of cigarettes between us. Jimmy Stokes had a '67 Chevy that we called 'The White Knight.' After football practice, we'd have to wait till we got out of the parking lot to light up so the coaches wouldn't see us. Chuck Johnson and Norman Grady, two of our black teammates, would get in the car with us. We all called Norman 'Pig.' We'd light a cigarette, passing it around and cupping it in our hands so nobody in town could see us and tell the coaches." In the huddles, when the games weren't close, they and the other white and black players would put their arms around one another's shoulders and talk about girls. They visited in one another's houses. At their graduation in 1977, the whole class, whites and blacks, went to Cash McCool's disco bar in Meridian. At the Junior-Senior Prom at the country club that year, all the whites and blacks in both classes came. There were two interracial marriages in that time, Sid said. The couples live away now, one of them at last report in Hawaii.

Salter and his friends talked about the "syndrome" of black graduates of Philadelphia High School. "They either go to college at Jackson State, Alcorn, Mississippi Valley, or East Central Junior College," Sid said, "or go to work at the U.S. Motors plant. That's it. You know that movie *Coal Miner's Daughter?* It's either coal mine, moonshine, or movin' on down the line."

\* \* \* \*

*One of my better games against Carthage. The offensive line started doing things right. We got our passing game down, and that opened up the running game.*

*We went to the "I" instead of the Wishbone, and threw the ball more. That really helped. Didn't seem like they were keying on me near as much. Passing kept them honest. As the deep back, I got to see what the defense was doing and had more time to cut.*

*Still playing defense. I like it. Nice to stick somebody instead of getting stuck all the time.*

*Nothing new recruiting. Went and saw Mississippi State and Miami. Enjoyed it a lot. I know State has a lot of good backs but that doesn't bother me.*

\* \* \* \*

The squirrel season opened, and on Friday night Philly was playing in the affable confines of Harpole Stadium against Louisville, a hill-and-prairie town and the seat of Winston County.

There had been a curious development that week. A black man appeared in a bank in Philadelphia and identified himself as an Ole Miss football coach. He asked to cash a seventy-five-dollar check so he could take Marcus Dupree to supper, he told the teller, left a new suede coat at

Marcus' house with the message that he wanted him to attend Ole Miss, then located Marcus at the school and promised to give him three thousand dollars if he did so. Then the elusive philanthropist disappeared. Marcus told Coach Wood.

I drove down to the Louisville game with five or six friends from Oxford, including Ed Morgan of Shine Morgan's Furniture Store, known as The Sage of the Square. In the shadowy afternoon, the leaves turning on the trees, Ed Morgan gazed out at the dark landscape south of Eupora and pointed with his cup of eleven-year Old Charter: "Them's *squirrel* woods, boys." We went down in an honored vehicle called The Love Van, which for years had carried this group to the out-of-town football games all over Dixie. In the spacious cabin were captain's chairs, a bar, and a poker table, under which Pete slept on this journey. The van got its name because it was once owned by a doctor who used it as a rendezvous with nurses.

During the week Temple Drake had given me a piece of information, which several others confirmed at the ball game. A gentleman named Bud Holmes, a lawyer, sports agent, and University of Southern Mississippi advocate from Hattiesburg, had flown Marcus, his father, and his uncle Curlee Connor to New Orleans for a Saints' game, taking them into the locker room afterward to meet some of the players. "A violation," Temple Drake said. "But I ain't tellin'."

Before the game we dropped Pete off at the Downtown, then I took my companions on a tour of metropolitan Philly, ending in Independence Quarters, where there were signs everywhere:

BIG DISCO GET-DOWN
PIPE MAN FROM LOUISVILLE
BOOKER T. GYM

There was another overflow crowd at Harpole. Louisville was favored, with a strong offensive line and several players over 200 pounds. In the game program Number 77, Willie Porter, a tenth grader, was listed at 344 pounds. (I accosted Willie Porter on this after the game. "Aw, naw. It's a, you know, *error*.")

Marcus was running smoothly again out of the "I," with several substantial gains in the early minutes. The Wildcats of Louisville scored first. Then, in the closing seconds of the first quarter, Marcus got one good block on a right sweep, ran over a linebacker, and outran the secondary for a thirty-three-yard touchdown, putting the Tornadoes ahead for the only time in the game, 7–6.

For some time now I had noticed a little black boy, perhaps ten years old, who would position himself just beyond the north end zone every time a team scored at that end of the field. Only a short distance beyond this end zone there was a tall hedge with a hole in it, then a sharp incline, out of sight for anyone in the stadium, which dropped down into Possum Hollow, a terrain which opened into a whole backyard locale of gardens and glades and chicken coops; I was familiar with this secret ground because of my strolls there with Pete. Once, a number of years before, Frank Trapp, who later played for Ole Miss, kicked a point-after-touchdown so long into the hollow that it broke the breakfast-room window of Mrs. Alice Walker's house. The little black boy had a serious responsibility, for after every place-kick for a point-after-touchdown, it was he who had been appointed to descend into Possum Hollow and retrieve the football. I watched him now, after Marcus' touchdown. He climbed slowly through the hole in the hedge and disappeared down the incline into the darkness. There was an interval. Then, thirty seconds later, I saw the top of his head, then all of him, as he emerged triumphantly through the hedge again with the ball.

Watching this sedate drama, I nearly missed my most serious scare of the season. Marcus was hurt, and he was coming off the field holding one hand in the other.

Momentarily the loudspeaker said: "Will Dr. Ross Smith come to the Philadelphia sidelines?" Had the one thing I had truly feared all year come to pass? The doctor came down, and I observed him as he examined the hand. Then Marcus and the doctor walked toward the gymnasium. They got into the ambulance which always waited near there, and with blinking lights the vehicle sped out the driveway toward the hospital.

I had been watching most of the game with my young Philadelphia friend Jaybird,* the six-year-old son of Laura and Max Kilpatrick. I stood up to leave.

"Where you goin'?" Jaybird asked.

"To the hospital."

"I'll go with you."

Jaybird took my hand and we rushed out of the stadium toward The Love Van, which was parked near the Downtown Hotel. I had a spare set of keys, but The Love Van was hopelessly blocked by several cars.

"You think he's hurt bad?" the little boy asked.

"Let's pray he's not."

He began to bow his head right there on Myrtle Street, but I led him again back down the hill to the stadium. We waited there by the door to the gymnasium for a long time, watching from that distance as Louisville kicked a field goal on the last play of the first half to go ahead.

As the teams disappeared into the gym for the halftime break, I saw the ambulance turning into the driveway. When it stopped, Marcus got out.

* No relation to Faulkner's grand-nephew Jaybird in Oxford.

"Are you okay?" I asked.

"I'm okay," he said, pointing to his hand, which was heavily taped. "Took X rays." Then he walked away to the gym.

"Well, he's *okay!*" Jaybird Kilpatrick said. We lingered by the gymnasium, where others too had gathered.

The visiting band performed, and then the home band came onto the field, executing a flag-waving routine. Near the end of this, the Philly team filed through the doorway of the gym and waited in the end zone. When the crowd saw Number 22 among them, there was relieved applause. He stood to the side with his helmet off, moving the damaged hand, waiting with his teammates for the band to finish. Many eyes in that moment were on him.

> *These vagabond shoes,*
> *Are longing to stray,*
> *And step around the heart of it*
> *New York, New York . . .*

In the third quarter he carried nine times for forty-five yards, including a niggardly one-yard gain when five tacklers cracked him at the line of scrimmage. The visitors scored on the first play of the final quarter and led, 15–7. Shortly after that, the Tornadoes were on the Louisville thirty-eight-yard line. Justy Johnson pitched out to him. Running sideways he threw a spiral pass to Terry Hoskins, who caught it near the goal line and ran in for the touchdown. A pass by Justy for the two-point conversion failed and Louisville led, 15–13.

Philly got the ball back late in the game near their forty. Marcus ran for 13, 12, 6, 8, 10. But a defender broke through and hit his arm on a pitchout, resulting in a fumble recovery with one minute to play. Louisville won, 15–13, evening the Philly record at 4–4. Marcus carried twenty-seven times for 174 yards, one touchdown running and one passing. He was thirteen away from Herschel with three games to go.

As The Love Van rattled up Highway 9 in the October night, I sat down in one of the captain's chairs. Pete lay at my side. I leaned back and watched the lights of the little Mississippi towns go past. I fell into a driftless reverie.

# 16
# *Possum in the Hollow*

*Louisville was our best game so far. We should have beaten them. We were on their 10 late in the game, and I was supposed to sweep left. Somebody missed a block, and one of their players caught my arm just as soon as the ball got there. Knocked it loose and they recovered.*

*Their linebacker (highly regarded Keith Jordan), he's fair. I didn't think he was that good. He's big, but not that physically tough. Once in a while he'd get in a cheap shot. Long as you stick him, he's not that tough.*

*I've got a little abuse about the Bulldog Blitz stickers on my car. I got two of them. I stuck them there. Plan to go see Alabama and Mississippi State game this weekend. Watched Jackson State and Grambling last weekend. I'm a little interested in Jackson, but not much.*

*Not much new recruiting-wise. I'm not interested in USC, but they keep calling. Also heard from Southern, Mississippi State, Oklahoma, Ohio State, Michigan, UCLA and Tennessee.*

*Plan to visit Texas and UCLA. Not sure about the rest.*

Long before Marcus came into this vale of sadness, I was no stranger to sports. I was never addicted to the horses like, say, Jack Whitaker or Gloria Jones or Danny Lavezzo of P. J. Clarke's, or to boxing like Norman Mailer or Budd Schulberg or Wilfred Sheed, and until the American ice-hockey team whipped the Soviets I was frigid to that unruly exercise. Even tennis left me largely unmoved, possibly because we had no place to play it in Yazoo in those days. Arthur Ashe and I once gave a joint speech to the law students at the University of Virginia; I asked Ashe why he, a Virginian, went to Southern Cal rather than UVA, and he replied: "Because when I was growing up they didn't let me use the courts." In my Hemingway years as a student in Europe I nurtured a haunted obsession with the bulls (I once almost got into a fight at the ring in Madrid, when a righteous Scotsman demanded to know why I was yelling for the toreador), which lasted until I saw three or four atrocious *corridas* along the Texas-Mexico border. The University of Texas was a magnificent place for track and field, which appealed to me greatly in college. But, since I was, like Marcus, a small-town Southern boy, my three favorite sports were football, basketball, and baseball; and these, of course, were the ones I played. They have remained with me into adulthood—so that my experiences with the Philadelphia High Tornadoes in the 1981 season were a vivid conjuring of my own past for me.

The most precious consort of the writer, and the most elusive, is memory. Where does memory begin? How does old time itself shape it, render it, distill it, fuse the moments of childhood, so delicate and ethereal, into the hard retrospect of one's middle years? Memory is surely the most unfathomable of the human gifts.

I was afforded a forthright reminder of these mysteries when John Logue of *Southern Living* asked me to write, in that autumn I was with the Tornadoes, a reminiscence of the first college football game I ever saw.

The first college football game I ever saw . . . on the long drive to Philly one day, it came back to me in disconnected images—of the first real journey I ever made; of an immense stadium; of my father at the wheel of a big green DeSoto. Most of all, curiously, it was the *rain* which had recurred to me over the years, and the abiding moment my father wrapped me in his raincoat so I could watch the enigmatic proceedings far below while he withdrew for shelter.

First, then, the rain, and the drenched overcoat, and the black umbrellas all around me. And I was in the second grade there in Yazoo City, because I brought back a game program to my teacher, Mrs. Lois Page. That would have been 1941. And one of the teams was the Ole Miss Rebels, for I remembered that also, and Junie Hovious and Merle Hapes, the names *Hovious* and *Hapes* having inexplicably survived adolescence, young manhood, many loves and deaths, a few adulteries, several recessions, and three or four wars. And Memphis, that was the place, not easily forgotten when you were seven years old, good old Memphis, for I recalled too with remarkable clarity the enthralling bustle of it, its enormous buildings, its throngs of people, its clanging trolleys, the River from its bluffs. It was bigger than Yazoo and Philly put together.

With these imperishable clues, what game was it? I wracked my head from Eupora to Noxapater. On a yellowing schedule of the 1941 Ole Miss football season, I found three Saturday afternoon Ole Miss games in Memphis that year. I went to the Ole Miss library, giving these three dates to the pretty co-ed who worked in the microfilm collection, asking her to locate these issues of *The Memphis Commercial Appeal*. Just a moment, I said in afterthought—what I needed was the *next* day's issues, which would have the Sunday football coverage. In a large filing cabinet she found the right containers. She inserted one of the rolls into a microfilm machine. The first date was November 23, 1941. The reproductions of aging newsprint flickered before us on the screen.

There, suddenly, at the top of the very first page for November 23, an image leaped out at me. It was an eight-column photograph, the old-fashioned kind with a wide view of the football field and all the players in miniature with name tags under each figure. Superimposed on the photograph was a large headline:

## OLE MISS 18, ARKANSAS 0

"Hold it there, miss," I said. I examined the picture more closely. "Is that mud?"

The girl too peered down. "It looks like mud to me."

"That's it, by God!" I exclaimed. "We got it on the first try. I'm there, somewhere up in those umbrellas." She looked up at me. I suspect she thought me somewhat deranged.

Why is it that the pages of old newspapers always make me sad? Is it their reminder of how transient all things are, of life ever so poignantly slipping by—of death itself? At home I studied the printouts of those pages. "Ole Miss Submerges Arkansas in Rain-Soaked Game" . . . "Sinkwich Runs Wild in Georgia Success" . . . "Vanderbilt 7, Alabama 0. Tennessee 20, Kentucky 7. Florida 14, Georgia Tech 7. Auburn 13, Villanova 0. Notre Dame 20, Southern Cal 18. Oklahoma 61, Marquette 14" . . . "Germans Launch Greatest Drive of War Against Moscow" . . . "How Near Are We to War?"

These pages of the faithful *Commercial Appeal* opened the floodgates of remembrance for me, inundating me with those distant moments of my past. It was an eerie, nearly mystical feeling, as if some immemorial obstacle had abruptly dissolved and memories flowed out in waves, evoking for me in a rush the sights and sounds and smells of that childhood day of forty-one years ago.

It was, indeed, the first genuine journey of my life. My father had promised me for weeks. I was lying in my front yard one night that fall, in the grass wet with dew, my head resting on a football as I looked up at the sky, when my father came out of the house and said, simply: "I'm going to take you to Memphis to see Ole Miss play."

My mother led me down to Ingram's Shoe Store on Main Street to buy me some new shoes. The day came to leave. I must have been enraptured by the spirit of the adventure, for I vividly recall retreating to the kennel in the backyard to pay a lengthy, ritualistic goodbye to our three hunting dogs, the affectionate companions of my early childhood. My father had been waiting in the car. Just before I got in, I asked if Tony, Sam, and Jimbo could go with us. His words now reverberate down the concourse of time. "They'd get lost in Memphis," he said.

Faint physical presences, wisps of perception, returned to me in my reminiscing journey to Philly about this long drive north—stretches of gravel roads in the Delta, black crosses ever so often on the shoulders of the main highways which my father explained were where people had been killed in car accidents, the Negroes waving at us from the yards and porches of their unpainted shacks, the sea of dead cotton stalks under a dark and expansive sky, the unrelieved flatness of the black earth, my father peering through the windshield at the unhurried rain.

When we reached our destination we checked into the Chisca Hotel, because that is where we would always stay in Memphis, a rather weary and forlorn establishment off Union with pinball machines and cuspidors in the lobby; only later would I comprehend, of course, that we stayed in the Chisca because it was inexpensive. The big hotel room on one of the top floors was a wonderful revelation. It had the first bathroom shower I ever saw, and a view of the River all dusky in the rain, and of the bustling streets below. I absorbed Memphis in a trance. Is the world really this big? Do the lights stay on all night everywhere but in Yazoo? It must have been that first afternoon that my father took me by the hand and we walked up the broad boulevard with the trolleys moving back and forth to the Peabody Hotel. The grand lobby greeted me—ducks parading to a fountain, majestic chandeliers, people drinking at tables encircled by large potted plants or waving flags and pennants with OLE MISS on them as they shouted and embraced and staggered madly about—and hovering over all this an aura of mystery and glitter that both frightened and titillated me.

The rain had stopped for a while the next morning; the traffic to Crump Stadium was heavy. The view of the stadium itself, once we had walked up a ramp inside, took my breath away—the immense field pooled with water; the row upon row of seats ascending, it seemed, to the murky heavens; the thousands of spectators with their umbrellas; the players of one team running about and exercising in all postures. A band was playing a song I later learned to know as "Dixie." Players from the other team raced onto the field and removed their red jackets to disclose unsoiled white jerseys and white pants. "That's Arkansas," my father said, although I must not have comprehended precisely what *Arkansas* was.*

I could only reconstruct that long-ago contest as a sequence of

* I still don't.

dreams—long, towering kicks into the misty gray sky; strange men in striped shirts who blew whistles and little boys who dried off the footballs with towels; the players covered from head to foot with mud, constantly slipping and falling or dropping the slippery ball, clawing and fighting one another in that ocean of mire until they seemed grim phantoms struggling for their very lives.

The *Commercial Appeal* provided me now with the names of those haphazard heroes. For Arkansas they were Pitts and Bynum and Sutton, Cato and Clark and Coats, Ramsay and Adams and Scarborough, Tibbitts and Delmonego and Forte. For Ole Miss they were Davidson and Kozel and Hazel, Wood and Britt and Flack, Thorsey and Bennett and Sam, Poole and Hovious and Hapes. The gallant Hovious and Hapes! Why do they remain with me to this day? I remember their dancing about in the mud, treacherous gallops for most of the length of the field, the crowd rising and cheering as they ran, so that Marcus' long runs for touchdowns forty years later would summon Hovious and Hapes for me.

Then, indelible as yesterday, the rain began again, descending in torrents. I felt gentle hands on my shoulders. My father was draping me in his raincoat, telling me to watch the game and not to go anywhere while he went down to a dry place.

Suddenly I was by myself in that prodigious stadium, surrounded by the exceptional sights and the unfamiliar people. A most unlikely figure I must have been there, a seven-year-old from the Mississippi Delta all alone in a soggy raincoat, the first time I had been so alone and so far from home. What could I have been thinking in that faraway moment? That the world is passingly strange? That it must be observed and remembered? That there is sadness in exuberance? Or was I merely frightened again, as I had been in the lobby of the Peabody? Recognition failed me anew on such august scrutinies. I only recall the cluster of girls in white boots and raincaps sitting down the way, the boisterous strangers next to me passing a bottle among themselves and drinking from it in long gulps, the sounds of the band and the yells of "Hotty, Toddy!", the laughter when one of the men in striped shirts was run over by a player and skidded for yards in the mud, the jubilant chant of *Hovious, Hovious!* when the little silhouette abruptly moved and darted through the other phantoms trying to wrestle him to the earth—and, all about me as I gazed behind me to see if I could find my father, the eternal Southern rain.

Not too long ago I sought out Junie Hovious, who was retired now from coaching football at Ole Miss. "It's funny. I don't remember a thing about that game. Maybe I'm just gettin' old. Or maybe I only remember the close ones."

Billy Sam, the Rebel right halfback, was killed on the beaches of Saipan, Hovious remembered. Larry Hazel, the left tackle, perished when his parachute failed to open in flight training in Pensacola. He stays in touch with a few of the others from that day. "Some have been in real bad health," he said. "Some have retired. Some I haven't heard head or tails of. Some I'm not sure are alive or dead."

One thing I had not forgotten of the morning after the game when my father and I were about to leave. Nothing would deny me my vibrant memory of actually *thanking* our hotel room for showing me such a good time, of saying farewell to it and telling it I would return to it someday.

Two weeks later to the day was December 7, 1941. When the news came and was explained to me, I went to the kennel in the backyard. Sitting among Tony, Sam, and Jimbo as they gave me moist licks on the face, I began to cry, tears surely as torrential as the Memphis rain; the Japs were coming to Mississippi.


Pete Dawkins, among others, was essential to my memory of sports. He would later be a young general, but in 1959 he was the Heisman Trophy winner as a running back from West Point, as well as the honor graduate and Commandant of the Corps among the Black Knights of the Hudson. When he came to Oxford, England, as a Rhodes Scholar in the autumn of '59, we became friends, for I was the *Time-Life* stringer there in my last year, and the Luce people only desired information about Pete from England then for those publications. In the bland Eisenhower years Dawkins was an American hero. He made the Oxford rugby team after a month, an impossible phenomenon in England, much like an English rugby player making starting fullback for Ohio State. Pete was big and fast, though not physically overpowering as Marcus Dupree was two decades later. I was there for his very first rugby match, the Oxford "B Team," before he reached the varsity and played before eighty thousand people at Twickenham. Rugby was a game of finesse and lateral passes. When Pete, playing for the "B Team" of the Oxford Dark Blues in the stadium where Roger Bannister had broken the first four-minute mile only six years before, exercised his American halfback's instincts to run over the smaller English defenders for a goal rather than pass off easily to the "wing," the British spectators shouted, "*Shame, Dawkins, shame!*" Dawkins later became a British legend by learning these fine points of rugby, but I doubt if Marcus Dupree would have. Marcus would have kept running over them.

In New York City later, during my years there, the confluence of sports and the other eclectic worlds of Manhattan was the purview of George Plimpton. His perpetual *salon* in his apartment overlooking the East River softened the sharpness of the acerbic intellectual life of our

cultural capital in the 1960s. There the literary, political, theatrical, journalistic, and Wall Street environments mingled easily with the athletes
and the big-time athletic entrepreneurs. Plimpton, whose great-grandfather
Ames had been the Radical Republican Governor of Mississippi during
Reconstruction against whom my own great-grandfather Senator Harper
had brought impeachment papers, was offering a *modus vivendi*. So too
was Toots Shor on West Fifty-third, where I gathered with Dan Jenkins,
Bud Shrake, Pete Axthelm, and the *Sports Illustrated* and New York
*Times* crowd, and Howard Cosell before he got famous, on many an
afternoon for the incomparable sports talk.

In my memories of Manhattan days, long before I settled into
Neshoba County, Mississippi, Bill Bradley and the Knicks were important. Bradley, I sensed even then, might be President of the United States
someday. My son David and I went to see him often in the Garden in the
years the Knickerbockers were the finest *team*-playing squad in the history of basketball. A day came that I resigned from my magazine. By
chance that noon—it was March of '71, as I recall—I was lunching with
my friend and erstwhile competitor Mr. Manning, the editor-in-chief of
*The Atlantic Monthly*, for in our lengthy *mano a mano* we had gotten together often to compare stories and complain of ownership and feel each
other out, like old coaches long around the league. He consoled me in my
melancholy. I apologized that lunch would have to be brief, since Bill
Bradley of the New York Knicks had invited my ten-year-old son to work
out with the team in Madison Square Garden at one-thirty and I had to
meet him there. "God, I'd love to go with you," my rival said. "I've got
an appointment with Dean Rusk at the Century."

Later, in the vast deserted arena, I idled on a front row and watched
my son David shoot free throws with Frazier, Reed, and DeBusschere. I
had just left everything I ever wanted, I was thinking self-pityingly, and I
was filled now with a terrible sorrow and with the most tender waves of
memory. As the bouncing basketballs resounded to the arched roof high
above, and David weaved a fast break with Russell and Barnett, I thought
of my own father, on gray winter Mississippi afternoons years ago, just before his death, stopping on the way home from work to watch our team
practice in our cramped little gymnasium. Immersed in this, alone in my
conjurings in that empty palace, I barely heard the solitary footsteps coming my way. Suddenly the editor-in-chief of *The Atlantic Monthly* stood
before me. "I cut Dean Rusk short," he said. "Say, which one's Bradley?"

Elaine's Restaurant on Second Avenue likewise performed a role. I
was there at a front table one night in the 1960s with the Texans Bud
Shrake and Dan Jenkins of *Sports Illustrated*, along with two or three
Delta Airlines stewardesses and Don Meredith of the Dallas Cowboys.

Shrake and Jenkins had once told me Meredith was the brightest athlete they had ever known.

We were sitting before an impeccable white tablecloth. Shrake and Jenkins had just written on it in a heavy pen a couple of paragraphs from their works-in-progress. I told Meredith I was going to pose a question to him.

"Go ahead," he said.

I wrote on the cloth: "Having been a quarterback from Texas since age 9, what has this taught you about being a human?"

Meredith thought for a long moment, then wrote on the tablecloth:

"1. *All leaders are lonely.*
2. *There is an unexpected pleasure in continuing failure.*"

"My God," I said, "have you been reading Hemingway?"

"Shrake and Jenkins got me to read everything the man wrote," Meredith said.

In New York City there were many other memories—of my friends Jack Whitaker and Lindsey Nelson sharing their stories of war in Europe, of the spring trainings in Florida, of old forgotten football games. Of Michael Burke recalling the golden afternoons of '39 when he ran the ball for the University of Pennsylvania as an all-American. Of Irwin Shaw bargaining with the wine steward of the Sherry-Netherland for vintage cellar wine, as he and Michael Burke and I and some sophisticated ladies lunched on a matchless October noon, watching the Sunday Manhattan crowds drift past our window in the sunshine, before we journeyed to the Yankee Stadium for a box behind the home dugout at a World Series game.

I sometimes reminded myself, in Philadelphia, Mississippi, that I had not been a stranger to sports.

Marcus, of course, was a pretty good high school baseball player too, and with the same work he devoted to football might have been a distinguished first baseman. But the great Southern black athletes of our day gravitated to football and basketball. Watching the Ole Miss baseball team under its coach Jake Gibbs, who had been a catcher with the New York Yankees, one rarely saw a black player in the Southeastern Conference.

The game itself had changed. "When I started," a retired umpire named Ron Luciano lamented in *The Umpire Strikes Out*, "baseball was played by nine tough competitors on grass in graceful ballparks. By the time I finished, there were ten men on a side, the game was played indoors on plastic, and I spent half my time watching out for a man dressed in a chicken suit who kept trying to kiss me."

This was the television influence, of course. Yet more than anything to me, baseball was a game enmeshed in growing up: those boyhood summers, starting the mornings with a buddy, throwing the ball back and forth and lazily talking about the girls and games, the whole ritual as natural and familiar as the morning itself.

This, however, is a book about football, and it is to football that we now return, and to Marcus' quest for Herschel's touchdown mark.

The Tornadoes, in their next-to-last regular-season game of the year, were traveling to Ackerman, the seat of Choctaw County. This time I journeyed down with David Sansing, the Ole Miss historian who was just launching his biography of the irascible Theodore G. Bilbo, and Larry Wells, the owner of the Yoknapatawpha Press.

We had arranged to arrive in Ackerman late that Friday afternoon to visit with J. P. Coleman, the well-known Mississippian and federal district judge appointed by Lyndon Johnson. Coleman had been governor of Mississippi in the late 1950s and was noted for his moderate position on the issue of race, in contrast with his successor, Ross Barnett. He was also a writer and a student of history. He was a tall, graying, well-spoken man of leonine aspect, and the four of us sat in his offices with the autographed pictures of presidents on the walls and discussed the history of our state and of Choctaw County. His forebears had come here in the 1830s. His great-grandfather had been a large landowner; the property was still in the family. He wanted to show us the family land.

In the fading light in front of his office, the judge reached in his pocket for something.

"Judge," David Sansing said, "you've got my favorite brand."

"Well, have a chew, Professor."

As they shared the Levi Garrett, we drove around the county, the judge lecturing us on the history of the little hamlets, the routes of the old railroads, and Colonel Grierson's march through this neighborhood in 1863. We looped back toward his house in town. "I'd like to show you literary gentlemen my library," the judge said. He proudly led us inside to an impressive collection of history, including the only complete set of *The Official Records of the War of the Rebellion*, all 350 volumes, that I had ever seen in a private dwelling. Where might he have gotten them? From the estate sale of the heirs of a gentleman in Jackson who, as state treasurer in 1883, had absconded to Chicago with eighty thousand dollars in Mississippi gold. I had walked by his house every summer twilight to the Jackson Senators baseball games during my childhood visits to Jackson. "You know who lived there a long time ago?" my grandmother Mamie always asked me. "The man who *stole the money from the State*." Here was a piece of him now in J. P. Coleman's library. In Mississippi, as I have suggested, everything leads to everything else.

All roads that night led to the little football stadium in Ackerman. Although the Ackerman Indians and the Philly Tornadoes were both only 4–4 on the season, another large crowd was gathering; in the parking lot there were dozens of license plates from other counties—people having come to see Marcus. Behind one end zone there was a line of young magnolias, and the uprights on the goalpost were rusty.

It was a brisk, clear night, windless, under a Halloween Eve's quarter-moon. As the teams went through their pregame drills, there was loud, rhythmic clapping among the Philadelphia visitors in the bleachers. The Ackerman band broke into a march tune. "The brass section is flat tonight," Professor Sansing said; then, absorbing the Friday-night high school pageantry which had become habit to me, he added: "This may be the last athletic purity in America."

"A lot of these girls are still wearing the Farrah Fawcett look three years too late," publisher Larry Wells said.

The man on the public-address system was evangelistic. "We want to welcome our friends and neighbors from down Neshoba way," he said. "Tomorrow night there will be a haunted house sponsored by the band boosters at 305 East Cherry." During the game he actually gave a play-by-play, possibly because the scoreboard broke down even before the game started. With each penalty he would say: "We are awaiting the *preliminary indication*." He had gotten this from television.

The crowd at the little field was one of the most integrated I had seen all year. This was not lost on the historian Sansing. "If we had only known how easy it was going to be," he observed, "how easily we'd be able to forget how it used to be, we wouldn't have had to go through all that damned travail."

I knew what he meant, I said.

"I tried to tell 'em, and a lot of others did too. They wouldn't believe us. I guess we just had to go through it. We couldn't say, 'Okay, we'll change.' We just couldn't do it that easy."

Marcus was splendid on this night. As my companions, who had never seen him, marveled at his moves, now so familiar to me, he started the first quarter with runs of six, twelve, and ten yards and then raced twenty-six to the Ackerman five-yard line. On the next play he went through the middle for a touchdown. He continued to accumulate yardage in the second quarter, and also caught a twenty-eight-yard pass. With less than a minute left in the half, he scored from the two-yard line on another Herschel Walker dive high in the air over the defensive line.

On the first offensive play of the second period, he broke for thirty-two yards—then ten, five, and ten again, capping this drive with a five-yard power plunge for another touchdown. From the bleachers we could hear the bone-crushing thuds when he ran over the defenders. He made his final touchdown on a twenty-five-yard run in the fourth quarter, then sat out the rest of the game. Philly won, 28–7.

His statistics were 201 yards on twenty-one carries, two lengthy pass receptions, and four touchdowns, the last being the seventy-seventh of his career. He needed nine touchdowns to tie, and ten to break, Herschel Walker's record. On the following Friday, Philly would play its county rival, Neshoba Central, in the last regular game of the year. A victory in that one would get them a bid to one of the high school bowl games. This eventually happened; he would have two games, then, to try to score ten touchdowns.

\* \* \* \*

*I ran pretty good Friday night . . . Ackerman. I have a sore back from two weeks ago and it was still bothering me. I'm liking the "I." I'm doing better out of it.*

*Some of the Neshoba players or fans tied up a possum on our fence. We call them goats and hogs and they call us possums. Doesn't really bother me. Just keys me up to play.*

*I want to play well, and leave some memories.*

*Went to the Alabama-State game last weekend. Pretty good game. I was kind of pulling for State. Mostly I was just looking. Went to the Alabama dressing room. Didn't meet the Bear, just a couple of players. Still like both of them a good bit.*

*I realize the pressure is liable to get worse. But I'm ready to handle it.*

During the week Philly accepted an invitation to play in the Choctaw Bowl, in the stadium on the Indian reservation in Neshoba County.

On the Saturday after the Louisville game, Jackson State was playing Grambling in Jackson. About four hours before the kickoff, Marcus' mother telephoned Jimmy Lee Shannon, the black alderman, and asked if he would drive Marcus, Mark Burnside, Daran Jackson, and Rod Sutton to the game. W. C. Gordon, the Jackson State coach, had been at the Louisville game, and Shannon had overheard this conversation: "I hated to see you lose the game last night," Gordon had said to Marcus and his teammates in Jackson. "I'd like to offer all of you scholarships for next year. Just come with me."

Friday night against Neshoba Central would be Marcus' last appearance on his home field, and the team would be caught in the drama of that farewell. Billy Watkins of *The Meridian Star*, who had followed his career, expressed his thoughts on the eve of the game:

> PHILADELPHIA—This is where it all began, right here on the field underneath the hill in downtown Philadelphia.
>
> This is where Marcus Dupree ran for a million yards as a junior high player. Where he started making headlines as a freshman wide receiver and kick returner.
>
> And this is where for the last three seasons, Marcus Dupree has shown the world he just may be the best high school running back in the nation, gaining more than 5,000 yards, scoring 77 touchdowns and making every college recruiter's heart do handstands. . . .
>
> It's been a testing time for Marcus this season. Consider the evidence: his entire offensive line had to be rebuilt with young players this season and, of course, every opponent would key eleven people, a water boy, and one German shepherd dog on Marcus each and every time he went on the field.

The rivalry between Philadelphia High and Neshoba Central was malevolent. The tough country boys of Central attended school in a sprawling building at the edge of town. The Philly High people called this "Goat Hall" because it had been built in an old goat field, and the Central partisans called Philly High "Possum Hollow" after the vicinity behind the football stadium.

Although their team was only 1–7–1 for the season, the Central fans had been needling Marcus all week. When he arrived at school one morning he found the dead possum tied to a fence with the number 22 attached to it. They had also been saying things. "Stuff about I won't ever be able to play football again after this game," Marcus said. "It's fired me up. I was ready to play this one last week."

I drove down to this one in the dappled sunlight and deepening shadows of the Mississippi November. Cotton bolls still bordered the highway. Secondhand clothes were for sale in a front yard in Pittsboro, and in the empty square in Calhoun City several little black girls with pigtails were playing hopscotch.

My companion on this trip was Ron Borne, a lanky fellow of serene disposition who taught medicinal chemistry at Ole Miss, a native of New Orleans, the most devoted sports fan I had ever met, as well as one of the beloved professors of the university, one of its dedicated teachers. His interest in sports was a diversion from teaching and research, albeit a most intriguing one. He claimed to have read Doubleday's mammoth *Encyclopedia of Baseball* from cover to cover four times. He could name the Four Horsemen of Notre Dame and the midget who once came to the plate for the St. Louis Browns. He had never seen Marcus play, and as with the other distinctive figures who had accompanied me to Philly that autumn, I was curious to have his judgments.

Ron Borne lightened the long, familiar miles on this day with an accomplished monologue on a little-heeded topic: the names of football players. He had even brought along a few notes relating to this arcane study.

"Now take *Marcus Dupree*," Professor Borne said. "Doesn't that *sound* like a running back? With a name like that he couldn't be an offensive tackle."

He continued at length. "My interest in this began a long time ago," he said. "I'd try to associate a ballplayer's name with the position he played, you see. For instance, you'd never have expected Bronco Nagurski to have been a wide receiver, or Lance Alworth a linebacker."

"I see your logic there," I said.

"Look, some guys were born to be linebackers—Dick *Butkus*, Sam *Huff*, Larry *Savage*, Brian *Ruff*, Jeff *Skocko*. Some of 'em tried to play linebacker but never made it big: Sylvester Boler, Tony Sweet. Some surprise you in spite of their names. I'd never have predicted Bob Lilly to be very mean. One of my favorites was a fellow named Mel *Rideout*, who played for the Richmond Spiders in the late fifties. You knew he was a halfback. I used to collect phrases from *Street and Smith*. Things like 'Army's solid plunger, Larry Klawinski,' and 'Ken Wypysznski was switched from end to center in the spring and looked outstanding.' I wasn't at all astonished. I'd have had Wypysznski at center to begin with. I also like to try to predict the winners of games based on the names of the players. For instance, you know that a team quarterbacked by Roch Hontas would whip one quarterbacked by June Jones. I mean, can you imagine a huddle in a crucial moment and the players say, 'Come on, June, we need this one'?"

I had turned on my tape recorder back in Eupora. Borne went on: "How about a big tackle named *Ecomet Burley* for Texas Tech, or a running back named *Elphage Callioutte* for Tulane, who later died in some kind of hunting accident. Or a quarterback for McNeese named *Oliver Hadnot*. He never made it big either. Or real cute quarterbacks like *Kingsley Fink* of Army, or *Darly Woodring* of Villanova? My favorite wide receiver was *Cephus Weatherspoon* of Colorado State."

As we crossed the Natchez Trace, my companion reached in his satchel. His eyes were feverish. "Will you just listen to *these*? They're contemporaries. *Matt Vanden Boom*, defensive back, Wisconsin. *Boomer*

*Esiason*, southpaw passer, Maryland. *Vinnie Mini*, defensive tackle, Temple. *Jitter Fields*, defensive back, Texas. *Amero Ware*, halfback, Drake. *Falaniko Noga*, nose guard, Hawaii. *Prince McJunkins*, quarterback, Wichita State. Come on, Prince! But Texas Tech wins the prize this year. *Pat Hrncir*, offensive tackle. *Hasson Arbubakrr* and *Willie Reyneveld*, defensive tackles. *Kerry Tecklenburg*, linebacker. *Greg Womble*, safety. Hell, that's just a beginning."

Professor Borne paused now to rest. The weight of this disquisition may have depleted him. We drove silently for a time through the piny woods.

"I've always liked some of the names of the college *teams*," he continued after an interval. "The *Blue Hens* of Delaware. The *Salukis* of Southern Illinois. The *Gobblers* of Virginia Tech. The *Owls* of Rice. The *Gamecocks* of South Carolina."

"I always wondered what they called the *women's* teams at South Carolina," I said irreverently.

"The *Razorbacks* of Arkansas," my companion went on, undeterred. "The *Horned Frogs* of Texas Christian. The *Lobos* of New Mexico. The *Thundering Herd* of Marshall. The *Black Bears* of Maine. The *Bullets* of Gettysburg. The *Palladins* of Furman. The *Terrapins* of Maryland. There's a lot in that."

"Do you have an all-time favorite name of a player?" I asked, for this was my most boring stretch of road.

"Damn right I do. It has to be a running back for Fresno State in the early 1970s. He was also their punter. *Atomic Torosian*. Would Marcus Dupree want to be tackled by a guy named Atomic Torosian? I wouldn't.

"Now, I have a little true story I want to tell you. Back in about 1974, our chemistry department was involved in some meetings with faculty members from various universities in the Southeast. We chartered a Trailways bus from Memphis to Chapel Hill. We left at night and bought a lot of beer and got plenty of change for nickel-penny poker. By the time we got to Athens to pick up the Georgia guys, the group was pretty loose. We got started on sports trivia and, as you might suspect, the questions got more and more specific. After a while, I decided to ask a question that would stump everybody on the bus. 'Who did *Atomic Torosian* play for?' I asked. From the back of the bus somebody shouted, '*Fresno State!*' I was shocked. I turned around and looked. The fellow was a professor at Tennessee who'd never once expressed an interest in sports. I asked him how in the hell did he know the answer to that one. He said, 'I knew Atomic Torosian.' That Tennessee professor had a pretty good name too—Armen Millikian. He said he'd once met Atomic at an event in California called the Armenian Olympics—Atomic apparently broke all the Armenian records in the 100 and 220 dashes."

Professor Borne was silent again. We had just entered Neshoba County. "Say," he turned and asked me, "does Marcus Dupree have a nickname?"

By his own count, Marcus in the previous week had been averaging eight long-distance telephone calls a night from college coaches. Before the ball game Ron Borne and I dropped by the Downtown Hotel to confer with Roy Tingle behind the check-in counter.

Roy whispered to me. "The Texas Longhorn coach is in town. He got in last night. Gene Tolbert Chevy sent a car over to the Jackson airport to get him."

It was a chilly evening at Harpole Stadium. Again the crowd was at capacity long before the kickoff. It was obvious that this was the place to be on this night. The signs on the fences said: EAT GOAT MEAT and BURY THE POSSUMS.

The word was out that both the Texas and Southern Mississippi recruiters would watch the game. I went down to the end zone next to the gymnasium, where a sizable crowd had as usual gathered, to look for them. A hefty man wearing a knit sweater with a word embroidered on the pocket stood near the gymnasium door. Wishing to remain inconspicuous, I asked the resourceful Professor Borne to walk up close to him and read the word on his pocket to see what college he was from. Borne returned. "Weyerhaeuser," he said.

The Neshoba Central Rockets, about twenty-five white and twenty-five black boys, came onto the field, followed by Philadelphia. Each of the seventeen seniors on the Philly team was introduced on the loudspeaker and ran onto the gridiron individually. With the introduction of Number 22, there was a chorus of boos from the visiting bleachers and a standing ovation from the home side.

It had to be one of his finest games of an illustrious career. The blocking of his young offensive line, which had had such problems through much of the season, was more effective than it had ever been, and Marcus himself seemed confident and assured in his fifth game running from Joe Wood's "I," a formation which appeared to have been designed for him alone. As the game progressed, the taunts of the many Neshoba Central fans served apparently to encourage him.

On the first play from scrimmage he powered through the middle for nine yards, and as he lay on the ground two enemy defenders piled on. This drew a fifteen-yard penalty, and there were shouts of wrath from the Philly grandstand. The Tornadoes moved downfield. From the Central nineteen-yard line he ran over two tacklers and scored his first touchdown.

Shortly after this, he scored again on a beautiful twenty-yard sweep, but the play was nullified for holding. Early in the second quarter, from his own fifteen, he took a pitch, broke a tackle at the line of scrimmage, decked a linebacker, reversed his field, dodged three tacklers in the secondary, and outran the safety man in a burst of speed for an eighty-five-yard touchdown.

The crowd was seized now with that palpable electricity which I had felt before, several times that season, when his artistry was flourishing. Even the enemy partisans seemed to acknowledge they were in the presence of one of the great athletes of America. He picked up 5 yards, then 11, 15, 12, 10. On one play two defenders who had tried to stop him were helped off the field. Late in the second quarter, from the Central three-yard line, he took the ball, ran slowly to the right, suddenly increased his speed, leaped high into the air as his demigod and competitor, Herschel, had taught him against Ole Miss, and landed in the end zone for his third touchdown of the night. Philly led 26–0 at the end of the first half. Marcus has carried twelve times for 181 yards.

Just as with the little black boy who retrieved the extra-point kicks down in Possum Hollow, my attention on this night had been drawn to an unlikely apparition on the Philly sidelines—an actual Tornado mascot, brought out especially for the cross-country rivalry. It was a youngster completely encased in a sort of alabaster which was meant to be a tornado cloud funnel, but which in truth did not resemble much of anything. All you could see were his feet as he swirled and twisted in celebrative moments after Marcus' long touchdowns. I walked down to the sidelines and approached this unlikely figure. There were two holes in the alabaster for his eyes. I peered down through the top and saw the head of a small black boy.

"Is it hard work being a tornado?" I asked.

"Suh?"

"Is it hard work?"

"Well, it's hot down in here," he said.

"What did they tell you to do?"

"They said move around fast—circle around the way *Du*-pree do." And he proceeded to perform for me his brief dervish.

I strolled around the top of the grandstand during "New York, New York." "Are you a coach?" asked a man of about sixty in a navy blue sports jacket and whiskey on his breath.

"No," I replied, "just a writer."

"Writin' about Dupree, I guess. We call him 'Super-Nigger' but we love him. You're not gonna write about what happened in '64, are you?" I pled ignorance on the events of that year.

"Listen, that wasn't the majority. I don't think you should write about that. Say, do you know Bear Bryant is in the press box?"

I excused myself and went to the tiny press box, knocking on the door. A man opened it. "Is Bear Bryant in here?" I asked.

There was loud laughter. Another man spoke into a radio microphone: "Some fellow wants to know if Bear Bryant is in here. Anybody seen the Bear?"

The strong Philly blocking held in the second half. Early in the third quarter, with the ball on the Neshoba Central thirty-eight-yard line, Marcus took a pitchout and moved slowly to his left. There were two blocks near the line of scrimmage, then he faked a defensive back and outran the others for the touchdown.

Late in the quarter he threw a fourteen-yard pass completion, and made gains of eleven and nine. On the next series Philly was in possession on its own twenty-seven. His last touchdown on the home field was imminent. He broke through the middle, twisted and turned like the tornado mascot, headed for the near sidelines, and turned on the speed. As he crossed the goal on this seventy-three-yard score, there was not a defender within twenty yards. The Philadelphia fans stood in prolonged applause as he came off the field.

Central finally scored in the fourth quarter to make it 39–6, which would be the final count. On the squib kickoff which followed, he took a long lateral and raced fifty-five yards to the Central twenty, where four defenders trapped him at the sidelines. He sat out the rest of the game on the table behind the bench. At the final whistle, as the players congregated in the middle of the field, the Neshoba Central Rockets gathered to shake his hand.

His statistics for the night were 322 yards on nineteen carries. In addition to one 55-yard kickoff return and a 20-yard score which was called back, he had five touchdowns on runs of 19, 85, 3, 38, and 73 yards. The last touchdown was the eighty-second of his career. In the Choctaw Bowl on the following Friday he would need four touchdowns to tie and five to break Herschel's total.

My football savant, Professor Borne, and I got in the car for the drive back to Oxford.

"He was like a Greek god tonight," Borne said. "I've never seen a high school player with that strength and speed. He reminded me a lot of Jim Brown, not so much from the way he ran but his mannerisms when he didn't have the ball. He seemed to drag around in an uninspired way. When he sat by himself when he was out of the game, he appeared very aloof. The only time he was impressive was when he had the ball. And that was enough for me."

On the radio the local station was paying a tribute to him. In honor of his last home game, they played the theme from the movie *Rocky*.

# 17
# *Choctaw Bowl*

---

*Had my best game yet. It was my last home game and I was really pumped up for it.*

*We play a bowl game this week and I'd like to get Herschel's record and another 300-yard game. This really means a lot to me, my final one in a Philadelphia uniform.*

*Didn't make any recruiting trips last weekend. Stayed home to practice basketball. We open in a couple of weeks. The only trips I know for sure are UCLA and Texas. Not sure of the others.*

The Tornadoes, now 6–4 on the 1981 season, would face the Yellow-jackets of Union, 5–4, in the Choctaw Bowl, the last game of the year. In the week before the bowl game there was considerable press coverage on Marcus' bid against Herschel.

"If Philadelphia's All-World running back is going to eclipse Herschel Walker's career touchdowns," Bill Spencer of *The Jackson Clarion-Ledger* reminded his readers, "he'd better do it Friday night." United Press International, noting his challenge to Herschel, praised his accomplishments in high school, but added: "Some coaches concede that Dupree is a talented back but point out that much of his yardage was gained against weak teams and for three years he ran behind a great line . . . The jury will remain out on Dupree until at least next fall."

The date of the Choctaw Bowl was November 13. A little more than two weeks later—December 1—the college coaches under NCAA rules could begin making their personal contacts, leading to the February 10 national signing date. Few of them would have predicted that on the afternoon of the Choctaw Bowl there would be a bombshell in Philly.


I went down on Friday morning. It was a bright, warm autumn day; all along the way the farmers were burning grass and weeds, and a smoggy haze filled the air. My confrere on this trip would be Will Norton, the young chairman of the journalism department at Ole Miss, a Midwestern

Yankee and a former Chicago *Tribune* man who had spent his early years in Africa. Just as Professor Ron Borne had eased the long drive the previous week with the names of ballplayers, Norton and I spoke of Mississippi. Would Marcus play his college football in this state? What kind of state was it anyway?

A few miles into Calhoun County I was telling Professor Norton of my friend Dean Faulkner Wells, who lived in Oxford, inheritor of much of her uncle's wit and compassion. She and her husband Larry had come to visit me on eastern Long Island a few years back. I had taken them to a wedding reception at the Montauk Yacht Club. In a summer's twilight on a lovely, placid inlet we milled about on a perfectly manicured lawn drinking Dom Perignon and listening to a society band play "Fascination." The other guests, Manhattan people with weekend houses in the Hamptons, mingled casually among themselves. Their laughter, the light strains of the music, the shimmering colors on the water formed a most splendid tableau. Dean Faulkner Wells surveyed this scene on that day, and the words she said touched me. "Everyone here seems so untroubled," she said. "Back home people are troubled."

I told Professor Norton, too, of a recent drive Dean and Larry and I had made into the Mississippi Delta. We were on our way to a black wedding in Clarksdale, and we were gazing out the windows of the car at the disorder of the Delta landscape—the weeds, the abandoned shacks, the hulks of old cars, the sights of impoverishment on the rich earth. Dean and Larry had just returned from driving to Illinois. "The contrast between Mississippi and Illinois reminded me of crossing the border from France into Germany," Dean said, "the same kind of transition from all this," she gestured out the window, "and the contained, orderly German farmland. Going up from the Delta into the Midwest was as if I had crossed an ocean, entered another country. Every time I come into the Delta, I understand why we started that war, and why we lost it."

We had gone on to the wedding in Clarksdale—a young black woman who had been an honor graduate of Ole Miss. Professor Norton, who had been her favorite teacher, had also been at this wedding, and we talked of it now—the small church in the black section, the windows adorned with magnolia leaves, the pink gladiolas and carnations, the black Ole Miss football players who were the groomsmen in their tuxedos, the white women crying while the black ones exulted, the reception afterward in the Magnolia Room at a junior college where the encircling cotton grew right up to the campus. Professor Norton and I remembered, too, the lines of "The Lord's Prayer" as sung by the black Ole Miss tight end: "And forgive us our debts, as we forgive our debtors."

We had just gone through Slate Springs, last outpost of Calhoun County, the smoky haze all around us. His parents, Will Norton told me, had been missionaries in what was then the Belgian Congo, and before his brothers were born he was the only white child on the mission station. Until he was three years old his parents could not bring him into a room of white people because he was so frightened of them; almost all the people he was familiar with were black. When the family returned to the United States, he seldom saw a black person.

"Here in Mississippi black and white people know each other," he said. "In Chicago black people were mostly strangers. You didn't speak to strangers." He found little feeling of community in Chicago, or in Palatine, the small town where he lived in his junior high and high school years. Whatever community existed there, or in Iowa where he attended graduate school, seldom extended beyond the town or county. "If something happens in Paris, Illinois, or Mount Vernon, or Ellingham, most people don't even know where they are in the state.

"Mississippi is different. When two people from different towns meet, one of the first things they ask each other is, 'Where you from?' And then, 'Do you know so-and-so?' People seem to know where the little towns are all over the state. They know what roads to take to get there, how far it is, the major families in town. And the Delta! It's two hundred miles long and fifty or sixty miles wide, but when you go to a party everyone else from the Delta seems to be there and they know each other. This is true of the white community and becoming more so among the blacks."

We discussed Philadelphia, Mississippi, in the 1960s. Norton told me he had known a man named Tommy Tarrants, the leader of the most violent terrorist group in the country in the late sixties, after he was released from Parchman Prison for his part in a plan to dynamite a Jewish businessman's house in Meridian. Tarrants had gotten religion while in prison. He had argued with Norton, who was doing an article on him, that racism had been strongly tied to conservative Protestantism, to an anti-Semitic belief that Jewish people were left-wing in their thinking. They believed that Jews were an integral part of the Marxist revolution and, because they were so visible in the civil rights movement of the 1960s, that they were trying to undermine America and bring about a revolution through equality for blacks.

"I was impressed by the brilliant minds at work in white Southern racism," Norton said as we sped toward Philadelphia that morning. "I was impressed by the skewed base they reasoned from so logically. I've realized how quickly those days could return. What if the economy gets worse and worse? Look at Germany and the Jews under Hitler. Who of us can dare to say we'd stand up and be counted in the backyard of the White Knights of the Ku Klux Klan of Mississippi?

"I look at the people of Philadelphia of the sixties and feel I have to be understanding. If I'd lived there in those days I might've cowered in the shadows too. Thank goodness we live in a society now where racial equality is praised and rewarded. It's to the credit of Southern people, I think."

We agreed on that in the vermilion hills of upper Neshoba.

I had arranged with Coach Joe Wood to ride to the game on the team bus. Earlier that afternoon I went to the high school to talk with Principal Danny Gregory.

That was where I learned that Marcus had just narrowed his choices to twelve colleges. Two weeks before the open recruiting season, this culling of the dozens of alternatives had taken people by surprise.

We sat in Gregory's office drinking coffee. Marcus had been complaining a few days before, Gregory said, that the telephone in his house was now ringing early in the mornings even before he left for school and that it kept ringing long into the night. Also, schools like Kansas, Kansas State, TCU, Oklahoma State, and others were beginning to telephone and send questionnaires. "I told Marcus he could do one of three things—get an unlisted number, keep the phone off the hook, or announce his college now."

That morning Marcus had given Gregory and Wood his final twelve:

> Alabama
> Georgia
> Jackson State
> LSU
> Michigan
> Mississippi State
> Ohio State
> Oklahoma
> Pittsburgh
> Southern Mississippi
> Texas
> UCLA

The most interesting omission was not Southern Cal, which the prospect had not mentioned in a long time, but Ole Miss, which had been recruiting him for three years. I asked Gregory about this. "I told Assistant Coach Tom Goode about it a little earlier," Gregory said, "and he said, 'Marcus will have to tell me face to face.'"

This would be the first of five lists which he would announce, each shorter than the one before. In early January he would disclose his final eight choices, on January 7 his final five—then four on February 7 and three just before the national signing date.

The deletion of Ole Miss at this early date was a grievous blow to that school's athletic pride, especially since its in-state rivals, Mississippi State and Southern Mississippi (not to mention Jackson State, a predominantly black school which competed in Division 1-AA) were still in the running. "If you want to understand the state of Mississippi," a State graduate said, "you must first understand the Ole Miss–State rivalry. Here, football is used politically. The politicians and lawyers who make the decisions that affect this state economically all went to Ole Miss." The Ole Miss series with Southern Mississippi had grown almost as intense, and in some ways more bitter, and the competition for Mississippi football players among the three schools had become savage. Steve Sloan, the Ole Miss coach, was one of the good men of the game, but he was now in his fifth year and had yet to enjoy a winning season. The alumni were restless. It had been ten years since Ole Miss had won more than six games in a season.

What was wrong? Some continued to blame Ole Miss's difficulty in recruiting the best black ballplayers on the traditional symbols, especially the Confederate flag. Sloan himself privately admitted this might be the case. Tommy Limbaugh, the recruiting coordinator, later reported that another school in the state sent as many as seven letters to each black football prospect saying he should not go to Ole Miss because of "racial prejudices" there.

Limbaugh did not identify the rival school, but it was common knowledge among the recruiters that it was the University of Southern Mississippi. However questionable these allegations, it was well-known that Southern was using racial politics against the state university, often to telling effect. Although Ole Miss had had a head start in recruiting him, Marcus later said Ole Miss "wasn't the type of school I was looking for. It just wasn't the environment that I was interested in." He told me simply, "My mother didn't like Ole Miss." I learned early that her boss at West Kemper, the school where she taught, was a strong Southern Mississippi man who was vehement to her about Ole Miss. Bernard Fernandez of The Jackson Daily News was a voice of rationality: "There are bigoted students at Ole Miss, both white and black, just as there are at State, Southern Mississippi, Jackson State, and also at such a supposedly enlightened institution as Harvard. Racial prejudice in America is a diminishing but unfortunate reality, and hardly confined to one college's campus. Black athletes, and students in general, are for the most part treated as evenhandedly at Ole Miss as they are at any other predominantly white institution in Mississippi. White supporters of other schools in the state who suggest otherwise ought to examine their own civil rights records before throwing rocks at someone else's glass house."

Whatever the reasoning, on the afternoon of the Choctaw Bowl, the Ole Miss Rebels were out of it, to the profound dismay of their partisans, although they kept trying.

"After most of the Indians moved to Oklahoma," Florence Mars said, "oil was struck out there. We had a joke that we should have taken the land in Oklahoma and let them keep Neshoba County."

I was looking forward to the Choctaw Bowl. I had read something of the Choctaw history, a tragic history in many ways, and the Choctaws I saw every day on the Square in Philadelphia never failed to intrigue me. Without them the streets of the town would have been bereft for me. I knew they spoke their own language, which Clayton Rand had described as "euphonious and epigrammatic, elemental like the sounds of the forest." I had absorbed some of the Anglo-Saxon stories—of the old Choctaw who cured warts on the children of Philly, of another who would buy Dr. Tischner's Antiseptic at Yates Drugs on the Square, filter it through light bread, then sell the residue to his fellow Indians as alcohol. I had seen the Pow Wow Drive-In on Highway 16 near the reservation, a reported beer place frequented by the Choctaws, and I had heard too of the Choctaws' problem with alcoholism, which they were dealing with in a large new hospital on the tribal land. I had been told that after a past of terrible neglect, the 1960s with the Civil Rights Act and other social legislation was a time of remarkable progress for the Mississippi Choctaws and that a visit to the reservation six miles west of town was requisite to an understanding of the tripartite racial composition of the county.

Pete and I had driven out there one morning a couple of weeks before. I had an appointment with the Chief. I had a craving to meet him. What did he look like? Did he wear a headband and feathers and carry a blow-gun? "What do I call him?" I asked Sid Salter, the new associate editor of The Neshoba Democrat. "You call him Chief," Salter said, adding: "He's a sharp, sharp man." I had been impressed that day by the modern building complexes on the Choctaw land, the industrial park, the school and the stadium where the bowl game would be played and where Pete mingled with the Choctaw dogs, the office buildings and federal housing units risen from the red-clay hills.

I had found the tribal headquarters that morning with its sign: OFFICE OF THE CHIEF. In an anteroom I admired a lovely Choctaw secretary who reminded me of Debra Paget in The Broken Arrow. Her little daughter was pecking on a typewriter.

In a moment I was ushered into the inner office. The Chief, whose name was Philip Martin, was an ample man in his forties, nattily dressed, with a tan trenchcoat that might have come from Neiman-Marcus. In my notes of our casual conversation I see now: "Looks like a modern Chief. Talks with Southern accent." We spoke of recent tribal history, of the more amiable relationship than before among the whites, blacks, and Indians of Neshoba. His records showed that eighty-five Choctaw veterans of World War II from this reservation were still alive, and that twenty had served in Vietnam. He spoke of his goal on the reservation of economic self-determination through various manufacturing operations, that this was not merely a myth but was actually working. "We employ 350 people today who otherwise would be out of work. It makes income for the tribal government and reduces our dependency on the federal government."

He strolled about the room, looking briefly out the window at a Choctaw boy trying to get a kite up in the windless sky. "I can tell you our dependency on the federal government isn't based on its generosity or good heart. It's because of the historical relationship. Vast amounts of land were taken from us, hardships inflicted on us. Long-standing deprivations. Bad relationships with the government. We've done everything to comply with the Constitution and to defend our country. In the last twenty years, with the help of the government, we're educating our children and developing our economic base. We've risen from a downtrodden people."

The secretary's little daughter wandered into the office, fondled a pottery ashtray, then retreated. Our talk drifted to lighter things, and then of course to football. "Marcus Dupree!" the Chief said. "He brings pride to our community. He makes us proud. I hope we can get him to the Choctaw Bowl."


The empty Philadelphia stadium was in shadows as I walked across it to the gymnasium. The team, already dressed in the red-and-white uniforms, was beginning to board two buses. I found Coach Joe Wood alone in his office. He welcomed me with his usual vivacity. We talked about Marcus' twelve final choices, and then about the Herschel record. "If he can get close," Wood said, "we'll let him have it." He pointed toward the locker room. "Go see the ol' fellow. He's meditatin'."

The room was deserted except for Marcus. He was sitting there alone in a chair, red hairnet over his Afro, silent, head bent, as if in supplication. When he saw me, he immediately rose and walked over.

"Hello," he said, and extended his hand.

"Will you break it tonight?" I asked.

"I'm sure gonna try." He lowered his head in a characteristic gesture. "Say, did Reggie get those other photographs I sent of my dog Pete?"

"He sure did." He laughed, possibly at the thought of a middle-aged man sending pictures of a ten-year-old dog to a ten-year-old boy.

"Well, we're pulling for you."

"All right. You goin' on the bus with us?"

We got on the first bus and I sat in a seat directly behind him, next to a big tenth-grade center, a white boy named Harold Blocker. "We're sure hopin' for him to break Herschel's touchdowns," the young man said. "He can do it." Joe Wood was in a front seat, and the bus driver was an assistant coach, Neil Hitchcock, who once told me he had played football and worked his way through Delta State University as a part-time guard at Parchman Prison.

From the back a black voice shouted: "*Du*-pree, we gonna make you look like *Herschel* tonight!"

"*Du*-pree! *Du*-pree!"

There was an eruption of black talk, black shouts. Then someone yelled: "Get quiet! Get your mind on the game."

Marcus and his quarterback, blond-headed young Justy Johnson, were conferring on the seat in front of me. "I'm gonna wait till you get over by the sidelines," Justy said, "and see if you get the break on the outside. Then I'll pitch. You be ready."

"Okay."

We were on the outskirts of town. Suddenly the bus swerved into a driveway in front of a business establishment and scraped against a signpost.

"Watch it, Hitchcock!" a black player shouted.

"Don't wreck it, Coach! Dupree'll have to *run* to the reservation."

Hitchcock had forgotten the box with the money in it from the advance ticket sales. Joe Wood told him where it was in his office. The disgruntled Hitchcock got off the bus and caught a ride back to the school with Professor Will Norton of Ole Miss, who had been following in our car.

Joe Wood was standing at the front of the bus. "Don't mind ol' Hitchcock," he addressed the team. "Let's get our minds on this thing now." Then he sat down at the wheel and with jerks and tremors the bus pulled away again.

There was silence. We were surrounded by the dark Mississippi woods in their deep autumn shadows. The earthen dam was not far from us now.

Then Marcus said something in a normal voice, a tender exhortation: "Think about the seniors."

As we bounced through the night, I remembered similar rides on our team bus to ball games more than a quarter of a century ago. Except for the blacks, we might have been the Yazoo High Indians, speeding into the Delta for a rendezvous with Belzoni. On one such long-ago journey, returning home with our hurts and bruises in the Delta quiet, a valiant little halfback with a broken hand had stood and shouted dramatically: "*Boys, we won . . . We won, by God! We won away from home in the last minute!*"

The stadium on the reservation was the finest I had seen all year, with excellent lights, and a large concrete grandstand on one side and bleachers on the other. A gymnasium–field house was adjacent to the grandstand with—what else?—WARRIORS in sizable letters on the façade. Although the game was more than an hour away, it was obvious there would be a big crowd.

As the team went into the gymnasium, I wandered about the stadium. The grandstand and bleachers were lively with talk about Marcus' challenge to Herschel. Governor William Winter, I learned, had planned to be in attendance, but had a last-minute meeting in the other Philadelphia—the one in Pennsylvania.

It had suddenly grown cold after the hot, smoke-filled day. There was a full moon, partly covered in thin, hazy clouds. The Union Yellowjackets were already on the field for their pregame exercises. They were representing an old, settled town in an adjoining county which had been burned by Sherman in 1863. The signs on the fence in front of their bleachers, which were already filled, said: FREAK OUT PHILLY! and DOWN WITH DUPREE!

I was witness that night to one of the most distinctive crowds I had ever seen at a sports event. The four thousand or so people seemed almost an equal mix of whites, blacks, and Indians. There were Indian boys in Choctaw Central letter jackets. Many of the Choctaw men wore boots and black felt hats. The older Choctaw women wore handmade, full-skirted gingham dresses with bright aprons, ribbons, and beaded necklaces. Some of the men were dressed in colorful shirts and beaded sashes. The younger women had their hair in long braids. Here and there groups of black children were waving pompons. On a swathe of level ground behind the grandstand, little white, black, and Indian boys were playing a brand of football which resembled a rugby scrum.

The Philly Tornadoes came onto the field for their practice. How many times that autumn had I observed the eyes of the spectators turn to Number 22 as he casually caught punts and ran his patterns? On this night he seemed bigger than life on the tribal ground under the full Neshoba moon.

I went back down on the field. The Philadelphia and Union teams were returning to the locker rooms. The other players had disappeared, but Marcus, strangely, lingered. On a grassy incline leading to the gymnasium he tossed a football back and forth with a couple of small Indian boys. The little boys departed. "Good luck, Marcus," one of them said. I stood there with him on the grass of the hill. We looked down at the sweep of the gridiron and the enveloping red earth. An honor guard of little Indian Boy Scouts in uniform and red berets was marching in step with the American flag along the sidelines. The Philly band was playing "Hail to the Varsity." "Well . . ." he said, then moved away toward the gymnasium.

"Get 'em, son," I said.

"All right."

Shortly before the kickoff I felt a hand on my shoulder and turned to see Tom Goode, the Ole Miss assistant coach. He looked immensely tired. The lines of scars on his face from old football encounters seemed more pronounced than ever, his eyes more piercing. Ole Miss was playing Tennessee the next afternoon in Knoxville. He told me he had come to watch the first half, after which he would make the three-hour drive to Oxford, then take a small plane the four hundred or so miles to Knoxville to get there in time for the team meeting.

He had been recruiting Marcus for three years. We talked about his final twelve choices, just announced that day.

"I don't know," Goode said. "I called him on the phone this afternoon. I said, 'Marcus, everybody says you've ruled us out.' He said, 'Shoot, naw.' 'Well, if you have, you'll have to tell me to my face.' "

Would he see him again?

"Steve and I have an official visit with him the Monday after Thanksgiving. We'll see what happens." When the team came out of the gym for the start of the game, he merely wanted Marcus to know he was there.

In the Texas Relays of 1954 I saw Wes Santee miss the four-minute mile by half a second. I watched the Miracle Mets of 1969 and the great Knicks-Lakers contests of those years. The Choctaw Bowl of 1981, in a little stadium in western Neshoba County, would likewise be one of the interesting sporting events of my experience.

Hundreds of yellow balloons were set loose when the Union squad raced onto the field. The Philly team dashed through another papiermâché banner with the words "Blunt the Yellowjackets." Marcus and Daran Jackson were the co-captains. Philly won the toss of the coin, and then the Indian Boy Scouts marched to midfield for "The Star-Spangled Banner."

On the first play from scrimmage Marcus was racked for a four-yard loss. Was this an omen? He gained eight, then was again thrown for a five-yard loss. He slapped down the ball in disgust. The Union players embraced ecstatically, their partisans roaring with delight. "What's wrong, Dupree?" Moments later he broke away for a twenty-five-yard gain, but the big Union line continued to hit hard, and the Philly offense stalled.

Late in the first quarter the Tornadoes began to move. Marcus accumulated fifty yards on this long drive. Then, on a fourth and goal from the one, with four seconds remaining in the first quarter, he negotiated yet another Herschel Walker dive for his eighty-third touchdown.

Early in the second quarter, however, he came out of the game with an injured shoulder, obviously in pain. The trainers were examining him, and Number 18, Cecil Price, Jr., brought him a cup of water. This, coupled with a lengthy Union drive which ended on the Tornado six-yard line, cast a pall over the Philadelphia crowd. He returned, with 4:03 left in the half, favoring his right shoulder. Daran Jackson fumbled and Union recovered on its own forty, and the half ended with Philly ahead, 7–0.

Marcus had not carried the ball a single time in the second period. It would be difficult now for him to score three touchdowns to tie Herschel's mark, four to surpass it, in a second half of twelve-minute quarters and with the way the Union team was hitting. Some of the drama had gone out of the evening, and the Philly band could not retrieve it at halftime, even with "New York, New York."

I drifted up to the concession stands, where long-haired Choctaws were selling soft drinks and hotdogs. A group of old Choctaw women in their full-length dresses were chatting in their language among themselves. Might they have been discussing the intricacies of the "I" formation? Several merchants from Philadelphia admitted they were pessimistic about his chances against Herschel. "Four touchdowns in twenty-four minutes?" one said.

Sid Salter was talking with Principal Gregory when he saw me. "Well, at least Mississippi State's in his final twelve," this dauntless Bulldog said. He then described to me a scene he had witnessed in the first half. After

Marcus scored his touchdown, he saw Cecil Price, Sr. "He was jumping up and down and cheering as hard as anyone," Salter said. "Ain't that a kick in the pants?"

A slight mist was gathering about the field and a cold wind came in from the north as the second half started. Union took the kickoff and consumed four minutes with running plays.

Philly had the ball on its own eighteen-yard line. The quarterback, Justy Johnson, pitched out to Marcus, moving to his right. He paused for an instant, studying the defensive secondary. Far down the field Number 24, Terry Hoskins, was breaking into the clear. Marcus threw a long spiral pass which went almost fifty yards in the air. Hoskins caught it on target and sped the rest of the way for a touchdown. The pass covered eighty-two yards, and the Tornadoes led, 14–0.

One could feel the restiveness in the crowd. With 5:35 left in the third quarter, he had not run with the ball in eighteen minutes. Philly took possession again on its own forty-yard line. Marcus crashed through the middle for twenty-five-yards. Now the Tornadoes were moving with short gains.

Time was running down. With 2:53 remaining in the third period, Philly had the ball on the Union twenty. Marcus was positioned at split end. Justy Johnson faded to pass. He threw to Marcus on the five. He caught the ball on the swing pass and ran over the safety man into the end zone for the touchdown.

Union was forced to punt on its next possession. From his own forty-five Marcus ran for nine, then seven. A long pass from Justy to Marcus was overthrown.

As the fourth quarter began, a series of penalties had moved Philly back to its own forty-eight. Marcus took a thirty-four-yard pass to the Union seventeen. He carried for three to the fourteen.

The scoreboard clock showed 11:40 left in the game when he took a pitch to the left, broke two tackles near the line of scrimmage, ran toward the sidelines, cut sharply, tightroped the line, and scored standing up. The public-address man announced this as his eighty-fifth touchdown, one short.

After the kickoff Union scored on a long run. Philly led 28–8.

The Tornadoes had the ball, first and ten on their own thirty with 9:39 left. Marcus on a sweep carried twenty yards until he was forced out of bounds by several defenders. The whistle had blown and the clock was stopped when a huge black tackle for Union knocked him over an empty bench. He went sprawling onto the concrete track just beyond the sidelines. There were rabid boos, followed by a fifteen-yard penalty. As he lay there motionless on the concrete for a moment, I said to myself, "Lord, not now!" I came out of the grandstand onto the concrete track and caught myself shouting at the culprit in a terse, florid language I had not been taught in the Yazoo County Methodist Youth Fellowship. Then I caught myself in this middle-aged spasm.

I walked down to the goal line, for I sensed a spectacular retribution. A large number of adult men and children were also gathering at the Union goal. Some of them carried cameras.

There was 8:53 left in the game. Now, after the penalty, Philly had the ball on the Union thirty-five.

A silence fell on the crowd as Marcus took a pitchout to the right, slowed for the briefest instant, swerved toward the sidelines, deceived a linebacker with a motion of his head, reversed his field, and sped unmolested into the end zone.

The entire stadium was joyous. I believed I heard war whoops. Even the Union people across the way stood and cheered. Over the pandemonium, the loudspeaker announced that this touchdown, number eighty-six, had tied Herschel's figure. The referee gave the football to Marcus. He ran off the field with it, holding it in one hand high in the air. The band played the fight song, and his coaches and teammates embraced him at the bench. Two white and two black cheerleaders embraced and kissed him. Another white cheerleader sat on his lap and hugged him. Cameras recorded these scenes. The crowd continued to stand, and little white, black, and Choctaw children ran down out of the stands and surrounded him for his autograph.

The referee had to clear the field. Union took the kickoff and ran two plays. With 7:32 remaining, Union fumbled and Philly recovered. Another series of penalties and long losses moved the Tornadoes back deep into their own territory. With 5:03 to play they faced a fourth down and forty-eight to go for the first down from their own twenty-eight-yard line.

A memorable moment was at hand. "We lined up in punt formation," Joe Wood would reminisce a long time after the night of the Choctaw Bowl, "and we already had the punter on the field. But I said to myself, 'What the hell, let's go for a fake.' So I tell the boys to get the ball to ol' Marcus."

I was standing again on the Union goal line when the play evolved. The punter faked, then passed to him in the flat. It was one of his finest runs of that autumn as he overpowered several tacklers, almost fell, then galloped down the sidelines, coming within a stride of going all the way before four defenders angled him out of bounds on the Union thirteen-yard line. It was a fifty-nine-yard play.

Four minutes, thirty-five seconds remained. Philly got an off-sides on the next play, moving the ball to the Union eighteen.

The handoff went to Marcus. He crashed down the middle for sixteen to the Union two-yard line, 4:24.

A hush descended once more on the spectators, about a hundred of whom were at the goal line. Everyone was standing.

He carried up the middle to the six-inch line. There was 3:57 left when the Philly team came out of the huddle.

The silence was eerie now as Number 22 ran the ball for the last time in his high school career. There was nothing spectacular about this play. He merely bulled his way across the double-stripe for the touchdown.

There was a re-enactment of the impassioned scene of five minutes before. Once again he ran off the field and was engulfed in children, and the crowd applauded for long minutes.

Union scored with thirty-one seconds left, making it 42–14.

"Marcus," Joe Wood said at the bench, "you want to go in for one last one?"

"Naw, Coach."


Long after the game the crowd remained. The Philly players celebrated. "*Du*-pree! *Du*-pree!" The Union team came over. There were the final sweet strains of the fight song.

For the game he carried twenty-one times for 171 yards, scored five touchdowns on runs of 1, 12, 35, and 1, and a 20-yard pass reception, passed for an 82-yard touchdown, and gained 86 yards on pass completions. He had just finished his high school career with eighty-seven touchdowns and 5,284 yards rushing, an average of 8.3 yards a carry. He had scored fourteen touchdowns in his last three games and missed by 45 yards gaining 2,000 in his senior season. Philly completed the year with a 7–4 record.

Justy Johnson was presented with the sportsmanship award and Marcus the most valuable player; Joe Wood was carried off the field with the Choctaw Bowl trophy. People continued to surround Marcus for autographs in the parking lot near the buses. Two Jackson State coaches stood at the edge of the throng and watched with bemusement. Jimmy Lee Shannon, who had been the Dupree of his pre-integration generation, came up to me and said, "He put on a *clinic* tonight."

"I give up on it," Joe Wood said. "I thought he might still pull it off on ol' Herschel, but I didn't expect it until that fake punt I called."

We all got on the bus for the ride back to town. Marcus was called out again to sign autographs for some white girls sitting in a car. "Come on, Marcus!" Joe Wood yelled. "This bus is goin'."

"Let's go, Du-pree," a white player said. "You can sign tomorrow." He kissed four or five Indian girls, then was whisked onto the bus by three Philly High teachers.

The vehicle departed into the abrupt darkness. With the trustworthy Coach Hitchcock at the wheel, it rambled off the reservation onto the main road.

"All right, men!" Joe Wood shouted from the front of the bus. "You seniors can keep your jerseys."

"Everybody except Du-pree!" someone yelled from the back.

"The rest of you turn in your shorts and jerseys," Wood continued. "We got a lot of laundry work to do tomorrow. I'm mighty proud of you. You went out winners. Be that way in life."

The celebration was under way. Charles Summers, a sophomore lineman, led the team in yells.

> *Philly own this territory,*
> *We rule this Mother Hubbard,*
> *Who say? We say?*
> *Who say? We say?*
> *Who dat? Who dat?*
> *Who dat tryin' to beat our Philly?*

There was another shout from the backseat: "Du-pree, he gonna whip some ass!"

As the bus moved haltingly into the driveway behind the Philly gymnasium, dozens of students waited at the door. I remembered Housman:

> *The time you won your town the race*
> *We chaired you through the market place,*
> *Man and boy stood cheering by,*
> *As home we brought you shoulder-high.*

# 18

# *Open Season for Courtiers*

*Really hard to describe my feeling about the record. I didn't think I was going to get it. I hurt my shoulder in the first quarter scoring the first touchdown, and when I got to the bench it felt like it was out of place.*

*I tried to suck it up, but it was really hurting. My fullback Mark Burnside told me I wasn't going to be able to play. . . .*

*This record is something I've been dreaming about for two years.*

*Now it's time to get down with the recruiting. I'm looking forward to it. Starting the first of December everything will pick up. Right now Texas and UCLA are visits. Those two for sure. Thinking about Georgia and Pittsburgh.*

*Narrowed my list to 12 schools this week. I thought about cutting it even more, but I'd look at six I like, then find another six I liked. I could expand the list by two or three more schools.*

*I'm looking highly on Southern right now. They've got a young offensive line and their tailbacks are leaving after this year. I really like their coaching staff. I'm leaning that way, but it's a long time until I sign.*

In late November, I learned in Oxford, Marcus strained some ligaments in a basketball game against East Kemper. I wrote him a note that he had gone through a difficult football season without a serious injury and not to challenge his good fortune playing basketball. He went to a specialist who advised the same thing. "I'm not going to jeopardize my career," he said.

Under NCAA rules a recruit was allowed six "official visits" to campuses for forty-eight hours with all expenses paid. On the last weekend in November he visited on his own the University of Southern Mississippi, whose team was playing Lamar University. "Seemed like the best place for me," he said. "I really like the people."

December 1 was the first day the college recruiters could see him at his home or at the school. The first to come in after the opening date were Ohio State and Texas A&M. "I told the man from A&M that wasn't the school for me," he said. "We didn't talk long at all." Wayne Stanley, the offensive backfield coach for Ohio State, "basically said the same stuff as all the other recruiters. I'm not sure about a visit. I don't like the cold weather." The talk around town was that Ohio State had offered Mark Burnside, his friend and fellow running back, a scholarship also. Joe Wood began to get more and more telephone calls. One day that week three assistant coaches, George Pugh of Pittsburgh, Bobby Fields of UCLA, and Tom Goode of Ole Miss were at the school at the same time. Fields was talking with Wood when Pugh arrived. "You see, Fields had coached Pugh at Alabama," Wood said. "They had a big time talkin'. They all seem to know each other. They're mighty friendly, but sometimes they look at each other funny."

"Everyone is being nice to each other this first week," the principal, Danny Gregory, told me. "There was someone here to see Marcus every day during his free period and two visits every night at his house. Michigan State and Texas Tech came in unannounced. The next week was exams, and his mother just told 'em not to come." One morning he was ten minutes late to school. "He'd never done that before," Gregory said. "He said the phone had kept ringing that morning."

Steve Sloan and Tom Goode of Ole Miss visited him that week, undeterred apparently by their exclusion from his list of twelve. "It went all right," Marcus said. "They talked about how they need a good back and how they're changing to the 'I.'" Sloan brought out a list of Heisman Trophy winners, arguing that most of them went to their state universities. Marcus' mother told them she had heard that Sloan might not be at Ole Miss the next year.

The Christmas decorations were up that week around the Square and in Independence Quarters, and when I dipped down for a four-day visit I could hardly avoid the festive spirit. One day, although he did not like it at all, I bought a red ribbon at Thompson's Drug Store and put it on Pete's collar for our strolls around the Square. The deer season was over, but some of the fellows around the Square were still wearing their camouflage hats and shirts. Pete and I were at home again in the Downtown Hotel. I admired the Christmas trinkets on the magnolias around the courthouse, and in front of the stores and churches of the Quarters. Sometimes the holiday luster of the town seemed far removed from the big-time gambits of football recruitment.

"I'm getting a little tired of it," Marcus said in the second week of the open season, "talking to coaches and reporters. A bunch of schools are still sending me literature, and I don't understand why." As the campaign for him progressed, leading to the February 10 signing date, I would see him grow more and more uncomfortable. "I don't like being the spotlight all the time," he would say to me. "I walk into a store or a restaurant and all anybody wants to do is talk about football. But I guess that's the way it is."

At the end of the first week of December, he said, his three main choices of his twelve were Southern Mississippi, Texas, and UCLA.

Some of the people of Philly believed 'Bama, only 160 miles away in Tuscaloosa, was decidedly in the running. Who could refuse to play under Bear Bryant, the best coach in America, the gruff yet tender man whose players loved him? "Don't kid yourself," a local man said. "Look at the stats on their running backs last year. The Bear don't believe in overwhelming running backs. His most prolific one gained 380 yards." Would Marcus choose such a team-oriented offense? Marcus' mother complained that the 'Bama recruiter had been worrying them to death. Also, the Bear himself had recently said on a television show that no halfback of his would ever win the Heisman Trophy because he would never give one player the ball thirty times a game.

In the second week recruiters from 'Bama, Pittsburgh, and Michigan came by, as well as Mississippi State and Ole Miss again. Coach Jerry Stovall of LSU arrived to see him, and so did an SMU recruiter. Coach Terry Donahue of UCLA stopped in. Donahue's UCLA obviously had a special appeal to the young man, ever since his trip to the West Coast the previous summer.

The telephone at 274 Davis Street in the Quarters now had an answering service.


On the eighteenth day of December Marcus flew out to Los Angeles for his official visit with UCLA. "It's pretty nice," he said. "Everybody is so friendly. Even if they don't know you, they speak." It was twelve degrees when he left home and seventy-eight or eighty out there. "The grass was green. It's different." He went to the house of the mayor of Los Angeles and was presented a baseball autographed by Roy Campanella. He watched the UCLA team practice for their Bluebonnet Bowl game and was introduced to some of the players he had not met the previous summer. Irv Eatman, the all-American tackle, showed him around. "He's six-seven, 270, and all muscle. We got along pretty well." He was a guest at the UCLA-DePaul basketball game at Pauley Pavilion and went to a party in Beverly Hills. "Friday night turned into Saturday morning," he said.

It was against NCAA rules for a school to pay the expenses of a member of the family or a high school coach or principal on an official visit. A UCLA man had met him in Jackson and flew with him to Los Angeles. "Anyone who's not flown a lot will be a little tense," Principal Danny Gregory told me. Marcus' mother was concerned about his flying to California alone, Gregory said. Bobby Fields, the UCLA assistant coach, had telephoned and said no one would fly back to Mississippi with Marcus after his UCLA visit. Donahue was worried that if she did not want him to fly alone, it might not be wise for him to go to college way out there.

Marcus' mother drove to the Jackson airport to meet him when he returned Sunday night. He was on neither the 7 P.M. nor the 9:30 flight from Los Angeles. He had missed connections in Houston and came in around midnight. "There was no problem," Gregory said, "other than a concerned mother. The flights don't bother Marcus at all. His mother has become more protective during all this. It's understandable. But Marcus has always been fairly independent—driving a car, taking trips to Ole Miss and State."

"Planning to visit Pittsburgh in January," he said on his return, "and thinking about LSU. I guess it's time to start clearing my mind about these things."

One afternoon in late December a small jet landed at the Philadelphia airport. Several police cars drove up and parked in front of the Dupree house on Davis Street. All the neighbors started telephoning to see what Marcus had done wrong.

The visitor whom the police escorted to the Quarters was thirty-six-year-old Jackie Sherrill, the head coach at the University of Pittsburgh. His team was practicing on the Gulf Coast in preparation for the Sugar Bowl against Herschel Walker and Georgia on New Year's Day. Sherrill was a native Mississippian, from Biloxi, who had played under Bear Bryant at Alabama. He had succeeded Johnny Majors at Pitt when Majors returned to his alma mater, Tennessee, and in his five years as head coach he had compiled a 58–9–1 record, including two straight 11–1 seasons and an 11–0 showing in 1981. It was Sherrill who had recruited Tony Dorsett, the Heisman Trophy running back who held the collegiate record for yards rushing. He also had a reputation for signing eminent black ballplayers from Mississippi, such as Hugh Green and Rooster Jones. "While the assistants usually handle the groundwork on prospective players," Inside Sports once reported, "the head coaches are counted on to close the deals. With his sincere, no-hype approach that reassures athletes and makes mothers swoon, Sherrill is considered the best closer in the business."

After the furor over the police cars abated, Sherrill discussed with Marcus his playing in the same backfield with Dan Marino, the versatile Pitt quarterback. "That interests me," Marcus said. "Besides that, we just talked about the basics." Given his formidable presence, Jackie Sherrill would be an exceedingly difficult man to refuse.

One day right after the Christmas holidays, Marcus waited until everyone had left the speech class of his favorite teacher, Sarah McKay, and walked up to her desk. "Miz McKay, I thought you'd want a souvenir." It was a Sugar Bowl fountain pen.

"Marcus, where did you get this? You didn't go to the Sugar Bowl."

"The Pittsburgh coach gave it to me."

"If the Pittsburgh coach gave you this, you should keep it."

"He gave me five. I want you to have one."

"He was always so inconspicuous about these things," Sarah McKay said. "He never made anything out of it. He waited until no one was around. He gave me this that day too." She handed me a newspaper which had been distributed at the Southern Mississippi football game when he made an informal visit there—a mock-up of *The Jackson Clarion-Ledger*. On the front page was a photograph of Number 10, Southern's quarterback Reggie Collier, giving the ball on a running play to Number 22. The caption said: "Dynamic Duo: Heisman candidate Reggie Collier, Golden Eagle quarterback, hands off to freshman sensation and future Heisman candidate Marcus Dupree for a touchdown against Florida State." The newspaper was signed to Sarah McKay "from Marcus Dupree, ⚡22."

# 19
# *Snowbound in Neshoba*

As 1982 began, Marcus received several honors. The influential Joe Terranova of Michigan, the most respected analyst of high school football talent in the nation, selected him the best high school running back in America. "To paraphrase the Budweiser slogan," Terranova wrote in his *Blue Chips*, the recruiters' Holy Book, "when you've said Marcus Dupree, you've said it all. Remember, this is the kid that shattered all of Herschel Walker's prep records." *Parade* magazine named him to its nineteenth annual All-American team for the second year in a row, citing him and another runner, Kevin Wilhite of Rancho Cordova, California, as the two finest high school players in the country. Dr. Charles Holland of Oak Ridge, Tennessee, a computer expert in the nuclear industry who performed his wizardry each year in listing America's "Top One Hundred," chose him Number One.* *The Jackson Clarion-Ledger and Daily News* gave him the Mississippi Player of the Year Award. "I think the year really helped me," he said in accepting. "I matured a lot as a person and a player. Things didn't go as well as planned and I learned to take the bad with the good."

Less than six weeks remained before the national signing date on February 10. Marcus had already told me he might wait two or three days after that to announce his decision. On New Year's night Temple Drake telephoned me from a bar in Dallas where he was carousing with some football people. "Watch out for Texas and Oklahoma," he said. "Before long they're gonna bring in the heavy artillery."

The out-of-state reporters were beginning to drift into Philly, their assignment now a felicitous relief to the townspeople with their memories

---

* The doctor's exuberant contemporary methods titillated me. "To arrive at his selections," *Athlon* reported, "Holland gathers data from a variety of sources (even newspaper clippings) and feeds it into a computer. He has a formula that predicts a success factor for a Pennsylvania all-state, for example, as compared with the best players in Kansas or Kentucky. His system has room for personal information, such as determination and toughness. He gets input from selected scouts and especially values the judgment of college recruiters . . . Size, speed, and strength, especially bench-press figures, are vital to Holland's computer rating." I was happy he did not rank American writers, poets, and literary critics.

of the national journalists of '64 and the events which had brought them there. On the question of whether Marcus would choose to stay in his native Mississippi just as Herschel Walker had remained in Georgia, John McGrath wrote for the sports pages of *The Atlanta Journal*:

> The lure, obviously, exists for Marcus Dupree to step outside Mississippi for a more glamorous backdrop with which to demonstrate his skills. That wouldn't be difficult.
>
> On the other hand, the same sort of familial ties which kept Walker in Georgia are apparent here, too. Dupree's third-grade brother, moreover, has cerebral palsy; Marcus is his hero, a role—unlike that of the weary bystander at McDonald's—played with consummate heart and soul.
>
> And what of the hauntingly persistent beckoning of Mississippi itself? This is a compelling land, little understood, less celebrated, but no better demonstrated than near the empty football field at Philadelphia High one overcast morning last week. Hickory smoke hovered in the air, and in the distance echoed the disparate sounds of life in the small town: a rooster screamed, and a dog barked.
>
> Then, for a second, you could almost hear the fans, jammed next to each other on the concrete bleachers, cheering on a Friday night. Philadelphia? It could be Wrightsville; it could be anywhere.
>
> Same game. Same dreams.

A local merchant would say to me: "When it's all over, will the State, Ole Miss, and Southern people in town remain bitter, or will they come together in pride over Marcus?"


On the fifth day of the New Year 1982, my son David, my dog Pete, and I drove down for a fortnight's stay. David was twenty-two and in his last year at Hampshire College, Amherst, Massachusetts—"taller and somewhat more handsome," the women always said, "than the father"— his looks apparently deriving more from his mother than from Pete and me. He and I had lived through much together on the planet. He, too, was no stranger to sports. In New York City, when he was young, he and I were habitués of the Knicks, Mets, and Yankees. Sometimes, on frosty Saturday afternoons, we were even so adventurous as to take the subway to Baker Field to observe the unfortunate Columbia Lions. When he grew older he was the centerfielder on our championship softball team of Eastern Long Island, the Bridgehampton Golden Nematodes, a team of unusual ethnic diversity which was held together by Jeffersonian democracy and the double-steal. David cared for Pete as much as I, but sometimes complained that they were sibling rivals. He was a photographer, and was engaged now in a project that would take him all over the country photographing Vietnam veterans, of whom there were several in Philadelphia. As with my other diverse and unconventional comrades in this story who had accompanied me to Philly, I was looking forward to seeing the town through his eyes.

The town was preparing now for the serious recruiting onslaught. The NCAA investigator Mike Glazier had been there to talk with Marcus and Joe Wood to see if any coaches had been unduly bothering the prospect. "Marcus told him there were a couple that wouldn't quit calling him," Wood said, "even though he'd indicated to them that they were wasting their time." Barry Switzer, the head coach of Oklahoma, had come into Philly, and the word was that Marcus' mother, for whatever reason, had been a little cool toward him. Marcus had been wearing a University of Pittsburgh baseball cap to school. A Mississippi State recruiter had visited the school again and gotten him out of a class,·the first time that had happened. A television crew from a Mississippi station had also come to the school and descended on Sarah McKay's first-period speech class with Marcus in tow. "Miz McKay, there are some *men* here," Marcus said, and they shot some footage. He returned for her third-period class. "Miz McKay, they're comin' back." The girls brought out their combs and mirrors. "Miz McKay," one of them said, "let me sit close to Marcus Dupree today." But Principal Gregory learned of this intrusion of the media into the ivory tower of Philly High and chased the TV men out.

It was announced that week that the town would have an Appreciation Day for Marcus on February 7, three days before the national signing, under the auspices of several black organizations in cooperation with the city government, and that signs would be erected on the highways saying: PHILADELPHIA, MISSISSIPPI . . . HOME OF MARCUS DUPREE.

In the first days of our sojourn there were two noteworthy developments. To ease the pressure, Joe Wood and Danny Gregory had advised Marcus to narrow his list of twelve preferences to four or five. He came into Gregory's office in early January and pruned the roster from twelve to eight. In alphabetical order

> Alabama
> Mississippi State
> Ohio State
> Oklahoma
> Pittsburgh
> Southern Mississippi
> Texas
> UCLA

From his original list of twelve he had dropped Georgia, Jackson State, LSU, and Michigan.

Then, on January 7, he narrowed the field to his final five:

Oklahoma
Pittsburgh
Southern Mississippi
Texas
UCLA

Now he had cut Alabama, Mississippi State, and Ohio State.

His various lists did not seem to discourage the most tenacious recruiters from schools he had long turned down. Ole Miss returned to town that week for one last try. Coach Darrell Moody of LSU telephoned Principal Gregory to discuss the latest list. "He was not pleased at all," Gregory told me. Doug Matthews, the Tennessee recruiter, arrived at the school and asked to see Marcus with Gregory present. "If Johnny Majors came, would you see him?" the Tennessee coach asked. "Yessir," Marcus said. He listened quietly as Matthews described the colossal Tennessee stadium, which seated more than ninety thousand people, and other aspects of their football program. When Marcus left, the coach said to Gregory, "Coach, I'd appreciate if you'd call and tell us if Marcus is interested and if Tennessee's still in the running." Marcus later told Gregory, however, that his mother had already told the Tennessee people he did not want to see them. And so it went through the early days of January.

Long after it was all over he would tell me, in his cryptic and underspoken way, precisely why he had cut the various schools from his list of preferences. *Southern Cal:* "I never seriously considered it. They got too many running backs." *Ole Miss:* "It was never in the running. I just didn't like it. Sometimes I didn't like the symbols." *Jackson State:* "They don't get the recognition. You don't see 'em on TV." *Michigan, Ohio State:* "They're too far from home and too cold." *Mississippi State:* "I didn't want to play wingback in the Wingbone." *Georgia, LSU, Tennessee:* "After a while, I never really considered 'em all that much." *Alabama:* "I really liked Alabama at first. But they got too many backs."

His deletion of Alabama more than a month before the signing date was the subject of much talk in the town. In the restaurant of the Downtown one afternoon, four of the steady patrons discussed this development until closing time. Back in August, they said, they thought Alabama was in the best position to get him. After all, he had visited Tuscaloosa several times in high school and had once gone there to be treated for his hamstring injury. He had talked with Bear Bryant in his famous tower at the practice field, and there had been a persistent rumor, which proved to be unfounded, that Alabama had bought him his car. A reporter from Birmingham even came to town that week to find out about Marcus and 'Bama. "How can someone win the Heisman Trophy and a rushing championship if they go there?" he told the reporter. "They just don't give you a chance to run the ball. They just run too many backs, just keep switching them in and out. A runner can't get his rhythm that way." And the Bear himself, he said, had not pushed him all that vigorously.

My son David wanted to get some photographs of people in the Hill section of Independence Quarters. On a bitterly cold morning we drove over to see Lillie Jones, the ninety-one-year-old black woman who had been a leader in the civil rights struggle, and Larry Walker of the Busy Bee. I introduced David to Mrs. Jones; we sat around the hot stove and talked. I asked if she thought Marcus should stay in Mississippi.

"I think he might be better off goin' away," she said.

I asked why.

"Oh . . ." she replied, with the same benevolent inflections again of my grandmother Mamie, "I don't know. He just might be better off."

I left the two of them together and crossed the street to the Busy Bee. This time the sign on the big marquee out front said:

MARCUS DUPREE DATE FEB. 7
ALL AMERICAN 87 TD's
GOING FOR HEISMAN

As usual the interior was astir with motion and Larry Walker, the owner, bestowed an ardent welcome. A red-and-white Number 22 jersey was on prominent display behind the counter. "We wanted to say 'Four Consecutive Years' on the next line after 'Heisman,'" he said, "but we ran out of letters. We also want to put on this sign ten or fifteen years from now: '*Marcus Dupree and the Busy Bee. What a Combination!*'"

As we leaned against the counter drinking coffee, Walker outlined for me his dreams for the future. "Marcus Dupree will be worth at least five million dollars a year in five years. Magic Johnson signed a contract with the Los Angeles Lakers for one million dollars a year for the next twenty-five years. When he gets through he'll be ownin' half of California."

He began walking around the counter, waving his cup of coffee. Three little children, poised to buy some bubble gum, stopped to listen. "I'm the entrepreneur of the Hill. I intend to rent a big bus and drive Marcus Dupree's followers to see him play in college, even if it's out there in California.

"I'm thinkin' ahead, you know, ten or fifteen years, when he's stopped playin'. Marcus Dupree will be good for the town. He's a born leader. He'll be good for business, good for industry." Someday, he said, he would buy the old Evers Hotel next door—the building which had been the COFO headquarters in 1964—and call it The Marcus Dupree Hotel. "Everybody who's anybody will come from miles around to stay in it. I plan to bet on Marcus Dupree's college team and raise the necessary ten thousand dollars."

I went to the school to get the latest information from Principal Gregory and Coach Wood and to find out what might be on people's minds. In the hallway the janitor, Henry Moore, briefly engaged me. "He had a mighty good time in California," he said. "Long way, though. Ain't he a runnin' fool?"

Gregory was in a talkative mood. This was one among many visits which made me feel how fortunate the young man was to have men like the principal and the coach overseeing his interests. At this stage both seemed to be enjoying much of the ritual; it was an emotion that would not last.

"He's been real nervous, having so many visitors," Gregory said. "I can tell he's a little tense, a little quieter than usual. Joe and I are simply trying to do what he asked us to do as he goes along. I hope he'll cut down one school a week now until signing."

He got his ACT score a couple of days before in Gregory's office. He scored 16.† "He had an expression of sheer joy," Gregory said. "I've never seen him so emotional. I asked, 'Do you feel better?' and he said, 'You'd better believe it.'"

The visit of Glazier, the NCAA representative, was "routine," but he planned to return. The NCAA man said the guidelines which the school had issued before the football season on recruiters' dealings with Marcus had helped, that with such a sought-after prospect there were usually all kinds of disturbing rumors—but few from here so far.

"The thing that's surprised me is the negative recruiting the alumni have done," Gregory said. "Alums are writing Marcus letters. Bellard can t score touchdowns. Sloan will get fired. Ole Miss plays 'Dixie.' That sort of thing. I guess you have to take the good with the bad. Some of the letters I've gotten, with requests to give them to Marcus, I've just thrown away. I can't understand why he'd need to see them. One Ole Miss alum wrote, 'We'll fire our coaches and get you some new ones.'"

We leaned over the desk and examined the list of the five schools Marcus said he was still considering—Oklahoma, Pittsburgh, Southern

† Most major "football colleges" required a minimum of 15.

Mississippi, Texas, and UCLA. "Well, as of today, those are his five. But it's still subject to change. Who knows? It may be like telling the insurance guy the first time that you don't want it."

The bells rang, and from the corridors outside came the resounding clamor of teenagers on the move. The principal gave me the most candid of appraisals.

"Of the five he's still looking at, in my opinion four of them would give him every opportunity to achieve what he wants—being an all-American, TV exposure, a national championship. If you can be the best running back for each of these four schools, your chances of being all-American are very great.

"Quite frankly, of these four to me, Texas would be my choice. It has a stable coaching staff, fine support, a favorable climate, and it's the closest of the four to here. The University of Texas people have been very honest and open from the beginning. They've been down-to-earth and low-keyed. They had first shot on the scheduling of the official visit and picked it late. They've used one visit at the house and one at school. They got the door open early and made the right moves. They haven't been pushy."

Fred Akers, the Texas head coach, came to town back in July with his assistant, a black man named Tommy Reaux. They arrived on a UT jet and drove to the school in the middle of the afternoon. "Akers wore an orange blazer," Gregory recalled. "I immediately knew who he was. We had a nice visit. He said, 'I'm here with one of my assistants to meet Marcus.' He's a much sharper, more articulate person than I'd thought from TV. I took them down to the weight room to meet Marcus and Joe Wood."

Tommy Reaux watched two of the Philly games during the season, although he could not talk formally with Marcus. Gregory was highly impressed with him also. "He's just one of those likable fellows who blends right in. He was a high school coach. I think he's got his kids' interests at heart. He makes me think he's concerned about Marcus—even if he didn't go to Texas, he'd advise him if he went somewhere else. If Marcus went to Austin, he'd have somebody who'd give him guidance."

Marcus' official visit to Texas would be the last weekend of the month. "I feel they'll try to get some kind of commitment while he's there," Gregory predicted.

As for Southern Mississippi, the principal was equally forthright. "In my opinion Southern can't offer him the opportunities of Texas, Pitt, Oklahoma, or UCLA. Southern's advantage is that it's in easy driving distance. Bobby Collins is a class person. His assistant, Bootsie Larsen, has been very honest. Their program is on the way up. But they don't have the exposure."

When Marcus narrowed his list to five, Gregory looked over his choices. "How is Southern still on your list?" he asked him. Marcus replied, "Coach, they've been very impressive."

He would visit the University of Pittsburgh the weekend after next. Daran Jackson, the Philly running back, would go with him.

"Maybe the Longhorns should pray that it's snowing with a twenty-below windchill factor when he visits up there," I said.

"I'll tell you what worries me about Pitt," Gregory said. "I think Jackie Sherrill will leave for one of the big schools in the South. He wants to come home. You're right. It's a cold climate."

Why not Oklahoma?

"It's just a gut feeling. I don't think Marcus would enjoy it. They use the Wishbone out there. To me Marcus isn't that quick off the ball. It's on about his third step that he gets moving. The 'I' formation is just better designed for him. He's tall, lanky, and you can turn and give him the ball and let him choose his moves. The Wishbone doesn't give him that opportunity."

And UCLA?

"It's too far from home. I don't think the Southern California life style would be right for him. Bobby Fields, their assistant coach, is a fine man. I knew him at State. He's honest and forthright. Again, I just don't believe Marcus would be happy there."

He predicted, too, that Marcus would not sign on the February 10 date, but would likely wait two or three more days. "I think he'll be ready to end it, more than anyone else. He's heard everything that everybody wants to say. And he can't get it over till he signs."

We talked of the past season, and of his remaining in Mississippi. "There were times when he wouldn't have a good game, or we'd get beat," Gregory said. "People would say he played poorly—he'd gained 196 yards—and then there were the fine articles, the recruiters coming in, and this caused our people to realize all over again how truly talented he is. If Marcus had the great ability all these men who know assure us he has, then there has to be a place where he can take advantage of it. Still, I'm a Mississippian and wanted him to stay in the state. If he came in here right now and said he'd decided to stay in Mississippi and wanted my advice on where to go, I'd be very confused. Southern doesn't get the attention. Ole Miss doesn't have the quality athletes. State doesn't have the right offense."

"Hasn't this been somewhat enjoyable for you and Joe Wood?" I asked. "Won't it be a little quiet around here next year? Unless you've got another Marcus Dupree hiding out somewhere."

The principal laughed. "No more Marcuses for a *long, long* time," he said. "I want it to go well, for him to be happy. It's been exciting and good for the town. At the Choctaw Bowl, when he was about to break Herschel's record, I'd never seen black and white Philadelphia people standing and applauding and being absolutely together that way. It was something to watch. And sure, I've immensely enjoyed meeting Coach Donahue of UCLA, Akers, and the others, and the conversations I've had with them. I told Coach Donahue when he left that it'd been fun meeting him, that he wouldn't ever be back in Philadelphia, Mississippi, again. He smiled and said, 'That's probably right.' "

In the piercing cold I walked down the hill to the gymnasium. Bobby Collins, the Southern Mississippi head coach, and Bootsie Larsen, his assistant, were in Coach Wood's office. There was a diagram of an offensive play on the blackboard, which Larsen was examining. As usual Wood was busy playing host and tending his telephone.

Collins was a nice-looking, companionable young man of forty-eight. He might have passed for the new bank president in a medium-sized city on the rise who was in charge of the keys to the vault.

"Why are you in Philadelphia, Coach?" I asked. "Are there any ballplayers here?" Joe Wood giggled gleefully.

"We were passing through," Collins said, "and just dropped in to see if there might be any."

I congratulated him on his successful season, in which he had finished 9–2–1, defeated Mississippi State and tied Alabama, and played in the Tangerine Bowl.

"Well, thank you. We only lose five starters." He gestured with his thumb and forefinger: "We're only *that* much away from being there."

They were using an official school visit that afternoon, but could not find Marcus. After a few moments they departed to look for him. The Mississippi State coaches were also expected later in the day, although they had been excluded from the final list.

"I think he may've put Ohio State back on his list," Wood said with a twinkling eye. "I guess you've heard the Touchdown Club of Columbus, Ohio, has just named him the outstanding high school player of the year." I was glad to see that the slightly intimidated coach of our first meeting many weeks before had developed a certain irreverence. "Any one of these teams—that's pretty good football. He'd have a chance of a good pro contract out of any of those five—or maybe *six*. Everything Herschel Walker does, he wants to do better, break all of Herschel's records, and you know why?—because Herschel don't let any *flies* land on *him*." He swiveled about in his chair. "Next time you talk to him, ask him what his ambitions are." He giggled again, this time moderately.

"Listen, I really think he's narrowed it to one. He's made up his mind." But he was suddenly all enigma and would not venture what that choice might be.

Why did he think Mississippi State had not survived on the list? "He doesn't like the offense." And Ole Miss? "His mother."

Marcus and his mother had asked him to sit in on a number of the official visits with recruiters at the house on Davis Street. "They all try to get across that he'll get a good education, that he'll be able to play a good schedule which attracts national attention, that they have a lot of starters comin' back. Also, they talk a lot about their school *tradition*. And they all try to get him to come to their campus on an official visit, on the grounds that if they get him there, he'll sign. They want him to make up his mind on the people he'll be around for four years. They always call these people *the family*. You know Marcus. He don't say much in these meetings. His mother asks some questions, like 'If he got hurt, would he still get a good education?' He seems to be makin' it real well. The pressures are gettin' to him a little bit, narrowin' the schools down from a long list to a few. He hasn't lost his temper yet. The main thing that still gets to him is the phone calls. A lot of people won't give up. Since he got that answerin' service, he just ignores the calls he don't want to return."

He himself leaned down to take a telephone call. It was not Barry Switzer, nor Fred Akers, nor Jackie Sherrill, but his young daughter telling him to bring home something from the grocery store. As soon as he put down the receiver, the phone rang again. "They're around here somewhere," he said. It was Marcus, wanting to know where Bobby Collins of Southern Mississippi was.

He turned to me again. "It's been a unique experience, I'll tell you, seein' how so many colleges wanted this kid as wanted him. I knew he was a great ballplayer, but I had no idea all these colleges would be after him this way. During the season it was both bad and good. Teamwise, it put some strain on the team, although I think we had very little jealousy, as little as could be expected. I believe they feel fortunate now to have played with him." He spoke again of his inexperienced offensive line, the injuries, the penalties and fumbles, the installation of the "I" formation which "really meant we'd just turn around and flip it to Marcus a little deeper than usual. But the most unfortunate thing of all was that the other teams were sky-high for us because of him. That hurt us a lot right there." He contemplated these reflections. "Hell, I'd take another one like him next year. I'd take the same problems. Wouldn't *you?*"

So far the actual recruiting had not been quite so bad as he had expected. The new rules prohibiting personal contact during the football season had helped. The coaches until now had been careful about not exceeding the three visits to the school and the three to his house. The close attention of the NCAA investigators, of course, may have been responsible. "There's one month to the signing date," he said. "It's gonna be real busy. It'll be worse than it's been, everybody makin' the last pitch. I just hope it's not as bad as I *think* it'll be."

That afternoon, while the coach and I were talking, Marcus had been in Herbert's, the men's store just off the Square, browsing among the ties and chatting casually with Steve Wilkerson, the young town alderman who worked there.

After a long silence, still looking at the ties, he said: "I can't believe they're gonna put up signs that say, 'Welcome to Philadelphia, Home of Marcus Dupree.'"

"Well, the San Diego Chargers sure needed you in that game in Cincinnati the other day," Wilkerson said.

"I don't want to play with San Diego *or* Cincinnati. It was too cold up there."

"You don't want to be playing with the University of Pittsburgh, then," Wilkerson said.

"I'm supposed to fly up there this weekend, but I don't know if I'm goin'."

"Why not?"

"It's too *cold*."

At that moment the front door opened and Neil Hitchcock, the assistant coach who had forgotten the money box on the way to the Choctaw Bowl, rushed in. "Doggone it, Marcus, Bobby Collins is down at the school. He's been waitin' on you for an hour."

"I didn't know he was comin'," Marcus said. He telephoned Joe Wood and went down for yet another assignation.

He was in Joe Wood's office the next afternoon leaning against the desk and listening to two Mississippi State recruiters. He saw me outside and waved. When his meeting was over he came out and said hello. We retired to Wood's private hideaway across the hall from the basketball court.

With the Afro, the glasses, the gold-capped tooth, wearing blue jeans and sneakers and the Pittsburgh cap which he had on the night before when I had talked with him at the Philly basketball game, he was

THE COURTING OF MARCUS DUPREE

different as always from the terrible behemoth of the football field. He looked tired, but, as usual, seemed rather glad to see me. His manner was, as ever, shy, almost bemused, with the calm, diffident gaze, and the occasional low chuckle to emphasize something he had said. I gave him a copy of *Pete and Me*, some poems my neighbor wrote about her walks on the Ole Miss campus with my dog. "Give this to Reggie. Tell him Pete can type with his tail." "Yeah?" He laughed and politely thumbed the pages.

We discussed the recruiting. "It's pressure if you let it get to you," he said. He was getting fifteen or more telephone calls a day now from coaches. "I couldn't count 'em earlier, before we cut down the list—maybe twenty-five a day. I got away from home. You have four or five people come to the school and then to your house every day. The answering service helps. I can sleep more. It's kind of all right. You get all this attention. But I didn't do all this on my own. I had teammates. It's a real God-given talent. I thank God a lot."

Sounds of basketball practice, bouncing balls echoing on wood, shouted commands, echoed from the gym. "Anybody who don't get this right," the coach yelled, "five times up and down the floor!"

Had he put back Ohio State on his list? "Oh, naw. I'm just goin' up there with Mark Burnside, I think. They're recruitin' him as a defensive back."

"Well, Coach Wood tells me he suspects you've really narrowed it down to one."

"He *did?*" He laughed again at this proposition, got up and walked around the tiny office. "I've been thinkin', but I really haven't. It's early right now. I've got to get things straight." He said this in the ambiguous tone of one who was reminding himself to do something he himself knew was impossible. He definitely planned to sign, he said, two or three days after the February 10 date.

One by one we went down the list of his final five choices, the attractions to him of each. Every now and then young students would curiously dip their heads inside the door, mumble "Hi, Marcus," and breeze away.

UCLA. "The weather, the players, the coaches, the people were all nice. It's a good environment all the way around. L.A.'s kind of a fast-goin' town."

Were there any problems in a small-town boy's living in such a big city? "Well, I guess any place you go, no matter where it's at, you got to know where you're goin', that's all."

*Texas.* "I'd have a chance to start. It gets cold sometimes, but not much, and it's a good traditional team that wins all the time. It's always in there for the national championship. I'm goin' out there this month. They say they really need a tailback, that they're hungry for one and that I could be another Earl Campbell."

"I graduated from the University of Texas," I said.

"Yeah?" He opened his eyes widely and looked straight at me.

"They have a main building thirty stories high."

"All *right.*"

*Pittsburgh.* "Not the weather, not this time of year anyway. They're just like Texas, always up for the national championship. I'd have a chance to play my freshman year. They get the ball to their backs a lot."

*Oklahoma.* "Like Texas and Pittsburgh, they're always in the top ten. I liked Oklahoma even when I was a little boy. I like the way they run the Wishbone." The Oklahoma recruiters had advised him that their outstanding running back of the '81 season, a versatile fellow named Buster Rhymes, would be moved to split end.

*Southern Mississippi.* "It's close to home, and they have a tailback spot open next year. All the offensive linemen are comin' back except one, I think. I know a lot of friends there. They're not in a conference, but they play SEC teams. They're movin' up. They're dominatin' the state right now."

He added: "If I work hard, and if the recruiters are tellin' me the truth, I think I can start next year at any of these schools."

We talked about all the children who surrounded him for his autograph after the Choctaw Bowl. "That was great. At the same time, my hand was gettin' pretty tired, but I didn't want to say no. So I kept on signin'. I was waitin' on somebody to come rescue me."

A pair of young black girls peered through the door. "Oh, he's talkin' to one of the *coaches*," one of them whispered as they hastened on.

"Joe Wood suggested I ask you what your ambitions are," I said. "What are they?"

His features brightened. He stood up again, walked around a little, and answered with spirit. "To try to break all of Herschel's freshman records. And try to become the first freshman to win the Heisman Trophy. People should look at how good a person is, not what grade he's in. That's what people should do." He paused, eyes toward the floor. "I want to sign with a good school and play a lot. I want to graduate and play in the pros. Then I can take care of my mama and Reggie. College football is important to me."

What was he learning from all this?

"Well—I've learned to meet a lot of people. It's teachin' me who to trust and who not to trust. After this is all over, I'll know who my friends are." He was thoughtful again. "The main thing, it's makin' me grow up."

We left the office and walked down the corridor with its display case of past Tornado trophies. On the basketball court the players were running sprints, and their heavy footfalls thundered through the empty building.

"Oh!" he said. "I forgot that book about your dog." And he sprinted away down the hall as I had seen him against the Ackerman Indians, the Union Yellowjackets, and the Neshoba Central Rockets.

A couple of nights later the neon temperature sign in front of the Bank of Philadelphia showed zero. There was an ominous feeling in the air which presaged some great act of nature.

My son David, Sid Salter of the *Democrat*, and I decided on a respite from nocturnal Philly. David had been moving about town with his cameras taking pictures of white, black, and Indian veterans of Vietnam in town, in the Quarters, and on the reservation. As a son of New York City, he had not become readily accustomed to a town closing down at 6 P.M. We drove south on the Meridian highway, past Rock Cut Road. In Mississippi the surest way to ascertain that one has crossed a county line is the sight of the bar and roadhouse signs. Only a few yards into Lauderdale County was "Ed's Beer Joint," where two generations of Philadelphia teenagers had by tradition stolen away from town to get drunk for the first time.

"At age eighteen?" I asked Sid Salter.

"Fourteen," he replied.

There was a long bar, a pool table, and a roaring fire in an open fireplace. It was an authentic Mississippi country honky-tonk, ever so proudly run-down. The only deference to modernity was the video games in the back room. There was a mammoth photograph of Mr. Ed on the wall. He had died six years ago. "You should've *seen* the flowers at his funeral," the bartender said.

Only the three of us were out on this bitter night. David and Sid were settled in at the bar talking about the Indians; I had never known a New Yorker so intrigued with Choctaws.

"It's a bad night," the bartender said. "We open at 7:30 A.M. and it's been this way all day. People around here are scared of the cold. They spent all their money on Christmas anyway." While the two young men discussed Nanih Waiya and the exodus to Oklahoma, the bartender explored the phenomenon of Marcus Dupree. "Everybody comes in here and talks about him. They say he's somethin' else again. Ain't that wonderful? You a coach?"

That was the night Sid Salter and I decided we would establish a Command Post in the last days of the football recruiting, pooling our intelligence, monitoring the Downtown Hotel and the motels and the school, making surreptitious forays into the Quarters, utilizing our command telephone, and relying when necessary on Pete's primal Labrador intuitions.

"We'll know before the coaches know," Salter said.

"I wish I didn't have to go back to Massachusetts," David said.

The bartender returned from studying the outdoors. His nose had turned pink. "Boys," he warned, "it feels like snow."

It arrived quite early the next morning. I was with Pete on his walk around the stadium and Possum Hollow when the first snowflakes descended from the murky purple skies. The seven or eight country Dixie dogs who had come out as usual to tease my Yankee dog did not quite know what to make of the phenomenon. One of them kept biting at the flakes. From the school building, after a while, there were exuberant whoops and shouts. School was letting out. From a distance I saw Marcus and Daran Jackson joyously striding toward his Olds parked behind the gymnasium.

Southern snow! It was Philly's first in five years, and the first heavy one in more than fifteen. The schoolchildren, so suddenly emancipated, were reveling in it. Pete and I walked toward the Square. Flakes gathered on his furry black coat and there was snow on his nose from rummaging in some shrubs. Did this bring back for him his Long Island youth? A woman stood in front of the Patio Ice Cream Parlor and Sandwich Shoppe with her little boy, who was mesmerized.

"Ain't it pretty, honey?" she asked.

The flakes were coming down thickly now. Several black children sat on the ground in front of the courthouse letting the snow fall on their faces. One seemed to be biting at them like the Possum Hollow dog. In the wind the frozen leaves of the magnolias on the Square hummed and tinkled, like the carousels I remembered from the playgrounds of Europe. Tom Turner was observing the intoxicating scene from the doorway of Turner Hardware. "I hope Marcus makes his trip to Pittsburgh in weather like this," he said. "That'll get him to Ole Miss."

In the restaurant of the Downtown, for the first time in weeks, there was a moratorium on the football talk. Roy Tingle, Morgan Hardy, and the others gazed out the windows at the falling snow and the cars spinning on Byrd Avenue. A black girl burst through the door and described a solitary snowflake. "I looked at it comin' down. It flittered and fluttered, and then it landed right in my hand!"

By midafternoon the Square was deserted. Even the courthouse was closed. David was out taking pictures of the storm, and I returned to my room, where later I had an interview with a black preacher. I sat by the window in the early dark and watched the unrelenting snow as it descended on the Philadelphia Motor Company, Sears, and Park's Furniture. Pete lay curled on the rug. I bent down and petted him on his ears, remembering our times together in the snowstorms of the North. He nuzzled my hand with his nose. It seemed on this day that Pete and I had been together forever. It saddened me to see him growing old. Near the stadium that morning a man had shouted: "Say, your dog get hit, or is it the arthritis?" His old legs were slowly giving out.

Why had snow always driven me to thought? Inexplicably I recalled the Irwin Shaw novel, *Two Weeks in Another Town.* The title had once captured my mood here.

"Have you ever seen such snow?" the black preacher asked when I answered the knock on the door. He was a husky man in his forties wearing a gray suit under his raincoat. He was known for his emphatic and articulate views. Our interview had been arranged by mutual friends; I would not use his name. He knew I wanted to talk about Marcus and the town. He was now living in the North after long years in Neshoba and adjoining counties, but he planned to return home shortly to stay. His manner was intense. Sometimes he tugged distractedly at his goatee.

"The blacks are very politically active here," he said. "There's a black alderman—something people thought would never happen. As far as having any strength in the city, it's very minute if anything at all. All you have to do is go into the courthouse, the stores, and you can tell the black authority in Neshoba's at a minimum. This won't stop us from tryin'."

There was a quote from Martin Luther King, I said, about how real integration meant that blacks in America would share responsibility and power: "Often when they merge, the Negro is integrated without power," King had said. "The two or three positions of power which he did have in the separate situation passed away altogether, so that he lost his bargaining position, he lost his power, and he lost his posture where he could be relatively militant and really grapple with the problems. We don't want to be integrated *out* of power; we want to be integrated *into* power."

"That's true," the preacher said. "Most of the political positions are *created* for blacks, from Washington on down. We merely carry the balance as a swing vote. The whites come along and say, you have the power to win the runoff. Only in the runoffs can we apply pressure in Neshoba. When the election's over, that power's gone. We've gotten a few deadbeats out by exacting our power in the first primaries. We can determine who'll get into the runoffs." In 1972 and '76, he said, for the first time there was a solid black voting bloc in the local, state, and presidential elections. There were efforts to buy the black vote. "When you're talkin' about politics in Neshoba, you're talkin' about blood and sweat."

I had ordered coffee. From outside there was the high whine of motors trying to negotiate the hill.

In '64, although he had not been active in COFO, the preacher had talked with Schwerner, Goodman, and Chaney when they came to adjoining Leake County. "We talked about the problems of black people, the shame of it—being taxed and not represented." He was stopped two or three times by the police. There were the bombings in Neshoba and Leake. "We couldn't get any butane gas for our houses. The homes of friends were shot into. Some do-gooder in the North sent several rifles and walkie-talkies. We took turns guardin' the houses at night."

In Neshoba, he said, "The light-skined and dark-skinned Negroes are different. When you're talkin' with a white man around here, he might be one of our cousins."

He turned the talk to Marcus. "I think your economic sector here needed a face-lift," the preacher said, "and that's what he's bein' used for. I'm not sure he's as good as they say he is. He's a *symbol*. If what I say they've done is true, he's not guilty. Let take Weyerhaeuser, Molpus, U.S. Motors, Wells Lamont, the others. These are national. Economically, socially, the whites here didn't give a damn, period, until these industries came in here.

"What does Marcus Dupree know about '64? What do his white friends know? We've got millionaires from other parts of the country comin' in here. It was the town where the three civil rights workers were killed. But we have to pull in management from Chicago and California. 'This is the town that produced Marcus Dupree.' It makes sense. It's a brand-new thing. We're talkin' about money. The town can't afford to have the old image for these new industrialists, the engineers, the computer people. They can't afford the image of lazy, uneducated, downtrodden blacks."

I had been reading that remarkable biennial volume, *The Almanac of American Politics*, published in Washington. I got it from my suitcase and read this passage about Mississippi to the preacher:

> Since the beginning of the 1970s, black outmigration has slowed way down and the long-term trend, for the first time since the 1870s, is for the black percentage in Mississippi to increase as the years grow on. The primary reason is that the state's economy has been taking off. Is this due to integration? No one is sure, but it is becoming increasingly clear that the number of jobs started rising just as Mississippi lost its segregationist ways. Part of the reason may be that investors don't like putting up plants and buildings where there is racial strife; part of the reason may be that people here have become better educated and more skilled; part of the reason may be that wage levels in many northern states got so much higher than those in the south that states like Mississippi became more at-

tractive. Another reason—not mentioned by those who focus only on the motives of white businessmen and the performance of state government—is that Mississippi's blacks themselves, finally free to express themselves and to make their livings as they wish, have been more and more likely, whether skilled or not, to work harder and to put out more effort than they were in the days when it seemed that anything they might accomplish would only be to the advantage of the white man.

"Yes. Well, I think that's pretty true too," he said. "That kind of thing makes Marcus all the more important as a symbol."

Does not his argument, however, place too much expectation on a seventeen-year-old boy? I asked.

The preacher had been sitting in an easy chair sipping coffee. He stood now and walked about the room, pausing ever so often at the window to look out at the storm. The snow was piling up on the hotel balcony.

"Look. Integration was forced on blacks in Mississippi on the white man's terms. What you hear about Marcus is this—he's a good guy, he's one of the few guys I know who can talk with a white girl. I've seen the times here when you couldn't do that. It's not being accepted here. It's being *tolerated*. But I'd rather be tolerated than rejected. If I'm tolerated to wash the windows in a hotel, then I can move up to bellhop.

"Two years ago a black graduate of Philadelphia High, an athlete, went to Jackson State and they found out he couldn't read on a fourth-grade level. Marcus is not only an athlete, he makes good grades—he's able to read and to take a college entrance exam."

With all this, I asked the preacher, why had he lived so long in Mississippi, and decided now to return?

"I have a deep love," he said, "for this part of the country. I feel this is the best place for my children. We can get an education here. We can own land here. There's time to breathe here. My family here is close and united. They can call on so many people for help. There's somethin' real here that doesn't exist in Milwaukee or Chicago. The white man here is either your friend or your enemy. He'll help you up front or hurt you up front. In Milwaukee the white man will use you and pat you on the back at the same time. Here the white man is *real*. If he meets you and shakes your hand, you know what he feels. In Mississippi, if a white man likes you, he'll help you. Even though Mississippi gets more federal money than any state, you'll find more black people ownin' land and houses than in Chicago. The white people here have a lot of feelin' for blacks who are *able*. That didn't used to be so, you know. They give you an awful lot of respect for havin' come up hard and done somethin' with yourself. I like that.

"We were integrated before the North ever *thought* about it. White and black kids have been livin' together here forever. Compare that with New York, where you don't know your next-door neighbor. You'll find more black people in Chicago wantin' to come to Mississippi with all its problems than black people in Mississippi wantin' to go to Chicago. If you look at the black people in Mississippi my age, we're more stable. What worries me are the youngsters gettin' out of school now. How many thousands can you turn out without the chance of a job? How long can you say that good's comin' while they walk down the road with their stomachs growlin'?"

It had been a compelling soliloquy. He was quiet for a moment, as if hypnotized by the falling snow, then he spoke again of young Marcus.

"I want him to stay in Mississippi. Mississippi could take care of him. A Mississippi school would allow him to fail and then try again. It's like a nice figurine fallin' off the table and breakin'. You glue it back together because you like it. It's yours. You have sentiment about it. You'll take care of a home product better. I don't know if they'd take care of him that way in some other state like Oklahoma or Texas or California.

"I wish somebody who's black could sit down and talk about the long-range things he could do for his people in Mississippi. These people from the colleges who've come to talk to him are white to the toenails."

Three recruiters from a predominantly white Mississippi university came to the preacher's house not too long ago to discuss Marcus, he said. "They're dreamers. They weren't talkin' sense to him. They were talkin' about an athletic program. They didn't so much as bring up the effect he could have on his black brothers and sisters. They should've said, 'Hey, man, look what Philadelphia's done for you. Stay here.' They should've been tellin' him he wouldn't be playin' football forever, that he could hurt his knees any time, that he had a responsibility to his people here, that he could do so much for them.

"The Mississippi schools don't know how to get home to him," the preacher said. "They don't give him reasons other than runnin' a ball and catchin' a pass. Now Mississippi may be sayin': *There goes Marcus Dupree!*"

After a few hours' respite, a second severe snowstorm whipped in from the Texas Panhandle the next day; Philadelphia, in fact, was in the very eye of it. After the first exhilaration, the expressions of the citizens were dubious. The men in the restaurant of the Downtown brought out the dominoes. One country woman known to the players came in and lamented: "I'm about *froze*. We got no electricity, no heat, not even a fireplace. My neighbors told me to stay with them, but all *they* got is a fireplace, and it don't draw. I may stay right here in this hotel. How much is a room?" The Square was even more deserted than before, and the heat and even the television in our rooms were not functioning at all. Interstate 55 and the other highways were closed, the streets of the town precarious. While David and Pete grew a little cranky with the lassitude, I used the telephone for several conversations. There were, of course, no recruiters in town. Marcus still planned to fly to Pittsburgh that weekend, and he had just decided to make official visits on the following three to Southern Mississippi, Texas, and Oklahoma, in that order. He would not visit Ohio State. His telephone was ringing more than ever.

Late that night the snow was still falling as Pete and I walked around the Square. When he relieved himself on the shrubs in front of the Peoples Bank the ice on the leaves steamed and melted. Suddenly I heard two boisterous voices shouting ny name, which echoed across the frozen façades. I turned to see two of my Philly friends in a prodigious van with a four-wheel drive. They motioned for me to climb in the back. Pete and I did so.

They had been cruising around town absorbing the unfamiliar wintry landscape and drinking bourbon whiskey, of which they had obviously partaken in considerable quantity. They resumed this journey now. The two of them were old friends, but they became involved for a time in a vehement argument as to which of the two made more money. They continued this aimless persiflage until we met two jeeps on a steep hill leading to the Square. The driver lowered the window. A young man wearing a cowboy hat got out of one of the jeeps. "We're spinnin'," he explained. He and his comrades had been hooking together the bumpers of the jeeps and dragging each other through the snow. Farther on we sighted a couple of pickup trucks in an alleyway. A party was in progress, and we were invited to take swigs from a large jug of Neshoba home brew. The fiery liquid curled my toes.

As we drove through the ghostly streets, Pete and I sat on a bench in back gazing out at the lovely scenes. "God, ain't it beautiful?" the driver said. The town, spectral and remote, was different altogether from the one I had known. I remembered one bitter Sunday night in 1969, after a blizzard, when I had walked alone down the middle of Fifth Avenue with not a soul in sight—no moonshine parties there on that evening.

The snow had caught in the pines and half-covered the tombstones in the cemetery. The icicles on the magnolias around the Square were like tinsel on a Christmas tree. In the affluent white neighborhoods the ranch-style dwellings appeared like mansions in the eerie whiteness.

We drove now toward Independence Quarters. The Busy Bee was closed tight, as was every other establishment. There were snowdrifts on the porches of the little shacks, and woodsmoke filled the air. There was snow also on the front steps of Marcus' house—might the telephone have been ringing inside at that moment?—and on the memorial in front of the Mount Nebo Church. As the Quarters drifted past, I recalled the words of the black preacher the day before, about symbols and face-lifts, success and despair.

Pete huddled against my shoulder, looked up at me, wondered no doubt where I might be taking him this time. My friends passed around their bottle as we turned once more toward the white section. "Ain't it lovely?" the driver repeated. "I've never seen it this way. It's my pretty ol' town."

We were snowbound in Philly. "All quiet on the Western Front," Sid Salter telephoned from the *Democrat* to report. The son, the dog, and I languished in our rooms for three more days. I had appointments in Oxford and David was expected in Massachusetts. David protested the incarceration with a thirty-six-hour fast, Pete by urinating on the bathroom floor. Then, suddenly, Charles Henry called from Oxford. Interstate 55 had just reopened. We had the car loaded in ten minutes. As I started the motor, the people in the Downtown lobby had their faces pressed against the plate-glass windows observing our departure. When we moved haltingly down Byrd Avenue, they waved their farewells.

Marcus took his trip to Pittsburgh. "It's pretty good schoolwise," he said. "I know there you'd have a chance for a national championship. They've got a bunch of *big* offensive linemen. I made a tour of the school, went to the cathedral, and things like that. I talked to Hugh Green [a black from Mississippi and an all-American defensive end] who said he really liked it up there. He said it was a good opportunity, kind of hard on you at first but you get adjusted."

When he got off the plane in Pittsburgh it was fourteen below zero. Later he told one of his teachers: "I ain't goin' there. My hair froze."

# 20

# *Big Money*

---

In the third week of January 1982, there were three swift occurrences which might affect his forthcoming decision. One of them suggested much of the rampant commercialism of collegiate football.

First, Bobby Collins, the head coach of Southern Mississippi, resigned to become the coach at Southern Methodist University, filling the vacancy left by Ron Meyer, who had departed for the New England Patriots of the National Football League. Collins, who had produced six winning teams in seven seasons at Southern Mississippi, would take with him to Dallas most of his assistants, including Bootsie Larsen, who had been the recruiter assigned to Marcus.

Second, Southern announced the next day the appointment of Jim Carmody to succeed Collins. Carmody, forty-five, a Tulane graduate, was noted in the football trade as an aggressive defensive tactician. For the past season he had been an assistant with the Buffalo Bills of the NFL. Before that he had served three years as an assistant at Southern and four at Ole Miss. "He knows the territory," a Mississippi football man said, "and the territory knows him."*

Southern Mississippi was one of the five schools left on Marcus' list, but he had had no inkling that Collins, whom he liked, was leaving. He was surprised. "He and Coach Larsen were up here last Monday and they told me they weren't going anywhere. I don't know what to think. Coach Collins was a major reason I was thinking about Southern. I don't know anything about the new coach. I guess I'll have to check it out. I still like Southern. I'm going to take an official visit this weekend. I should know more after that."

Collins was taking over a team at SMU which had compiled a 10–1 record in 1981, ranked fifth in the country, and won the Southwest Conference championship. With almost all of its players returning, it was ex-

---

* The NCAA had disclosed the previous September that it was beginning an investigation into football recruiting at Southern. Carmody later said: "I know I'm the first coach to report for work and on the first day have the NCAA show up. My first day—January 15—the NCAA had a man here on campus."

pected to be a contender for the national championship in '82. Would Collins try now to bring Marcus to SMU? "Right now I don't know what we're going to do," Collins said. "We aren't going to recruit anybody who isn't on the present SMU list." His predecessor, Ron Meyer, had been one of the many pilgrims to Philadelphia. SMU, however, had had two running backs the previous season, named Dickerson and James, who gained more than a thousand yards each, and they had almost never been in a game at the same time. Both were returning. "Don't predict anything," one newspaper said. "The status of Marcus Dupree remains unclear."

Three days after Collins' defection to SMU, Jackie Sherrill, the Mississippian who was head coach at the University of Pittsburgh, announced that he was moving to Texas A&M. The speculation over whether Sherrill might induce Marcus to become an Aggie, just as he had hoped he might sign with Pittsburgh, was drowned in the national debate concerning his contract.

The circumstances were questionable at best. The A&M coach, Tom Wilson, had a year left on his contract after a 7–5 season and had been led to believe he would be retained. Sherrill accepted an offer from the A&M regents of $267,000 a year, the highest payment for any position at an American college or university. The six-year figure, to be paid both by Texas A&M and privately by its alumni, was for $1,602,000 in cash and fringe benefits. These latter included insurance policies and investments, the usual television and radio shows, private club memberships, cars, and help in buying a house. The contract would be renewed each year, which meant that if the Aggies ever grew disenchanted with the new coach they would have to pay him $1.4 million. The president of Texas A&M, who had no responsibility in the hiring, was so disturbed by these phantasmagoric figures he almost resigned.†

† Bo Schembechler, the head coach at Michigan, was offered the position at A&M before Sherrill and turned it down. Doug Looney of *Sports Illustrated* noted that he was offered about $2.25 million over ten years. "He was on the brink, then backed off, but his base salary at Ann Arbor quickly jumped from $60,000 to $85,000." He was also given a large interest in a pizza parlor in Columbus, Ohio.

Interestingly, a detailed study by *The Miami Herald* during this period reported that Sherrill's salary at A&M was only the third highest in college sports. According to the *Herald*, Bear Bryant of Alabama was the highest wage-earner with a base salary and benefits totaling $450,000 a year, with Barry Switzer of Oklahoma second at $270,000. The *Herald* listed Lou Holtz of Arkansas fourth at $226,000, followed by Kentucky's Jerry Claiborne at $152,500, Miami's Howard Schnellenberger at $150,000, Colorado's Chuck Fairbanks at $150,000, Michigan's Schembechler at $147,500, Nebraska's Tom Osborne at $140,500, and Florida State's Bobby Bowden at $140,000. The Associated Press looked into fringe benefits, which included speaking engagements, courtesy cars,

The reaction in the American academic community was acute. Howard R. Swearer, president of Brown University, was one among many voices:

> It is so far beyond reason or imagination, I have never heard of a salary like that in colleges. It also begins to make the connection between intercollegiate sports and professional sports when they are throwing around that kind of money. Just think of the other uses for $2 million—financial aid to students, starting new and important programs, making sure your faculty has decent salaries.
>
> I believe salaries should be kept within the scales set by a university. This does seem to raise the question of how much influence a booster club may have over a university's football coach. I would not like to see an employee of Brown University paid directly by another group.
>
> It is really appalling.

Joe Restic, the football coach at Harvard, said: "I look at the direction we're going in college sports and it's a tragedy. It's no longer education, it's big business. And television controls it. That's where the money comes from."

As one sportswriter noted, Sherrill "was a chip, although an expensive chip, off the grand old sequoia of coaching." His mentor, Bear Bryant, had come to Texas A&M from Kentucky in 1954 and in two years transformed a 1–9 team into one which compiled a 9–0–1 record and won the Southwest Conference championship. Then he went back to his alma mater, Alabama. He also left the Aggies on NCAA probation.

Having attended the University of Texas, I was not unfamiliar with the impenitent traditions of the Aggies. My father-in-law had even been an Aggie, a gruff and wonderful man named Rudy Buchan, sardonic about many things of this world but not about genuflecting before Aggie shrines. I never told an Aggie joke around him. I had been all too familiar with the Corps of Cadets, the Aggie War Hymn, and the Twelfth Man. There was a ferocious religiosity to all this, born of the Texas boondocks. One afternoon many years ago, after an Aggie-Texas baseball game in Austin, I witnessed the largest mass fistfight I had ever seen—about two thousand Aggies and Longhorns mauling one another from Clark Field to Texas Memorial Stadium. I myself took a hard blow to the nose, and when I later wrote my story of this catastrophic event for *The Daily Texan*, there was blood on my copy paper.

As Doug Looney of *Sports Illustrated* reported, some 250 Aggie alumni gave $2,000 a year to the athletic department; 75 had donated

---

TV and radio shows, commercials, deals on houses, memberships in country clubs, lucrative summer camps, investments, annuities. Oklahoma State's Jim Johnson had six working oil wells. Lou Holtz owned part of a cable television franchise. Barry Switzer was in the oil business and owned an insurance company.

$30,000 each to a permanent endowment for athletic scholarships. There was a $750,000 practice field with the grass designed by Aggie agronomists. The stadium seated 73,500 and had a 3,600-square-foot training room. When forty-eight luxury suites were built at the stadium and offered at rentals from $10,000 to $50,000 for eight years, they were taken in little more than two hours.

Would all this appeal to the prospect from Philadelphia, Mississippi? Personally I could not conceive of Marcus Dupree as an Aggie.

"Football pays for a lot of things here," Jackie Sherrill said that week. "It pays for the other sports. The salaries and the facilities come from gifts, the scholarship fund, our fund-raising apparatus. Professors who complain, why, they don't spend their summers raising money for the school. Football is a business. Let's get our heads out of the sand."

"Who the hell can blame him?" a friend said to me. "Would *you* have turned down that kind of money? Besides, he's just an ol' Mississippi boy tryin' to make his way in this world." One can imagine the pressures he would encounter if he failed to win. Patience had never been an Aggie virtue. "If Sherrill starts losing," Beano Cook of ABC said, "he's going to feel like Rommel in Africa, with Hitler calling him all the time wondering what's going on." Withal, this development in mid January 1982 provided another insight among many into the importance of America's number one high school recruit in the exigent world of college football.


The day after Jackie Sherrill announced he was leaving Pittsburgh for the Texas Aggies, Marcus dropped Pittsburgh from his Final Five. "I thought about them seriously till Coach Sherrill left," he told me later. On January 22 he made his official visit to Southern Mississippi, the third of the six allowed by the NCAA. He had already been to UCLA and Pittsburgh. The departure of Bobby Collins for SMU and the appointment of Jim Carmody had no apparent effect on his interest in Southern. "I had a good time during my trip," he said. "I still like the school—still thinking about going there." His list now was down to four:

> Oklahoma
> Southern Mississippi
> Texas
> UCLA

Despite his regard for Bobby Collins, he said he did not plan to visit SMU. As for Texas A&M, no one, least of all the recruit himself, was especially surprised when Jackie Sherrill, in the cold bleak days of early February in Philly, and in the tenacious spirit of the Aggie Twelfth Man, would try to ambush them all.

Bobby Fields, the UCLA recruiter, was back in town after Marcus' trip to Southern. One afternoon that week Coach Dave Driscoll of Michigan State was in Joe Wood's office. Apparently he had not been following the prospect's various lists. Scott Hill, the recruiting coordinator at Oklahoma, came in. Wood, Driscoll, and Hill were talking casually. Hill wanted to make absolutely sure that Marcus was coming to Norman, Oklahoma, on his official visit.

"You'll have to see Marcus," Wood said. "I'll go check with him." When he returned, Hill had his feet propped up on Wood's desk.

"Coach Driscoll, he doesn't want to talk to you," Wood said. "Coach Hill, he doesn't want to visit Oklahoma."

"Hill's feet came down real quick," Wood said. "I just happened to have a fungo bat in my hand. Hill said, 'Hit me between the eyes with the bat, but don't tell me *that*.' "

A new and impressive personage also entered the narrative in these last days of January. "Lucious Selmon, the Oklahoma assistant, was by here yesterday," Marcus said. "He was an all-right guy." On his schedule he had two more announced official visits—the University of Texas on January 29–31, and the University of Oklahoma on February 5–7. He could make one more official trip elsewhere if he wished.

"America's Most Wanted must wait until February 10 officially to sign for his future," one sportswriter wrote on the eve of Marcus' weekend trip to Austin. "Still, he seems to be prolonging the decision much the way a hemophiliac might ponder a contribution to a local blood drive. Dupree has pared the list down, achingly . . . On Friday he was to leave town for his official visit to Texas. On the itinerary is a trek to Oklahoma, with UCLA and Southern Mississippi seemingly in the fray, although the whims of recruitment are legend. Anything can happen. Anything still might."

# 21
# Sojourn in Texas

I had been as neutral as the Swiss Red Cross, but secretly, if he did not remain in our native Mississippi, I wished him to choose my alma mater, the University of Texas. There was a touch of selfishness to this, involving what I supposed might be a mutual sense of belonging. I had gone to Austin at his age, and although the university had frightened me at first (its student population was sixteen thousand, or twice as large as Yazoo City), it eventually had given me a deep and liberating sense of values and, in curious ways, of loyalty. It had educated me.

Austin had been a lovely town then, with its rolling green hills descending to the banks of the Colorado River, and the muted blue ridges of the Great Balcones Divide in the distance which had led O. Henry to call it the City of the Violet Crown. It was a blend of the South and the West; it was both and it was neither. The close proximity of the campus and the state capital with its circumference of government buildings endowed it with a pointed urgency from time to time—its cyclic political controversies from which it always seemed somehow to recover. To this day the university filled me with the tenderness a man has when he gets a little drunk late at night and starts telling his dog how much he loves him.

Before I had settled down to become editor of *The Daily Texan*, the great newspaper of college journalism, I had indulged in the usual undergraduate enthusiasms. As a sophomore I had driven all the way to South Bend, Indiana, with the university's mascot, a savage fifteen-hundred-pound Longhorn steer named Bevo V, for a Texas–Notre Dame game. His caretaker was an imperturbable ranch boy named Dean Smith, who had placed fourth in the 100-meters in the 1952 Olympics. Through the night we took turns driving across the dry and lonesome Oklahoma plains, the bugs splattering on our windshield. Bevo was so big that every time he shifted his weight in his orange-and-white trailer, our station wagon would move with him. Eventually we stopped at a motel on the outskirts of St. Louis. "Madam," Dean Smith said to the woman behind the counter, "we're from Texas and we're on our way to the Texas–Notre Dame game. We need a room to rest in."

"We've got plenty of vacancies," she replied.

"We'll take one. The only problem is, we got a fifteen-hundred-pound Longhorn steer out there tied to one of your trees."

"I'm sorry," the woman said, "but we don't allow pets."


I journeyed out from Mississippi to Austin a few months ago for a sentimental return to the mother university. By chance, that weekend was the twenty-fifth anniversary of my graduation. I had not been there in a very long time. The enrollment was now forty-six thousand. My visit helped me know what Mark Twain meant when he returned after many years to Hannibal: "I had a sort of realizing sense of what the Bastille prisoners must have felt when they used to come out and look upon Paris after years of captivity and note how curiously the familiar and the strange were mixed together before them." The Tower was still there, of course, with its inscription in the stone which had so titillated me as a youngster: YE SHALL KNOW THE TRUTH AND THE TRUTH SHALL MAKE YOU FREE. So was the football stadium, where on a sweltering September afternoon of 1952 I saw another Notre Dame team walk listlessly on the field for the pregame drills in T-shirts and shorts, and a Longhorn fan yelled: "Next time they'll come out naked!" Here too, in '54, I witnessed the first black player ever to perform in the stadium, a second-string halfback named Duke Washington for the lowly Washington State Cougars, as he broke free on a long touchdown and the entire student section rose spontaneously and applauded. Now the stadium was twice the size it had been, as was the campus with its dozens of glittering new buildings—symbolic of this rich and restless society—and I became hopelessly lost on the very terrain of my young manhood.

In the sad disorientation of that day, I had wandered to the older parts of the campus. Without warning I would stumble upon some quiet corner which had not changed at all—the little park of live oaks behind Hogg Auditorium, and breezeways and dogleg paths that greeted me with a calming reassurance. Here, on this bench by the grooved steps, on an evanescent spring afternoon, I had told a beautiful girl I loved her. A little farther on, near this mossy terrace, a professor had advised me I should apply for a scholarship to Europe. Under these very trees, one long-ago midnight, I had composed my "thirty" column for The Daily Texan. In this shady courtyard, I had retreated one day to read the words of Jefferson on freedom of expression. Beneath these statues of mustangs, as part of some forgotten rite, I had been thrown into the waters of Littlefield

Fountain. I had sat here one morning with the baseball players as they readied their cheat notes for an examination, one of them writing a chemical formula in ink on his ankle. Adjacent to this pleasant lane, in the old Experimental Science Building, I was introduced to Byron, Shelley, and Keats by Dr. Sackton to the heady smell of chemicals wafting down the lengthy halls, and his Romantics brought that incomparable spring of my eighteenth year alive for me, and I would emerge into the dappled sunshine under the oak trees with the pink-granite capitol out at the horizon, oblivious to everyone around me, reading from the textbook to myself:

> When old age shall this generation waste,
> Thou shalt remain, in midst of other woe
> Than ours, a friend to man, to-whom though say'st,
> "Beauty is truth, truth beauty—that is all
> Ye know on earth, and all ye need to know."

The University of Texas! Perhaps over the years, and even in the unsettling odyssey into the past on this particular day, I must have forgotten my profound affection and love for this place.

Yet amid these pleasing rediscoveries of its unchanging aspects, the awareness of this emotion gratified me immeasurably, as if this comprehension of affection were part of an old debt repaid, a gesture of continuity, an affirmation of the heart. I know too in that moment that this campus with its prosperous new appurtenances, its symbols of enormous wealth and power, was beautiful to the young who now inhabited it, just as in its more placid times it had been beautiful to my own generation. Perhaps Marcus, another small-town Mississippi boy, could grow to care for it as I had.


The Texas Longhorn football team over the years had won three national championships and appeared in twenty-nine bowl games. Fred Akers, the head coach, age forty-three, had succeeded to the tradition of Dana X. Bible and Darrell Royal.

Akers had come to Philadelphia, Mississippi, the previous summer. "We're looking all over the country to find a top breakaway back," he said then. "Jam Jones, our tailback, is graduating next year and we need someone to take his place."

Akers was a native of Blytheville, Arkansas, and was a quarterback, defensive back, and place-kicker under Frank Broyles at Arkansas. He was an assistant coach at Texas for nine years before becoming head coach at the University of Wyoming. In 1977 he returned to Austin to take over from Darrell Royal, who had said he wanted to retire "while there's still some meat on the bones." Royal was a smart, colorful figure, hard to dislike, a poor Okie who had developed a rich Texas veneer, a friend of Willie Nelson, John Connally, and LBJ. "They didn't come in on a load of wood," he would say, or "There's a lot of snot knocking between the okra."

Akers could not match that poetry, and seemed rather bland in comparison, but he knew he could win. He espoused the running game. In his first season at Texas, Earl Campbell won the Heisman Trophy and the Longhorns were ranked number one in the country until they lost to Notre Dame in the Cotton Bowl. He followed with two consecutive 9-3 seasons, then 7-5. There was grumbling among the Texas alumni, who were as skittish a breed, almost, as the Aggies. But in 1981, Marcus' senior year in high school, his team compiled a 10-1-1 record, including a 14-12 victory over Alabama in the Cotton Bowl, and finished second in the nation behind Clemson in the final Associated Press poll. In five seasons at Texas he had won forty-six games and lost only thirteen for a .775 percentage.

He was noted for his fiery locker-room orations, and he was persuasive with recruits, more the suave older brother than the father. One such prospect arrived from Mississippi in the City of the Violet Crown by jet on Friday, January 29, twelve days before the national signing date.

"I really liked Texas for several reasons," he said later. "They've got a lot of people back, the crowd really gets off on football, and two of their tailbacks, Jones and Tate, are leaving. The campus isn't as big as everybody thinks. All the guys seem happy there. It's a place to get a good education. Most all their athletes graduate."

He spent some time with Earl Campbell's brother, Tim, a Texas player, and talked with the offensive linemen, who said they needed him. He was chauffeured about the campus in a private limousine. He attended the football awards banquet Friday night and toured the campus and the awesome football facilities the next day. That night he was a guest at the Texas–Texas A&M basketball game in the Super-Drum.

A Longhorn linebacker, Jeff Leiding, told *The Dallas Times Herald*: "The kid wouldn't say much to me. It seemed like he got along better with the black athletes than he did with me. I don't know if it was because I'm white or what. He was a quiet person. He never let you know what was on his mind, like he had something going on in his head and he didn't want to tell anybody about it. He did tell [fullback Terry] Orr that he was coming here."

He met privately with Fred Akers Sunday morning, and that after-noon he flew back to Mississippi.

Shortly before noon the next morning, Monday, I was sitting in my bungalow in Oxford working on a speech I was to give in Memphis that night. Pete and I had just returned from a brisk walk through Bailey's Woods, where he had made a number of ritualistic though not especially menacing moves against the squirrels, and he was exhausted. He was doz-ing now under my desk.

The telephone rang. It was Sid Salter calling from *The Neshoba Democrat.*

"Guess what?" he said.

"What?"

"Well, *guess.*" Sid saw things dramatically, I had learned, and en-joyed prolonged tension.

"I don't have any idea."

"He just committed to Texas."

"Are you serious?"

"Damned right I'm serious. Joe Wood just announced it."

I yelled in delight, causing Pete to leap from his slumber, like a character in a dawn battle scene from Shakespeare.

"Of course you know a verbal commitment isn't binding," Salter said. "He has to sign the papers, and he can't do that till February 10. But he's really going to Texas."

"I'll be damned."

We talked a little more. I would be down on Thursday, I told him, and I planned to stay until he formally signed.

When I hung up the telephone I was still pleased, yet at the same time strangely disappointed. I was normally as theatrical as Sid Salter, and there had been no real *dénouement.* I had not even been there for the conclusion. Nelson Doubleday was not going to like this at all. So be it. Marcus Dupree had announced as a Texas Longhorn, which had been my covert wish.

I began to reconstruct what had happened.

On Sunday morning in Austin, in their private meeting, Fred Akers had asked him how he liked Texas. "I told him I liked it fine," he said later. "He asked me if I liked their offense, and I told him I did. Then he asked me what the chances were of signing me. I told him they were pretty good. I told him I was pretty sure I was going to Texas."

Shortly after he got back to Philadelphia Sunday night, he went to the youth center in the old Booker T. Washington School in Independence Quarters. He told his friend and fellow running back, Daran Jackson, that he had decided on Texas.

"For real?" Jackson asked.

"Yeah."

He told his mother Sunday night. "She didn't say anything," he said.

On Monday morning at eight-fifteen he came into Coach Joe Wood's office and told him he wanted to go to Texas. He was wearing a Texas jersey under his coat. "He really didn't have a whole lot to say about it," Wood said. "He just said he liked what he saw, and he decided to commit. He told me they have big offensive linemen and are always a contender for the national championship. My personal feeling is the factors that influenced him are Texas' winning tradition and the fact that they run the 'I.' I'd have liked to see him stay in the state, but if he had to go somewhere else, I think he made the best choice in Texas. I certainly believe Marcus will be good for Texas." Wood noticed that he was wearing a beautiful new pair of cowboy boots.

He left Joe Wood and went to Danny Gregory's office, where he told the principal of his decision. "It seemed to me that he was really impressed by Texas," Gregory said. "I have a feeling he's comfortable with that decision. However, he does have the right to change his mind." Since he had committed to Texas, Gregory said, he would likely not visit Norman, Oklahoma, the following weekend.

In Sarah McKay's speech class that morning, three of the students were out sick, so only Marcus and another youngster were in the classroom. He was wearing the burnt-orange jersey with Number 22. He talked about how much he loved the University of Texas.

"Those big linemen are gonna take care of me, Miz McKay."

"Marcus," she said, "you've put me through so much uncertainty on all this, I want you to promise me one thing."

"What's that?"

"When you get out to Texas, I want you to send me a Number 22 in that orange color with Texas on it." Later, in the hallway after the next class, he held up his fingers in a circle and said, "I'll give you a Texas jersey, Miz McKay. You can count on it."

His decision was prominent news for the Monday afternoon papers, especially in the Deep South and Texas. One headline in Texas said: "Dupree Chooses Texas, Bypasses Sherrill." *The Jackson Daily News* did a quick story for its home edition and Billy Watkins of *The Meridian*

*Star* ran a copyright piece on the front page, including the information that Marcus had already canceled his weekend visit to Oklahoma. The wire services sent out the word, and radio stations throughout the South and Southwest got it on the air. By early Monday afternoon everyone on the Square in Oxford, Mississippi, had heard, and a cadre of football people gathered in Shine Morgan's Furniture Store for a discussion.

In his Monday afternoon column, under the headline "Dupree's Exit a Sad Affair," Orley Hood, the literate and whimsical sports editor of *The Jackson Daily News*, expressed sentiments which were shared by Mississippians:

> Well, it has happened again. The news came in at 10:40 Monday morning. It is, as the little green letters on the video display terminal hop, around 10:47. This won't wait.
>
> Marcus Dupree is packing up his talent and lugging it off to Austin to become a Longhorn . . .
>
> The state I love has lost another fine athlete—maybe the best we've had.
>
> This is a continuing tragedy. Remember Natchez' Hugh Green? He went to Pittsburgh. How about James Berry? Tennessee. Lancaster Gordon and Charles Jones, the basketball players, ended up at Louisville; Kevin Magee to Cal-Irvine; Carey Kelly to Arkansas. Calvin Smith, the world-class sprinter, runs his 100s in Tuscaloosa, Alabama.
>
> Why are the kids leaving home?
>
> Marcus Dupree is much more than a football player. He has become a symbol of progress in our state. He is a hero in Philadelphia, an east central Mississippi town that provided the setting for one of the darker moments in our history . . .
>
> I went up there in late October of 1980 to see Dupree and Joe Wood and to wander around the town that begat such enormous tragedy and talent. It is an old town, Philadelphia, and stagnant in the cruel economy of the 1980s.
>
> But I was told that a new grocery store would be opening the next week and the lady, a white lady, at the Chamber of Commerce fairly gushed when she spoke of Marcus Dupree.
>
> He was, at the time, a 16-year-old boy whom 18-year-old boys couldn't seem to tackle. He wore large black-rimmed glasses, hung around the locker room, talked easily and intelligently . . .
>
> To criticize Marcus Dupree for leaving Mississippi would be comically provincial. It is his life, his decision, and if he thinks Texas will serve his needs and his future better than Mississippi, fine.
>
> Besides, losing a football player to one of the surrounding 49 states in no way compares with future doctors fleeing to Memphis and Atlanta and Dallas. Football players don't add that much to quality—or length—of life.

Still, there are questions that require answers. Why do they leave? Is it better over there? Is somebody doing something wrong around here?

We can figure that Mississippi State lost because a man can't win a Heisman Trophy on six carries a game in the triple-option offense. Ole Miss lost because its program crumbled into ruins in the 1970s and shows no sign of improvement. Southern Mississippi lost because the coach who recruited him, Bobby Collins, also fled to chicken-fried steak land.

And all the other schools in the state, to a world-class recruit, are just an order of small fries.

It is sadness I'm feeling, not bitterness. Marcus Dupree, from all I've ever heard, is a wonderful kid who loves his mother and grandmother and little brother. Folks glow when they speak his name.

I've never seen him play and I'm sorry we won't be able to watch him run on a regular basis . . .

All for nothing!

By midafternoon of this Monday, February 1, only a few hours after Coach Wood's public announcement on his behalf, the young man had temporarily withdrawn his verbal commitment to the Texas Longhorns.

I found out about this in another telephone call from Sid Salter just before I was leaving for Memphis. "He's pulled back," Salter said.

"What happened?"

"A lot."

The events of that afternoon were very difficult for Marcus. They made me recognize anew that he was only a seventeen-year-old boy, that the pressures on him were enormous and, perhaps by the standards and priorities of a wholly rational society, unforgivable.

He was lifting weights in the gym when his uncle, Curlee Connor, came in and said he wanted to talk with him outside. Connor was wearing a Southern Mississippi baseball cap.

Uncle Curlee—his father's brother—was an abrupt new figure in this story. As the townspeople acknowledged, he had not really been in the picture until now. He was a tall, solid man who had played college basketball in the early 1970s with McNeese State in Louisiana. He was an eighth-round selection in the National Basketball Association draft and spent two years with the Cleveland Cavaliers. He had been living in Meridian and had returned recently to Philadelphia, where he had a small service station and grocery store in Independence Quarters.

Marcus talked with his uncle for fifteen or twenty minutes, then came back into the gym. "I just got word that my mother is upset about me making the decision without first talking it over with her," he said.

"Whatever decision is made, I want it to be a happy one for everyone concerned."

He elaborated later: "Both of us will kind of make the decision because I don't want her to be unhappy about anything. I'm close to my mother and I want to do what she thinks is best. We'll start talking about it tonight."

"In the afternoon he returned and said his mother didn't like the idea," Joe Wood said.

"I don't care where Marcus goes to school," Curlee Connor told Billy Watkins of *The Meridian Star*. "The main thing I'm concerned with is that Marcus take all his visits, then sit down and talk it over with his mother. Then they can decide what school is best for him. What I tried to tell him is that all the planes and cars and all the big shots ain't gonna be there every morning when he walks out of that dormitory."

The uncle added: "If he wants to go to Texas, that's fine. We just want Marcus to get the whole picture, take all his visits. He's a young boy. This is all a big fantasy right now for him."

Watkins of the *Star* wrote: "It was too easy, too quiet an ending to such a dramatic story."

The next day, Tuesday, February 2, Marcus for the first time that year did not come to school at all. Also for the first time in a long while, his coach, Joe Wood, did not know where he was. His telephone was off the hook all day. Lucious Selmon, the Oklahoma recruiter, came to the school looking for him. Tommy Reaux, the Texas assistant coach, paid a visit to Uncle Curlee's service station.

Tuesday's newspapers were detailed on the turnabout. The banner headline in *The Jackson Clarion-Ledger* said: "Mother Knows Best: Dupree May Not Play at Texas." *The Meridian Star*: "Dupree Saga Resumes Again." The Texas papers purported to be baffled. Under the headline "Dupree Is Causing Undue Excitement," Paul Borden, sports editor of the *Clarion-Ledger*, wrote:

> Marcus should have heeded Bear Bryant's advice and called his momma first . . .
>
> If he wants to wait a few days before announcing where he's going to school, that's fine with me. The first day prospects may sign letters-of-intent is February 10. Just let me know when Marcus' name is on that dotted line, please. Until then, let's hold the excitement.
>
> Of course, we're all at fault in making a fuss, we the media for making Marcus Dupree a football Superman, you the public for feeding that image by constantly phoning our office to ask for his latest words.
>
> What's it get us?
>
> One caller is told, "Yes, Marcus is going to Texas."

The next gets a different answer. "Marcus is waiting to make a final decision."

What's it all mean?

In many instances, it's much ado about nothing.

If you reflect on the box score on Mississippi prep running backs of recent years, guys who got the same kind of attention Dupree received this past fall, the hoopla is overdone.

Pascagoula's Rooster Jones turned out to be just an average back at Pitt, James Berry of Natchez was average at Tennessee, and, after a splashy debut, Buford McGee of Durant has been less than average at Ole Miss. Paul Carruth of McComb starts at Alabama, but then, if you make the traveling squad there you get to play a lot.

Maybe Marcus Dupree will be the best back in Texas (or UCLA or Oklahoma or Southern Mississippi) history. But he'll prove it on the field, not with a stroke of the pen.

Lee "Scoop" Ragland of the *Daily News* speculated in a lengthy piece that he would still sign with Texas. Coach Reaux of the Longhorns agreed; he talked with Marcus' mother that night. Joe Wood said: "He may change his mind, but I don't think so. I think Texas is where he wants to play football." Still, the careful *modus operandi* which had been established by Wood and Principal Gregory to ensure that everything went smoothly during the mad chase seemed to be unraveling a bit, as I had sensed all along it might.

Marcus returned to school on Wednesday. Sarah McKay saw him in the hall.

"*Marcus?*" she said, a questioning look on her face.

"Miz McKay," he said, "I'm goin' to *Texas.*"

Later that week he reflected: "My mother wants me to wait until next week. I don't know why. I might have made a mistake to commit, but Texas is still my first choice."

He added: "Still thinking about the other schools. I believe I'll go to Oklahoma this weekend. Hopefully, I'll know what I want to do next weekend."

It was, however, as Temple Drake advised me by the long-distance telephone, just starting.

# 22
# *Football Fratricide*

Pete and I arrived in Philly on Thursday, the day before his flight to Norman, Oklahoma. It was cold and gray when we checked into the hotel. From his station behind the counter, Roy Tingle reported that the whole town was mystified by the events of three days ago and was anxious for an end to the affair. After all, Roy said, they had been behind him for four years, and they deserved some sensible end to all of it. Sid Salter telephoned from the *Democrat* and said later on he would bring me a copy of the special "Marcus Appreciation Day" issue.

The town's Appreciation Day for him would be Sunday afternoon, February 7, which meant he would have to return from Oklahoma by 4 P.M. that day. All the coaches from the schools still in the competition would be there. Herschel Walker was also expected to come, as well as other sports celebrities and outside reporters. The national signing date would be the following Wednesday. I knew that much would transpire in the next several days.

For this reason I desired a little quiet distance and perspective on the hyperboles of collegiate football. So Pete and I walked over to the town cemetery; I wished to spend part of the afternoon with the other generations. Around the Square human beings were coming and going in their eternal commerce, seeming so purposeful and busy, but I did not doubt they would finish the mysterious journey sooner or later on these sloping gray hills.

The cemetery was only a few blocks from the Square; Pete and I had been here often at the end of an arduous day. It seemed at once remote from the town and an integral part of it, not only for this proximity with the town's daily rituals but because of the narrow access road which ran through it, so that drivers occasionally used this lane for their detours and shortcuts. We paused again before the tombstones with the names of the people of the town whom I knew and had talked with: Turner, McKay, Mars, Hester, Posey, King. Some might have considered our pursuits lugubrious, but they seemed natural enough to me, and Pete found this landscape perfect for his ceaseless investigations.

I remembered, not too long before in Oxford, having been invited by my friends Patty and William Lewis to go with them and their children to the cemetery there to help choose their burial plot. That graveyard, like this one in Philadelphia, was also not far from the Square, and was touched with the same blend of seclusion and activity. My friends were in the heartiest prime of life and did not anticipate departing the Lord's earth immediately, and hence, far from being funereal, our search had had an adventurous mood to it, rather like picking out a Christmas tree. It was that hour before twilight, and the marvelous old graveyard with its cedars and magnolias and flowering glades sang with the Mississippi springtime. The honeysuckled air was an affirmation of the tugs and tremors of living. My companions had spent all their lives in the town, and the names on even the oldest stones were as familiar to them as the people they saw every day. "Location," the man of the family said, laughing. "As the real estate magnates say, we want *location*." At last they found a plot in the most venerable section which was to their liking. I knew the caretaker would soon have to come to this place of their choice with a long, thin rod, shoving it into the ground every few inches to see if it struck forgotten coffins. If not, this plot was theirs. Our quest had been a tentative success, and we retired elsewhere to celebrate with catfish and wine.

Their humor coincided with mine, for graveyards had never frightened me. As on this day in Philadelphia, Pete and I had gone out into many cemeteries, not only to escape the telephone and those living beings who placed more demands on us than the dead ever would, but to feel a continuity with the flow of generations. I reminded myself to quote the words of Faulkner to the college football recruiters in Philly this week: "Living is a process of getting ready to be dead for a long time."

Now the clouds lay heavy overhead. In the quiet of late afternoon I could almost hear the long-ago Neshoba voices. I came across the grave of Zealous Graham McNeil, born in 1900, died in 1964, less than a month before Marcus' birth, less than two before the tragedy of that summer. At a distance I saw Pete near the Turner plot, rolling around in the grass scratching his back, a sure sign from our many years together that he felt mischievous and content. I came across a solitary Confederate marker:

> J. M. Schumaker
> Gamblin's Co.
> Hodges Miss. Cav.
> CSA

I recalled Marty Gamblin of this town, who had taken Marcus on his first trip to Los Angeles to meet the TV starlets and to stay in a house in Malibu. Surely he would be here this week representing UCLA's Golden Bruins. Was this Gamblin his great-grandfather?

I remembered now how the great urban cemeteries of New York City had always filled me with horror, the mile after mile of crowded tombstones which no one ever seemed to visit, as if one could *find* anyone in there even if he wished to. Likewise, the suburban cemeteries, North and South, of this generation with their carefully manicured lawns and bronze plaques embedded in the ground, all imbued with affluence and artifice, were much too ethereal for me. I supposed it was the graveyards of Mississippi, like this one, which were the most moving for me, having to do, I believed, with my belonging here. Pete and I once found an isolated graveyard in the hills far north of Oxford, with photographs on many of the stones, some nearly a century old, the women in bonnets and Sunday dresses, the men in faded shirts and overalls: "The short and simple annals of the poor." I was drawn there to the tiny grave of a little girl. Her name was Fairy Jumper, and she lived from April 14, 1914, to January 16, 1916. There was a miniature lamb at the top of the stone, and the words: "A fairer bud of promise never bloomed." There were no other Jumpers around her, and there she was, my Fairy, in a far·corner of that country burial ground, so forlorn and alone that it was difficult to bear.

I had arrived now in the Philadelphia cemetery at the crest of the hill. Pete joined me again and sat down to rest. He looked up at me with his bright liquid eyes, tail wagging, as he always did when we were on an adventure together. "I am with you," he seemed again to say. Down below us on one side were the rows of the dead of the town, this town of pride and adversity. I thought of how each generation lives with its own exclusive solicitudes—the passions, the defeats, the victories, the sacrifices, the names and dates and faces belong to each generation in its own passing, for much of everything except the most unforgettable is soon forgotten. On the opposite side below the hill were acres of empty land, an area large enough to accommodate the next two or three generations. The Philadelphia cemetery was expanding.

I wondered if they would ever begin to believe me, if one could somehow tell them, Zealous Graham McNeil and these other vanished souls, that on the next afternoon a seventeen-year-old black boy of their town, with an Afro and eyeglasses and a warm-up jacket, would be on his way to his courting in Oklahoma—the land of the departed Neshoba Choctaws—in a private jet airplane, accompanied by a white oil executive and a young black millionaire wearing a cowboy hat, a silver belt buckle, and gold chains around his neck.


*The Neshoba Democrat* was printed on Wednesdays and distributed to subscribers and newsstands on Thursdays. The special Marcus Dupree edition was sold out by early Thursday morning and immediately went into a substantial second printing. *The Dallas Morning News,* which had a reporter in town, said the issue "looks more like a Marcus Dupree scrapbook than a newspaper." Across the front page was an eight-column banner and subhead:

MARCUS DUPREE APPRECIATION DAY SUNDAY, FEB. 7
Philadelphia is Proud of You

Right underneath this were reproductions of congratulatory letters from the governor of Mississippi and the president of the Neshoba County Board of Supervisors, as well as a resolution passed by the City of Philadelphia and signed by the mayor. There were a number of stories on his high school career and speculations on where he might go to college. Practically every business establishment in town ran advertisements in his honor, many of them with photographs of him in various poses and postures while playing football, basketball, baseball, and track—all told, some sixty-five ads.

One wondered what other small-town paper in America would publish a special issue like this one on a seventeen-year-old, white or black. Its most arresting feature was a lengthy perspective by Sid Salter, under the headline: "A Measure of Progress—How Wide the Tracks?" I wish to quote it almost in its entirety:

> The lifetime of this 17-year-old has seen the most dramatic events in our city's history unfold. He is a child of those events, and a shining product of this community's heroism in interpreting those events, and in utilizing the lessons learned as building blocks for our future.
>
> The phrase "crossing the tracks" needs no lengthy explanation. It has long been used as a euphemism in Southern literature, and in our slang as a symbol of the division between rich and poor, social pillars and social outcasts, and black and white.
>
> The tracks, that 10-foot expanse of wood, steel and stone, was at one time in this community thought to be an impregnable barrier, a gulf that could and would not be traversed.
>
> Never did those tracks loom wider than in the hot, turbulent, seemingly eternal summer of 1964. The deluge of negative national media attention, focused on our town, both deserved and undeserved, threatened to strangle the social growth of this community for decades thereafter.
>
> But that growth was not strangled. We, as a people, refused to allow those grave events to destroy our community from without, or better yet, from within. We persevered.
>
> Marcus Dupree was born in that cataclysmic year of 1964.
>
> The tracks again became a potential battle line in 1969, when the philosophy of the United States Supreme Court regarding the landmark 1954 *Brown vs. The Board of Education of Topeka, Kansas,* school deseg-

regation decision changed from one of "integrate with all deliberate speed" to one of "integrate now."

Even in the midst of heated local debate on the issue, we did integrate our public schools in January of 1970.

As television cameras rolled and writers made hurried notes on that first day of integration, our community calmly accepted the federal mandate, and we joined each other in the classroom without internecine feuds . . .

And now, 12 years later, he is a member of the first class of Philadelphia youngsters who will soon graduate from a totally-integrated school system.

He will take that rite of passage on graduation night with his classmates, black and white, in which we tell our children that we have done all that we can do in preparing them for the world and all its trials and opportunities.

Those young people have but one direction, their future.

Their future, though not accompanied with the glitter and fanfare of their famous classmate, is no less significant or vital as an indicator of the growth of our community's social consciousness. The sense of direction that we impart to them must, as in the case of an outstanding running back, be keen.

On February 7, we once again have an opportunity to cross those ideological, social and political tracks that we have individually and collectively worked so hard during Marcus's lifetime to narrow.

It would be naive to assume that our community has all its problems behind us, but the prospects for solving our future problems as a unified, harmonious community appear bright.

That Thursday morning Jackie Sherrill once more arrived at the Philadelphia airport by private jet. With him was George Pugh, his assistant, who had been in charge of recruiting Marcus for the University of Pittsburgh and who had gone with Sherrill to Texas A&M. They borrowed a car and drove to Kemper County to talk with Marcus' mother at her school. Sherrill had conferred with her a month before when he was still with Pittsburgh.

Sherrill and Pugh came to the Philadelphia High gym early that afternoon. Marcus arrived half an hour later. He shook Sherrill's hand. "Can I see you about five minutes?" the Aggie coach asked. He, Pugh, and Marcus closeted themselves in Joe Wood's office for ten minutes or so.

When the conference was over, Pugh said he thought Marcus would make his sixth and last official visit at some point to A&M. Then he and the dapper Sherrill departed.

"Coach Sherrill didn't put any pressure on me," Marcus said. "He told me that if I wanted to visit to just call him."

The NCAA was in town that day, too, in the person of Dave Didion. Didion and Mike Glazier, the two young investigators, had been diligently following the developments in Philadelphia because of the exceptional interest in Marcus across the country. He was one of fourteen high school seniors whom the NCAA was especially watching. "We could see that it could get very interesting here," Didion said, "so we decided to come down and hang around and monitor the situation." One had the impression, rightly or not, over the next several days leading to the signing date, that this vigilant NCAA presence in the recruitment of the nation's foremost prospect might serve to discourage any major, or minor, transgressions.

There was a happening in Joe Wood's office late Friday morning. Two young men were sitting in those familiar cramped quarters in a relaxed mood. The imperturbable Wood introduced me first to Lucious Selmon, a husky black man with pleasant, handsome features. Then he gestured to the other visitor, a white fellow. "He's an oil millionaire," Joe said, "and he flies his own jet. They've come to take ol' Marcus to Oklahoma."

In a moment, a third figure appeared in the doorway, another young black. From his photographs I knew him to be the great Billy Sims.

Billy Sims was from Hooks, Texas, where Barry Switzer of Oklahoma had recruited him as a running back. He was in the lineage of the distinguished Sooner runners. He was an all-American for two years, and in 1978 he won the Heisman Trophy. As the first player chosen in the 1980 professional draft, he signed a stunning contract with the Detroit Lions of the National Football League. In his first pro game he ran for 153 yards and three touchdowns. He led the league in touchdowns that season and was named Rookie of the Year. There was a story about him in his second game as a pro. He caught a short pass against Green Bay and outran everyone 87 yards for a score. As he crossed the goal line, two players from the opposing teams looked at one another in disbelief. "You think that sonuvabitch isn't worth the money?" the Lion center said to the Packer linebacker.

Billy Sims drifted away from Wood's office and was immediately surrounded by high school students asking for his autograph. He was wearing Calvin Klein jeans, a cowboy hat with feathers around the brim, cowboy boots that must have cost five hundred dollars, a purplish-gray shirt with metallic silver thread running through it, an OU national championship ring, a gold-and-diamond stud displaying the name "Billy," several gold chains around his neck, and a silver belt buckle with a gold oil derrick on it. He greeted each high school kid with a soul-slap. "How you doin', man? What's *happenin'*?" He spoke in a deep East Texas drawl. Some of Marcus' teammates, on the fringe of the group, began whistling "The Eyes of Texas" while looking mock-innocently at the ceiling.

"Billy, why did you come all the way to Philadelphia to pick up Marcus?" someone asked.

"I was shown first-class treatment at the University of Oklahoma. That's what we do with recruits."

"What will you talk with Marcus about on the plane?"

"I ain't gonna pressure him. I just want to tell him what Oklahoma's done for me."

"What've they done for you?"

"They've given me the opportunity to provide the things for a family that I'd never been able to give 'em without football. My family has a nice home, nice cars, and a future that we'd have never had without football. Look, that future began at Oklahoma."

He left to walk up to the main building to fetch the prospect. A few minutes later Sarah McKay noticed Marcus at the door of her classroom.

"Miz McKay, can I see you?"

"Just a minute, Marcus," she said. "I'm talking with someone."

When she came out into the hall, he said, "I want you to meet somebody. This is Billy Sims."

"So nice to meet you. Are you from around here?" She thought he might be a relative who had arrived early for the Appreciation Day.

"No, but I'm from a little town like this one. I'm takin' Marcus Dupree to Oklahoma."

I was walking with Pete on the football field when I saw the two of them strolling along the end zone to the gym. Two or three dogs and several of the smaller boys were following them. Marcus was wearing blue jeans, white shoes, and a blue warm-up jacket with DUPREE on the back. He dwarfed his older companion. As they walked swiftly by, Marcus waved. An air of heightened reality seemed to envelop the two of them.

Joined by Lucious Selmon and the oilman, they moved toward a car parked near the gym.

"Have a good time, Marcus!" a white boy shouted.

He turned around, still in stride. "I'm goin' somewhere for a change!" he shouted back. The car pulled away and vanished up the hill.

A couple of hours later the telephone rang in Joe Wood's office. He picked it up.

"Coach, this is Marcus."

"Marcus? Where in heck are you?"

"They told me I could call you from the plane. They say I'm 41,000 feet in the air somewhere over Oklahoma. It seems like I'm almost to the moon."

Sid Salter and I established our Command Post in a house he was renting on Poplar Avenue. It consisted largely of a spacious room equipped with a color television, telephones, and a bar, and a kitchen which never had anything in it. As the recruiting drama evolved, the Command Post became more and more disarranged—empty beer cans, pizza cartons, old socks, overflowing ashtrays, newspapers from three or four states. When Sid's fiancée, Paula Jones, came to town one day, she forthwith went to Wal-Mart to buy a broom. These quarters, nonetheless, had the force of human history about them.

We gathered there on Saturday night. Marcus was in Oklahoma, and the town was for the moment quiescent. Barry Horne of *The Dallas Morning News* and Brad Bucholtz of *The Austin American-Statesman* were there, as were Sarah McKay of the high school and Sleepy Posey, proprietor of the Western Auto Store. Pete was eating pretzels in the kitchen and from time to time joined the conference. Horne, a native of New York and the only sportswriter I ever knew who did not drink, was working on a story at a table in the corner and listening at the same time to the conversation. The Texas visitors were getting much talk about families, graveyards, dogs, whites, blacks, and the more elusive Neshoba landmarks, and one could only wonder what they were making of it. Sleepy Posey of Western Auto, for instance, spoke eloquently and at some length about the crossroads community of Deemer. Many of the towns-people knew of these headquarters, and the telephone rang every now and again with requests for information. We told them nothing was happening on this night.

Sid was explaining to the outsiders what Marcus' grandfather, Reverend Major Dupree, did for a living. He drove a truck for Cole Wholesale and was also a part-time preacher. In the South, he was saying, black preachers were often bricklayers, carpenters, farmers, or truck drivers during the day.

Horne had just written a seventy-inch piece on Marcus and the town which would be published on the front page of his Dallas paper the next day. He read something his subject had told him: "I hope I helped bring blacks and whites together some. There is a way to go here. But there is a way to go everywhere. I like Philadelphia. It's a nice little town. Every-body knows each other. And everybody gets along. I'm going to go away to college. But maybe someday I'll return. I wouldn't mind settling here."

Sarah McKay reached in her purse and withdrew a colored photograph of Marcus and Daran Jackson. On the back they had written: "Marcus, ✗22 . . . Daran, ✗30. Love ya!" Then she admitted she did not have the slightest notion who Billy Sims was when she had met him the day before.

We stopped to listen to a report on one of the national sports networks: "Marcus Dupree of Philadelphia, Mississippi, America's most acclaimed high school running back, is at the University of Oklahoma this weekend on an official visit. Four days before the national signing date his choices are Texas, Oklahoma, Southern Mississippi, and UCLA." Nothing was new there, and Pete returned to the kitchen for more pretzels.

"When Marcus was in the seventh grade," Sid told the group, "I was a senior. My teammates and I walked around school wearing our letter jackets with three stripes. We'd give our girlfriends our letter jackets to wear, but only for two or three days at a time. We'd say to ourselves, 'Yeah, we're *bad*.' It took us till after graduation to realize the letter jacket wouldn't last forever, that the carrousel would stop. Marcus looked up to us back then because he was a little kid and felt we'd done something, well, important. But I think he felt early on that he was destined for more. You've got to know he feels that now."

"Does anyone ever sense that sometimes he's laughing at us?" someone asked.

"Well, I think he's smart as hell," Sid said. "Of course, he's a player in a grand chess game now."

A young woman of the town had told me she was sitting in the Pizza Hut the other night and at the next table were Marcus and a white man in his thirties. This man was telling him about a bed one could lie on in a certain house in San Diego and push a button on the headboard and the whole roof would open up.

"Sounds like Marty Gamblin—the UCLA connection," Salter surmised.

In between telephone calls the conversation turned to the Appreciation Day the next afternoon. It would be held in the Westside Community Center in the Quarters, where every day the white and black "senior citizens" got together for lunch.

"It'll be a semi-religious event," Salter predicted "—the black people giving him their blessing, and a lot of whites." It would likewise be, he said, the biggest social event in the town since Archie Manning married Olivia Williams, when there were twelve bridesmaids, twelve groomsmen, and the smell of mothballs from the ladies' fur coats.

Barry Horne of *The Dallas Morning News* had just finished his article. He stood up at the work table and stretched. "I'll tell you this," he said. "Whoever signs him had better be clean. Because if he promises to go somewhere else and doesn't go there, you can bet that school will turn him in. Everybody knows what everybody else is doing."

The talk got around to Texas vs. Oklahoma. The prospect had obviously been most impressed that Oklahoma dispatched Billy Sims to get him. Why had Texas not sent Earl Campbell the previous weekend? Lucious Selmon, the Oklahoma assistant, was OU's "hit man" on the important recruiting. Tommy Reaux, the Texas recruiter, was enormously persuasive. Coach Akers of the Longhorns must be damned worried right now, someone said, what with the young man being in Norman, especially after the strange contretemps over his verbally committing to Texas. Would Akers be a "father figure" for him, as Joe Wood and Danny Gregory had been for him in Philly? "No," one of the Texans said, "he's kind of aloof. But he's a motivater, a positive-thinking type."

During this conversation, I quietly considered the situation. It struck me as plausible that Texas and Oklahoma were the frontrunners now, with Southern and UCLA (and perhaps Texas A&M?) waiting in the wings, like dark horses hoping for a locked convention.

There was a mad rationale to this, after all—Texas vs. Oklahoma, Longhorns vs. Sooners, in all their historic, inchoate bloodletting over the decades, having found their latest battleground in a small hamlet in the red hills of east-central Mississippi. "The oilmen are back in town," someone once observed of them. "Evacuate the women and children first." Since 1950, I remembered, there had been only three years in which neither had finished in the top ten in the country. It was one of the most bitter collegiate rivalries of America, their annual meetings in Dallas having always been marked with riot, anarchy, and rapine. For years the arrests in Dallas on the night before the game averaged six hundred people. One night some years ago, with fifty thousand fans from both schools swaying around Commerce and Akard, someone started throwing desks and tables out of the top floors of the Baker Hotel. This became known in the Texas-OU series as "The Night It Rained Furniture."

In my files I had recently reread the words of my Texas friend Gary Cartwright about this venomous feud. (In one of his early assignments as a young Texas sportswriter, Cartwright, a grandiloquent figure known to us then as "The Jap," had in the course of an interview thrown up all over Duffy Dougherty, the football coach of Michigan State.) No one comprehended the historical context of Texas vs. Oklahoma more expertly than Jap Cartwright, and, sitting now with my thoughts in the Command Post, I recalled his analysis:

> Texas and Oklahoma are neighbors only by a quirk of geography. They are separated by the Red River, which used to separate New France from New Spain. What really separates them is a century and a half of

history, the Alamo as opposed to the Dust Bowl. When you hear a Texan or an Oklahoman call the other neighbor, it just means they share ownership in an oil well. They are like tribes connected by a common hatred, two people who look on one another with the special loathing usually reserved for cannibalism. Oil and football prescribe the characters of the two universities, and to a degree the states. Longhorns see themselves as big, fast, wealthy, wily, capable, cultured and anointed by the Almighty. The good guys. They see Okies as poor, ignorant, Bible-thumping outlaws. Okies see Texans as loud, arrogant, smartass bullies. They see themselves as big, fast, wealthy, wily Bible-thumping outlaws. Jesus and football are one-two, but the order depends on the year and which side of the Red River you occupy.

There is something else in this rivalry, something harder to define but something that has to do with the times in which we live. Just as Army-Navy symbolized all that was glorious and traditional during World War II, Texas and Oklahoma are two states of the here and now. Strange to say, trendy. Witness Texas chic, a disease in which people wear cowboy boots, ride mechanical bulls and talk about the last time they saw Willie Nelson at the Lone Star Cafe. Witness the popularity of such shows as *Dallas* or *The Best Little Whorehouse in Texas*. Somehow, *The Best Little Whorehouse in New Jersey* just doesn't sound right. There are many who would contend that the words Okie chic are mutually exclusive, but there is no denying the popularity of Oral Roberts and his message to the Masses of Unhealed.*

Of the games in Dallas, Darrell Royal, who participated in twenty as the Texas coach, once said: "It's strange how you can go down that ramp in perfect health, then a few minutes later actually be physically hurting just from making decisions on the sideline. Every play is so vital, every foot of Astroturf. A fumble, an interception. One soft block and a yard less gained, that can be the difference." Barry Switzer of Oklahoma always said he looked upon the Texas game as the national championship. No surprise, then, that Royal and Switzer became hardened enemies who eventually refused to speak with one another, nor that Royal once accused Oklahoma of sending spies to watch his practices from a distance with binoculars.

Our young hero was at this moment in Norman, Oklahoma, although he must return the next afternoon, Sunday, for the Appreciation Day. Was he having a good time out there among those thirty thousand OU students? As fine a time as he had had in Austin, Texas, when he committed to the Longhorns the weekend before? What, pray, was going through the young man's thoughts? Had the big-time, frantic collegiate football of the day disoriented him? To whom could he turn for counsel? Where were Joe Wood and Danny Gregory, who had served him so well

* *Inside Sports*, October 1981.

until now? Where was his favorite teacher, Sarah McKay? (At that moment sitting right across from me.) Where was the NCAA? Would his mother, Cella, who loved him beyond his nimble feet, seize the day? Would Tommy Reaux of the Texas Longhorns come in again and advise him on what to do? Reaux—a large, generous man of black middle-class Texas parentage who had grown to care for him and considered him the finest running back in America. Might the lovable Reaux show him the way? Or Carmody, the tenacious new coach of Southern Mississippi? Or Donahue, the famous inspirational leader of UCLA? Or Sherrill, the persuasive millionaire parvenu of the Texas Aggies? Who would help our young man? Who might come forward now?

Or would Marcus himself, who, after all, comprehended his own talent, prove smarter than anyone?

As my companions in the Command Post on this evening dwelled on the competition, I considered too what I knew about Oklahoma. I knew it from more than Rodgers and Hammerstein. I had read about the Indian migrations and the Trail of Tears, and the great land rush of 1889, when the homesteaders crossed the territorial line in their wagons sooner than the federal government wanted them—hence "The Sooners." I had heard about the southern part of the state, Little Dixie, which, having been settled by white Mississippians, had many of the place names of Mississippi. John Steinbeck's descriptions of the Dust Bowl of the Depression still haunted me. I had driven across its plains at night and briefly visited the oil-rich environs of Tulsa and Oklahoma City; I remembered the oil derricks on the very grounds of the state capitol. It was a *driven* state, I felt, given to turmoil and extremes, yet there were bedrock things there too, and I had even liked most of the Oklahomans I had known.

As for football itself, I knew Lucious Selmon at twenty-nine was the eldest of the three Selmon brothers. They were legitimate folk heroes in the state. They were born of a poor black family in the town of Eufaula, and all of them had gone on to play football for the Sooners. In Oklahoma's undefeated 1973 season the three of them, Lucious, Dewey, and Lee Roy had lined up side by side. In 1982 Lee Roy and Dewey were still playing professional football with Tampa Bay. Lucious, an all-American guard and co-captain who finished second in the balloting for the Outland Trophy given to the outstanding lineman in the country and seventh for the Heisman Trophy, later played briefly with Memphis in the old World Football League. Now he was the Oklahoma coach in charge of the defensive ends under Barry Switzer. He was likewise known in the tight world of college football, where everyone knew everything about everybody, as the "troubleshooter" in Oklahoma's recruiting.

The Oklahoma team was an expression of a wealthy, restless university. One of its presidents had once promised, in 1951, to "build a university the football team can be proud of." Ever since the postwar boom years in the Southwest the oilmen of Oklahoma, as with their counterparts in Texas, would expect nothing less. In that period Oklahoma had won five national championships and nineteen Big Eight titles, sharing in four others and forfeiting one because of an ineligible player, often paying the price in NCAA probations. At one point under Bud Wilkinson, Oklahoma had forty-seven straight victories.

Wilkinson became the head coach in 1947 and quickly acquired his reputation as a Caesar among recruiters, particularly in Texas, which explained much of the poison in the rivalry. Since 1950, eighteen of Oklahoma's thirty-seven all-Americans had been natives of Texas. The latter-day Oklahoma teams usually had twenty or more Texans on their rosters. "Texans playin' for Oklahoma?" a former Longhorn fullback once said. "That's just like somebody from the United States playin' for Nazi Germany." Wilkinson was also noted for his relationship with black athletes. Oklahoma recruited its first black player as early as 1958, ten years before the University of Texas. The powerful and conservative regents of Texas (J. Frank Dobie once said they cared as much about intellectual enlightenment as a razorback sow about Keats's *Ode on a Grecian Urn*), who refused to allow any black Longhorns, would joke among themselves that the reason blacks were such swift runners was because "the lions and tigers got all the slow ones."

Barry Switzer, known as one of the free spirits of the game, was named head coach in 1973, succeeding Chuck Fairbanks. He was born and raised in Crossett, Arkansas, a little lumber town, where he read books under kerosene lamps and shot copperheads with a .22 pistol in the backyard so his mother and grandmother could go to the privy. He played center and linebacker for Arkansas in the late fifties; Fred Akers of Texas was a teammate. In his first three seasons as Oklahoma's head coach, he had lost only one game and had won two national titles. At forty-five, with a record through nine seasons of 90–13–3, he had the highest winning percentage among active coaches.

"Who is Barry Switzer?" Tom Shatel of *The Kansas City Times* once asked. "He is a vibrant man. A politician. A good ol' boy. A riverboat gambler who brings a touch of Vegas to the plains. A recruiter who relates to rich and poor, black and white. His players sign autographs on the sideline—during games. They return after graduation to drink with him and recruit for him." He liked good-looking girls. Who didn't? He knew how to speak at alumni banquets and solicit the hundred-thousand-dollar checks for his "program," and how to get along with young Negroes. "Blacks know that Oklahoma was the first major college team in the South and Southwest to integrate," he had said, "and that we've had seven black captains. They appreciate that and so do we." He once telephoned Billy Sims in Hooks, Texas, during the halftime of an Oklahoma-Colorado game in which OU was well in the lead. Sims, like Marcus Dupree now, was seventeen years old, and pumping gas at a service station in Hooks on Saturday afternoons.

Switzer's Oklahoma teams became famous for their efficacious Wishbone offense. Since incorporating this offensive attack Alabama and Oklahoma had had the highest winning percentages of any teams in college football. "We're more a true triple-option football team," Switzer once said. "Alabama sometimes gets away with it. We line up in the Wishbone and run the Wishbone offense. We may break the Wishbone, but we still run the triple option. My offensive philosophy is that the team with the best rushing attack is the most consistent winner. I believe that history and statistical facts prove this point. The best rushing teams are the biggest winners in college football." Switzer's Wishbone was prone, however, to fumbles. He once lost thirteen in one game and still won by forty points. Precise pitchouts and handing off the ball close to the line of scrimmage had led to these numerous errors.

How would Marcus, who under the resourceful farm boy Joe Wood had switched from the Wishbone to the "I" in his senior year in high school with such extraordinary success, fit into the exciting yet doctrinaire Wishbone of Barry Switzer? With powerful runners like Herschel Walker and Marcus Dupree, who seemed fated to run deep and alone behind the line of scrimmage to choose their moves and accelerate speed at their own private momentum, had the Wishbone seen its day? Surely Marcus was aware that the Texas Longhorns had been running more or less consistently out of the "I" since Earl Campbell's senior year, and with much glory.

Further, Switzer's OU team of the '81 season, Marcus' senior year in high school, had been his poorest ever. "Say it ain't so, Barry," the Oklahoma papers had complained. His Wishbone backs had fumbled fifty-two times on the way to a 7-4-1 season, including disastrous trouncings by Texas and Nebraska. It was the first time since 1972 that OU had neither won nor shared the Big Eight Conference championship. In addition to this, although he likely was the most popular figure in the state, Switzer had accumulated a number of vociferous critics because of his complicated and flamboyant outside business interests.

How might Marcus adapt to all this? Was Switzer's blithe personality too exotic for an Independence Quarters boy? Compared with the majestic University of Texas, surely the University of Oklahoma out on its windswept terrain seemed terribly remote and unreal. What were they doing with him out there right now? Better Southern Mississippi in down-to-earth Hattiesburg, only a few dozen miles from home. Or the golden boulevards of L.A.

In the midst of these ruminations and conjecturings, I noticed that Pete had opened the back door of the Command Post with his nose and vanished into the night. I went in search of him down the empty streets. It took me a long time to find him, three blocks away rolling about in some bushes. We walked back toward the Post in the gloomy cold. All about us on the eve of the Appreciation Day were the dark, solemn old houses of Poplar Avenue. Behind their drawn curtains was the dead bluish glow—the nocturnal American retreat. The little town of Philly had withdrawn into television.

# 23
# *Philly Appreciates Him*

Sunday dawned sunny and frigid. The chimes of the churches in the white section played "Rock of Ages," "Abide with Me," "Faith of Our Fathers." In Independence Quarters little black boys were shooting baskets. Someone had put twigs of holly on the memorial in front of Mount Nebo, and cars were parked four-deep before all the churches. There was activity in Uncle Curlee Connor's service station, and the hand-painted sign out front still said:

GAS
BREAD
MILK
OIL AND GREASE JOB

The wash on the fences near the houses was frozen and still. At the sawmill the water from the sprinklers had formed mammoth icicles, and a photographer from *The Dallas Morning News* was snapping pictures of them. "Aren't they fantastic?" he said. There were five or six new graves with fresh wreaths in the little cemetery near Westside. As always, young blacks in leather jackets lounged outside the Busy Bee. Its marquee proclaimed:

MARCUS DUPREE
GOING TO
TEXAS LONG HORN

Half an hour before the Appreciation Day ceremonies were to begin, the auditorium of the Westside Community Center was overflowing with people. Eventually they would line the walls, sit on the floor, and spill far out onto the lawn—some six hundred of them, about 60 percent black and 40 white, and more than a few Choctaws.

The official program noted that the event was sponsored by such local black organizations as the Ebonee Unique B & P Women's Club, the Black Progressive Women's Club, Today Black Women's Club, Sophisticated Ladies' Club, Philadelphia Men's Club, and Young Black Businessmen's Club. A banner behind the stage said: "Black Awareness Month," and huge signs along both sides: "We Still Have a Dream." On each end of the stage were big black stars in gold lettering: "Marcus Dupree."

I was taken with the dozens of smaller black stars in the same gold script motif all along the auditorium walls—front, sides, and back—with these names prominently on each: *Barbara Jordan, Pélé, Nat Turner, Stevie Wonder, Malcolm X, Benjamin Mays, Miles Davis, Frederick Douglass, Crispus Attucks, Harriet Tubman, James Baldwin, Andrew Young, Toussaint L'Ouverture, Henry Aaron, Sojourner Truth, Vernon Jordan, Mahalia Jackson, W. C. Handy, Joseph Cinque, Adam Clayton Powell, Duke Ellington, Martin Luther King, Jr., Benjamin Hooks, Sidney Poitier, Floyd McKissick, Charles R. Drew, Alex Haley, Paul L. Dunbar, Scott Joplin, Ralph Bunche, Thurgood Marshall, Ray Charles, Coleman Young, Gwendolyn Brooks, Bessie Smith, Aretha Franklin, Muhammad Ali, Arthur Ashe, Roy Wilkins, Shirley Chisholm, Alexandre Dumas, Oscar Robertson, Count Basie, Bill Russell, Earl Hines, Diana Ross, Alexander Pushkin, Althea Gibson, Phillips Randolph, Sammy Davis, Jr., Joe Louis, W. E. B. DuBois, Lena Horne, Rosa L. Parks, Julian Bond, Jackie Robinson, Willie Mays, Jesse Jackson, Louis Armstrong, Jesse Owens, Pearl Bailey, Langston Hughes,* and the Mississippians—*Leontyne Price, Medgar Evers, Walter Payton, Richard Wright, Charles Evers,* and *James Meredith.* I was surprised there was no star for another Mississippian: James Earl Chaney.

It was overheated inside, and people were cooling themselves with the old-style cardboard funeral home fans. Black and white children ran up and down the crowded aisles. Many babies were crying in unison, a capella. People were in their best, with much polyester among the men and little leather; the young blacks almost looked preppy. White and black adults of the town mingled with animation. I sighted Lillie Jones in a polka-dot dress and long gold earrings, and I remembered what she had told Barry Horne of *The Dallas News:* "When I heard the whole town, black and white, was going to give Marcus a day, it was hard to believe. But I always believed if we struggled along we'd get there. Now we're honoring one of our babies."

There were several television cameras and numerous photographers, and the press table was crowded with representatives from the Jackson and Meridian papers, *The Houston Post, The Houston Chronicle, The Dallas News, The Dallas Times-Herald,* and *The Austin American-Statesman.* A copy of *Three Lives for Mississippi* by William Bradford Huie lay on the table. The Texas papers were here in abundance. Were they expecting an announcement?

Among the whites in the crowd I noticed many of the school people, elected officials, and Square merchants—the local establishment. Stan Dearman, the editor of the *Democrat*, found a seat next to mine. "You wouldn't have seen this ten or fifteen years ago," he said. High school students were in evidence, including Cecil Price, Jr., wearing a corduroy jacket with elbow patches.

People were craning toward the back of the auditorium, for word had arrived that the honoree had just flown in from Oklahoma and that an august assemblage was with him.

He was walking down the aisle now with his mother and Reggie. He was wearing a shirt and tie, a blue pullover sweater, and a corduroy jacket with patches like Cecil Price's. Reggie, slowly hobbling along with his crutches, wore a navy blue suit. They sat in chairs on the stage.

From the wings came the visitors, and they too took chairs. There was Fred Akers; his assistant, Tommy Reaux; Billy Joe DuPree of the Dallas Cowboys, a distant cousin of the family who had come to help represent the Longhorns; Albert Jackson of the Atlanta Falcons, another Texas alumnus; Terry Donahue, the head coach of UCLA; Jim Carmody, the new head coach of Southern Mississippi; Marty Gamblin of Los Angeles; and Walter Reed, the athletic director of Jackson State. Standing in the rear of the auditorium was Lucious Selmon of Oklahoma, who was not on the stage because he had used all his "official visits" with the prospect and chose not to risk a violation by appearing with him now. Only Herschel Walker was absent. The crowd, especially the younger ones, suddenly became agitated over the entrance of such notables, and there was an undercurrent of the nervous talk of small-town people when they find themselves in the presence of recognizable celebrities.

Mrs. Glenda Faye Greer, a black woman and mistress of ceremonies, welcomed the audience to "a ceremony given in honor of a talented high school young man, who has broken the high school record of Mr. Herschel Walker of Georgia." Mrs. Marion Cook, wife of the black Philadelphia coach Kenneth Cook, announced that she would lead in the singing of the Black National Anthem. I had never heard this song, nor, apparently, had many of the blacks in the auditorium, a number of whom did not stand. There was no singing of the U.S. National Anthem.

During the singing, Terry Donahue had been chatting amiably with Jim Carmody, a rather intense figure whose public countenance was sinewy, lean-spirited, and hard-nosed, a man with whom one would not have wished gratuitously to challenge, on whose face seemed to have settled the accumulated fratricides of collegiate football. Donahue turned from him and looked out quizzically at the mixed crowd. He wore a powder-blue sports jacket and was unexpectedly young; without the sartorial grace, he could have passed for a junior high algebra instructor, about whom the matrons of the PTA might have had secret fantasies. I wondered what might be wafting through his mind in this moment—this sudden visitor with the well-known TV face interspersed so often among the Texaco and Lite Beer commercials, from the alien universe of Southern California, set here now in the poor red Deep Dixie hills. Was he touched? Intrigued? Baffled? Worried sick about getting his man? A vein of secret recognition seemed to pass across his clean American features, as if he had momentarily divined some fragile regional truth.

Reverend Major Dupree, Marcus' grandfather, was introduced to deliver the benediction. He was a large man with an equally large voice, and his words boomed down in bass from the podium: "Pray our blessings on this town of Philadelphia and that our coming together will not be in vain . . . Bless our President of the United States, our senators and congressmen, the officials of this town."

Two black women with piano accompaniment sang "My Living Shall Not Be in Vain," prompting several of the babies in the audience to try their lungs also. When they and the infants had finished, Mitchell Meredith, a black man in policeman's uniform who had once coached at Booker T. Washington, cited the honoree's athletic accomplishments from age ten until the present. "Last and not least," he concluded to laughter and applause, "he's an outstanding citizen of our county, because he has had no dealings with my department as of yet."

On the stage now I took note of Fred Akers, a television personage on an equal footing with Donahue, tanned and deftly chiseled, but with an ambivalence about his eyes. Like Donahue, with his Beverly Hills looks, he seemed consciously detached from the Okie-Texan-country western-Willie Nelson directness of his predecessor, Darrell Royal, whom I once had known. I had seldom seen a man with such a stricken expression. Ashen-faced and glum, Akers appeared in the tremors of some dyspeptic unease, as if he had recently mistaken a jalapeño pepper for an anchovy. He turned briefly to whisper with Tommy Reaux, then retreated again to his solitary enigmatic suffering. What might this be? What was going on?

Several of Marcus' teammates, all nervous to the point of self-conscious giggles, gave testimonials—Michael Smith and Tree McAfee, now of the Ole Miss Rebels; Mark Burnside and Rod Sutton, Daran Jackson and Justy Johnson. "I've seen him squat over five hundred pounds, bench press over six hundred pounds, then run the forty in 4.3," Jackson said. "Marcus, we wish you the best in collegiate football, but also to put God first in everything you do." And Justy Johnson: "As his quarterback, he always did what was best for the team. We knew even in the fifth grade he'd be one of the best. I remember him runnin' touchdowns with five-pound leg weights on when the rest of us couldn't even lift them."

The mistress of ceremonies introduced his mother, his grandmother, and then his brother—"The most dedicated admirer of Marcus Dupree, little Reginald." Reggie struggled to his feet and beamed at the applause.

The distinguished visitors were recognized to loud cheers. Fred Akers was mistakenly introduced as the head coach of the University of Southern Mississippi—"Oh, I mean the Texas Longhorns!" Billy Joe DuPree of the Cowboys had been observing the afternoon's scene with the silken equilibrium of celebrityhood; he wore a sweater with black and white stripes and a red cap. When he was acknowledged, he received the most spirited response of all.

Then came brief speeches from Joe Wood, Kenneth Cook, Superintendent Therrell Myers, and Jimmy Lee Shannon. "I've coached Marcus, Daran, Michael, Mark, and all the young boys," Shannon said. "Marcus, be yourself at all times and always respect one another . . . This is something I never dreamed would come to Neshoba County—showing love to one another." Mrs. Beatrice Hampton, the president of Ebonee Unique and a schoolteacher, presented a letter from the Goodway Baptist Church: "The path to success, Marcus, is just as narrow as the path to Jesus Christ." The president of the Chamber of Commerce read an honorary resolution. Two telegrams were read, one from Governor William Winter, the other from Earl Campbell, the former Heisman Trophy winner from Texas. The latter said: "Congratulations. Hope you Become a Longhorn. Peace and Love." Charles McClain, the mayor, introduced the city aldermen and their wives. "I stand here representing all the citizens of Philadelphia, Mississippi," he said. "We're behind you, Marcus!"

Marcus rose to a prolonged standing ovation, the kind he had heard time without number ever since he was fourteen on his magical touchdown runs. He spoke simply: "It's hard to believe the whole county is honoring me today. As most of you know, football is a big part of my life. Without your support, I couldn't have made it through the last four years. Without my teammates, I couldn't have made one touchdown. My coaches and my family supported me no matter what. But most of all I'd like to give credit to God, Who's the head of my life."

Until now the afternoon had been alternately festive and evangelic, but what ensued was nothing but pandemonium.

While the children of the town surrounded Billy Joe DuPree on the stage for autographs, and the coaches stood there as if dubious of their next move, Sid Salter and I managed to get Marcus around to the back of the building outside. Was his prior commitment to Texas still valid?

"I found out some things I needed to know out at Oklahoma," he said, "and I'm definitely gonna sign with them."

"With Oklahoma?"

"Yeah."

"Are you sure?"

"Yeah, I'm sure."

The reporters had found him now, and a television crew, and a crush of well-wishers. He was not repeating to them his words about Oklahoma. In the early darkness he was as trapped by human flesh as his distant cousin Billy Joe on the stage.

Inside the auditorium again, the tumult had intensified. No one left. The coaches had descended from the platform and were all looking for Marcus. Gazing about desperately, they in their turn were engulfed by autograph hounds of all races and ages. The television crews likewise had moved in for the assault, and people began tripping over their tangle of wires. The television interviewers snared Akers, then Donahue and Carmody. The white and black women of the town had gathered together to socialize and were chattering loudly. Children dashed among the rows of seats, one of them displaying the black star with Nat Turner's name on it.

Stan Dearman of the *Democrat* came up to me. The wife of an important Klan member during "The Troubles" had asked him to get Marcus' autograph.

Fred Akers had been talking with Marcus' mother. He had the same haunted look as before—the hunter without his quarry, an unhappy Francis Macomber. He confronted a Texas reporter. "Do you know where Marcus is going when he leaves the auditorium?" he asked. A few feet away Carmody of Southern was asking Coach Cook of Philly High: "Where is Marcus going when he leaves?" On the stage Billy Joe DuPree was still hopelessly ensnarled. From the back of the arena Lucious Selmon of Oklahoma was observing the moment's extravaganza with an amused eye.

I had been talking casually with Fred Akers when another television camera abruptly took over with him. Tommy Reaux was standing alone to the side. I asked if I might talk with him in a moment of calm.

"Are you staying at the Colonial?" I inquired.

He looked direly apprehensive. Then he laughed, a huge black man with a defensive lineman's girth. "I may be stayin' in a ditch," he said mysteriously. But we arranged to meet the next day in the Downtown.

Terry Donahue of UCLA was signing autographs. Several of the youngsters slipped away from him toward me. "Are you a coach?" A black voice shouted: "Where's Marcus *Du*-pree? Where's he at?"

Now Donahue was all alone, looking about uncertainly. I introduced myself. "This was *some* afternoon," he said. "I've never quite seen anything like it. Three people killed here just a few years ago. It shows the power of football—what football can do to bring about change." Had he ever attended an occasion like this for a recruit? "Not an official *day*. Of course, we recruit all over the country. But you never have anything like this in California. The high schools out there aren't built around towns."

Another Texas reporter wandered by. Donahue asked him if he had heard when Marcus might sign. "Just outside there a minute ago he said Wednesday, Thursday, or Friday," the reporter said. "And his final choices are still Texas, Oklahoma, Southern Miss, and you."

"Where is he now?" Donahue asked. The reporter did not know.

Donahue had come to Philadelphia by himself that day. "We had some recruits in this weekend," he said, turning back to me. "But I felt I ought to be here. I just dropped in to be here. I should probably be getting on back right now." He departed graciously, coolly. But he had the look of a man who might stay around.

The crowd was sparser now. I heard someone shouting my name. It was Marcus' brother Reggie. He extended a high-five. "Where's your dog Pete?" he asked.

"He's in the hotel. He's watching television."

"Pete's watchin' television," Reggie said to his mother, who had just joined us.

"I'm so glad you came," she said, taking my hand.

"I wouldn't have missed it."

"When all this is over," she said, "I want to write a book about recruiting."

Billy Joe DuPree had now escaped most of his young admirers and was moving surreptitiously toward the door. Billy Watkins of *The Meridian Star* was talking with him. "I chose Michigan State for football," he was saying. "I grew up in West Monroe, Louisiana, a small town. No knock against it, but there really wasn't much to keep me around home."

Where did he think Marcus would go?

"I think he'll go to Texas," he said. "Man, Texas is where it's at. Texas just has more to offer. If you're good, they make sure they highlight that, and you'll get the recognition you deserve. Texas was special-sent from heaven." Then he too was gone.

Marcus had indeed informed the reporters that he still held to his final four choices. Obviously Jackie Sherrill was at last out of it. Neither he nor the Texas Aggies had been represented that day. "I just don't like Texas A&M," he later told me. "Too many boys."

I walked past the black stars displayed on the wall and into the darkness outside. From all over the Quarters there were shouts of celebration. They were even shooting firecrackers.


A white woman later said to me: "You'd think with this fantastic outpouring of love in his hometown today, he'd stay in Mississippi to go to college. What other small town in America ever had something like that for a seventeen-year-old kid?"

To me the ceremony served in a measure to refute my black preacher friend's contention that the white establishment in town was only using him as a "symbol." With the Black National Anthem and the whole decorative motif, the blacks seemed to be saying, "This is our turf. This is our boy. Look what we've done. You can come to us."

But Stan Dearman of the *Democrat* said: "He wasn't black or white. He was a young athlete whose townspeople were proud of him."

# 24
# *Nocturnal Disguises*

*Sunday Night, February 7*

Sid Salter and I conferred at the Command Post. We agreed that Oklahoma might have taken the slight edge, with Texas second, but that Southern was moving up hard in the homestretch. Donahue of UCLA had left town. What credence to put on Marcus' remark that he would sign with Oklahoma? He had said the same thing about Texas after returning fom Austin only a week before. There were three days to the signing date, and with representatives of all four principals on the premises, who could predict anything?

Sid and I decided to cruise about the Quarters to see what was happening. We donned disguises—he a dirty cowboy hat, I a maroon-and-white Mississippi State baseball cap. Pete jumped into the back seat of my Plymouth. We had already ascertained that the University of Texas contingent was driving a silver four-door Pontiac Bonneville with a Rankin County license plate and that Lucious Selmon had a black Mercury with a silver top and a Rankin plate also. We believed that Jim Carmody of Southern was in a red car, unidentified make, with a Neshoba plate. Tommy Reaux was registered in the Pines Motel and Selmon in the Colonial. There were no recruiters at the moment in the Downtown.

A full moon shone brightly over the Quarters as we drove past Marcus' house. The silver Pontiac was parked in front. Fred Akers was sitting in the back seat and Tommy Reaux was knocking on the front door. On our second loop around the block Akers, Reaux, Billy Joe DuPree, and Albert Jackson of the Atlanta Falcons were standing on the porch.

We circled again—past the Mount Nebo Church, Latimer Metropolitan Funeral Home, Lillie Jones's house, and the old COFO quarters. Just beyond the Busy Bee we noticed for the first time a mysterious red car with a long radio aerial and a Neshoba plate. It too was going around and around the block, slowing each time it went by Marcus' house. Two shadowy figures were in the front seat. The Texans were now inside the house, but Marcus, Albert Jackson, and a girl were standing near the road.

In front of us, the red car continued across Carver on Davis. "Follow it!" Salter said. It was traveling fast as it turned another corner. It had disappeared. Suddenly it pulled out of a driveway behind us and began following our Plymouth. Salter, Pete, and I turned our heads to see what was happening. At that moment our pursuers swerved into another side street and vanished. I believed I had seen a "Golden Eagle" decal on the back window. "It certainly wasn't Yale," Sid said.

Sid concluded that the best way to find out what was transpiring at the house was for him, a local reporter, to walk by there. "Casually walking through the Quarters?" I said. "It won't work."

"I'll think of something," he said.

I parked the car a few yards from the Mount Nebo Church. Salter got out and departed down Davis Street. From the back seat Pete nudged me with his cold, wet nose. "What have you got us into now?" I knew he was asking. I was forty-six years old. What was I doing in a Mississippi State baseball cap playing cloak-and-dagger games under a full winter moon in the black precincts of Philadelphia, Mississippi? From a vehicle coming by, someone shined a flashlight on us, then went on. It was the same red car.

After ten minutes or so, Sid returned. Marcus, standing in front of his house with Albert Jackson and the girl, had laughed when he saw him walking up the road and asked him what he was doing in the neighborhood.

"Just wanted to holler at you a minute if you've got the time."

He excused himself from his companions and they retreated a few feet.

"Who's your company, Marcus?"

"Texas, man. They're really comin' on strong tonight."

He was wearing a University of Oklahoma sweatsuit and a cap with "OU" on it.

"Are you sure about what you told me about Oklahoma?" Sid asked.

"Yeah. I found out they're movin' Buster Rhymes to split end next year. They lost another back for disciplinary reasons, and that opens up a spot for me. Everybody else, includin' the Texas people, say they won't move Buster. But they told me they would." He said Akers and the other Texans were in the house talking with his mother and that he was about to leave and get away from it all for a while.

"So you're definitely going to OU?"

"Yeah. That's what I told you today. I'll probably wait to announce Wednesday or Thursday."


The Colonial Motel was about three miles from town on Highway 19. We drove out there, past a tall silo where, Sid informed me, a teenaged boy of the town had jumped off a few years before because of troubles with his girl.

Lucious Selmon's rented Mercury was parked in front of Room 17. Selmon was alone and warm in his greetings. He seemed to welcome a little brief company.

"I thought you might be able to clear up a few things about Marcus."

He laughed. "Well, I was hopin' you might do the same for me."

He had no idea, he said, where Marcus was going to school, but he planned to be in Philadelphia "for the duration." We agreed to compare notes the next day.

Back at the Post, I learned after a couple of calls that Tom Goode of Ole Miss had telephoned Joe Wood that night expressing concern that "the kid might get in trouble." Goode told Wood he was not at the appreciation ceremony because his presence would have counted as an official visit and he wanted to save one just in case. The Rebels had not given up.

# 25

# And Then
# There Were Four

The jury was in session at the courthouse. Among the cases were a wife-beating, a murder of a man by an old friend, a marijuana possession, and a theft of 5,500 pounds of soybeans from Illinois Central Gulf. The jury, mostly women, was staying in the Downtown. As our elevator opened, one of the women standing in the lobby said, "I'd hate to get caught in a dark alley with *him*." I was relieved to learn she was referring, not to me, but to Pete.

There was no activity that morning at Joe Wood's office at the school. "You tell *me* where he's goin'," Joe said.

I telephoned Lucious Selmon at the Colonial to set up an appointment. "Say, have they got dial phones in the rooms at the Downtown," he asked, "so you don't have to go through the switchboard?"

I told him you could even dial direct on long distance and that Roy Tingle took messages at the desk.

"No kidding? I'm gonna move in over there."

Later that morning there was a knock on the door of my room. It was Tommy Reaux. "What do you hear?" he asked. When he walked in and saw Pete, he said: "Wow, we could use *him*."

Tommy Reaux put his huge frame in a chair. He was instantly lovable. He was a warmhearted man who, I was soon to discover, liked company and talk. Both Joe Wood and Danny Gregory had spoken highly of him to me—"a man of honor," Gregory had said. Sometimes his eyes shone with mirth; his laughter was contagious. But on this day he was nervous and tense, and he seemed near exhaustion.

"Say. You got a dial phone. I'm gonna move into this hotel."

We managed to avoid the subject of Marcus for a few minutes. Reaux, I learned, had played his football at Baylor, where he was an all-Conference defensive lineman in 1969. He had coached for three years at

Smiley High School in Houston. He was a bachelor. He had joined Freddie Akers at Texas the previous summer and was the running-back coach. His father was a school principal in Houston.

Sid Salter came into the room. "What do you hear?" he asked. There was much banter all around.

Reaux and Akers had made their first visit to Marcus here last June 23. Reaux remembered the date because it was his thirty-second birthday. Their first "phone contact," he said, was June 15, right after he had taken his job with Texas. They had heard about Marcus from a national scouting service. "We told him we'd been watchin' him, that he could be a great running back anywhere, even at East Central Junior College. We said we thought Texas was the best place for him. We told him we'd sign one running back this year." Subsequently, Reaux had seen him in four games during the past season.

Our visitor was obviously frustrated. He fidgeted in his chair and occasionally lapsed into morbid silence; he asked questions about Marcus which Sid and I were unable to answer. Every now and again he would say, "What goes round, comes down." He had been on the road almost constantly since December 1. "The flying is sometimes more tiring than the driving," he said.

"As of today," he said, "if I were a betting man, I'd say we're not gonna get him." Akers, Billy Joe DuPree, and Albert Jackson had left last night. "We used all our house visits after last night. I've got one more school visit. I may use it this afternoon. Oklahoma says they've got one more house visit. I think they're all used up."

He got up for a moment and walked about the room. Pete, who apparently had likewise developed a swift liking for the big Longhorn, walked around with him.

He was not sure whether he would leave town that afternoon after seeing Marcus. "I'm not gonna baby-sit him," he said. "The signing date is day after tomorrow, and I've got recruits I may have to sign in Washington, D.C.; Fort Smith, Arkansas; and East Texas."

He seemed exceedingly upset with Marcus and his mother. When Marcus committed to Texas a week ago today, he said, Fred Akers informed the best running back in Texas, a young black from Newton, Texas, named Anthony Byerly, in whom the Longhorns were highly interested, that Marcus Dupree had chosen to go to college in Austin. So unless young Byerly were told otherwise, and unless the Longhorns made a successful last-minute effort for his services, he was going to sign with the University of Nebraska Cornhuskers.

Reaux said they had spent considerable time at the university working out a curriculum in communications for Marcus, since he had told them this would be his major. Mike Quinn, a classmate of mine from student days and now the associate dean, had devised a course list based on whether he wished to graduate in four years with two summers, four and a half years, and so forth. When Marcus came into his house the night before, wearing the Oklahoma sweatsuit, Coach Akers handed him this material. "Marcus just laid it on the table," Reaux said, "and walked out." Also, Marcus had told them he wanted Billy Joe DuPree to come to the appreciation ceremonies. He worked hard signing autographs at the community center, Reaux said, and he signed quite a few last night for Marcus' mother to give out at her school. "Marcus walked out of the house without talking to him."

He sank back in his chair, tapping his foot on the carpet to the cadences of his words. "What goes round," he repeated, "comes down."

It was the noon recess, and the shouts of the high school students resounded up Byrd Avenue. From the window I noticed a horde of young scholars entering Wizard's World for the video games.

"Cella's on an ego trip," Reaux continued. "Every time the phone rang last night, she was eager to pick it up on the first ring. She didn't take it off the hook."

Then, emphatically: "I smell a rat."

Both Southern and Oklahoma, he predicted, would be investigated by the NCAA if Marcus went to either place. So would UCLA because of the visit with Marty Gamblin last summer.

He outlined the turn of events, his kindly features turning sour with his catalogue. On his official visit to Austin last weekend, Marcus told them he liked Texas and that he was committing. "The only thing we promised him was the chance to get a good education. We didn't even make any promises about him playing as a freshman." Previously, he said, Marcus' mother had told Barry Switzer to his face that she respected Akers above all other coaches. They had planned to make the formal announcement yesterday, after the ceremonies at Westside.

Last Monday morning, Marcus authorized Joe Wood to announce his commitment to the press. "I know for a fact Uncle Curlee Connor came to the school that Monday afternoon without tellin' Cella," Reaux said. "Marcus and Cella had conferred the night before, after he got back from Austin, about his decision." He telephoned Marcus' mother the following Thursday. "She was abrupt. She said she'd learned some things about Texas—that a lot of players were unhappy, other things. I spoke to her frankly. I was outspoken with her. The next day Marcus told somebody that I hadn't been nice to his mother on the phone. I know somethin' happened between Marcus' announcement for Texas last Monday and the following day."

Uncle Curlee, he said, arrived in Norman, Oklahoma, Friday, the same day Marcus did. He said he had come on his own.

He was quiet again. He leaned down and rubbed Pete's nose, then sighed. I wondered to myself now whether the Texas-Oklahoma conflict was merely a smoke screen for Southern to pick up the pieces at the last moment. I remembered Agatha Christie's *And Then There Were None*.

The Longhorn coach spoke gently, turning philosophical now. He had stressed to Marcus and his mother the high percentage of Texas football players who get their degrees. "We've got a clean program," he said. "We've never been on probation. I've seen this same situation a hundred times, and nothing surprises me any more. We've got a good product to sell at Texas, and if the young man doesn't know that by now, then I'm wasting my time and his. The University of Texas speaks for itself. It's a great institution, maybe the best university in the South. The guys we want are the guys who recognize that. I'll tell you one thing, and you can take this to the bank. Marcus couldn't find a better program in the country. It's just like a Hershey candy bar. They don't have to advertise it, 'cause they know it's the best there is. What Marcus needs to look at is what Marcus will be doin' fifteen years from now. He needs to have a competitive education."

I had learned something, I said, about the strains of football recruiting.

"Everybody that's for you is not for you," he replied. "Everybody that's against you is not against you." He continued: "If I don't get a good word today, by God, I'm goin' back to Texas. We made a commitment to him and his family to be here, but we didn't spend no $543 an hour on a Lear jet to come sit on our thumbs. I sent him a letter three weeks ago sayin' he should be happy wherever he goes. We don't want him if he's not happy."

Sid Salter, who had said little until now, asked him if signing Marcus would be "a feather in your cap?"

"Hell, I'm at one of the best programs there is. I don't need to sign this or any other kid to get a better job. I've got the best job there is. The people here are handling it well. Joe Wood and Danny Gregory have done just right. I just hope they don't drag it out and make a circus of it. I spent almost ten of my twelve years as a coach in high school, and I know the most important thing for a kid is goin' where he'll be happy. I'll tell you one thing. We made a promise to be here with him and his family for his Appreciation Day when he announced last week he was comin' to Texas. By God, Fred Akers was here. Where was Barry Switzer?"

By now it was nearly one o'clock, and the three of us decided to drive out to the Shorewood Inn for lunch.

We were waiting for the elevator on the second floor. Suddenly the elevator doors opened. There, without warning, was Coach Lucious Selmon, on his way with his bags to move into his room on the third floor.

For the most transitory instant, before the doors closed again, Selmon and Reaux stood facing one another, two imposing young black men, Longhorns vs. Sooners, in the Downtown Hotel. Stunned, they gazed directly at one another for a moment, then, just as the elevator doors closed again, they smiled at each other knowingly.

Tommy Reaux punched Sid Salter on the arm. "Sid, life sure does get interestin' sometimes, don't it?"

At the Shorewood, Reaux only ordered a cup of coffee. "Coach, how are you going to keep that 280-pound body in shape on just coffee?" Sid asked.

"My appetite is dictated by the success of the day," Coach Reaux said, "and today I can't eat a bit."

The conversation loosened. He talked about how much he loved Austin, of how he went to the athletic dormitory at UT all the time to visit with the boys. Hearing his jolly laughter, the ladies seated across the room from us turned to look. Then: "I've been after that kid since June 15. When Marcus left our campus after his visit, I would've bet you a dollar to a doughnut he'd sign with us. But now," he repeated, "I've got a bad feeling we've lost him."

Sid told him what the prospect had said outside the Westside auditorium yesterday, fresh back from Oklahoma: "I found out some things I needed to know."

"Is there a phone in this place?" Reaux quickly asked. He excused himself and was away for ten minutes. He returned and sat down.

"I'm gonna stay," he said.

*Monday Afternoon*

Reaux checked into the Downtown in the room next to mine. Selmon's room was directly above Reaux's on the third floor.

Selmon was at the school gym talking with Joe Wood. He appeared confident but cautious. "I don't know what he'll do at this point. I'm just here to monitor the situation. I think UCLA's still in the running. I'm more worried about Jackie Sherrill and Texas A&M now than I am about Southern."

Joe Wood said he was convinced that Marcus would not sign this week and would make his last official visit on the weekend to A&M.

"I'm not countin' anybody out," Selmon said.

Marty Gamblin, one of two UCLA advocates in town, was working out in the weight room. He too believed UCLA was still in the running. As he lifted weights, his eyes did not miss anyone walking through the room.

As Pete and I walked around the Square, everyone wanted to know what was happening. Tom Turner came out from his hardware store. "What's goin' on?" he asked.

With his acute perception, Pete had adopted an interesting mannerism. For some time now, whenever he heard the words *Marcus Dupree* he lifted his ears, then wagged his tail in the familiar circle.

In the Downtown Restaurant, a man from Leake County bet his friends five dollars on Southern. There were no takers. In the lobby Roy Tingle said, "Let's get this ol' stuff over with."

*Monday Night*

I heard heavy footsteps in Tommy Reaux's room next door. He was pacing the floor between telephone calls. I gave him a call and we arranged to meet at the Command Post a little later in the evening.

Sid Salter and I were exchanging intelligence and watching *Superman II* on Home Box Office in a desultory way when Reaux came into the Post. He sank into an easy chair and with alacrity accepted Sid's offer of a Cutty Sark. He had had his last official visit with Marcus in the afternoon, and apparently it had not gone well.

"Sid, you married?" he asked, looking about at the wreckage.

"Gonna be soon," Sid said.

"Good."

Our affable new friend was more restless than ever. Although he was trying to relax, he was tapping his foot on the floor as he had done that morning in my hotel room. From time to time he glanced at the movie. Superman just then was flying over Gotham. "I wish Akers and I could get a runnin' back like that," he said.

We chatted about football and recruiting. He told us what effective recruiters the UCLA people were. He got up three or four times and went into the kitchen to telephone Marcus' mother, but each time the line was busy. He intermittently watched *Superman II*.

"I smell a rat," he repeated.

After a while he reached in his billfold and withdrew a telephone credit card. Several times he retreated into the kitchen and placed calls to the running back in Newton, Texas, named Byerly—the one who had said he was going to the Nebraska Cornhuskers. The line was busy there too.

Finally he got the call through to young Byerly. I could hear him talking softly from the kitchen. Then he returned to the room. "He has an upset stomach," Reaux said.

He declined a mushroom pizza which we had ordered from the Pizza Hut and watched thoughtfully as Pete ate a slice. "I have some work to do," he said. "I'll see you fellas tomorrow." With a burst of false cheer he departed.

That night Tommy Reaux returned to the Downtown and placed

more long-distance calls. Then he drove to Independence Quarters. He went into the pool hall catty-corner from the Busy Bee. It was crowded with the denizens of the Quarters. He tried to ascertain what was going on with Marcus, Uncle Curlee Connor, Oklahoma, and Southern. In the early light he came back to the Downtown—shaved, showered, and had breakfast.

# 26
# Puzzlements and Déjà Vu's

*Tuesday Morning, February 9*

On the day before the national signing, Southern Mississippi was back in town. Coach Jim Carmody and his assistant, Keith Daniels, had scheduled an official house visit later in the day.

Tommy Reaux and Joe Wood were sitting in Wood's office at 8:30 A.M. Both looked tired. "I spent the rest of the night over on 'the Hill' talking to folks," Reaux said.

*Tuesday Afternoon*

Horace Johnson, a tall, immaculately dressed black man, was at the school gym. As an alumnus of UCLA he was here representing his alma mater. He was pleasant and courteous. He also had the trenchant look about him of money, the feel and ambience of money, the predisposed casuistry of a man who had made money and knew how to carry it. He lived in two places, he told me—Tyler, Texas, and Los Angeles. He thought UCLA was very much in it. "He's a fine young man. Whoever gets him will have a great citizen and a great athlete. I'll be a friend of his forever. He's that kind of fellow."

Joe Wood categorically predicted he would not sign tomorrow.

I had an appointment in the Downtown with Lucious Selmon. Sid Salter said he would wait around the school to try and corner Marcus. He had parked his pickup truck next to Marcus' Olds behind the gym. Usually Marcus stopped at Wood's office every day after class, but today he walked straight to his car. Sid invited him to drive around for a while in his pickup truck.

They left the school and went out the Highway 15 bypass. "Marcus, what's the word?"

"Well, I've narrowed it down to OU and UCLA," he said.

"I thought UCLA was out of it."

"I made a lot of friends out there, and I've got to think about that. I don't know anyone at Oklahoma."

He continued: "I've been hearin' bad rumors all week about me and my momma and my uncle. I swear to you, we're clean."

Sid warned him to be careful.


Early in the afternoon Tommy Reaux drove to DeKalb to see Marcus' mother in her school. From all he had gathered, and for whatever reason, he felt Texas was no longer in the competition. By the time he reached the school she had already left for the day. He was driving back to Philadelphia on the main road when he saw her car ahead of him. He blew his horn and gestured that he wanted to talk with her. At first she did not see him. "Finally, I pulled up beside her and waved and she pulled over."

They had a cordial talk, he said. He informed her that unless she told him differently, he was returning that afternoon to Texas. "All I wanted to do was thank her for her time and wish them well. I knew we were out of it. We exchanged pleasantries and said our goodbyes."

Reaux was about to leave town, but decided to talk with Marcus in private and to say goodbye. He found him at Uncle Curlee's station. Marcus agreed to go outside to talk, but Curlee said no. Someone suggested they go in the back room, but again the uncle was adamant. "Two or three old drunks sittin' in the corner thought this was funny as hell," Reaux said.

"I told Curlee that UT was out of it and that I just wanted to say goodbye. I'd run out of visits, but there ain't no such thing as an illegal visit to a nonrecruit. So I had to say my goodbyes right there in the station with no privacy."

Reaux must have been finding it difficult to leave town after all the emotion he had invested in it. Like the dying man before the mirages of the Sahara, had he one last, lingering hope? He packed his bags and an hour or so later drove to the Dupree house. The ubiquitous Uncle Curlee met him at the front door. Joe Wood was there also. "I thought you Texas people had class," Curlee said. He said he was going to report them to the NCAA.

"What do you mean?" Reaux asked.

The uncle accused Reaux of making mean telephone calls to Marcus' mother and of trying to run her off the road earlier that afternoon. "If you hang around this town," he said, "you're gonna get hurt."

"It wouldn't have bothered me," Reaux would later reflect, "if someone in the family had told me, 'Hey, you're out of it, Oklahoma outrecruited you.' But no one told me anything. The kid does a complete 180-degree, and I don't know sure to this day why."

As he was leaving Philadelphia, he dropped by *The Neshoba Democrat* looking for Sid and me. "I just came by to thank you for everything and to say goodbye," he said. "I'm fixin' to go back to Texas and find me a running back."

"Tommy, you've spent eight months on this kid," Sid said.

"Well, I've done it before and I'll probably do it again. But you know I did my best." He almost looked relieved.

Just before he left, he said: "The only thing Marcus is guilty of is being seventeen years old.

Lucious Selmon opened the door of Room 333 and invited me in. The television was turned on to a rerun of "The Flintstones." On a table was a container of Kool-Aid. He wore blue jeans, a brown sweater, and brown cowboy boots, and beneath the short beard and mustache was the doleful look of a man who had settled into many a solitary hotel room. Like Reaux the day before he seemed nervous.

Just as we sat down in chairs at the table the telephone rang. He moved toward it with a feline dexterity, getting it on the first ring, as if his fate rested on that very call. I heard the staccato voice on the other end, an interrogative, but could not make out the words.

"Twiddlin' my thumbs," Selmon said. "Watchin' 'The Flintstones.' I may get a block of wood and whittle."

The voice again.

"Yeah, he checked out about forty-five minutes ago . . . Of course I'm sure. I *guarantee* you." He then discussed with the caller a report in the Pittsburgh and Houston papers about Marcus coming to Oklahoma.

When he had finished we talked incidentally about OU. I told him I still remembered the oil wells on the campus from a visit there years ago. One of his brothers, he said, was now doing graduate work in ancient philosophy there between the professional football seasons.

The telephone rang again, and again he leaped for it. "Can't talk now," he said. "Things are okay, I guess."

He had first heard about Marcus, he told me, in his junior year from a national recruiting service. "Some people in Atlanta also contacted us." He had only seen him play on film. "It took us about three minutes of film to tell how great he is. Marcus is one of the greatest high school running backs we've ever seen, and we've seen a few. His speed and size set him out from all the rest."

How did he compare with Herschel Walker?

"Herschel's got great speed, the ability to stop and start real quick. He and Marcus compare in that way, and in size. Statistically he's better than Herschel, and he's just as fast or faster. He's got the kind of quick speed to get out on the corner of the Wishbone that Herschel doesn't have. Once he's done that, he's got the ability to run away from the defensive backfield, or to run over you. He'll be the best back we recruit this year. We'd line him up at right halfback. He's got all the capabilities to start as a freshman." What playing weight would they want from him? "Well, we know what he weighed during the high school season. We'd like him to report in good condition, and the weight will take care of itself. Two hundred twenty to two twenty-two would be fantastic."

His first contact was a telephone call shortly after Christmas. Their recruiting coordinator, Scott Hill, came to Philadelphia in December, and Barry Switzer visited in early January.

"I believe we impressed him with our facilities on his visit last weekend, with the happiness of our players. The Wishbone's impressed him, knowin' how much we like to run. We took him to a recruiting banquet with nineteen or twenty others. We showed him our place. He liked the relaxed atmosphere of the coaches and players." They left the date of the official visit to Marcus. "The last visit has to weigh very heavily. The in-between schools are sometimes looked over."

Their offensive line, he said, was depleted this year. They would have two returning, and the average weight would be 286 pounds. "We used variations on the 'I' when we had Billy Sims. If a team is vulnerable to the outside, we'll put him in the 'I' and sweep him to the right or the left. He never had to do much blockin' in high school. That's important in the Wishbone, and we'll probably have to work with him on it. But I'll tell you one thing—his runnin' ability won't have to be coached. We'll just sit back and watch."

The television murmured in the background. My mannerly host had been speaking in the affirmative, as if his prospect had already signed the papers, but this formal self-assurance was belied by his occasional skittish gestures and expressions—fingers drumming gently on the table, apprehensive glances my way, a drowsy-eyed prudence. I could tell he felt he had to be cautious with me, and well-spoken, as if he feared that relaxing with me as a human being might open a cataract of professional uncertainties. He was plainly a decent fellow, and his easy smile was ingratiating. The warm volubility of Tommy Reaux seemed not in his nature, but there were serene and solid qualities, I sensed, and a Christian sweetness which must have appealed to young athletes from the small towns, especially blacks. Only later, under the pressures which were to come, would he reveal himself as a sentient, likable figure with a rueful comprehension of the absurdities.

"I'll tell you, it might be 'a feather in my cap' getting Marcus, but basically I see it as a team effort. I wouldn't expect any recognition. Just seein' him happy and successful would be enough. Marcus can go as far as he wants to in football, and on to a lucrative pro career."

Why, then, should he choose Oklahoma? "He says he wants to break Herschel's freshman record and win the Heisman someday. We're a run-oriented team, and we've had the caliber of backs in the past who've won the Heisman—Billy Sims, Steve Owens, Billy Vessels. Sims carried twenty-five times or more a game. Marcus could too."

He had one house visit left, he said, but none at the school. Barry Switzer might fly in if necessary. They had reserved one more visit just in case. This was the first time Texas and Oklahoma had been after the same Mississippian. "Now the rivalry's carried a long way." How did this situation compare with his own experience as a high school football recruit? "All the Big Eight schools were after me," he said, "but it was nowhere this intense—*nowhere!* The pressure to make the right decision was just as intense, though. Two small-town boys tryin' to make up their minds."

What were his plans now? I asked. For the first time he grinned, as if he had been pondering just this while drinking strawberry Kool-Aid. "Well, I'll go down to the school. Knock around a little. Lift some weights. Keep my eyes open. Then come back here and wait for the phone to ring. I'll call the house tonight."

Did he know that Southern Mississippi was in town at this moment?

All of a sudden, quick as could be, he opened up with me. "I feel very nervous, just sittin' by the phone. It's lonesome too. I'll tell you somethin'—I'm worried about Southern Mississippi. They make me *very, very* nervous. It's a gut feeling I have. Very, very nervous.

"I'll stay here through the rest of the week if it takes that long. Or till this time next week. By then my money will have run out."

"Come on, Coach," I said. "Oklahoma money running out?"

We laughed, then stopped to listen to the television announcer for a news program on a Jackson channel: "Marcus Dupree, Philadelphia's great running back and the most recruited football player in the nation, said earlier today he's leaning to Oklahoma, but may change his mind. He says Texas is out of it, but UCLA is still in, and of course Southern Mississippi. He says he probably won't sign on tomorrow's national signing date."

Selmon and I looked at each other. "See what I mean?" he said. "That lifted me up, then put me down."

I suggested he come over to the Command Post to be with Sid Salter and me that night. "I may do it," he said. "Doubt if I have nothin' else to do."

*Tuesday Night*

Tomorrow was not only the signing day, but the Philadelphia schools would not be in session because of a teachers' conference. Sid and I learned that the Southern coaches, Carmody and Daniels, were going to Marcus' house later that night. Lucious Selmon, who arrived now at the Command Post, knew it too.

We told Selmon of Tommy Reaux's departing words as he had left town not long before. Sid informed him that Marcus had told him in midafternoon that his choices were UCLA and Southern.

Lucious Selmon seemed less than pleased. "I know it," he said. "But it's really Southern." He took an iced tea and settled into the same easy chair occupied by Tommy Reaux the night before.

"I'm profoundly worried," he said. Marcus was a good kid, he felt, who was getting unsound advice. The central figure, he believed, was Uncle Curlee. He repeated: "I'm profoundly worried."

As the telephone rang from time to time from townspeople desiring information, Selmon sat there tensely with his thoughts. The evening was a striking *déjà vu*. Selmon tapped the floor with his cowboy boots just as Reaux had done twenty-four hours earlier, and he spoke in the same tones of melancholy resignation. "It's driftin' away," he said.

From the very beginning last summer people in town had told me Southern would be in the competition against the major collegiate powers right to the end. Temple Drake had said as much. Their advice to the prospect to stay home in the state, to be the player to lead them to the national championship, had had its effect. They were a stubborn group. Mickey Spagnola of *The Jackson Daily News* would say it well:

> If you're going to war, and if you get to pick first, choose Southern Mississippi. Always choose Southern Mississippi. You want those folks over in Hattiesburg on your side at all times.
> If they're on the other side, then change sides. Don't fight Southern Mississippi. No matter how hard you fight, those folks will fight harder. They are that way, as if this Hattiesburg, this school of 11,800 is some sort of transplanted inner-city core in the state of Mississippi.
> Blue collar types, you know. Hard hats. Tattoos. Cigarettes in the shirt-sleeve. Beer. These people know sweat. They know work. They know nothing ever came easy, nor will it ever come easy. They are hard . . . hard, I'm telling you.

Lucious Selmon knew this. He got up and telephoned Marcus' house to talk with his mother. The line was busy. He kept trying. "They got it off the hook," he said. He returned to the chair and gazed at the ceiling, exhaling deeply.

Finally he reached her. He carried the telephone into the kitchen and talked for a long time. He rejoined Sid and me with the look of a man who had just talked with the governor and lost the last reprieve. I truthfully thought—I do not exaggerate—that this big ex-lineman would at any moment break into tears.

"She says she still hasn't made up her mind," he said. "That means Southern's got him."

"How do you know, Coach?" I asked.

"From my long experience with all this."

Sid Salter graciously made our guest some more iced tea, then left to get a six-pack of beer at Conn's Mini-Mart.

"It's driftin' away," he repeated, and sighed again. "Driftin', driftin'." Good old Pete had been lying on the carpet, observing the scene with eyes as dolorous as Selmon's. With his intuition of human sorrow, he walked up to the coach and put his chin on the arm of the chair, wagging his tail in the circle. Selmon patted his head but did not have his heart in it.

Knowing full well as I did that they both represented incredibly wealthy and resourceful football Goliaths, I was nonetheless feeling as unaffectedly sorry for Selmon as I had for Reaux the night before.

"You'll get him, Coach."

"I wish I could believe that."

"When do you think he'll sign now?"

"He can wait till the summer if he wants to. No rules against it."

Sid came back in. He had just run into Marcus and his girlfriend, Katrina, at Conn's. The coach leaned forward to listen. Sid had told Marcus he had to go to press with his story in the *Democrat* the next day and wanted to know what his headline should be.

"Dupree narrows choice to OU and Southern," Marcus replied.

"What about UCLA?" Sid asked.

"They're out of it."

"But that's not what you said this afternoon. What changed your mind so fast?"

"Southern just told me a lot of people wanted me to stay in the state. I have to consider that."

Sid wanted to know where he could be reached tomorrow. He said he would be out of town. Where was he going? "To Jackson to get my hair done."

When Sid had finished, Selmon stood up and said: "He's going to Jackson to sign with Southern."

"What makes you think so?" I asked.

"He could get his hair done better here in the Quarters than in Jackson," Selmon said, "unless he wants a jerry-curl."

"How do you know?" Sid asked.

"Because it makes sense. Get him out of town. Go to Jackson, the media center. Get him away from here."

A poignant silence fell on the room. Pete looked curiously from one to the other of us.

"Unless he's really gettin' a jerry-curl," the Sooner coach said with hope.

"He could get one of those here," Sid said.

"What's a jerry-curl?" I asked.

While Sid and Selmon discussed this sudden change of events, I went to the telephone and called a prominent Southern man in town. "What do you hear?" he asked. I wanted to know if Marcus would sign with Southern tomorrow. "I'm out of it," he said. "I don't know nothin'."

I telephoned Danny Gregory. "What's happening?" he asked. What did *he* know? "I'm out of it," he said. This was quickly becoming the most shopworn expression in Philly. For the first time since I had known him, Gregory was upset. "Marcus avoided me today," he said. "The situation has completely deteriorated in the last five or six days, ever since he announced for Texas and then withdrew it. I don't have the faintest idea what's going on." He said he was in the Jackson airport that afternoon and saw Marty Gamblin waiting for a flight to Los Angeles. Gamblin had said goodbye to Marcus earlier in the day, wished him well, and emphasized how much UCLA wanted him. Horace Johnson, the other UCLA representative, was still very much in town.

"Where's Tommy Reaux?" Gregory asked.

"He's gone back to Texas," I said. "He rode off into the sunset this afternoon."

I noticed that Selmon, sitting in the easy chair, had heard this. Despite everything, he smiled faintly. At least the rival Longhorns, on the opposite side of the Maginot Line, had given up first.

The three of us resumed our speculations. "If he's goin' to Jackson tomorrow to sign with Southern," Selmon said, "his mother will be there. The only way we'll know is if Cella doesn't go to her school tomorrow."

We thought out this newest consideration with all the seriousness of assistant professors of English at Rutgers discussing what Yvor Winters had said about T. S. Eliot.

Sid and I talked about a stakeout near 274 Davis Street at six the next morning. If Cella drove east toward Kemper County, there would be no signing in Jackson. If she drove west toward Jackson, there would be.

Lucious (by now it seemed we were fellow conspirators—hence the first name) was considering telephoning Marcus' mother to see if he could have coffee with her in the morning at her school. Then he dismissed this strategy. She might say yes and *still* go to Jackson, leaving him empty-handed and bereaved in the farthest reaches of Kemper County, a somber prospect for anyone.

"I may just go to Jackson and catch the plane tomorrow," he said. He reminded me of Fred Akers at the Appreciation Day ceremony. If a black man had ever been ashen-faced, I was looking at one now.

"There's a running back in Newton, Texas, Lucious," I could not help saying.

"If I showed up there," he replied, "Tommy Reaux would murder me."

He was quiet again. "Something's going on," he finally said, trance-like. "I smell something very bad. He's listened to his uncle."

A telephone call snapped this mood. "Southern is over at Marcus' house right now!" the caller said.

"Let's go to the Quarters," Sid suggested.

The trip in Sid's pickup truck took less than five minutes. Davis Street lay just ahead. A maroon car was pulling out of the Dupree drive-way. The license plate was from Forrest County—Hattiesburg. Lucious scrunched down in the seat. Sid sped up, trailing closely behind the Southern car for four or so blocks until it turned onto Beacon Street headed west. Sid turned east.

Suddenly the maroon car turned around and began following Sid's truck. Sid hit a back street, turned onto another, and switched off the headlights. The Southern recruiters went down Beacon again moving west and appeared to be going to Carthage—or was it Jackson?

"I'm goin' back to the hotel and go to sleep *under* the bed," Lucious said.

It was now 11 P.M. at the Command Post. Sid, Lucious, and I wondered if the maroon car was really going on to Jackson.

My friend, Tom Turner, my Ole Miss connection in town, came into the house. "What do you hear?" he asked. "The town's gettin' a little tired of all this." He was apprised of the late developments. What was *his* prediction?

"Ole Miss," he said, "waitin' in the wings."

We tried to comprehend how Southern had gotten back in the picture so quickly. "What does all this mean?" Sid asked rhetorically. "I've been getting calls at the office from as far away as Anchorage, Alaska." We had no answers, only the deepening riddle.

The coach was more crestfallen than ever. "He's goin' to Jackson tomorrow to sign," he said. "Wait and see. If Cella doesn't go to her school tomorrow, I'm packin' my bags and goin' back to Oklahoma."

He spoke wistfully now of his elderly parents, who had moved from

Eufaula to Oklahoma City. "When this is all over, I'm goin' off with my
wife and not tell anybody where. I may go to Tampa, Florida, for a week
and a half to rest up."

Then he departed in the night for the Downtown. At the door he
said again: "I'm gonna sleep *under* the bed."

Sid and I opened a beer and assessed the situation. His keen sense of
the dramatic had not failed him yet.

"He's in the same boat Reaux was," he said. "Why do these guys talk
to us? Why do they want to see us?"

"Because they're lonely and in a strange town. And they want to
share their desperation," I suggested.

Sid was impressed, he said, with the intelligence web of the big-time
recruiters. "Unlike the wire services, Reaux and Selmon never bought that
first Texas commitment. That's when people in town began feeling
Marcus wasn't so much the poor, confused black kid. They felt something
else was in the works."

"If Texas had brought in Earl Campbell the way Oklahoma did Billy
Sims," I said. ". . . If his last visit had been to Texas instead of Oklahoma . . ."

"Texas and Oklahoma fighting with swords," Sid said with a flourish,
"UCLA and Southern fighting with needles. This story has layer after
layer, like a pomegranate."

"No," I said. "Like an artichoke."

"Even the Appreciation Day, with all the black emphasis," he said,
"was *pure* Mississippi."

"So why should this be any different?" I said avuncularly.

At that moment the telephone rang. I picked it up. It was Tommy
Reaux.

"Where are you, Tommy?"

"In the Virginia Courts in Meridian."

"I thought you'd gone back to Texas."

"Not yet. What's goin' on?"

I described as succinctly as possible the Southern-Oklahoma confrontation.

"It's Oklahoma!" he said. "Look, even after I had my fallin' out with
Cella on the phone last Thursday, Marcus told me on the phone the next
day he was still goin' to Texas. It was a setup. Everything Uncle Curlee
said about the mean calls to Cella and then runnin' her off the road today
—it was set up by Oklahoma. That's why Lucious is so nervous tonight. It
wasn't Lucious, it was somebody else. An alum in the area, maybe. The
only thing Marcus is guilty of," he repeated, "is being seventeen years old.
Eighty-five percent of the blacks I talked to in the Quarter last night were
with me."

Marcus was going to Jackson tomorrow, Reaux predicted, to sign with Oklahoma. He would probably announce tomorrow and sign on Thursday.

"Is there a payoff in the making?" I asked.

"You said it, not me."

Sid got on the phone to talk.

"If all that's true," he said when he had hung up, "Lucious Selmon's a damned good actor."

The time had come to confer long-distance with Temple Drake. He was at home drinking whiskey and playing poker. He listened carefully as I described what was happening, interrupting occasionally with a terse, hoarse question. I finished.

"It's Oklahoma," he said emphatically.

If there was a payoff, what should I look for?

"Is there an airport in Philadelphia?" he asked.

"A small one."

"Can it handle Lear jets?"

"It can in good weather."

"What's the weather forecast for tomorrow down there?"

"Clear and cold."

"Phone the airport in the morning and see if any little jets are expected from Oklahoma. If so, get your tail out there. Then look for some guy in a cowboy hat gettin' off with a heavy satchel."

# 27

# *Where Is He?*

National Signing Day. No planes from Oklahoma.

People in the Quarters reported that Marcus was indeed in Jackson. His mother was at her school in Kemper.

I called Lucious Selmon in his room. He had checked with Wade Walker, his athletic director, in Norman late last night. The NCAA prohibited a prospect from officially signing outside the city limits of his hometown. "He *can* announce, though. I don't know what's goin' on in Jackson," he said wearily.

Pete and I went to the stadium. All was quiet with school not in session because of the teachers' meeting.

One must admit, with Marcus out of town on this day, the melodrama went with him. I was reminded of Yazoo the day after the Clyde Beatty circus departed. How much would the town miss all this when it was finally over, and especially when the young man left for college next summer?

I ran into Danny Gregory outside the gym. The principal had dark circles under his eyes and was extremely perplexed. He was awakened from a sound sleep at one in the morning by a call from Norman, Oklahoma. The caller was Scott Hill, the Oklahoma recruiting coordinator, saying he was afraid Marcus might be getting into trouble and that he should be careful. Hill said that if Marcus did not choose Oklahoma, for his own good he would not mind if he signed with Texas.

"He's visited four schools and committed to three," Gregory said. Neither he nor Joe Wood knew what was happening. He had heard that Marcus was on the Southern campus in Hattiesburg today. Marcus had told him only last week that he was not signing with Southern because it did not have what he was looking for. He was worried now, he said, about who might be advising Marcus. We arranged to have coffee that afternoon in the Downtown.

Lucious Selmon was in the lobby of the Downtown, gazing dejectedly out the window onto Byrd Avenue. "I don't have anything to do," he said. Marcus and his uncle, he suspected, were in Jackson "cutting the deal" with Southern. The man was not play-acting. Either that or he was the Lionel Barrymore of college football. He said he would remain in town until that night or tomorrow, and if he had failed by then to work out something with Marcus, "I'm gonna wash my hands of all this. I don't want to be involved in a situation like this any more."

Behind the counter Roy Tingle said the telephone rang all last night from Oklahoma. "I mean *all* night! I'd hate to see their phone bill."

*Wednesday Afternoon*

Still no planes from Oklahoma.

Coach Wood and Neil Hitchcock, his assistant, were waiting outside the school as if they, like Selmon, had nothing to do. "What's goin' on?" Joe asked, jangling his five pounds of keys.

At 1:30 A.M. he also had received a call from Scott Hill in Norman saying the same things he had told Danny Gregory—that if Marcus did not choose Oklahoma he should go to Texas or UCLA, "or some other big school for his own sake."

We talked about Reaux's departure from town. "And Marcus told me he really liked Texas," he said, shaking his head. "I don't even know where he is. It was all fine till five or six days ago. Then the uncle got in on it. Marcus's not talkin' to me. If he says he's gonna sign tomorrow, I couldn't believe him. He hasn't asked my advice on anything in a week."

There was talk, he said, that the Texas-Oklahoma showdown was being exercised as a ploy for a Southern signing at the last moment. He felt Texas had been used. He was in front of Marcus' house yesterday, Wood said, when Reaux came to say goodbye and when the uncle criticized Reaux for his telephone calls and for running Marcus' mother off the road. When the uncle told Reaux he might get hurt if he stayed around town, the Texas coach said he did not want any trouble and left.

Marcus had told him yesterday at 5 P.M. that his choice was Oklahoma or UCLA. He did not know that Marcus was officially seeing Carmody of Southern last night until later. He talked with Curlee yesterday. "Curlee said he was only protectin' Marcus. He sounded sincere. Then I found out about the meeting with Southern."

Joe was ruminative. "The ol' boy don't know *what* he wants."

We were standing about on the deserted school grounds in the crisp, invigorating afternoon. We watched Pete make a halfhearted move toward a squirrel.

Kenneth Cook, the black assistant coach, pulled his car into the driveway. When he saw us he let down his window.

"What's goin' on?" he asked.

"Notre Dame," Joe Wood said.

"*Notre Dame?*"

"Yeah. He and his momma flew up today to South Bend."

Cook considered this. "Aw . . ." he scoffed, "you're lyin'," and drove away with a rattle of gears.

"Let's go over to the hotel and see Lucious Selmon," Wood said.

Wood, Hitchcock, Pete, and I took the elevator to the third floor. Lucious had his curtains drawn and was once again watching television.

"What's happenin'?" Joe Wood asked.

"You got me."

As we took chairs, he stretched out on the bed, hands behind his head. "It's just become a joke. I'll stick around a couple more days. I've run out of visits. We've got one more we're savin' in case we sign him. The NCAA is watchin' this so close, I wouldn't want to get caught on some minor regulation."

Between the small-town Mississippi coaches and the celebrated Oklahoma recruiter the conversation became jocular.

Wood glanced around the room, pale in the afternoon light filtering through the curtains. "It looks like you've got the good life, Coach," Joe said. "Loungin' around lookin' at TV. 'The Flintstones.'"

"I'm impressed," Coach Hitchcock said.

"It makes me feel like a child again," Lucious said.

"Well, the ol' boy don't know *what* he wants," Wood repeated. "I wouldn't be surprised if he went out to Texas A&M and saw Jackie Sherrill this weekend."

"I'd rather the kid go to *any* big school—Texas, UCLA, or another school in Mississippi—over Southern," Selmon said. "The rumors goin' around. Everybody's got a rumor. This has been more drawn out than any kid I've ever been involved with." He sighed now as he had the night before. "A man has to get his priorities straight. I've got a wife and kids. No recruit is worth more priority than my family."

"How do you spend your day?" Wood asked.

"Waitin' on the telephone."

I later met Danny Gregory in the restaurant. "I'll bet a dressed hog he signs with Southern," a man at the domino game at the next table was saying.

I had known Gregory for several months and he had never equivocated with me. "He's as honest as the day's long," one local had put it.

He reconstructed some of the events of the previous week. Last Thursday, three days after he had withdrawn his commitment to Texas, Marcus came into his office and said he was ready to do something, that the recruiting process had become too difficult for him. He told Gregory that he and his mother had talked the night before—Wednesday—and still liked Texas. He was not sure he would make the visit to Oklahoma after all. "I want to go to Texas," he said to Gregory last Thursday. Jackie Sherrill of A&M was arriving that day to see him. When Marcus told Gregory he did not want to talk with Sherrill, Gregory said he would find him a place in the school where he could be alone. But at 2 P.M. he did come out and visit with Sherrill.

"Tommy Reaux's been perfectly honorable throughout all this," Gregory said. "He always informed me what he was doing. I think he's been a credit to Texas."

He added: "Our guidelines were working so well. Then it all started falling apart."

*Wednesday Night*

There was little activity at the Command Post. Sid, who was finishing his piece, "The Battle of 274 Davis Street," for the *Democrat*, had received a copy that day of Barry Horne's lengthy article in *The Dallas Morning News*. "He got it right," Sid said. It ran on page one. Under "A Philadelphia Story" there was a large color photograph of Marcus in front of the memorial to Schwerner, Goodman, and Chaney at the Mount Nebo Church.

Pete and I took the requisite cruise through the Quarters. Marcus was still out of town. The words on the marquee in front of the Busy Bee, out of date now, still proclaimed him to be a "Texas Long Horn." A raucous party was under way at Guys and Dolls.

Lucious Selmon remained in his room at the Downtown. His line had been busy for an hour.

On the television at the Post, a psychiatrist from Manhattan Island for Home Box Office was discussing the clitoral orgasm. On another channel was a report on the football signings in Mississippi. It had been a successful day for the University of Southern Mississippi. "Where is Marcus Dupree?" the reporter asked.

There was nothing to tell the telephone callers. Tom Turner phoned. "Right now Ole Miss is about to make its move," he said.

My son David called from Amherst, Massachusetts. "What's going on?" he asked.

He listened with interest as I told him at length.

"Is it still snowing down there?" he asked.

At midnight Tommy Reaux telephoned again. He had his shoes off in his apartment in Austin and was sipping some ten-year-old scotch. "What's the word?" he asked Sid.

He too listened. He had changed his mind. "The OU-UT thing was a bluff," he surmised. "He'll go with Southern now.

"The greatest problem facin' the Negro is the Negro. Your town has changed, but then it hasn't."

He had telephoned Marcus early that morning before he left for the Jackson airport and talked with him for fifteen minutes. "Can you believe he'd talk to me fifteen minutes if he thought I'd run his mother off the road? I said, 'Marcus, do you think I ran your mom off the road?' 'Well, that's what they say.' 'But do *you* believe it?' 'No.' I told him I thought he was a class act, and just be strong."

"How are your spirits?" Sid asked.

"I'm fine. You win some and lose some."

"Did you get your running back in Newton, Texas?"

"Not yet. He's gonna wait a few days to sign. He's a good kid, but he's got a bad case of Dupree."

# 28

# Between the Walls

*Thursday Morning, February 11*

Marcus was back in town, and at this moment in school. There had been no announcement for Southern in Jackson. Southern, however, was in town again. Keith Daniels, their offensive coordinator, would visit Marcus' mother at her school in the afternoon. A visit with the prospect was scheduled for Friday morning.

The morning papers reported Southern's recruiting successes. Jim Carmody said: "We feel Marcus is very interested in our school and we've been very low-keyed in the recruiting of him and remaining there all the time. We've not beaten down his door and constantly called him in any way. We just liked him to know we were around. We tried to impress on him the chance to play in a winning program, to get a quality education, and to be near home where his family and friends can see him play."

"Looks like Southern vs. Oklahoma," Joe Wood said in his office. "Who knows?" He and Marcus had been sitting in the coach's pickup truck before classes started. "Coach, I really like Oklahoma," he had said, "and I really like their Wishbone. But, gosh, that's a long way from home."

Pete was with the Philly dogs down in the hollow. I was whiling away the time around Wood's office, sitting in a chair in the weight room. A young black man in his late twenties walked in. "I want to be in a book," he said. He was Toab Gill, who helped Wood and the other coaches with odd assignments. "I'm on the staff," he said. "I help when the players get hurt. I go to the doctor with 'em." He was the grandson of Glover Gill, a respected handyman around town; when his house burned down in '77, the Jaycees rebuilt it. The grandson, Toab, told me he drove in the same car with Ronald Reagan when he visited in '80. "We talked about different things comin' up this year and all that. He wanted my advice." As for Marcus, "I'm sure he's gonna be one of the greatest of all time, but he's gonna get hisself in trouble if he don't sign today or tomorrow." That pleased me. I could now see myself waiting around Wood's office all spring.

The noon bell rang. Through the open doorway I saw Marcus

rushing by toward his car. I went to the door. "I'm signin' tomorrow," he turned and shouted. His hair was shorter. He had his jerry-curl.

I was talking with Joe Wood when a tall, preppy young man strolled in. With his blue dress shirt, tie, and khakis and his relaxed and amiable manner he reminded me startlingly of a somewhat younger George Plimpton.

Wood introduced me to Mike Glazier, an official representative of the NCAA. I had expected the NCAA man to be more rabbinical, or at the least to resemble a Secret Service agent or an FBI investigator.

He had just come in from Tallahassee, he said. He and Wood exchanged breezy solicitudes. "Say, Coach, I heard coming over on the radio that you think he's going to Southern Miss."

"Well, I never said that," Joe replied.

Glazier told me his background. He was from Kankakee, Illinois, originally. He had played football for Northeast Oklahoma A&M and later attended Indiana University and John Marshall Law School in Chicago. He was not allowed to discuss Marcus with me, he said apologetically. He was associated with the NCAA's "Big Brother" program, which involved the country's top twelve or fifteen prospects with the purpose of preventing recruiting violations before they occurred. As Marcus' "Big Brother," Glazier had spent time with him and his family, made him aware of the rules, and answered his questions. So he was, in effect, "watching out" for him.

Another NCAA man, Dave Didion, was arriving that night or early tomorrow, and Glazier himself planned to meet at length with Marcus and his mother later that afternoon. The federal marshals were riding into the badlands.

*Thursday Afternoon*

The boys having coffee in Stribling's were philosophically detached. This temper, however, did not discourage them from their usual garrulous speculations. Sid Salter and I had arrived at the point where we were beginning to hear rumors which we ourselves had started.

Lucious Selmon was in the offices of the *Democrat* conversing with Sid. "I'm layin' low," he said. It occurred to me again that both he and Tommy Reaux had arrived in town confident, proud, and aggressive, and each had grown increasingly pessimistic, dejected, and defeated. Where was the glamour of the calling?

He had telephoned Marcus' mother again, he said, and had gone through his entire presentation. "She was polite, but curt. When I finished what I had to say, she said 'All right.' I was left with a negative feeling. I want you and Sid to tell me anything you hear. I'm booked on a five-thirty flight out of Jackson tomorrow afternoon. I'm goin' home."

"Coach, you seem a little emotionally removed."

"I guess I am. I'll go on back to the hotel now and watch 'The Flint-stones.'"

At about 2:30 P.M. at the school, Molly Turner—Tom's wife and one of Marcus' teachers—had a talk with Marcus and Daran Jackson. Marcus was wearing a black-and-gold Southern Mississippi football jersey with Number 22 on it. "I gave him some pretty stiff advice," she said. "Then he told me he was definitely signing with Southern."

Billy Watkins of *The Meridian Star* and Lee "Scoop" Ragland of *The Jackson Daily News* checked into the Downtown and came to my room. "The recruitment of Dupree has been full of strange occurrences," Ragland had written in that afternoon's edition. The three of us discussed the various alternatives in the story. After all that had happened, I felt strongly now, out of the instincts of my newspaper past when I was their age, something would break in the next several hours. The two enterprising young reporters rushed out into the streets.

"It's between the two," Uncle Curlee Connor, wearing a Southern cap, said later in the afternoon. "Oklahoma offers him the publicity and a chance to win the Heisman. Southern Miss is on the rise, and he's the player they need to get into national prominence." His name, he admitted, had been involved in various talk. "I've heard all the rumors, but there's no amount of money in the world that could buy Marcus after the seventeen years Cella Ruth and I spent raising him."

A few minutes later, someone saw Marcus in the front yard of the house on Davis Street wearing his Southern jersey. "Would look good, wouldn't it?" he asked.

Marcus got in a car with Mike Glazier. They began riding around town.

*Thursday Night*

It was 6 P.M. Tom Goode had just called long-distance. He knew I was a "neutral," he said, but he had been unable to reach Marcus. When I saw him, would I please get him to telephone him collect? I told Goode that Marcus was with the NCAA.

I opened a can of chicken-and-liver Alpo and put it in Pete's bowl. Then I sat back, contemplating all the moments I had spent in this town, the things I had learned, the people I had come to know, the countless drives with Pete from Oxford to here, the incalculable pressures on a teenaged boy stalked like a quarry, with the hunters becoming quarry in their turn, the desperation of grown men for his services.

From the room above I heard a loud thumping on the floor. Pete turned from his cuisine and barked.

Momentarily there was an urgent knock on my door. I opened it to find my collaborator, Sid Salter, standing in the hallway. He entered the room and closed the door behind him.

"Guess what?" he asked. He looked as Ribbentrop must have in front of the Western diplomats after he had negotiated the Nazi-Soviet Pact.

"What?" I asked.

"He's signing with Oklahoma tomorrow."

"No!"

"Yes!"

"Are you sure?"

"Totally."

So it was over, the long months, the fighting for position, the rumors, the various lists, the telephone calls, the mind-changings, the "house visits" and "school visits" and "official visits," the "recruiting coordinators," the computer assessments, the denigrations, the announcements and withdrawals, the relentless jargon, the town gossip. The young man was going to the Oklahoma Sooners.

"Well, I'll be damned!" I said. "What happened?"

"Wait till I tell you," Sid said. "I just told Lucious Selmon—pledged him to secrecy. He can't even tell Barry Switzer. He's the happiest man in America now. He shook my hand five times and started jumping up and down on the floor. Did you hear him from upstairs? He wants to see you."

Mike Glazier of the NCAA and Marcus rode around town talking in Glazier's car all through the early afternoon. In the meantime, as a friend of the family, Sid had gone out to the house to talk with Marcus' mother and try to advise her. They were sitting in the front room. The grandmother, Mrs. Dupree, was wandering about the house listening in.

There were footsteps on the front porch. The door opened. In came Marcus, wearing the Southern Mississippi jersey, with Mike Glazier and Joe Wood.

Sid and Marcus' mother stopped talking.

Glazier asked Marcus: "Is there anyone here in this room not aware of this situation?"

Marcus' mother: "Better tell Sid."

Marcus: "I'm signin' with Oklahoma tomorrow."

There was cheerful handshaking all around. "We can't let this out till tomorrow," someone said. "This is secret."

Wood, Glazier, Marcus, and Marcus' mother concluded that Sid, as a friend of the family, should organize the press conference for tomorrow at 1 P.M. at the school. He would sign the official papers right after the announcement.

"Go ahead," Marcus' mother said to Sid. "I'll talk to you later."

"This is a secret till the press conference tomorrow," Joe Wood repeated.

Now, in my room, Sid was working for the Dupree family. He needed my telephone to contact the media in Jackson, New Orleans, and Meridian about the press conference.

Pete and I got the elevator to the third floor. I knocked on the door of Room 333. Lucious Selmon appeared.

"You know, don't you?" he at once said.

"I do."

As Pete and I went inside the now familiar room, he shook my hand once, then again. "Pete, how *about* it?"

He was swinging his arms all around. "Hey, what a super, super feelin'! Just like winnin' a big football game. When I found out a minute ago, I slapped my hands and jumped in the air. It's not a selfish feeling— I know Marcus will feel it at OU. And he'll give the fans there and people all over the country that same good emotion."

He walked around the room now with his unabashed grin. He shook my hand again. "Hey," he said, "you and Salter are good guys."

It had been some months since I had seen a fellow human so undisguisedly happy; his joy was encompassing. Life was hard enough, I knew, and to witness someone so overcome with honest elation made me feel better than I had in a very long time. Also, he had been so cautious and circumspect at first; his simple pleasure in this moment was reassuring.

Pete, too, caught the mood. After Lucious' sadness of the night before at the Command Post, Pete was standing in front of the exuberant Oklahoma coach now with twinkling eyes and a wagging tail.

"I was watching 'Happy Days' on the TV when I found out. I'll tell you how glad I was. I was so glad I got a *headache*."

We sat down for a moment in the chairs by the table where he had scrutinized me so carefully only two evenings before; he was thoughtful now.

"The first time I met him down at the school, I said 'Marcus, I think you're gonna like me.'

"I felt I could identify with him from the start, because he's very shy, soft-spoken, a small-town black kid like me. He has such a great personality about himself. We just talked, the two of us, and he let me know he has goals he wants to accomplish. I trust him very much, and I think he trusts me. It makes me feel I want to take part of his life in my hands and shape and mold it."

"You were depressed last night, and in the *Democrat* office this afternoon," I said.

"For the last two days I thought I'd lost him. On the plane back from Norman Sunday, before his Appreciation Day, I said, 'Marcus, I really like you.' I told him what I was about to say to him was in the Good Book: 'If you make one step toward Him, I'll make two steps toward you.' I said, 'If you make one step toward me, Marcus, I'll make two toward you.' "

Pete and I got up to leave. We would see him tomorrow at the signing, I said. We stood for a moment in the doorway.

"You'll take care of him out there, won't you?" I asked.

"Yes."

"How good will he be?"

He thought for a moment. "Not getting hurt—and with luck?"

"Yes."

"One of the best of all time."

Sid and I went to a dinner at Carolyn and Stan Dearman's. Stan, the editor of the *Democrat*, was the only other person in town who had been secretly apprised that Marcus would sign with Oklahoma the next day. It was a gracious gathering of "old-line" Philadelphia people. The wire services already had the story that Marcus would sign at 1 P.M. tomorrow at the school. The Dearmans' guests kept wondering whether his choice would be Southern or Oklahoma. "And where is UCLA?" A black maid of one of the guests had come to work that morning and asked: "Did you hear that Texas coach ran Marcus' mother off the road?" One of the guests, an elderly lady named Ellen Spendrup, Florence Mars's aunt, who had stood up during "The Troubles," told of touring Europe in 1940, where she saw men, women, and children being herded along the streets by German soldiers with guns. Another, Herbert Garrett of Herbert's Men's Wear, described helping liberate one of the death camps as an American soldier. This served to put a certain perspective on football recruitment.

Back at the Downtown at 10:30 P.M., the Southern Mississippi assistant coach, Keith Daniels, had just checked in. Roy Tingle had put him in Room 332, right next to Lucious Selmon.

"You've got plenty of empty rooms," I said to Roy. "Why did you put the Southern coach next door to the Oklahoma coach?"

"Well, there's been so much drama around here for such a long time," Roy said. "It's centered on this hotel. I hear it's finally gonna end tomorrow. We're proud of this town and Marcus, but we're all gettin' a little jumpy. I put the Southern coach next to the Oklahoma coach because I want 'em to talk to each other between the walls."

Keith Daniels, who had been hired by Jim Carmody only the week before, was lying in his bed in a white T-shirt and blue boxer shorts. He was a thin, balding man in his middle thirties with knobby knees. He was smoking Merit cigarettes from a near-empty package. All the lights were off in his room except for the silent glare of the television. The telephone rang frequently between the walls from Lucious Selmon's room next door. "That could be bad news," Daniels said.

"Coach Carmody and I visited with Marcus and his mother and left with the impression we were in good shape," he said. "That was Tuesday night. I felt we were in good shape to sign the kid when we left, he sure led us to believe it, but something happened and they told me to get back up here tonight. I talked with Marcus' mother on the phone tonight and tried to go to their house, but she said it was too late. So I'm just here if they need me."

The telephone rang from next door again. Coach Daniels raised his eyes widely to the ceiling.

Might Marcus sign with Southern?

"I sure hope so. I sure hope so."

If not, where would he go?

"Looks like Oklahoma to me," the Southern coach said. "Selmon's the only one still in town."

On the eve of the signing, there were reporters at work in the Downtown, especially Scoop Ragland of the *Daily News*. Ragland was a diligent young man of considerable flourish. He was an Oxford boy, and his uncle-in-law, Motee Daniel, was a friend of mine, a formidable country entrepreneur who had been Faulkner's bootlegger. Motee, Mayor Leslie, and I had once been the judges in a Halloween costume contest at an ambiguous local bar; when we chose Sex Symbol over Mrs. Frankenstein, the patrons threw beer bottles at us.

We were in Ragland's room just down from Selmon's and Daniels'. He was composing a story on his portable word processor,* which was plugged into an outlet in the wall.

"I don't know what to say!" he complained. "I don't know what to say! Help me. I've been workin' for an hour and haven't really said anything yet." Given my long-ago newspaper background, I felt guilty in not being able to share what I knew with a man named "Scoop."

"Give me some words," he said. I pulled up a chair next to him and peered at the characters on the screen. My only contribution was to get

---

* The technical word for Scoop Ragland's machine was "Tele-Ram," which hooked into the central newsroom through telephone lines. The "Tele-Ram" would soon become obsolescent as the B-17, to be replaced by the "Porta-bubbles," which was lighter and more sensitive. Never mind what happened to the typewriter.

him to push the input button and send my salutations to his boss in Jackson, the sports editor Orley Hood.

Roy Tingle came up from the lobby. He had just gotten off work for a while. He carried a percolator of coffee. "I thought you hard-workin' boys might need this," he said. He went over to the wall and mindlessly unplugged the cord to Ragland's machine, substituting the plug to the percolator.

"Hot-damned!" Scoop Ragland shouted.

"I'll just go get some cups," Roy said, and departed.

"He just erased my story!" Ragland said plaintively. "The whole thing. I got to start all over."

The loyal Roy Tingle returned and poured the coffee. He gestured to Ragland hunched over his screen. "I try to think like the young people," he said, "because they're the leaders of tomorrow. Ain't that right, Pete? Pete's your best buddy, ain't he?"

"Give me a quote, Roy," Ragland said.

Roy told the reporter why he had put the Southern coach next to the Oklahoma coach—so they could talk to each other between the walls.

"Hey, I can use that!"

"The Southern coach's only got eight or ten calls since he checked in," Roy said. "But he's just got started. I started work at 5 P.M. and just got off. I bet you a dollar to a doughnut that Oklahoma coach has had fifty calls between now and then. Morgan Hardy just said to me, 'He don't get no sleep.'" He shook his gnarled old head in disbelief, as if he needed a different Darwinian taxonomy to describe these visitors. "When the Southern coach checked in, I told him, 'You ain't got a prayer.'"

He returned to the subject of Lucious Selmon's telephone calls in Room 333. "They was just givin' me fits. That switchboard's been lit up like a Christmas tree. Mr. Scott Hill, one of the Oklahoma coaches, phoned for about the umpteenth time from Oklahoma a little while ago. I told him Lucious Selmon's line was busy. So while he waited he and I struck up a little talk."

"Where do you want him to go to school?" Hill asked Roy.

"I want him to stay right here in ol' Mississippi," Roy replied.

"Well, why?"

"I think we got just as good schools as y'all got," Roy said.

"You sure are taking up for Mississippi, aren't you?"

"Just like you are for Oklahoma."

"Yeah, but we've got more prestige," Hill said. "We're going to have a national championship."

"If we had the money you got," Roy Tingle said, "we would too."

# 29

# *The End of the Affair*

---

"Pete, we've been in this town too long. Is this an important day for us?" I dressed and went down to breakfast, to memories of the night's vivid dreams of—of all things—my first glimpse of Paris on an April morning of many years ago, the grand boulevards, the girls along the Champs Élysées, the first buds in the trees in the Tuileries.

I was ready for an end to the little tale, which seemed to me now to have drawn itself out too much. Lucious Selmon of Oklahoma must have felt as dislocated as I. He had been here for many days, except for a trip in a private jet to Oklahoma and back again, away from his family in a raw provincial town without restaurants, bars, or the minimal appurtenances. I saw him in the lobby. "I'm *still* not convinced," he said. "I just talked to him on the phone and he didn't seem happy."

"Let's get it over," I said.

"Let's do," he replied.

It was a gray, rainy morning, with a wind slipping in from the east. For the hundredth time, it seemed, I walked Pete around the Square. The people knew him to say hello, to reach down and rub his shiny black coat. I took him to the empty stadium for his leisurely constitutional. Then I brought him back to the room in the hotel and promised him we would go home to Oxford as soon as Marcus signed.

At the noon recess, an hour before the press conference, many high school adolescents had gathered around the gym. On the basketball court they were playing pickup games with their ear-rending black and Caucasian screams. There was solace in realizing they would someday be old, although they themselves did not know it.

Mike Glazier, Marcus' "Big Brother," was sitting in the bleachers by the basketball court. He introduced me to Dave Didion, his fellow NCAA investigator. Didion was as young as Glazier, and as innocently groomed. They should have had beards, graying hair, bowler hats, flecks of Yankee dandruff.

I sat down next to them. I learned from Didion that he was a native of Sandusky, Ohio, and had attended Ohio State. The two of them played in an amateur basketball league in Johnson County, Kansas.

"We got beat in our last game by the Mark Twain Bank in overtime," Glazier said.

"Mark Twain will get you every time," I said. "Even the NCAA."

Sid Salter, recently arrived in the gymnasium, overheard this. "We're putting your basketball team on probation," he said.

I posed a question to Glazier: "What did you tell Marcus when you drove around with him and talked yesterday afternoon?"

"I'm sorry," he replied. "I can't talk about that."

"Did you advise him not to sign with Southern Mississippi because they might be going on probation, and that this would jeopardize his future?"

"I'm sorry," he repeated. "I can't discuss it."

Sid wore a coat and tie and was uncharacteristically distracted. The Duprees had put him in charge of the whole press conference; he had summoned the reporters and television people. "If he changes his mind now," Sid said, "I'll have to leave Mississippi; maybe go in exile in Arkansas." We walked toward a corner of the gym. He confided to me that he had granted a scoop to a close friend, a young woman named Leah Cole, to put the story of Marcus' signing with Oklahoma on the local radio station where she worked ten minutes before the formal announcement, and also to telephone the wire services then.

"He *is* signing with Oklahoma, isn't he?" I asked.

"He'd better," Sid said. "I'm much too young to die."

It was 12:30 P.M. The press conference was scheduled for 1 P.M. in a hallway next to the gym. Joe Wood looked uncommonly sophisticated in a brown leather jacket. There were television crews from Oklahoma, Meridian, and Jackson, but none from Texas, and a multitude of newspaper people, including the unfaltering Billy Watkins and Scoop Ragland. Cars were streaming into the parking lot outside.

Horace Johnson, representing UCLA, was waiting in the hallway. "A big day!" he said to me. Perfectly tailored, cool, and impeccable, he must have been the best-dressed man in Neshoba on this day. Keith Daniels looked rather tousled and sleepy, no match for the sartorial elegance of UCLA. Lucious Selmon's telephone calls must have kept him up. Contrasted with the affluent nonchalance of this mysterious black man representing the L.A. Golden Bruins, Daniels unexpectedly drew from me a Mississippi tenderness and solicitude. Daniels had tried to visit with Marcus earlier that morning, to no avail. The prospect was apparently through talking. Selmon had isolated himself on the steps just outside the door to the gym. He did not wish to jeopardize another "official visit." He was holding a small briefcase.

A table with a long bank of microphones had been set up in the hall-way, in front of a large trophy case and a sign which said: PHILADELPHIA TORNADOES. The klieg lights were already on. Stan Dearman of the *Democrat* milled about with the others. His neck was draped in cameras. "This is some kind of relief," he said. "Plez" Tinsley, the vice-mayor of Philadelphia, was there, as was Bobby Posey of Southern and "Good Time Charlie" Henson, a black disc jockey and former alderman. Many local whites had congregated, including two or three former Klansmen. Several of Marcus' teammates were standing on the edges of the crowd— Justy Johnson, Cecil Price, Jr., Daran Jackson, and the others. A group of pretty high school co-eds came in, many of them wearing their beaux' foot-ball-letter jackets. I noticed some of the black and white cheerleaders in mufti. A black television cameraman was wearing a Kappa Alpha Theta cap. Glazier and Didion stood in the doorway, as British courtiers might have during the signing of the Treaty of Ghent.

At 12:55 P.M. Sid motioned me aside again. "The radio station put the news on the air and told the wire service," he said. "The station has al-ready got twenty calls from all over the country."

Amid this air of expectancy, I was standing behind the crowd near a small office off the hallway. The door to the office was open and a tele-phone inside kept ringing. I went into the office and picked up the phone. The line was apparently linked with Danny Gregory's extension in the main school building, for I could hear Principal Gregory's familiar voice on the other end. In quick succession I eavesdropped on calls from re-porters in Oklahoma City, New York, Houston, and Los Angeles. Gregory told each caller an announcement was about to be made. My mood was mischievous. As Gregory hesitated in his conversation with the Los An-geles man, I said on the extension: "*He has just signed with Swarth-more.*"

Then, from the hallway, I saw Marcus and his mother walking slowly across the basketball court in our direction. "Here they come!" someone shouted. Marcus was wearing the jacket with "Dupree" on it. He looked younger without the Afro and sporting the new "jerry-curl."

Something strange happened. Halfway across the basketball court he and his mother stopped short and whispered to one another. Then they retraced their steps back toward Joe Wood's office. What was this?

"His mother said she wanted to talk to him a few more minutes," Wood told me. A student came up to Wood and summoned him to this conference. "They want me," he said, and swiftly departed. In this unexpected lull on the basketball court, Uncle Curlee and several of the visitors shot baskets.

Sid confronted me again, a study in apoplexy. "It's all going down the drain," he said, as Selmon had three nights before. "Oh, my God! They're changing their minds. My name is mud."

Marcus, his mother, Joe Wood, and the NCAA men were now closeted in Wood's office. Their last-minute retreat had not gone unnoticed by Keith Daniels of Southern Mississippi. "The longer they talk," he said, "the more chance I've got."

Selmon was standing outside the main door, peering inside with an expression of stricken apprehension. "What's happenin'?" he asked me. "What's goin' on?" The press conference was already late.

"By God, it's *Southern!*" a man shouted, and among the crowd there was a flurry of applause. "*Southern!*" someone else exclaimed.

At last Marcus, his mother, and Joe Wood were walking across the basketball court again. When they finally entered the hall and sat down at the table under the glaring lights there was loud clapping. The TV cameras were grinding away, and people stood on tiptoe to get a better look. A silence fell as Marcus leaned into a microphone.

There was a span of eternity to me from that midnight of seventeen years ago on Rock Cut Road to this hallway of Philly High on this day when he said: "Next year you'll see me at the University of Oklahoma."

The applause echoed down the corridor. Several people dashed out the door.


The reporters asked their questions. "Why did you choose Oklahoma?"

"They have a winnin' tradition. They'll be on TV a lot. They'll be a national contender. I can win the Heisman. I enjoyed the trip. I believe I can fit in there."

"When did you make up your mind?"

"Last night."

"Why not Southern Mississippi?"

"I felt like I had to go to a better program."

There were other questions. Then Marcus' mother, her eyeglasses reflecting the hard artificial light, her voice husky and emotional, said, "I'd just like to say to the people of Mississippi and especially to the people of Philadelphia that we appreciate very much the support they've shown. It was a difficult decision for Marcus. Very difficult."

"Let's make it official," Joe Wood said. Someone brought in the papers from Lucious Selmon outside, and Marcus and his mother began signing them one by one.

When they had finished, the surging crowd—old Klansmen and young teammates, wizened reporters and nubile cheerleaders—seemed flooded with relief, engaging themselves in a spontaneity seldom seen since the young survivors danced in the Berlin bunker right after Hitler shot himself in the mouth. Selmon, free now to come inside, shook Marcus' hand and embraced his mother. A television cameraman chanted "*Boomer Sooner!*" A pretty girl shouted "*Go Tornadoes!*"

The reporters moved about for separate interviews. "I felt I might want to stay in-state," Marcus said to one of them. "All the people gave me support in-state and I appreciated that. But I just felt like I had to go to a better program to achieve the goals I want to achieve."

To another inquisitor, he said he had ruled out the Texas Longhorns "because of some incidents that came up. I probably would've gone to Texas if they'd just said 'whenever you make up your mind, just call us up.' But they kept pressuring me. They really upset a lot of people here in Philly. And there were phone calls, too. I don't know if they were from Texas alums or what, but we were gettin' bad calls. They said stuff like, 'You'd better sign with Texas or else.' That really turned me off."

Marcus' mother: "The stories about Texas, sayin' that Marcus said yes and that I said no, simply weren't true. I just felt he needed more time. He needed to take some more visits. I never once said I didn't want him to go to Texas."

Why not Southern Mississippi, another wanted to know. Did the possibility that Southern, under the preliminary investigation by the NCAA, might be placed on severe probation for past recruiting violations have a part in his decision?

"It had a lot to do with it," Marcus replied. "I want to play on television." He said he asked the Southern coaches about the possibility of probation.

"They told me they won't be," he said. "But ask this guy right here." He pointed to the nearby Mike Glazier, who had driven him around town and talked with him at length the day before.

Keith Daniels was gracious in adversity. The scholarship papers in his pocket remained unsigned. "Marcus made the decision he felt was right," he said, "and I know it'll turn out well for him. As for us, the world keeps spinning. We'll keep winning at Southern Mississippi."

The throngs were dispersing now, into the gray February afternoon. I congratulated Marcus and embraced his mother. Lucious Selmon was standing alone. He had to leave to catch a plane to Oklahoma.

"*Whew!*" he said. "Come out and see us."

"Don't forget that other running back in Newton, Texas," I said. We looked at each other and laughed.

"A close damned call," Sid Salter said.

I stopped at the florist's to send Valentine flowers to Marcus' mother. Then I went to the Downtown to fetch Pete. We drove the road home by memory.

# 30

# Soon the Town
# Would Watch Him Go

Soon the people of the town would watch him go, their pride and hope clouded with a subtle disquiet. Ever since his childhood he had touched on every aspect of the community, and at age seventeen he was already its most famous son. But how good was he really? Many boys, black and white, had left Mississippi with grand expectations and were never heard from again. And what might his failure mean to a town which itself had once failed so disastrously?

His choice of colleges was greeted at first with the expected elation and bitterness. "As far as recruiting goes," Scott Hill, the Oklahoma recruiting coordinator who had engaged in the switchboard conversation with Roy Tingle was swift to say, "he was the best football player in the country. This shows the best football players in America are recruited by the University of Oklahoma. Potentially he's a great player, a superb player. The great thing about Marcus Dupree is that he's an intelligent kid, he's got all the tools, and his best playing days are ahead of him."

Oklahoma's numerous detractors, in the days after the signing, were not hesitant to point out that the team had just suffered a 7–4–1 season, the first time it had lost more than two games since the installation of the Wishbone offense in 1970. Furthermore, there were severe problems for '82, which would be Marcus' freshman season. The Sooners were weak at quarterback and would not return a single starter in the offensive line. Ironically, they would have the most splendid array of running backs in many years. Foremost was the gifted senior Stanley Wilson, an all-American candidate whom *The Sporting News* was calling "the best *pure* running back" in the nation. There were Fred Sims, Weldon Ledbetter, Steve Sewell, Chet Winters, and others, as well as a new recruit from Tulsa named Spencer Tillman, ranked only slightly below Marcus in the country's first ten running prospects. Small-town aspirations might not last very long in the midst of this talent.

There was the lingering ambivalence, too, about the young man's "mental toughness" and durability. He would be moving from a small Mississippi school to the major leagues of collegiate competition. "He's not gonna make it," one white man in town told me that spring without any twinge of doubt. "He'll be too homesick. He'll get hit like he's never been hit before. Wait and see. He'll come home." Would his life follow the downward path of Christian Darling in *The Eighty-Yard Run?*

"The expectations are too high," Temple Drake reminded me. "He's up for grabs. It mainly depends on how much he wants it way down in the gut." Temple Drake likewise reported from the intelligence network what I myself had divined, that the prospect had been about to sign with Southern Mississippi when the NCAA representative warned him that Southern was facing probation. "He won't really appreciate that till he's forty," Temple Drake said. There was a brief spell of uncharitableness at Southern, State, and Ole Miss, where some people expressed bafflement about precisely why he was taking his skills to the far steppelands of Oklahoma. An assistant coach at Ole Miss grinned sarcastically and said: "He must have grown up all his life wanting to run for the Sooners."

The bitterness at Texas in the days after the signing was no surprise. "I've been dying to call Cella and just ask her flat out what happened," Tommy Reaux said on the telephone from Austin. "I think we ended up getting hurt for trying to be honest and helpful. I've never been accused of anything shoddy before this deal. Never before was I ever accused of lying, of smearing other folks. Hell, it was in every paper in Texas that I tried to run her off the road. My response was that Oklahoma did a better job recruiting the kid, period. And later I just quit talking. The last call I got on the subject was late at night. A reporter asked, 'What can you tell me about Marcus?' I said: 'Marcus who?'"

Fred Akers was similarly undelighted. "Akers talks about an uncle who suddenly emerged and became involved in the recruiting process after Marcus announced he was going to Texas," *The Dallas Times-Herald* wrote in a postscript. "Akers believes the uncle had something to do with Dupree's changing to Oklahoma." The Texas coach had assumed he would choose a place that used the "I" formation. "That's why I figured either we'd get him or he'd go to Southern Mississippi. The last place I figured he'd go was a school that runs the Wishbone."

Paul Borden, the incisive *Clarion-Ledger* sports editor, ran into Akers at an NCAA meeting in Kansas City a week or so after the signing and found him critical of the "carnival atmosphere" surrounding the recruitment of the Marcus Duprees. "I don't think it's hard for the coach," he said, "but it's hard for the player." As for Marcus himself, "He's a fine football player, an outstanding football player. I wish I could say he was coming to the University of Texas, but I cannot. That's a personal choice each youngster must have to make. I don't ever want to coach someone who doesn't want to be at our school. If I have to twist his arm to get him to come here, that's not what I want."

Borden blamed the press and the recruiters for much of the brouhaha and concluded with a dampening assessment:

So much was made over Dupree that it was little wonder he became somewhat of a national celebrity, in Akers' words. As good a prospect as he is, to put him in a class with Herschel Walker is a disservice to Dupree. In two college seasons, Walker has proved his worth at Georgia, where he turned an average club into a two-time Southeastern Conference champion. Dupree has yet to play a down in college.

Had Dupree been allowed to function as a normal recruit, he would not have created the stir with his premature announcement concerning Texas, and he probably would have signed the first day permitted by the rules, a Wednesday. By waiting two days he did not have to share publicity with the other signees that day.

He may have been signed with Texas. But I don't think Akers will lose any sleep over it.

It remained for Billy Watkins of *The Meridian Star*, who had followed the young recruit more closely than any of the newspaper reporters, to remind Mississippians of his human qualities. I would concur in his words:

For Marcus' sake, I'm glad the burden is off his shoulders. And glad he handled the situation as smoothly as he did.

The only goof-up during the entire ordeal was when he committed to Texas, then uncommitted. He told me later, "I think I was just trying to get this thing over with. I'm tired of all the attention."

I've gotten to know Marcus pretty well over the last eight months, and there are a few things I think you ought to know about him:

He loves little kids, and he's good with little kids. He's not too busy for them, not too big-shot for them. How many 17-year-olds can you say that about?

He's never been short, never been too busy, never been anything but class in my dealings with him during a trying time for him in recent weeks. How many athletes can sports writers say that about?

He speaks from his heart. I was going over the notes I've kept on Marcus for the past eight months. Everything he's told me, every quote I've taken from him, was right on the money. Never did he say one thing, then pull another, except for the Texas mistake. If a team was in it, he said so. If a team was out, he said so. If a team called on a certain night, he said so. How many people can you say that about?

In time, of course, many of the ill feelings would dissipate, to be replaced by the emotion of human curiosity: How good was he?

Three weeks after the signing, on a balmy afternoon in March, Pete and I went down there for one last time. Spring comes early in Mississippi; the familiar hills and fields were alive with wildflowers, and there was a tranquil softness in the air. It occurred to me that I had absorbed this landscape of my journeyings through the four seasons.

Roy Tingle was in the Downtown as always, and out the windows of the room was a magnificent riotous sunset, the everlasting echo of the train horns, and the sounds of dogs barking far away. The snow and ice of January seemed distant now, and the town was dreamlike in the serene orange glow. I cared for this place which had suffered and come up from adversity. I recalled the words I had recently read by Theodore H. White, of the questions modern Americans were asking of themselves "in their search to find again an old civility of life, and communities in which that civility can reign." I prayed that the hard-earned civility of the town might grow and deepen and endure.

The Command Post was cleaner and more orderly now because of Sid Salter's fiancée ("Ole Miss girls have to take care of Mississippi State men," she said) and the telephone was not ringing there as much as before. Tommy Reaux and Lucious Selmon were hundreds of miles away, doing whatever football coaches do when the recruiting season ends. "People are glad it's all over," Sid said. "I really think they'd grown tired of it." The State, Southern, and Ole Miss people were being reasonably polite to one another again, and even Tom Turner had at last acknowledged that Marcus was not going to be a Rebel after all. There were no more celebrities at the school, and Joe Wood was mapping new plays for a black running back named Nathan Horne. Down at the House of Barbeque the one-eyed waitress finally mustered the nerve to tell me she had once known a Choctaw Indian named Willie Morris. In the Quarters, Lillie Jones was feeding her chickens and taking the wash off the line. The marquee in front of the Busy Bee said: BOOMER SOONER! and there had been one shooting and two stabbings at Guys and Dolls since my last visit. Sid told me of his conversation the day before with the old white garbage collector. "Just because this little colored boy who plays football is gettin' all this publicity," the old man had said while emptying a garbage can, "don't mean things have changed." Although an outsider from, let us say, Westchester County, might find this hard to fathom, Sid thought the fellow did not say this maliciously. In fact he had smiled when he said it, as if he felt it was expected of him, and as if all things in life would sooner or later pass away.

I had come down really to see three people, three of the main actors in the drama.

Danny Gregory was more relaxed than I had ever seen him. He leaned back in an easy chair in the den of his house, while outside on the front lawn his little boy was wearing a football jersey with the numerals 22 and pulling a red wagon.

He remembered the day Marcus signed with Oklahoma. The school had three incoming telephone lines. In less than half an hour, one hundred calls came in from all over the nation. "Then, all of a sudden, it stopped. I haven't had a single call since that day concerning Marcus."

Everything went as smoothly as he had hoped until the last five or six days before the signing, he said. And there were some nasty letters addressed to Marcus at the school afterward. Quite a few came from Texas alumni. "You're not a man of your word." Southern Mississippi: "You should have stayed in the state. Out there you'll just be somebody's boy." He threw the bad ones away. By Gregory's count he was recruited by more than one hundred schools, but he doubted if there were ever more than twelve seriously in the running.

What had he learned from all this? He responded without pause.

"If this had happened while I was still a football coach," he said, "I'd have been amazed by the distortions, the half-truths, the rumors. But as a principal, I suppose I've had more experience with things. In all honesty, it wasn't as difficult as I'd expected. If anybody was more"—he hesitated for the word—"*persistent* than I had thought, it was the reporters and TV people. The college recruiters were much more respectful of us than the reporters. Both Tom Goode of Ole Miss and Emory Bellard of State, for instance, were above board from the start. Whether all the rumors were right, I just don't know. When you have a TV crew drive all night from Norman, Oklahoma, to get to a seventeen-year-old's press conference, it makes you wonder about priorities. Marcus is more loose now than he's been in months. He's made his decision and he seems comfortable with it. He's enjoying being a senior now."

Gregory said he had never told him where he thought he should go, but he felt that if he stayed in Mississippi he should have gone to State. Out of the state he favored Texas. "But something happened. What, I guess we'll never know."

He spoke of the recruiting process. "It puts far too much pressure on the youngster. There must be a better way of doing it. The six visits—three at school, three at home—are atrocious. The NCAA needs to do a great deal of simplification. They should take their manual of rules and turn them into one eight-by-eleven-inch sheet so everybody can understand them. The whole thing is hard on everybody. You saw the emotions of two guys, Reaux and Selmon. They're football coaches. Coaching and recruiting are two different functions. Their emotions went from one gamut to another. Staying in a Downtown Hotel doin' nothing for days would drive *me* crazy."

He turned now to Marcus. What would he predict?

"There won't be an in-between with him. He'll either go out to Oklahoma and achieve instant stardom real quick, or he won't stay at all. He can't go out there and be an ordinary freshman ballplayer. He has the physical abilities to achieve great stardom. But what if he pulls a hamstring early on, and sits there in the training room with the team on the road? He wouldn't stay. With all his publicity, they expect him to go right in and be a Herschel Walker. He has close family ties. For the first time in his life he's going to be far away from his family and friends. It's going to be difficult for him."

And his advice? He got up from the chair and moved around the room. "You've made a hard decision and there are going to be hard times. Keep the strong religious faith you've had. Approach the challenge one hundred percent. If you make it, great. I'd remind him of the constant media pressure. I'd tell him to show the same attitude and character he's always had."

As I was leaving, he paused amiably at the door. He said: "I'm just glad the number one recruit in the nation next year won't be from Philadelphia, Mississippi."

One had grown accustomed to action around Joe Wood's office. He was reclining in the chair enjoying his dip of snuff. Several pretty girls and athletes in letter jackets were dallying about the doorway. "Tell 'em up North that Philadelphia's famous for its beautiful women and its ballplayers," he said.

He closed the door so we could talk. There were frequent intrusions from boys coming in to get their new baseball uniforms out of a closet. Two boys burst in to tell him a friend had just hurt himself in the gym. "I think he'd done broke his collarbone on the water pipe!" one of them said. "Bring him in here," Wood said. "Take off your shirt," he told the victim. "Naw, it ain't a break, it's just a bad bruise." "Well, I'm gonna suit out tomorrow no matter what," the boy said petulantly.

Shortly after this there was a knock on the door, and a pair of eyeglasses peered in. It was the recently acquired running back for the Oklahoma Sooners.

"Come on in here, Marcus," Wood said. "Get your baseball suit."

He went to the closet and put on a shirt with the number 22.

"Justy Johnson gets number 22," I said.

"What? Oh no he don't!"

"Don't he look pretty?" Wood said. "These uniforms cost me sixty dollars apiece. They may not win, but they're gonna look good."

Wood pointed to Marcus' brand-new red and white sneakers with "OU" on them. "How about that? Get them from Tommy Reaux, son?"

Marcus chuckled, scowled, chuckled again, then left to go outside.

"How many times do you think we've talked, Coach?"

"Many, many times, under all conditions." He spit gingerly into the wastebasket.

He told me he had only gotten one telephone call about Marcus since the signing—from a newspaper. "To tell you the truth, all this quiet is *nice*. I got so far behind, I ain't caught up yet. All I was doin' was answerin' the telephone. I met a lot of people and made some friends out of this thing, though. I got to know the Texas and Oklahoma coaches better than any of the others because they were so much around at the end. Good folks! Tommy Reaux's called a couple of times just to shoot the breeze. So has Didion of the NCAA. He says he'll be comin' back to see us, but I doubt it. I swear I don't know what happened with Texas. I think Marcus got on the outs with Coach Reaux for some reason or another. That's all I've been able to get out of all that."

What had *he* learned? "That people will do crazy things for a football player," he said. "I knew college football was a big-time sport, but not *that* big. Them guys are serious. I *never* realized as many colleges would get after him as hot and heavy as they did."

"Will he make it?"

He contemplated this. There was another knock on the door. He opened it slightly and said, "Go away," then he sat down again. "I really believe he will, I honestly do—for one reason. He's got the speed that it takes, and the acceleration. The size and strength too. And he *wants* to make it. I truly believe he'll make it big. If he doesn't I'll be tremendously surprised. People say he'll be up against faster and bigger guys, that he didn't have the competition here. But one thing you got to remember— he'll be playin' *with* faster and bigger boys. We didn't have an offensive line last year, you know that. If he can get past the line of scrimmage with his speed, he's gonna break a lot of long runs. He's gonna make it big. Tell 'em up North I told you.

"Also, he can play with pain. He played most of the eleventh grade with a hip-pointer. He's had a lot of sore hamstrings. He hurt his shoulder so bad in the Choctaw Bowl that he missed almost an entire quarter. It was an awful bruise. He came back and scored four touchdowns in the second half and threw another one for eighty yards. In the Louisville game right out here I thought he'd broken his arm or hand. We sent him to the hospital in the ambulance. Remember what he did in the second half?

"Of course he's gonna have to get *adjusted*. Sure it's a different brand of football. He's got to make the adjustment from high school to college. He's got the tools. He'll do it."

I repeated what I had asked Principal Gregory. What would his parting advice be?

"I'd tell him to do more listenin' than talkin'," he said, "to mingle in and get to know the other players. He don't need to go in and get the others mad at him. He wouldn't do that anyhow. He's not the boastful kind. The coaches out there won't hear him say three words in the first month. Remember what I told you? I coached him for a month before he even said a word. All he did was nod his head."

The coach of the Philly Tornadoes stood up, then sat down again. He was thinking.

"We're gonna miss the ol' boy," he finally said. "He wouldn't want to be called *boy*, but you know what I mean. Some people are good human beings and not good athletes. Some are good athletes and not good human beings. Marcus is both. I know him better than almost anybody. You get to know somebody coachin' him three years. I really and truly hope he does good. I hope he don't get hurt. That's the only thing that could stop him. I think the world of ol' Marcus. He's a good ol' boy."

The object of this ultimate Mississippi compliment was at that moment jostling with Neil Hitchcock, the big white assistant coach, in the sunshine outside the gym. He still wore the new baseball shirt. He gave Hitchcock a friendly bear hug, then a shove. "I told him to sign a baseball contract two years ago," Hitchcock said to me. "He'd have a hundred thousand now and could leave baseball and play college football. He didn't take my advice. Of course, he probably got a hundred thousand from Oklahoma *anyway*. Just look at them Oklahoma sneakers he's got on!" To dramatize the thought, he knocked him back two or three feet with another shove.

Marcus and I drifted over to the bleachers on the visitors' side of the football stadium and sat down. Pete was rolling around on his back in the end zone, and when he sighted us he indolently walked our way. Some of the high school kids were tossing a ball near the fifty-yard line. The daffodils were out, and the grass was turning green again on the football turf. The shrubs and bushes down by the hollow were just beginning to flower. It was a soft afternoon of sunshine and breezes.

He and I had a long and meandering conversation, mellow almost as the day's promise of spring. He was nothing if not a relaxed seventeen-year-old three months from high school graduation. From time to time one of the white or black boys on the field would shout a teenage witticism at him. He chuckled frequently and looked at me intently when I asked a question. As usual he was not one for elaborate talking. I realized how fond I had grown of him.

He gazed across the football field toward the familiar concrete grandstand steeply inclined on the hill. "We ain't lost much here," he said. They had lost only twice here since Coach Wood came in '79, and not once to the Goats of Neshoba Central. "I've had some fun here."

I reminded him that he had once told me, a number of weeks before, that he wished he could be himself and not be noticed so much, that every time he went into a store people would pay too much attention to him. "Well, it feels a lot better now," he said. "It's all back to normal. It's the same ol' town of Philadelphia again. I'm back to my old self, I guess. The phone's not ringin'. The mailbox's kinda empty." Lucious Selmon and Scott Hill telephoned from Oklahoma once a week, but he did not really need his answering service any more.

"I think if I wasn't an athlete," he said, "I'd be goin' to work in a factory or somethin'."

Once he left his hometown, I asked, did he think he would find it difficult to return? "It might be hard to come back," he said, "but if I do the things I think I'm capable of doin', the people of Philadelphia will always accept me—because I'm tryin' to do something with myself. It's my home. It's a pretty good ol' town. When I was at Oklahoma, they asked me, 'Are you from Mississippi?' I said yes. They said, 'You don't *talk* like you're from Mississippi. You don't talk like Herschel in that thick Southern accent.'"

"You sound enough like Mississippi to me," I said.

"I guess so."

We talked about the Appreciation Day in his honor, and the irony of "The Troubles." Did he ever view himself as a symbol?

"I felt great about the whole thing. It really made me feel good. I never did think about what happened back then in the 1960s. I never thought about bein' a symbol till everybody started talkin' about it. I guess maybe I am. I never thought it'd be like this when I was comin' up in elementary school and junior high. I just thought I'd be another regular runnin' back. The kids in school look up to me, I know that. But I honestly never thought about all this other—the symbol and things. I guess it just happened."

The boys on the field were getting rough now, and Pete retreated from them to the sidelines and lay down. A black Philly Tornado split end named Cleveland McAfee yelled in our direction: "You put me in that book about *Du*-pree now, you heah?" Marcus laughed.

Did he still believe God had allowed him to achieve what he had?

"I feel this very strongly, yes. Before every game I used to think if it wasn't for Him I wouldn't be out here—what God gave me and didn't give Reggie. I'll always think about that. It makes me work harder. I want Reggie to go see me play."

The echo of the train horn reverberated from down the hill. High above us a big passenger liner was flying south—to New Orleans? Mexico City?—leaving immaculate little puffs of smoke in the azure sky. Outside the gym Joe Wood was standing under the goal post gazing across his suzerainty, then casually began throwing a football with a couple of diminutive black boys. Marcus stretched his legs on the bleacher seats and waved at his coach.

What, after all of it, did he have to say now about college football recruiting?

"It's fun for a while, but then it starts to get a little tiresome. When you come down to it, a lot of people are gonna hate you and a lot are gonna like you." Later, when he had settled into Oklahoma, he would tell Ish Haley of *The Dallas Times-Herald:* "I just wish the schools wouldn't bother the players so much. I think recruiting should be done by letter and the coaches should be limited to one visit. Let the recruit meet the coach, visit the school, and make up his own mind. There were so many people putting pressure on me. I was trying to write a research paper for school. Every time I went out people were asking me where I was going to college."

His final four choices had been UCLA, Texas, Southern Mississippi, and Oklahoma. What, briefly, had decided him against the first three?

UCLA: "It's too far away. It's pretty out there. But they don't contend for the national championship. They just want to win the Rose Bowl."

Texas: "After I announced that day, my mom said I needed to go ahead and take my other visits. Some people had been tellin' me Oklahoma wasn't gonna move Buster Rhymes to split end. But the Oklahoma people told me they were. Texas is a pretty big school. I might have chosen them till all the incidents came up, the way Coach Reaux was actin' toward people around here—my uncle and my mom."

Southern: "I asked myself, if Oklahoma and Southern both went ten and zero, which would be picked number one in the country? But I *like* Southern. I almost went there."

He went on: "Norman, Oklahoma, is kind of like Philadelphia. Norman's bigger than Philadelphia, you know, but it's a quiet little town that loves its football and its football players."

I admired Lucious Selmon, I told him.

"He's a guy like me," he replied. "He came up poor like me. We think on the same level. When we were comin' back from Oklahoma after my visit, we landed in Meridian and were drivin' over to here. Coach Selmon saw a nice house on a hill and said he'd like to have a place like that someday. I said that's exactly what I want too."

He hesitated. Then, wistfully, he said: "I wish I could stay in Mississippi. I'd love to stay in Mississippi. Sometimes you just have to give up the finer things in life to get what you want."

Shadows were falling now across the football field. The boys who had been playing had gone home, and Pete was asleep in the grass.

"Sometimes we have to leave home, Marcus, before we can really come back," I said.

This tale had come full circle for me. Almost thirty years ago I too, at age seventeen, had left a small town in Mississippi, and everything I ever knew and cared for and honored, for another strange, teeming university of the American Southwest. It had been a lonely departure. "The leave-takings of the children of youth," I remembered from Thornton Wilder, "are like first recognitions."

He listened thoughtfully as I told him now of these things. I was not a great athlete, as he was, I said, but I did discover of myself, out there in the Southwest a generation ago, that I was a writer. There would be a time in the first two-a-day practices in the August heat of the Oklahoma plains, I suggested, surrounded by 250-pound strangers, hurting, questioning his own talent, and a long way from home, when he would want to be anywhere on the Lord's earth but there. I was not talking about mere mundane homesickness, I said, but about the very bedrock qualities of his own existence—belonging, fortitude, faith, ability. Who was he? Time and again that year, I said, I had seen him get up after being tackled by six, seven, or eight defenders. Never turn back. Never lose faith in your gifts. Courage was sometimes more than physical. Learning this in his heart, I told him, he would be one of our great ones.

"I'm really gonna try," he said.

We parted in the fading sunshine near the bleachers. Pete was next to us, looking at us and wagging his tail. The next time I was to see Marcus personally, many months hence, would be in a hotel in Lincoln, Nebraska.

# 31
# *The Reckoning*

On an oppressively hot morning of August,* he loaded his car, said goodbye to his mother and Reggie, and drove down to the school to bid his farewell to Coach Wood. Wood took him to a service station off the Square and bought him a tank of gas. "I was sad, brother," Wood remembered. "I said a little prayer." The town knew he was going. Some of the townspeople may have seen his black Olds with the tinted windows and the "22" decal on the window as he drove to the highway, headed toward whatever destiny awaited him on the dry plains of Oklahoma.

It was not going to be easy for him at first.

Barry Switzer, who had coached some of America's most talented running backs, watched him closely in the first practice. He had never seen him play. "I tell you," Switzer would later say, "the first time he practiced in shorts, I wasn't much impressed. I thought he was out of shape. He weighed 233 pounds. When I watched him run, he looked lazy, like he wasn't putting out. He gave the impression of not having much speed. I thought we'd recruited a big back who had just 4.7 or 4.8 speed, and that's not fast enough for us. I was thinking about getting him down to a playing weight of 215."

The next day Switzer himself timed Marcus in the forty-yard dash. He was in for a surprise. "It was amazing," he said. "He did 4.5 both times and still didn't look like he was running hard. I raced him against one of our 9.4 sprinters. Marcus chested him out at the wire. Hell, he was our fastest player. Unbelievable speed with his size. To see a kid that big move that fast just doesn't give you the illusion of speed. I decided to let him play at 233."

* Earlier that month he had performed in the North vs. South Mississippi high school all-star game in Jackson. The opposing defenders, many of whom had football scholarships to Ole Miss, State, and Southern, had promised, in the words of one sportswriter, "to break him in half, stop him cold, make him wish he'd gone off to Oklahoma a week or so sooner." In a torrential rainstorm which lasted the entire game, playing for the last time in Mississippi in a red and white Oklahoma helmet, he gained 112 yards, scored the only touchdown of the game, and was named Most Valuable Player. Afterward the enemy defenders gathered around him and gave him the soul shake.

In the first team scrimmage, he ran 70 yards for a touchdown on his first carry. He scored three touchdowns that afternoon and had 154 yards rushing. In the second scrimmage he gained 140 yards, and in the third 118.

In Norman, however, there seemed a purposeful campaign, official as *Pravda*, to underplay his promise. "I like the way he runs," Switzer said in those days, "but he still has a lot of work to do on his blocking and learning the system." The system, of course, was the famous Oklahoma Wishbone, and he was running at the Number 3 right halfback. "They plan to bring him along slowly," one of the Oklahomans said. "They don't want to project him into the limelight too soon. They don't want him to think it's too easy. As he learns the system, his playing time will increase. Right now he isn't projected in a starting role. That isn't likely to come any time soon. He's one of our better signees. We have three who are doing well and he's one of them."

As the 1982 Oklahoma season was about to begin, he was down to about 231 pounds. Here was the '82 schedule:

*Sept* 11  W *Virginia*†
Sept 18  Kentucky
*Sept* 25  *USC*
Oct   2  Iowa St
*Oct*   9  *Texas*
Oct 16  Kansas
*Oct* 23  *Oklahoma St*
Oct 30  Colorado
*Nov*  6  *Kansas St*
*Nov* 13  *Missouri*
Nov 26  Nebraska

Memorial Stadium, still known to many as Owen Field, in Norman was filled to capacity, 75,992 against the University of West Virginia on September 11. It was in this game, early in the second quarter, that he carried the football for the first time as a collegian. He went to the left side for five yards. He only carried one other time that day for no gain. Worse, the Sooners were stunned by a 41–27 upset.

On the following Saturday, against the University of Kentucky in Lexington, he carried the ball six times for fifteen yards. Oklahoma won, 29–8.

The Southern California Trojans came to Norman the next week in a renewal of one of the country's spectacular intersectional rivalries. Once more the Oklahoma partisans were shocked. The Sooners failed to score

† Home games in italics.

for the first time in 181 games. Southern Cal won, 12–0, and Marcus carried the ball only four times for a mere seven yards. He did have a twenty-three-yard pass reception.

After this second loss in three games, an unknown failing in the recent history of Oklahoma football, E. L. Gaylord, publisher of *The Daily Oklahoman* in Oklahoma City and a longtime critic of Coach Barry Switzer, wrote an editorial suggesting that Switzer should resign because he had too many outside business interests, in insurance, oil, and trucking. "As a winner [Switzer] may have been tolerable to some," Gaylord wrote, "as a loser maybe it's time for him to move on."

What, indeed, was going on? The vaunted Oklahoma Wishbone, which had terrorized college football for years, seemed in its final decline. The two early defeats, following as they did the unheroic 1981 season, were prompting widespread complaints across the state. Further, where was Marcus Dupree? The most heralded high school player in the country, running as a lowly substitute, had gained only twenty-seven yards in three games. Was he, as some had predicted he might be, merely another overpublicized small-town failure? Did Switzer and the other Oklahoma coaches regard him so lightly that they only gave him the ball twelve times in three games? Had the whole chronicle of Marcus, conceived in such irony and drama, been an illusion?

The mood in Philly was perplexed. The high school crowd still gathered at the Pizza Hut. J. W. Roebuck brought a five-foot-six-inch chicken snake to the *Democrat* office and had it photographed. The snake had been eating Mr. Roebuck's hen eggs and mistakenly swallowed a light bulb that was in the nest. Another moonshine still had been discovered. The Tornadoes had won two of their first three games, but Sid Salter reported that the new quarterback kept turning to hand off the ball to Marcus, who was not there; he was a ghostly presence in Harpole Stadium. An old Kluxer came up to Sid one day and said, "I told you that nigger was no good." "What's wrong with Marcus?" the townspeople were asking. Some seemed actually embarrassed that he had not become an overnight success. "Much ado about nuthin'," Sid overheard a gentleman say in Stribling's. Certain Ole Miss, State, and Southern Mississippi people wore knowing smirks.

It was, I would learn, the most difficult time of young Marcus' life. He was baffled and homesick. He was telephoning his mother and Reggie every day—also Joe Wood. "He calls me all the time," Wood said. "I don't know how happy he is out there." Weeks after this Marcus himself, reflecting on this painful and challenging period, said he was seriously thinking of quitting and coming home after the Southern Cal game. "I wasn't carryin' the ball very much and I was disappointed the way things were goin'. I was ready to go home. But then I figured things were goin' to be like that with me comin' in as a freshman. You have to work your way up through the ranks. So I decided to stick it out." It was pride that would see him through. Yet there was the seed here of later misunderstandings with Barry Switzer.

A consequential moment for Marcus and his team took place on the practice fields of the University of Oklahoma Sooners on the Monday after the Southern Cal game. Barry Switzer made the most important strategic change of his coaching career. Just as Joe Wood had done in a different setting a year before, he scuttled the Wishbone and installed the "I" formation for Marcus.

"Change for a freshman?" one sportswriter asked. "Unheard of." Switzer himself said later: "In the Wishbone, we just weren't getting him the ball enough. In the 'I,' Marcus was an instant success. The first scrimmage, he carried the ball six times for 148 yards. The coaches all looked at each other. We knew we had something."

Although he had experimented with the "I" in spring practice a few months before, it must have been a difficult move for Switzer, for his illustrious career had been synonymous with the Wishbone and the succession of swift runners who operated from it. In eleven years, the OU offense had produced six national rushing titles. He would continue to use that formation sporadically, but the crucial move had nonetheless been made. *Sports Illustrated* soon took note: "Dupree's style is best suited to the tailback position in the 'I', but despite the intensifying heat [on him], Switzer was understandably reluctant to abandon the Wishbone. In the '70s, Alabama and Oklahoma, Wishbone teams both, were the only Division I teams to accumulate 100 victories. But while Alabama tinkered with its Wishbone—flanking its backs, throwing play-action passes, even dropback passes—Oklahoma remained classic, or stoic, with gradually less impressive results."

For the next two games, Marcus would alternate with Stanley Wilson, the great senior all-Big Eight runner, at the tailback position. The Sooners were on the road that week against Iowa State in Ames, Iowa, in their Big Eight Conference opener. On a luminous October afternoon before a sell-out gallery of 52,770 Marcus carried the ball thirteen times for sixty-two yards. He returned a kickoff for thirty-two yards and had a twenty-two-yard run from scrimmage, the longest of his brief collegiate career, picking up the last eight by pummeling a tackler with his shoulder. He was about to fulfill the success he had promised in the red clay hills of Mississippi.

On the following Saturday, October 9, Oklahoma was to play the Texas Longhorns in the Cotton Bowl in Dallas, the seventy-seventh renewal of that brilliant and envenomed rivalry. Sid Salter and I decided to drive out there and to take with us my friend Squirrel Griffing, the former all-American quarterback for Ole Miss who had watched Marcus with me in the Philly-Newton game a year before and called him the finest running back he ever saw. I left Pete with friends, saying as I departed: "Pete, I'm going to see Marcus." In recognition, he wagged his tail again in a circle.

As we drove through northeast Louisiana Friday afternoon, past Poverty Point and Industry and Winnsboro, Squirrel Griffing recalled the 1962 Cotton Bowl game in which he had quarterbacked Ole Miss against Texas. "The field was frozen as hard as this highway. Those cleat marks on the ground would freeze, and, man, when you fell on them they'd cut you like a knife. Texas had an ol' runnin' back named Saxon that was some kind of good." He talked about playing in that magnificent stadium. "When you come out of the tunnel, your knees get a little wobbly, your stomach hurts, and you keep runnin' back and forth to the restroom. But once you get out there and run a play or two you don't notice the fans, the noise, or the size of the stadium. You just play football." Then The Squirrel launched into a story about a trip he and some pipeline workers had made to Mexico through Texas during his summer college days that lasted from Ruston, Louisiana, to the Texas line.

We spent the night in Longview in East Texas. At a Mexican restaurant named Chico's, Sid Salter telephoned home to learn that the Philly Tornadoes had just defeated Kosciusko.

Early the next morning we headed on Interstate 20 toward Dallas. Cars with Texas and OU pennants sped past us. We had bought the Dallas papers in Longview and perused their bulky coverage of the day's game as we drove. Much was made of the fact that Oklahoma had won out over Texas for Marcus Dupree's services. In one of the stories Coach Joe Wood described a telephone conversation with his former running back. "I told him, 'Those Texas players will be after you.' I'd sure like to see that game. But I'll tell you this: Marcus will have a great game against Texas. He'll do better against them than anybody else he plays against all year. That's just the way he's put together."

Texas, ranked number thirteen in the nation, was undefeated in three games against Utah, Missouri, and Rice, and had won four of the last five contests against Oklahoma. The Sooners were 2–2, the worst record they had brought into the Texas game since 1965. Sam Blair, who years ago taught me about writing on *The Daily Texan*, and his colleagues discussed the theatrics of the UT-OU series in *The Dallas Morning News*. A banner headline over Danny Robbins' by-line in *The Dallas Times-Herald* proclaimed: "The Big Question: Will a Star Be Born?" The story said: "And if so, will he be a tailback or the offense he lines up in? . . . The starting tailback, the meal ticket, is expected to be Marcus Dupree. Call him a freshman with acquaintances on both coaching staffs. Billed by many as the No. 1 running back prospect in the nation and even another Herschel Walker, Dupree has been little more than a struggling backup on an OU team that hasn't had a back crack 100 yards on the ground this year."

A large photograph of Marcus accompanied another piece in the *Times-Herald* by Ish Haley, in which Barry Switzer spoke of Marcus, saying he remembered seeing such a prototype three other times—Earl Campbell, Herschel Walker, Eric Dickerson. "He can be good in any offense, but we can get the ball to him more in the 'I' formation. Marcus hasn't had the opportunity to get into the open field, but we know from watching him in practice he can make people miss him." Pete Martinelli, the Oklahoma "strength coach," said: "For sure he's the strongest freshman running back I've ever seen." Marcus himself was quoted in the Texas papers that morning at length: "I'm still not running the way I want. I haven't been able to break loose the way I want to. Maybe the 'I' formation will help us. I don't care what offense we run as long as we win."

As we journeyed past the small towns and farmlands of East Texas, Squirrel Griffing was taken with some of the observations of the Texas players. Craig Curry, the strong safety, said: "All I've heard is he's the Number one recruit. Well, I'm gonna see just how much of a blue chip he is." The Texas defense, which had allowed its opponents only 1.9 yards per rush, was led by a middle linebacker named Jeff Leiding, whom Switzer called "another Dick Butkus." He was from Tulsa and had chosen Texas over Oklahoma, and he too was ready for Marcus. "I felt sorry for him at first," he said. "But when he decided to go to Oklahoma, I knew what happened. They try to make you go to Oklahoma last, so they can have that final psychological input." And so it went from Longview to the Big D.

Against the expansive Texas horizon the skyline of Dallas loomed before us. We were drawn magnetically to Dealy Plaza and the old Book Depository, haunted ground for Americans, where three years before the assassination, one muggy afternoon during the campaign of '60, I had preceded Jack Kennedy's car in an open truck full of photographers over the same immemorial route.

Then we fought the traffic out to the Cotton Bowl.

Sid Salter, covering the game for the persevering *Neshoba Democrat*, would roam the Oklahoma sidelines with his cameras. Squirrel Griffing and I had high fifty-yard-line seats, acquired from Coach Tommy Reaux of Texas, among the Longhorn partisans. The spectacle as it greeted me now, with the 75,587 spectators equally divided between the Orange and the Red, was a song to remember. More than a quarter of a century ago, as a Texas undergraduate, I had come to these games.

The two teams were going through their pregame drills. I looked down, across the deep green turf. After a while I saw the familiar figure. He was wearing Number 22 and he was standing among a group of other running backs catching punts.

All of a sudden, gazing down at him, I was overcome by emotion. What was it?—a wistful sadness, a curious disbelief. The historic stadium was already packed to capacity. All around it the State Fair of Texas was in full swing, and the ferris wheels and roller coasters whirled madly amid the shows and exhibits and concessions on that vast ground. In the distance the skyscrapers of Big D were silhouetted against the glittering blue horizon. Every now and again a helicopter would descend on a greensward outside, bringing in the late-arriving oil people. The Texas and Oklahoma marching bands, hundreds strong, were massing for their grand entrance beyond the tunnelway, and soon in their numbers would cover the whole length of the field. Texas students were leading the world's largest bass drum around the track, and beyond an end zone was the mascot Bevo, the longhorn steer in lineal descent from the one I had accompanied to South Bend, Indiana, many years ago. Not far from Bevo was the Sooner Schooner, the miniature Conestoga wagon drawn by a pair of sleek Welsh ponies. Beautiful women in the Neiman-Marcus fashions escorted by their men in expensive ten-gallon hats milled among the crowds shouting twangy salutations. All about me was the ebullient, mindless affluence of the Great American Southwest, the mementos of the incandescent parvenu rich. And from all sides now, as the marching bands came onto the field with their impeccable resounding brass, a deep, nearly erotic hum of anticipation rose from the assembled thousands.

I thought in that moment of the forlorn little football fields of Mississippi where I had gone to see Marcus play. I remembered the raw enveloping earth, the old yellow school buses parked behind the sagging bleachers, the dim lights and broken scoreboards and off-key fight songs, the black and white people in sweaty work clothes in the concrete grandstand, the tractor caps and T-shirts, the little boys forever playing in the end zones, the dogs from Possum Hollow who interrupted the play, the smell of talcum and drugstore perfume, the dry autumnal dust rising up from the moiling heat, the black child retrieving the footballs in the deep incline behind the goal post, "New York New York," the crickets chirping from the thicket, the sad echo of the train's horn from the Quarters. I watched Marcus as he left the field far below. He had come a long way.

When the two teams returned to the mighty roar, Sid Salter came up to him on the Oklahoma sidelines. To Sid he looked even bigger than he had at Harpole Stadium in Philly. He had shed his glasses for contact lenses. "Anybody else from Philadelphia come with you?" he asked. He left the sidelines to go through his drills with the starting offense. Soon the bands were playing "Boomer Sooner" and "The Eyes of Texas." I spotted Lucious Selmon on one side of the field, Tommy Reaux on the other, and I remembered their fortuitous confrontation at the elevator in the Downtown Hotel those many weeks ago.

Alternating with Stanley Wilson at tailback, Marcus was gaining yardage in the first quarter. On one play up the middle, running low, he plowed over the garrulous 240-pound Texas linebacker, Jeff Leiding, and knocked him a couple of yards. "You can't teach that," Squirrel Griffing said. "He got down and took ol' Leiding home." The two teams kept alternating possessions. Texas was throwing the ball more than any Longhorn team in memory. The first quarter ended in a scoreless tie.

A quintessential moment was approaching. Early in the second quarter he carried for eight to the Oklahoma thirty-seven. On the next play he took a pitch from quarterback Kelly Phelps and moved to his right. He faked a handoff to Steve Sewell on a reverse. Then he accelerated speed, crushed a defender near the line of scrimmage, outmaneuvered a linebacker, raced toward the sidelines, and outran the Texas secondary for a touchdown. Squirrel Griffing embraced me amid the Texas partisans; if the truth be known, with my Longhorn roots I did not even feel guilty in that gratifying instant. We had just witnessed the first touchdown of Marcus' collegiate career—sixty-three yards from scrimmage. Suddenly he was mobbed on the sidelines by his teammates, coaches, and photographers.

"That was worth the trip and the Mexican food last night," Squirrel said.

It was a keenly contested game between two enthusiastic rivals, likely the only college football game in America where at any given moment precisely half of the people in the stadium were on their feet yelling "Kill . . . Kill . . . Kill!" The lead fluctuated. The Oklahoma running game carried the day. With the young Oklahoma offensive line opening cunning little apertures, Marcus, Stanley Wilson, and the "I" fullbacks Weldon Ledbetter and Fred Sims cracked the Texas defense for 384 rushing yards that day. Marcus carried for 35 more yards, but lost a fumble in the fourth quarter, only the third time I had seen him do so. Oklahoma won a thriller, 28–22, and the Sooners carried an ecstatic Barry Switzer, who had for the moment stifled the critics, off the field on their shoulders. Marcus finished with 98 yards on nine carries.

Sid Salter walked with Marcus through the tunnel toward the locker room. As the bands played in the distance, he was besieged for autographs, as in the Choctaw Bowl.

"How did Philadelphia do last night?" he asked Sid.

"We beat Kosciusko, 25–14."

"All *right!*"

Sid asked him what to tell the people back home.

"I've got a lot of work to do, but I'm gettin' better every day. Tell them to look for four more years of games like today."

In the Oklahoma locker room Barry Switzer told the press and television: "I've had better teams, but I don't know when I've had a better victory. Tell the folks back home that the big boy from Philly did super . . . As long as we've got Number 22 in the backfield, we'll run from the 'I.' He's a natural in that formation and is getting better every week. But we remember enough of our Wishbone plays that I think we can keep our opponents honest." Lucious Selmon commented: "There's no doubt in my mind that he's a Heisman Trophy caliber back. Dupree is for real. He proved today he's capable of exploding on one of the finest teams in the country. He's got a lot of work to do, but barring injury he'll be a great, great football player."

On the Texas side, Fred Akers told the reporters of Dupree: "This young man is a difference-maker." And our gentlemanly friend from the Neshoba recruiting season, Tommy Reaux, added: "I'm proud for the kid. He was everything I thought he could be in this class of football. It killed me for him to break one on us like that, but I want him to be successful in all he does. I wish Marcus all the best."

The triumphs began to mount for him now, and with them the fortunes of his Oklahoma team. Against the University of Kansas in Lawrence the following Saturday, on his first carry of the game he sprinted 75 yards for a touchdown—"pausing along the way," *Sports Illustrated* reported, "to plant the final defender with a stiff arm so stunning that Switzer said later, 'It's not fair for a guy to be 6′3″, 233, 9.5, and know karate too.'" He had two other touchdowns that day on runs of 13 and 7 yards in a 38–14 Oklahoma victory. He gained a total of 158 yards on 9 carries and was named the Big Eight Offensive Player of the Week. *The Sporting News*, the trusty gray lexicon of American sports, observed: "Many people have conceded the Big Eight Conference championship and the host role in the Orange Bowl to the Nebraska Cornhuskers. But don't count out Oklahoma. The Sooners, after a slow start, are showing some of the firepower to which their fans have become accustomed. . . . Freshman Marcus Dupree looks like a future superstar at tailback."

It was about then that I began tuning in to the sports call-in programs on the Oklahoma City and Tulsa radio stations. From these I deduced he was soon on his way at age eighteen to becoming something of a folk hero in that state. By now Pete's conditioning was such that when he heard "Marcus Dupree" on the Oklahoma airwaves he got up and moved about the room. The young man from Neshoba was likewise beginning to receive the national television coverage. The film of his long "stiff-arm" run against the Kansas Jayhawks was shown several times on the national networks.‡

The Sooners, 4 and 2 now on the year, were at home next against Oklahoma State. That week Switzer moved Stanley Wilson, the senior All-Big Eight selection and three-year starter, from left half-tailback to fullback; Marcus would no longer alternate with the distinguished Wilson. "Marcus has won the job," the head coach said, "because of his abilities and his talents being the best on the football team. He didn't inherit it by default or by injury." Switzer added: "We knew we had a good athlete, but we didn't know he would come along this fast."

Against the Cowboys of Oklahoma State before 76,406 fans in Memorial Stadium, he carried the ball sixteen times for eighty-three yards. He scored a thirty-yard touchdown on a fourth-and-one and had another from two yards out in a 27–9 victory. At one point in the game he and an Oklahoma State linebacker rolled into the sideline near the Oklahoma bench and knocked down Barry Switzer, who suffered a bruised wrist and a broken watch. Someone helped Switzer to his feet and inquired about the watch. "Heck with the watch," Switzer said. "How's Marcus?"

The Sooners made it five straight, and 4–0 in the conference, in a 45–10 win over the University of Colorado in Boulder. He was held to

‡ It was during this week that the NCAA placed the University of Texas on "mild probation" without penalties involving a $143 pair of cowboy boots someone bought Marcus during his official recruiting visit to Austin the previous January, although he was not wearing them as he entered the Kansas Jayhawk end zone that day.

fifty-three yards in twelve carries, but returned a punt seventy-seven yards for a touchdown, in the description of *Sports Illustrated*, "after shrugging off an attempted necktie tackle that might have turned even a good back into a soprano." Switzer asked: "Can you imagine? Two hundred and thirty pounds, running back punts?"

The following Saturday Oklahoma was at home again against Kansas State. The game would be on ABC Television. It was a bright, crisp November day in Oxford, and Pete and I took a few turns around the deserted Ole Miss stadium and the woods beyond before the two of us returned to settle in before my TV set.

Before the kickoff, the network showed films of his long runs. Lee Grosscup, the "color commentator," observed: "You have to say, is he another Herschel Walker? You've got to think of Earl Campbell, Walker, Chuck Muncie, Eric Dickerson." Al Michaels, the play-by-play man, added: "Keep in mind that he's 6 feet 3 inches, 230 pounds, with 9.5 speed."

Leaves of a dozen colors drifted from the big trees in my front yard. Pete was dozing at my feet. Once again I felt the same wistful emotion of the Cotton Bowl in Dallas a month before. With my memories of the games in the little stadiums in Ackerman, New Hope, Newton, and Philly, it was strange watching him now on national television, before seventy-five thousand people in an ocean of red on the Oklahoma plains. Remembering too the small, inexperienced Philly Tornado offensive line of his senior year, I was reassured to learn that the Oklahoma blockers from tackle-to-tackle weighed 280, 275, 275, 270, and 267.

Early on Kansas State's Wildcats took a 3–0 lead. They kicked off and Marcus downed the ball in the end zone. Oklahoma lined up in the "I" from its own twenty-yard line.

Swift as could be, he struck. He took a pitch to the right from quarterback Phelps, ran slowly, raced then to the inside behind three blocks near the line of scrimmage, weaved through the secondary with tacklers all around him, paused again, eluded two more defenders who bounced off him, then cut again toward the sidelines. I caught myself standing and shouting so energetically that Pete leaped to his feet in surprise and retreated momentarily out the front door. There was Marcus' familiar gliding movement, the unearthly speed, as he outran another defensive back and scored on his eighty-yard run.

Having forgiven me my outburst, Pete returned again for the second quarter. Kansas State went ahead again 10–7, and then an interesting thing happened. With Marcus in the deep receiving position on the kickoff, Kansas State deliberately made a shallow kick to deprive him of the ball. How many times had I seen that against Eupora, Winona, Northwest Rankin, and Carthage?

Switzer was using the Wishbone only about 20 percent of the time. Running mainly from the "I," he and Stanley Wilson at fullback were accumulating substantial yardage. Later in the second period the Sooners reached the Kansas State one-yard line. From there he negotiated a high dive into the end zone for a touchdown, as he had learned it from Herschel Walker in the '81 Georgia–Ole Miss game and perfected it on the playing grounds of east-central Mississippi.

When he came off the field the television cameras focused on him as he took off his helmet and sat on the bench. Only the red hair net was missing, and the little kids who used to congregate behind the wire fence in Harpole. "Hi, Mom," he said. "Hi, Reggie."

The momentum turned to the Sooners in the second half. Marcus and Wilson were getting four, six, eight, five, twelve on slicing runs through the line. He gained six on an important fourth-and-one from the Kansas State forty, but then failed on another fourth-and-one from the enemy three.

Oklahoma won, 24–10. Marcus had scored two touchdowns, gained 118 yards on fourteen carries, and along with Darrell Dickey of Kansas State was named Player of the Game. From the television studio in New York, Ara Parseghian, the former coach of Notre Dame, said: "This is the young player destined to go after Herschel Walker's records." Oklahoma's showing was now 7–2 and 5–0 in the Big Eight. After switching to the "I" formation to accommodate Marcus' skills, the Sooners had won six straight games; since that move he had scored nine touchdowns and carried the ball for a 6.9 average.

ESPN, the sports television network, featured him in films the next week. *Sports Illustrated* came out with an impressive spread of photographs and an article by Ralph Wiley. He had "put the long, brilliant run back into football," Wiley wrote. "It ain't the alignment," Barry Switzer said, "it's the alignee. And Marcus Dupree is the best freshman ever to set foot on this campus. I don't know if any freshman ever went to school with his equipment."

Wiley of *Sports Illustrated* continued:

> With each subsequent dash, the cheers for Dupree grow louder, the comparisons grander, the attention greater . . . The comparisons abound. Dupree is Herschel Walker II, Sooner fans say. "He's Earl Campbell all over again," says Williams. Switzer says that Dupree is "unlike any back we've had here. Bigger, but still a runner." No one has mentioned Jimmy Brown yet, but the similarity is obvious . . .
>
> Perhaps in anticipation of the Nov. 26 showdown with the [Ne-

braska] Cornhuskers, Dupree ran an option run-pass sweep at the Thursday practice before the Kansas State game and fired a 40-yard bullet completion. A bespectacled 13-year-old named Kathy, sheltered against evening shadows and prairie winds by her father's arms, said, "Look, Daddy! He's the quarterback, the runner, the tank, everything!" Her father, Barry by name, adjusted the tobacco in his lip, squinted, and said, "Yep."

The Tigers of the University of Missouri came into Memorial Stadium on November 13 for a regionally televised game. He established a new Oklahoma total yardage record for freshmen—756 yards. He scored two touchdowns that day on runs of 70 and 7 yards and gained 166 yards on nineteen carries. Oklahoma won, 41–14. Asked if his Missouri players were discussing Dupree after the game, Coach Warren Powers said: "Yeah, especially the ones who had his cleat marks all over them."

Going into the final regular season match of '82 against the University of Nebraska two weeks hence—the game that would determine the Big Eight championship and an Orange Bowl invitation—the Sooners had now won seven in a row and had an 8–2 record. After the Missouri game he was second in the nation in average yards per carry at 7.3.

Just before I departed for dinner at the Taylor catfish place that night, leaving Pete with visions of hushpuppies to come, I got KRMG on the radio dial from downtown Tulsa. In the setting sun, when the distant radio stations of America spring to life, Marcus' name was wafting without surcease through the southwestern airwaves. The radio host, I believe, was named Joe.

"Joe, you've got to remember," one female telephone caller emphasized, "this guy is just a freshman. He's just eighteen and from Mississippi."

"You're right on," Joe replied. "He'll be the best back OU ever had."

"I'm Sylvia, Joe. Best *America* ever had."

"Joe, this is Mike in Ardmore. Marcus Dupree deserves silver shoes. He don't have none yet."

"In a couple of years," Joe philosophized, "he'll have *gold* shoes."

As such things sometimes happen in our land, he was suddenly a national figure now, fed by the insatiable injunctions of television. Here, for instance, was a national wire-service story two days after the Missouri game:

Oklahoma freshman tailback Marcus Dupree has been hospitalized suffering from a chest cold. Spokesmen at the OU football office and the Goddard Health Center on the Oklahoma campus said Dupree, suffering from chest congestion, was admitted Monday night. Officials said Dupree was admitted to the hospital for rest and to get over the infection.

Dupree, from Philadelphia, Miss., has set an Oklahoma freshman record with 756 yards and 10 touchdowns while averaging 7.3 yards per carry. He told reporters last Saturday he felt like he had the flu when he gained 166 yards against Missouri.

With an open date that Saturday before the Nebraska game, he flew home for a couple of days. In the old school the students flocked around him for his autograph. Some of the football players got him to sign their letter jackets. "Same ol' Marcus," one of them said.

While there, he may have heard the announcement that the NCAA had ended a fourteen-month investigation by placing Southern Mississippi, with whom he had nearly signed the previous February, on stringent probation for two years for recruiting violations. These violations included "improper recruiting inducements, unethical conduct, meals, improper campus visits, transportation, recruiting contacts, and improper commitment to attend the university." Offers of cash and an automobile were involved. The penalties included banning Southern from television and bowl appearances for two years. The mayor of Hattiesburg presented Jim Carmody, the Southern coach, with a trophy for the GATA Bowl—"Get After Their Ass." The players chose the regular season game against Alabama as their bowl and won, 38–29.

Shortly before the Nebraska game, *The Sporting News* published a lengthy article on him as an outstanding freshman with a glittering future. A panel of sportswriters and sportscasters named him to the first team All-Big Eight Conference squad. A record about him called *Mr. Marvelous*, written by an Oklahoma drama professor, made its debut on radio stations throughout the state. The vocalist, accompanied by exuberant background vocals, electric guitar, keyboards, bass, and drums, exclaimed:

> And then you're down on the field
> And what do you see?
> A red-and-white blur of Sooner history,
> A mean motor-scooter from Mississippi,
> Marvelous Marcus Dupree.

In the cold Southern autumn air my friend Pete was hurting. There were times around Rowan Oak and the bare Confederate cemetery behind the Ole Miss Coliseum that I knew he was drifting away from me. After a few steps he would lie down in the dry fall leaves. I would lie next to him for a while. Then I would have to coax him back into the car and lift him in the back seat.

Pete and I had been together for so many years that I did not want to leave him. But I had to. The Oklahoma Sooners were playing the Nebraska Cornhuskers in Lincoln, Nebraska. Nebraska, having lost only one game all season, and this to mighty Penn State in the closing seconds, was ranked Number 4 in the nation; Oklahoma with its seven-game winning streak was Number 11. The Sooners had begun the '82 college football season with their worst start in fourteen years, but having changed to the "I" formation they were now among the exciting teams in America. The game would be played before the national television cameras and an audience of many millions. The OU-Nebraska series was one of the most extravagant in the country. For the twenty-first consecutive year the Sooners and the Cornhuskers could either win or share the Big Eight Conference championship. It suggested much about the bitter OU-Nebraska rivalry that for the eighteenth time in the last twenty-one games the title would be determined by this contest. The winner would go to the heralded Orange Bowl in Miami on New Year's Night, the loser to the Fiesta Bowl in Tempe, Arizona, on New Year's Day. Both squads were 6–0 in the league. Further, the Cornhuskers, the defending league champions, were averaging 42.8 points a game, the highest in the conference since the Sooners averaged 45 points in 1971. Nebraska and Oklahoma were the top two rushing teams in the nation as they entered this game. Barry Switzer's ingenuity in switching to the "I" was now at its apex. He had perennially won over the opposing Nebraska coach, a tough-eyed figure named Tom Osborne, whose very visage seemed synonymous with the barren and icy Nebraska landscape, a man who considered winning in college football a moral equivalent of the survival of the earth, in an American state where many nuclear-headed missiles were aimed toward the susceptible gray interstices of Soviet Russia.

Nebraska had an outstanding all-American running back named Mike Rozier, who had rushed for 1,482 yards in the '82 season. Yet, as the pertinacious *Sports Illustrated* reported, he had been limping about all week with a strained ankle, and "Oklahoma's sensational freshman tailback, Marcus Dupree, had spent several days in the hospital with a nagging cold." Marcus had scored one run of at least 63 yards in five of the six previous contests. As *Sports Illustrated* reported, "Switzer had seen fit to declare the 6'3", 233-pound freshman better than Billy Sims, Oklahoma's '78 Heisman Trophy winner. Switzer also announced that 'Marcus Dupree came in here with E.T. He's from another world.' Which may be true, depending on what one thinks of Philadelphia, Miss."

Despite my sadness over Pete's condition, I had arranged in this late November of 1982 to drive the thousand miles from Mississippi to Nebraska, with my trusted Philadelphia collaborator Sid Salter and Joe

Wood. We were joined by young Dan Turner, an Ole Miss student from Philly and the brother of Tom Turner. On a viciously cold Thanksgiving morning I again left Pete with friends, and my comrades and I were off to the Great Midwest to see our boy.

"Where are your keys, Joe?" I asked.

"They were too heavy to bring along," he said.

The car was laden with heavy clothes, fur-lined hats, boots, pens, pads, cameras, thermal underwear, Skoal snuff containers, a gingerbread cake, and a sack of candied orange slices which Joe Wood called "the poor man's caviar."

The Philly Tornado coach from the empty stretches of Choctaw County who, as a boy, got up at 4 A.M. to milk the cows was visibly excited. As we sped through the flat delta land of Arkansas and the cape of Missouri, past Cooter, Tyronza, Luxora, and Hayti, he told us he had not made too many trips. He had never flown in an airplane before, he said, and this was about the longest drive he had ever taken. He talked with his running back on the telephone about once a week, he reported. In fact he had called him in Oklahoma the night before to get passes for us to sit on the Oklahoma bench during the ball game. "Y'all comin' up?" Marcus had asked enthusiastically. "I just hope the big fellow does good," Joe Wood said. "He always comes through on the big 'uns. If I didn't think he could do the job," he said, as he spit a little snuff into a paper cup, "I'd have stayed home with Momma and the girls."

The Mississippi River in its perpetual twistings and turnings often came into view. This was Mark Twain country. The day was gray and cold, and woodsmoke curled from the chimneys of farmhouses where Missouri people were having their Thanksgiving dinners. I remembered the Thanksgivings of my childhood with my parents and grandparents and great-aunts, all of them long dead. The solitary hitchhikers, forlorn and shivering, were out on this day. I felt as I always did on long drives such as this the loneliness of America.

From time to time Joe Wood passed around the package his wife Renee had packed for him—chocolate-covered cherries, Nabs, cheese and crackers, and the poor man's caviar. Sometimes I heard him singing country songs. Sid Salter had switched on the radio. "Turn that one up, Sid!" the coach said. He sang with T. G. Sheppard:

> *War is hell on the home front too,*
> *God only knows what a woman goes through . . .*

He changed the last line, singing: "God only knows what Marcus can't do."

In Marston, Missouri, we stopped at a dubious roadside place for our Thanksgiving meal, greasy cheeseburgers and french fries. Norman Rockwell was absent from this institution. As we rose to leave, Joe Wood paused at the jukebox and inserted three or four quarters for Loretta Lynn, Willie Nelson, and Conway Twitty. "We can at least leave these folks with a little culture," he said.

A few miles south of Cape Girardeau we saw several huge irrigation machines at work. "That's what I need for my football field right there," Joe said.

Football was on his mind again. "I got another one comin' along. A black kid in the seventh grade named Deion Talley. He scores every time he gets the ball, the way Marcus did back then. I guess I better tell these Oklahoma people about him." He reminisced about the recruiting back home. "You hear all these stories about high school *coaches* gettin' paid off. Why didn't somebody offer *me* a hundred thousand dollars? I'd have been hard put to turn down a hundred thousand dollars, but nobody offered it." He described taking some students on a class trip to the Parchman Prison in Mississippi, where one of his former players was an inmate. Once during the early recruiting of Marcus, Coach Steve Sloan, and his assistant, Tom Goode, asked if they could go to Wood's house to meet his wife. The three of them stood at the front door. "'Renee, you decent?' I said. 'I got Steve Sloan and Tom Goode out here.' Renee thinks I'm pullin' her leg. 'Well,' she says in an exaggerated voice, 'you just tell ol' Steve and Tom to come on in.' When she sees them she almost faints."

Then, in the lingering autumn twilight he grew philosophical. He was developing a plan for world peace, he said, which he called Operation Wishbone. "I think we should introduce football to Russia," he said. "The Russkies would vent all their hostility on the coaches and referees, like American people do here. Then there wouldn't be any war. The Orange Bowl should be played every year in Moscow."

He added by way of punctuation: "*Hot* dog! Goin' to Lincoln, Nebraska, to see my boy! I hope he has as good a game as he did against Neshoba Central." As the Midwestern night descended, and the lights of the houses along the way glittered in the frosty mist, the coach's enthusiasm for the next afternoon's game grew more and more palpable.

After the day's interminable drive, we spent the night in St. Joseph, Missouri. Lincoln was four hours away. The temperature the next morning was below freezing, and there was a searing, frigid wind. At the car we drew in deep breaths of the cold. There were scant signs of life in northwest Missouri on this day. We traveled past endless miles of wheat and barley on the prairies, and even the occasional rambling farmhouse seemed deserted. The Christmas decorations were already up in the bleak little hamlets. Holly wreaths were on the doors, and tinsel on the trees. There were patches of hard snow and ice between the rows in the fields. Overhead vast numbers of ducks flew southward in majestic symmetry. "I taught general science, but I never figured out how they know to fly that way," Joe Wood said. I felt again the mysterious pull of the Midwest, the darkness of its long winters, the strange ambivalent curiosity which the Southerner has for its implacable sweep and isolation. One could dissolve indistinguishably into this gray American land. I remembered Irwin Shaw's words: "America is a country of many cultures, some clashing with each other, some complementary, some a volatile combination of simultaneous attraction and rejection." This remote landscape had a haunting appeal to me, yet it was almost too much to absorb easily. This emotion was confirmed for me by Marcus' coach. "I'm tellin' you boys," he said, "this is funny country. I ain't seen nobody yet. How far are we from Canada?"

The ground became craggy. Then the steep bluffs of the Missouri River came into view. "I'd like to have one of them for my boys to run up," he said. "Wouldn't the big ol' tackles love it?"

We touched upon a frosty little finger of Iowa. "This is the first time I've ever been in this state."

Sid Salter had been silent before these solemn vistas. "You're a world-traveling kind of fellow, Coach," he said.

We crossed the Missouri River into Nebraska and drove through Nebraska City, Syracuse, and Unadilla. Immense barns dotted the horizon, and the earth now was black. "Look at this soil!" the Tornado coach said. "That red land around home won't grow nothin' but a pine tree. There ain't much to this, is there? Half the towns I've seen in Nebraska to this point look like Ethel, Mississippi."


The Oklahoma team was staying at a Holiday Inn not far from the stadium. The game was a little more than two hours away. We entered the hotel to be greeted by an unusual scene. Seated at tables around a large indoor swimming pool surrounded by green carpeting were a hundred or so Oklahomans. Most of them were dressed in red—red tam-o'-shanters, bandannas, pantsuits, leisure suits; they were drinking bloody marys. There was a festive vacation air about this milieu, and the people moved from table to table chatting mindlessly, as they would on such a moment in Mississippi. Big money was present here. One elderly fellow mingling among his compatriots wore a red-and-white cowboy suit, a red hat, and red boots. Inexplicably he walked up to me. "We're gonna *whup* 'em today," he said, then went on about his errands.

At the far side of this arena, Lucious Selmon was playing Ping-Pong with a little black girl. When he sighted us, he came our way with an energetic welcome. I remembered our February days in the Downtown Hotel in Philly.

"We've come from Mississippi with some Kool-Aid and films of 'The Flintstones,'" I said.

"How did you get here?"

"We drove," Joe Wood said.

"You *drove* from Mississippi?"

We asked how Marcus was doing.

"I can't tell you how pleased we are with him. I have absolutely no doubt if we'd put in the 'I' for him in the first game of the season, we'd be undefeated now, and maybe Number 1 in the country."

"I got another one just like him comin' up right now," Joe Wood said. "Except he's even bigger and faster."

Selmon's eyes brightened. "You *do*?"

"Where's the big fellow now?" Joe asked.

Lucious Selmon had his room number. "Go see him. You're gonna be with us on the bench, you know."

We found him in a room off the mezzanine overlooking the spirited Oklahoma party. He was talking with his mother and Reggie on the telephone. "They've written a song about me," he was saying. When he saw us he grinned and waved, then warmly shook hands.

"Us and you are gonna be the only people from Mississippi in the stadium," Wood said.

"All *right*."

"Looks like they're feedin' you pretty good."

"Hey, Coach, look at these pictures they took of me for *Sports Illustrated*." He reached in his suitcase and withdrew two large mounted color shots from the recent spread.

"I'm really glad y'all came," he said.

We chatted about home.

"I want you to go out there and do a good job today," the coach said. "We're gonna be right down there on that field with you."

"I think we can beat 'em. I'm really glad you're here, Coach," he repeated.

As we departed for the stadium, he came out of the room and leaned against the railing, gazing down at the extravagant scene around the swimming pool. "There's *Marcus!*" one of the Oklahomans shouted from below. "Get 'em, Marcus!" I paused momentarily to talk with him. The shy young boy of the Neshoba days was relaxed and self-assured. He even called me by my first name.


It was a marvelous old stadium, with a patina about it of grim, wind-swept Midwestern time. It had been added onto over the years, and I admired its ancient seams and junctures and conjoinings. I was reminded a little of the Yale Bowl, Notre Dame Stadium, Franklin Field.

There would be 76,398 people in attendance on this day. By the time we got there with the Oklahoma team the seats were already three-quarters filled. Standing on the field with Joe Wood, I was colder than I had been in years, colder even than I was when the Freedom Train stopped at Vicksburg at 8 A.M. in the winter of 1946. There was a sharp, wild brace in the air which settled in the very marrow of one's bones.

The stadium was alive with color. Red banners and pompons were everywhere, and the Nebraska band was playing "Dear Ol' Nebraska U." On the loudspeaker Gordon Macrae sang "Oklahoma." There were numerous signs draping the railings beyond the end zones, including a huge one with a drawing of Oklahoma's Number 22 sitting on a toilet. In reference to Nebraska's great running back Mike Rozier, the caption said: WHEN I GROW UP I WANNA BE LIKE MR. ROZIER.

Sid Salter and Dan Turner were walking about taking pictures; I saw them down the way talking with the Oklahoma cheerleaders. I mingled among the Nebraska cheerleaders as they did their dexterous pyramids and pirouettes. One of the girls was so beautiful that she reminded me of the cheerleader from Northwest Rankin High in Philly many months before. She must have been freezing in her short skirt.

"Aren't you cold?" I asked her between her routines.

"I'm used to it. You have to move around a lot."

"*I'm* cold. I drove all the way from Mississippi."

"*Mississippi!* You've got to be kidding."

Joe Wood was wearing a baseball cap with "P" on it. He gazed around the massive stadium. "Ol' Hitchcock, my defense coach, don't know what he's missin'," he said.

By the time the Nebraska and Oklahoma teams came on the field for the pregame practice, the stadium was filled to capacity. The OU contingent, numbering no more than five hundred, were sitting together in a section behind us. After a time they began a chant: "Marcus! Marcus!"

Wherever his pupil went on the field, Joe Wood ambled along the sidelines to be close to him. Receiving a punt, Marcus ran to within a yard of his old coach and stopped before him. They grinned at each other.

The Nebraska squad across the way was big and menacing, more so than Kosciusko, New Hope, Eupora, or Neshoba Central had ever been. The home fans, denizens of an immense and underpopulated state where college football was an existential faith, were sending forth a stupendous roar. Someone told us that the stadium on this afternoon was the third most populated place in all of Nebraska, and one believed it from the diabolic noise. In the midst of this, the television crews from Oklahoma City and Tulsa discovered the presence of Marcus Dupree's high school coach. One by one they came down the sidelines to interview him. When they had finished, he turned to me. "She had the prettiest eyes," he said of the last interviewer. "The other side of her family is from Carroll County, Mississippi."

Marcus was running plays with the starting offensive team. During a short break he casually walked over to us on the sidelines again. "Is it too cold for you, Coach?" he asked, then dashed away.

A small pep band from Oklahoma launched into "Boomer Sooner." The outnumbered partisans were chanting again for Marcus as their team left the field through the tunnel toward the locker room.

Marcus was the last player on the field. In the most poignant of gestures he walked over to his old coach again and tarried there, touching him lightly on the arm. The Oklahoma coaches were about to disappear through the tunnel. Barry Switzer turned around. "What are you doing, Marcus?" he shouted. "Come on in here!" One of his assistants whispered in his ear. Switzer bounded back onto the field with Scott Hill and approached Marcus and Wood. "The 'P' on your hat gave you away, Coach," he said. "We're glad to have you. Come see us in the dressing room after the game."

The sun broke through for the first time that day as the Nebraska band, which seemed to number in the thousands, marched onto the field playing "Grandioso." "Our band plays that!" Joe Wood exclaimed. "It's our song. We ain't too far from home." With that a CBS cameraman came by and took some shots of the Philly coach.

As the game began, the awesome thud of bodies as seen and heard at the field level reminded me of what the coach of the University of Iowa had recently said: "I don't know but that ten years from now football will be so violent it'll be outlawed." Joe Wood and I stood on the sidelines in the early minutes with the bearded 275-pound offensive guard, Steve Williams, a professional wrestler in the off-season who was better known as "Dr. Death."

Dr. Death growled and muttered to himself as the Nebraska

Cornhuskers moved down the field. Following the blocking of an offensive line led by a 293-pound all-American named Dave Rimington, Rozier, who would later sit out the second half with an injury, broke for slashing gains. Nebraska went ahead 7–0 on this first possession.

With this touchdown, a curious thing happened. The Nebraska fans began barraging the field with hundreds of oranges. They descended on us from all directions, an exercise which served to remind us that the victor in this game would go to the Orange Bowl on New Year's. Two or three of these hellborn missives whizzed inches away from Joe Wood and me. "Look at that!" he shouted. "They got us up here, and then they started *throwin'* at us!" Across the field a policeman was struck in the head by one of them from a high upper tier and had to be carried away. "Let's stand in front of some of these big ol' players," Wood said.

Now it was Marcus' turn. He carried the ball on eight of the first twelve Oklahoma plays, as John Papanek, writing for *Sports Illustrated* would later describe it, "running around defenders, through defenders, and carrying them on his back." He gained thirty-one of Oklahoma's sixty-two yards on this sustained drive, ending with his two-yard run for a touchdown. "That," *Sports Illustrated* was to say, "proved just a teaser for what was to come."

Coach Barry Switzer had a reputation, in the description of the trade, for conducting a "relaxed bench." I spotted a couple of Indians among the Oklahoma players on the sidelines, and a middle-aged man in Saville Row tweeds, a fine leather trenchcoat, and a hound's tooth hat, who savored of many oil millions.

Marcus had hurt his hand on the first set of plays. As he had in high school, he sat alone now on a small elevated bench behind the longer one. A portable heater next to him was blowing out warm air. He sat there staring at the ground in a pose of prayerful meditation, just as I had found him that afternoon before the Choctaw Bowl in the Philadelphia locker room.

I was touched now by this scene: Joe Wood was sitting next to him on the bench, examining his hand, patting him on the shoulder. A thousand miles from home, before seventy-six thousand impassioned strangers throwing oranges in a freezing November cold, they sat there wordlessly together.

Marcus carried for substantially more yardage on the next Oklahoma possessions, as did the redoubtable fullback Stanley Wilson. The Sooners went ahead, 10–7, on a field goal in the second quarter. But Nebraska, displaying why it was the nation's Number 4 team with the best offense in the country, retaliated with two touchdowns and led 21–10 at the end of the half.

The small cadre of Oklahoma loyalists were solemn and dejected during the halftime ceremonies. Joe Wood and I sat shivering on the OU bench. "We're sittin' ducks for the flying objects," he said.

Oklahoma took the kickoff to begin the second half. On the first play from scrimmage, Marcus was viciously decked by a Nebraska tackler for a one-yard loss to the Sooner fourteen-yard line.

Wood and I were standing on the sidelines now near the Nebraska thirty-five-yard line, away from the action at the distant end of the field. Our view of the two teams was almost wholly obscured by the Oklahoma players and coaches standing in front of the bench.

"I hope he gets a lot of yards this half," I said.

"Don't worry," Wood said, spitting out his snuff. "He'll be down this way before not too very long."

There was no gain on the next try, and Oklahoma faced third down and eleven from its own fourteen-yard line.

Craning beyond the players at the bench, we could barely see the next play unfold. We managed to watch Marcus take the ball from quarterback Phelps and head off-tackle toward the left sidelines. After that we could see nothing.

It was an odd moment, one of the most curious I had ever experienced at a sporting event. The vast old stadium crammed with Midwesterners suddenly fell into a ghostly silence. Then the Oklahoma people immediately behind us in the lower rows gradually began to shout, barely audible in the sepulchral quiet. The Oklahoma players in front of the bench to our right started jumping up and down. So did the coaches. One of the players was shouting, "Go, Marcus, go!"

Our line of vision was directly in front of us. In mere seconds we were witness to a bizarre sight. A large figure raced by us all alone with the football. He was moving as swiftly as a human being can move. We could have reached out and touched him.

Joe Wood pounded me on the back. "That was him!" he exclaimed. "That was ol' Marcus!"

Sure enough, as we turned now to the left and moved slightly onto the field for a better view, he was sprinting just inside the farther sidelines into the end zone for a touchdown. He had come eighty-six yards, and when he crossed the Nebraska goal there was not a defender within range.

He was surrounded by his teammates and coaches as he returned slowly to the bench. That touchdown made it 21–17, Nebraska.

Once more he sat on the smaller bench alone. Wood and I sat next to him in front of the portable heater. His hand was covered with a glove and hurting badly, and he was winded from his recent bout with bronchitis.

Nebraska returned with another quick touchdown, then Wilson scored for Oklahoma. The Cornhuskers led 28–24 as the final quarter was winding down. Both defenses stiffened, and the game could go either way now, perhaps to the team which last got the ball.

With 2:56 left in the fourth quarter, Marcus went for six, then four, but with second and six from the Nebraska thirty-five, Oklahoma's questionable passing game failed. There was a string of incomplete passes, and eventually an interception which preserved the Nebraska victory. The oranges descended again, and with them the fans themselves.

Marcus had finished with 149 yards on twenty-five carries and the two touchdowns. Oklahoma ended the regular season with eight wins and three losses.

On the sidelines I looked down at my shoes. They were covered with snuff.

In the locker room afterward, Marcus apologized to Coach Wood because Oklahoma did not win. "Don't worry about it, son. You did a good job out there today. I wouldn't have missed it for the world."

We drove southward in the bleak Midwestern night. Joe Wood was driving; our companions were asleep on the back seat. "It was just about the best day of my life," he said. "I didn't know I was important." On the radio we picked up the powerful Oklahoma stations. One of them dedicated a song by Lefty Frizzell to Marcus Dupree. It was called "You're the Reason God Made Oklahoma."


Limited to twenty carries in his first three games, he ended the season rushing for 905 yards on 129 tries, an average of 7 yards. This was a school record for freshmen by 246 yards. He was Oklahoma's leading scorer with thirteen touchdowns, and the leading rusher (the first freshman ever to lead OU in rushing) as well as punt and kick returner. Both the Associated Press and UPI named him Big Eight Newcomer of the Year. He made the AP's first-team All-Big Eight squad, and UPI's second. As for the home people, *The Jackson Clarion-Ledger* and *Daily News* chose him Mississippi's Male Athlete of the Year.


The student from Philly High got his first-semester grades. He made A in Astronomy, B in Mythology, B in English, and C in Political Science. Later, despite a 2.23 average, he would be named co-winner of the award presented each year to the freshman athlete who combines excellence in scholarship and sports.

His final appearance of the season would be in the Fiesta Bowl in Tempe, Arizona, on New Year's Day. He and Barry Switzer flew to New

York to be on the "Today" show in December. NBC, which was televising the game, announced it would introduce "The Dupree Camera" for high aerial shots of the Mississippi boy as he ran with the football.

Arizona State, ranked eleventh in the nation, was statistically the Number 1 defensive team in America, having allowed its opponents an average of only ninety-five yards rushing a game. In the ample pregame coverage, Darryl Rogers, the Arizona State coach, observed: "Dupree looks like Chuck Muncie when Muncie was at the University of California a while back. It's hard enough trying to tackle a 230-pound back, but Dupree can flat-out run. He's never been caught from behind. I keep telling our linebackers that." "I don't know how fast their linebackers are," Marcus said in response. "And I don't really know how fast I am yet. I'm still learning a lot of things. I didn't think I could run over people in college like I did in high school. But I am."

I watched the action, Dupree Camera and all, in a bar in Oxford, as Pete lay in a shadowy corner. Before 70,553 spectators Arizona State won it, 32–21, with a fourth-quarter rally, but Marcus shone. Although he left three times with rib and leg injuries, broke his finger, suffered a hamstring pull, and played no more than half the game, he gained 239 yards on seventeen carries, including runs of 56 and 48 yards, established a new rushing record for the Fiesta Bowl, and was named Most Valuable Player. "The freshman of the century," Charlie Jones of NBC said. "Eighteen years old, 230 pounds, 239 yards—and a rib injury? Oh boy!" Darryl Rogers of Arizona State commented: "I don't know if we've played any back like Marcus Dupree. The outcome would've been different if he'd been in there."

Barry Switzer, however, chastised his young runner for eating too much over the Christmas holidays and accused him of being caught from behind twice. "He'd have scored us two more touchdowns if he played at 228 instead of 240 like he did today," Switzer said. "It's entirely obvious he's a tremendous football talent, but as a freshman he still has to learn how to best prepare to play his game. He'll have to discipline himself in order to best utilize his talents. It's obvious that when he's playing his game he's a class by himself."

"The injuries I got today were freak injuries that I've never had before," Marcus said. In high school I had always feared for this, and his cracked ribs and damaged ankle and his grimacing with pain on the bench in the Fiesta Bowl gave me additional pause for concern. In the increasingly violent world of football, he had only just begun. Bert Jones, the professional quarterback, said on his retirement with injuries: "I think only the players really realize it, that when you play, you're always just one hit away from the end of your career." Herschel Walker had taken out a million-dollar insurance policy with Lloyd's of London on an annual premium of twelve thousand dollars, the first college football player to insure himself. By Lloyd's estimate, one-and-a-quarter college players out of every hundred would suffer a career-ending injury each season. The hazards for great running backs had to be much higher. Subsequently Marcus would sit out the '83 spring practices with the hamstring pull he had suffered in the Fiesta Bowl.

Off the field "I try to treat everybody right and be nice to everybody," Marcus would say. But on the field, "You have to get rough with them, because if you don't you'll probably get knocked crazy."

As in high school, in the future years the opposition's defenses would "key in" on him more and more now. He would live with further pain before it was over. I hoped he would survive it.

Oklahoma finished sixteenth in the national polls, Texas seventeenth. The two archenemies would not likely finish that far down for many years.

Marcus completed the total season with 1,144 yards on 146 carries for an average of 7.8 yards per carry. This included his famous long runs of 63, 75, 30, 77, 80, 70, 86, 56, and 48 yards. The national *Football News* selected him Freshman of the Year. When polled, six of the eight Big Eight Conference football coaches said they would choose him if they could have only one player from the conference for a new team.

Three days after the Fiesta Bowl game, I made my last visit to Philadelphia. Marcus was home briefly for the end of the winter vacation. My son David was down from the North to take the jacket photograph of Marcus and Reggie for this book.

We met in a familiar place, the school gymnasium. Pete was taking his final stroll around the football field, searching about for the country dogs from the hollow. Although his ribs were taped, Marcus was not hurting too much from the game, he said. He helped Reggie up the steps of the gym, and Joe Wood led us into his hideaway office to show us a television cassette of a color film the Oklahoma people had made. The film was a mélange of Marcus' greatest runs of the '82 season. As Barry Switzer had suggested, there was a touch of magic in them. The background music was from the song "Fame," with the lyrics "I'm gonna live forever." The narrator said: "The dream can be real when you're good enough."

I noticed Marcus combing his Afro as he and Reggie walked onto the empty football field for the pictures. It was a bright, cold winter's day. The two brothers posed with the concrete grandstand and the two water towers of the town in the background. Pete limped over to us and sat watching with his usual curiosity. Marcus' friends Michael Smith and Tree McAfee, the black players from Philly High who had gone elsewhere to play college football, watched too.

We went to the little house in the Quarters for more pictures. First Marcus, and then he and Reggie, posed on the front porch. When we had finished, Marcus and his friends got in their car to visit the old high school gang at the Pizza Hut.

Reggie lingered on the porch. We were about to drive back to Oxford, and I told him I would help Pete out of the car so they could say goodbye. Reggie stood on his crutches on the steps as Pete walked toward him on the lawn. Pete's back legs collapsed, and he sprawled on the grass. The little boy looked down at the old, crippled dog. "Bye, Pete!" Reggie said.

The icy Mississippi winter descended again. The world took a couple of turns. Among the cast in the recruiting, Steve Sloan departed Ole Miss for Duke, to be replaced by "Dog" Brewer. Temple Drake left football for what he called "the private segment." Bear Bryant died in Tuscaloosa.

In February Herschel Walker left the University of Georgia to sign with the New Jersey Generals of the new United States Football League. The contract was five million dollars for three years, the richest in the history of professional football. Walker had one year of college eligibility remaining; his decision provoked a storm in college football. The policy of the established National Football League was not to seek college players until they had completed their eligibility. What was to prevent the renegade league, a creature of market research and television which would play its games in the spring and summer from taking any college player it wanted?

National attention immediately turned to Marcus. Coach Barry Switzer expressed concern that the USFL would cast its eye toward his running back because "Marcus Dupree is the best running back in America. He's better than Herschel Walker."

"I think it was a great deal for Herschel," Marcus said in a new video arcade called Corridor IV, a door down from Stribling's Drug Store in Philly. "He's won the national rushing title and the SEC championship. There was nothing else for him to do but take the money and run. It would be a hard decision for me, but if I win the Heisman I can't walk in the store and put a Heisman Trophy on the counter and buy something. I'd have to think about my mother and Reggie. Herschel made $1.5 million just to sign, more than most folks make in a lifetime."

Switzer sought safeguards to protect Marcus' remaining three years of college eligibility. The threat abated when representatives of the new league met with the college football coaches and the NCAA and promised that the case of Herschel Walker was exceptional and that they would not entice any more collegians. Despite this uneasy compromise, the commissioner of the league, when asked later if the USFL might someday sign Marcus as they had Herschel, admitted: "We won't entice a kid to do it. But if I face the same challenge again, how do I defend it?"

Tony Dorsett, the fabulous runner of the Dallas Cowboys, stated his feelings candidly. Walker was within 823 yards of breaking Dorsett's all-time college record of 5,259 yards rushing while at the University of Pittsburgh. "That's the first thing I thought about," he said. "I'll be at the top for a while. Well, at least until Marcus Dupree gets there."

Marcus himself, as the seasons changed again, was looking ahead to his sophomore year at the University of Oklahoma. He told the press in the Sooner State: "I think we're going to the 'I' more next year. We're recruiting seven quarterbacks who are all good passers, and we'll try to mix up the pass with the run, but we'll be running the Wishbone, too. We lose only one starter off the offensive line and two starters on defense and we have a lot of experience. We should be looking at a national championship next year."

He had told me: "Philadelphia's my home and I love it. But I kind of like it out there too."

As his second collegiate year was about to begin, he was being mentioned as a leading candidate for the Heisman Trophy. The realities of this challenge—of the swift national fame of a young black from a small Mississippi town, of the pressures on him to succeed as no running back ever had, of a certain naïveté and an uneasiness with established Northern reporters—would be accentuated by a cover story on him in *Sports Illustrated*. He was portrayed there for the nation as a slovenly, malicious prima donna who barely got along with Barry Switzer, who could care less about school, and who would likely leave Oklahoma after one more year. The young man so described bore scant resemblance to the one I had grown to know. I was gratified that many sports people around the country who also knew and cared for him and for the drama which enveloped him came to his defense, and none more so than his fellow Mississippians. The Jackson papers cited his work with white and black children, his self-discipline as an athlete, his role in the emerging decency of his town and state.

Yet such exigencies would mount for him, for they had always accompanied the burden of precocious success, no matter how hard-earned, in America. All of us struggle; all of us *respond* to struggle. In our deepest being we are all tormented by the uncertainty: What if I fail? We secretly may ask: What do I do when they find out I'm me?

The demands on him, at age nineteen, were more acute than ever. As with Herschel Walker, fewer than three touchdowns a game might be a symptom of failure. From the first moment I saw him play, my faith in Marcus had never wavered; nor, I sensed, had he ever lost faith in himself. "Pressure is only what you make it," he said a long time ago, long before he performed before crowds of 75,000 and on national television. "I've always had pressure on me, but you only feel it if you let it bother you. It means nothing." Or as a young hometown white who knew him well observed: "When one of our own gets attacked from the outside, we Mississippians always rally to him. Also, there's something about growin' up in Philadelphia, Mississippi—white or black. When things get difficult and there's more on the line, you don't quit. You get mean. He ain't worried. He's thinkin' right now about goin' on the field and *doin' good*."

And so the story of Marcus continued much in ourselves. And someday—I hope only in the infinitely distant future—his skills would inevitably fail him. Perhaps the way he coped with that would prove the final measure not of the boy, but of the man. He had not faced the half of it yet, the pain and discouragement. He was going to be with us for a long time—a name of our generation to be remembered. Perhaps through his struggles and hopes to fulfill his monumental promise, we Americans could understand much in ourselves.

I had been taking Pete to Dr. Shivers two or three times a week. From his suffering I knew he was fading from me.

I found him one morning gasping for breath. His eyes were heavy with pain. I lay on the floor next to him. I held him in my arms and told him I loved him. He looked at me and weakly wagged his tail. After a time he stood and limped out the door. He lay down near the house. I sat with him there for a while. I left for a moment. When I came back he was dead.

Our friends made him a small pine coffin. Late that afternoon, in a dark and gloom-filled rain, we buried him on a serene old hill he had known. A few people he had loved gathered there. The rain tapped on their umbrellas. One of his friends read from the Episcopal Book of Common Prayer:

> Unto Almighty God we commend the soul of our brother departed, and we commit his body to the ground; earth to earth, ashes to ashes, dust to dust . . .
>
> Therefore are they before the throne of God, and serve Him day and night in His temple: and He that sitteth on the throne shall dwell among them.
>
> They shall hunger no more, neither thirst any more; neither shall the sun light on them, nor any heat.
>
> For the Lamb which is in the midst of the throne shall feed them, and shall lead them unto living fountains of waters: and God shall wipe away all tears from their eyes.

I thought of our inseparable days on the earth. He and I had come together at the right time, just perhaps as young Marcus and I had; and he, too, had been at Marcus' courting. There was immortality in Pete's gentleness, as there was in the way Marcus ran.

Something of me was gone with Pete, so much of my deluded youth and vanity, my loves and fears as a writing man, my American comings and goings. Marcus' boyhood in Neshoba, and everything Neshoba meant to me, his destiny on the Oklahoma plains, were an inextricable part of my strange, bittersweet return. Laying Pete there in the Mississippi ground evoked for me the blue immemorial mists of Fitzgerald, for I see now that this has been, after all, a tale about the South. It was Pete who came home with me.

# ACKNOWLEDGMENTS

My debt to Florence Mars is greater than to anyone else in Philadelphia, Mississippi. Her memoir, *Witness in Philadelphia,* was indispensable to me. I have drawn on her recollections time and again in these pages, not merely for her decent perception of life, but for her extraordinary abilities as an observer. I thank her.

Don Whitehead's *Attack on Terror: The FBI and the Ku Klux Klan in Mississippi,* a fine book by an American reporter of the old school, was essential. So was William Bradford Huie's *Three Lives for Mississippi.* Huie was one of the first reporters on the scene in the summer of 1964. I am grateful to Whitehead and Huie, and I do not think they would have minded my drawing liberally from their reportage of that earlier time.

Clayton Rand's *Ink on My Hands,* a wonderfully engaging memoir which illuminates a time and a place but which unfortunately is out of print and seldom read, was of great help to me in understanding the Neshoba of the 1920s.

My gratitude goes also to Stanley Dearman, the editor and publisher of *The Neshoba Democrat* since 1968. His Centennial issue, published in 1981, was a fount of information about the town and the county, as were his regular weekly issues.

I am grateful to *The Jackson Daily News* for the brief entries from Marcus Dupree's notes on the 1981 football season and afterward. Under Lee Ragland's purview, the *Daily News* published these informal notes on February 7, 1982.

I wish to express my appreciation to the following sportswriters whose reportage and comments helped me immeasurably:

Foremost, Billy Watkins of *The Meridian Star.* Watkins was based only thirty-eight miles from Philadelphia, and his writings and personal assistance were invaluable to me. Paul Borden, Rick Cleveland, Jerry Potter, Roscoe Nance, Barry Lasswell, Bill Spencer, and their colleagues on *The Jackson Clarion-Ledger.* Orley Hood, Lee Ragland, Bernard Fernandez, and others on *The Jackson Daily News.* Bill Ross of *The Tupelo Journal.* Al Dunning and Bobby Hall of *The Memphis Commercial Appeal.* George Lapides of *The Memphis Press-Scimitar.*

Art Carey's piece in the Sunday magazine of *The Philadelphia Inquirer* in the summer of '81 was especially helpful in providing a knowledgeable

Northerner's perspective on Neshoba.

My distinguished editor at Doubleday, Carolyn Blakemore, and her assistant, Bob Frese, were unfailingly encouraging and insightful, as was my friend there, Gloria Jones. Sarah Garner, a lovely Southern belle of Oxford, aided me along the way in research and typing.

On this new edition, I wish to thank my friend and editor at the University Press of Mississippi, Seetha Srinivasan.

Finally, I want to thank the dozens of people in Philadelphia, Mississippi, who were kind and helpful to me.

*W. M.*

# POSTSCRIPT
by Billy Watkins

He lasted a year and a half at the University of Oklahoma. Coach Barry Switzer, six years before his disciplinary and recruiting violations forced his own departure, said Marcus had eaten too many late-night snacks, had too little discipline. Marcus said there were too many expectations, too much Switzer. Marcus also said he should have listened to his mama. "When Barry came to the house recruiting me, Mama couldn't stand him. Me, I like cocky people sometimes. I just didn't think he would be cocky with his players."

The beginning of the end for Marcus as an OU Sooner was an article in *Sports Illustrated* in June 1983, reporting for a national audience that Marcus and Switzer were feuding. Part of the story read: "The awful truth is, Dupree . . . hates it at Oklahoma, and his relationship with Switzer, which was barely cordial to begin with, has seriously deteriorated."

The story, according to Marcus, was only partially correct. He did not hate Oklahoma. "I always liked Oklahoma. I still do," he said. But, yes, he and the volatile Switzer had their differences. Their discord started when Switzer claimed that Dupree reported for his freshman year in 1982 soft and out of shape. It got worse near the end of that season when Switzer criticized Marcus for not giving his offensive linemen their proper credit. "He said that when I made a touchdown I'd run to the sidelines instead of going over and giving my blockers high-fives. I went to see Coach Selmon. He knew that wasn't true. He knew I was giving the folks around me credit. Marcus felt Switzer favored Spencer Tillman, another touted young running back, though not as celebrated in the national media as Marcus. "It was always 'Spencer this, Spencer that.' But Spencer wasn't starting. I was." Marcus considered not going back for his second season, 1983, even though as only a sophomore he was the leading candidate in the United States for the Heisman Trophy. But he decided to give it another try.

After gaining 138 yards in a 27-14 victory over Stanford in the 1983 season-opener, he suffered a minor knee injury against Ohio State. "That's when I began saying: 'I don't know about this,' " he said. After sitting out the Tulsa game, he returned to gain 151 yards and score three touchdowns against Kansas State. That was to be his last glorious moment at Oklahoma. In a 28-16 loss to Texas in Dallas the next week, he rushed for 50 yards on 14 carries and left the game with a concussion. Because the Sooners would not play the next weekend, Switzer gave the players permission to go home for a couple of days.

"I wasn't feeling too good," Marcus recalled. "My head wasn't feeling good. I said, 'Forget this. I ain't getting paid to play this game, and I think it's about time I did.' Players can't have a job when they're on scholarship. Where is the money going to come from—gas money, money to wash clothes? Plus, we brought in so much money to the college. That stadium holds 80,000 and it was packed every game." He decided not to go back.

Marcus hid out in Hattiesburg, Mississippi for about a week. A missing person's report was filed with the authorities. The media, both national and local, dug hard to uncover his whereabouts. He was an item on the NBC Nightly News. His mother said even she did not know where he might be and told the Jackson *Clarion-Ledger* she was worried to death. Some people even went so far as to suggest jokingly that Willie Morris, who was teaching at Ole Miss at the time, had Marcus hidden in the basement of his house on Faculty Row to elicit publicity for his book, which was to be released nationally that same week.

"I just wanted some time to think," Marcus said. "After a few days, I had no bad feelings about it, so I knew I had done the right thing." In October 1983 he enrolled at the University of Southern Mississippi in Hattiesburg, about one hundred miles from Philadelphia, but left Southern three months later when he learned he would have to sit out the 1984 season under the NCAA rules. In March 1984 he signed a five-year, $6 million contract with the new, short-lived United States Football League's New Orleans Breakers. He was nineteen years old, likely the youngest player in the history of professional football, and one of six players at the time earning more than $1 million a year. And he appeared to be worth it, gaining 681 yards and scoring nine touchdowns his rookie season.

Call it what you will—a premonition, a vision, a visceral feeling—but Marcus always knew that one day he would suffer a serious knee injury while playing football. "I used to think about it all the time, especially in college," Marcus said one day in July 1986. "I didn't have any insurance on my knees then, and I just kept wondering every day, 'When is it going to happen?' " Many times during his year-and-a-half at Oklahoma, he telephoned his agent, Ken Fairley (who entered the story after the publication of *The Courting of Marcus Dupree*) and admitted he was afraid. "I kept telling Ken I felt like I needed to leave," Marcus said. "Something kept dawning on me that I was going to get hurt."

Finally, on February 24, 1985, while playing for the Breakers, who had moved to Portland, Oregon, his nightmare was transmitted into eerie, painful reality. Only a few days earlier, during a telephone conversation with Fairley, Marcus predicted something bad would happen in that weekend game. "I knew I was gonna get hurt in that game," Marcus said. "I just knew it. It was something I felt." Great athletes, not unlike soldiers in combat, sometimes have such hunches.

Fairley said: "He called me right before the game and said, 'Man, this game is gonna be it.' It was the strangest thing I've ever heard. But I took him seriously. It was nothing to hear Marcus say, 'I'm gonna score twice this weekend.' Then he'd go out and do it."

Marcus laughed when I asked if it bothered him to talk about the injury. "The play was 25 Lag Draw, and I was the fullback," he said. "It was a good play. We were driving. I went around the end, and, really, I don't know what happened at the time. I just started hurting, and I told them it was my knee. They couldn't understand because everything happened so quickly."

Television replays showed that his left knee had been hit from the side while his cleats were firmly planted. The anterior cruciate ligament and the bicep tendon were torn. "I promise you it hurt," Marcus said. "I was screaming. It was pain like I had never felt before. It didn't swell at the time, and they said they weren't sure if anything was torn or not. But when I tried to stand up, I couldn't."

He underwent surgery and was in a cast for two months. His long road to recovery was filled with obstacles. An examination a year and a half after the injury revealed that his knee was not improving. He could jog and play softball, but he could not cut at full speed like a professional running back must. At the age of twenty-two, when most super-talented running backs are just beginning their professional careers, Marcus was forced to retire.

He received two years' pay from the Breakers. At the time of the injury, his knee was insured by Lloyds of London for several million dollars. Marcus, on advice from Fairley, refused to discuss the settlement. "Are you rich?" I asked him in July of 1986. "Yeah," he answered without hesitation. "Very rich?" I asked. "Yeah. I'm where I've always wanted to be, on top financially. Being secure means a lot. It means I don't have to go out there and scuffle like my mom had to do to take care of me. I'll be able to give my mom and my grandparents nice things. They were always there when I needed them, and now I have the chance to give something back."

He said his personal life was good. He had married his high school sweetheart, Katrina McGowan, in June of that year, and they had two sons, Marquez, 3, and Landon, 1. Although football seemed to be over for him, Marcus's life was a busy one. He played on softball teams in Hattiesburg and Philadelphia and coached a Pony League baseball team in Philadelphia. He planned to build neighborhood youth centers across Mississippi. He hoped to establish a hamburger chain, possibly named "Heisman's," and to bring professional wrestling to Philadelphia. "I wake up every morning with new ideas," he said. He seemed happy.

"But believe me," Fairley said then, "he's going through a lot of withdrawal pains right now. It's that time of year. All these guys are getting ready for the season. He sees these guys going off to training camp, and he has nowhere to go. He's like a boxer who keeps wanting to come back for one more fight."

Marcus found it hard to watch games on television because his mind kept telling him he could be out there playing; he could do it better than the men he watched on the tube. Too often he was reminded of the good times: the day before the game, the pre-game meal, those runs when he was chased but not caught. "I used to love the fact that people thought they could hit me but couldn't," he said.

He said the best time of his life was playing high school football. Not the touchdowns or the victories, just the playing. "Playing with your friends. All through elementary and junior high, you all set goals about what you're gonna do when you get to high school. You hang out after practice. You look forward to Thursdays when you get to practice in shorts. After games, there are parties. Just being in high school, period, was fun. Kids need to enjoy it while they're young."

He paused, put his hands behind his head, and drew a deep breath. "All this has been hard to swallow. But sooner or later, I knew it would all come to an end. Running backs just don't last. I'm not sure I can quit, but it's to the point where if I get the knee hurt again, where will I be? Will I be able to walk? Will I have to have a knee replaced? How bad do I really want to play? I don't know if it's worth taking the chance."

The next time I tried to contact Marcus was the summer of 1990. Find Marcus Dupree, my editors at the *Clarion-Ledger* said, and tell us what he's doing. Easier said than done. Phone calls to the Dupree domicile were usually answered by Reggie Dupree, Marcus's younger brother. "He's not here," was the standard response, followed by: "He's gone running" or "He's gone to Hattiesburg" or "He's down in Jackson somewhere" or "I don't know where he is." Since his days at Philadelphia High School, there always had been an incalculable mystery about Marcus Dupree, and his elusiveness now was only enhancing the image. Finally, one day in late July 1990 he answered the phone. "Marcus, is that really you?" I asked. "Yeah," he said. "I've tried calling you back, but I could never reach you." I explained that I wanted to write an update on his life. "Great," he said. "Come on up Monday. One o'clock."

When I arrived there on Monday, Marcus was not around. "He's in Hattiesburg," Reggie said, standing in the doorway of the expanded trailer he occupied with Marcus and their mother, Cella Conners. "I'm not sure when he'll be back." I drove around Philadelphia for three hours, went back to Marcus's house, and still he was not there. I called the office and gave them the news: No Marcus. No story, again. "Fine," Billy Turner, the executive sports editor, said, "Come on home and forget Marcus. We've tried. It's obvious he's snubbing us."

This bothered me. I had known Marcus since he was a junior at Philadelphia High School. I trusted him; he seemed to trust me. More than once, I defended Marcus against those who said they knew all along he would wind up not only without fame and fortune but back in Philadelphia, penniless and without a job. I wondered now if I had been wrong in arousing myself professionally to his defense.

A week later, the phone rang at my house. "Billy, this is Marcus. I need you to come up here."

"Marcus, I *did* come up there. Remember? Monday, one o'clock?"

"I know, man, I forgot. I had to go to Hattiesburg to get some stuff worked out, and I thought I'd be back. I really need to see you."

"What's going on?"

"I'm in jail. I'm serious. It's a long story. But I'm telling you, there are some good stories in here. They've got guys locked up here who have no business being here. And they want to talk, to tell the whole story of what's going on in Neshoba County these days."

The Neshoba County sheriff's office confirmed that Marcus Dupree, indeed, was in jail for non-payment of alimony and child support. He was three months behind on his $1,200-per-month payments, and another payment was due soon. We ran a brief piece in the sports section about it.

A week later, Marcus telephoned me again. "I'm out," he said. "I spent eight days in jail. I didn't have the money. My mom wound up borrowing $3,600 to get me out. Another $1,200 is due next week. I have no idea where it's coming from."

"Let me come up there and do a story with you about this whole mess," I said. He agreed: "Tomorrow, eleven o'clock."

When I arrived at 274 Davis Street, Marcus walked out the front door and met me in the yard. We shook hands. I could not believe my eyes. Marcus was wearing a pair of blue walking shorts and a black New Orleans Saints cap. He looked fit and powerful, much like he did as a high school star nine years earlier. His stomach was flat. His chest, arms and legs bulged at all the right places.

"I want you to see this," he said, walking over to a set of doctors' scales he had placed in the shade of his driveway. The needle on the scales circled twice, then vibrated back and forth for a couple of seconds before settling on 226. "Too high," he said, shedding his shorts and stepping back on the scale in his bikini underwear. "Hurry up, Dupe," his friend

Spuds said. "A couple of girls are coming around the corner." Patiently, Marcus waited for the scales to come to rest. "Two-twenty-five," he said, "Two weeks ago, I weighed 219. A lot of it is water weight. I drunk a lot of fluids yesterday. I'll lose three pounds working out today." Marcus slipped his pants back on and walked toward the trailer. "Four months ago, I weighed 270 pounds. Should've seen me."

Hanford Dixon, the former NFL cornerback, had invited him down to Hattiesburg to work out with him. That was April 28. Bud Holmes, Dixon's agent, had a 3,000-acre ranch down there, with a one-mile road they ran on. "Hanford ran five or six miles," Marcus said. "I couldn't even run an 880. It was sickening. The next day, Hanford told me, 'Marcus, you could play in the NFL if you'd just get yourself in shape.' Bud had been saying it all along. So I said I'd give it one last shot. I'm 26 years old, I thought, and if I'm ever going to do it, I'll have to do it now. I just made up my mind to start working out, and I made a vow to be consistent with it."

Marcus had lived a relatively sedate life during the five years since his knee injury with the Breakers. He had tried several careers—rap artist, professional wrestling promoter, night club entrepreneur. He played a little softball, but he rarely worked out. Now, almost inexplicably, he had labored himself into the best shape of his life. He limited his diet to baked chicken, baked fish, and salads. For three months, he exercised as he never had before.

"I started out running on the track over here at Northside Park," he said. "I'd run the straightaways, walk the curves. It was torture. Running was never easy for me. Even in high school, I couldn't run a mile. Anything longer than a 220, and I just couldn't make it." By mid-June he was running five miles a day. Five days a week, he spent at least two hours in a portable building that he converted into a weight room. "My cousin Rocky worked out with me. We'd cut the heaters on in there, and the thermometer would read 110 or 120 degrees. We'd see just how much we could stand."

"I feared for the boy's life he had it so hot in here," Marcus's grandmother Gladys Dupree said. On May 22, he weighed 250. He dropped 13 more pounds by June 1. And on August 15, he weighed 219, the least since his sophomore year in high school. I kept wondering whether a simple talk with a former NFL comeback could really inspire this sort of dedication.

No, he said. It was more than that. "I think the biggest reason I've worked so hard is for my kids," he said, referring to his sons, Marquez, now 7, and Landon, 5. "Seeing them sit for hours and watch the videotapes of me running the football—that's what really did it. Maybe I can be an inspiration to them. They love their father, and I just want them to be able to come to a game, to experience the feeling. I think they have a right to experience that. And all I want is a chance. If I get into an NFL training camp, somebody's going to lose his job."

He invited me inside. "I want to show you something," he said, and slipped a videotape into the VCR. On the screen was a short, chubby teenager acting as a surrogate quarterback and Dupree, dressed in shorts, a cutoff T-shirt, cleats, and a Dallas Cowboys helmet, running plays. He took handoffs. He caught passes. He dodged and cut and dipped and sprinted. We watched this for fifteen minutes. Marcus sat, nervously rubbing the remote control with his right thumb. He seemed to be waiting for my approval. "You look great," I said. "Quick. No limp."

"I'm telling you," he said, "I can play if somebody will give me a chance. My knee is fine."

At that point, his knee was in much better shape than his bank account. Just five years earlier, he was a self-proclaimed millionaire. Now, after numerous bad investments and a nasty court battle with Fairley, he claimed to be broke. "Me and his mother had to give him spending money for gas and things like that," his grandmother volunteered.

Why, I asked Marcus, had he not gotten a steady job since his retirement from football? His wife Katrina has been asking the same thing, Marcus said. "Her lawyer wants to know why I don't get a job pumping gas. Well, pumping gas isn't my profession. Playing football is. And that's what I'm trying to do." I reminded him that he already had been rejected by several NFL teams since the knee injury. The Tampa Bay Buccaneers gave him a physical exam during the 1987 strike season, and ruled his knee permanently disabled. "I tried to tell them I hadn't worked the knee, that it would get better," he said. "They wouldn't listen."

Marcus sat down on the sofa and began rummaging through a laundry basket of clothes, looking for a pair of socks. Had he given much thought to how it might feel to play football again? "Aw man," he said. "There's nothing like playing ball, hearing the cheers. Nobody knows what it's like to make a long run and have 80,000 people stand and scream."

The phone rang. It was one of Marcus's friends, and he stretched the phone cord into the next room. His grandmother, shelling peas for supper, took this moment to say certain things to me, as if she had waited a long time to say them:

I'll tell you what I always think. Marcus has never had no peace. When he was in flag football, when he was playing baseball, they always had to take his birth certificate wherever they went to prove he wasn't over age. 'Cause every where they went, his team brought home the trophy. He never got a chance to play junior high football. They moved him right up to high school. His mama had a fit when she found out. Then when he was at Philly High, it was always something. Kosciusko said they were gonna gang up on him and do something to hurt him. When they played Neshoba Central, they'd have to have the police down there because they were threatening to do something to him. He's just never had no peace from one thing to another. His life has always been lived at a hustle. And I know what people might think of Marcus. But I also know how good he's been to his boys. Even after he and Katrina separated, I've seen him give her a blank check to buy them boys things. Marcus bought all their school clothes. He bought all their school supplies. But when the money runs out, it runs out.

At my office the next day, I reported my findings in Philadelphia. "I've never seen him look this good," I told Turner and sports editor Rick Cleveland. "I think we'll see him signed to an NFL contract sometime this season. Somehow his knee seems to be healed." Turner and Cleveland laughed out loud, and I could hardly blame them. Marcus had not played football since 1985. His knee had been ruled a permanent wreck by several NFL teams. Four years earlier, he had said he did not think football was worth the physical risk. One year earlier, he had weighed nearly 300 pounds. A few days before, he was in jail. And now I was claiming that he looked like he did in high school, that his knee was fine, and that he suddenly loved football again. My claims did not gather much support when Butch John, our New Orleans Saints beat writer, began calling NFL teams to see if they were interested in signing Dupree. Each one said the same thing: You're talking about a guy who has been out of football for five years. Forget it.

I telephoned Marcus's agent, Bud Holmes, who was also the agent for several NFL stars, including the great Mississippian Walter Payton of the Chicago Bears, the leading rusher in league history, and former Saints assistant coach Bob Hill, who was advising Marcus. Both said they believed he could get an NFL tryout before the regular-season began in less than two weeks. "What they've told us," Holmes said, "is that they're in the process of making cuts. They asked us to let them get that done, let the smoke clear, then they'll bring Marcus in for a tryout. Whether or not he makes it depends on a lot of things. But I believe this: if somebody will give him a chance, they'll wind up with a starter."

I told Holmes he was talking about a great comeback. "One of the greatest of all time," he agreed. "And I'm not talking about just football here. I'm talking about coming back as a person. I've told Marcus many times that he was a victim of his own talent. God gave him this wonderful body and tremendous talent, and Marcus never had to put anything into it. Football was easy for him. And when you really think about it, football has caused him nothing but grief and misery. It's a wonder he doesn't hate the game." Holmes had gotten a notion Marcus still missed football when they attended a Saints game the year before at the Superdome in New Orleans. "Marcus was sweating all over, like a racehorse waiting for the race to begin. He was way out of shape then, but was drooling to get out on that field. I'd never seen him like that before."

So Holmes began planting seeds in Marcus's mind. He took him to visit Walter Payton in Hattiesburg. "Marcus would say that he'd like to try a comeback," Holmes said, "and Walter would say, 'Oh yeah? Well, come down to the ranch and run the hills with me. We'll find out how bad you want it.' Walter really rode him. Marcus saw Payton and Dixon, and he saw a different side of life, something more than all the glitter and gold. He finally understood what I meant when I said that in order to take a nickel out of your pocket, you first have to put one there. He finally realized he had to put something into football. 'Get yourself in shape, get your weight back down to about 220, run me a 4.5 40-yard dash, and I'll go to bat for you.' But I told him he had to take the first step. He did that."

I asked Holmes what Marcus's chances were of making an NFL team in 1990. "Probably zero," he said. "He hasn't taken any licks in about five years. There's more to football than just running a track meet. He can show them the track meet side. Now he's got to show them the other side. Believe me, there are teams that need a Marcus Dupree-type running back. But the NFL is one big happy fraternity. Teams are already talking about who they're going to pick up when another team cuts them. Marcus is not part of those conversations right now. He's been out of football for so long, it's probably hard for them to come to grips with the fact that Marcus does love football and can come back after a layoff like that. But I really believe he can make it. If not this year, then maybe next."

One month later, Marcus called my house. "I'm signing tomorrow with the Los Angeles Rams," he said, adding that his contract was worth "about $50,000." We spoke a long time. I gave him a spirited pep talk. "Somebody in the Rams backfield," he said, just before hanging up, "is fixin' to lose his job."

He signed on October 3, 1990, and spent four weeks on the "injured reserve" list. He was activated on November 7, in time for the Rams's home game in the Coliseum with the New York Giants. The game was a blowout for the Giants. So with less than two minutes left, Rams coach John Robinson inserted Marcus for the first time and used the final seconds of that game to reintroduce him to real football. On his first carry, Marcus gained nine yards, running over a Giants defensive back four strides into the run. He carried three more times for 13 yards. "I just want to help the team," he told the press after the game.

Robinson used Marcus only sparingly the rest of the season. He finished with 19 carries for 52 yards. The Rams finished 5-11. "We simply wanted
to bring him along slowly," Dick Coury, the Rams's running backs coach
that season, said. "People were expecting so much from Marcus, and we
just didn't want him in a situation to fail. He needed to be successful."

In 1991, Marcus had won a starting position in training camp. Then
in the Rams's final preseason game, against Atlanta, he injured his left
big toe, and the injury cost him the first seven regular-season games and
his starting position. He finished the year with 179 yards on 40 carries
and one touchdown, and 6 pass receptions for 46 yards. The Rams had
a disappointing 3-13 record. This hard-earned comeback from rock-bottom
in Neshoba, broke and in jail, and 280 pounds, may not have been as
graphic as the running back Gayle Sayers' in the movie *Brian's Song*, but
it was nonetheless deeply affecting, and gave one pause for remembrance.

He departed Anaheim after the final game, unsure if he would get
another chance with the fabled but losing Rams. There were major changes
ahead—Robinson was being replaced by Chuck Knox—and Marcus did
not know if he would be welcomed by the new regime. So his chronicle
lingered.

It was a beautiful spring day in April 1992. Other business had
brought me to Philadelphia, and I decided to stop by and see Marcus
as I had so many times over the years. When I arrived at 274 Davis Street,
things had not changed much since my last visit nearly two years before:
the shade trees, his grandmother's house in front, his mother's trailer in
the back, the workout room in the side yard, the BMW with California
license plates parked in the driveway alongside the 740 GLE Volvo and
the Lincoln Town Car.

One of Marcus's cousins answered my knock at the door. When I
asked if Marcus was home, he closed the door halfway and disappeared.
A couple of minutes later he returned. "Naw, I think he's gone running."

I thanked him, and drove away. I knew Marcus was there. And I
made up my mind I would not leave Philadelphia until I had seen him.
An hour later I pulled back into his driveway expecting the runaround
once again. Instead, as I walked toward the trailer, Marcus opened the
door and met me with a big smile. We sat down on the porch. He was
wearing a T-shirt, shorts, tennis shoes, and a Chicago White Sox cap.
He had a chew of tobacco in his right cheek and two earrings—one stud,
one loop—in his left ear.

"You look like you're in good shape," I said. "I weigh 235, but I
want to get down to 215," he said. "I'm just working on my speed right
now, trying to get my time down where it should be. It hasn't been hot
enough yet to really work out and lose some weight."

His contract with the Rams was up. "I thought I might sign a Plan

B contract with the Saints, but that didn't work out. Right now I'm not under contract to anyone. But I got a letter today from the Rams, inviting me to their minicamp in May. I guess that means they're still interested in me."

How were things going for him off the field? "Good," he said. "Me and Katrina are getting along okay. She doesn't bother me, I don't bother her. Me and Walter Payton have opened up a country and western bar in Hattiesburg, and that's doing well. Everything is okay. I can't complain. Only thing I have to gripe about is losing. I had forgotten how much losing hurt. If you think about it, I probably hadn't lost a dozen football games in my life before going to the Rams. Then the last two years, it's been miserable. I want that respect, that feeling that comes from being a winner."

I reminded him of two years ago, when he simply wanted to play again in the NFL, to hear the roar of the fans, to feel the pre-game butterflies and the post-game pains, to play football with his sons sitting in the stands, to prove he could come back. Now, he had done all that. "That hasn't been enough?" I asked.

Marcus laughed. "I feel some satisfaction to a certain degree. But losing just takes all the fun out of everything. I hate losing. I hate it. And I wouldn't care if I sat on the bench as long as we won. I really mean that. As long as we win, I don't care what role I play."

I realized as I sat there listening to Marcus that he no longer was the kid from Philly High I knew those years ago, no longer the superstar with the incredible future. And perhaps for the first time since I had met him in 1978, I was not talking to him adult-to-boy. It was adult-to-adult. I had my fears. He had his. And he was laying his life on the table: he was not sure how much longer he could play football.

He had seen Johnie Cooks of Leland, Mississippi, the former linebacker, a couple of weeks before. "I asked him if he ever woke up the day after a game hurting as much as I do," Marcus said. "He told me that he usually wouldn't stop aching until it was time to go to training camp the next year. I'm just now getting over some of the bumps and bruises from last season, and I'm about to go back to minicamp. Who knows? One morning I might just wake up and say, 'I've hurt enough. It's over.' "

Billy Watkins is with the *Clarion-Ledger* in Jackson, Mississippi.